Criminal Justice in Action
The Core

9e

Larry K. Gaines
California State University San Bernardino

Roger LeRoy Miller
Institute for University Studies Arlington, Texas

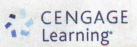

CENGAGE Learning®

Australia • Brazil • Japan • Singapore • United Kingdom • United States

CENGAGE
Learning®

Criminal Justice in Action
The Core, 9th Edition
Larry K. Gaines
Roger LeRoy Miller

SVP for Social Science, Humanities, & Business: Erin Joyner
Sr. Product Director: Marta Lee-Perriard
Sr. Product Manager: Carolyn Henderson Meier
Associate Content Developer: Jessica Alderman
Product Assistant: Timothy Kappler
Marketing Manager: Mark Linton
Marketing Director: Jennifer Levanduski
Marketing Coordinator: Quynton Johnson
Production Director: Brenda Ginty
Sr. Content Project Manager: Ann Borman
Digital Content Specialist: Michelle Wilson
Manufacturing Planner: Judy Inouye
Sr. Inventory Analyst: Jessica Sayers
Sr. IP Director: Julie Geagan-Chavez
IP Analyst: Jennifer Bowes
IP Project Manager: Reba Frederics
Photo Researcher: Nisha Bhanu Beegum, Lumina Datamatics
Text Researcher: Magesh Rajagopalan, Lumina Datamatics
Sr. Designer: Helen Bruno
Interior Designer: tani hasegawa
Cover Designer: Irene Morris Design
Cover Images: Alexander Spatari/Getty Images, inhauscreative/Getty Images, Masterfile, XiXiXing/Shutterstock.com, ra2studio/Shutterstock.com
Compositor: Lachina
Copyeditor: Sue Bradley
Indexer: Terry Casey

Design elements: abstract background (all features): Shutterstock/13Imagery;
A Question of Ethics, goddess of justice: Felix Pergande/Dreamstime.com;
Discretion in Action, female police officer: Rachel Donahue/Shutterstock.com
CJ Controversy: M Dogan/Shutterstock.com;
CJ & Technology: Shutterstock;
Comparative Criminal Justice,
Myth v. Reality: Shutterstock/saicle; world map: Pable631/Dreamstime.com
Landmark Cases: Shutterstock/kentoh

For product information and technology assistance,
Cengage Learning Customer & Sales Support, 1-8

For permission to use material from this text or
submit all requests online at **www.cengage.com/p**
Further permissions questions can be email
permissionrequest@cengage.com

Library of Congress Control Number: 2016950157

Student Edition ISBN: **978-1-337-09214-2**
Looseleaf Edition ISBN: **978-1-337-09216-6**

Cengage Learning
20 Channel Center Street
Boston, MA 02210
USA

Cengage Learning is a leading provider of customized learn
with employees residing in nearly 40 different countries and
than 125 countries around the world. Find your local repres
www.cengage.com.

Cengage Learning products are represented in Canada by Nelson Education, Ltd.

To learn more about Cengage Learning Solutions, visit **ww**

Purchase any of our products at your local college store or
preferred online store **www.cengagebrain.com**

Printed in the United States of America
Print Number: 03 Print Year: 2017

Contents in Brief

Contents

PART TWO : THE POLICE AND LAW ENFORCEMENT

PART THREE : CRIMINAL COURTS

PART FIVE : SPECIAL ISSUES

Special Features

Chapter Opening Stories

Comparative Criminal Justice

Careers in CJ

Landmark Cases

Mastering**Concepts**

CJ & Technology

Discretion in ACTION

Myth vs Reality

CJ Controversy

Preface

Continuing a tradition established by its eight predecessors, the Ninth Edition of *Criminal Justice in Action, The Core* provides students with all the facts, analyses, and real-life examples they will need to be successful in this course. Relying on the help and advice of the many criminal justice professors who have adopted this best-selling textbook over the years, we are confident that we have established an invaluable introduction to the field.

Pushed by the constantly changing, constantly challenging world of crime and justice, however, we feel that we have upped the ante for ourselves and for those who study and teach this book. In this edition, we offer the criminal justice system not simply as a subject to be learned and taught, but as a crucial American institution to be critiqued and held to the highest moral and ethical standards.

Ethics, Discretion, and Public Policy

Criminal Justice in Action, The Core provides students not only with the tools to understand how the criminal justice system *does* work, but also the opportunity to express their opinions on how the criminal justice system *should* work. This opportunity presents itself primarily in the following three components, the first two of which are new to the Ninth Edition:

- **Ethics Challenges.** Each chapter contains three of these short challenges, placed at the end of a section. As well as reinforcing an important concept from that section, the challenges allow students to explore their own values in the context of the criminal justice system. Subjects covered include the use of deception during police interrogations (Chapter 6), for-profit bail (Chapter 8), and the ability of juvenile suspects to understand their *Miranda* rights (Chapter 13).
- **CJ Policy—Your Take.** This chapter-specific margin feature engages students by asking them to critique a hot-button criminal justice policy issue. Examples include Oregon's Death with Dignity Act (Chapter 1), state "stand-your-ground" self-defense laws (Chapter 3), and the disenfranchisement of ex-convicts (Chapter 11).
- **Discretion in Action.** As in previous editions, this feature asks students to step into the shoes of a criminal justice professional or other CJ participant and make a difficult decision. Nine new *Discretion in Action* features drive home the pivotal role that discretion plays in the criminal justice system, a subject that we have expanded upon over the past several editions of *Criminal Justice in Action, The Core.*

This expanded coverage of ethics, policy, and discretion allows us to present a *panoramic* view of important criminal justice issues. Chapter 5, for example, opens with an account of a disputed police shooting in Bexar County, Texas, that spurred local authorities to purchase body-worn cameras for local law enforcement officers. Throughout the chapter, the issue is revisited as we discuss policies that limit a police officer's discretion regarding the operation of body-worn cameras, how such cameras may influence a police officer's ethical decision making, the role of the cameras in ensuring police accountability, and the legal ramifications of use-of-force evidence gathered by this new technology.

Careers in Criminal Justice

We are well aware that many students using this text are interested in a criminal justice career. Consequently, as in previous editions, each chapter of *Criminal Justice in Action, The Core, Ninth Edition* includes a Careers in CJ feature in which a criminal justice practitioner presents a personal account of his or her occupation. These features also include a **Social Media Career Tip**, designed to help students succeed in today's difficult labor market by successfully navigating the opportunities and pitfalls of searching for employment online.

To this same end, each chapter of the Ninth Edition also includes a **new** feature entitled **Getting LinkedIn.** These items focus on a profession such as computer forensics, victim advocacy, or homeland security, providing students with information on how to best research the profession while visiting the popular business-oriented social networking website.

Further Changes to the Ninth Edition

Each chapter in the Ninth Edition begins with a new "ripped from the headlines" vignette that introduces the themes to be covered in the pages that follow. Furthermore, the text continues to reflect the ever-changing nature of our topic, with hundreds of new references to **research involving crime and criminal behavior** and **real-life examples describing actual crimes.** The Ninth Edition also includes dozens of **new features and figures,** as well as **discussions of every relevant United States Supreme Court decision** that has been handed down since the previous edition.

Three other extensive changes to the Ninth Edition involve topics crucial to the American criminal justice system:

- **Mental Illness.** We have significantly increased our coverage of the **challenges facing the criminal justice system involving the mentally ill.** Six chapters of *Criminal Justice in Action, The Core* now include in-depth discussions of this subject, covering a variety of issues such as the link between mental illness and offending and victimization, law enforcement strategies for managing mentally ill criminal suspects, and the impact of mentally ill inmates on American prisons and jails.
- **Public Trust in Law Enforcement.** A series of high-profile incidents in which law enforcement agents have either injured or killed unarmed civilians has led to **increased public scrutiny of police use of force.** We examine this controversial topic from the point of view of community members who feel they are unfairly targeted by police violence, and from the point of view of police officers who feel they are placed in a "no win" situation when it comes to use-of-force law and practice.
- **Privacy versus Security.** Chapter 14 of the Ninth Edition includes a new section that covers the **controversies surrounding the federal government's efforts to balance civil liberties and homeland security.** The section focuses on **complex issues of mass surveillance and privacy in the age of terrorism,** and discusses how far we, the people, should allow the government to stretch the Fourth Amendment when it comes to collecting our personal data.

Concentrated Critical Thinking

As with previous editions, the Ninth Edition of *Criminal Justice in Action, The Core* focuses on developing critical thinking. Almost every feature and photo caption in the textbook includes a critical thinking question, and students are provided with five additional such questions at the end of each chapter. Chapter-opening vignettes are followed by three critical analysis questions, which relate back to the vignette and introduce themes important to the upcoming chapter. Other critical-thinking tools in *Criminal Justice in Action, The Core, Ninth Edition,* include:

- **Learning Objectives.** At the beginning of each chapter, students are introduced to up to ten learning objectives (LOs) for that chapter. For example, in Chapter 10, "The Criminal Trial," Learning Objective 2 (LO2) asks students to "Explain what 'taking the Fifth' really means." The area of text that furnishes the information is marked with a square LO2 graphic, and, finally, the correct answer is found in the chapter-ending materials. This continuous active learning will greatly expand students' understanding of dozens of crucial criminal justice topics.
- **CJ Controversy.** Each chapter of the textbook includes one of these features, which start with a short summary of a controversial criminal justice topic, followed by general "for" and "against" arguments concerning that topic. Then, students are asked to go online and research a specific issue, event, or policy related to the controversy surrounding the topic. Finally, students have the opportunity to analyze the results of their research in a short writing assignment of at least two paragraphs. These features not only help students improve writing and critical thinking skills, but they also act as a review of important material in the chapter.

Chapter-by-Chapter Organization of the Text

This edition's fourteen chapters blend the principles of criminal justice with current research and high-interest examples of what is happening in the world of crime and crime prevention right now. What follows is a summary of each chapter, along with a description of some of the revisions to the Ninth Edition.

Part 1: The Criminal Justice System

Chapter 1 provides an introduction to the criminal justice system's three major institutions: law enforcement, the courts, and corrections. The chapter also answers conceptual questions such as "what is crime?" and "what are the values of the American criminal justice system?"

- Students are introduced to a number of **social justice issues** that will be revisited throughout the textbook, including **law enforcement's relationship with minority communities** in the United States, efforts to **help ex-inmates reintegrate into society**, and the problem of **wrongful convictions**.
- A **new** CJ Controversy feature ("Encryption and Terrorism") that addresses the balancing act between protecting personal information on the Internet and on devices such as smartphones, and the government's need to access such information to prevent and investigate terrorist attacks.

Chapter 2 furnishes students with an understanding of two areas fundamental to criminal justice: (1) the various methods of measuring crime, including the FBI's Uniform Crime Report and the U.S. Department of Justice's National Crime Victimization Survey, and (2) criminology, providing students with insight into why crime occurs. Then, in later chapters, they shift their attention toward combating it.

- A **new** Myth vs. Reality feature ("'Black on Black' Violence") explores several misconceptions concerning the intersections between race, offending, and victimization in the United States.
- A **new discussion** on **the rapidly evolving drug landscape** in this country, including a description of **widespread destruction caused by prescription drug and heroin abuse** and a **new** CJ Policy—Your Take feature asks students to consider a federal law **legalizing marijuana** throughout the United States.

Chapter 3 lays the foundation of criminal law. It addresses constitutional law, statutory law, and other sources of American criminal law before shifting its focus to the legal framework that allows the criminal justice system to determine and punish criminal guilt.

- A **new** chapter-opening vignette ("No Good Deed . . .") uses the example of Eddie Ray Routh, who was convicted of murdering "American Sniper" Chris Kyle, to highlight the difficulties of successfully offering a not-guilty-by-reason-of-insanity defense under American criminal law.
- The three **new** Ethics Challenges in this chapter confront the morality of criminal laws that promote the good of the community over the wishes of the individual, punish parents who negligently allow their children access to firearms, and allow federal law enforcement officers to trick suspects into raiding non-existent "stash houses" full of nonexistent weapons and illegal drugs.

Part 2: The Police and Law Enforcement

Chapter 4 acts as an introduction to law enforcement in the United States today. This chapter offers a detailed description of the country's numerous local, state, and federal law enforcement agencies and examines the responsibilities and duties that come with a career in law enforcement.

- A **new** Discretion in Action feature ("Handle with Care") asks students to put themselves in the shoes of two police officers who must decide what level of force to use against a mentally ill suspect who may or may not pose a threat to herself, themselves, and others.
- A new discussion of **"hard"- and "soft"-power strategies** being implemented by **local police departments to combat domestic terrorism**—the "hard" strategies focusing on **"hostile surveillance" and militaristic weaponry**, and the "soft" strategies relying on **community outreach**.

Chapter 5 puts students on the streets and gives them a gritty look at the many challenges of being a law enforcement officer. It starts with a discussion of the importance of discretion in law enforcement and then moves on to policing strategies and issues in modern policing, such as the "thin blue line," corruption, and the use of force.

- Throughout the chapter, the emergent issue of **police accountability** is given panoramic coverage, including a **new** chapter-opening vignette ("First Impressions") about the impact of two citizen cell phone videos on media coverage of a fatal police shooting in Texas, a **new** Discretion in Action feature ("Deadly Force") based on the real-life killing of twelve-year-old Tamir Rice by a police officer in Cleveland, and a **new** section entitled **"Issues of Race and Ethnicity,"** which covers topics such as how **police use of force** has impacted relations with **minority communities** in the United States and how the federal government uses **civil rights investigations** to combat misbehavior by local law enforcement agencies.
- A **new** discussion of **crisis intervention teams**, or partnerships with mental health professionals, used by a growing number of local police departments to improve local law enforcement's response to the challenges posed by mentally ill suspects.

Chapter 6 examines the sometimes uneasy relationship between law enforcement and the U.S. Constitution by explaining the rules of being a police officer. Particular emphasis is placed on the Fourth, Fifth, and Sixth Amendments, giving students an understanding of crucial concepts such as probable cause, reasonableness, and custodial interrogation.

- A **new** section on **cell phones and the Fourth Amendment** features discussions of the legality of law enforcement efforts to track these devices and the Supreme Court's recent decision that police officers need a warrant to search the content of a suspect's cell phone.
- A **new** section discusses the role that police interrogation tactics may play in the **troubling phenomenon of false confessions.**

Part 3: Criminal Courts

Chapter 7 takes a big-picture approach in describing the American court system, giving students an overview of the basic principles of our judicial system, the state and federal court systems, and the role of judges, prosecutors, and defense attorneys in the criminal justice system.

- The court system's ability to live up to societal expectations of truth and justice, a running theme of the third part of this textbook, is explored in the chapter's **new** chapter-opening vignette ("Minor Threat?") on the fate of Anthony Elonis, whose challenge of his conviction for posting violent rap lyrics on the Internet eventually reached the United States Supreme Court.
- A **new** discussion of the **community pressures faced by public prosecutors**, including an examination of State's Attorney Marilyn Mosby's decision to charge six Baltimore police officers following the death of Freddie Gray while in custody and a **new** CJ & Technology feature explaining the ramifications of American's glut of untested rape kits.

Chapter 8 provides students with a rundown of pretrial procedures and highlights the role that these procedures play in America's adversary system. Chapter materials also place the student in the courtroom and give her or him a comprehensive understanding of the steps in the criminal trial.

- To help students understand recent attempts to improve the effectiveness of **pretrial detention** strategies, a **new** figure lists the risk factors used by courts in certain Colorado jurisdictions to determine whether a defendant will "jump bail" before trial, along with a **new** Ethics Challenge that focuses on the ethical implications of America's "for-profit bail industry."
- Three **new** figures use excerpts from actual court records to give students a first-hand understanding of three crucial aspects of the criminal trial: jury selection, the opening statement, and the art of the cross-examination.

Chapter 9 links the many different punishment options for those who have been convicted of a crime with the theoretical justifications for those punishments. The chapter also examines punishment in the policy context, weighing the public's desire for ever-harsher criminal sanctions against the consequences of such governmental strategies.

- The subject of mandatory minimum sentencing arises several times in this chapter. First, a **new** chapter-opening vignette ("A Long Time Gone") introduces the growing national concern caused by such sentences for nonviolent offenders. Then, a **new** discussion of efforts to **repeal state mandatory minimum sentencing laws** shows how these laws have fallen into some disrepute.
- An **updated** overview of the declining use of the death penalty in the United States includes **new** discussions of problems surrounding lethal injection drugs and the Supreme Court's recent decision concerning capital punishment of the mentally ill.

Part 4: Corrections

Chapter 10 makes an important point, and one that is often overlooked in the larger discussion of the American corrections system: not all of those who are punished need to be placed behind bars. This chapter explores the community corrections options, from probation to parole to intermediate sanctions such as intensive supervision and home confinement.

- A **new** chapter-opening vignette ("Family Ties") compares two possible sentencing options—prison or probation—for a young woman who killed her cousin while driving drunk.
- Recognizing trends of innovative thinking among corrections officials, we include a **new** discussion of **risk assessment tools** and **"swift and certain"**

punishments designed to keep probationers from recidivating.

Chapter 11 focuses on prisons and jails. Record-high rates of incarceration have pushed these institutions to the forefront of the criminal justice system, and this chapter explores the various issues—such as overcrowding and the emergence of private prisons—that have resulted from the prison population boom.

- Continuing our focus on mentally ill offenders and the criminal justice system, we have **updated** our section on the **challenges facing jail administrators** because of **high rates of mental illness among inmates** to include a **new** figure describing Miami-Dade County's Criminal Mental Health Project.
- Three **new** Ethics Challenges ask students to comment on ethical issues surrounding low wages for inmate employment, health care in private prisons, and the practice of charging pretrial detainees for their meals behind bars.

Chapter 12 is another example of our efforts to get students "into the action" of the criminal justice system, putting them in the uncomfortable position of being behind bars. This chapter also answers the crucial question, "What happens when the inmate is released back into society?"

- As part of our panoramic examination of the roles of correctional officers in prisons and jails: a **new** Getting LinkedIn feature that highlights the profession, a **new** Discretion in Action feature ("Downing a Duck") that focuses on how inmates are sometimes able to manipulate correctional officers, and a **new** discussion of the recent Supreme Court decision that makes correctional officers more susceptible to civil rights violation lawsuits for excessive use of force against inmates.
- A **new** section entitled **"What Works in Reentry"** describes strategies developed by corrections officials to **help ex-convicts succeed following release from prison,** including reentry courts and various laws designed to aid offenders in the difficult task of finding post-incarceration employment.

Part 5: Special Issues

Chapter 13 examines the juvenile justice system, giving students a comprehensive description of the path taken by delinquents from first contact with police to trial and punishment. The chapter contains a strong criminological component as well, scrutinizing the various theories of why certain juveniles turn to delinquency and what steps society can take to stop them from doing so before it is "too late."

- A **new** CJ Policy—Your Take margin feature addresses whether juvenile sex offenders should be treated the same as adult sex offenders when it comes to lifelong legal constraints such as residency restrictions and inclusion on sex-offender registries.
- A **new** Discretion in Action feature ("Juvenile Drunk Driving") asks students to decide whether a seventeen-year-old who commits vehicular homicide should be charged as a juvenile or as an adult.

Chapter 14 concludes the text by taking an expanded look at four crucial criminal justice topics: (1) privacy in the age of terrorism, (2) cyber crime, (3) gun conrol, and (4) white-collar crime.

- Starting with a discussion of four decades' worth of crucial antiterrorism legislation, a **new** section entitled **"Security vs. Liberty"** gives students a comprehensive look at the current state of civil liberties in the context of homeland security. The section includes discussions of the constitutionality of governmental mass surveillance techniques and the use of Internet speech to ensnare potential "known wolf" domestic terrorists.
- A **new** CJ & Technology feature ("Hacking the 'Internet of Things'") examines the cyber crime–related risks that emerge when hundreds of everyday objects such as automobiles, refrigerators, and televisions are connected to the Internet via tiny, weakly protected computer chips.

Special Features

Supplementing the main text of *Criminal Justice in Action, The Core, Ninth Edition,* are more than one hundred eye-catching, instructive, and penetrating special features. These features, described below with examples, have been designed to enhance the student's understanding of a particular criminal justice issue.

Careers in CJ: As stated before, many students reading this book are planning a career in criminal justice. We have provided them with an insight into some of these careers by offering first-person accounts of what it is like to work as a criminal justice professional. Each Career in CJ feature also includes a **Social Media Career Tip** to help students succeed in today's competitive labor market for criminal justice professionals.

- In Chapter 13, Carl McCullough, a former professional football player, provides an inside look at his duties as a resident youth worker at a juvenile detention center in Hennepin County, Minnesota.

Mastering Concepts: Some criminal justice topics require additional explanation before they become crystal clear in the minds of students. This feature helps students to master many of the essential concepts in the textbook.

- In Chapter 6, this feature helps students understand the legal differences between a police stop and a police arrest.

Discretion in Action: This feature puts students in the position of a criminal justice actor in a hypothetical case or situation that is based on a real-life event. The facts of the case or situation are presented with alternative possible outcomes, and the student is asked to take the part of the criminal justice professional or lay participant and make a decision. Students can then consult Appendix B at the end of the text to learn what actually happened in the offered scenario.

- "The 'Sexting' Scandal" (Chapter 1), a **new** feature, requires students to play the role of a prosecutor who must decide whether to expend scarce resources by charging a large group of high school students with crimes related to child pornography for sharing inappropriate images of themselves with each other online.

CJ & Technology: Advances in technology are constantly transforming the face of criminal justice. In these features, which appear in nearly every chapter, students learn of one such emergent technology and are asked to critically evaluate its effects.

- This **new** feature in Chapter 3 describes how American criminal law is responding to the challenges posed by the increased civilian use of Unmanned Aerial Vehicles, or drones.

Comparative Criminal Justice: The world offers a dizzying array of different criminal customs and codes, many of which are in stark contrast to those accepted in the United States. This feature provides dramatic and sometimes perplexing examples of foreign criminal justice practices in order to give students a better understanding of our domestic ways.

- "The Great Firewall of China" (Chapter 14), an **updated** feature, describes China's efforts to limit and control the use of the Internet through criminal laws to an extent that is unimaginable to most Americans.

CJ Controversy: Each one of these features introduces students to a controversial topic related to the text of the chapter in which it appears. Following a short introduction, students are provided with arguments "for" and "against" a particular aspect of the topic, to give them a better idea of the basis for the controversy. Then, they are asked to research the topic online and write a short essay outlining their own opinions on the relevant controversy. Not only do these features highlight an interesting aspect of the criminal justice system, but they also help students improve their research, writing, and critical thinking skills.

- In Chapter 3's **new** feature, "Hate Crime Laws," students are asked to decide whether society benefits from laws that punish those who commit crimes motivated by bias more harshly than if no bias were present.

Landmark Cases: Rulings by the United States Supreme Court have shaped every area of the criminal justice system. In this feature, students learn about and analyze the most influential of these cases.

- In Chapter 12 "*Brown v. Plata*" (2011), the Supreme Court ordered California corrections officials to reduce the state's prison population after deciding that overcrowding was denying inmates satisfactory levels of health care.

Myth vs Reality: Nothing endures like a good myth. In this feature, we try to dispel some of the more enduring myths in the criminal justice system while at the same time asking students to think critically about their consequences.

- "Are Too Many Criminals Found Not Guilty by Reason of Insanity?" (Chapter 3) dispels the notion that criminal justice is "soft" because it lets scores of "crazy" defendants go free due to insanity.

Extensive Study Aids

Criminal Justice in Action, The Core, Ninth Edition, includes a number of pedagogical devices designed to complete the student's active learning experience. These devices include the following:

- Concise **chapter outlines** appear at the beginning of each chapter. The outlines give students an idea of what to expect in the pages ahead, as well as a quick source of review when needed.
- Dozens of **key terms** and a **running glossary** focus students' attention on major concepts and help them master the vocabulary of criminal justice. The chosen terms are boldfaced in the text, allowing students to notice their importance without breaking the flow of reading. On the same page that a key term is highlighted, a margin note provides a succinct definition of the term. For further reference, a glossary at the end of the text provides a full list of all the key terms and their definitions.
- Each chapter has at least four **figures,** which include graphs, charts, and other forms of colorful art that reinforce a point made in the text. This edition includes eleven new figures.
- Hundreds of **photographs** add to the overall readability and design of the text. Each photo has a caption, and most of these captions include a critical-thinking question dealing with the topic at hand. This edition includes nearly one hundred new photos.
- At the end of each chapter, students will find five **Questions for Critical Analysis.** These questions will help the student assess his or her understanding of the just-completed chapter, as well as develop critical-thinking skills.

Acknowledgments

Throughout the creation of the nine editions of this text, we have been aided by hundreds of experts in various criminal justice fields and by professors throughout the country, as well as by numerous students who have used the text. We sincerely thank all who participated on the revision of *Criminal Justice in Action, The Core.* We believe that the Ninth Edition is even more responsive to the needs of today's criminal justice instructors and students alike because we have taken into account the constructive comments and criticisms of our reviewers and the helpful suggestions of our survey respondents.

We continue to appreciate the extensive research efforts of Shawn G. Miller and the additional legal assistance of William Eric Hollowell. Product Manager Carolyn Henderson-Meier supplied crucial guidance to the project through her suggestions and recommendations. At the production end, we once again feel fortunate to have enjoyed the services of our content project manager, Ann Borman, who oversaw virtually all aspects of this book. Additionally, we wish to thank the designers of this new edition, tani hasegawa (interior) and Irene Morris (cover), who have created what we believe to be the most dazzling and student-friendly design of any text in the field. We are also thankful for the services of all those at Lachina who worked on the Ninth Edition, particularly Dane Torbeck. The eagle eyes of Sue Bradley and Beverly Peavler, who shared the duties of copyediting and proofreading, were invaluable.

A special word of thanks must also go to those responsible for creating the MindTap that accompanies *Criminal Justice in Action, The Core*, including content developer Jessica Alderman. We are also grateful to Jessica for ensuring the timely publication of supplements, along with content development services manager Joshua Taylor. A final thanks to all of the great people in marketing who helped to get the word out about the book, including marketing manager Mark Linton, who has been tireless in his attention to this project.

Any criminal justice text has to be considered a work in progress. We know that there are improvements that we can make. Therefore, write us with any suggestions that you may have.

L. K. G.
R. L. M.

Dedication

This book is dedicated to my good friend and colleague, Lawrence Walsh, of the Lexington, Kentucky Police Department. When I was a rookie, he taught me about policing. When I became a researcher, he taught me about the practical applications of knowledge. He is truly an inspiring professional in our field.

L.K.G.

For Lorraine,

Your positive outlook about life keeps you on top.

Stay there.

R.L.M.

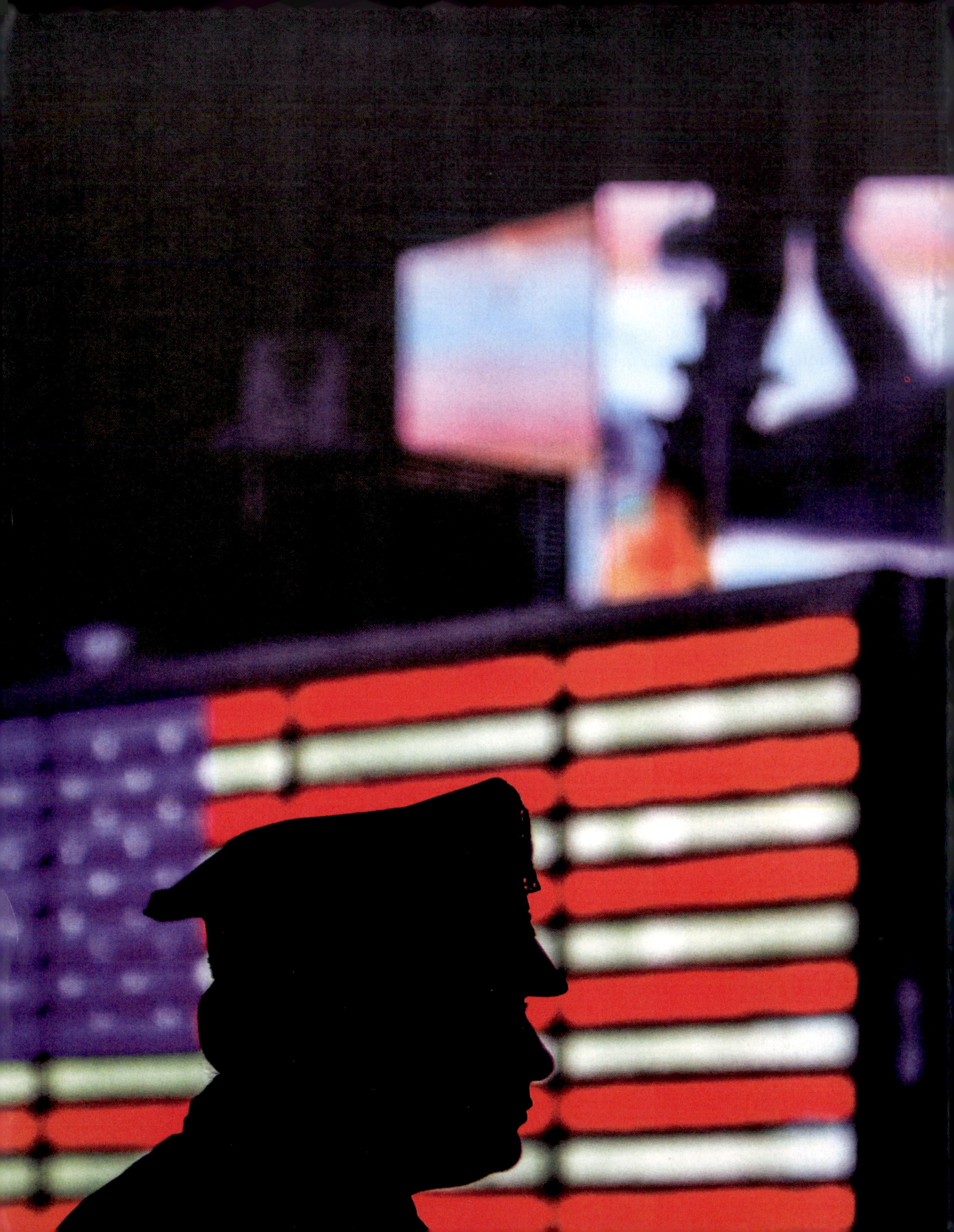

SAM HODGSON/*The New York Times*/Redux Pictures

1

Criminal Justice Today

Chapter Outline		Corresponding Learning Objectives
What Is Crime?	1	Describe the two most common models of how society determines which acts are criminal.
The Purpose of the Criminal Justice System	2	Explain two main purposes of the criminal justice system.
The Structure of the Criminal Justice System	3	Outline the three levels of law enforcement.
	4	List the essential elements of the corrections system.
Discretion and Ethics	5	Explain the difference between the formal and informal criminal justice processes.
	6	Define ethics, and describe the role that it plays in discretionary decision making.
Criminal Justice Today	7	Contrast the crime control and due process models.
	8	List the major issues in criminal justice today.

To target your study and review, look for these numbered Learning Objective icons throughout the chapter.

the Echo Chamber

leading up to his death, Elton Simpson hardly kept his support for the Islamic State, an extremist terrorist group operating out of the Middle East, a secret. In particular, Simpson's Twitter contacts included Mohammed Hassan, who used social media to promote the Islamic State (also called ISIS or ISIL) from a base in the African country of Somalia. On April 23, 2015, Hassan went on Twitter to condemn an upcoming cartoon contest in Garland, Texas, which was to feature drawings of the Prophet Mohammed, images that are considered taboo by many Muslims. Referring to a recent deadly attack on a French satirical newspaper that had printed the prophet's likeness, Hassan encouraged "our brothers in the #US to do their part."

Ten days later, Simpson, who had expressed online approval of Hassan's call to arms, and a partner were killed by law enforcement when they opened fire on the Garland cartoon contest with assault rifles. Before driving to the event, Simpson posted a message on Twitter using #texasattack as a hashtag. Even though the Islamic State took responsibility for the incident, U.S. authorities could not establish any direct contact between Simpson and the foreign organization. Rather, counterterrorism investigators believe that Simpson was an Internet enthusiast who got caught up in the "echo chamber" of recruitment propaganda on social media. "The ISIS guys are talking to these wannabes on Twitter all day long," said one expert. "It's like the devil is sitting on their shoulder."

The difficulty for America's counterterrorism infrastructure is determining which of "these wannabes" are merely spouting fantasies and which are planning actual violence. In fact, Simpson had been the subject of intermittent Federal Bureau of Investigation (FBI) surveillance for several months before the Garland event. FBI agents could not, however, find any hard evidence that he intended to make good on his various threats. With hundreds of suspects in the United States constantly expressing online sympathy for various extremist ideologies, authorities do not have the resources to keep them all under control. In the words of one senior law enforcement official, "There are so many like [Simpson] that you have to prioritize your investigations."

Ben Torres/Stringer/Getty Images

▲ Federal law enforcement agents work the crime scene after Elton Simpson and an accomplice opened fire on the Muhammad Art Exhibit and Cartoon Contest in Garland, Texas.

1. Would you be in favor of a federal law that allowed law enforcement authorities to arrest any person who expressed support for violent terrorism on social media? Why or why not?
2. What are the arguments for and against requiring that social media companies such as Twitter and Instagram monitor their users for possible terrorist activity and report any suspicious behavior to law enforcement?
3. Suppose that Jaylen, an American citizen, drives a friend to the airport so that the friend can travel to Syria and join the Islamic State in the Middle East. Has Jaylen committed a crime? Explain your answer.

What Is Crime?

Members of the public often wonder why terrorist sympathizers such as Elton Simpson are allowed to operate with impunity on the Internet. The answer is relatively straightforward: American criminal law does not prohibit individuals from making anti-American statements or expressing sympathy with extreme terrorist organizations. At the same time, our laws *do* prohibit individuals from making threats that pose a "clear and present danger" of harm to others.[1] So, in November 2015, federal authorities arrested Ohio hospital worker Terrence J. McNeil after he reposted a "kill list" on Tumblr that contained detailed personal information about one hundred U.S. military members earmarked for death by the Islamic State.

Had McNeil been content with making posts such as, "Somebody should park a car bomb in front of a church, school, or mall" on Facebook, he likely would have avoided arrest. By reposting the Islamic State's list of targeted military personnel with an exhortation to "kill them wherever you find them," McNeil crossed a legal line, and was charged with solicitation of a crime of violence.[2] As this example shows, a *crime* is not simply an act that seems dishonest or dangerous or particularly appalling. A **crime** is a wrong against society that is *proclaimed by law* and that, if committed under specific circumstances, is punishable by the criminal justice system.

crime An act that violates criminal law and is punishable by criminal sanctions.

consensus model A criminal justice model in which the majority of citizens in a society share the same values and beliefs. Criminal acts are acts that conflict with these values and beliefs and that are deemed harmful to society.

Determining Criminal Behavior

One problem with the definition of crime just provided is that it obscures the complex nature of societies. A society is not static—it evolves and changes, and its concept of criminality evolves and changes as well. On December 2, 2015, a married couple apparently radicalized by online extremist Islamic propaganda killed fourteen people and wounded twenty-one other victims in San Bernardino, California. Following this attack, some legal experts called for a loosening of the "clear and present danger" requirement. Eric Posner, a professor of law at the University of Chicago, even suggested that it should be a crime to access websites that "glorify, express support, or provide encouragement for" the Islamic State.[3]

Furthermore, different societies often have differing ideas of criminal behavior that reflect local customs and norms. Several years ago, for example, a court in the Southeast Asian country of Myanmar sentenced three men to two years in prison for posting an image of the Buddha wearing headphones. It is highly unlikely that American courts, bound by American traditions of free speech, would allow criminal sanctions for acts that "offend the majority religion." (See the feature *Comparative Criminal Justice—No Hate Allowed* to learn about another foreign custom that runs counter to our legal traditions.)

To more fully understand the concept of crime, it will help to examine the two most common models of how society "decides" which acts are criminal: the consensus model and the conflict model.

Learning Objective

1 Describe the two most common models of how society determines which acts are criminal.

The Consensus Model

The term *consensus* refers to general agreement among the majority of any particular group. Thus, the **consensus model** rests on the assumption that as people gather together to form a society, its members will naturally come to a basic agreement with regard to shared norms and values. Those individuals whose actions deviate from the established norms and values are considered to pose a threat to the well-being of society as a whole and must be sanctioned (punished). The society passes laws to control and prevent unacceptable behavior, thereby setting the boundaries for acceptable behavior within the group.[4]

Comparative Criminal Justice

Central Intelligence Agency

No Hate Allowed

After reading an online article about sexual violence against women in Egypt, Swedish politician Michael Hess felt compelled to offer his opinion on the subject. "When are you journalists going to realize that it is deeply ingrained in Islamic culture to rape and mistreat those women who do not abide by the teachings of Islam?" Hess wrote. He then claimed that higher-than-normal rates of sexual assault in certain areas of Sweden were caused by the presence of Islamic immigrants.

In the United States, with its long tradition of freedom of expression, such comments would not be subject to punishment. In Sweden, however, criminal law prohibits any speech that threatens or expresses disrespect for groups or individuals based on ethnicity, race, nationality, creed, or sexual orientation. Consequently, Hess was convicted of "hate speech" and fined about $5,000.

Swedish law protects a citizen's right to make "hateful" statements in private. Such speech only becomes a crime when it is expressed publicly or, as in Hess's case, on the Internet. In recent years, Swedish courts have fined a woman $560 for yelling "Death to Jews" in a crowd and sentenced an artist to six months behind bars for exhibiting a poster that showed three African men with nooses around their necks.

For Critical Analysis

Besides Sweden, Western democracies such as Canada, Britain, Denmark, and Germany have criminal laws that punish hate speech. Do you think that the United States should criminalize public hate speech that "threatens" or "disrespects" members of minority groups? What would be some of the consequences—both intended and unintended—of such a law?

The consensus model, to a certain extent, assumes that a diverse group of people can have similar **morals**. In other words, they share an ideal of what is "right" and "wrong." Consequently, as public attitudes toward morality change, so do laws. In seventeenth-century America, a person found guilty of *adultery* (having sexual relations with someone other than one's spouse) could expect to be publicly whipped, branded, or even executed. Furthermore, a century ago, one could walk into a pharmacy and purchase heroin. Today, social attitudes have shifted to consider adultery a personal issue, beyond the reach of the state, and to consider the sale of heroin a criminal act.

The Conflict Model Some people reject the consensus model on the ground that moral attitudes are not constant or even consistent. In large, democratic societies such as the United States, different groups of citizens have widely varying opinions on controversial issues of morality and criminality such as abortion, the war on drugs, immigration, and assisted suicide. These groups and their elected representatives are constantly coming into conflict with one another. According to the **conflict model**, then, the most politically powerful segments of society—based on class, income, age, and race—have the most influence on criminal laws and are therefore able to impose their values on the rest of the community.

Consequently, what is deemed criminal activity is determined by whichever group happens to be holding power at any given time. Because certain groups do not have access to political power, their interests may not be served by the criminal justice system. For instance, nearly eight of every ten elected prosecutors in the United States are white men, while only five percent of these posts are held by members of minority groups.[5] Given the authority of prosecutors to decide which charges will be brought against defendants, this lack of diversity can contribute to mistrust of law enforcement in many minority communities.

morals Principles of right and wrong behavior, as practiced by individuals or by society.

conflict model A criminal justice model in which the content of criminal law is determined by the groups that hold economic, political, and social power in a community.

An Integrated Definition of Crime

Considering both the consensus and conflict models, we can construct a definition of crime that will be useful throughout this textbook. For our purposes, crime is an action or activity that is:

1. Punishable under criminal law, as determined by the majority or, in some instances, by a powerful minority.
2. Considered an *offense against society as a whole* and prosecuted by public officials, not by victims and their relatives or friends.
3. Punishable by sanctions based on laws that bring about the loss of personal freedom or life.

▲ Lawmakers are scrambling to devise regulations for the hoverboard, a relatively new form of personal transportation that has become popular, particularly among young people. **What are the arguments for banning the use of such devices on city sidewalks and school hallways? Why might using a hoverboard be considered deviant behavior?** Timothy A. Clary/AFP/Getty Images

At this point, it is important to understand the difference between crime and **deviance**, or behavior that does not conform to the norms of a given community or society. Deviance is a subjective concept. For example, some segments of society may think that smoking marijuana or killing animals for clothing and food is deviant behavior. Deviant acts become crimes only when society as a whole, through its legislatures, determines that those acts should be punished—as is the situation today in the United States with using certain drugs but not with eating meat. Furthermore, not all crimes are considered particularly deviant—little social disapprobation is attached to those who fail to follow the letter of parking laws. In essence, criminal law reflects those acts that we, as a society, agree are so unacceptable that steps must be taken to prevent them from occurring.

Ethics Challenge

In this section, we used the example of killing animals for clothing and food as behavior that, although deviant to some, is generally accepted by the majority. What is a widespread activity that, although considered "normal" in modern American society, goes against your personal values or morals? What is the likelihood that this activity eventually will become illegal in the United States?

The Purpose of the Criminal Justice System

Defining which actions are to be labeled "crimes" is only the first step in safeguarding society from criminal behavior. Institutions must be created to apprehend alleged wrongdoers, to determine whether these persons have indeed committed crimes, and to punish those who are found guilty according to society's wishes. These institutions combine to form the **criminal justice system**. As we begin our examination of the American criminal justice system in this introductory chapter, it is important to have an idea of its purpose.

deviance Behavior that is considered to go against the norms established by society.

criminal justice system The interlocking network of law enforcement agencies, courts, and corrections institutions designed to enforce criminal laws and protect society from criminal behavior.

Careers in CJ

FASTFACTS

Youth intervention specialist/ gang investigator

Job description:

- Conducts assessments and refers at-risk youth to appropriate activities, programs, or agencies.
- Serves as a liaison between the police department, schools, other agencies, and the community regarding gang and other youth-related matters.

What kind of training is required?

- A bachelor's degree in counseling, criminal justice, or other social science–related field. Bilingual (English/ Spanish) skills are desired.

Annual salary range?

- $60,000–$80,000

F. W. Gill
Gang Investigator

Courtesy F. W. Gill

The problem, for most of these kids, is that nobody cares. Their parents don't, or can't, get involved in their children's lives. (How many times have I heard parents deny that their son or daughter is a gang banger, even though it's obvious?) Teachers are in the business of teaching and don't, or can't, take the time to get to know their most troubled students. So, when I'm dealing with gang members, the first thing I do is listen. I don't lecture them, I don't tell them that they are throwing away their lives. I just listen. You'd be amazed how effective this can be—these kids, who look so tough on the outside, just want an adult to care.

Not that there is any magic formula for convincing a gang member to go straight. It is very difficult to get someone to change his or her lifestyle. If they don't want to change—really want to change—then nothing I can say or do is going to make much of a difference. Unfortunately, there are many lost causes. I've even had a couple of cases in which a juvenile was afraid to leave the gang because his father was a gang member, and he insisted that the boy stay in the gang. I have had some success in convincing gang members to turn their lives around by joining the military. The military provides discipline and a new outlook on life, things that these kids badly need. The way I look at it, in some cases, war is the best shot these kids have at saving their own lives.

SOCIAL MEDIA CAREER TIP When you are posting on Facebook, assume that your post will be published in your local newspaper and read by a potential employer. So, if you think the post might reflect poorly on you as a potential employee, keep it offline.

Learning Objective 2

Explain two main purposes of the criminal justice system.

Maintaining Justice

As its name implies, the explicit goal of the criminal justice system is to provide *justice* to all members of society. Because **justice** is a difficult concept to define, this goal can be challenging, if not impossible, to meet. Broadly stated, justice means that all individuals are equal before the law and that they are free from arbitrary arrest or seizure as defined by the law. In other words, the idea of justice is linked with the idea of fairness. Above all, we want our laws and the means by which they are carried out to be fair.

Justice and fairness are subjective terms, which is to say that people may have different concepts of what is just and fair. If a woman who has been beaten by her husband retaliates by killing him, what is her just punishment? Reasonable persons could disagree, with some thinking that the homicide was justified and that she should be treated leniently. Others might insist that she should not have taken the law into her own hands. Police officers, judges, prosecutors, prison administrators, and other employees of the criminal justice system must decide what is "fair." Sometimes, their course of action is obvious, but often, as we shall see, it is not.

justice The quality of fairness that must exist in the processes designed to determine whether individuals are guilty of criminal wrongdoing.

Protecting Society

Within the broad mandate of "maintaining justice," Megan Kurlychek of the University at Albany, New York, has identified four specific goals of our criminal justice system:

1. To protect society from potential future crimes of the most dangerous or "risky" offenders.
2. To determine when an offense has been committed and provide the appropriate punishment for that offense.
3. To rehabilitate those offenders who have been punished so that it is safe to return them to the community.
4. To support crime victims and, to the extent possible, return them to their pre-crime status.[6]

drug Any substance that modifies biological, psychological, or social behavior. In particular, an illegal substance with those properties.

psychoactive drugs Chemicals that affect the brain, causing changes in emotions, perceptions, and behavior.

Again, though these goals may seem straightforward, they are fraught with challenges. Throughout this textbook, we will be discussing the role that the criminal justice system plays in controlling the use of *illegal drugs* in the United States. The broadest possible definition of a **drug**, which includes alcohol, is any substance that modifies biological, psychological, or social behavior. In the context of criminal law, the primary focus is on **psychoactive drugs** such as cocaine and heroin, which affect the brain and alter consciousness or perception.

Recently, our society has significantly changed its attitude toward one psychoactive drug in particular: marijuana. Although marijuana production and use is still illegal under federal law, state legislatures and voters across the nation have taken steps to lessen criminal punishments associated with the drug. As Figure 1.1 shows, thirty states now allow the use of marijuana or THC—an active ingredient in marijuana—for medicinal purposes. The drug has also been *decriminalized* in sixteen states, meaning that its use is treated as an infraction similar to a traffic violation rather than as a crime. Finally, in 2014, Alaska, Oregon, and Washington, D.C., joined Colorado and Washington State by *legalizing* small amounts of marijuana sale and possession, a trend that is expected to continue in the near future.

Proponents of this trend contend that society benefits when the criminal justice system is no longer required to expend scarce resources on arresting, trying, and incarcerating nonviolent marijuana users. Opponents, however, point to the negative consequences of liberalized marijuana laws. These include a dramatic increase in the number of Americans using the drug, which has led to a concurrent rise in problems such as marijuana addiction and driving under the influence of the drug.[7] Both Colorado and Washington State reported a surge in marijuana-related calls to state poison control centers in the first year of legalization.[8] Thus, the question of whether permissive marijuana laws benefit or harm society is, like so many questions relating to criminal justice, complex and difficult to answer.

Figure 1.1 Marijuana and Criminal Law

As this map shows, at the beginning of 2016 most states—representing about three-fourths of the population of the United States—allow for the use of marijuana under certain circumstances. Remember that *any* use of the drug is outlawed under federal law.

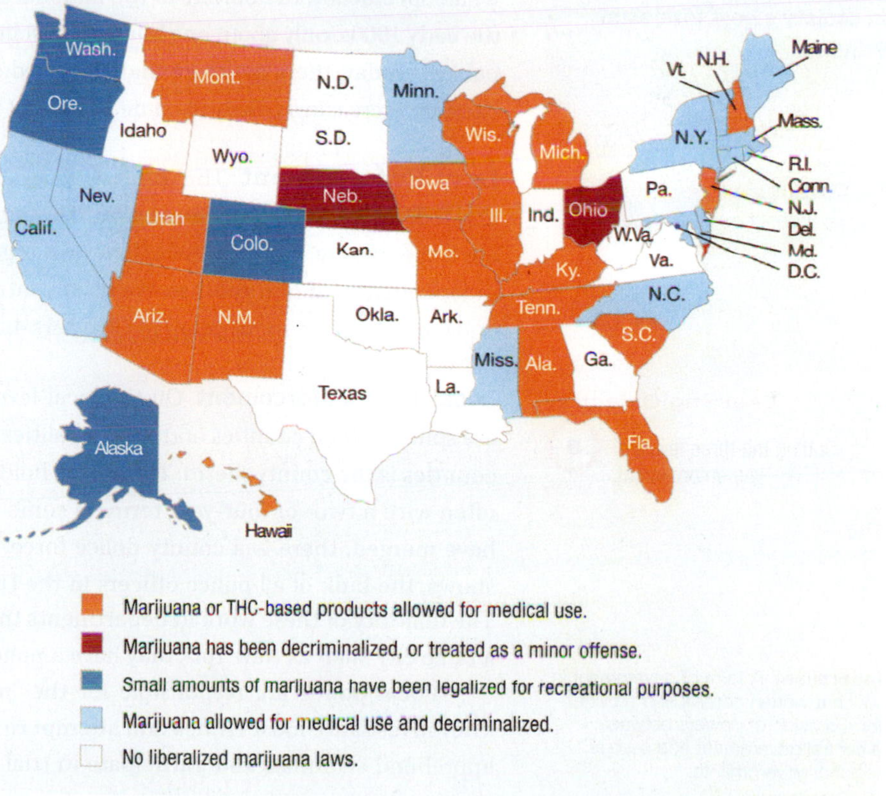
Wash.
Ore.
Calif.
Idaho
Nev.
Mont.
Wyo.
Utah
Colo.
Ariz.
N.M.
N.D.
S.D.
Neb.
Kan.
Okla.
Texas
Minn.
Iowa
Mo.
Ark.
La.
Wis.
Ill.
Mich.
Ind.
Ohio
Ky.
Tenn.
Miss.
Ala.
Ga.
Fla.
S.C.
N.C.
Va.
W.Va.
Pa.
N.Y.
Vt.
N.H.
Maine
Mass.
R.I.
Conn.
N.J.
Del.
Md.
D.C.
Alaska
Hawaii
Marijuana or THC-based products allowed for medical use.
Marijuana has been decriminalized, or treated as a minor offense.
Small amounts of marijuana have been legalized for recreational purposes.
Marijuana allowed for medical use and decriminalized.
No liberalized marijuana laws.

The Structure of the Criminal Justice System

Society places the burden of maintaining justice and protecting our communities on those who work for the three main institutions of the criminal justice system: law enforcement, the courts, and corrections. In this section, we take an introductory look at these institutions and their role in the criminal justice system as a whole.

The Importance of Federalism

To understand the structure of the criminal justice system, you must understand the concept of **federalism**, which means that government powers are shared by the national (federal) government and the states. The framers of the U.S. Constitution, fearful of tyranny and a too-powerful central government, chose the system of federalism as a compromise.

The appeal of federalism was that it established a strong national government capable of handling large-scale problems while allowing for state powers and local traditions. For example, in 2015, California became the fifth state—after Montana, Oregon, Vermont, and Washington—to legalize physician-assisted suicide for certain terminally ill patients. About a decade ago, the federal government challenged the decision made by voters in Oregon and Washington to allow the practice. The United States Supreme Court sided with the states, ruling that the principle of federalism supported their freedom to differ from the majority viewpoint in this instance.[9] (See this chapter's *CJ Policy—Your Take* feature to express your own opinion of this highly controversial topic.)

CJ Policy—Your Take

Oregon's **Death with Dignity Act** permits physicians to prescribe lethal drugs to competent, adult patients who have been diagnosed with a terminal illness and want to end their lives. In most other states, if a doctor takes such a step on behalf of a patient, that doctor commits a crime. **Which approach do you think is in society's best interests? Why?**

The Constitution gave the national government certain express powers, such as the power to coin money, raise an army, and regulate interstate commerce. All other powers were left to the states, including police power, which allows the states to enact whatever laws are necessary to protect the health, morals, safety, and welfare of their citizens. As the American criminal justice system has evolved, the ideals of federalism have ebbed somewhat. Specifically, the powers of the national government have expanded significantly. In the early 1900s, only about one hundred specific activities were illegal under federal criminal law. Today, there are more than 4,500 federal criminal statutes, meaning that Americans are increasingly likely to come in contact with the federal criminal justice system.[10]

Law Enforcement

The ideals of federalism can be clearly seen in the local, state, and federal levels of law enforcement. Though agencies from the different levels cooperate if the need arises, they have their own organizational structures and tend to operate independently of one another. We briefly introduce each level of law enforcement here and cover them in more detail in Chapters 4, 5, and 6.

Learning Objective 3

Outline the three levels of law enforcement.

Local Law Enforcement

On the local level, the duties of law enforcement agencies are split between counties and municipalities. The chief law enforcement officer of most counties is the county sheriff. Those who hold the position of sheriff are typically elected, often with a two- or four-year term. In some areas, where city and county governments have merged, there is a county police force, headed by a chief of police. As Figure 1.2 shows, the bulk of all police officers in the United States are employed on a local level. The majority of these work in departments that consist of fewer than 10 officers, though a large city such as New York may have a police force of about 34,500.

Local police are responsible for the "nuts and bolts" of law enforcement work. They investigate most crimes and attempt to deter crime through patrol activities. They apprehend criminals and participate in trial proceedings, if necessary. Local police are

federalism A form of government in which a written constitution provides for a division of powers between a central government and several regional governments.

Figure 1.2 Local, State, and Federal Employees in Our Criminal Justice System

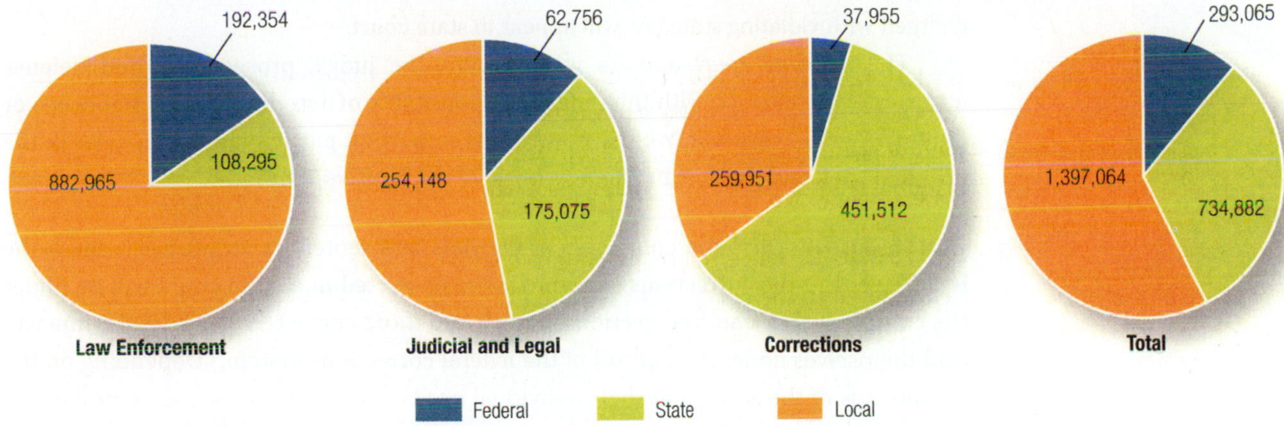
192,354
108,295
882,965
Law Enforcement
62,756
254,148
175,075
Judicial and Legal
37,955
259,951
451,512
Corrections
293,065
1,397,064
734,882
Total
Federal
State
Local

Source: Bureau of Justice Statistics, *Justice Expenditure and Employment Extracts, 2012 - Preliminary* (Washington, D.C.: U.S. Department of Justice, July 2015), Table 2.

also charged with "keeping the peace," a broad set of duties that includes crowd and traffic control and the resolution of minor conflicts between citizens. In many areas, local police have the added obligation of providing social services such as dealing with domestic violence and child abuse.

State Law Enforcement Hawaii is the only state that does not have a state law enforcement agency. Generally, there are two types of state law enforcement agencies: those designated simply as "state police" and those designated as "highway patrols." State highway patrols concern themselves mainly with infractions on public highways and freeways. Other state law enforcers include fire marshals, who investigate suspicious fires and educate the public on fire prevention; and fish, game, and watercraft wardens, who police a state's natural resources and often oversee its firearms laws. Some states also have alcoholic beverage control officers, as well as agents who investigate welfare and food stamp fraud.

Federal Law Enforcement The enactment of new national anti-terrorism, gun, drug, and violent crime laws over the past forty years has led to an expansion in the size and scope of the federal government's participation in the criminal justice system. The Department of Homeland Security, which we will examine in detail in Chapter 4, combines the police powers of twenty-four federal agencies to protect the United States from terrorist attacks. Other federal agencies with police powers include the Federal Bureau of Investigation (FBI), the Drug Enforcement Administration (DEA), the U.S. Secret Service, and the Bureau of Alcohol, Tobacco, Firearms and Explosives (ATF). In fact, almost every federal agency, including the postal and forest services, has some kind of police power.

Federal law enforcement agencies operate throughout the United States and often work in cooperation with their local and state counterparts. There can be tension between the different branches of law enforcement, however, when state criminal law and federal criminal law are incompatible. For example, even though states such as Alaska, Colorado, Oregon, and Washington have legalized the sale and possession of small amounts of marijuana, the drug is still illegal under federal law. Consequently, federal officers are authorized to make marijuana arrests in those states, regardless of any changes to the states' criminal codes.

The Courts The United States has a *dual court system*, which means that we have two independent judicial systems, one at the federal level and one at the state level. In practice, this translates into fifty-two different court systems: one federal court system and fifty different state court systems, plus that of the District of Columbia. In general, defendants charged with violating federal criminal law will face trial in federal court, while those charged with violating state law will appear in state court.

The *criminal court* and its work group—the judge, prosecutors, and defense attorneys—are charged with the weighty responsibility of determining the innocence or guilt of criminal suspects. We will cover these important participants, their roles in the criminal trial, and the court system as a whole in Chapters 7, 8, and 9.

Corrections Once the court system convicts and sentences an offender, she or he is delegated to the corrections system. (Those convicted in a state court will be under the control of that state's corrections system, and those convicted of a federal crime will find themselves under the control of the federal corrections system.) Depending on the seriousness of the crime and their individual needs, offenders are placed on probation, incarcerated, or transferred to community-based correctional facilities.

Learning Objective

List the essential elements of the corrections system. **4**

- *Probation,* the most common correctional treatment, allows the offender to return to the community and remain under the supervision of an agent of the court known as a probation officer. While on probation, the offender must follow certain rules of conduct. When probationers fail to follow these rules, they may be incarcerated.
- If the offender's sentence includes a period of *incarceration,* he or she will be remanded to a correctional facility for a certain amount of time. *Jails* hold those convicted of minor crimes with relatively short sentences, as well as those awaiting trial or involved in certain court proceedings. *Prisons* house those convicted of more serious crimes with longer sentences. Generally speaking, counties and municipalities administer jails, while prisons are the domain of federal and state governments.
- *Community-based corrections* have increased in popularity as jails and prisons have been plagued with problems of funding and overcrowding. Community-based correctional facilities include halfway houses, residential centers, and work-release centers. They operate on the assumption that all convicts do not need, and are not benefited by, incarceration in jail or prison.

▲ America's state and federal prisons hold just over 1.5 million inmates, while, on any given day, about 740,000 inmates are locked up in the nation's jails. **What are the basic differences between prisons and jails?** View Apart/ Shutterstock.com

The majority of those inmates released from incarceration are not finished with the corrections system. The most frequent type of release from a jail or prison is *parole,* in which an inmate, after serving part of his or her sentence in a correctional facility, is allowed to serve the rest of the term in the community. Like someone on probation, a parolee must conform to certain conditions of freedom, with the same consequences if these conditions are not followed. Issues of probation, incarceration, community-based corrections, and parole will be covered in Chapters 10, 11, and 12.

The Criminal Justice Process

In its 1967 report, the President's Commission on Law Enforcement and Administration of Justice asserted that the criminal justice system is not a hodgepodge of random actions. It is rather a continuum—an orderly progression of events—some of which, like arrest and trial, are highly visible and some of which, though of great importance, occur out of public view.[11]

The commission's assertion that the criminal justice system is a "continuum" is one that many observers would challenge.[12] Some liken the criminal justice system to a sports team, which is the sum of an indeterminable number of decisions, relationships, conflicts, and adjustments.[13] Such a volatile mix is not what we generally associate with a "system." For most, the word **system** indicates a certain degree of order and discipline. That we refer to our law enforcement agencies, courts, and correctional facilities as part of a "system" may reflect our hopes rather than reality. Still, it will be helpful to familiarize yourself with the basic steps of the *criminal justice process,* or the procedures through which the criminal justice system meets the expectations of society. These basic steps are provided in Figure 1.3.

system A set of interacting parts that, when functioning properly, achieve a desired result.

Figure 1.3 The Criminal Justice Process

This diagram provides a simplified overview of the basic steps of the criminal justice process, from criminal act to release from incarceration. Below each step, you will find the chapter of this textbook in which the event is covered.

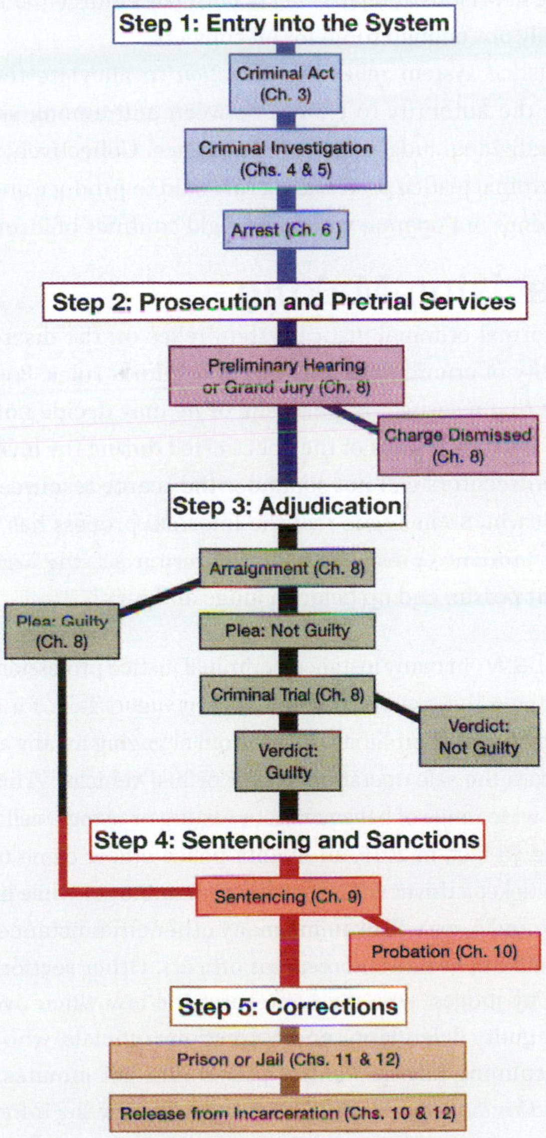

Step 1: Entry into the System
Criminal Act (Ch. 3)
Criminal Investigation (Chs. 4 & 5)
Arrest (Ch. 6)
Step 2: Prosecution and Pretrial Services
Preliminary Hearing or Grand Jury (Ch. 8)
Charge Dismissed (Ch. 8)
Step 3: Adjudication
Arraignment (Ch. 8)
Plea: Guilty (Ch. 8)
Plea: Not Guilty
Criminal Trial (Ch. 8)
Verdict: Not Guilty
Verdict: Guilty
Step 4: Sentencing and Sanctions
Sentencing (Ch. 9)
Probation (Ch. 10)
Step 5: Corrections
Prison or Jail (Chs. 11 & 12)
Release from Incarceration (Chs. 10 & 12)

In his classic study of the criminal justice system, Herbert Packer, a professor at Stanford University, compared the ideal criminal justice process to an assembly line "down which moves an endless stream of cases, never stopping."[14] In Packer's image of assembly-line justice, each step of the **formal criminal justice process** involves a series of "routinized operations" with the end goal of getting the criminal defendant from point A (his or her arrest by law enforcement) to point B (the criminal trial) to point C (if guilty, her or his punishment).[15] As Packer himself was wont to point out, the daily operations of criminal justice rarely operate so smoothly. In this textbook, the criminal justice process will be examined as the end product of many different decisions made by many different criminal justice professionals in law enforcement, the courts, and corrections.

Discretion and Ethics

Practically, the formal criminal justice process suffers from a serious drawback: it is unrealistic. Law enforcement agencies do not have the staff or funds to investigate *every* crime, so they must decide where to direct their limited resources. Increasing caseloads and a limited amount of time in which to dispose of them constrict many of our nation's courts. Overcrowding in prisons and jails affects both law enforcement agencies and the courts—there is simply not enough room for all convicts.

The criminal justice system relies on *discretion* to alleviate these pressures. By **discretion**, we mean the authority to choose between and among alternative courses of action, based on individual judgment and conscience. Collectively, the discretionary decisions made by criminal justice professionals are said to produce an **informal criminal justice process** that does not operate within the rigid confines of formal rules and laws.

Informal Decision Making

By its nature, the informal criminal justice system relies on the discretion of individuals to offset the rigidity of criminal statutes and procedural rules. For example, even if a prosecutor believes that a suspect is guilty, she or he may decide not to bring charges against the suspect if the case is weak or the police erred during the investigative process. In many instances, prosecutors will not squander the scarce resource of court time on a case they might not win. Some argue that the informal process has made our system more just. Given the immense pressure of limited resources, the argument goes, only rarely will an innocent person end up before a judge and jury.[16]

Interpreting the Law In many instances, criminal justice professionals must use their discretion to interpret laws that are overly broad or even vague. Take, for example, Georgia's distracted-driving statute, which prohibits drivers from engaging in "any actions which shall distract such driver from the safe operation of [her or his] vehicle."[17] This statute could be interpreted to cover a wide range of behavior, from texting or using a cell phone to listening to music while driving. In fact, in 2015, an Atlanta police officer came under criticism for using his discretion to ticket a driver who was eating a hamburger while behind the wheel.[18]

In Chapters 4, 5, and 6, we will examine many other circumstances that call for discretionary decision making by law enforcement officers. Other sections of the textbook will cover discretion by judges, who must interpret the law when overseeing criminal trials and sentencing guilty defendants, and corrections officials, who have a great deal of discretion in determining how to control prison and jail inmates. (See the feature *Discretion in Action—The "Sexting" Scandal* for insight on how the informal criminal justice process applies to a distinct form of child pornography.)

formal criminal justice process The model of the criminal justice process in which participants follow formal rules to create a smoothly functioning disposition of cases from arrest to punishment.

discretion The ability of individuals in the criminal justice system to make operational decisions based on personal judgment instead of formal rules or official information.

informal criminal justice process A model of the criminal justice system that recognizes the informal authority exercised by individuals at each step of the criminal justice process.

Discretion in ACTION

The "Sexting" Scandal

Rachel Donahue/Shutterstock.com

Learning Objective

5 Explain the difference between the formal and informal criminal justice processes.

The Situation The first hint of a serious problem came from an anonymous tip on the high school's Safe2Tell hotline. According to the tipster, numerous students were using a photo vault app to share inappropriate images of each other. Following a lengthy investigation by school officials and local law enforcement, the full extent of the "sexting" activity was revealed: more than one hundred students, both male and female, had contributed photos of themselves posing nude or in their underwear. As far the investigators could determine, none of these images had been posted on the Internet or shown to adults, and no coercion or bullying was involved.

The Law Under state law, any person who takes, receives, or shares a photo of a "naked body part" of someone under the age of eighteen has committed a Class C felony child pornography offense. Under the law, the fact that such activity is consensual is irrelevant. A conviction for a Class C felony is punishable by four to twelve years in a state prison and a fine of up to $750,000.

What Would You Do? You are the prosecutor responsible for deciding the fate of the students involved in this "sexting" scandal. With nearly unlimited discretion, you have several choices: (1) you can charge the students with committing crimes involving child pornography; (2) you can require that they undergo counseling; or (3) you can do nothing, relying on the students' parents to "straighten them out." Note that any student convicted of child pornography charges will be required to register as a sex offender, making it difficult for her or him to find or keep a job and secure affordable housing in the future. How would you use your discretion in this situation?

To see how a prosecutor in Cañon City, Colorado, reacted in similar circumstances, go to Example 1.1 in Appendix B.

The Pitfalls of Discretion Unfortunately, the informal criminal justice system does not always benefit from measured, rational decision making. Individual judgment can be tainted by personal bias, erroneous or irrational thinking, and plain ill will. When this occurs, discretion becomes "the power to *get away* with alternative decisions [emphasis added]."[19] Indeed, many of the rules of the formal criminal justice process are designed to keep its employees from substituting their own judgment for that of the general public, as expressed by the law.

Recently, federal investigators found that law enforcement officers in Ferguson, Missouri, were disproportionately detaining African Americans for offenses that hinge on police discretion. For instance, ninety-five percent of all arrests in that city for disturbing the peace and jaywalking (illegally crossing the street) involved black residents.[20] In Chapter 6, you will learn more about *racial profiling*, which is the police practice of improperly targeting members of minority groups based on personal characteristics such as race or ethnicity. Furthermore, the late associate Supreme Court justice Antonin Scalia (1936–2016) criticized discretion in the courts for its tendency to cause discriminatory and disparate criminal sentences, a subject we will discuss in Chapter 9. According to Scalia, the need for fairness and certainty in the criminal justice system outweighs the practical benefits of widespread and unpredictable discretionary decision making.[21]

Ethics and Justice

How can we reconcile the need for some sort of discretion in criminal justice with the ever-present potential for abuse? Part of the answer lies in our initial definition of discretion, which mentions not only individual judgment but also *conscience*. Ideally, actors in the criminal justice system will make moral choices about what is right and wrong based on the norms that have been established by society. In other words, they will behave *ethically*.

Ethics in criminal justice is closely related to the concept of justice. Because criminal justice professionals are representatives of the state, they have the power to determine whether the state is treating its citizens fairly. If some law enforcement officers in fact make the decision to issue a jaywalking citation on the basis of the offender's race, then they are not only acting unethically but also unjustly.

Ethics and the Law The line between ethics and justice is often difficult to discern, as ethical standards are usually not written into criminal statutes. Consequently, individuals must often "fill in" the ethical blanks. To make this point, ethics expert John Kleinig uses the real-life example of a police officer who refused to arrest a homeless person for sleeping in a private parking garage. A local ordinance clearly prohibited such behavior. The officer, however, felt it would be unethical to arrest a homeless person under those circumstances unless he or she was acting in a disorderly manner. The officer's supervisors were unsympathetic to this ethical stance, and he was suspended from duty without pay.[22]

Learning Objective

6 Define ethics, and describe the role that it plays in discretionary decision making.

Ethics and Critical Thinking Did the police officer in the preceding example behave ethically by inserting his own beliefs into the letter of the criminal law? Would an officer who arrested peaceful homeless trespassers be acting unethically? In some cases, the ethical decision will be *intuitive,* reflecting an automatic response determined by a person's background and experiences. In other cases, however, intuition is not enough. *Critical thinking* is needed for an ethical response. Throughout this textbook, we will use the principle of critical thinking—which involves developing analytical skills and reasoning—to address the many ethical challenges inherent in the criminal justice system.

EthicsChallenge

Refer back to this section's discussion of the police officer who refused to arrest the nonviolent homeless person for ethical reasons. Did the officer act properly in this situation, or should he have carried out the law regardless of his personal beliefs? Explain your answer.

Criminal Justice Today

Learning Objective

7 Contrast the crime control and due process models.

In describing the general direction of the criminal justice system as a whole, many observers point to two models introduced by Professor Herbert Packer: the *crime control model* and the *due process model.*[23] The underlying value of the **crime control model** is that the most important function of the criminal justice process is to punish and repress criminal conduct. The system must be quick and efficient, placing as few restrictions as possible on the ability of law enforcement officers to make discretionary decisions in apprehending criminals.

Although not in direct conflict with crime control, the underlying values of the **due process model** focus more on protecting the rights of the accused through formal, legal restraints on the police, courts, and corrections. That is, the due process model relies on the courts to make it more difficult to prove guilt. It rests on the belief that it is more desirable for society that ninety-nine guilty suspects go free than that a single innocent person be condemned.[24] (This chapter's *Mastering Concepts* feature provides a further comparison of the two models.)

ethics The moral principles that govern a person's perception of right and wrong.

crime control model A criminal justice model that places primary emphasis on the right of society to be protected from crime and violent criminals.

due process model A criminal justice model that places primacy on the right of the individual to be protected from the power of the government.

Crime and Law Enforcement: Core Concerns

It is difficult to say which of Packer's two models has the upper hand today. As we will see throughout the textbook, homeland security concerns have brought much of the criminal

Mastering**Concepts** Crime Control Model versus Due Process Model

trekandshoot/Shutterstock.com

American Spirit/Shutterstock.com

Crime Control Model	Due Process Model
Goal	**Goal**
• Deter crime by arresting and incarcerating criminals as quickly and efficiently as possible.	• Protect individuals charged with a crime against the immense and sometimes possibly unjust power of the state.
Methods	**Methods**
• Allow the police to "do their jobs" by limiting the amount of judicial oversight of law enforcement tactics.	• Assure the constitutional rights of the accused when they are arrested by law enforcement officers and prosecuted in criminal court.
• Limit the number of rights and protections enjoyed by defendants in court.	• Whenever possible, allow nonviolent convicts to serve their sentences in the community rather than behind bars.
• Incarcerate criminals for lengthy periods of time by imposing harsh sentences, including the death penalty.	• Protect the civil rights of all inmates, and focus on rehabilitation rather than punishment in prisons and jails.

justice system in line with crime control values. At the same time, decreasing arrest and imprisonment rates suggest that due process values are strong, as well. Indeed, national rates of violent and property crimes are at historically low levels.[25] In Chapter 2, we will discuss some of the reasons for this phenomenon, as well as concerns on the part of some experts that, when it comes to crime rates, "what goes down generally comes back up."[26]

Smarter Policing Just as law enforcement inevitably gets a great deal of the blame when crime rates are high, American police forces have received much credit for the apparent decline in criminality. The consensus is that the police have become smarter and more disciplined over the past two decades, relying, like many other criminal justice institutions, on **evidence-based practices**, or those strategies that demonstrably result in positive outcomes.

For example, *predictive policing,* sometimes also known as *intelligence-led policing,* employs statistical models to anticipate which locations are at the highest risk of criminal activity. Once these high-risk locations, or *hot spots,* are identified, law enforcement agencies can direct resources toward preventing crime in the area. Another, more controversial, strategy called *proactive policing* promotes rigorous enforcement of minor offenses—such as drunkenness and public disorder—with an eye toward preventing more serious wrongdoing. We will explore a wide range of these innovative policing strategies more fully in Chapter 5.

evidence-based practices Approaches or strategies that have been extensively researched and shown consistently to produce the desired outcomes.

biometrics Methods to identify a person based on his or her unique physical characteristics, such as fingerprints or facial configuration.

Identifying Criminals Technology has also played a significant role in improving law enforcement efficiency. Police investigators are enjoying the benefits of perhaps the most effective crime-fighting tool since fingerprint identification: DNA profiling. This technology allows law enforcement agents to identify a suspect from body fluid evidence (such as blood, saliva, or semen) or biological evidence (such as hair strands or fingernail clippings). As we will also see in Chapter 5, by collecting DNA from convicts and storing the information in databases, investigators have been able to reach across hundreds of miles and back in time to catch wrongdoers.

Law enforcement's ability to identify criminal suspects is set to receive another boost with the increased use of **biometrics**. This term refers to the measurement and analysis of a person's unique physical characteristics and, in the context of law enforcement, the technological ability to identify if that person is a criminal suspect. The most well-known biometric is the fingerprint, which has been used for decades by police to establish and authenticate suspects.

Today, with mobile ID technology, police officers in the field use handheld devices to match a suspect's fingerprints against those stored in state and federal databases. These devices allow law enforcement to accomplish a task that used to take hours or even days in as little as forty-five seconds. Other important forms of biometric identification are provided by hand geometry, facial features, and the minute details of the human eye.

CJ & Technology

iStockPhoto.com/labsas

Facial-Recognition Software

Recently developed facial-recognition software makes even the most technologically advanced fingerprint-matching systems seem sluggish in comparison. This software distinguishes 16,000 points on a person's face—such as the shape of the lips and the distance between the eyes—and compares them with similar points within photos in law enforcement databases at a rate of more than 1 million faces a second. Designed by the U.S. military to identify potential terrorists in Iraq and Afghanistan, this technology is linked to surveillance cameras in cities such as Chicago and New York for purposes of fighting street crime. It was also used more than 20,000 times from 2011 to 2015 by San Diego patrol officers hoping to establish the identity of suspects in the field.

For all its speed, this technology does have its limitations. The error rate is as high as 20 percent, which suggests the possibility of regular misidentifications. In San Diego, the software succeeded in finding a criminal record match only a quarter of the time, meaning that police officers were, for the most part, photographing noncriminals. Boston recently decided not to link the software to surveillance cameras because, in the words of its police commissioner, "I don't want people to think we're always spying on them."

Thinking about Facial-Recognition Software

Suppose a convenience store manager was able to use her smartphone to take a picture of someone robbing the store. How could facial-recognition software help solve the crime? What are some of the potential drawbacks of allowing citizens with smartphone cameras to help identify criminal suspects?

gun control Efforts by the federal government or state governments to regulate the sale of firearms.

Continuing Challenges: Gun Violence Despite the positive news regarding crimes rates in general, certain trends continue to worry law enforcement and the public. In particular, gun violence in the United States remains a significant concern. Overall, about 300,000 violent firearm crimes are reported to police each year in this country, including over 9,000 murders.[27]

Even though these numbers have been steadily decreasing, they are considerably higher than those in Canada and most European democracies. In Germany, the Netherlands, and Austria, for example, about two of every million residents are victims of gun homicides. In the United States, by contrast, the death rate from gun homicides is about 31 per million people.[28]

Mass Shootings Another violent firearm crime category in which America surpasses other developed nations is the occurrence of *mass shootings*. Definitions of this phenomenon vary, but using the broad measurement of "an incident in which four or more people (not including the shooter) are killed or wounded," more than one mass shooting a day took place in the United States in 2015.[29]

Using the more conservative definition of a shooting in which four or more victims died, Professor James A. Fox of Northeastern University in Boston believes that the rate of mass shootings in the United States has held steady for several decades. What has changed, Fox believes, is fear of concentrated gun violence, driven by the media. "In the 1970s and 1980s, we didn't hear about [mass shootings] on the Internet—because there was no Internet—and we didn't have cable news channels that would devote twenty-four hours of coverage [to the topic]," says Fox.[30]

Gun Control For many supporters of **gun control**, the blame for mass shootings generally lies in the easy access to firearms in the United States. Gun control refers to the policies that federal and state governments implement to limit access to firearms in this country. Proponents of stricter gun control call for expanded *background checks*, designed to keep firearms out of the possession of certain groups of people, such as convicted felons, those with a history of certain types of violence, and the mentally ill.

Opponents of gun control counter that someone who is planning to commit a crime with a gun is probably going to obtain that firearm illegally. Consequently, stricter gun control "prevents only law abiding citizens from owning handguns."[31] Furthermore, one study shows that more than 60 percent of people who carried out mass shootings between 2009 and 2015 were not prohibited from possessing firearms by law, bringing into question the usefulness of background checks in preventing these incidents.[32] Generally speaking, increased scrutiny of mass shootings has served to enflame the controversy surrounding gun control, and we will take a much closer look at this issue in Chapter 14.

Police and Use of Force: The Video's Glare

In the words of James Comey, director of the FBI, "something has changed in policing."[33] The "change" to which Comey refers involves a number of dramatic developments in modern American policing over the past several years, including viral videos of actual or alleged officer misconduct, growing mistrust of law enforcement in minority communities, and on-the-job pressures that may impact the future of crime fighting in the United States.

A "Ferguson Effect?" For many, the origins of this turmoil can be found in the fatal shooting of an unarmed African American teenager by a white police officer in the St. Louis suburb of Ferguson, Missouri. The incident spurred weeks of nationwide protests,

▲ A pile of guns confiscated by the Los Angeles County Sheriff's Department is displayed before the weapons' destruction. **Do you think law enforcement agencies would be for or against stricter gun control measures? Why?**
David McNew/Getty Images

which continued when, in November 2014, a grand jury determined that the police officer, Darren Wilson, was justified in using deadly force against the teenager, Michael Brown. The national debate over the use of police deadly force against minority suspects intensified after a series of similar incidents—often captured on video—took place in cities including Baltimore; Cleveland; and North Charleston, South Carolina.

Some law enforcement experts believe that, as a result of the increased negative attention, many police officers are less aggressive in confronting potential criminals for fear of becoming the "latest racist cop of the week."[34] These experts point to rising violent crime rates in certain American metropolitan areas as evidence of a "Ferguson Effect." For example, arrests in St. Louis decreased by one-third in the two months following Brown's death, while homicides increased by 47 percent and robberies by 82 percent.[35] Nationwide, more than thirty cities saw increases in violent crime in 2015 compared to 2014.[36]

Video and Excessive Force The "Ferguson Effect" is not universally accepted in policing circles. As we will see in Chapter 2, many factors contribute to fluctuations in crime rates. Furthermore, the theory relies on an implied—and cynical—assumption that police officers rely on excessive force to do their jobs effectively. Whether or not a "Ferguson Effect" exists, there is little doubt that the behavior of law enforcement agents is under a national microscope, thanks in no small part to civilians with smartphone video cameras.

Police Credibility Every year, about 44 million face-to-face contacts between police and civilians take place.[37] The vast majority of these interactions are routine and fail to generate any public interest. On the extremely rare occasions when the police-civilian contact does involve force, it has become increasingly likely that the incident will be caught on a smartphone video. "The video camera has become omnipresent," says Richard Aborn, president of Citizens Crime Commission of New York City, "and it has become an absolute check on police credibility."[38]

Two factors generally tend to command public attention with regard to videos of police misconduct. First, whether the incident involves a white police officer and a minority suspect. Second, whether the contents of the video contradict the official version of the incident. Both factors were present in a fatal encounter that started when Michael Slager, a white police officer, pulled over an African American driver named Walter Scott for a broken headlight in North Charleston, South Carolina.

Initially, Slager claimed that he fatally shot Scott when Scott tried to grab the officer's stun gun, known as a Taser. A smartphone video taken by a passerby, however, showed Slager shooting a fleeing Scott in the back and then apparently planting the Taser near Scott's body. As a result of this video evidence, in June 2015, local authorities began the process of trying Slager for murder.

Body-Worn Cameras Following Michael Slager's shooting of Walter Scott, authorities in North Charleston decided that all the city's police officers would start wearing body cameras. Many police administrators feel that these devices, worn on an officer's uniform or behind the ear, will produce a record of police conduct that, unlike many smartphone videos, is complete and unbiased. While the number of local police departments turning to body-worn cameras is increasing dramatically, the impact of this technology on day-to-day law enforcement is still unclear. We will discuss body-worn cameras and other elements that impact police strategies regarding police use of force in greater detail in Chapter 5.

Issues of Trust and Race It seems that, because of the negative media attention generated by alleged police misconduct and the resulting street protests, public support for law enforcement has waned. In a June 2015 Gallup Poll, only 52 percent of the respondents expressed confidence in the police, the lowest level since 1993.[39] (It should be noted that, according to the same poll, the police remain one of the most trusted institutions in American society.)

In some minority communities, videos such as the one involving the death of Walter Scott have, according to one observer, "provided corroboration of what African Americans have been saying for years" about racial bias in law enforcement.[40] According to a survey following the shooting of Michael Brown in Ferguson, nearly half of African American respondents said that they had experienced racial discrimination by a police officer. (Virtually none of the white respondents responded in the same manner.)[41]

Examining racial tensions between blacks and law enforcement in Cleveland, a recent federal report stated that the city's police force sees itself as an "occupying force" and that the various local departments "must undergo a cultural shift at all levels to change an 'us-against-them' mentality."[42] In Chapters 4 and 5, we will take a comprehensive look at the possible root causes of this climate and explore some of the ways in which tensions between police and members of minority groups might be defused. In particular, we will focus on diversity in law enforcement, a crucial issue in today's criminal justice system.

Domestic Terrorism and Homeland Security

Was it an act of terrorism? Or was it a mass shooting? Is there a difference between the two phenomena, and, if so, does this difference matter? These were the questions being asked immediately after Syed Farook and his wife, Tashfeen Malik, killed fourteen people and wounded twenty-one others at a rented banquet room in San Bernardino, California, in December 2015. To some, the controversy seemed superficial—following such a tragedy, what do words and definitions matter? The debate did, however, reflect a national uncertainty concerning the criminal justice policy decisions needed to prevent similar attacks in the future.

Terrorism Defined The morning after the San Bernardino shootings, the cover headline of the *New York Post* read, "Muslim Killers: Terror Eyed as Couple Slaughters 14 in Calif." This reaction, shared by many, was based on the ethnic and religious backgrounds of Syed Farook, a U.S. citizen of Pakistani descent, and Tashfeen Malik, a lawful resident of this country born in Pakistan. By all accounts, the couple, eventually killed in a shootout with law enforcement agents, were practicing Muslims.

▲ An officer salutes during funeral services for University of Colorado police officer Garret Swasey, who was killed when Robert Dear opened fire at a Planned Parenthood clinic in Colorado Springs on November 27, 2015. In describing his anti-abortion motivation for the attack, Dear later told a court, "I'm a warrior for babies." **Why are Dear's actions considered an example of domestic terrorism?** Justin Edmonds/Getty Images

In fact, according to traditional definitions of **terrorism**, the demographic traits of the actors are irrelevant. Under federal law, for instance, terrorism is described as any dangerous act intended to influence government policy or intimidate a civilian population by "mass destruction, assassination, or kidnapping."[43]

Domestic Terrorism Defined Relatively quickly, the FBI began investigating the San Bernardino shootings as an act of terrorism. The agency had uncovered evidence that Farook and Malik shared an extremist past, and, on the day of the attack, Malik declared her allegiance to the Islamic State—a terrorist organization described earlier in the chapter—on Facebook.[44] This ended any uncertainty over terminology and placed the event squarely in the realm of **domestic terrorism**, an umbrella term that covers acts of terrorism that are carried out within one's own country and against one's own people.

A Variety of Causes Domestic terrorists are driven by a number of different causes. Besides religious extremism, these motivations have included antigovernment beliefs, white supremacy, animal rights, and opposition to abortion.[45] For example, after Dylan Roof fatally shot nine African American parishioners in their church in Charleston, South Carolina, local authorities cited a website in which Roof spouted white supremacist views as proof that he was a domestic terrorist. In fact, according to the research organization New America, since 2001, the number of murders committed in the United States by Islamic extremists (forty-five) is about the same as the death toll in attacks carried out by white supremacists and antigovernment ideologues (forty-eight).[46]

Protecting the Homeland

There is no specific federal law or state law against "domestic terrorism." For killing the African American parishioners, Dylan Roof was charged with murder. Had they lived, Syed Farook and Tashfeen Malik would almost certainly have faced similar charges. Categorizing an attack as terrorism, however, does make it more likely that the FBI, the federal government's primary crime-fighting agency, will lead the investigation.

The FBI's shift in focus from traditional crimes to counterterrorism is one of the hallmarks of the homeland security movement that started on September 11, 2001 (9/11). That day, terrorists hijacked four commercial airlines and used them to kill nearly three thousand people in New York City, northern Virginia, and rural Pennsylvania. In the fifteen years since, **homeland security** concerns have, as we will see throughout this textbook, touched nearly every aspect of the American criminal justice system.

"Crowdsourcing" Terrorism Immediately following 9/11, homeland security efforts in the United States concentrated on preventing large-scale assaults carried out by foreign terrorist operatives. More recently, however, the terrorist threat seems to have shifted to homegrown, self-radicalized individuals who attempt to operate undetected

terrorism The use or threat of violence to intimidate civilian populations or achieve political objectives.

domestic terrorism Acts of terrorism that take place on U.S. territory.

homeland security A concerted national effort to prevent terrorist attacks within the United States and reduce the nation's vulnerability to terrorism.

on U.S. soil. (Elton Simpson, whose failed attack on a Texas community center was described in the chapter opening, is an example of this threat.) In many cases, these "lone wolf" domestic terrorists do not have direct contact with any known terrorist organizations. Rather, groups such as the Islamic State and al Qaeda seek to "crowdsource" their terrorism goals by inspiring followers in the United States and other nations.

Such crowdsourcing efforts mostly take place on social media sites such as Twitter and Instagram, as well as other Internet platforms. The Islamic State, for example, produces thousands of Internet videos designed to recruit foreign adherents. The terrorist group also maintains a twenty-four-hour online recruiting operation, buoyed by volunteers affirming the group's viewpoint. "By assimilating into the Internet world instead of the real world, I became absorbed in a 'virtual' struggle while disconnecting from what was real," said a Virginia teenager who was arrested in 2015 for driving a friend to the airport so the friend could join the Islamic State in Syria.[47]

Going Dark As noted earlier in the chapter, it is often difficult for counterterrorism investigators monitoring the Internet to determine which terrorism supporters are "talkers" and which are "doers." One common strategy requires an undercover law enforcement officer or informant to work alongside a "doer," so as to apprehend that person in the early stages of his or her plot. While this tactic—discussed more fully in Chapter 5—has been responsible for numerous terrorism-related arrests, it does have one major flaw. That is, it is of limited value against those potential domestic terrorists who are savvy enough to keep their viewpoints and their intentions off the Internet.

Security versus Privacy "We've created the world's most powerful terrorism hindsight machine," insists one critic of U.S. counterterrorism efforts.[48] In order to develop more foresight in this area, homeland security officials have relied on various electronic methods of gathering information on possible terrorist plots. In particular, over the past decade the federal government has conducted *metadata surveillance* operations in which the phone records of Americans are collected in bulk and analyzed to uncover any links with or between suspected terrorists.

As we will discuss in Chapter 14, when details of the federal government metadata surveillance program came to light in 2013, it raised the ire not only of American Muslims, who felt they were unfairly targeted, but also of *civil liberties* groups. The term **civil liberties** refers to the personal freedoms guaranteed by the U.S. Constitution, particularly the first ten amendments, called the Bill of Rights. Concerns about balancing personal freedoms and personal safety permeate our criminal justice system. In fact, an entire chapter of this textbook—Chapter 7—is needed to properly examine the rules that law enforcement must follow to protect the civil liberties of crime suspects.

In this instance, critics felt that the government's "snooping" program infringed on the rights of American citizens to keep information about their phone and Internet activity private unless such activity could be linked to criminal activity. As a result of this criticism, in June 2015, Congress passed the USA Freedom Act,[49] which limits the federal government's megadata surveillance abilities. Needless to say, the legislation angered those who feel that metadata collection is a crucial weapon in our homeland security arsenal. (To learn more about another technology designed to keep communications private—including communications by terrorists—see the feature *CJ Controversy—Encryption and Terrorism.*)

civil liberties The basic rights and freedoms guaranteed by the U.S. Constitution, particularly in the Bill of Rights.

CJ Controversy
·EQUAL·JUSTICE·UNDER·LAW·

M Dogan/Shutterstock.com

Encryption and Terrorism

Using a process called *encryption,* companies such as Apple, Google, and Facebook insert complicated computer codes on their messaging services to protect these communications from being read by third parties. In the words of one observer, "Without encryption, Internet traffic might as well be written on postcards." The drawback, at least according to many homeland security officials, is that terrorists often take advantage of these encrypted services to keep their electronic correspondence hidden from authorities. The result is a "big problem," says James Comey, director of the FBI.

The Government Should Ban Private Message Encryption Because...

- Encryption makes it nearly impossible for government officials to access and collect early warning clues about future terrorist attacks.
- Terrorist groups openly favor the technology, as demonstrated by the Islamic State providing its supporters a guide to the best encrypted messaging apps.

The Government Should Not Ban Private Message Encryption Because...

- Encryption keeps data safe from both cybercriminals and government officials who would otherwise be able to gain access to private data by illegal hacking or through a lawful court order.
- If the government banned encryption, consumer confidence in products such as Apple's popular iPhone would suffer, and terrorists would simply find alternative methods to continue communicating "in the dark."

Your Assignment

The encryption issue came to national prominence in late 2015, when the federal government asked Apple to help FBI investigators gain access to an iPhone used by Syed Rizwan Farook during the mass shooting in San Bernardino, California. Apple refused, on privacy grounds. To better understand this dispute, go online and search for the terms **Apple, FBI,** and **encryption.** Then, write at least two paragraphs that explain your position concerning whether Apple should comply with the federal government's wishes in this matter.

Prison Population Trends

After increasing by 500 percent from 1980 to 2009, the prison population in the United States decreased in four of the five following years.[50] Certainly, these decreases have been small, and the American corrections system remains immense. More than 2.2 million offenders are in prison or jail in this country, and another 4.7 million are under community supervision.[51] Still, the new trend reflects a series of crucial changes in the American criminal justice system.

The "Deincarceration" Movement There is no question that economic considerations have played a role in the nation's shrinking inmate population. Federal, state, and local governments spend $80 billion a year on prisons and jails, and many corrections officials are under pressure to decrease costs.[52] Many state officials have also embraced the concept of **justice reinvestment**, an umbrella term for policies that redirect funds saved by lowering a state's inmate population into strategies that improve community safety. For instance, policymakers in Alabama hope to reduce that state's inmate rolls by nearly five thousand over the next decade, freeing up $26 million to hire additional parole officers and increase behavioral health treatment services for ex-offenders.[53]

In addition to economic concerns, downsizing efforts increasingly reflect "the message that locking up a lot of people doesn't necessarily bring public safety," says Joan Petersilia, co-director of Stanford University's Criminal Justice Center.[54] To reduce prison populations, therefore, federal and state correctional officials are implementing programs designed to curtail the *recidivism* rate of ex-convicts. **Recidivism** refers to the

justice reinvestment A corrections policy that promotes (a) a reduction in spending on prisons and jails and (b) reinvestment of the resulting savings into programs that decrease crime and reduce reoffending.

recidivism The act of committing a new crime after a person has already been punished for a previous crime by being convicted and sent to jail or prison.

act of committing another crime (and possibly returning to incarceration) after a person has already been punished for previous criminal behavior.

To further promote deincarceration, federal and state corrections systems are making efforts to (1) keep nonviolent offenders from being sent to prison, and (2) when possible, release qualified inmates from prison before the end of their terms.

diversion An effort to keep offenders out of prison or jail by diverting them into programs that promote treatment and rehabilitation rather than punishment.

Diversion Over the past several years, Texas has spent millions of dollars to fund programs that provide low-level drug offenders with treatment rather than sending them to prison. This strategy is known as **diversion** because it reroutes offenders from incarceration to the community through special courts that advocate rehabilitation rather than punishment. As we will see in Chapter 10, numerous states have developed diversion programs to lower their prison populations.

Release and Reentry Under pressure from federal courts to reduce prison overcrowding, California has decreased the number of inmates in its state prisons by 51,000—over 30 percent—since 2006.[55] Nationwide, this trend has focused on early release for offenders that Stanford's Joan Petersilia characterizes as "triple-nons": nonserious, nonviolent, and nonsexual. In October 2015, for example, the U.S. Justice Department released about six thousand nonviolent drug offenders from federal prisons. Indeed, as Figure 1.4 highlights, releases have begun surpassing admissions in federal prisons, a key factor in the overall decline in the number of federal prisoners in the United States.

Some observers feel that this aspect of the deincarceration movement inevitably will lead to increased crime rates, as the newly freed ex-offenders revert to their "old ways." To lessen this possibility, the corrections system has embraced *reentry programs* that provide ex-offenders treatment for drug and alcohol addictions and mental illness, as well as help in finding housing and employment. We will examine the deincarceration movement, including policies that promote diversion and reentry, in much more detail in Chapters 10, 11, and 12.

Figure 1.4 Federal Prisons: Admissions and Releases

From 2012 to 2014, the number of inmates released from federal prisons has been greater than the number of inmates admitted to federal prisons, an important factor in the overall reduction of federal inmates in the United States.

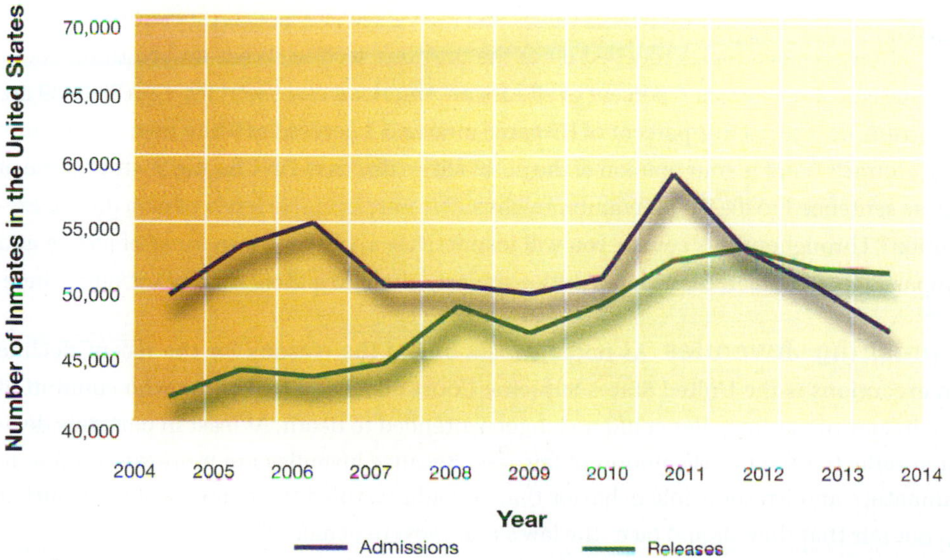

Source: Bureau of Justice Statistics, *Prisoners in 2014* (Washington, D.C.: U.S. Department of Justice, September 2015), Appendix table 2, page 29.

capital crime A criminal act that makes the offender eligible to receive the death penalty.

Declining Use of the Death Penalty Another interesting corrections trend involves death row inmates who are in prison awaiting execution after having been found guilty of committing a **capital crime**. Near the end of 2015, the death row population in American prisons stood at just under 3,000, down from 3,653 in 2000.[56] During that same time period, the number of annual executions in this country dropped from eighty-five to twenty-eight, a twenty-three-year low. Since 2002, the United States Supreme Court has barred executions of people with intellectual disabilities, juvenile offenders under the age of eighteen, and those convicted of crimes other than murder.[57]

In addition, it seems that judges and juries have become less willing to sentence the "worst of the worst" criminals to death. In 2014, only forty-nine offenders were sentenced to death, down from seventy-two the previous year and 315 in 1996.[58] Furthermore, Nebraska recently became the seventh state since 2007 to abolish the death penalty. We will further explore *capital punishment*, one of the most controversial areas of the criminal justice system, in Chapter 9.

Incarceration and Race One troublesome aspect of capital punishment is that a black defendant is much more likely to be sentenced to death for killing a white victim than a white defendant is for killing a black victim.[59] Indeed, looking at the general statistics, a bleak picture of minority incarceration emerges. Even though African Americans make up only 13 percent of the general population in the United States, the number of black men in state and federal prisons (497,000) is larger than the number of white men (468,000).[60]

In federal prisons, one in every three inmates is Hispanic,[61] a ratio that has increased dramatically over the past decade as law enforcement and homeland security agencies have focused on immigration law violations, a subject we will consider in Chapter 4. The question of whether these figures reflect purposeful bias on the part of certain members of the criminal justice community will be addressed at various points in this textbook.

Justice and Crime

To a certain extent, every important issue that we examine in this textbook will be approached from two directions. In each instance, we will look at the objective, legal framework that defines the issue's place in the criminal justice system. In addition, we will inevitably explore more subjective concerns about the issue. Is it applied fairly and impartially? Does it reflect our individual values and the values of American society as whole?

Consider two topics touched on in the previous section. What do you think about the statistical reality that 6 percent of all African American men from the ages 30 to 39 are in prison, compared to 2 percent of Hispanic men and 1 percent of white men in the same age group?[62] What is your opinion of the possibility—discussed in Chapter 9—that some of those sentenced to die in this country might suffer unreasonable levels of pain during execution? Throughout this course, you will instinctively apply your own sense of justice and impartiality to numerous criminal justice subjects, including three that we introduce here.

Getting Linked in™

Juvenile violent offenders seeking reduced sentences and inmates who feel they have been wrongly convicted often seek help from **civil rights lawyers**, who specialize in protecting the rights guaranteed by the U.S. Constitution. **You can connect with these criminal justice professionals on LinkedIn by searching for "civil rights lawyers," or, alternately, by entering the search term "legal aid."**

Punishing Juveniles As noted earlier, one of the reasons for the recent decline in executions is the United States Supreme Court's decision that those who committed capital crimes as juveniles could no longer sentenced to death. At least in part, this decision reflected the Court's notion of fairness. Because juveniles are more susceptible to immature and irresponsible behavior than are adults, ruled the majority of the Court, it is not fair that they should face "the law's most severe penalty."[63]

As we will see in Chapter 13, the Supreme Court has applied similar reasoning to the sentence of life in prison without parole for juvenile offenders. Though the Court did not ban the possibility of this penalty for violent juvenile offenders, it did, in 2012, rule that the sentence could not be mandatory under state law.[64] This decision impacts the future of about 2,500 inmates across the country presently serving life-without-parole sentences for crimes committed as juveniles. Ten states have started the process of resentencing these defendants, taking into consideration factors such as the offender's family background and potential for rehabilitation in deciding whether a release from incarceration at some point is appropriate.

▲ In July 2015, Jansen Young speaks to the media in Centennial, Colorado, after James Holmes was found guilty of murdering twelve people at a nearby movie theater three years earlier. Jansen was injured in the shooting spree, and her boyfriend was killed. **Why might some observers feel that victims should not have any role in criminal justice proceedings? Do you agree with this viewpoint? Explain your answers.** Theo Stroomer/Getty Images

The Role of Victims

Many observers do not believe it is fair that violent juvenile offenders be treated more leniently. In particular, *victims' rights* advocates generally are opposed to the policy changes described in the previous section. For our purposes, a **victim** is any person against whom a crime has been committed or who is directly or indirectly harmed by a criminal act. "When I started thinking of the possibility that we'd have to go back to court, I couldn't sleep for four months," said a women whose pregnant sister was murdered by a sixteen-year-old over two decades ago.[65]

Widespread recognition of crime victims is a relatively recent phenomenon. It was not until the 1970s that victims' rights supporters began addressing what they perceived to be an imbalance in favor of criminal defendants in the criminal justice system. These activists pointed out that crime victims had virtually no rights under state or federal law. Therefore, they were forced to deal with the physical, emotional, and financial consequences of victimization on their own. Over the past twenty years, all fifty states have redressed the situation by providing legal rights to victims through their statutory codes or state constitutions. In Chapter 2, we will take a close look at whether these legislative efforts have succeeded in making the criminal justice system a safer, and fairer, place for crime victims.

victim Any person who suffers physical, emotional, or financial harm as the result of a criminal act.

Wrongful Convictions

In 1993, Juan Rivera was convicted of raping and murdering an eleven-year-old girl in Waukegan, Illinois. Twenty years later, he was released from prison after DNA evidence cleared him of the crime. In 2015, a jury awarded Rivera $20 million, the largest settlement yet for someone who had been wrongfully convicted in an American criminal court.

Court reversals of *wrongful convictions,* covered more extensively in Chapter 9, are becoming more commonplace thanks to technological advances in DNA testing. For many, this disturbing trend of wrongful convictions has wide implications. The possibility that an innocent person can be found guilty—due to either human error or human misconduct—strikes at the heart of our society's belief in the criminal justice system as an institution governed by fairness and impartiality.

Learning Objective

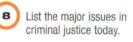

8 List the major issues in criminal justice today.

EthicsChallenge

Do you think that sentencing juveniles to life in prison without the possibility of parole is an ethical practice? Explain your answer, keeping in mind that these offenders have generally committed violent crimes such as murder. ■

Summary

For more information on these concepts, look back to the Learning Objective icons throughout the chapter.

1 **Describe the two most common models of how society determines which acts are criminal.** The consensus model argues that the majority of citizens will agree on which activities should be outlawed and punished as crimes. It rests on the assumption that a diverse group of people can have similar morals. In contrast, the conflict model argues that in a diverse society, the dominant groups exercise power by codifying their value systems into criminal laws.

2 **Explain two main purposes of the criminal justice system.** The first purpose of the criminal justice system is to provide justice to society by ensuring that all individuals are treated equally under criminal law. The second purpose is to protect society, a far-reaching objective that involves the fair treatment of crime victims and those who may or may not have committed criminal acts.

3 **Outline the three levels of law enforcement.** Because we have a federal system of government, law enforcement occurs at the (a) national, or federal, level and the (b) state level and within the states at (c) local levels. Because crime is mostly a local concern, most employees in the criminal justice system work for local governments. Agencies at the federal level include the FBI, the DEA, and the U.S. Secret Service, among others.

4 **List the essential elements of the corrections system.** Criminal offenders are placed on probation, incarcerated in a jail or prison, transferred to community-based corrections facilities, or released on parole.

5 **Explain the difference between the formal and informal criminal justice processes.** The formal criminal justice process involves the somewhat mechanical steps that are designed to guide criminal defendants from arrest to possible punishment. For every step in the formal process, though, someone has discretion, and such discretion leads to an informal process. Even when prosecutors believe that a suspect is guilty, they have the discretion not to prosecute, for example.

6 **Define ethics, and describe the role that it plays in discretionary decision making.** Ethics consists of the moral principles that guide a person's perception of right and wrong. Most criminal justice professionals have a great deal of discretionary leeway in their day-to-day decision making, and their ethical beliefs can help ensure that they make such decisions in keeping with society's established values.

7 **Contrast the crime control and due process models.** The crime control model assumes that the criminal justice system is designed to protect the public from criminals. Thus, its most important function is to punish and repress criminal conduct. The due process model presumes that the accused are innocent and provides them with the most complete safeguards, usually within the court system.

8 **List the major issues in criminal justice today.** (a) Falling violent and property crime rates; (b) improved policing strategies; (c) the videotaping of alleged police misconduct; (d) social justice and law enforcement; (e) defining and preventing domestic terrorism; (f) homeland security and civil liberties; (g) America's shrinking, though still massive, inmate population; (h) fewer executions; (i) possible bias against minorities in the criminal justice system; (j) leniency in juvenile justice; (k) victims' rights; and (l) wrongful convictions.

Questions for Critical Analysis

1. How is it possible to have a consensus about what should or should not be illegal in a country with several hundred million adults from diverse races, religions, and walks of life?
2. What would be some of the drawbacks of having the victims of a crime, rather than the state (through its public officials), prosecute criminals?
3. Relate the concept of federalism to the proliferation of different state laws regarding the possession, use, and sale of marijuana. Do the principles of federalism support each state's ability to make its own laws regarding the drug? Or, do the principles of federalism suggest that federal law regarding marijuana should supersede state-level efforts? Explain your answers.
4. Using the Internet or the news media, find three recent examples of domestic terrorism. What factors do these examples have in common? How are the incidents different?
5. As noted earlier in the chapter, corrections officials are reducing prison budgets by releasing nonviolent offenders before their sentences are finished. What is your opinion of this strategy? What might be some of the consequences of large-scale early release programs for drug dealers and those convicted of property crimes?

Key Terms

biometrics 18
capital crime 26
civil liberties 23
conflict model 6
consensus model 5
crime 5
crime control model 16
criminal justice system 7
deviance 7
discretion 14
diversion 25
domestic terrorism 22
drug 9
due process model 16
ethics 16
evidence-based practices 17
federalism 10
formal criminal justice process 14
gun control 19
homeland security 22
informal criminal justice process 14
justice 8
justice reinvestment 24
morals 6
psychoactive drugs 9
recidivism 24
system 13
terrorism 22
victim 27

Notes

1. *Schenck v. United States,* 249 U.S. 47 (1919). Many United States Supreme Court cases will be cited in this book, and it is important to understand these citations. *Schenck v. United States* refers to the parties in the case that the Court is reviewing. "U.S." is the abbreviation for *United States Reports,* the official publication of United States Supreme Court decisions. "249" refers to the volume of the *United States Reports* in which the case appears, and "47" is the page number. The citation ends with the year the case was decided, in parentheses. Most, though not all, Supreme Court case citations in this book will follow this formula.
2. Eric Lichtblau, "Ohio Man Arrested after Social Posts Urging Killing of Military Members," *New York Times* (November 13, 2015), A16.
3. Eric Posner, "ISIS Gives Us No Choice but to Consider Limits on Speech," *Slate .com* (December 12, 2015), at **www.slate .com/articles/news_and_politics /view_from_chicago/2015/12/isis_s _online_radicalization_efforts_present _an_unprecedented_danger.html.**
4. Herman Bianchi, *Justice as Sanctuary: Toward a New System of Crime Control* (Bloomington: Indiana University Press, 1994), 72.
5. "Justice for All?" *The Reflective Democracy Campaign* (July 2015), at **wholeads.us/ justice.**
6. Megan Kurlychek, "What Is My Left Hand Doing? The Need for Unifying Purpose and Policy in the Criminal Justice System," *Criminology & Public Policy* (November 2011), 909.
7. Elahe Izadi, "Marijuana Use More than Doubles in Just 12 Years," *Washington Post* (October 21, 2015), at **www.washingtonpost .com/news/to-your-health/wp/2015 /10/21/marijuana-use-more-than-doubles-in-just-12-years.**
8. Gene Johnson, "After Legalization, Pot-Related Emergencies Spike," *Associated Press* (January 25, 2015), 10.
9. *Gonzales v. Oregon,* 546 U.S. 243 (2006).
10. Steve Nelson, "Bipartisan Task Force Looks to Cut List of 4,500 Federal Crimes," *U.S. News & World Report* (June 14, 2013), at **www.usnews .com/news/newsgram/articles/2013/06 /14/bipartisan-task-force-looks-to-cut -list-of-4500-federal-crimes.**
11. President's Commission on Law Enforcement and Administration of Justice, *The Challenge of Crime in a Free Society* (Washington, D.C.: Government Printing Office, 1967), 7.
12. John Heinz and Peter Manikas, "Networks among Elites in a Local Criminal Justice System," *Law and Society Review* 26 (1992), 831–861.
13. James Q. Wilson, "What to Do about Crime: Blaming Crime on Root Causes," *Vital Speeches* (April 1, 1995), 373.

14. Herbert Packer, *The Limits of the Criminal Sanction* (Stanford, Calif.: Stanford University Press, 1968), 154–173.

15. *Ibid.*

16. Daniel Givelber, "Meaningless Acquittals, Meaningful Convictions: Do We Reliably Acquit the Innocent?" *Rutgers Law Review* 49 (Summer 1997), 1317.

17. O.C.G.A. Section 40-6-241 (2010).

18. Alan Blinder, "A Cheeseburger, a Suburban Traffic Stop and a Ticket for Eating While Driving," *New York Times* (January 21, 2015), A10.

19. George P. Fletcher, "Some Unwise Reflections about Discretion," *Law & Contemporary Problems* (Autumn 1984), 279.

20. "Civil Rights Division, *Investigation of the Ferguson Police Department* (Washington, D.C.: United States Department of Justice, March 4, 2015), 4.

21. Antonin Scalia, "The Rule of Law as a Law of Rules," *University of Chicago Law Review* 56 (1989), 1178–1180.

22. John Kleinig, *Ethics and Criminal Justice: An Introduction* (New York: Cambridge University Press, 2008), 33–35.

23. Packer, *op. cit.*, 154–173.

24. Givelber, *op. cit.*, 1317.

25. Federal Bureau of Investigation, *Crime in the United States 2014* (Washington, D.C.: U.S. Department of Justice, 2015) at **www.fbi.gov/about-us/cjis/ucr/crime-in-the-u.s/2014/crime-in-the-u.s.-2014.**

26. James Alan Fox, quoted in Henry Gass, "Spike in Violent Crime: Why You Shouldn't Worry," *Christian Science Monitor* (June 4, 2015), at **www.csmonitor.com/USA/Justice/2015/0604/Spike-in-violent-crime-Why-you-shouldn-t-worry-video.**

27. *Crime in the United States 2014, op. cit.*, at Violent Crime and Table 12.

28. Kevin Quealy and Margot Sanger-Katz, "Gun Deaths: Rare Elsewhere, Common in U.S.," *New York Times* (December 6, 2015), SR3.

29. Gun Violence Archive, "Mass Shootings—2015," at **www.gunviolencearchive.org/reports/mass-shootings/2015?page=8.**

30. Quoted in Sharon LaFraniere, Sarah Cohen, and Richard A. Oppel, Jr., "How Often Do Mass Shootings Occur?" *New York Times* (December 3, 2015), A1.

31. Quoted in David Nakamura and Robert Barnes, "Appeals Court Rules D.C. Handgun Ban Unconstitutional," *Washington Post* (March 10, 2007), A1.

32. Everytown for Gun Safety, "State Background Check Requirements and Mass Shootings" (November 12, 2015), at **everytownresearch.org/state-background-check-requirements-mass-shootings.**

33. Quoted in "Paralysed by YouTube," *The Economist* (October 31, 2015), 28.

34. Heather Mac Donald, "America's Legal Order Begins to Fray," *Wall Street Journal* (September 13, 2015), at **www.wsj.com/articles/americas-legal-order-begins-to-fray-1442182979.**

35. Heather Mac Donald, "The New Nationwide Crime Wave," *Wall Street Journal* (May 29, 2015), at **www.wsj.com/articles/the-new-nationwide-crime-wave-1432938425.**

36. Monica Davey, "Murder Rates Rising Sharply in Many U.S. Cities," *New York Times* (September 1, 2015), A1.

37. Bureau of Justice Statistics, *Police Use of Nonfatal Force, 2002–11* (Washington, D.C.: U.S. Department of Justice, November 2015), 1.

38. Quoted in Pervaiz Shallwani, Ana Campoy, and Valerie Bauerlein, "Prevalence of Video Puts Police Under the Lens," *Wall Street Journal* (April 10, 2015), at **www.wsj.com/articles/prevalence-of-video-puts-police-under-the-lens-1428708033.**

39. Gallup, "In U.S., Confidence in the Police Lowest in 22 Years" (June 19, 2015), at **www.gallup.com/poll/183704/confidence-police-lowest-years.aspx.**

40. Quoted in Richard Pérez-Peña and Timothy Williams, "Glare of Video Is Shifting Public's View of Police," *New York Times* (July 31, 2015), A1.

41. Tanzina Vega and Megan Thee-Brenan, "Polls Show National Unease with Missouri Unrest," *New York Times* (August 22, 2014), A14.

42. Quoted in Richard A. Oppel, Jr., "National Questions over Police Hit Home in Cleveland," *New York Times* (December 9, 2014), A16.

43. Federal Bureau of Investigation, "Definitions of Terrorism in the U.S. Code," at **www.fbi.gov/about-us/investigate/terrorism/terrorism-definition.**

44. Michael S. Schmidt and Richard Pérez-Peña, "F.B.I. Treating San Bernardino Attack as Terrorism Case," *New York Times* (December 5, 2015), A1.

45. Jerome P. Bjelopera, *The Domestic Terrorist Threat: Background and Issues for Congress* (Washington, D.C.: Congressional Research Service, January 17, 2013), 2.

46. New America, "Deadly Attacks Since 9/11," at **securitydata.newamerica.net/extremists/deadly-attacks.html.**

47. Quoted in Scott Shane, Matt Apuzzo, and Eric Schmitt, "Online Embrace from ISIS, a Few Clicks Away," *New York Times* (December 9, 2015), A1.

48. Quoted in Philip Shishkin and Patrick O'Connor, "San Bernardino Shooting Shows How U.S. Terror Defenses Are Tested," *Wall Street Journal* (December 6, 2015), at **www.wsj.com/articles/san-bernardino-shooting-tests-u-s-terror-defenses-1449452604.**

49. H.R. 3361—113th Congress: USA FREEDOM Act," January 11, 2016.

50. Bureau of Justice Statistics, *Prisoners in 2014* (Washington, D.C.: U.S. Department of Justice, September 2015), Table 1, page 2.

51. Bureau of Justice Statistics, *Correctional Populations in the United States, 2014* (Washington, D.C.: U.S. Department of Justice, December 2015), Table 1, page 1.

52. "One Nation, Behind Bars," *The Economist* (August 17, 2013), 12.

53. *Justice Reinvestment in Alabama: Analysis and Policy Framework* (Washington, D.C.: Bureau of Justice Assistance, March 2015), 1–2.

54. Quoted in Erica Goode, "U.S. Prison Populations Decline, Reflecting New Approach to Crime," *New York Times* (July 26, 2013), A11.

55. "The Right Choices," *The Economist* (June 20, 2015), 26.

56. Death Penalty Information Center, "Size of Death Row by Year—1968 to Present," at **www.deathpenaltyinfo.org/death-row-inmates-state-and-size-death-row-year?scid=9&did=188.**

57. *Atkins v. Virginia,* 536 U.S. 304; *Roper v. Simmons,* 543 U.S. 551 (2005); and *Kennedy v. Louisiana,* 554 U.S. 407 (2008).

58. *The Death Penalty in 2015: Year End Report* (Washington, D.C.: Death Penalty Information Center, December 2015), 1.

59. Death Penalty Information Center, "National Statistics on Death Penalty and Race," at **www.deathpenaltyinfo.org/race-death-row-inmates-executed-1976?scid=5&did=184.**

60. Bureau of Justice Statistics, *Prisoners in 2014* (Washington, D.C.: U.S. Department of Justice, September 2015), Appendix table 4, page 30.

61. Federal Bureau of Prisons, "Inmate Ethnicity," at **www.bop.gov/about/statistics/statistics_inmate_ethnicity.jsp.**

62. *Prisoners in 2014, op. cit.*, 1.

63. *Roper, op. cit.*

64. *Miller v. Alabama,* 567 U.S. _____ (2012).

65. Quoted in Erik Eckholm, "A Murderer at 14, Then a Lifer, Now a Man Pondering a Future," *New York Times* (April 11, 2015), A1.

Chapter 1 Appendix

1A

How to Read Case Citations and Find Court Decisions

Many important court cases are discussed throughout this book. Every time a court case is mentioned, you will be able to check its citation using the endnotes on the final pages of the chapter. Court decisions are recorded and published on paper and on the Internet. When a court case is mentioned, the notation that is used to refer to, or to *cite*, the case denotes where the published decision can be found.

Decisions of state courts of appeals are usually published in two places: the state reports of that particular state and the more widely used *National Reporter System* published by West Group. Some states no longer publish their own reports. The *National Reporter System* divides the states into the following geographic areas: Atlantic (A. or A.2d), North Eastern (N.E. or N.E.2d), North Western (N.W. or N.W.2d), Pacific (P., P.2d, or P.3d), Southern (So., So.2d, or So.3d), and South Western (S.W., S.W.2d, or S.W.3d). The 2d and 3d in these abbreviations refer to the *Second Series* and *Third Series*, respectively.

Federal trial court decisions are published unofficially in West's *Federal Supplement* (F.Supp. or F.Supp.2d), and opinions from the circuit courts of appeals are reported unofficially in West's *Federal Reporter* (F., F.2d, or F.3d). Opinions from the United States Supreme Court are reported in the *United States Reports* (U.S.), the *Lawyers' Edition of the Supreme Court Reports* (L.Ed.), West's *Supreme Court Reporter* (S.Ct.), and other publications. The *United States Reports* is the official publication of United States Supreme Court decisions. It is published by the federal government. Many early decisions are missing from these volumes. The citations of the early volumes of the *United States Reports* include the names of the actual reporters, such as Dallas, Cranch, or Wheaton. *McCulloch v. Maryland*, for example, is cited as 17 U.S. (4 Wheat.) 316. Only after 1874 did the present citation system, in which cases are cited based solely on their volume and page numbers in the *United States Reports*, come into being. The *Lawyers' Edition of the Supreme Court Reports* is an unofficial and more complete edition of Supreme Court decisions. West's *Supreme Court Reporter* is an unofficial edition of decisions dating from October 1882. These volumes contain headnotes and numerous brief editorial statements of the law involved in a given case.

Citations to decisions of state courts of appeals give the name of the case; the volume, name, and page number of the state's official report (if the state publishes its own reports); and the volume, unit, and page number of the *National Reporter*. Federal court citations also give the name of the case and the volume, name, and page number of the reports. In addition to the citation, this textbook lists the year of the decision in parentheses. Consider, for example, the case *Miranda v. Arizona*, 384 U.S. 436 (1966). The Supreme Court's decision in this case may be found in volume 384 of the *United States Reports* on page 436. The case was decided in 1966.

POLICE
INE DO NOT

Ringo Chiu/Getty Images

2

Measuring and Explaining Crime

Chapter Outline		Corresponding Learning Objectives
Types of Crimes	1	Identify the six main categories of crime.
Measuring Crime in the United States	2	Identify the publication in which the FBI reports crime data, and list the two main ways in which the data are reported.
	3	Distinguish between the National Crime Victimization Survey (NCVS) and self-reported surveys.
Crime Trends in the United States	4	Explain why income level appears to be more important than race or ethnicity when it comes to crime trends.
What Causes Crime	5	Discuss the difference between a hypothesis and a theory in the context of criminology.
	6	Explain the theory of the chronic offender and its usefulness for law enforcement.
	7	Describe the importance of early childhood behavior for those who subscribe to self-control theory.
Victims of Crime	8	Explain the routine activities theory of victimization.
The Link between Drugs and Crime	9	Discuss the connection between the learning process and the start of an individual's drug use.

To target your study and review, look for these numbered Learning Objective icons throughout the chapter.

by the Numbers

the headlines were terrifying, particularly for high school seniors about to go to college. "1 in 4 Women Experience Sex Assault on Campus," declared the *New York Times.* "More than 1 in 5 Female Undergrads at Top Schools Suffer Sexual Attacks," stated the *Washington Post.* And, in fact, a survey of more than 150,000 students from twenty-seven universities released in September 2015 by the Association of American Universities (AAU) did paint a dire picture. According to the study, 23 percent of female college students reported experiencing some form of unwanted sexual contact on campus.

While the AAU survey highlighted a crucial safety issue for American higher education, it also highlighted the inherent difficulties in accurately measuring unlawful and unacceptable behavior. Immediately following its release, the study's authors cautioned that to conclude that 23 percent of female students are victims of "sexual attacks" would be "oversimplistic, if not misleading." The study's definition of sexual assault includes both unwanted penetrative sex *and* unwanted sexual touching and groping. Defining sexual assault in a way that is consistent with criminal rape statutes, the survey showed that 11 percent of females have been victimized—a number that, while still high, is not as high as the headlines suggested.

Experts also point out that the AAU survey may suffer from "nonresponse bias." Though 150,000 students participated in the study, 780,000 students had been asked to participate, via e-mail. It is possible that the 19 percent of students who responded were more likely to have experienced unwanted sexual contact than the 81 percent who did not. This could be one reason why the AAU study's results are inconsistent with those released by the federal government just nine months earlier. Using the National Crime Victimization Survey, which we will examine later in the chapter, the federal government found that 6.1 of every 1,000 female college students had suffered a sexual assault. Those numbers, however, are so low as to have generated their own criticism, with many wondering if the government's definition of sexual assault is too narrow or too confusing for survey respondents.

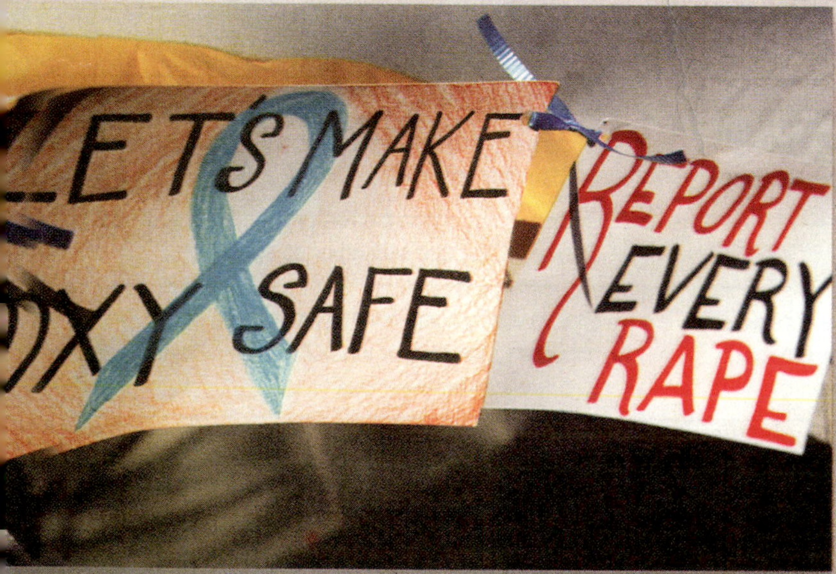

Patrick Fallon/Bloomberg/Getty Images

▲ Students protest the high incidence of campus rape during a sexual assault awareness night campout at Occidental College ("Oxy") in Los Angeles.

1. A decade ago, the federal government surveyed 4,000 college women about their experience with rape (coerced or unwanted sex) and found that one in four had survived a rape or attempted rape *at any point in their lives.* Compared with the AAU survey just discussed, which study is more useful? Why?
2. Explain the reasoning behind "nonresponse bias." Do you think it is a valid criticism of the AAU survey, as described above?
3. In 2015, several universities considered banning female students from fraternity houses to lessen the risk that these women would be sexually assaulted. What is your opinion of this policy?

Types of Crime

Learning Objective

1 Identify the six main categories of crime.

Statistical measurements such as the AAU's survey of unwanted sexual contact on college campuses are important because they often spur policy change.[1] For example, reacting to numerous studies detailing the magnitude of this particular problem, in 2013 Congress passed the Campus Sexual Violence Elimination Act. This legislation requires American secondary schools to, among other things, educate incoming students on the risks of dating violence and sexual assault.[2]

Legal definitions of criminal acts also matter. One first-year university student was surprised to learn, in a class designed to lessen the risk of rape, that a person who is incapacitated by alcohol cannot legally give consent to sex. Reflecting on a high school sexual incident during which she was drunk, she said, "I no longer felt shame and guilt about it being my fault."[3] In this chapter, we will examine the crucial role that definitions, statistics, and research play in answering broad questions such as, "How common is crime in United States?" and "Why do people commit crimes?" We start our discussion of measuring and explaining crime with a description of the six basic categories of criminal behavior in the United States: violent crime, property crime, public order crime, white-collar crime, organized crime, and high-tech crime.

Violent Crime

Crimes against persons, or *violent crimes,* have come to dominate our perspectives on crime. There are four major categories of violent crime:

- **Murder**, or the unlawful killing of a human being.
- **Sexual assault**, or *rape,* which refers to coerced actions of a sexual nature against an unwilling participant.
- **Assault** and **battery**, two separate acts that cover situations in which one person physically attacks another (battery) or, through threats, intentionally leads another to believe that he or she will be physically harmed (assault).
- **Robbery**, or the taking of funds, personal property, or any other article of value from a person by means of force or fear.

As you will see in Chapter 3, these violent crimes are further classified by *degree,* depending on the circumstances surrounding the criminal act. These circumstances include the intent of the person committing the crime, whether a weapon was used, and (in cases other than murder) the level of pain and suffering experienced by the victim.

Property Crime

The most common form of criminal activity is *property crime,* or those crimes in which the goal of the offender is some form of economic gain or the damaging of property. There are three major forms of property crime:

1. Pocket picking, shoplifting, and the stealing of any property without the use of force are covered by laws against **larceny**, also known as theft.
2. **Burglary** refers to the unlawful entry of a structure with the intention of committing a serious crime such as theft.
3. *Motor vehicle theft* describes the theft or attempted theft of a motor vehicle. Motor vehicles include any vehicle commonly used for transportation, such as a motorcycle or motor scooter, but not farm equipment or watercraft.

murder The unlawful killing of one human being by another.

sexual assault Forced or coerced sexual intercourse (or other sexual acts).

assault A threat or an attempt to do violence to another person that causes that person to fear immediate physical harm.

battery The act of physically contacting another person with the intent to do harm, even if the resulting injury is insubstantial.

robbery The act of taking property from another person through force, threat of force, or intimidation.

larceny The act of taking property from another person without the use of force with the intent of keeping that property.

burglary The act of breaking into or entering a structure (such as a home or office) without permission for the purpose of committing a felony.

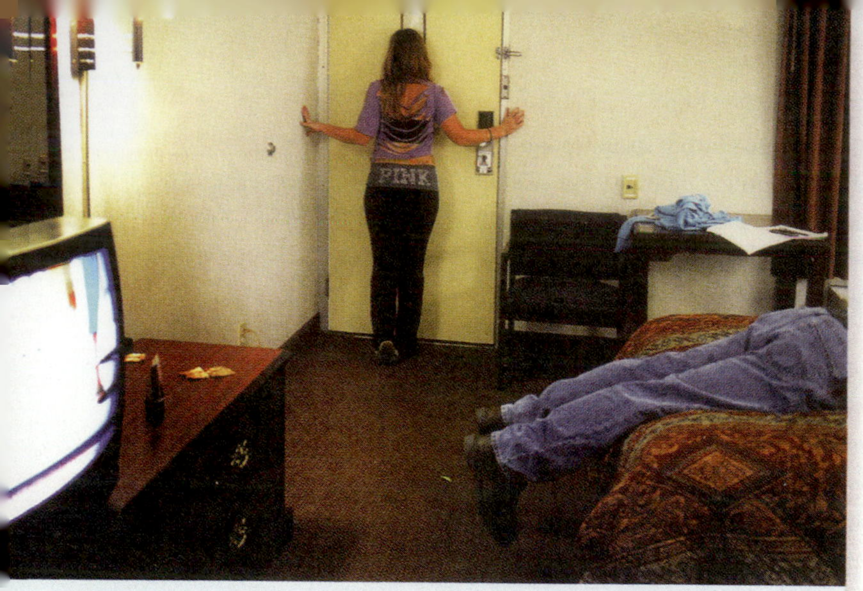

▲ A female member of the Prince George's County Police Department poses as a prostitute as part of an operation to crack down on the illegal activity in College Park, Maryland. Do you agree with the characterization of prostitution as a victimless crime? Why or why not? Bill O'Leary/*The Washington Post*/Getty Images

Arson is also a property crime. It involves the willful and malicious burning of a home, automobile, commercial building, or any other construction.

Public Order Crime

The concept of **public order crime** is linked to the consensus model discussed in Chapter 1. Historically, societies have always outlawed activities that are considered contrary to public values and morals. Today, the most common public order crimes include public drunkenness, prostitution, gambling, and illicit drug use. These crimes are sometimes referred to as *victimless crimes* because they often harm only the offender. As you will see throughout this textbook, however, that term is rather misleading. Public order crimes may create an environment that gives rise to property and violent crimes.

White-Collar Crime

Business-related crimes are popularly referred to as **white-collar crimes**. The term *white-collar crime* is broadly used to describe an illegal act or series of acts committed by an individual or business entity using some nonviolent means to obtain a personal or business advantage. As you will see in Chapter 14, when we consider the topic in much greater detail, certain property crimes fall into this category when committed in a business context. Although the extent of this criminal activity is difficult to determine with any certainty, the Association of Certified Fraud Examiners estimates that white-collar crime costs businesses worldwide as much as $3.7 trillion a year.[4]

Organized Crime

White-collar crime involves the use of legal business facilities and employees to commit illegal acts. For example, a bank teller can't embezzle unless he or she is first hired as a legal employee of the bank. In contrast, **organized crime** describes illegal acts by illegal organizations, usually geared toward satisfying the public's demand for unlawful goods and services. Organized crime broadly implies a conspiratorial and illegal relationship among any number of persons engaged in unlawful acts. More specifically, groups engaged in organized crime employ criminal tactics such as violence, corruption, and intimidation for economic gain.

The hierarchical structure of organized crime operations often mirrors that of legitimate businesses, and, like any corporation, these groups attempt to capture a sufficient percentage of any given market to make a profit. For organized crime, the traditional preferred markets are gambling, prostitution, illegal narcotics, and loan sharking (lending funds at higher-than-legal interest rates), along with more recent ventures into counterfeiting and credit-card scams.

High-Tech Crime

The newest variation on crime is directly related to the increased presence of computers in everyday life. The Internet, with approximately 3.2 billion users worldwide, is the vehicle for

public order crime Behavior that has been labeled criminal because it is contrary to shared social values, customs, and norms.

white-collar crime Nonviolent crimes committed by business entities or individuals to gain a personal or business advantage.

organized crime Illegal acts carried out by illegal organizations engaged in the market for illegal goods or services, such as illicit drugs or firearms.

numerous *cyber crimes*, such as selling pornographic materials, soliciting minors, and defrauding consumers through bogus financial investments. The dependence of businesses on computer operations has left corporations vulnerable to sabotage, fraud, and embezzlement.

Both corporations and individuals are susceptible to the theft of private information via the Internet—annually, nearly 170 million personal records are stolen through online data breaches.[5] The issue of cyber security will become even more important in the near future as tiny computers wirelessly connected to the Internet are placed in cars, kitchen appliances, and other objects of everyday use. We will address cyber criminality in much greater detail in Chapter 14.

Uniform Crime Report (UCR) An annual report compiled by the FBI to give an indication of criminal activity in the United States.

Measuring Crime in the United States

The six general categories of criminal behavior act as a frame for this country's crime picture. To fill in the frame's interior, experts rely on numerous measurements and studies of criminality, carried out by an array of government agencies, academic institutions, and individual researchers. The most widespread and best known of these surveys tries to answer the broadest of questions: How much crime is there in the United States?

The Uniform Crime Report

One of the more troubling aspects of sexual assault on college campuses is how infrequently these offenses are reported to law enforcement. According to the federal study referenced in the opening of this chapter, only 20 percent of student sexual assault victims communicate with the police.[6] Among these students, the most common reason given for keeping silent is, "I did not think [the incident] was serious enough to report."[7]

This trend almost certainly leads to the underreporting of sex crimes in the nation's most far-reaching and oft-cited set of national crime statistics. Each year, the U.S. Department of Justice releases the **Uniform Crime Report (UCR)**. Since its inception in 1930, the UCR has attempted to measure the overall rate of crime in the United States by organizing "offenses known to law enforcement."[8] To produce the UCR, the Federal Bureau of Investigation (FBI) relies on the voluntary participation of local law enforcement agencies. These agencies—approximately 18,400 in total, covering most of the population—base their information on three measurements:

1. The number of persons arrested.
2. The number of crimes reported by victims, witnesses, or the police themselves.
3. Police employee data.[9]

Once this information has been sent to the FBI, the agency presents the crime data in two important ways:

1. As a *rate* per 100,000 people. So, for example, suppose the crime rate in a given year is 3,500. This means that, for every 100,000 inhabitants of the United States, 3,500 *Part I offenses* were reported to the FBI by local police departments. The crime rate is often cited by media sources when discussing the level of crime in the United States.
2. As a *percentage* change from the previous year or other time periods. From 2005 to 2014, there was a 20 percent decrease in violent crime and a 24.3 percent decrease in property crime. Thus, according to the UCR, that decade saw a significant reduction in criminal behavior in the United States.[10]

Learning Objective

2 Identify the publication in which the FBI reports crime data, and list the two main ways in which the data are reported.

Part I offenses Crimes reported annually by the FBI in its Uniform Crime Report. Part I offenses include murder, rape, robbery, aggravated assault, burglary, larceny, and motor vehicle theft.

Part II offenses All crimes recorded by the FBI that do not fall into the category of Part I offenses. These crimes include both misdemeanors and felonies.

The Department of Justice publishes its data annually in *Crime in the United States*. Along with the basic statistics, this publication offers an exhaustive array of crime information, including breakdowns of crimes committed by city, county, and other geographic designations and by the demographics (gender, race, age) of the individuals who have been arrested for crimes.

Part I Offenses The UCR divides the criminal offenses it measures into two major categories: Part I and Part II offenses. **Part I offenses** are those crimes that, due to their seriousness and frequency, are recorded by the FBI to give a general idea of the "crime picture" in the United States in any given year. For a description of the seven Part I offenses, see Figure 2.1.

Part I violent offenses are those most likely to be covered by the media and, consequently, inspire the most fear of crime in the population. These crimes have come to dominate crime coverage to such an extent that, for most Americans, the first image that comes to mind at the mention of "crime" is one person physically attacking another person or a robbery taking place with the use or threat of force.[11] Furthermore, in the stereotypical crime, the offender and the victim usually do not know each other.

Given the trauma of violent crimes, this perception is understandable, but it is not accurate. According to UCR statistics, a relative or other acquaintance of the victim commits at least 43 percent of the homicides in the United States.[12] Furthermore, as is evident from Figure 2.1, the majority of Part I offenses committed are property crimes. Notice that 62 percent of all reported Part I offenses are larceny/thefts, and another 18 percent are burglaries.[13]

Part II Offenses Not only do violent crimes represent the minority of Part I offenses, but Part I offenses are far outweighed by **Part II offenses**, which include all crimes recorded by the FBI that do not fall into the category of Part I offenses. While Part I offenses are

Figure 2.1 Part I Offenses

Every month, local law enforcement agencies voluntarily provide information on serious offenses in their jurisdiction to the FBI. These serious offenses, known as Part I offenses, are defined here. (Arson is not included in the National Crime Report data, but it is sometimes considered a Part I offense nonetheless, so its definition is included here.) As the graph shows, most Part I offenses reported by local police departments in any given year are property crimes.

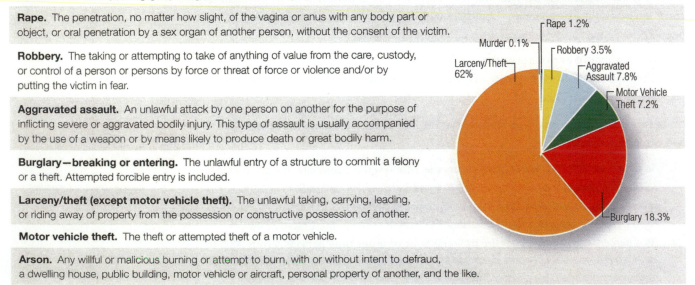

Murder. The willful (nonnegligent) killing of one human being by another.

Rape. The penetration, no matter how slight, of the vagina or anus with any body part or object, or oral penetration by a sex organ of another person, without the consent of the victim.

Robbery. The taking or attempting to take of anything of value from the care, custody, or control of a person or persons by force or threat of force or violence and/or by putting the victim in fear.

Aggravated assault. An unlawful attack by one person on another for the purpose of inflicting severe or aggravated bodily injury. This type of assault is usually accompanied by the use of a weapon or by means likely to produce death or great bodily harm.

Burglary—breaking or entering. The unlawful entry of a structure to commit a felony or a theft. Attempted forcible entry is included.

Larceny/theft (except motor vehicle theft). The unlawful taking, carrying, leading, or riding away of property from the possession or constructive possession of another.

Motor vehicle theft. The theft or attempted theft of a motor vehicle.

Arson. Any willful or malicious burning or attempt to burn, with or without intent to defraud, a dwelling house, public building, motor vehicle or aircraft, personal property of another, and the like.

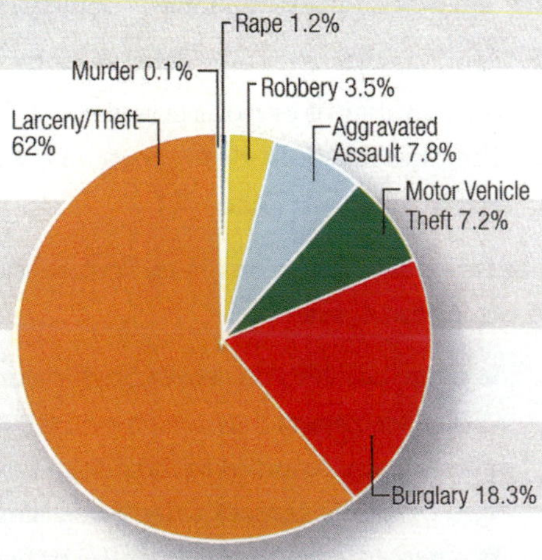
Rape 1.2%
Murder 0.1%
Robbery 3.5%
Larceny/Theft 62%
Aggravated Assault 7.8%
Motor Vehicle Theft 7.2%
Burglary 18.3%

Source: Federal Bureau of Investigation, *Crime in the United States. 2014* (Washington, D.C.: U.S. Department of Justice, 2015), **at www.fbi.gov/about-us/cjis/ucr/crime-in-the-u.s/2014/crime-in-the-u.s.-2014/resource-pages/offense-definitions and www.fbi.gov/about-us/cjis/ucr/crime-in-the-u.s/2014/crime-in-the-u.s.-2014/tables/table-1.**

almost always felonies, Part II offenses include criminal behavior that is often classified as a misdemeanor. Of the nineteen categories that make up Part II offenses, the most common are drug abuse violations, simple assaults (in which no weapons are used and no serious harm is done to the victim), driving under the influence, and disorderly conduct.[14]

Information gathered on Part I offenses reflects those offenses "known," or reported to the FBI by local agencies. Part II offenses, in contrast, are measured only by arrest data. In 2014, the FBI recorded about 2.2 million arrests for Part I offenses in the United States. That same year, about 10.2 million arrests for Part II offenses took place.[15] In other words, a Part II offense was four and one-half times more common than a Part I offense. Such statistics have prompted Marcus Felson, a professor at Rutgers University School of Criminal Justice, to comment that "most crime is very ordinary."[16]

The National Incident-Based Reporting System

About three decades ago, the Department of Justice began seeking ways to improve its data-collecting system. The result was the National Incident-Based Reporting System (NIBRS). In the NIBRS, local agencies collect data on each single crime occurrence within twenty-three offense categories made up of forty-nine specific crimes called Group A offenses. These data are recorded on computerized record systems provided—though not completely financed—by the federal government.

The NIBRS became available to local agencies in 1989. By 2014, about 6,300 law enforcement agencies were submitting all their crime data to the federal government using this program. Crime experts are responding enthusiastically to the NIBRS because the system provides information about four "data sets"—offenses, victims, offenders, and arrestees—unavailable through the UCR. The NIBRS also presents a more complete picture of crime by monitoring all criminal "incidents" reported to the police, not just those that lead to an arrest. For example, the 2014 NIBRS, which recorded more than 4.7 million criminal incidents, found that sex offenses were most likely to take place between midnight and 12:59 A.M., and that 121 murders and 12,567 aggravated assaults were the result of a "lovers' quarrel."[17] (See Figure 2.2 to get a clearer sense of the differences between the UCR and the NIBRS.)

Figure 2.2 Comparing the UCR and the NIBRS

As the following scenario shows, the process of crime data collection under the NIBRS is much more comprehensive than the reporting system of the UCR.

At approximately 9:30 p.m. on July 26, 2016, two young males approach a thirty-two-year-old African American woman in the parking garage of a movie theater. The first man, who is white, puts a knife to the woman's throat and grabs her purse, which contains $180. The second man, who is Hispanic, then puts a gun to the woman's temple and rapes her. When he is finished, he shoots her in the shoulder, a wound that does not prove to be serious. The two men flee the scene and are not apprehended by law enforcement.

	UCR	NIBRS
Crime reported to FBI	One rape. Under the UCR, when more than one crime is involved in a single incident, only the most serious is reported. Also, attempts are not recorded.	One rape, one robbery, and one attempted murder.
Age, sex, and race of the victim	Not recorded.	Recorded.
Age, sex, and race of the offenders	Not recorded.	Recorded.
Location and time of the attack	Not recorded.	Recorded.
Type and value of lost property	Not recorded.	Recorded.

Source: U.S. Department of Justice.

Figure 2.3 Sample Questions from the NCVS (National Crime Victimization Survey)

36a. Was something belonging to YOU stolen, such as

a. Things that you carry, like luggage, a wallet, purse, briefcase, book
b. Clothing, jewelry, or cell phone
c. Bicycle or sports equipment
d. Things in your home—like a TV, stereo, or tools
e. Things outside your home, such as a garden hose or lawn furniture
f. Things belonging to children in the household
g. Things from a vehicle, such as a package, groceries, camera, or CDs?

41a. Has anyone attacked or threatened you in any of these ways?

a. With any weapon, for instance, a gun or knife
b. With anything like a baseball bat, frying pan, scissors, or stick
c. By something thrown, such as a rock or a bottle
d. Include any grabbing, punching, or choking
e. Any rape, attempted rape, or other type of sexual attack
f. Any face to face threats OR
g. Any attack or threat or use of force by anyone at all? Please mention it even if you are not certain it was a crime.

43a. Incidents involving forced or unwanted sexual acts are often difficult to talk about. Have you been forced or coerced to engage in unwanted sexual activity by

a. Someone you didn't know
b. A casual acquaintance OR
c. Someone you know well?

45. During the last six months, did anything you thought was a crime happen to YOU, but you did NOT report it to the police?

a. Yes b. No

Source: Adapted from U.S. Department of Justice, *National Crime Victimization Survey 2009* (Washington, D.C.: Bureau of Justice Statistics, 2013).

Victim Surveys

To avoid the distortions caused when criminal behavior is not reported to the police, mentioned earlier in the context of campus sexual assaults, crime experts often prefer to go straight to the source. In **victim surveys**, these researchers ask the victims of crime directly about their experiences, using techniques such as interviews or e-mail and phone surveys. The first large-scale victim survey took place in 1966, when members of 10,000 households answered questionnaires as part of the President's Commission on Law Enforcement and the Administration of Justice. The results indicated a much higher victimization rate than had been previously expected, and researchers felt the process gave them a better understanding of the **dark figure of crime**, or the actual amount of crime that occurs in the country.

Crime experts were so encouraged by the results of the 1966 experiment that the federal government decided to institute an ongoing victim survey. The result was the National Crime Victimization Survey (NCVS), which started in 1972. Conducted by the U.S. Bureau of the Census in cooperation with the Bureau of Justice Statistics of the Justice Department, the NCVS conducts an annual survey of approximately 90,000 households with about 160,000 occupants over twelve years of age. Participants are interviewed twice a year concerning their experiences with crimes in the prior six months. As you can see in Figure 2.3, questions are quite detailed in determining the experiences of crime victims.

Learning Objective 3

Distinguish between the National Crime Victimization Survey (NCVS) and self-reported surveys.

victim surveys A method of gathering crime data that directly surveys participants to determine their experiences as victims of crime.

dark figure of crime A term used to describe the actual amount of crime that takes place. The "figure" is "dark," or impossible to detect, because a great number of crimes are never reported to the police.

self-reported survey A method of gathering crime data that relies on participants to reveal and detail their own criminal or delinquent behavior.

Self-Reported Surveys

Based on many of the same principles as victim surveys, but focusing instead on offenders, **self-reported surveys** are a third source of information for crime experts. In this form of data collection, persons are asked directly—through personal interviews or questionnaires, or over the telephone—about specific criminal activity to which they may have been a party. Self-reported surveys are most useful in situations in which the group to be studied is already gathered in an institutional setting, such as a juvenile facility or a prison.

One of the most widespread self-reported surveys in the United States, the Drug Use Forecasting Program, collects information on narcotics use from arrestees who have been brought into booking facilities. Because there is no penalty for admitting to criminal activity in a self-reported survey, subjects tend to be more forthcoming in discussing their behavior. This honesty often leads researchers to a striking conclusion: the dark figure of crime, referred to earlier as the *actual* amount of crime that takes place, appears to be much larger than the UCR or NCVS would suggest.

EthicsChallenge

In a recent one-year period, the Los Angeles Police Department misclassified about 1,200 violent crimes as minor offenses. Why might law enforcement officials feel pressure to "doctor" crime statistics in this manner? What steps could police administrators take to discourage this clearly unethical behavior?

Crime Trends

According to the UCR and the NCVS, the two most extensive measurements of national crime rates, the United States is presently enjoying historically low levels of crime. Since the early 1990s, the violent crime rate has declined by more than 50 percent (see Figure 2.4) and the property crime rate has dropped about 45 percent.[18] James Alan Fox, a crime expert and law professor at Northeastern University, points to four factors that likely have contributed to this trend:

1. Longer prison terms for offenders since the 1990s, when a sentencing reform movement that we will cover in Chapter 9 took hold in many state legislatures.
2. Continued improvement in law enforcement, including intelligence-based policing techniques that focus crime prevention tactics on "hot spots" of criminal activity and technology that improves the rapidity with which police respond to citizen reports of crime.
3. An aging population, meaning that older Americans—who are statistically less prone to criminal behavior—are having a greater influence on overall crime rates.
4. More lenient marijuana laws in many states (covered in Chapter 1) and lower nationwide heroin prices, which reduce the amount of violent and property crime associated with these drugs.[19]

One problem with relying on large-scale crime surveys to determine such trends is that the surveys are usually out of date. The 2014 UCR, for example, was released near the end of 2015. So, in the autumn of 2015, when many American cities were reporting increases in violent criminal activity, the FBI—relying on 2014 figures—was about to pronounce, officially, that violent crime rates had continued to drop.[20]

Figure 2.4 Violent Crime in the United States, 1990–2014

According to statistics gathered each year by the FBI, American violent crime rates dropped steadily in the second half of the 1990s, leveled off for several years, and now have begun to decrease anew.

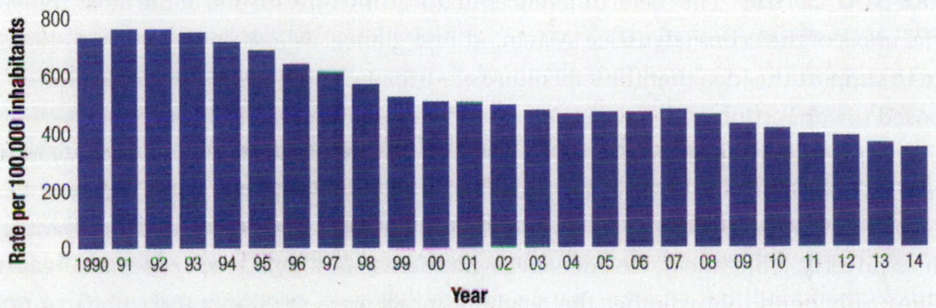

Source: Federal Bureau of Investigation.

Myth vs Reality

"Black on Black" Violence

The Myth According to the latest federal statistics, about 90 percent of African American homicide victims are killed by other African Americans. This data, along with disproportionately high rates of both violent offending and violent victimization in African American communities, is evidence of a "black on black" crime epidemic that is sweeping the United States.

The Reality Numerous references in the media to the spread of "black on black" crime has several consequences. First, it implies that African Americans are inherently lawless when compared to other racial and ethnic groups. Second, it suggests that African American communities have a greater tolerance for criminal and immoral behavior than do other segments of American society.

In fact, the vast majority of *all* homicides and violent crimes are intra-racial and intra-ethnic. In 2014, for example, white offenders killed about 82 percent of white homicide victims, and the relative number was 72 percent for Hispanic offenders and victims. This trend is largely a result of demographics. That is, most criminals commit crimes against victims who live nearby, and most Americans live in racially and ethnically homogeneous neighborhoods. Furthermore, violent crime victims and offenders often share a prior relationship, and such relationships are more likely to occur within racial and ethnic groups. By focusing on "black on black" crime, the media, politicians, and police officials not only give credence to stereotypes that create fear of African Americans, particularly young black men. They also ignore other causes of criminality, such as disadvantaged neighborhood conditions, that we will explore later in the chapter.

For Critical Analysis
What are some of the ways in which "black on black" crime rhetoric might influence policing strategies in African American neighborhoods?

Crime, Race, and Poverty

Although crime and victimization rates have decreased across racial lines over the past twenty years, the trends have been less positive for African Americans than for whites. For example, blacks are 6.3 times more likely to be homicide victims than whites,[21] and significantly more likely to be homicide offenders.[22] African Americans are particularly susceptible to gun violence, with firearm murder rates of 14.6 per 100,000 adults, compared to 1.9 for whites and 4.0 for Hispanics.[23] Chicago's West Garfield Park neighborhood, which is 96 percent black, has a homicide rate of 116 per 100,000 people. Honduras, the worldwide leader in murders, has a homicide rate of 90 per 100,000.[24]

Race and Crime Homicide rates are not the only area in which there is a divergence in crime trends among the races. Official crime data seem to indicate a strong correlation between minority status and crime: African Americans—who make up 13 percent of the population—constitute 38 percent of those arrested for violent crimes and 29 percent of those arrested for property crimes.[25] In five states that recently reformed their drug laws, the Center of Juvenile and Criminal Justice found that African Americans were still five times more likely than all other races and ethnicities to be arrested for marijuana-related crimes.[26] Furthermore, a black juvenile in the United States is more than twice as likely as a white juvenile to wind up in delinquency court and 30 percent more likely to have his or her case transferred to adult criminal court.[27] (See the feature *Myth vs Reality—"Black on Black" Violence* to further consider the intersection between crime and race.)

Learning Objective 4
Explain why income level appears to be more important than race or ethnicity when it comes to crime trends.

Class and Crime The racial differences in the crime rate are one of the most controversial areas of the criminal justice system. At first glance, as just noted, crime statistics seem to support the idea that the subculture of African Americans in the United States is disposed toward criminal behavior. Not all of the data, however, support that assertion. A recent research project led by sociologist Ruth D. Peterson of Ohio State University gathered information on nearly 150 neighborhoods in Columbus, Ohio. Peterson and her colleagues separated the neighborhoods based on race and on levels of disadvantage such as poverty, joblessness, lack of college graduates, and high levels of female-headed families. She found that whether the neighborhoods were predominantly white or predominantly black had little impact on violent crime rates. Those neighborhoods with higher levels of disadvantage, however, had uniformly higher violent crime rates.[28]

Peterson's research suggests that, regardless of race, a person is at a much higher risk of violent offending or being a victim of violence if he or she lives in a disadvantaged neighborhood. Given that African Americans are two times more likely than whites to live in poverty and hold low-wage-earning jobs, they are, as a group, more susceptible to the factors that contribute to criminality.[29] Indeed, a considerable amount of information suggests that income level is more important than skin color when it comes to crime trends. Recent victim surveys show that persons living in households at or below the federal poverty level have more than double the violent victimization rates as persons living in high-income households.[29] Lack of education, another handicap most often faced by low-income citizens, also seems to correlate with criminal behavior. Forty-one percent of all inmates in state and federal prisons failed to obtain a high school education, compared with 18 percent of the population at large.[30]

Ethnicity and Crime In the past, crime experts and statisticians have tended to focus on race, which distinguishes groups based on skin color, rather than *ethnicity*, which denotes national or cultural background. Given that Americans of Hispanic descent are the largest minority group in the United States, however, this bias against ethnic crime research is quickly diminishing. The FBI recently incorporated ethnicity into the UCR, finding, for example, that nearly a quarter of all arrests in this country involve a Hispanic or Latino suspect.[31] Furthermore, even though the firearm victimization rate of Hispanics in this country is more than twice that of whites,[32] the NCVS shows that their overall violent victimization rates are somewhat lower.[33]

The research treatment of other minority categories, such as Asian Americans, Native Americans, and Native Hawaiians, is mixed. The UCR has separate offense categories for these groups, with Native Americans arrested at a rate consistent with their population numbers and Asian Americans arrested at a much lower rate than their percentage of the country's overall population.[34] For its part, the NCVS refers to these disparate races and ethnicities collectively as "other," and shows them having similar victimization rates to whites and Hispanics.[35]

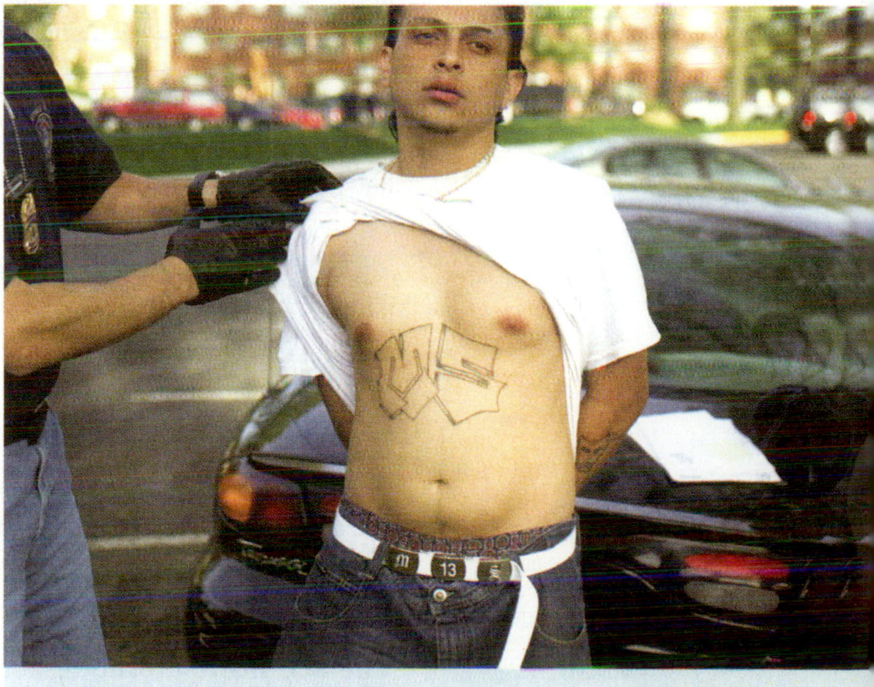

▲ A member of Prince George's County's Anti-Gang Unit makes an arrest during a crackdown on Hispanic gangs in Langley Park, Maryland. **Why is it likely that crime experts will increase their focus on issues of Hispanic offenders and victims in the United States over the next few decades?**
Robert Nickelsberg/Getty Images

Women and Crime

To put it bluntly, crime is an overwhelmingly male activity. Sixty-one percent of all murders involve a male victim and a male perpetrator, and in only 2.6 percent of homicides are both the offender and the victim female.[36] Only 15 percent of the national jail population and 7 percent of the national prison population are female, and in 2014 only 26 percent of all arrests involved women.[37]

These statistics fail to convey the startling rate at which the female presence in the criminal justice system has been increasing. Between 1991 and 2014, the number of men arrested each year declined about 35 percent. Over that time

criminology The scientific study of crime and the causes of criminal behavior.

correlation The relationship between two measurements or behaviors that tend to move in the same direction.

causation The relationship in which a change in one measurement or behavior creates a recognizable change in another measurement or behavior.

theory An explanation of a happening or circumstance that is based on observation, experimentation, and reasoning.

period, annual arrests for women remained about the same.[38] In 1970, there were about 6,000 women in federal and state prisons, while today, there are nearly 113,000.[39]

It appears that these statistics are the result of a change in the criminal justice system's attitude toward women, rather than a dramatic change in female misbehavior. A significant percentage of women arrested in the United States are involved in a narrow band of wrongdoing, mostly drug- and alcohol-related offenses or property crimes.[40] Research shows that as recently as the 1980s, many of the women now in prison would not have been arrested or would have received lighter sentences for their crimes.[41] Consequently, more scholars are convinced that rising female criminality is the result of a criminal justice system that is "more willing to incarcerate women."[42]

What Causes Crime?

David Kirk, a professor of sociology from Oxford University in England, knew that, on release from prison, most convicted criminals go back to their home neighborhoods. What happens, Kirk wondered, if those offenders are unwilling or unable to go back home after being released? He suspected that the rearrest rates of these ex-cons would be lower than the rearrest rates of ex-cons who returned to the often-negative influences of their families and social networks.[43]

The study of crime, or **criminology**, is rich with different explanations for why people commit crimes. These reasons range from bad social influences to mental illness to violent video games. In this section, we discuss the most influential of these explanations put forth by *criminologists* such as David Kirk who study the causes of crime.

Correlation and Cause

In the study of criminology, it is important to first understand the difference between *correlation* and *causation*. **Correlation** between two variables means that they tend to vary together. **Causation**, in contrast, means that one variable is responsible for the change in the other. As we will see later in the chapter, there is a correlation between drug abuse and criminal behavior: statistically, many criminals are also drug abusers. But drug abuse does not cause crime. Not everyone who abuses drugs is a criminal.

So, correlation does not equal cause. Such is the quandary for criminologists. We can say that there is a correlation between many factors and criminal behavior, but it is quite difficult to prove that the factors directly cause criminal behavior. Consequently, the question that is the underpinning of criminology—what causes crime?—has yet to be definitively answered.

The Role of Theory

Learning Objective 5

Discuss the difference between a hypothesis and a theory in the context of criminology.

Criminologists have, however, uncovered a wealth of information concerning a different, and more practically applicable, inquiry: Given a certain set of circumstances, why do individuals commit criminal acts? This information has allowed criminologists to develop a number of *theories* concerning the causes of crime.

The Scientific Method

Most of us tend to think of a *theory* as some sort of guess or a statement that is lacking in credibility. In the academic world, and therefore for our purposes, a **theory** is an explanation of a happening or circumstance that is based on observation, experimentation, and reasoning. Scientific and academic researchers observe facts and their consequences to develop *hypotheses* about what will occur when a similar fact pattern is present in the future. A **hypothesis** is a proposition that can be tested by researchers or observers to determine if it is valid. If enough authorities find the hypothesis valid, it will be accepted as a theory. See Figure 2.5 for an example of this process, known as the *scientific method*, in action.

Theory in Action To test his hypothesis about released inmates and recidivism discussed above, David Kirk turned to data involving ex-offenders from New Orleans. In 2005, the aftermath of Hurricane Katrina destroyed a number of residential areas in that city. Kirk decided to compare the recidivism rates of freed inmates from New Orleans who were able to return to their home neighborhoods and freed inmates who were not, because their neighborhoods were no longer inhabitable due to flooding from the storm. As it turned out, Kirk's hypothesis had some basis in fact. Over a period of eight years, the recidivism rate of those ex-convicts who returned home to New Orleans was 15 percent higher than the recidivism rate of those who moved away.[44]

As you read this chapter, keep in mind that theories are not the same as facts, and most, if not all, of the criminological theories described in these pages have their detractors. Over the past century, however, a number of theories of crime have gained wide, if not total, acceptance. We now turn our attention to these theories, starting with one that relies on freedom of choice.

Figure 2.5 The Scientific Method

The scientific method is a process through which researchers test the accuracy of a hypothesis. This simple example should provide an idea of how the scientific method works.

Observation: I left my home at 7:00 this morning, and I was on time for class.

Hypothesis: If I leave home at 7:00 every morning, then I will never be late for class.
(Hypotheses are often presented in this "If . . . , then . . ." format.)

Test: For three straight weeks, I left home at 7:00 every morning. Not one time was I late for class.

Verification: Four of my neighbors have the same morning class. They agree that they are never late if they leave by 7:00 A.M.

Theory: As long as I leave home at 7:00 A.M., I don't have to worry about being late for class.

Prediction: Tomorrow morning I'll leave at 7:00, and I will be on time for my class.

Note that even a sound theory supported by the scientific method, such as this one, does not *prove* that the prediction will be correct. Other factors not accounted for in the test and verification stages, such as an unexpected traffic accident, may disprove the theory. Predictions based on complex theories, such as the criminological ones we will be discussing in this chapter, are often challenged this manner.

The Brain and the Body

Perhaps the most basic answer to the question of why a person commits a crime is that he or she makes a willful decision to do so. This is the underpinning of the **rational choice theory** of crime, summed up by criminologist James Q. Wilson (1931–2012) as follows:.

> At any given moment, a person can choose between committing a crime and not committing it. The consequences of committing a crime consist of rewards (what psychologists call "reinforcers") and punishments; the consequences of not committing the crime also entail gains and losses. The larger the ratio of the net rewards of crime to the net rewards of [not committing a crime], the greater the tendency to commit a crime.[45]

In other words, a person, before committing a crime, acts as if she or he is weighing the benefits (which may be money, in the case of a robbery) against the costs (the possibility of being caught and going to prison or jail). If the perceived benefits are greater than the potential costs, the person is more likely to commit the crime.

"Thrill Offenders" Expanding on rational choice theory, sociologist Jack Katz has stated that the "rewards" of crime may be sensual as well as financial. The inherent danger of criminal activity, according to Katz, increases the "rush" a criminal experiences on successfully committing a crime. Katz labels the rewards of this "rush" the *seduction of*

hypothesis A possible explanation for an observed occurrence that can be tested by further investigation.

rational choice theory A school of criminology that holds that wrongdoers weigh the possible benefits of criminal or delinquent activity against the expected costs of being apprehended.

crime.[46] For example, one of the three teenagers charged with randomly and fatally shooting a jogger in Duncan, Oklahoma, in 2013 told police that he and his friends were "bored and didn't have anything to do, so we killed somebody."[47] Katz believes that such seemingly "senseless" crimes can be explained by rational choice theory only if the intrinsic (inner) reward of the crime itself is considered.

Rational Choice Theory and Public Policy The theory that wrongdoers choose to commit crimes is a cornerstone of the American criminal justice system. Because crime is seen as the end result of a series of rational choices, policymakers have reasoned that severe punishment can deter criminal activity by adding another variable to the decision-making process. Supporters of the death penalty—now used by thirty-one states and the federal government—emphasize its deterrent effects, and legislators have used harsh mandatory sentences to control illegal drug use and trafficking.

Trait Theories of Crime If society is willing to punish crimes that are the result of a rational decision-making process, what should be its response to criminal behavior that is irrational or even unintentional? What if, for example, a schoolteacher who made sexual advances to young girls, including his stepdaughter, could prove that his wrongdoing was actually caused by an egg-sized tumor in his brain?[48]

Somewhat in contrast to rational choice theory, *trait theories* suggest that certain *biological* or *psychological* traits in individuals could incline them toward criminal behavior given a certain set of circumstances. **Biology** is a very broad term that refers to the scientific study of living organisms, while **psychology** pertains more specifically to the study of the mind and its processes. "All behavior is biological," pointed out geneticist David C. Rowe. "All behavior is represented in the brain, in its biochemistry, electrical activity, structure, and growth and decline."[49]

Genetics and Crime Criminologists who study biological theories of crime often focus on the effect that *genes* have on human behavior. Genes are coded sequences of DNA that control every aspect of our biology, from the color of our eyes and hair to the type of emotions we have. Every person's genetic makeup is determined by genes inherited from his or her parents. Consequently, when scientists study ancestral or evolutionary developments, they are engaging in **genetics**, a branch of biology that deals with traits that are passed from one generation to another through genes.

Research has shown a genetic basis for such traits as attention deficit hyperactivity disorder (ADHD) and low self-control, both of which have been linked to antisocial behavior and crime.[50] Keep in mind, however, that no single gene or trait has been proved to cause criminality. As a result, the best that genetics can do is raise the possibility for a predisposition toward aggression or violence in an individual based on her or his family background.

The Brain and Crime The study of the nervous system and brain activity, or *neurophysiology*, has also found a place in criminology. Indeed, Jessica Wolpaw Reyes, an economist at Amherst College in Massachusetts, uses neurophysiology to help explain the drop in crime rates over the past twenty-five years (discussed earlier in the chapter).

Numerous studies have shown that exposure to lead damages the brains of children, causing them to have lower IQs, less impulse control, and a propensity for violent behavior. In the late 1970s, the federal government banned lead in gasoline and many types of paint. A generation of lead-free children has reached adulthood since then, and, Reyes believes, its nonviolent tendencies are responsible for half of the recent drop in violent crime rates.[51]

biology The science of living organisms, including their structure, function, growth, and origin.

psychology The scientific study of mental processes and behavior.

genetics The study of how certain traits or qualities are transmitted from parents to their offspring.

CJ & Technology

Repeat Offender Tracking

Nearly a half century ago, researchers found that a small number of juvenile offenders—6 percent—were responsible for a disproportionate amount of the violent crime attributed to a group of nearly 10,000 individuals. Further studies have supported the idea of a "chronic 6 percent," and, in the process, provided law enforcement with one of the most useful concepts in the history of criminology: the *chronic offender.*

Numerous law enforcement agencies have devised technological strategies to control and apprehend these chronic, or repeat, offenders. The Niagara County, New York, Sheriff's Department, for example, employs a Repeat Offender Tracking (ROTIN) system to keep tabs on individuals who have been arrested more than five times during a three-year period. Using special software, ROTIN provides local officers with a quick update every time one of these chronic offenders is arrested, booked into jail, or released from jail. ROTIN also helps law enforcement keeps track of chronic offenders with outstanding arrest warrants thought to be laying low in the Niagara County region.

Thinking about Repeat Offender Tracking

In theory, why should law enforcement agencies want the ability to track the movements of chronic offenders? In practice, do you think this ability prevents future crimes? Why or why not?

Learning Objective

6 Explain the theory of the chronic offender and its usefulness for law enforcement.

John Roman Images/Shutterstock.com

Mental Illness and Crime According to the federal government, more than half of all prison and jail inmates in the United States have mental health problems, with smaller percentages suffering from severe brain disorders.[52] In recent years, thanks to several high-profile murders, violent crime has been linked to *schizophrenia*, a chronic brain disorder that can lead to erratic, uncontrollable behavior. Persons suffering from this and other mental diseases are at an unusually high risk for committing suicide or harming others. Evidence culled from news reports suggests that more than half of mass shooters in the United States displayed symptoms ranging from depression to schizophrenia at the time of their violent outbursts.[53]

Further research shows that even moderate use of alcohol or drugs increases the chances that a schizophrenic will behave violently.[54] Still, it is important to note that about 3.5 million Americans—1 percent of the adult population—have been diagnosed with schizophrenia, and the vast majority of them will never become criminal offenders. Overall, according to Richard Friedman, a professor of clinical psychiatry at New York's Weill Cornell Medical College, only about 4 percent of violence in the United States can be attributed to those with mental illnesses.[55] Consequently, there may be a correlation between mental conditions such as schizophrenia and violence, but such conditions cannot be said to cause violent behavior.

Psychology and Crime Like biological theories of crime, psychological theories of crime operate under the assumption that individuals have traits that make them more or less predisposed to criminal activity. One crucial branch of psychology—*social psychology*—focuses on human behavior in the context of how human beings relate to and influence one another. Social psychology rests on the assumption that the way we view ourselves is shaped to a large degree by how we think others view us. Generally, we act in the same manner as those we like or admire because we want them to like or

▲ After a shooting rampage in which ten people were killed and another seven wounded at Umpqua Community College in Roseburg, Oregon, on October 2, 2015, local law enforcement officers urged the media not to name the shooter. The publicity that surrounds these events, they reasoned, makes it more likely that others will seek attention by carrying out similar acts. **Do the tenets of social psychology support this premise?** Scott Olson/Getty Images

admire us. Thus, to a certain extent, social psychology tries to explain the influence of crowds on individual behavior.

More than four decades ago, psychologist Philip Zimbardo highlighted the power of group behavior in dramatic fashion. Zimbardo randomly selected some Stanford University undergraduate students to act as "guards" and other students to act as "inmates" in an artificial prison environment. Before long, the students began to act as if these designations were real, with the "guards" physically mistreating the "inmates," who rebelled with equal violence. Within six days, Zimbardo was forced to discontinue the experiment out of fear for its participants' safety.[56] One of the basic assumptions of social psychology is that people are able to justify improper or even criminal behavior by convincing themselves that it is actually acceptable behavior. This delusion, researchers have found, is much easier to accomplish with the support of others behaving in the same manner.[57]

Trait Theory and Public Policy Whereas rational choice theory justifies punishing wrongdoers, biological and psychological views of criminality suggest that antisocial behavior should be identified and treated before it manifests itself in criminal activity. Though the focus on treatment diminished somewhat in the 1990s, rehabilitation practices in corrections have made, to some degree, a comeback over the past decade. The primary motivation for this new outlook, as we will see in Chapters 9 through 12, is the pressing need to divert nonviolent offenders from the nation's overburdened prison and jail system.

Bad Neighborhoods and Other Economic Disadvantages

For decades, the neighborhood of Liberty City in Miami, Florida, has endured one hardship after another. In the 1980s, it was racked by riots. In the 1990s, it was decimated by crack cocaine and AIDS. In the first decade of the 2000s, it was burdened by recession. Today, the area is marked by high levels of poverty, unemployment, and—not surprisingly—crime. After fifteen people were recently wounded during a shootout at a local nightclub, one resident reacted with resignation. "It's a shame," he said. "You hear gunshots every night and every day, and it becomes the norm."[58] Indeed, criminologists focusing on **sociology** have long argued that neighborhood conditions are perhaps the most important variable in predicting criminal behavior.

sociology The study of the development and functioning of groups of people who live together within a society.

social disorganization theory The theory that deviant behavior is more likely in communities where social institutions such as the family, schools, and the criminal justice system fail to exert control over the population.

Social Disorganization Theory In the early twentieth century, juvenile crime researchers Clifford Shaw and Henry McKay popularized sociological explanations for crime with their **social disorganization theory**. Shaw and McKay studied various high-crime neighborhoods in Chicago and discovered certain "zones" that exhibited high rates of crime. These zones were characterized by "disorganization," or a breakdown of the traditional institutions of social control such as family, school systems, and local businesses. In contrast, in the city's "organized" communities, residents had developed certain agreements about fundamental values and norms.

strain theory The assumption that crime is the result of frustration felt by individuals who cannot reach their financial and personal goals through legitimate means.

Shaw and McKay found that residents in high-crime neighborhoods had to a large degree abandoned these fundamental values and norms. Also, a lack of social controls had led to increased levels of antisocial, or criminal, behavior.[59] According to social disorganization theory, factors that lead to crime in these neighborhoods are:

1. High levels of high school dropouts
2. Chronic unemployment
3. Deteriorating buildings and other infrastructures
4. Concentrations of single-parent families

(See Figure 2.6 to better understand social disorganization theory.)

Strain Theory Another self-perpetuating aspect of disorganized neighborhoods is that once residents gain the financial means to leave a high-crime community, they usually do so. This desire to escape the inner city is related to the second branch of social structure theory: **strain theory**. Most Americans have similar life goals, which include gaining a certain measure of wealth and financial freedom. The means of attaining these goals, however, are not universally available. Many citizens do not have access to the education or training necessary for financial success.

This often results in frustration and anger, or *strain*. Sociologist Robert K. Merton (1910–2003) believed that strain is caused by a social structure in which all citizens have similar goals without equal means to achieve them.[60] One way to alleviate this strain is to gain wealth by the means that are available to the residents of disorganized communities: drug trafficking, burglary, and other criminal activities.

Figure 2.6 The Stages of Social Disorganization Theory

Social disorganization theory holds that crime is related to the environmental pressures that exist in certain communities or neighborhoods. These areas are marked by the desire of many of their inhabitants to "get out" at the first possible opportunity. Consequently, residents tend to ignore the important institutions in the community, such as businesses and education, causing further erosion and an increase in the conditions that lead to crime.

Source: Adapted from Larry J. Sigel, *Criminology*, 10th ed. (Belmont, CA: Thomson/Wadsworth, 2009), 180.

▲ Two law enforcement officers investigate a burglary in Camden, New Jersey—one of the poorest cities in the United States. **How would a criminologist who advocates social conflict theories of criminal behavior explain high crime rates in low-income communities such as Camden?** Spencer Platt/Getty Images

In the 1990s, Robert Agnew of Emory University in Atlanta, Georgia, updated this line of criminology with his *general strain theory,* or GST.[61] Agnew reasoned that of all "strained" individuals, very few actually turn to crime to relieve the strain. GST tries to determine what factors, when combined with strain, actually lead to criminal activity. By the early 2000s, Agnew and other criminologists settled on the factor of *negative emotionality,* a term used to cover personality traits of those who are easily frustrated, quick to lose their tempers, and disposed to blame others for their own problems.[62] Thus, GST mixes strain theory with aspects of psychological theories of crime.

Social Conflict Theories Strain theory suggests that the unequal structure of our society is, in part, to blame for criminal behavior. This argument forms the bedrock of **social conflict theories** of crime. These theories, which entered mainstream criminology in the 1960s, hold capitalism responsible for high levels of violence and crime because of the disparity of income that it encourages.

According to social conflict theory, the poor commit property crimes for reasons of need and because, as members of a capitalist society, they desire the same financial rewards as everybody else. They commit violent crimes because of the frustration and rage they feel when these rewards seem unattainable. Laws, instead of reflecting the values of society as a whole, reflect only the values of the segment of society that has achieved power and is willing to use the criminal justice system as a tool to keep that power.[63] As FBI Director James Comey pointed out in a recent speech, "At many points in American history, law enforcement enforced the status quo, a status quo that was often brutally unfair to disfavored groups."[64]

Life Lessons and Criminal Behavior

Some criminologists find class theories of crime overly narrow. Surveys that ask people directly about their criminal behavior have shown that the criminal instinct is pervasive in middle- and upper-class communities, even if it is expressed differently. Anybody, these criminologists argue, has the potential to act out criminal behavior, regardless of class, race, or gender.

Social Process Theories Philip Zimbardo, mentioned earlier in the context of social psychology, also conducted a well-known, if rather unscientific, experiment to show the broad human potential for misbehavior. The psychologist placed an abandoned automobile with its hood up on the campus of Stanford University. The car remained in place, untouched, for a week. Then, Zimbardo smashed the car's window with a sledgehammer. Within minutes, passersby had joined in the destruction of the automobile, eventually stripping its valuable parts.[65]

Zimbardo's "interdependence of decisions experiment" highlights the basic premise of **social process theories**: the potential for criminal behavior exists in everyone. This potential is more likely to be realized depending on an individual's interaction with various institutions and processes of society. Social process theory has two main branches: (1) learning theory and (2) control theory.

social conflict theories A school of criminology that views criminal behavior as the result of class conflict.

social process theories A school of criminology that considers criminal behavior to be the predictable result of a person's interaction with his or her environment.

Learning Theory Popularized by Edwin Sutherland in the 1940s, **learning theory** contends that criminal activity is a learned behavior. In other words, a criminal is taught both the practical methods of crime (such as how to pick a lock) and the psychological aspects of crime (how to deal with the guilt of wrongdoing). Sutherland's *theory of differential association* held that individuals are exposed to the values of family and peers such as school friends or co-workers. If the dominant values one is exposed to favor criminal behavior, then that person is more likely to mimic such behavior.[66] Sutherland's focus on the importance of family relations in this area is underscored by research showing that sons of fathers who have been incarcerated are at an increased risk of delinquency and arrest.[67]

learning theory The theory that delinquents and criminals must be taught both the practical and the emotional skills necessary to participate in illegal activity.

More recently, learning theory has been expanded to include the growing influence of the media. In the latest in a long series of studies, researchers released data in 2013 showing that children or adolescents who watched "excessive" amounts of violent television content faced an elevated risk of exhibiting antisocial behavior such as criminality in early adulthood.[68] The issue of whether academic and anecdotal evidence can be used to conclusively link such games to violent behavior has been addressed by the United States Supreme Court, as shown in the feature *Landmark Cases*—Brown v. EMA.

Landmark Cases

Brown v Entertainment Merchants Association (EMA)

Reacting to studies linking violent video games to violent behavior in children, in 2006 then–California governor Arnold Schwarzenegger signed a bill prohibiting the sale or rental of games that portray "killing, maiming, dismembering or sexually assaulting an image of a human being" to people younger than eighteen years old. The law imposed a $1,000 fine on violators. Immediately, video game sellers sued the state, saying it had violated their constitutional right to freedom of speech. After two lower courts accepted this argument and invalidated California's law, the issue finally arrived before the United States Supreme Court.

Brown v. EMA
United States Supreme Court
559 S.Ct. 1448 (2010)

In the Words of the Court . . .

Justice Scalia, Majority Opinion

* * * *

Like the protected books, plays, and movies that preceded them, video games communicate ideas—and even social messages—through many familiar literary devices (such as characters, dialogue, plot, and music) and through features distinctive to the medium (such as the player's interaction with the virtual world). That suffices to confer First Amendment protection. Under our Constitution, "esthetic and moral judgments about art and literature * * * are for the individual to make, not for the Government to decree, even with the mandate or approval of a majority."

* * * *

No doubt a State possesses legitimate power to protect children from harm, but that does not include a free-floating power to restrict the ideas to which children may be exposed.

* * * *

California relies primarily on * * * research psychologists whose studies purport to show a connection between exposure to violent video games and harmful effects on children. These studies have been rejected by every court to consider them, and with good reason: They do not prove that violent video games *cause* minors to act aggressively (which would at least be a beginning). Instead, "[n]early all of the research is based on correlation, not evidence of causation * * * ." They show at best some correlation between exposure to violent entertainment and minuscule real-world effects, such as children's feeling more aggressive or making louder noises in the few minutes after playing a violent game than after playing a nonviolent game.

Decision

In the absence of any provable negative effects on minors from violent video games, the Court ruled that California's ban was unconstitutional and therefore could not be enforced.

For Critical Analysis

If states have the "legitimate power" to "protect children from harm," why did the Court invalidate California's violent video game law? How did the late Justice Scalia use the concepts of *cause* and *correlation* to support the Court's decision? (You can review those terms from our discussion earlier in the chapter.)

control theory A series of theories that assume that all individuals have the potential for criminal behavior, but are restrained by the damage that such actions would do to their relationships with family, friends, and members of the community.

life course criminology The study of crime based on the belief that behavioral patterns developed in childhood can predict delinquent and criminal behavior later in life.

Control Theory Criminologist Travis Hirschi focuses on the reasons why individuals do not engage in criminal acts, rather than why they do. According to Hirschi, social bonds promote conformity to social norms. The stronger these social bonds—which include attachment to, commitment to, involvement with, and belief in societal values—the less likely that any individual will commit a crime.[69] **Control theory** holds that although we all have the potential to commit crimes, most of us are dissuaded from doing so because we care about the opinions of our family and peers.

Janet Lauritsen, a criminologist at the University of Missouri–St. Louis, contends that familial control is more important than run-down surroundings in predicting whether crime will occur. Lauritsen found that adolescents residing in two-parent households were victims of crime at similar rates, regardless of the levels of disadvantage in the neighborhoods in which they lived. By contrast, adolescents from single-parent homes who lived in highly disorganized neighborhoods were victimized at much higher rates than their counterparts in more stable locales. In Lauritsen's opinion, the support of a two-parent household offers crucial protection for children, whatever the condition of their neighborhood.[70]

Life Course Theories of Crime If crime is indeed learned behavior, some criminologists are asking, shouldn't we be focusing on early childhood—the time when humans do the most learning? Many of the other theories we have studied in this chapter tend to attribute criminal behavior to factors—such as unemployment or poor educational performance—that take place long after an individual's personality has been established. Practitioners of **life course criminology** believe that lying, stealing, bullying, and other conduct problems that occur in childhood are the strongest predictors of future criminal behavior and have been seriously undervalued in the examination of why crime occurs.[71]

Self-Control Theory Focusing on childhood behavior raises the question of whether conduct problems revealed at a young age can be changed over time. Michael Gottfredson and Travis Hirschi, whose 1990 publication *A General Theory of Crime* is one of the foundations of life course criminology, think not.[72] Gottfredson and Hirschi believe that criminal behavior is linked to "low self-control," a personality trait that is formed before a child reaches the age of ten and can usually be attributed to poor parenting.[73]

In general, someone who has low self-control is:

1. Impulsive,
2. Thrill-seeking, and
3. Likely to solve problems with violence rather than her or his intellect.

Learning Objective 7

Describe the importance of early childhood behavior for those who subscribe to self-control theory.

Gottfredson and Hirschi think that once low self-control has been established, it will persist. In other words, childhood behavioral problems are not "solved" by positive developments later in life, such as healthy personal relationships or a good job.[74] Thus, these two criminologists ascribe to what has been called the *continuity theory of crime,* which essentially says that once negative behavior patterns have been established, they cannot be changed.

The Possibility of Change Not all of those who practice life course criminology follow the continuity theory. Robert Sampson and John Laub have gathered a great deal of data showing, in their opinion, that offenders may experience "turning points" when they are able to veer off the road from a life of crime.[75]

Mastering**Concepts** The Causes of Crime

Rational Choice Theories

Key Concept: Crime is the result of rational choices made by those who decide to engage in criminal activity for the rewards—financial and otherwise—that it offers.

Example: Montgomery County, Maryland, prosecutors charged Daniel Cleaves, who is HIV-positive, with a crime for having unprotected sex. In court, Cleaves apologized for knowingly placing his victim at risk of infection.

Biological and Psychological Trait Theories

Key Concept: Criminal behavior is explained by the biological and psychological attributes of an individual.

Example: A forty-year-old married schoolteacher in Virginia inexplicably began exhibiting aberrant sexual conduct, including trying to molest his stepdaughter. When a tumor in the part of the teacher's brain associated with social behavior was removed, his deviant actions stopped.

Sociological Theories

Key Concept: Crime is not something one is "born to do." Rather, crime is the result of the social conditions such as poverty, poor schools, unemployment, and discrimination with which a person lives.

Example: Researchers at the University of Texas at Dallas found that teens who expect to die young are more likely to commit serious crimes. In addition, these early-death expectations strongly correlate with adverse neighborhood living conditions.

Social Conflict Theories

Key Concept: Through criminal laws, the dominant members of society control the minority members, using institutions such as the police, courts, and prisons as tools of oppression.

Example: When making automobile stops from 2002 to 2013, police in Durham, North Carolina, searched African American male drivers at more than twice the rate of white male drivers. There was no difference in how often illicit materials such as illegal drugs were found on white and black drivers.

Social Process Theories

Key Concept: Family, friends, and peers have the greatest impact on an individual's behavior, and it is the interactions with these groups that ultimately determine whether a person will become involved in criminal behavior.

Example: According to the U.S. Department of Justice, nearly 50 percent of inmates in state prisons have relatives who have also been incarcerated.

Life Course Theories

Key Concept: Criminal and antisocial behavior is evident at each stage of a person's life. By focusing on such behavior in early childhood, criminologists may be able to better understand and predict patterns of offending that emerge as a person grows older.

Example: Following the life course of more than seven thousand adolescents through adulthood, the American Psychological Association found that those repeatedly bullied as children were much more likely to go to prison than those who did not suffer repeated bullying.

Much of the research in this area has concentrated on the positive impact of getting married, having children, and finding a job,[76] but other turning points are also being explored. John F. Frana of Indiana State University and Ryan D. Schroeder of the University of Louisville argued that military service can act as a "rehabilitative agent."[77] Several researchers have studied the role that religion and spirituality can play as "hooks for change."[78] Furthermore, particularly for drug abusers, the death of a loved one or friend from shared criminal behavior can provide a powerful incentive to discontinue that behavior. (See this chapter's *Mastering Concepts* for a review of theories discussed so far in this chapter.)

Ethics Challenge

Suppose that a woman who harmed or even killed her newborn baby could be proven to be suffering from postpartum psychosis, a temporary illness caused by hormonal changes following childbirth. Would it be ethical to punish her for a criminal act that she may not have had control over? Do you agree with the prosecutor who said, "The mere fact that you have a mental condition is not an excuse for a criminal act"? Explain your answers.

Victims of Crime

For many years, criminologists have assumed that victims of childhood sexual abuse are more likely to commit sex offenses as adults. In 2015, Cathy Spatz Widom, a professor of psychology at the John Jay College of Criminal Justice in New York City, released a study that challenged this assumption. According to Widom's research, childhood *sexual* abuse does not lead to greater risks of later sexual offending. Young victims of *physical* abuse, however, do appear to be at an increased risk for being arrested of a sex crime as adults.[79]

Since its founding, criminology has focused almost exclusively on one-half of the crime equation: the offender. If you review our discussion of criminology up to this point, you will find little mention of the other half: the victim. Indeed, only in the past several decades has *victimology* become an essential component of criminology. Victim-oriented studies such the one overseen by Widom have had a profound impact on the police, the courts, and corrections administrators in this country, as well as on policymakers in fields not directly related to criminal justice.

The Risks of Victimization

Anybody can be a victim of crime. This does not mean, however, that everybody is at an equal risk of being victimized. For instance, residents of neighborhoods with heavy concentrations of payday lending businesses, which loan funds at burdensome interest rates on short notice, are targeted by criminals at unusually high rates.[80] To better explain the circumstances surrounding this type of victimization, criminologists Larry Cohen and Marcus Felson devised the *routine activities theory.* According to Cohen and Felson, most criminal acts require the following:

Learning Objective 8
Explain the routine activities theory of victimization.

1. A likely offender.
2. A suitable target (a person or an object).
3. The absence of a capable guardian—that is, any person (not necessarily a law enforcement agent) whose presence or proximity prevents a crime from happening.[81]

When these three factors are present, the likelihood of crime rises. Cohen and Felson cite routine activities theory in explaining the link between payday lenders and crime. People who use payday lenders often leave those establishments with large sums of cash late at night or during weekends, when there is less street traffic. Consequently, they act as suitable targets, attracting likely offenders to neighborhoods where the payday lenders are located.[82]

Repeat Victimization Cohen and Felson also hypothesize that offenders attach "values" to suitable targets. The higher the value, the more likely that target is going to be the subject of a crime.[83] A gold watch, for example, would obviously have a higher value for a thief than a plastic watch and therefore is more likely to be stolen. Similarly, people who are perceived to be weak or unprotected can have high value for criminals.

Careers in CJ

Courtesy Anne Seymour

Anne Seymour
National Victim Advocate

The aspect of my job that I enjoy the most is my direct work with crime victims and survivors. These are people who have been severely traumatized by pain and suffering and loss, and I consider it a true honor to be able to assist them. I'll never forget the day I met a young survivor who had been abducted, beaten within an inch of her life, raped, and then left to die in the forest. This young woman became one of my closest friends, and I helped her to speak out in her state and at the national level. Every time she does so, she has a powerful impact on our society. So my help in turning a victim/survivor into a stellar victim advocate/activist began on the day I met her, and it continues.

Victim advocacy is one of the most exciting and rewarding careers you could ever embark on, though it is not one that you should get into because of the money. (Few victim advocates become rich doing this work!) Every day is unique and different, reflecting the people I assist and the colleagues with whom I interact. I am never, ever bored and never will be. AND I go to bed every single day knowing that I have done at least one thing—and often many more than one!—to promote social justice and to help someone who is hurting. It's an amazing feeling!

SOCIAL MEDIA CAREER TIP Social media technologies are about connecting and sharing information—which means privacy is an important issue. Make sure you understand who can see the material you post and how you can control it. Facebook has numerous privacy settings, for example, as does Google+.

FASTFACTS

National victim advocate

Job description:

- Provide direct support, advocacy, and short-term crisis counseling to crime victims.

What kind of training is required?

- Bachelor's degree in criminal justice, social work/psychology, or related field.
- A minimum of two years' experience in the criminal justice system, one year of which must have involved direct services with victims.

Annual salary range?

- $31,000–$63,000

Law enforcement officials in southern Florida, for example, believe that undocumented immigrants in the area have elevated victimization rates because criminals know that these potential targets are afraid to report crimes to authorities for fear of being removed from the country.

Resources such as the National Crime Victimization Survey provide criminologists with an important tool for determining which types of people are most valued as potential victims. Statistics clearly show that a relatively small number of victims are involved in a disproportionate number of crimes. These findings support an approach to crime analysis known as **repeat victimization**. This theory is based on the premise that certain populations—mostly low-income residents of urban areas—are more likely to be victims of crimes than others and, therefore, past victimization is a strong predictor of future victimization.[84] Further criminological research shows that factors such as drug and alcohol use and mental illness also increase the possibility that a crime victim will be revictimized.[85]

The Victim-Offender Connection Not only does past victimization seem to increase the risk of future victimization, but so does past criminal behavior. "The notion that [violent crimes] are random bolts of lightning, which is the commonly held image, is not the reality at all," says David Kennedy, a professor at New York's John Jay College of Criminal Justice.[86]

repeat victimization The theory that certain people and places are more likely to be subject to repeated criminal activity and that past victimization is a strong indicator of future victimization.

Figure 2.7 Crime Victims in the United States

According to the U.S. Department of Justice, minorities, residents of urban areas, and young people are most likely to be victims of violent crime in this country.

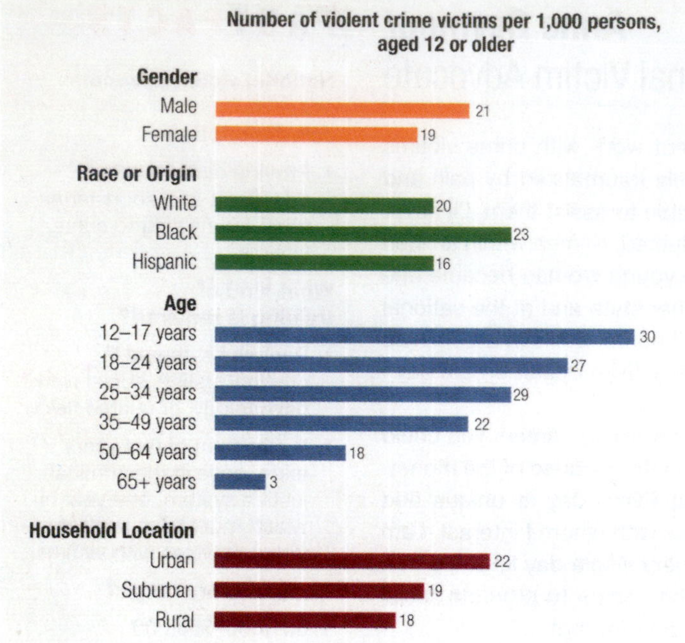

Number of violent crime victims per 1,000 persons, aged 12 or older
Gender
Male 21
Female 19
Race or Origin
White 20
Black 23
Hispanic 16
Age
12–17 years 30
18–24 years 27
25–34 years 29
35–49 years 22
50–64 years 18
65+ years 3
Household Location
Urban 22
Suburban 19
Rural 18

Source : Bureau of Justice Statistics, *Criminal Victization, 2014* (Washington, D.C.: U.S. Department of Justice, August 2015), 9, 10.

Kennedy's point is further made by Figure 2.7, which identifies young African American males from urban neighborhoods as the most common victims of crimes. This demographic, as we have discussed, is also at the highest risk for criminal behavior. Increasingly, law enforcement agencies are applying the lessons of repeat victimization and other victim studies to concentrate their attention on "hot spots" of crime, a strategy we address in Chapter 5.

Women as Crime Victims

Figure 2.7 also shows that men and women are victims of violent crimes at almost the same rate. The most striking aspect of women as victims of crime is the extent to which such victimization involves a prior relationship. According to the National Crime Victimization Survey, a male is twice as likely as a female to experience violence at the hands of a stranger.[87] With regard to intimate partner violence—involving a spouse, ex-spouse, boyfriend, girlfriend, ex-boyfriend, or ex-girlfriend—the gender difference is even more pronounced. Women are about five times more likely than men to be victims of intimate partner violence.[88]

Sexual Violence In general, about six of every ten crimes in the United States are committed by someone known to the victim. Those crimes that usually involve strangers, such as robbery and assault, most often target male victims. In contrast, women have a greater chance of being victimized in nonstranger crimes, such as sexual assault.[89] Indeed, women are the victims in 86 percent of all intimate partner violence prosecutions.[90] The highest rate of victimization occurs among women between the ages of twelve and thirty-four, and, as we discussed at the beginning of this chapter, a recent study estimates that about 23 percent of female college students have experienced some form of unwanted sexual contact, with 11 percent suffering from a serious sexual assault.[91]

Domestic Violence and Stalking Statistically, women are also at a greater risk of being victims of **domestic violence**. This umbrella term covers a wide variety of maltreatment, including physical violence and psychological abuse, inflicted among family members and others in close relationships. Though government data show that women are significantly more likely to be victims of domestic violence than are men,[92] these findings are not unquestioned. Men, many observers assume, are less likely to report abuse because of the social stigma surrounding female-on-male violence.[93] (The feature *CJ Controversy—Prosecuting Domestic Violence* explains how victims of this crime are often put in a difficult position when it comes to the punishment of their abusers.)

Another crime that appears to mainly involve female victims is **stalking**, or a course of conduct directed at a person that would reasonably cause that person to feel fear. Such behavior includes unwanted phone calls, following or spying, and a wide range of online activity that we will address in Chapter 14. Stalkers target women at about three times the rate they target men, and seven out of ten stalking victims have had some prior relationship with their stalkers.[94]

domestic violence The act of willful neglect or physical violence that occurs within a familial or other intimate relationship.

stalking The criminal act of causing fear in a person by repeatedly subjecting that person to unwanted or threatening attention.

M Dogan/Shutterstock.com

CJ Controversy

Prosecuting Domestic Violence

As you will see in Chapter 7, prosecutors have the ultimate authority to decide when to bring a case to court, regardless of the victim's wishes. In practice, domestic violence cases unfold somewhat differently. Because the victim is usually the only witness to the violence, if she or he refuses to participate, such cases can be very difficult to prosecute successfully. For a number of reasons, domestic violence victims frequently choose not to side with law enforcement against their abusers. These motivations include fear of retaliation, financial dependence on the offender, issues of custody and child support, and complex emotional ties.

The Wishes of Domestic Violence Victims Should Be Respected Because . . .

- Doing so rejects the paternalistic message that these victims cannot make rational choices about themselves and their futures.
- If a domestic violence victim chooses to cooperate with law enforcement officials, she or he often becomes more vulnerable to retaliatory attacks by the abuser.

The Wishes of Domestic Violence Victims Should Be Ignored Because . . .

- Crime victims should not have the power to determine whether public officials punish criminal activity.
- Prosecuting domestic violence offenders deters others from committing similar wrongdoing.

Your Assignment

To get a more nuanced idea of this issue, go online and research **no-drop policies and domestic violence.** When you feel you have a working knowledge of the subject, write at least two full paragraphs in which you explain why you support or reject these policies, which are designed to remove discretion when it comes to prosecuting alleged domestic violence offenders.

Mental Illness and Victimization

Those who suffer from mental illness are much more likely to be victims of crime than perpetrators. There are several reasons for this high victimization risk:

1. Mental illness often interferes with a person's ability to find and keep employment, and therefore leads to poverty, which, we have seen, correlates with victimization.
2. The mentally ill are more likely to be homeless, a circumstance that leaves them particularly susceptible to crime.[95]
3. Mental illness can interfere with a person's ability to make prudent decisions in potentially dangerous situations, increasing her or his chances of being assaulted.[96]

One review of the subject found that rates of victimization among people with mental illness are as much as 140 percent higher than in the general population.[97]

Mental health advocates insist that increasing services such as treatment and temporary housing for America's mentally ill will reduce the harm they cause themselves and others. The prohibitive costs of such services, however, seem to guarantee that mental illness will continue to be a problem for the criminal justice system, and for society at large.

The Link between Drugs and Crime

Earlier in this chapter, we discussed the difference between correlations and causes. As you may recall, criminologists are generally reluctant to declare that any one factor causes a certain result. Richard B. Felson of Penn State University and Keri B. Burchfield of Northern Illinois University, however, believe that alcohol consumption has a causal effect on crime victimization under certain circumstances.[98] Felson and Burchfield found

Figure 2.8 Illegal Drug Use in the United States

In 2014, about 27 million Americans reported using an illegal drug at least once in the previous twelve months. As this graph shows, marijuana is by far the most popular illicit drug in the United States.

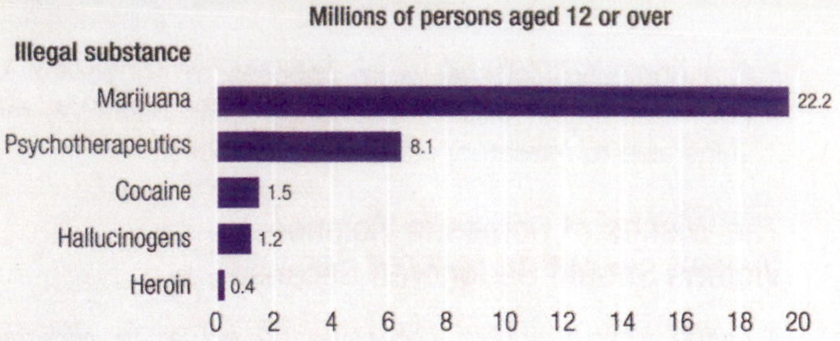

Millions of persons aged 12 or over
Illegal substance
Marijuana
Psychotherapeutics
Cocaine
Hallucinogens
Heroin
22.2
8.1
1.5
1.2
0.4
0
2
4
6
8
10
12
14
16
18
20

Marijuana: The most popular form of this drug is made using the dried, flowering tops of the cannabis plant, often mixed with tobacco, and smoked in the form of a cigarette. It primarily affects the central nervous system, causing feelings of relaxation, euphoria, and heightened sensory perception.

Psychotherapeutics: This term covers prescription drugs (pain relievers, tranquilizers, stimulants, and sedatives) used for nonmedical purposes. It includes methamphetamine, a highly addictive stimulant that is manufactured using prescription and over-the-counter drugs.

Cocaine: Derived from coca leaves, this stimulant is most commonly snorted as a powder, though it can be injected and, in a crystallized form known as "crack," smoked. Use of cocaine produces an instant euphoria, as well as numbness and feelings of increased energy and confidence.

Hallucinogens: A category that includes LSD, mescaline (from the peyote cactus), and PCP ("angel dust"). These drugs are known for their "psychedelic" effects, which cause users to experience reality in a distorted state.

Heroin: Derived from the poppy plant, this opioid is most commonly injected directly into the user's veins, though it can be snorted or smoked. Heroin use creates feelings of sedation and decreased anxiety, as well as a rush of euphoria.

Source : Sustance Abjuse and Mental Health Service Administration, Behavioral Health Trends in the United States: Results from the 2014 National Survey on Drug Use and Health (Washington, D.C.: National Institute of Drug Abuse, September 2015), Figure 1, page 4.

that "frequent and heavy" drinkers are at a great risk of assault when they are drinking, but do not show abnormal rates of victimization when sober. They hypothesize that consuming alcohol leads to aggressive and offensive behavior, particularly in men, which in turn triggers violent reactions from others.

According to the National Survey on Drug Use and Health, only 10.2 percent of those questioned had used an illegal drug in the past month. Even so, this means a significant number of Americans—about 27 million—are regularly using illegal drugs. That figure mushrooms when consumers of legal substances such as alcohol (140 million users) and tobacco (67 million users) are included.[99] (See Figure 2.8 for an overview of illegal drug use in the United States.) In this section, we will discuss two questions concerning these habits. First, why do people use drugs? Second, what are the consequences for the criminal justice system?

The Criminology of Drug Use

At first glance, the reason people use drugs, including legal drugs such as alcohol, is obvious: such drugs give the user pleasure and provide a temporary escape for those who may feel tension or anxiety. Ultimately, though, such explanations are unsatisfactory because they fail to explain why some people use drugs while others do not.

Theories of Drug Use Several of the theories we discussed earlier in the chapter have been used by experts to explain drug use. *Social disorganization theory* holds that rapid social change can cause people to become disaffiliated from mainstream society, causing them to turn to drugs. *Control theory* suggests that a lack of social control, as provided by entities such as the family or school, can lead to antisocial behavior.

Learning Objective 9

Discuss the connection between the learning process and the start of an individual's drug use.

Drugs and the "Learning Process" Focusing on the question of why first-time drug users become habitual users, sociologist Howard Becker sees three factors in the "learning process." He believes first-time users:

1. Learn the techniques of drug use.
2. Learn to perceive the pleasurable effects of drug use.
3. Learn to enjoy the social experience of drug use.[100]

Becker's assumptions are evident in the widespread view that positive images of drug use in popular culture "teach" adolescents that such behavior is not only acceptable but desirable. The entertainment industry, in particular, has been criticized for glamorizing various forms of drug use.

Drug Abuse and Addiction

Another theory rests on the assumption that some people possess overly sensitive drug receptors in their brains and are therefore biologically disposed toward drug use.[101] Though there is little conclusive evidence that biological factors can explain initial drug experimentation, scientific research has provided a great deal of insight into patterns of long-term drug use.

▲ A young woman prepares to use heroin under a bridge in Portland, Maine. **Do you think that drug abusers should be treated as criminals to be punished or as ill people in need of treatment? Explain your answer.** Cheryl Senter/*The New York Times*/Redux

Drug Use and Drug Abuse In particular, science has aided in understanding the difference between drug *use* and drug *abuse*. **Drug abuse** can be defined as the use of any drug—licit or illicit—that causes either psychological or bodily harm to the abuser or to third parties. Just as most people who drink beer or wine avoid abusing alcohol, most users of illegal substances are not abusers. Excluding cigarette smokers, only between 7 and 20 percent of all users suffer from compulsive abuse.[102] About 17 million Americans suffer from alcohol abuse, while another 7.1 million abuse illicit drugs and 2.6 million abuse both alcohol and an illicit drug.[103]

Addiction Basics The most extreme abusers are addicted to, or physically dependent on, a drug. To understand the basics of addiction and physical dependence, you must understand the role of *dopamine* in the brain. Dopamine is the neurotransmitter responsible for delivering pleasure signals to brain nerve endings in response to behavior—such as eating delicious food or engaging in sex—that makes us feel good. The bloodstream delivers drugs to the area of the brain that produces dopamine, thereby triggering the production of a large amount of the substance in the brain.

Over time, the continued use of drugs physically changes the nerve endings, called *receptors*. To continue operating in the presence of large amounts of dopamine, the receptors become less sensitive, meaning that greater amounts of any particular drug are required to create the amount of dopamine needed for the same levels of pleasure. When the supply of the drug is cut off, the brain strongly feels the lack of dopamine stimulation, and the abuser will suffer symptoms of withdrawal until the receptors readjust.[104]

Crime and Health: The Landscape of Drug Abuse

As we will see throughout this textbook, the prosecution of illegal drug users and suppliers has been one of the primary factors in the enormous growth of the American correctional industry. Of course, because many drugs are illegal, anybody who sells, uses, or in any way promotes any of these drugs is, under most circumstances, breaking the law. The drug-crime relationship goes well beyond the language of criminal drug statutes, however.

The Drug-Crime Relationship Studies that connect drug use to criminality can be problematic, mainly because such activity is likely one risk factor among many in a criminal user's life. Still, drugs and crime are related in three general ways:[105]

drug abuse The use of drugs that results in physical or psychological problems for the user, as well as disruption of personal relationships and employment.

Getting **Linked in**™

Teen drug abuse is a significant problem in the United States, and you can work toward alleviating it by becoming a **substance abuse counselor.** To learn more about this career path, enter the search term "substance abuse" on LinkedIn to access dozens of government and private health care organizations in this field.

1. *Drug-defined offenses*, or violation of laws prohibiting the possession, use, distribution, or manufacture of illegal drugs. Examples include possession of marijuana or methamphetamine production.
2. *Drug-related offenses*, such as crimes motivated by drug abuse or committed to further the illegal drug trade. Examples include gang violence between rival drug dealers and theft to get money to buy illegal drugs.
3. *The drug-using lifestyle*, experienced by many drug abusers who do not participate in the legitimate economy and thus rely on crime for the means of survival. These users often support short-term goals with illegal activities such as prostitution and welfare fraud.

According to the federal government, at least two-thirds of all persons arrested in this country have illegal drugs in their system when apprehended.[106] Legal drugs also play a role in the crime picture of the United States. About 37 percent of state prisoners and 33 percent of jail inmates incarcerated for a violent crime were under the influence of alcohol at the time of their arrest.[107]

Drugs and the National Health The laundry list of health problems associated with drug abuse is lengthy and sobering. It includes a weakened immune system, increased susceptibility to infection, heart conditions (including heart attacks), liver damage, brain damage, nausea, vomiting, and abdominal pain. Illegal drug users make about 525,000 emergency room visits each year.[108] Approximately 16,000 annual fatal overdoses in the United States are attributed to **prescription drugs**, or those drugs that can only be legally obtained with the permission of a licensed health care professional.[109]

In fact, drug overdoses are the driving force behind a surprising trend in this country: death rates for white adults ages twenty-five to thirty-four are rising for the first time since the AIDS epidemic took hold more than twenty years ago. The overdose death rate for this demographic group is five times higher today than it was in 1999, and heroin-related overdose death rates have quadrupled since 2002.[110] Many experts believe that the increased use and overdose rates of prescription drugs and heroin are linked. Three-quarters of heroin addicts previously used prescription drugs before switching to heroin, which is cheaper and more readily available on the black market.[111]

Marijuana Legalization

How would the link between certain illegal drugs and crime change if those drugs were legalized? That is, what if a particular illegal drug was treated in the same manner as alcohol and tobacco—heavily regulated, but available to persons over the age of twenty-one? While these questions are not being asked with regard to "hard" drugs such as heroin and cocaine, the **legalization** of marijuana—America's most-used illicit drug—has become an important policy issue. Indeed, as we noted in Chapter 1, in 2014 Colorado and Washington became the first states to legalize the sale, possession, and use of small amounts of marijuana. The next year, Alaska and Oregon followed suit, and the District of Columbia approved possession but not sale of the drug.

prescription drugs Medical drugs that require a physician's permission for purchase.

legalization The process of making a formerly illegal product or action lawful. In the context of marijuana, the process includes strict regulation, including a ban on sale to or use by minors.

Consequences of Legalization As we also discussed in Chapter 1, changing legal attitudes toward marijuana use seem to have had an impact on its popularity. Overall, marijuana use in the United States doubled between 2001 and 2013,[112] and college students now are more likely to be smoking marijuana than tobacco on a daily basis.[113] Given recent research showing a permanent negative impact of marijuana on the brain function of young (though not adult) frequent users, there is concern regarding the potential health impact of this national trend.[114] At the same time, many marijuana consumers in states where the drug is legal are frustrated that, under state law, they are limited to smoking it in private homes. In Denver, Colorado, advocates of the drug are pushing for the "the freedom to congregate and socialize to the same extent as alcohol users."[115]

The Future of Legalization Another foreseeable problem with marijuana legalization is *diversion.* This occurs when marijuana from states where it is legal inevitably begins supplying the black market for the drug in other, nonlegalized marijuana states. Of course, diversion would not exist if marijuana were legal throughout the United States, a contentious proposal we address in this chapter's *CJ Policy—Your Take.*

Practically speaking, whether or not the legalization movement spreads beyond Alaska, Colorado, Oregon, and Washington depends on what happens in those states. If they see a dramatic increase in underage pot use or drugged driving, or experience an unexpected rise in marijuana-related health problems, then the drug's "march toward the mainstream" could come to a halt. If, however, marijuana legalization has a primarily positive impact, particularly in areas such as tax revenue and crime reduction, then, in the words of one supporter, other states will "want to get rid of their prohibition laws, too."[116]

Ethics Challenge

In fiscal year 2015, the Colorado Department of Revenue brought in $70 million in taxes related to the sale of legal marijuana. Do you think there are any ethical issues with collecting taxes on a product that may have harmful health effects for users? Why or why not? (Note that Colorado also collected $42 million in taxes on alcohol that year.)

CJ Policy—Your Take

Several years ago, the **Ending Federal Marijuana Prohibition Act** was introduced before the U.S. Congress. Among other things, this bill, which never passed, would have legalized marijuana under federal law and led to its regulation in much the same manner as alcohol. **What would be the positive and negative consequences if marijuana were legalized throughout the United States and regulated like alcohol? Taking these factors into consideration, are you for or against such a dramatic change in criminal justice policy? Explain your answer.**

Summary

For more information on these concepts, look back to the Learning Objective icons throughout the chapter.

1 **Identify the six main categories of crime.** The six main categories of crime are (a) violent crime—murder, rape, assault and battery, and robbery; (b) property crime—pocket picking, shoplifting, larceny/theft, burglary, motor vehicle theft, and arson; (c) public order crime—public drunkenness, prostitution, gambling, and illicit drug use; (d) white-collar crime—business-related crimes such as fraud and embezzlement; (e) organized crime—illegal acts undertaken by illegal organizations, usually to satisfy the public's demand for unlawful goods and services; and (f) high-tech crime—theft of data from computer systems, as well as cyber crimes, such as selling child pornography over the Internet.

2 **Identify the publication in which the FBI reports crime data, and list the two main ways in which the data are reported.** Every year, the FBI releases the Uniform Crime Report (UCR), in which it presents different crimes as (a) a rate per 100,000 people and (b) a percentage change from the previous year.

3 **Distinguish between the National Crime Victimization Survey (NCVS) and self-reported surveys.** The NCVS involves an annual survey of more than 90,000 households conducted by the Bureau of the Census along with the Bureau of Justice Statistics. The survey queries citizens on crimes that have been committed against them. As such, the NCVS includes crimes not necessarily reported to police. Self-reported surveys, in contrast, involve asking individuals about criminal activity to which they may have been a party.

4 **Explain why income level appears to be more important than race or ethnicity when it comes to crime trends.** Criminologists have found that the most consistent indicators of criminal behavior are circumstances such as low family earning power and the absence of a parent. In addition, failure to obtain a high school diploma appears to have a positive correlation with criminal activity, regardless of the race or ethnicity of the individual.

5 **Discuss the difference between a hypothesis and a theory in the context of criminology.** A hypothesis is a proposition, usually presented in an "If . . . , then . . ." format, that can be tested by researchers. If enough different authorities are able to test and verify a hypothesis, it will usually be accepted as a theory. Because theories can offer explanations for behavior, criminologists often rely on them when trying to determine the causes of criminal behavior.

6 **Explain the theory of the chronic offender and its usefulness for law enforcement.** A chronic offender is a juvenile or adult who has committed multiple offenses in the past, and is therefore considered at risk to commit more offenses in the future. Using computer programs, some law enforcement agencies have devised strategies to track chronic offenders with the goal of preventing them from further criminality.

7 **Describe the importance of early childhood behavior for those who subscribe to self-control theory.** Advocates of self-control theory believe that violent and antisocial behavior in adulthood can be predicted, to a large extent, by low levels of self-control in early childhood. Therefore, a child who is impulsive and tends to solve problems with violence is at risk for adult offending.

8 **Explain the routine activities theory of victimization.** The routine activities theory holds that victimization becomes more likely to occur when the following three factors are present: (a) a likely offender; (b) a suitable target, in the form of either a person or an object to be stolen; and (c) the absence of a person who could prevent the crime, such as a law enforcement agent.

9 **Discuss the connection between the learning process and the start of an individual's drug use.** One criminologist believes that first-time illegal drug users go through a learning process in taking up the habit. That is, they learn the techniques of drug use from experienced drug users, they learn to perceive the pleasurable aspects of drug use, and they learn to enjoy the social experience of drug use.

Questions for Critical Analysis

1. For nearly eight decades until 2013, the federal government defined rape as sex with "a female forcibly and against her will." Compare this definition with the new definition in Figure 2.1. Which do you think is more representative of the crime, and why? What are the consequences of removing "forcibly" and "against her will" from the official definition?
2. Assume that you are a criminologist who wants to determine the extent to which high school students engage in risky behaviors such as abusing alcohol and illegal drugs, carrying weapons, and contemplating suicide. How would you go about gathering these data?
3. Why would someone who subscribes to rational choice theory believe that increasing the harshness of a penalty for a particular crime would necessarily lead to fewer such crimes being committed?
4. Research shows that when levels of single-family mortgage foreclosures rise in a neighborhood, so do levels of violent crime. Explain the correlation between these two sets of statistics. Why is it false to say that single-family mortgage foreclosures cause violent crimes to occur?
5. Consider the following statement: "The government should protect the public from mentally ill persons who are potentially dangerous, even if that means hospitalizing those persons against their will." Do you agree or disagree? Why?

Key Terms

assault 35
battery 35
biology 46
burglary 35
causation 44
control theory 52
correlation 44
criminology 44
dark figure of crime 40
domestic violence 56
drug abuse 59
genetics 46
hypothesis 45
larceny 35
learning theory 51
legalization 60
life course criminology 52
murder 35
organized crime 36
Part I offenses 38
Part II offenses 38
prescription drugs 60
psychology 46
public order crime 36
rational choice theory 45
repeat victimization 55
robbery 35
self-reported survey 40
sexual assault 35
social conflict theories 50
social disorganization theory 48
social process theories 50
sociology 48
stalking 56
strain theory 49
theory 44
Uniform Crime Report (UCR) 37
victim surveys 40
white-collar crime 36

Notes

1. David Cantor et al., *Report on the AAU Campus Climate Survey on Sexual Assault and Sexual Misconduct* (Rockville, Md.: Westat, September 21, 2015).
2. The Campus Sexual Violence Elimination Act of 2013, at **www.campussaveact.org.**
3. Quoted in Jan Hoffman, "College Rape Prevention Program Proves a Rare Success," *New York Times* (June 11, 2015), A15.
4. *2014 Report to the Nations: Occupational Fraud and Abuse* (Austin, Tex.: Association of Certified Fraud Examiners, 2014), 4.
5. *Data Breach Reports* (San Diego, Calif.: Identity Theft Resource Center, December 31, 2015), 4.
6. Bureau of Justice Statistics, *Rape and Sexual Assault Victimization among College-Age Females*, 1995–2013 (Washington, D.C.: U.S. Department of Justice, December 2014), 1.
7. Cantor et al., *op. cit.*, iv.
8. Federal Bureau of Investigation, *Crime in the United States 2014* (Washington, D.C.: U.S. Department of Justice, 2015), at **www.fbi.gov/about-us/cjis/ucr/crime-in-the-u.s/2014/crime-in-the-u.s.-2014.**
9. *Ibid.*
10. *Ibid.*, Table 1.
11. Jeffrey Reiman, *The Rich Get Richer and the Poor Get Prison*, 4th ed. (Boston: Allyn & Bacon, 1995), 59–60.
12. *Crime in the United States 2014, op. cit.*, Expanded Homicide Data Table 10.
13. *Ibid.*, Table 1.
14. *Ibid.*, Table 29.
15. *Ibid.*
16. Marcus Felson, *Crime in Everyday Life* (Thousand Oaks, Calif.: Pine Forge Press, 1994), 3.
17. Federal Bureau of Investigation, *National Incident-Based Reporting System 2014* (Washington, D.C.: U.S. Department of Justice, 2015), at **www.fbi.gov/about-us/cjis/ucr/nibrs/2014/tables/main.**
18. Federal Bureau of Investigation, *Crime in the United States 2010* (Washington, D.C.: U.S. Department of Justice, 2011), at **www**

.fbi.gov/about-us/cjis/ucr/crime-in-the-u.s/2010/crime-in-the-u.s.-2010/tables/10tbl01.xls; and *Crime in the United States 2014, op. cit.*, Table 1.

19. Quoted in Reid Wilson, "In Major Cities, Murder Rates Drop Precipitously," *Washington Post* (January 2, 2015), at **www.washingtonpost.com/blogs/govbeat/wp/2015/01/02/in-major-cities-murder-rates-drop-precipitously.**
20. Quoted in Devlin Barrett, "Inadequate Data Hampers Law Enforcement Fight against Rising Crime," *Wall Street Journal* (October 8, 2015), at **www.wsj.com/articles/inadequate-data-hampers-law-enforcement-in-fight-against-rising-crime-1444331310.**
21. Erica L. Smith and Alexia Cooper, *Homicide in the U.S. Known to Law Enforcement, 2011* (Washington, D.C.: U.S. Department of Justice, December 2013), 1.
22. *Crime in the United States 2014, op. cit.*, Expanded Homicide Data Table 3.
23. Michael Planty and Jennifer L. Truman, *Firearm Violence, 1993–2011* (Washington, D.C: U.S. Department of Justice, May 2013), 5.
24. Justin Glawe, "America's Mass Shooting Capital Is Chicago," *Daily Beast* (October 8, 2015), at **www.thedailybeast.com/articles/2015/10/08/america-s-mass-shooting-capital-is-chicago.html.**
25. *Crime in the United States 2014, op. cit.*, Table 43.
26. Mike Males and Lizzie Buchen, *Reforming Marijuana Laws: Which Approach Best Reduces the Harms of Criminalization?* (San Francisco, Calif.: Center of Juvenile and Criminal Justice, September 2014), 5–6.
27. Julie Furdella and Charles Puzzanchera, *Delinquency Cases in Juvenile Court*, 2013 (Washington, D.C.: Office of Juvenile Justice and Delinquency Prevention, October 2015), 2.
28. Ruth D. Peterson, "The Central Place of Race in Crime and Justice—The American Society of Criminology's 2011 Sutherland Address," *Criminology* (May 2012), 303–327.
29. Bureau of Justice Statistics, *Household Poverty and Nonfatal Violent Victimization*, 2008–2012 (Washington, D.C.: U.S. Department of Justice, November 2014), 1.
30. Caroline Wolf Harlow, *Education and Correctional Populations* (Washington, D.C.: Bureau of Justice Statistics, January 2003), 1.
31. *Crime in the United States 2014, op. cit.*, Table 43.
32. *Hispanic Victims of Lethal Firearms Violence in the United States* (Washington D.C.: Violent Policy Center, April 2014), i.
33. Bureau of Justice Statistics, *Criminal Victimization, 2014* (Washington, D.C. U.S. Department of Justice, August 2015), Table 9, page 9.
34. *Crime in the United States 2014, op. cit.*, Table 43A.
35. *Criminal Victimization, 2014, op. cit.*, Table 9, page 9.
36. *Crime in the United States 2014, op. cit.*, Expanded Homicide Table 6.
37. Bureau of Justice Statistics, *Jail Inmates at Midyear 2014* (Washington, D.C.: U.S. Department of Justice, June 2015), Table 2, page 3; Bureau of Justice Statistics, *Prisoners in 2014* (Washington, D.C.: U.S. Department of Justice, September 2015), Table 1, page 2; and *Crime in the United States 2014, op. cit.*, Table 33.
38. Federal Bureau of Justice, *Crime in the United States, 2000* (Washington, D.C.: U.S. Department of Justice, 2001), Table 33, page 221; and *Crime in the United States 2014, op. cit.*, Table 33.
39. *Prisoners in 2014, op. cit.*, Table 1, page 2.
40. *Crime in the United States 2014, op. cit.*, Table 42.
41. Jennifer Schwartz and Bryan D. Rookey, "The Narrowing Gender Gap in Arrests: Assessing Competing Explanations Using Self-Report, Traffic Fatality, and Official Data on Drunk Driving, 1980–2004," *Criminology* (August 2008), 637–671.
42. Meda Chesney-Lind, "Patriarchy, Prisons, and Jails: A Critical Look at Trends in Women's Incarceration," *Prison Journal* (Spring/Summer 1991), 57.
43. Malcolm Gladwell, "Starting Over," *New Yorker* (August 24, 2015), 32.
44. *Ibid.*
45. James Q. Wilson and Richard J. Hernstein, *Crime and Human Nature: The Definitive Study of the Causes of Crime* (New York: Simon & Schuster, 1985), 44.
46. Jack Katz, *Seductions of Crime: Moral and Sensual Attractions of Doing Evil* (New York: Basic Books, 1988).
47. Quoted in Matt Pearce, "Police: 'Bored' Oklahoma Teens Randomly Kill Australian Student," *Los Angeles Times* (August 20, 2013), A5.
48. Jeffrey M. Burns and Russell H. Swerdlow, "Right Orbifrontal Tumor with Pedophilia Symptom and Constructional Apraxia Sign," *Archives of Neurology* (March 2003), 437.
49. David C. Rowe, *Biology and Crime* (Los Angeles: Roxbury, 2002), 2.
50. Gail S. Anderson, *Biological Influences on Criminal Behavior* (Boca Raton, Fla.: CRC Press, 2007), 105–118.
51. Jessica Wolpaw Reyes, *Environmental Policy as Social Policy? The Impact of Childhood Lead Exposure on Crime* (Cambridge, Mass.: National Bureau of Economic Research, May 2007), at **www.nber.org/papers/w13097.pdf.**
52. Bureau of Justice Statistics, *Health Problems of Prison and Jail Inmates* (Washington, D.C.: U.S. Department of Justice, September 2006), 1.
53. "The Killing Contagion," *The Week* (September 11, 2015), 11.
54. Melissa S. Morabito and Kelly M. Socia, "Is Dangerousness a Myth? Injuries and Police Encounters with People with Mental Illness," *Criminology & Public Policy* (May 2015), 253–276.
55. Richard Friedman, "Why Can't Doctors Identify Killers?" *New York Times* (May 28, 2014), A21.
56. Philip Zimbardo, "Pathology of Imprisonment," *Society* (April 1972), 4–8.
57. David Canter and Laurence Alison, "The Social Psychology of Crime: Groups, Teams, and Networks," in *The Social Psychology of Crime: Groups, Teams, and Networks*, eds. David Canter and Laurence Alison (Hanover, N.H.: Dartmouth, 2000), 3–4.
58. Quoted in Lizette Alvarez, "Club Shooting in Rough Miami Neighborhood Continues a Cycle of Violence," *New York Times* (September 30, 2014), A15.
59. Clifford R. Shaw and Henry D. McKay, *Report on the Causes of Crime, Vol. 2: Social Factors in Juvenile Delinquency* (Washington, D.C.: National Commission on Law Observance and Enforcement, 1931).
60. Robert K. Merton, *Social Theory and Social Structure* (New York: Free Press, 1957). See the chapter on "Social Structure and Anomie."
61. Robert Agnew, "Foundation for a General Strain Theory of Crime and Delinquency," *Criminology* 30 (1992), 47–87.
62. Robert Agnew, Timothy Brezina, John Paul Wright, and Francis T. Cullen, "Strain, Personality Traits, and Delinquency: Extending General Strain Theory," *Criminology* (February 2002), 43–71.
63. Robert Meier, "The New Criminology: Continuity in Criminology Theory," *Journal of Criminal Law and Criminology 67* (1977), 461–469.
64. Quoted in Michael S. Schmidt, "F.B.I. Director Speaks Out on Race and Police Bias," *New York Times* (February 13, 2015).
65. Philip G. Zimbardo, "The Human Choice: Individuation, Reason, and Order versus Deindividuation, Impulse, and Chaos," in *Nebraska Symposium on Motivation*, eds. William J. Arnold and David Levie (Lincoln, Neb.: University of Nebraska Press, 1969), 287–293.
66. Edwin H. Sutherland, *Criminology*, 4th ed. (Philadelphia: Lippincott, 1947).
67. Michael E. Roettger and Raymond Swisher, "Associations of Fathers' History of Incarceration with Sons' Delinquency and Arrest among Black, White, and Hispanic Males in the United States," *Criminology* (November 2011), 1109–1147.
68. Lindsay A. Robertson, Helena M. McAnally, and Robert J. Hancox, "Childhood and Adolescent Television Viewing and Antisocial Behavior in Early Adulthood," *Pediatrics* (March 2013), 439–446.
69. Travis Hirschi, *Causes of Delinquency* (Berkeley: University of California Press, 1969).
70. Janet L. Lauritsen, *How Families and Communities Influence Youth Victimization*

(Washington, D.C.: Office of Juvenile Justice and Delinquency Prevention, 2003).

71. Francis T. Cullen and Robert Agnew, *Criminological Theory, Past to Present: Essential Readings*, 2d ed. (Los Angeles: Roxbury Publishing Co., 2003), 443.

72. Michael R. Gottfredson and Travis Hirschi, *A General Theory of Crime* (Stanford, Calif.: Stanford University Press, 1990).

73. *Ibid.*, 90.

74. *Ibid.*

75. Robert J. Sampson and John H. Laub, *Crime in the Making: Pathways and Turning Points through Life* (Cambridge, Mass.: Harvard University Press, 1993), 11.

76. *Ibid.*; John H. Laub and Robert J. Sampson, *Shared Beginnings, Divergent Lives: Delinquent Boys to Age 70* (Cambridge, Mass.: Harvard University Press, 2003); and Derek A. Kreager, Ross L. Matsueda, and Elena A. Erosheva, "Motherhood and Criminal Desistance in Disadvantaged Neighborhoods," *Criminology* (February 2010), 221–257.

77. John F. Frana and Ryan D. Schroeder, "Alternatives to Incarceration," *Justice Policy Journal* (Fall 2008), at **www.cjcj.org/files/alternatives_to.pdf.**

78. Peggy C. Giordano, Monica A. Longmore, Ryan D. Schroeder, and Patrick M. Seffrin, "A Life-Course Perspective on Spirituality and Desistance from Crime," *Criminology* (February 2008), 99–132.

79. Cathy Spatz Widom, "A Prospective Examination of Whether Childhood Sexual Abuse Predicts Subsequent Sexual Offending," *JAMA Pediatrics* (January 15, 2015), at **archpedi.jamanetwork.com/article.aspx?articleid=2086458.**

80. Chris E. Kubrin et al., "Does Fringe Banking Exacerbate Neighborhood Crime Rates?" *Criminology and Public Policy* (May 2011), 437–464.

81. Larry Cohen and Marcus Felson, "Social Change and Crime Rate Trends: A Routine Activity Approach," *American Sociological Review* (1979), 588–608.

82. Kubrin et al., *op. cit.*, 441.

83. Cohen and Felson, *op. cit.*

84. Marre Lammers et al., "Biting Once, Twice: The Influence of Prior on Subsequent Crime Location Choice," *Criminology* (August 2015), 309-326.

85. R. Barry Ruback, Valerie A. Clark, and Cody Warner, "Why Are Crime Victims at Risk of Being Victimized Again? Substance Use, Depression, and Offending as Mediators of the Victimization-Revictimization Link," *Journal of Interpersonal Violence* (January 2014), 157–185.

86. Quoted in Kevin Johnson, "Criminals Target Each Other, Trend Shows," *USA Today* (August 31, 2007), 1A.

87. Erika Harrell, *Violent Victimization Committed by Strangers*, 1993–2010 (Washington, D.C.: U.S. Department of Justice, Decemwber 2012), 2.

88. Shannan Catalano, *Intimate Partner Violence, 1993–2010* (Washington, D.C.: U.S. Department of Justice, November 2012), Table 1, page 2.

89. Harrell, *op. cit.*, Table 1, page 2.

90. Bureau of Justice Statistics, *Female Victims of Violence* (Washington, D.C.: U.S. Department of Justice, September 2009), Table 2, page 5.

91. Cantor et al., *op. cit.*, viii.

92. National Intimate Partner and Sexual Violence Survey, *Intimate Partner Violence in the United States—2010* (National Center for Injury and Prevention Control, February 2014), 1–2.

93. Eve S. Buzawa, "Victims of Domestic Violence," in eds. Robert C. Davis, Arthur Lurigio, and Susan Herman, *Victims of Crime*, 4th ed. (Los Angeles: Sage, 2013), 36–37.

94. Shannan Catalano, *Stalking Victims in the United States—Revised* (Washington, D.C.: U.S. Department of Justice, September 2012), 1, 5.

95. Arthur J. Lurigio, Kelli E. Canada, and Matthew W. Epperson, "Crime Victimization and Mental Illness" in *Victims of Crime, op. cit.*, 216–217.

96. *Ibid.*, 217–218.

97. Roberto Maniglio, "Severe Mental Illness and Criminal Victimization: A Systematic Review," *Acta Psychiactra Scandinavica* 119 (2009), 180–191.

98. Richard B. Felson and Keri B. Burchfield, "Alcohol and the Risk of Physical and Sexual Assault Victimization," *Criminology* (November 1, 2004), 837.

99. Substance Abuse and Mental Health Services, *Results of the 2013 National Survey on Drug Use and Health: Summary of National Findings* (Washington, D.C.: National Institute on Drug Abuse, September 2014), 1, 35, 47.

100. Howard S. Becker, *Outsider Studies in the Sociology of Deviance* (New York: Free Press, 1963).

101. David G. Myers, *Psychology*, 7th ed., (New York: Worth Publishers, 2004), 576–577.

102. Peter B. Kraska, "The Unmentionable Alternative: The Need for and Argument against the Decriminalization of Drug Laws," in *Drugs, Crime, and the Criminal Justice System*, ed. Ralph Weisheit (Cincinnati: Anderson Publishing, 1990).

103. Substance Abuse and Mental Health Services, *op. cit.*, 2.

104. Anthony A. Grace, "The Tonic/Phasal Model of Dopamine System Regulation," *Drugs and Alcohol* 37 (1995), 111.

105. Bureau of Justice Statistics, *Fact Sheet: Drug Related Crimes* (Washington, D.C.: U.S. Department of Justice, September 1994), 1.

106. *ADAM II: 2013 Annual Report* (Washington, D.C.: Office of National Drug Policy, January 2014), xi.

107. Bureau of Justice Statistics, "Alcohol and Crime: Data from 2002 to 2008," at **bjs.ojp.usdoj.gov/content/acf/29_prisoners_and_alcoholuse.cfm** and **bjs.ojp.usdoj.gov/content/acf/30_jails_and_alcohol use .cfm.**

108. Gateway Foundation, "Effects of Drug Abuse and Addiction," at **recovergateway.org/substance-abuse-resources/drug-addiction-effects.**

109. Centers for Disease Control and Prevention, "Prescription Drug Overdose Data Overview," at **www.cdc.gov/drugoverdose/data/index.html.**

110. Gina Kolata and Sarah Cohen, "Drug Overdoses Propel Rise in Mortality Rates of Young Whites," *New York Times* (January 17, 2016), A1; and Katharine Q. Seelye, "Obituaries Shed Euphemisms to Chronicle Toll of Heroin," *New York Times* (July 12, 2015), A16.

111. "A Hydra-Headed Scourge," *The Economist* (September 15, 2015), 28.

112. Elahe Izadi, "Marijuana Use More than Doubles in Just 12 Years," *Washington Post* (October 21, 2015), at **www.washingtonpost.com/news/to-your-health/wp/2015/10/21/marijuana-use-more-than-doubles-in-just-12-years.**

113. Lloyd D. Johnston et al., *Monitoring the Future: National Survey Results on Drug Use, 1975–2014*, Vol. 2 (Ann Arbor: The University of Michigan Institute for Social Research, July 2015), 86, 91.

114. Nora D. Volkow, "Marijuana Use by Youth Can Have Long-Term Consequences," *The Police Chief* (August 2015), 14.

115. Quoted in Jon Murray, "Activists Plan to Pull Denver Pot Consumption Initiative from Ballot," *Denver Post* (September 2, 2015), at **www.denverpost.com/politics/ci_28748511/activists-plan-pull-denver-pot-consumption-initiative-from.**

116. Quoted in Matt Ferner, "Recreational Marijuana Shops Open in Colorado," *The Huffington Post* (January 1, 2014), at **www.huffingtonpost.com/2014/01/01/marijuana-shops-open-colorado_n_4519506.html.**

sergign/Shutterstock.com

3

Inside Criminal Law

Chapter Outline		Corresponding Learning Objectives
Written Sources of American Criminal Law	1	List the four written sources of American criminal law.
The Purposes of Criminal Law	2	Explain the two basic functions of criminal law.
Classification of Crimes	3	Discuss the primary goals of civil law and criminal law, and explain how these goals are realized.
The Elements of a Crime	4	Explain how the doctrine of strict liability applies to criminal law.
Defenses under Criminal Law	5	List and briefly define the most important excuse defenses for crimes.
	6	Discuss a common misperception concerning the insanity defense in the United States.
	7	Describe the four most important justification criminal defenses.
Procedural Safeguards	8	Explain the importance of the due process clause in the criminal justice system.
	9	Describe the three ways that victims' rights legislation increases the ability of crime victims to participate in the criminal justice system.

To target your study and review, look for these numbered Learning Objective icons throughout the chapter.

no good Deed . . .

Eddie Ray Routh's mother knew former Navy SEAL and bestselling "American Sniper" author Chris Kyle often gave assistance to other veterans facing mental health problems. She asked Kyle to help her son, whom she believed to be suffering from post-traumatic stress disorder (PTSD) after serving in Iraq and Haiti. Kyle agreed, and he and a friend named Chad Littlefield took Routh to a shooting range near Chalk Mountain, Texas, as a form of therapy. During the drive over, Kyle texted Littlefield, "This dude [Routh] is straight up nuts." At the range, Routh fatally shot both Kyle and Littlefield while they were taking target practice.

During his murder trial, Routh pleaded not guilty to several counts of murder by reason of insanity. To back this claim, his lawyers presented evidence not only that Routh had been diagnosed with PTSD, but also that he was taking medication for schizophrenia and feared the world was being taken over by "pig people." Shortly before the shooting, Routh had been released from a local veterans hospital, where staff psychiatrists found that he was likely to harm himself or others. According to defense attorney J. Warren St. John, his client "killed [Kyle and Littlefield] because he had a delusion. He believed in his mind that they were going to kill him."

Under Texas law, a defendant who pleads not guilty by reason of insanity must prove that, "as a result of a severe mental disease or defect," he "did not know that his conduct was wrong." In other words, demonstrating mental illness is not enough. The defendant must convince a jury that, at the time of the crime, he or she did not realize the wrongness of his or her behavior. At Routh's trial, prosecutors argued that, despite any evidence of mental instability, the defendant was, in a legal sense, sane enough to be held responsible for the murders. After only about two hours of deliberation on February 24, 2015, the jury agreed and found Routh guilty. Whatever mental problems Routh may have been having, said a juror, "he knew the consequences of pulling the trigger."

Rodger Mallison/Fort Worth Star-Telegram/TNS/Getty Images

▲ Despite some evidence that he suffered from mental illness at the time of his crime, Eddie Ray Routh, shown here in a Stephenville, Texas, courtroom, was convicted of murdering Chris Kyle and Chad Littlefield.

1. One expert claims that Texas's legal standard for insanity is so difficult to meet that it is "virtually meaningless." Do you agree? Why or why not?
2. Prosecutors used Eddie Ray Routh's visit to a Taco Bell immediately following the murders as proof he was sane. Said Assistant District Attorney Jane Starnes, "You've got to go through the right lane; you've got to place your order; you've got to interact with the clerk; you've got to give them the money, get your change, get your food and go. It's not something that somebody who's just out-of-their-mind delusional does." What is your opinion of this reasoning?
3. Several decades ago, a Vietnam War veteran was found not guilty by reason of insanity for fatally shooting two suspected car thieves that he believed to be enemy soldiers on a Brooklyn street. Is the verdict in this case fair when compared to the verdict in Routh's case? Explain your answer.

Written Sources of American Criminal Law

Originally, American criminal law was *uncodified.* That is, it relied primarily on judges following custom, and the body of the law was not written down in any single place. Uncodified law, however, presents a number of drawbacks. For one, if the law is not recorded in a manner or a place in which the citizenry has access to it, then it is difficult, if not impossible, for people to know exactly which acts are legal and which acts are illegal. Furthermore, citizens have no way of determining or understanding the procedures that must be followed to establish innocence or guilt.

Consequently, American history has seen the development of several written sources of criminal law, also known as "substantive" criminal law. These sources include:

1. The U.S. Constitution and the constitutions of the various states.
2. Statutes, or laws, passed by Congress and by state legislatures, plus local ordinances.
3. Regulations, created by regulatory agencies, such as the federal Food and Drug Administration.
4. Case law (court decisions).

Combined, these written authorities (summarized in Figure 3.1) help ensure that our society is governed by the **rule of law**. This principle holds that all persons, as well as the government itself, must abide by the laws that reflect the values of the community at large. Furthermore, the law must be applied equally and enforced fairly, and must not be altered arbitrarily by any individual or group, no matter how powerful.

rule of law The principle that the rules of a legal system apply equally to all persons, institutions, and entities—public or private—that make up a society.

constitutional law Law based on the U.S. Constitution and the constitutions of the various states.

Learning Objective

1 List the four written sources of American criminal law.

Constitutional Law

The federal government and the states have separate written constitutions that set forth the general organization and powers of, and the limits on, their respective governments. **Constitutional law** is the law as expressed in these constitutions.

The U.S. Constitution is the supreme law of the land. As such, it is the basis of all law in the United States. Any law that violates the Constitution, as ultimately determined by the United States Supreme Court, will be declared unconstitutional and will not be enforced. The Tenth Amendment, which defines the powers and limitations of

Figure 3.1 Sources of American Law

Constitutional law	**Definition:** The law as expressed in the U.S. Constitution and the various state constitutions.	**Example:** The Sixth Amendment to the U.S. Constitution states that any person accused of a crime has the right "to be informed of the nature and cause of the accusation."
Statutory law	**Definition:** Laws or *ordinances* created by federal, state, and local legislatures and governing bodies.	**Example:** Illinois state law considers exposing a cat or dog to life-threatening weather to be a criminal act punishable by up to a year in jail.
Administrative law	**Definition:** The rules, orders, and decisions of federal or state government administrative agencies.	**Example:** U.S. Fish and Wildlife Service regulations make it a crime to kill a wolf in certain protected areas except when necessary for the immediate defense of human life.
Case law	**Definition:** Judge-made law, including judicial interpretations of the other three sources of law.	**Example:** A federal appeals court overturns a Michigan law criminalizing peaceable panhandling in public places on the ground that the statute violates the constitutional right of freedom of speech.

statutory law The body of law enacted by legislative bodies.

supremacy clause A clause in the U.S. Constitution establishing that federal law is the "supreme law of the land" and shall prevail when in conflict with state constitutions or statutes.

ballot initiative A procedure in which the citizens of a state, by collecting enough signatures, can force a public vote on a proposed change to state law.

the federal government, reserves to the states all powers not granted to the federal government. Under our system of federalism (see Chapter 1), each state also has its own constitution. Unless they conflict with the U.S. Constitution or a federal law, state constitutions are supreme within their respective borders. (You will learn more about how constitutional law applies to our criminal justice system throughout this textbook.)

Statutory Law

Statutes enacted by legislative bodies at any level of government make up another source of law, which is generally referred to as **statutory law**. *Federal statutes* are laws that are enacted by the U.S. Congress. *State statutes* are laws enacted by state legislatures, and statutory law also includes the ordinances passed by cities and counties. A federal statute, of course, applies to all states. A state statute, in contrast, applies only within that state's borders. City or county ordinances (statutes) apply only to those jurisdictions where they are enacted.

Legal Supremacy It is important to keep in mind that there are essentially fifty-two different criminal codes in this country—one for each state, the District of Columbia, and the federal government. Originally, the federal criminal code was quite small. The U.S. Constitution mentions only three federal crimes: treason, piracy, and counterfeiting. Today, federal law includes about 4,500 offenses that carry criminal penalties.[1] Inevitably, these federal criminal statutes are bound to overlap or even contradict state statutes. In such cases, thanks to the **supremacy clause** of the Constitution, federal law will almost always prevail. Simply put, the supremacy clause holds that federal law is the "supreme law of the land."

So, for example, hundreds of individuals have been charged with violating federal law for possessing or selling medical marijuana in states where such use is legal under state law.[2] As we discussed earlier in the textbook, marijuana use—for medicinal purposes or otherwise—remains illegal under federal law, and, in the words of one federal judge, "we are all bound by federal law, like it or not."[3] Along the same lines, any statutory law—federal or state—that violates the Constitution will be overturned. In the late 1980s, for example, the United States Supreme Court ruled that any state laws banning the burning of the American flag were unconstitutional because they impinged on the individual's right to freedom of expression.[4]

Ballot Initiatives On a state and local level, voters can write or rewrite criminal statutes through a form of direct democracy known as the **ballot initiative**. In this process, a group of citizens draft a proposed law and then gather a certain number of signatures to get the proposal on that year's ballot. If a majority of the voters approve the measure, it is enacted into law. Currently, twenty-four states and the District of Columbia accept ballot initiatives, and these special elections have played a crucial role in shaping criminal law in those jurisdictions. Crucial changes in state law regarding physician-assisted suicide and marijuana legalization, discussed earlier in this text, have been the result of ballot initiatives.

Like other state laws, laws generated by ballot initiatives are not immune from review by state and federal courts. Oklahoma and Nebraska recently filed a joint lawsuit asking the United States Supreme Court to find Colorado's recreational marijuana law, passed as a ballot initiative, unconstitutional. The two states claimed that marijuana flowing from Colorado over their borders has unfairly "stressed" state and local law enforcement resources.[5]

Administrative Law

A third source of American criminal law consists of **administrative law**—the rules, orders, and decisions of *regulatory agencies.* A regulatory agency is a federal, state, or local government agency established to perform a specific function. The Occupational Safety and Health Administration (OSHA), for example, oversees the safety and health of American workers. The Environmental Protection Agency (EPA) is concerned with protecting the natural environment, and the Food and Drug Administration (FDA) regulates food and drugs produced in the United States.

▲ In 2015, voters in Washington State passed a ballot initiative that outlawed sales relating to the trafficking of products made from ten endangered species, including elephants, marine turtles, lions, and tigers. Breaking the new state law could result in a maximum of five years in prison and a $10,000 fine. **What are some of the pros and cons of using ballot initiatives to create criminal law?** Csehak Szabolcs/Shutterstock.com

Disregarding certain laws created by regulatory agencies can be a criminal violation. Federal statutes, such as the Clean Water Act, authorize a specific regulatory agency, such as the EPA, to enforce regulations to which criminal sanctions are attached.[6] So, several years ago, following a criminal investigation led by EPA agents, a Longview, Washington, septic tank pumping business was found to have illegally dumped two million gallons of pollutants and waste into the city's sewage system. A federal judge sentenced the business's owner to twenty-seven months in prison and a fine of $250,000.

Case Law

Another basic source of American law consists of the rulings announced in court, or *precedents*. A **precedent** is a decision that furnishes an example or authority for deciding subsequent cases involving similar legal principles or facts. The body of law created by precedent is referred to variously as the common law, judge-made law, or **case law**.

Case law is the basis for a doctrine called ***stare decisis*** ("to stand on decided cases"). Under this doctrine, judges are obligated to follow the precedents established within their jurisdiction. For example, any decision of a particular state's highest court will control the outcome of future cases on that issue brought before all the lower courts within that same state. Per the supremacy clause, discussed earlier, all U.S. Supreme Court decisions involving the U.S. Constitution are binding on *all* courts, because the U.S. Constitution is the supreme law of the land.

The doctrine of *stare decisis* does not require the U.S. Supreme Court *always* to follow its own precedent, though the Court often does so. At times, a change in society's values will make an older ruling seem obsolete, at least in the eyes of the Supreme Court justices. In 1986, for example, the Court upheld a state law that banned certain homosexual acts that were lawful when performed by a man and a woman.[7] Seventeen years later, the Court overturned that decision, ruling that the government does not have the ability to treat one class of citizens differently from the rest of society when it comes to sexual practices between consenting adults. Wrote Justice Anthony Kennedy, the original case "was not correct when it was decided, and it is not correct today."[8]

administrative law The body of law created by administrative agencies (in the form of rules, regulations, orders, and decisions) in order to carry out their duties and responsibilities.

precedent A court decision that furnishes an example of authority for deciding subsequent cases involving similar facts.

case law The rules of law announced in court decisions.

stare decisis (pronounced *ster*-ay dih-*si*-*ses*). A legal doctrine under which judges are obligated to follow the precedents established under prior decisions.

The Purposes of Criminal Law

Learning Objective

Explain the two basic functions of criminal law. **2**

Why do societies need laws? Many criminologists believe that criminal law has two basic functions: one relates to the legal requirements of a society, and the other pertains to the society's need to maintain and promote social values.

The Legal Function of the Law

The primary legal function of the law is to maintain social order by protecting citizens from *criminal harm.* This term refers to a variety of harms that can be generalized to fit into two categories:

1. Harms to individual citizens' physical safety and property, such as the harm caused by murder, theft, or arson.
2. Harms to society's interests collectively, such as the harm caused by unsafe foods or consumer products, a polluted environment, or poorly constructed buildings.[9]

Because criminal law has the primary goal of protecting people from harm, new criminal laws are often passed in response to specific acts. For example, in May 2014, an otherwise healthy eighteen-year-old high school senior in LaGrange, Ohio, died from a caffeine powder overdose. By mid-2015, to prevent a similar tragedy, the Illinois legislature had passed a bill making the sale of caffeine powder to minors illegal within state limits.[10]

CJ & Technology

Unmanned Aerial Vehicles (UAVs)

Maria Dryfhout/Shutterstock.com

An estimated one million unmanned aerial vehicles (UAVs), commonly referred to as drones, are operating in the United States. Most of these models weigh only a few pounds and are "virtually toys," according to one enthusiast. These "toys" have, however, caused a multitude of problems. They have interfered with firefighters, crashed into buildings, and been used to smuggle contraband into prisons. Most seriously, pilots of passenger planes and other aircraft are reporting about one hundred sightings or close calls with UAVs each month.

The law is now trying to catch up with this emerging technology. In September 2015, the Federal Aviation Administration announced that recreational UAV owners must register their drones with the government. Any registered operator who interferes with air traffic will be subject to a fine. In addition, twenty states have passed criminal legislation related to UAVs. For example, New Hampshire prohibits the use of drones for hunting, fishing, or trapping, and in Mississippi it is a crime to engage in "Peeping Tom" activities with the aid of a UAV.

Thinking about UAVs

Should it be against the law to fly a camera-equipped drone onto or over another person's private property? Should the law punish someone who damages a drone that is flying over her or his property without permission, or is flying unreasonably close to her or his family? Explain your answers.

The Social Function of the Law

If criminal laws against acts that cause harm or injury to others are almost universally accepted, the same cannot be said for laws that criminalize "morally" wrongful activities that may do no obvious, physical harm outside the families of those involved. Why criminalize gambling or prostitution if the participants are consenting?

Expressing Public Morality The answer lies in the social function of criminal law. Many observers believe that the main purpose of criminal law is to reflect the values and norms of society, or at least of those segments of society that hold power. Legal scholar Henry Hart has stated that the only justification for criminal law and punishment is "the judgment of community condemnation."[11]

Take, for example, the misdemeanor of bigamy, which occurs when someone knowingly marries a second person without terminating her or his marriage to an original husband or wife. Apart from moral considerations, there would appear to be no victims in a bigamous relationship, and indeed many societies have allowed and continue to allow bigamy to exist. In the American social tradition, however, as John L. Diamond of the University of California's Hastings College of the Law points out, "Marriage is an institution encouraged and supported by society." Therefore, the immorality of bigamy, Diamond explains, "is not in choosing to do wrong, but in transgressing, even innocently, a fundamental social boundary that lies at the core of social order."[12]

▲ Many gun rights activists, such as these two demonstrators outside the Idaho State Capitol in Boise, support state "nullification" laws that aim to void federal gun legislation. **Why does the supremacy clause, discussed earlier in the chapter, make it unlikely that such state laws would survive a court challenge?** Chris Butler/*Idaho Statesman*/MCT/Getty Images

Local Values Of course, public morals are not uniform across the entire nation, and a state's criminal code often reflects the values of its residents. In Kentucky, for example, someone who uses a reptile as part of a religious service is subject to up to $100 in fines, and New Hampshire prohibits any person or agency from introducing a wolf into the state's wilds.[13]

Sometimes, local values and federal law will conflict with one another. Nine states, mostly in the western half of the country, have passed "nullification" laws that seek to void federal gun legislation within their borders.[14] For example, in 2014, Idaho passed a new law under which state law enforcement officers could be charged with a misdemeanor and fined up to $1,000 dollars for enforcing a federal gun law.[15]

EthicsChallenge

For a variety of reasons, many parents in this country are refusing to have their infant children vaccinated against measles and other infectious diseases. By doing so, according to the medical community, these parents are putting other children at a much greater risk of contracting a wide range of diseases, some of which are fatal. Would it be ethical for the government to pass a law forcing parents to have their children vaccinated for the good of society as whole? Why or why not? ■

Classification of Crimes

The huge body of the law can be broken down according to various classifications. Three of the most important distinctions are those between (1) civil law and criminal law, (2) felonies and misdemeanors, and (3) crimes *mala in se* and *mala prohibita*.

Civil Law and Criminal Law

Learning Objective 3

Discuss the primary goals of civil law and criminal law, and explain how these goals are realized.

All law can be divided into two categories: civil law and criminal law. These two categories of law are distinguished by their primary goals. As we have seen, the criminal justice system is concerned with protecting society from harm by preventing and prosecuting crimes. **Civil law**, which includes all types of law other than criminal law, is concerned with disputes between private individuals and between entities.

Proceedings in civil lawsuits are normally initiated by an individual or a corporation (in contrast to criminal proceedings, which are initiated by public prosecutors). Such disputes may involve, for example, the terms of a contract, the ownership of property, or an automobile accident. Under civil law, the government provides a forum for the resolution of *torts*—or private wrongs—in which the injured party, called the **plaintiff**, tries to prove that a wrong has been committed by the accused party, or the **defendant**. (Note that the accused party in both criminal and civil cases is known as the *defendant*.)

Guilt and Responsibility

A criminal court is convened to determine whether the defendant is *guilty*—that is, whether the defendant has, in fact, committed the offense charged. In contrast, civil law is concerned with responsibility, a much more flexible concept. For example, nearly a decade ago Adam Jones started a melee in a Las Vegas strip club by tossing hundreds of dollar bills into the air. During the ensuing brawl, doorman Tommy Urbanski was shot and paralyzed from the waist down. Jones did not pull the trigger nor was he charged with any crime. Nonetheless, in 2015 a civil appeals court decided that he was **liable**, or legally responsible, for Urbanski's injuries because of his irresponsible behavior.

Most civil cases involve a request for monetary damages to compensate for the wrong that has been committed. Thus, the civil court ordered Jones to pay Urbanski and his ex-wife, Kathy, about $11.2 million to cover medical costs and loss of earnings, as well as for infliction of emotional distress.

The Burden of Proof

Although criminal law proceedings are completely separate from civil law proceedings in the modern legal system, the two systems do have some similarities. Both attempt to control behavior by imposing sanctions on those who violate society's definition of acceptable behavior. Furthermore, criminal and civil law often supplement each other. In certain instances, a victim may file a civil suit against an individual who is also the target of a criminal prosecution by the government.

Because the burden of proof is much greater in criminal trials than civil ones, it is almost always easier to win monetary damages than a criminal conviction. The most famous (or infamous) example of such a situation in recent memory occurred about twenty years ago. After former professional football player O. J. Simpson was acquitted of murder charges in the deaths of his ex-wife, Nicole, and Ronald Goldman, the families of the two victims sued Simpson. In 1997, a civil court jury found Simpson liable for the wrongful deaths of his ex-wife and Goldman, and ordered him to pay their families $33.5 million in damages.

civil law The branch of law dealing with the definition and enforcement of all private or public rights, as opposed to criminal matters.

plaintiff The person or institution that initiates a lawsuit in civil court proceedings by filing a complaint.

defendant In a civil court, the person or institution against whom an action is brought. In a criminal court, the person or entity who has been formally accused of violating a criminal law.

liability In a civil court, legal responsibility for one's own or another's actions.

Mastering**Concepts** Civil Law versus Criminal Law

Issue	Civil Law	Criminal Law
Area of concern	Rights and duties between individuals	Offenses against society as a whole
Wrongful act	Harm to a person or business entity	Violation of a statute that prohibits some type of activity
Party who brings suit	Person who suffered harm (plaintiff)	The state (prosecutor)
Party who responds	Person who supposedly caused harm (defendant)	Person who allegedly committed a crime (defendant)
Standard of proof	Preponderance of the evidence	Beyond a reasonable doubt
Remedy	Damages to compensate for the harm	Punishment (fine or incarceration)

During the criminal trial, the jury did not find enough evidence to prove **beyond a reasonable doubt** (the burden of proof in criminal cases) that Simpson was guilty of any crime. In contrast, the civil trial established by a **preponderance of the evidence** (the burden of proof in civil cases) that Simpson had killed his victims in a fit of jealous rage. (See this chapter's *Mastering Concepts* feature for a comparison of civil and criminal law.)

Felonies and Misdemeanors

Depending on their degree of seriousness, crimes are classified as *felonies* or *misdemeanors*. **Felonies** are crimes punishable by death or by imprisonment in a federal or state prison for one year or longer (though some states, such as North Carolina, consider felonies to be punishable by at least two years' incarceration). For the most part, felonies involve crimes of violence such as armed robbery or sexual assault, or other "serious" crimes such as stealing a large amount of money or selling illegal drugs.

Types of Misdemeanors Under federal law and in most states, any crime that is not a felony is considered a **misdemeanor**. Misdemeanors are crimes punishable by a fine or by confinement for up to a year. If imprisoned, the guilty party goes to a local jail instead of a prison. Disorderly conduct and trespassing are common misdemeanors. Most states distinguish between *gross misdemeanors,* which are offenses punishable by thirty days to a year in jail, and *petty misdemeanors,* which are offenses punishable by fewer than thirty days in jail. Probation and community service are often imposed on those who commit misdemeanors, especially juveniles. As you will see in Chapter 7, whether a crime is a felony or misdemeanor can also determine in which criminal court the case will be tried.

Infractions The least serious form of wrongdoing is often called an **infraction** and is punishable only by a small fine. Even though infractions such as parking tickets or traffic violations technically represent illegal activity, they generally are not considered "crimes." Therefore, infractions rarely lead to jury trials and are deemed to be so minor that they do not appear on the offender's criminal record.

In some jurisdictions, the terms *infraction* and *petty offense* are interchangeable. In others, however, they are different. Under federal guidelines, for example, an infraction can be punished by up to five days behind bars, while a petty offender is only

beyond a reasonable doubt The degree of proof required to find the defendant in a criminal trial guilty of committing the crime. The defendant's guilt must be the only reasonable explanation for the criminal act before the court.

preponderance of the evidence The degree of proof required to decide in favor of one side or the other in a civil case. In general, this requirement is met when a plaintiff proves that a fact more likely than not is true.

felony A serious crime, usually punishable by death or imprisonment for a year or longer.

misdemeanor A criminal offense that is not a felony; usually punishable by a fine and/or a jail term of less than one year.

infraction In most jurisdictions, a noncriminal offense for which the penalty is a fine rather than incarceration.

mala in se A descriptive term for acts that are inherently wrong, regardless of whether they are prohibited by law.

mala prohibita A descriptive term for acts that are made illegal by criminal statute and are not necessarily wrong in and of themselves.

corpus delicti The body of circumstances that must exist for a criminal act to have occurred.

liable for a fine.[16] Finally, those who string together a series of infractions (or fail to pay the fines that come with such offenses) are in danger of being criminally charged. In Illinois, having three or more speeding violations in one year is considered criminal behavior.[17]

Mala in Se and *Mala Prohibita*

Criminologists often express the social function of criminal law in terms of *mala in se* or *mala prohibita* crimes. A criminal act is referred to as ***mala in se*** if it would be considered wrong even if there were no law prohibiting it. *Mala in se* crimes are said to go against "natural laws"—that is, against the "natural, moral, and public" principles of a society. Murder, rape, and theft are examples of *mala in se* crimes. These acts are generally regarded as crimes from country to country or culture to culture.

In contrast, the term ***mala prohibita*** refers to acts that are considered crimes only because they have been codified as such through statute—"human-made" laws. A *mala prohibita* crime is thought to be wrong only because it has been prohibited. It is not inherently wrong, though it may reflect the moral standards of a society at a given time. Thus, the definition of a *mala prohibita* crime can vary from country to country and even from state to state. Bigamy, or the offense of having two legal spouses, could be considered a *mala prohibita* crime.

Some observers question the distinction between *mala in se* and *mala prohibita.* In many instances, it is difficult to define a "pure" *mala in se* crime. That is, it is difficult to separate a crime from the culture that has deemed it a crime.[18] Even murder, under certain cultural circumstances, is not always considered a criminal act. In a number of poor, traditional areas of the Middle East and Asia, the law excuses "honor killings," in which men kill female family members suspected of sexual indiscretion.

Our own legal system excuses homicide in extreme situations, such as self-defense or when a law enforcement agent kills in the course of upholding the law. Therefore, "natural" laws can be seen as culturally specific. Similar difficulties occur in trying to define a "pure" *mala prohibita* crime. More than 150 countries, including most members of the European Union, have legalized prostitution. With the exception of seven rural counties of Nevada, prostitution is illegal in the United States.

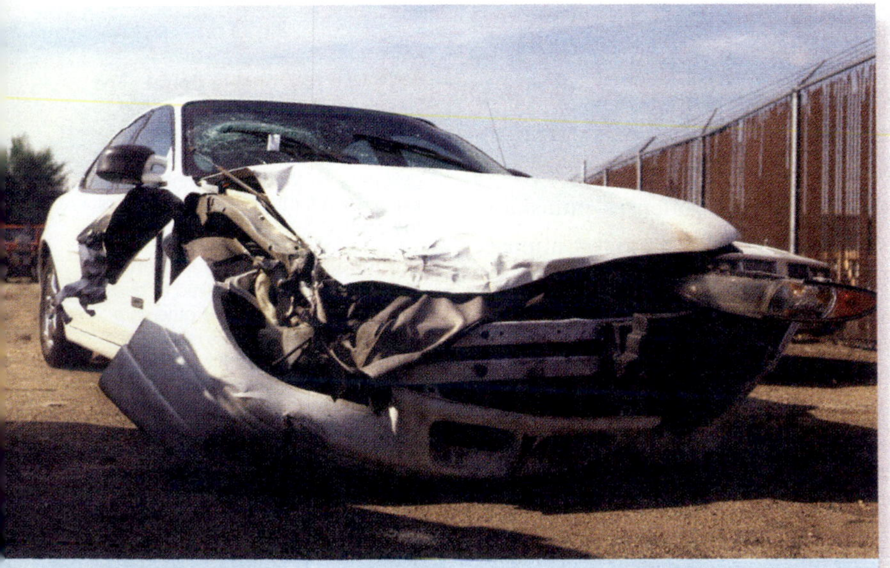

▲ Several years ago, in Longmont, Colorado, a drunk driver crashed into this car, killing the unborn child of its driver. **Do you consider driving while intoxicated to be a *mala in se* crime or a *mala prohibita* crime? Explain your answer.** Stephen Mitchell/*The Denver Post*/Getty Images

The Elements of a Crime

In fictional accounts of police work, the admission of guilt is often portrayed as the crucial element of a criminal investigation. Although an admission is certainly useful to police and prosecutors, it alone cannot establish the innocence or guilt of a suspect. Criminal law normally requires that the ***corpus delicti***, a Latin phrase for "the body of the crime," be proved before a person can be convicted of wrongdoing.[19]

Corpus delicti can be defined as "proof that a specific crime has actually been committed by someone."[20] It consists of the elements of any crime, which include:

1. The *actus reus*, or guilty act,
2. The *mens rea*, or guilty intent,
3. Concurrence, or the coming together of the criminal act and the guilty mind,
4. A link between the act and the legal definition of the crime,
5. Any attendant, or accompanying, circumstances, and
6. The harm done by the crime.

An explanation of each of these basic elements follows.

Criminal Act: *Actus Reus*

Suppose Mr. Smith walks into a police department and announces that he just killed his wife. In and of itself, the confession is insufficient for conviction unless the police find Mrs. Smith's corpse, for example, with a bullet in her brain and establish through evidence that Mr. Smith fired the gun. (This does not mean that an actual dead body has to be found in every homicide case. Rather, it is the fact of the death that must be established in such cases.)

Most crimes require an act of *commission*, meaning that a person must *do* something in order to be accused of a crime. The prohibited act is referred to as the ***actus reus***, or guilty act. Furthermore, the act of commission must be voluntary. For example, if Mr. Smith had an epileptic seizure while holding a hunting rifle and accidentally shot his wife, he normally would not be held criminally liable for her death.

A Legal Duty In some cases, an act of *omission* can be a crime, but only when a person has a legal duty to perform the omitted act. One such legal duty is assumed to exist based on a "special relationship" between two parties, such as a parent and child, adult children and their aged parents, and spouses.[21] Those persons involved in contractual relationships with others, such as physicians and lifeguards, must also perform legal duties to avoid criminal penalty. Hawaii, Minnesota, Rhode Island, Vermont, and Wisconsin have even passed "duty to aid" statutes requiring their citizens to report criminal conduct and help victims of such conduct if possible.[22] Another example of a criminal act of omission is failure to file a federal income tax return when required by law to do so.

A Plan or Attempt The guilty act requirement is based on one of the premises of criminal law—that a person is punished for harm done to society. Planning to kill someone or to steal a car may be wrong, but the thoughts do no harm and are therefore not criminal until they are translated into action. Of course, a person can be punished for *attempting* murder or robbery, but normally only if he or she took substantial steps toward the criminal objective and the prosecution can prove that the desire to commit the crime was present. Furthermore, the punishment for an **attempt** normally is less severe than if the act had succeeded.

Mental State: *Mens Rea*

A wrongful mental state—***mens rea***—is usually as necessary as a wrongful act in determining guilt. The mental state, or requisite *intent*, required to establish guilt of a crime is indicated in the applicable statute or law. For theft, the wrongful act is the taking of another person's property, and the required mental state involves both the awareness that the property belongs to another and the desire to deprive the owner of it.

actus reus (pronounced *ak*-tus *ray*-uhs). A guilty (prohibited) act.

attempt The act of taking substantial steps toward committing a crime while having the ability and the intent to commit the crime, even if the crime never takes place.

mens rea (pronounced mehns *ray*-uh). Wrongful mental state, or intent; usually as necessary as a wrongful act to establish criminal liability.

negligence A failure to exercise the standard of care that a reasonable person would exercise in similar circumstances.

recklessness The state of being aware that a risk does or will exist and nevertheless acting in a way that consciously disregards this risk.

The Categories of *Mens Rea* A guilty mental state includes elements of purpose, knowledge, negligence, and recklessness.[23] A defendant is said to have *purposefully* committed a criminal act when he or she desires to engage in certain criminal conduct or to cause a certain criminal result. For a defendant to have *knowingly* committed an illegal act, he or she must be aware of the illegality, must believe that the illegality exists, or must correctly suspect that the illegality exists but fail to do anything to dispel (or confirm) his or her belief.

Criminal **negligence** involves the mental state in which the defendant grossly deviates from the standard of care that a reasonable person would use under the same circumstances. The defendant is accused of taking an unjustified, substantial, and foreseeable risk that resulted in harm.

In 2015, for example, Greeley, Colorado, prosecutors charged Kristen Braig and her boyfriend, Dustin Blanchard, with negligent homicide after the death of Braig's three-year-old daughter in a mobile home fire. Just before the fire started, Braig and Blanchard, who had been drinking and smoking marijuana, left the child alone in the mobile home to visit a neighbor. The couple obviously did not intend for Braig's daughter to die. At the same time, there is a foreseeable risk in leaving a child of that age unattended for any amount of time, especially when one's judgment is impaired by alcohol and marijuana.

A defendant who commits an act recklessly is more blameworthy than one who is criminally negligent. The Model Penal Code, a general guide for criminal law, defines criminal **recklessness** as "consciously disregard[ing] a substantial and unjustifiable risk."[24] So, in 2015, Ryan Jorgenson pleaded guilty to reckless homicide in an Oshkosh, Wisconsin, court for causing the death of his fiancee's three-year-old daughter. Jorgenson, annoyed that the little girl would not stop crying, had fatally pushed her down a flight of stairs. Although Jorgenson—like Kristen Braig and Dustin Blanchard in the previous example—had no intention of killing his victim, the substantial risk of harm in treating a child in such a manner is evident to any reasonable person.

▲ During a recent concert in Chicago, rapper Travis Scott encouraged fans to climb over barricades set up to block access to the stage. In the resulting melee, a fifteen-year-old girl was injured. Scott later pleaded guilty to one count of reckless conduct. **Is recklessness the proper standard to describe Scott's behavior? Why or why not?** hurricanehank/Shutterstock.com

Degrees of Crime In the previous section, you learned that crimes are graded by degree. Generally speaking, the degree of a crime is a reflection of the seriousness of that crime, and is used to determine the severity of any subsequent punishment.

With many crimes, degree is a function of the criminal act itself, as determined by statute. For example, most criminal codes consider a burglary that involves a nighttime forced entry into a home to be a burglary in the first degree. If the same act takes place during the day and involves a nonresidential building, then it is burglary in the second degree. As you might expect, burglary in the first degree carries a harsher penalty than burglary in the second degree.

Willful Murder With murder, the degree of the crime is primarily determined by the mental state of the offender. Murder is generally defined as the willful killing of a human being. It is important to emphasize the word *willful*, as it precludes homicides caused by accident or negligence. A death that results from negligence or accident generally is considered a private wrong and therefore a matter for civil law.

In addition, criminal law punishes those who plan and intend to do harm more harshly than it does those who act wrongfully because of strong emotions or other extreme circumstances. First degree murder—usually punishable by life in prison or the death penalty—occurs under two circumstances:

1. When the crime is premeditated, or contemplated beforehand by the offender, instead of being a spontaneous act of violence.
2. When the crime is deliberate, meaning that it was planned and decided on after a process of decision making. Deliberation does not require a lengthy planning process. A person can be found guilty of first degree murder even if she or he made the decision to kill only seconds before committing the crime.

Second degree murder, usually punishable by a minimum of fifteen to twenty-five years in prison, occurs when no premeditation or deliberation was present, but the offender did have *malice aforethought* toward the victim. In other words, the offender acted with wanton disregard for the consequences of his or her actions. (*Malice* means "wrongful intention" or "the desire to do evil.")

The difference between first and second degree murder is illustrated by the case of Thu Hong Nguyen, a Kansas City woman who, in 2015, intentionally set fire to a spa business that she owned. This act of arson turned deadly when a wall of the burning building collapsed, killing two firefighters who were battling the blaze. Although Nguyen may have intentionally committed arson, there was no evidence that she planned to kill either of the two men. At the same time, she certainly acted with wanton disregard for the safety of others. Therefore, local authorities charged Nguyen with second degree murder, which carries a maximum penalty of life in prison, rather than first degree murder, which is punishable by death in Missouri.

Types of Manslaughter A homicide committed without malice toward the victim is known as *manslaughter* and is commonly punishable by up to fifteen years in prison. **Voluntary manslaughter** occurs when the intent to kill may be present, but malice is lacking. Voluntary manslaughter covers crimes of passion, in which the emotion of an argument between two friends may lead to a homicide. Voluntary manslaughter can also occur when the victim provoked the offender to act violently.

Involuntary manslaughter covers incidents in which the offender's acts may have been careless, but he or she had no intent to kill. In 2015, for instance, a jury found Griffin Campbell guilty of involuntary manslaughter after six people were killed when a building collapsed several years earlier in Philadelphia. Prosecutors proved that Campbell, a demolition contractor, had removed support beams and joists from the building to sell for salvage, thus causing the structure to collapse. Although Campbell certainly did not intend to kill anybody, the jury agreed with the prosecutor's argument that he was legally responsible for the deaths.

Comparing Campbell's case with the one involving Thu Hong Nguyen above, you can see that the distinction between malice aforethought and carelessness is not always clear. The feature *Discretion in Action—Murder or Manslaughter?* provides further insight into the differences between various homicide charges, with an emphasis on the importance of ascertaining the offender's intent.

voluntary manslaughter A homicide in which the intent to kill was present in the mind of the offender, but malice was lacking.

involuntary manslaughter A homicide in which the offender had no intent to kill her or his victim.

Discretion in ACTION

Murder or Manslaughter?

Rachel Donahue/Shutterstock.com

The Situation It is after midnight, and George, drunk and angry, decides to pay a visit to Yeardley, his ex-girlfriend. When Yeardley refuses to let George in her apartment, he kicks the door down, grabs Yeardley by the neck, and wrestles her to the floor before leaving. Several hours later, Yeardley's roommate finds her dead, lying face down on a pillow soaked with blood.

The Law George can be charged with one of three possible crimes: (1) first degree murder, which is premeditated and deliberate; (2) second degree murder, which means he acted with wanton disregard for the consequences of his actions; or (3) involuntary manslaughter, which involves extreme carelessness but no intent to kill.

What Would You Do? Further investigation shows that, two years prior to Yeardley's death, a jealous George put her in a chokehold in public. Furthermore, just days before breaking into her apartment, George sent Yeardley an e-mail in which he reacted to news that she was dating someone else by threatening, "I should have killed you." In his defense, George says that although he did have a physical confrontation with Yeardley, she did not seem injured when he left the apartment. George's lawyer claims that Yeardley died from suffocation, not from any injury caused by George. If it were your decision, would you charge George with first degree murder, second degree murder, or involuntary manslaughter? Why?

To see how a Charlottesville, Virginia, jury responded in this case, see Example 3.1 in Appendix B.

Strict Liability For some crimes, criminal law holds the defendant to be guilty even if intent to commit the offense is lacking. These acts are known as **strict liability crimes** and generally involve endangering the public welfare in some way.[25] Drug-control statutes, health and safety regulations, and traffic laws are all strict liability laws.

Learning Objective 4 Explain how the doctrine of strict liability applies to criminal law.

Protecting the Public To a certain extent, the concept of strict liability is inconsistent with the traditional principles of criminal law, which hold that *mens rea* is required for an act to be criminal. The goal of strict liability laws is to protect the public by eliminating the possibility that wrongdoers could claim ignorance or mistake to absolve themselves of criminal responsibility.[26] Thus, a person caught dumping waste in a protected pond or driving 70 miles per hour in a 55 miles-per-hour zone cannot plead a lack of intent in his or her defense.

Protecting Minors One of the most controversial strict liability crimes is **statutory rape**, in which an adult engages in a sexual encounter with a minor. In most states, even if the minor consents to the sexual act, the crime still exists because, being underage, he or she is considered incapable of making a rational decision on the matter.[27] Therefore, statutory rape has been committed even if the adult was unaware of the minor's age or was misled to believe that the minor was older.

Accomplice Liability Under certain circumstances, a person can be charged with and convicted of a crime that he or she did not actually commit. This occurs when the suspect has acted as an *accomplice,* helping another person commit the crime. Generally, to be found guilty as an accomplice, a person must have had "dual intent." This level of *mens rea* includes *both:*

1. The intent to aid the person who committed the crime, and
2. The intent that such aid would lead to the commission of the crime.[28]

strict liability crimes Certain crimes, such as traffic violations, in which the defendant is guilty regardless of her or his state of mind at the time of the act.

statutory rape A strict liability crime in which an adult engages in a sexual act with a minor.

So, assume that Jerry drives Jason to a bank that Jason intends to rob. If Jerry had no knowledge of Jason's criminal plan, he would not fulfill the second prong of the "dual intent" test. As for the *actus reus,* the accomplice must have helped the primary actor in either a physical sense (for example, by providing the getaway car) or a psychological sense (for example, by encouraging her or him to commit the crime).[29]

In some states, a person can be convicted as an accomplice even without intent if the crime was a "natural and probable consequence" of his or her actions.[30] This principle has led to a proliferation of **felony-murder** legislation. Felony-murder is a form of first degree murder that applies when a person participates in any of a list of serious felonies that results in the death of a human being. Under felony-murder law, if two men rob a bank, and the first man intentionally kills a security guard, the second man can be convicted of first degree murder as an accomplice to the bank robbery, even if he had no intent to hurt anyone.

Along these same lines, if a security guard accidentally shoots and kills a customer during a bank robbery, the bank robbers can be charged with first degree murder because they committed the underlying felony. These kinds of laws have come under criticism because they punish individuals for an unintended act or acts committed by others. Nevertheless, the criminal codes of more than thirty states include some form of the felony-murder rule.

Concurrence

According to criminal law, there must be *concurrence* between the guilty act and the guilty intent. In other words, the guilty act and the guilty intent must occur together. Suppose, for example, that a woman intends to murder her husband with poison in order to collect his life insurance. Every evening, this woman drives her husband home from work. On the night she plans to poison him, however, she swerves to avoid a cat crossing the road and runs into a tree. She survives the accident, but her husband is killed. Even though her intent was realized, the incident would be considered an accidental death because she had not planned to kill him by driving the car into a tree.

Causation

Criminal law also requires that the criminal act cause the harm suffered. In 1998, for example, thirteen-year-old Don Collins doused eight-year-old Robbie Middleton with gasoline and set him on fire, allegedly to cover up a sexual assault. Thirteen years later, after years of skin grafts and other surgeries, Middleton died from his burns. In 2014, a Montgomery County, Texas, judge ruled that, despite the passage of time, Collins could be charged with Middleton's murder.

Attendant Circumstances

In certain crimes, **attendant circumstances**—also known as accompanying circumstances—are relevant to the *corpus delicti.* Most states, for example, differentiate between simple assault and the more serious offense of aggravated assault depending on the attendant circumstance of whether the defendant used a weapon such as a gun or a knife while committing the crime. Criminal law also classifies degrees of property crimes based on the attendant circumstance of the amount stolen. According

felony-murder An unlawful homicide that occurs during the attempted commission of a felony.

attendant circumstances The facts surrounding a criminal event that must be proved to convict the defendant of the underlying crime.

Figure 3.2 Attendant Circumstances in Criminal Law

Most criminal statutes incorporate three of the elements we have discussed in this section: the act (*actus reus*), the intent (*mens rea*), and attendant circumstances. This diagram of the federal false imprisonment statute should give you an idea of how these elements combine to create the totality of a crime.

Intent | Act | Attendant Circumstances

Whoever **intentionally** **confines, restrains, or detains** another **against that person's will** is guilty of felony false imprisonment.

to federal statutes, the theft of less than $1,000 from a bank is a misdemeanor, while the theft of any amount over $1,000 is a felony.[31] (To get a better understanding of the role of attendant circumstances in criminal statutes, see Figure 3.2.)

Requirements of Proof and Intent Attendant circumstances must be proved beyond a reasonable doubt, just like any other element of a crime.[32] Furthermore, the *mens rea* of the defendant regarding each attendant circumstance must be proved as well. Consider the case of Ronald Thompson, who was charged several years ago with multiple crimes for taking underwater photos of children wearing swimsuits at a San Antonio, Texas, water park. Thompson had broken a state "upskirt" law prohibiting photography or video recordings taken "with the intent to arouse or gratify the sexual desire of the defendant."

In 2014, a Texas appeals court struck down the part of the law dealing with the defendant's intentions. The court ruled that it would be difficult, if not impossible, for prosecutors to prove beyond a reasonable doubt exactly what Thompson was thinking while he was taking the photos. Therefore, the *mens rea* requirement was unfair.[33] In general, if state legislatures want to ban "upskirting" or "downblousing" or other similar behavior, they must remove intent requirements. For example, a new Massachusetts law makes "the secret photographing, videotaping, or electronically surveilling of another person's sexual or other intimate parts" a crime.[34]

Hate Crime Laws In most cases, a person's motive for committing a crime is irrelevant—a court will not try to read the accused's mind. Over the past few decades, however, nearly every state and the federal government have passed *hate crime laws* that make the suspect's motive an important attendant circumstance to his or her criminal act. In general, **hate crime laws** provide for greater sanctions against those who commit crimes motivated by bias against a person based on race, ethnicity, religion, gender, sexual orientation, disability, or age.

In 2015, for example, Troy Burns pleaded guilty to violating a federal hate crime law for threatening three gay men in Seattle's Capitol Hill neighborhood with a knife while shouting homophobic slurs. Burns was sentenced to thirty months in prison for the assault, a tougher penalty than he would have received had the element of hate not been present. The United States Supreme Court has upheld the constitutionality of hate crime laws, as long as the attendant circumstance of the defendant's motive is proved beyond a reasonable doubt.[35] Still, this legal trend has its detractors, whose views are explored in the feature *CJ Controversy—Hate Crime Laws.*

hate crime law A statute that provides for greater sanctions against those who commit crimes motivated by bias against an individual or a group based on race, ethnicity, religion, gender, sexual orientation, disability, or age.

M Dogan/Shutterstock.com

CJ Controversy

Hate Crime Laws

When Dylann Roof killed nine African American parishioners at a historically black church in Charleston, South Carolina, on June 17, 2015, he was clearly motivated by hate. Before shooting his victims, the white twenty-one-year-old told them, "You are raping our women and taking over our country." South Carolina does not, however, have hate crime legislation, so Roof's racist motivations will not play a role in the state's case against him. Even though South Carolina is seeking Roof's execution, the federal government felt compelled to charge Roof as well, under the federal hate crime statute, to highlight the moral wrongness of his actions.

Hate Crime Laws Benefit Society Because . . .

- Such crimes target groups, not just an individual—if one African American is singled out for violence in South Carolina because of her or his skin color, for example, then all African Americans in South Carolina suffer intimidation and fear. Thus, such acts need to be punished more harshly.
- Historically, the groups listed in hate crime legislation have received inadequate protection from the American criminal justice system. Hate crime laws redress these shortcomings.

Hate Crime Laws Do Not Benefit Society Because . . .

- For the most part, motive is irrelevant in criminal law. Defendants are punished for what they did, not for why they did it.
- Hate crime laws indicate that some victims are worthy of more protection than others. It is unjust that Dylann Roof would receive a lesser sentence if his victims were not members of a minority group.

Your Assignment

Go online and learn the facts about **Craig Hicks's killing of three Muslim students in Chapel Hill, North Carolina.** Do the facts of this case support the legal argument that Hicks committed a hate crime? Do you think that Hicks, or any offender, should be punished more harshly when the underlying crime is motivated by prejudice? Write at least two paragraphs to explain your answers.

Harm

For most crimes to occur, some harm must have been done to a person or to property. A certain number of crimes are actually categorized depending on the harm done to the victim, regardless of the intent behind the criminal act. Take two offenses, both of which involve one person hitting another in the back of the head with a tire iron. In the first instance, the victim dies, and the offender is charged with murder. In the second, the victim is only knocked unconscious, and the offender is charged with battery. Because the harm in the second instance was less severe, so was the crime with which the offender was charged, even though the act was exactly the same. Furthermore, most states have different degrees of battery depending on the extent of the injuries suffered by the victim.

Many acts are deemed criminal if they could do harm that the laws try to prevent. Such acts are called **inchoate offenses.** They exist when only an attempt at a criminal act was made. If Jenkins solicits Peterson to murder Jenkins's business partner, this is an inchoate offense on the part of Jenkins, even though Peterson fails to carry out the act. Threats and *conspiracies* also fall into the category of inchoate offenses. In 2015, four teenage boys were arrested for **conspiracy** to commit assault with deadly weapons after local officials found evidence that they were planning a mass shooting at Summerville High School in Tuolumne County, California. The United States Supreme Court has ruled that a person could be convicted of criminal conspiracy even though police intervention made the completion of the illegal plan impossible.[36]

inchoate offenses Conduct deemed criminal without actual harm being done, provided that the harm that would have occurred is one the law tries to prevent.

conspiracy A plot by two or more people to carry out an illegal or harmful act.

EthicsChallenge

Consider a situation in which a father hands a .22-calilber rifle to his six-year-old daughter, asking her to take it to another room. As she does so, the six-year-old playfully points the gun at her eight-year-old sister and accidentally pulls the trigger. The eight-year-old, bleeding from a wound in her neck, dies on the way to the hospital. Would it be ethical to charge the father with a crime? If so, would it be manslaughter or murder, and what would be the category of *mens rea*? Explain your answers.

Defenses under Criminal Law

After Leslie Merritt, Jr., was arrested and charged in connection with a series of random shootings at cars on Phoenix-area freeways in 2015, his lawyers argued that he could not have possibly committed the crimes. They produced phone records indicating that Merritt was at home on the phone with his grandmother during at least two of the freeway shooting incidents.

In other words, the lawyers claimed that Merrit had an **alibi**, or evidence that a criminal suspect was elsewhere at the time of the crime, to prove his innocence. Alibis are just one of a number of established defenses for wrongdoing in our criminal courts. These defenses generally rely on one of two arguments: (1) the defendant is not responsible for the crime, or (2) the defendant was justified in committing the crime.

Learning Objective 5

List and briefly define the most important excuse defenses for crimes.

Excuse Defenses

The idea of responsibility plays a significant role in criminal law. In certain circumstances, the law recognizes that even though an act is inherently criminal, society will not punish the actor because he or she does not have the requisite mental condition. In other words, the law "excuses" the person for his or her behavior. Insanity, intoxication, and mistake are the most important excuse defenses today, but we start our discussion of the subject with one of the first such defenses recognized by American law: infancy.

Infancy Under the earliest state criminal codes of the United States, children younger than seven years of age could never be held legally accountable for crimes. Those between seven and fourteen years old were presumed to lack the capacity for criminal behavior, while anyone over the age of fourteen was tried as an adult. Thus, early American criminal law recognized **infancy** as a defense in which the accused's wrongdoing is excused because he or she is too young to fully understand the consequences of his or her actions.

With the creation of the juvenile justice system in the early 1900s, the infancy defense became redundant, as youthful delinquents were automatically treated differently than adult offenders. Today, most states either designate an age (eighteen or under) under which wrongdoers are sent to juvenile court or allow judges and prosecutors to decide whether a minor will be charged as an adult on a case-by-case basis. We will explore the concept of infancy as it applies to the modern American juvenile justice system in much more detail in Chapter 13.

Insanity After Robert Jaworski stabbed his parents while they were lying in bed watching a football game, the Cleveland resident told authorities he believed himself to be living in a computer simulation and that his victims were not "real." In 2015, a common pleas court judge ruled that Jaworski suffered from a severe mental illness

alibi Proof that the suspect was somewhere other than the scene of the crime at the time of the crime, typically offered to demonstrate that he or she was not guilty of that particular crime.

infancy A condition that, under early American law, excused young wrongdoers of criminal behavior because presumably they could not understand the consequences of their actions.

that prevented him from knowing his actions were wrong. As a result, he was sent to a psychiatric hospital rather than prison. Thus, **insanity** may be a defense to a criminal charge when the defendant's state of mind is such that she or he cannot be held legally responsible for her or his actions.

insanity A defense for criminal liability that asserts a lack of criminal responsibility due to mental instability

***M'Naghten* Rule** A common law test of criminal responsibility, derived from *M'Naghten's* Case in 1843, that relies on the defendant's inability to distinguish right from wrong.

Measuring Sanity The general principle of the insanity defense is that a person is excused for his or her criminal wrongdoing if, as a result of a mental disease or defect, he or she

- Does not perceive the physical nature or consequences of his or her conduct;
- Does not know that his or her conduct is wrong or criminal; or
- Is not sufficiently able to control his or her conduct so as to be held accountable for it.

Although criminal law has traditionally accepted the idea that an insane person cannot be held responsible for criminal acts, society has long debated what standards should be used to measure sanity for the purposes of a criminal trial. This lack of consensus is reflected in the diverse tests employed by different American jurisdictions to determine insanity. The tests include the following:

1. *The* M'Naghten *rule.* Derived from an 1843 British murder case, the ***M'Naghten* rule** states that a person is legally insane and therefore not criminally responsible if, at the time of the offense, he or she was not able to distinguish between right and wrong.[37] As Figure 3.3 shows, half of the states still use a version of the *M'Naghten* rule. One state, New Hampshire, uses a slightly different version of this

Figure 3.3 Insanity Defenses

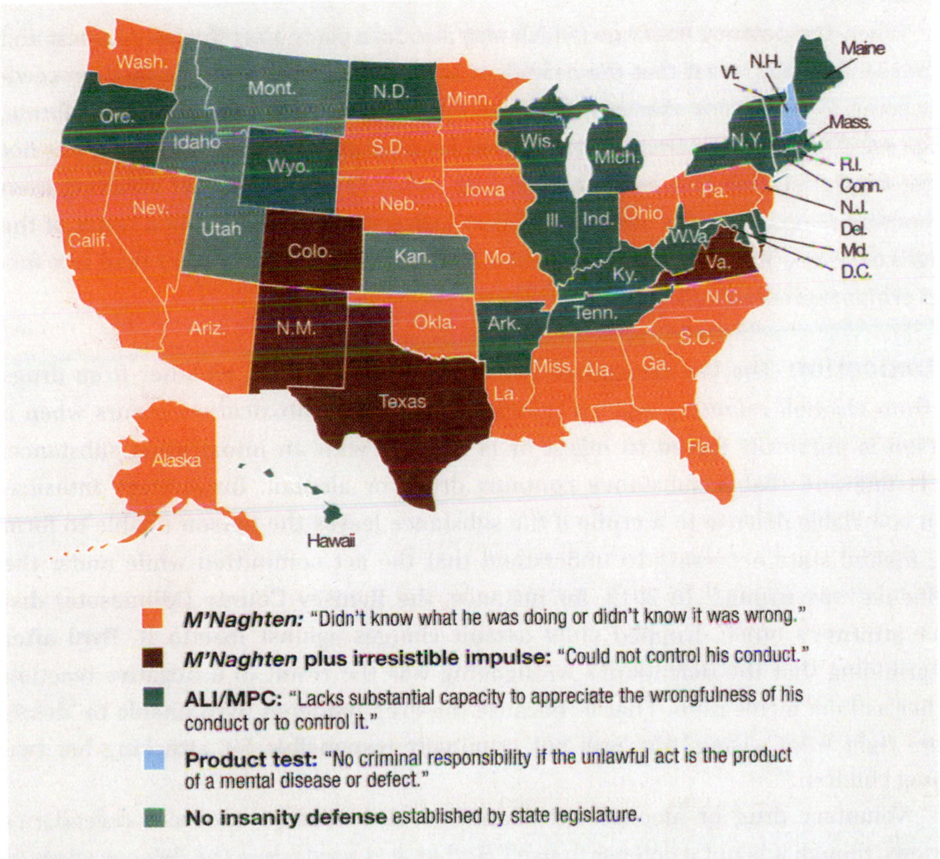

Source: Bureau of Justice Statistics, *The Defense of Insanity: Standards and Procedures, State Court Organization, 1998* (Washington, D.C.: U.S. Department of Justice, June 2000).

rule called the "product test." Under this standard, a defendant is not guilty if the unlawful act was the product of a mental disease or defect.

2. *The ALI/MPC test.* In the early 1960s, the American Law Institute (ALI) included an insanity standard in its Model Penal Code (MPC). Also known as the **substantial-capacity test**, the **ALI/MPC test** requires that the defendant lack "substantial capacity" to either "appreciate the wrongfulness" of his or her conduct or to conform that conduct "to the requirements of the law."[38]
3. *The irresistible-impulse test.* Under the **irresistible-impulse test**, a person may be found insane even if he or she was aware that a criminal act was "wrong," provided that some "irresistible impulse" resulting from a mental deficiency drove him or her to commit the crime.[39]

The ALI/MPC test is considered the easiest standard of the three for a defendant to meet because the defendant needs only to show a lack of "substantial capacity" to be released from criminal responsibility. Defense attorneys generally consider it more difficult to prove that the defendant could not distinguish "right" from "wrong" or that he or she was driven by an irresistible impulse.

Determining Competency Whatever the standard, the insanity defense is rarely entered and is even less likely to result in an acquittal, as it is difficult to prove.[40] (See the feature *Myth vs Reality—Are Too Many Criminals Found Not Guilty by Reason of Insanity?)* Psychiatry is far more commonly used in the courtroom to determine the "competency" of a defendant to stand trial. If a judge believes that the defendant is unable to understand the nature of the proceedings or to assist in his or her own defense, the trial will not take place.

When **competency hearings** (which may also take place after the initial arrest and before sentencing) reveal that the defendant is in fact incompetent, criminal proceedings come to a halt. For example, in December 2015, an Alameda County, California, judge ruled that because One L. Goh suffered from paranoid schizophrenia, he was not fit to stand trial. Goh had been charged with seven counts of murder resulting from a shooting rampage on the campus of Oikos University in Oakland. As a result of the judge's decision, Goh will be held at mental institution indefinitely rather than face further criminal proceedings.

Intoxication The law recognizes two types of **intoxication**, whether from drugs or from alcohol: *voluntary* and *involuntary.* Involuntary intoxication occurs when a person is physically forced to ingest or is injected with an intoxicating substance, or is unaware that a substance contains drugs or alcohol. Involuntary intoxication is a viable defense to a crime if the substance leaves the person unable to form the mental state necessary to understand that the act committed while under the influence was wrong.[41] In 2015, for instance, the Ramsey County (Minnesota) district attorney's office dropped child assault charges against Jozetta R. Byrd after determining that the defendant's wrongdoing was the result of a negative reaction to her asthma medication. That is, because the drug rendered Byrd unable to "determine right from wrong," she was not criminally responsible for attacking her two young children.[42]

Voluntary drug or alcohol intoxication is also used to excuse a defendant's actions, though it is not a defense in itself. Rather, it is used when the defense attorney wants to show that the defendant was so intoxicated that *mens rea* was negated. In

substantial-capacity test (ALI/MPC test) A test for the insanity defense that states that a person is not responsible for criminal behavior when he or she "lacks substantial capacity" to understand that the behavior is wrong or to know how to behave properly.

irresistible-impulse test A test for the insanity defense under which a defendant who knew his or her action was wrong may still be found insane if he or she was unable, as a result of a mental deficiency, to control the urge to complete the act.

competency hearing A court proceeding to determine whether the defendant is mentally well enough to understand the charges filed against him or her and cooperate with a lawyer in presenting a defense.

intoxication A defense for criminal liability in which the defendant claims that the taking of intoxicants rendered him or her unable to form the requisite intent to commit a criminal act.

other words, the defendant could not possibly have had the state of mind that a crime requires. Many courts are reluctant to allow voluntary intoxication arguments to be presented to juries, however. After all, the defendant, by definition, voluntarily chose to enter an intoxicated state. Thirteen states have eliminated voluntary intoxication as a possible defense, a step that has been criticized by many legal scholars but was upheld by the United States Supreme Court in *Montana v. Egelhoff* (1996).[43]

Mistake Everyone has heard the saying, "Ignorance of the law is no excuse." Ordinarily, ignorance of the law or a *mistaken idea* about what the law requires is not a valid defense. Such was the case when retired science teacher Eddie Leroy Anderson and his son dug for arrowheads near their favorite campground site in Idaho, unaware that the land was a federally protected archaeological site. Facing two years in prison for this mistake, they pleaded guilty and were given a year's probation and a $1,500 fine each. "Folks need to pay attention to where they are," said U.S. attorney Wendy Olson.[44]

Myth vs Reality

Are Too Many Criminals Found Not Guilty by Reason of Insanity?

The Myth Because of the publicity surrounding the insanity defense, many people are under the impression that it is a major loophole in our criminal justice system, allowing criminals to be "let off" no matter how heinous their crimes.

The Reality In fact, the insanity defense is raised in only about 1 percent of felony trials, and it is successful only one out of every four times it is raised. The reason: it is extremely difficult to prove insanity under the law. For example, during the 2015 trial of James Holmes, who killed twelve people and injured seventy others in an Aurora, Colorado, movie theater three years earlier, prosecutors essentially conceded that the defendant was mentally ill. They also argued, successfully, that a heavily armed Holmes knew his actions were wrong when he walked into the showing of a Batman movie and began shooting. The jury found Holmes guilty of numerous counts of murder and attempted murder. The trial of Eddie Ray Routh for killing "American Sniper" Chris Kyle, covered in the opening of this chapter, similarly showed that mental illness does not equal legal insanity.

Even if Holmes and Routh had succeeded with the insanity defense, they would not have been "let off" in the sense that they would have been set free. Many defendants found not guilty by reason of insanity spend more time in mental hospitals than criminals who are convicted of similar acts spend in prison.

For Critical Analysis

What if a defense attorney simply was able to show that her client would not have committed the underlying crime if not for the client's mental illness? Do you think that such a strategy should lead to a successful "not guilty by reason of insanity" defense? Why or why not?

Learning Objective 6
Discuss a common misperception concerning the insanity defense in the United States.

Mistake of Law As the above example suggests, strict liability crimes specifically preclude the *mistake of law* defense, because the offender's intent is irrelevant. For practical reasons, the mistake of law defense is rarely allowed under any circumstances. If "I didn't know" was a valid defense, the courts would be clogged with defendants claiming ignorance of all aspects of criminal law. In some rare instances, however, people who claim that they honestly did not know that they were breaking a law may have a valid defense if (1) the law was not published or reasonably known to the public or (2) the person relied on an official statement of the law that was erroneous.[45]

Mistake of Fact A *mistake of fact*, as opposed to a *mistake of law*, operates as a defense if it negates the mental state necessary to commit a crime. If, for example, Oliver mistakenly walks off with Julie's briefcase because he thinks it is his, there is no theft. Theft requires knowledge that the property belongs to another. The mistake-of-fact defense has proved very controversial in rape and sexual assault cases, in which the accused claims a mistaken belief that the sex was consensual, while the victim insists that he or she was coerced.

Careers in CJ

FASTFACTS

Crime scene photographer

Job description:

- Photograph physical evidence and crime scenes related to criminal investigations.
- Also must be able to compose reports, testify in court, and understand basic computer software and terminology.

What kind of training is required?

- One year in law enforcement or commercial photography OR a degree or certificate in photography and darkroom techniques OR some combination of the above training or experience totaling one year.

Annual salary range?

- $30,000–$63,000

Diana Tabor
Crime Scene Photographer

Photo courtesy of Diana Tabor

iStockPhoto.com/Vozks

A crime scene photographer's job is invaluable to those who are not present at the scene, yet need to be able to observe the scene as accurately as possible. I like the variety of my work. No two scenes are exactly alike, and the conditions pose different challenges. I have photographed scenes in cramped mobile homes, spacious homes, and out in the woods where we had to hike because there were no roads leading directly to the scene. I've been really hot and sweaty, fogging up the viewfinder. Then I have been so cold that I had to go sit in the van to let my hands and the camera warm up because they had stopped working.

I do wonder what the people at the gas stations think when we come in there after we're done to clean up and get something to drink. Fingerprint powder gets everywhere—I have found that nothing less than a shower really gets rid of it completely. It is sometimes difficult to accept that there is nothing to prevent the crime that has already happened, but I take pride in representing the victim when he or she cannot speak.

SOCIAL MEDIA CAREER TIP Don't forget about your phone! Every week, call at least three people from your social media networks and talk with them about your career interests. This kind of personal contact can be far more useful than an online exchange.

Justification Criminal Defenses

Learning Objective 7 Describe the four most important justification criminal defenses.

In certain instances, a defendant will accept responsibility for committing an illegal act, but contend that—given the circumstances—the act was justified. In other words, even though the guilty act and the guilty intent were present, the particulars of the case relieve the defendant of criminal liability. In 2014, for example, there were 721 "justified" killings of those who were in the process of committing a felony: 444 were killed by law enforcement officers and 277 by private citizens.[46] Four of the most important justification defenses are duress, self-defense, necessity, and entrapment.

Duress **Duress** exists when the *wrongful* threat of one person induces another person to perform an act that she or he would otherwise not perform. In such a situation, duress is said to negate the *mens rea* necessary to commit a crime. For duress to qualify as a defense, the following requirements must be met:

1. The threat must be of serious bodily harm or death.
2. The harm threatened must be greater than the harm caused by the crime.
3. The threat must be immediate and inescapable.
4. The defendant must have become involved in the situation through no fault of his or her own.[47]

duress Unlawful pressure brought to bear on a person, causing the person to perform an act that he or she would not otherwise perform.

Note that some scholars consider duress to be an excuse defense, because the threat of bodily harm negates any guilty intent on the part of the defendant.[48]

When ruling on the duress defense, courts often examine whether the defendant had the opportunity to avoid the threat in question. Two narcotics cases illustrate this point. In the first, the defendant claimed that an associate threatened to kill him and his wife unless he participated in a marijuana deal. Although this contention was proved true during the course of the trial, the court rejected the duress defense because the defendant made no apparent effort to escape, nor did he report his dilemma to the police. In sum, the drug deal was avoidable—the defendant could have made an effort to extricate himself, but he did not, thereby surrendering the protection of the duress defense.[49]

In the second case, a taxi driver in Bogotá, Colombia, was ordered by a passenger to swallow cocaine-filled balloons and take them to the United States. The taxi driver was warned that if he refused, his wife and three-year-old daughter would be killed. After a series of similar threats, the taxi driver agreed to transport the drugs. On arriving at customs at the Los Angeles airport, the defendant consented to have his stomach X-rayed, which led to discovery of the contraband and his arrest. During his trial, the defendant told the court that he was afraid to notify the police in Colombia because he believed them to be corrupt. The court accepted his duress defense, on the grounds that it met the four requirements listed above and the defendant had notified American authorities when given the opportunity to do so.[50]

Justifiable Use of Force—Self-Defense A person who believes he or she is in danger of being harmed by another is justified in defending himself or herself with the use of force, and any criminal act committed in such circumstances can be justified as **self-defense.** Other situations that also justify the use of force include the defense of another person, the defense of one's dwelling or other property, and the prevention of a crime. In all these situations, it is important to distinguish between deadly and nondeadly force. Deadly force is likely to result in death or serious bodily harm.

The Amount of Force Generally speaking, people can use the amount of nondeadly force that seems necessary to protect themselves, their dwellings, or other property or to prevent the commission of a crime. Deadly force can be used in self-defense if (1) there is a reasonable belief that imminent death or bodily harm will otherwise result; (2) the attacker is using unlawful force (an example of lawful force is that exerted by a police officer); (3) the defender has not initiated or provoked the attack; or (4) there is no other possible response or alternative way out of the life-threatening situation.[51]

Deadly force normally can be used to defend a dwelling only if the unlawful entry is violent and the person believes deadly force is necessary to prevent imminent death or great bodily harm. In some jurisdictions, it is also a viable defense if the person believes deadly force is necessary to prevent the commission of a felony (such as arson) in the dwelling. Authorities will often take an expansive view of lawful deadly force when it is used to protect another person. So, several years ago, a New Orleans man was not charged with any crime after he fatally shot an offender who was sexually assaulting a woman—the first man's companion—at gunpoint.

The Duty to Retreat When a person is outside the home or in a public space, the rules for self-defense change somewhat. Until relatively recently, almost all jurisdictions required someone who is attacked under these circumstances to "retreat to the wall" before fighting back. In other words, under this **duty to retreat** one who is being assaulted may not resort to deadly force if she or he has a reasonable opportunity to "run

self-defense The legally recognized privilege to protect one's self or property from injury by another.

duty to retreat The requirement that a person claiming self-defense prove that she or he first took reasonable steps to avoid the conflict that resulted in the use of deadly force.

CJ Policy—Your Take

At 4 A.M., Ronald Westbrook, lost and suffering from Alzheimer's disease, tried to open Joe Hendrix's front door. Armed with a handgun, Hendrix, unaware of the intruder's condition, came outside and shouted at Westbrook, who was carrying an unlit flashlight. Westbrook did not respond, but instead began walking toward the other man. Hendrix fatally shot Westbrook. Citing Georgia's **"stand your ground" law,** prosecutors decided not to charge Hendrix with any crime. **What is your opinion of the prosecutors' decision in this case, and of "stand your ground" laws in general?**

away" and thus avoid the conflict. Only when this person has run into a "wall," literally or otherwise, may deadly force be used in self-defense.

Recently, however, several states have changed their laws to eliminate this duty to retreat. For example, a Florida law did away with the duty to retreat outside the home, stating that citizens have "the right to stand [their] ground and meet force with force, including deadly force," if they "reasonably" fear for their safety.[52] The Florida law also allows a person to use deadly force against someone who unlawfully intrudes into her or his house (or vehicle), even if that person does not fear for her or his safety.[53] More than thirty states now have passed legislation that removes the duty to retreat before using force in self-defense.

"Stand your ground laws" have come under a great deal of criticism. According to one opponent, they have created a "nation where disputes are settled by guns instead of gavels, and where suspects are shot by civilians instead of arrested by the police."[54] In Texas, which passed its version of this legislation in 2007, the number of justifiable homicides increased from eighteen in 1999 to sixty-two in 2013.[55] Proponents of "stand your ground" laws contend that they allow people who face serious bodily harm or death the opportunity to defend themselves without first having to retreat as far as possible. Supporters also argue that the laws strengthen the concept of self-defense by making it less likely that a person defending him- or herself will be charged with a crime. In this chapter's *CJ Policy—Your Take* feature, you can make up your own mind about "stand your ground" laws.

Necessity The **necessity** defense requires courts to weigh the harm caused by the crime actually committed against the harm that would have been caused by the criminal act avoided. If the avoided harm is greater than the committed harm, then the defense has a chance of succeeding. A San Francisco jury, for example, acquitted a defendant of illegally carrying a concealed weapon because he was avoiding the "greater evil" of getting shot himself. The defendant had testified that he needed the gun for protection while entering a high-crime neighborhood to buy baby food and diapers for his crying niece.[56] Murder is the one crime for which the necessity defense is not applicable under any circumstances.

Entrapment **Entrapment** is a justification defense that criminal law allows when a police officer or government agent deceives a defendant into wrongdoing. Although law enforcement agents can legitimately use various forms of subterfuge—such as informants or undercover agents—to gain information or apprehend a suspect in a criminal act, the law places limits on these strategies. Police cannot persuade an innocent person to commit a crime, nor can they coerce a suspect into doing so, even if they are certain she or he is a criminal.[57] For an overview of justification and excuse defenses, see Figure 3.4.

necessity A defense against criminal liability in which the defendant asserts that circumstances required her or him to commit an illegal act.

entrapment A defense in which the defendant claims that he or she was induced by a public official—usually an undercover agent or police officer—to commit a crime that he or she would otherwise not have committed.

Ethics Challenge

Over the past decade, federal law enforcement agents have conducted more than 350 "stash-house stings." In these operations, an undercover agent pretending to be a drug courier tells a group of suspected criminals about a fictitious, heavily guarded warehouse filled with illegal drugs. When the suspects arm themselves to raid the stash house and steal the contraband, they are arrested. Is this entrapment? Is it an ethical way to round up criminal conspirators? Explain your answers.

Figure 3.4 Excuse and Justification Defenses

Excuse Defenses: Based on a defendant's admitting that she or he committed the criminal act, but asserting that she or he cannot be held criminally responsible for the act due to lack of criminal intent.

	The defendant must prove that:	Example
INFANCY	Because he or she was under a statutorily determined age, he or she did not have the maturity to make the decisions necessary to commit a criminal act.	A thirteen-year-old takes a handgun from his backpack at school and begins shooting at fellow students, killing three. (In such cases, the offender is often processed by the juvenile justice system rather than the criminal justice system.)
INSANITY	At the time of the criminal act, he or she did not have the necessary mental capacity to be held responsible for his or her actions.	A man with a history of mental illness pushes a woman in front of an oncoming subway train, which kills her instantly.
INTOXICATION	She or he had diminished control over her or his actions due to the influence of alcohol or drugs.	A woman who had been drinking malt liquor and vodka stabs her boyfriend to death after a domestic argument. She claims to have been so drunk as to not remember the incident.
MISTAKE	He or she did not know that his or her actions violated a law (this defense is very rarely even attempted), or that he or she violated the law believing a relevant fact to be true when, in fact, it was not.	A woman, thinking that her divorce in another state has been finalized when it has not, marries for a second time, thereby committing bigamy.

Justification Defenses: Based on a defendant's admitting that he or she committed the particular criminal act, but asserting that, under the circumstances, the criminal act was justified.

	The defendant must prove that:	Example
DURESS	She or he performed the criminal act under the use or threat of use of unlawful force against her or his person that a reasonable person would have been unable to resist.	A mother assists her boyfriend in committing a burglary after he threatens to kill her children if she refuses to do so.
SELF-DEFENSE	He or she acted in a manner to defend himself or herself, others, or property, or to prevent the commission of a crime.	A husband awakes to find his wife standing over him, pointing a shotgun at his chest. In the ensuing struggle, the firearm goes off, killing the wife.
NECESSITY	The criminal act he or she committed was necessary in order to avoid a harm to himself or herself or another that was greater than the harm caused by the act itself.	Four people physically remove a friend from her residence on the property of a religious cult, arguing that the crime of kidnapping was justified in order to remove the victim from the damaging influence of cult leaders.
ENTRAPMENT	She or he was encouraged by agents of the state to engage in a criminal act she or he would not have engaged in otherwise.	The owner of a boat marina agrees to allow three federal drug enforcement agents, posing as drug dealers, to use his dock to unload shipments of marijuana from Colombia.

Procedural Safeguards

To this point, we have focused on **substantive criminal law**, which defines the acts that the government will punish. We will now turn our attention to **procedural criminal law**. (The section that follows will provide only a short overview of criminal procedure. In later chapters, many other constitutional issues will be examined in more detail.)

Criminal law brings the force of the state, with all its resources, to bear against the individual. Criminal procedures, drawn from the ideals stated in the Bill of Rights, are designed to protect the constitutional rights of individuals and to prevent the arbitrary use of this power by the government.

substantive criminal law Law that defines the rights and duties of individuals with respect to one another.

procedural criminal law Rules that define the manner in which the rights and duties of individuals may be enforced.

The Bill of Rights

For various reasons, proposals related to the rights of individuals were rejected during the framing of the U.S. Constitution in 1787. The need for a written declaration of rights of individuals eventually caused the first Congress to draft twelve amendments to the

Bill of Rights The first ten amendments to the U.S. Constitution.

due process clause The provisions of the Fifth and Fourteenth Amendments to the Constitution that guarantee that no person shall be deprived of life, liberty, or property without due process of law.

procedural due process A provision in the Constitution that states that the law must be carried out in a fair and orderly manner.

Constitution and submit them for approval by the states. Ten of these amendments, commonly known as the **Bill of Rights**, were adopted in 1791. Since then, seventeen more amendments have been added.

The Bill of Rights, as interpreted by the United States Supreme Court, has served as the basis for procedural safeguards of the accused in this country. These safeguards include the following:

1. The Fourth Amendment protection from unreasonable searches and seizures.
2. The Fourth Amendment requirement that no warrants for a search or an arrest can be issued without probable cause.
3. The Fifth Amendment requirement that no one can be deprived of life, liberty, or property without "due process" of law.
4. The Fifth Amendment prohibition against *double jeopardy* (trying someone twice for the same criminal offense).
5. The Fifth Amendment guarantee that no person can be required to be a witness against (incriminate) himself or herself.
6. The Sixth Amendment guarantees of a speedy trial, a trial by jury, a public trial, the right to confront witnesses, and the right to a lawyer at various stages of criminal proceedings.
7. The Eighth Amendment prohibitions against excessive bails and fines and cruel and unusual punishments. (For the full text of the Bill of Rights, see Appendix A.)

The Bill of Rights initially offered citizens protection only against the federal government. Over the years, however, the procedural safeguards of most of the provisions of the Bill of Rights have been applied to the actions of state governments through the Fourteenth Amendment.[58] Furthermore, the states, under certain circumstances, have the option to grant even more protections than are required by the federal Constitution. As these protections are crucial to criminal justice procedures in the United States, they will be afforded much more attention in Chapter 6, with regard to police action, and in Chapter 8, with regard to the criminal trial.

Due Process

Learning Objective 8
Explain the importance of the due process clause in the criminal justice system.

Both the Fifth and the Fourteenth Amendments provide that no person should be deprived of "life, liberty, or property without due process of law." This **due process clause** basically requires that the government not act unfairly or arbitrarily. In other words, the government cannot rely on individual judgment and impulse when making decisions, but must stay within the boundaries of reason and the law. Not surprisingly, disagreements as to the meaning of these provisions have plagued courts, politicians, and citizens since this nation was founded, and will undoubtedly continue to do so.

To understand due process, it is important to consider its two types: procedural due process and substantive due process.

Procedural Due Process

According to **procedural due process**, the law must be carried out by a *method* that is fair and orderly. It requires that certain procedures be followed in administering and executing a law so that an individual's basic freedoms are not violated. Several years ago, for example, the University of Michigan ruled that a sophomore named Drew Sterrett had engaged in sexual intercourse with another student without her consent. This ruling resulted in his suspension. Sterrett responded by suing the university in federal court, claiming that it violated his due process in coming to a conclusion that would limit his future "education, employment, and career opportunities."

In his lawsuit, Sterrett claimed that he was never provided with the charges against him in writing. In addition, he was not given a chance to question his accuser, or to know the names of the witnesses who had testified against him regarding the alleged sexual assault. These procedural due process rights, as we will see in Chapter 8, are bedrocks of the American criminal justice system, and in 2015, following judicial proceedings, the University of Michigan vacated all its findings against Sterrett.[59]

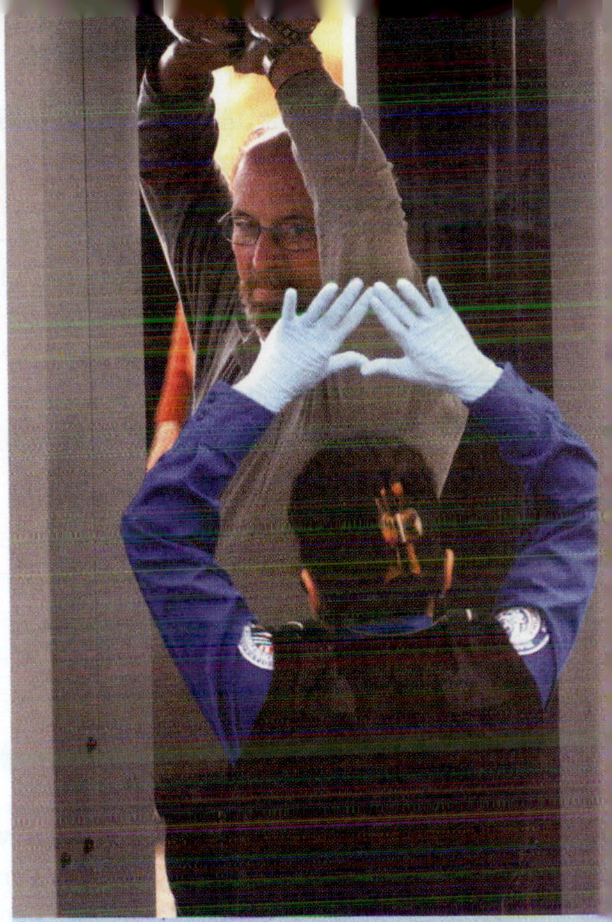

▲ Why do most Americans accept security precautions taken by the federal government—such as full body scans at airports—that restrict our individual freedom or compromise our privacy? John Moore/Getty Images

Substantive Due Process Fair procedures would obviously be of little use if they were used to administer unfair laws. For example, suppose a law requires everyone to wear a red shirt on Mondays. You wear a blue shirt on Monday, and you are arrested, convicted, and sentenced to one year in prison. The fact that all proper procedures were followed and your rights were given their proper protections would mean very little because the law that you broke was unfair and arbitrary.

Thus, **substantive due process** requires that the laws themselves be reasonable. The idea is that if a law is unfair or arbitrary, even if properly passed by a legislature, it must be declared unconstitutional. In the 1930s, for example, Oklahoma instituted the Habitual Criminal Sterilization Act. Under this statute, a person who had been convicted of three felonies could be "rendered sexually sterile" by the state (that is, the person would no longer be able to produce children). The United States Supreme Court held that the law was unconstitutional, as there are "limits to the extent which a legislatively represented majority may conduct biological experiments at the expense of the dignity and personality and natural powers of a minority."[60]

The Judicial System's Role in Due Process As the last example suggests, the United States Supreme Court often plays the important role of ultimately deciding when due process has been violated and when it has not. (See Figure 3.5 for a list of important Supreme Court due process cases.)

The Court is also called on from time to time to determine whether a due process right exists in the first place. For example, in Figure 3.3 from earlier in the chapter, you will notice that four states—Idaho, Kansas, Montana, and Utah—do not provide defendants with access to the insanity defense. In 2007, John Delling killed two men in Idaho whom he believed had conspired to steal his soul. Because Idaho does not allow the insanity defense, Delling pleaded guilty to the murders and was sentenced to life in prison. In 2012, his lawyers asked the United States Supreme Court to rule that the insanity defense was a constitutional right that should be available to all defendants. The Court refused to do so, allowing individual states to prohibit the insanity defense if they so wish.[61]

Victims' Rights in the Criminal Justice System

In 2013, several members of Congress introduced a proposed Victims' Rights Amendment to the U.S. Constitution.[62] Indeed, victims' rights supporters have been trying, without success, to amend the Constitution in favor of victims for nearly two decades. The problem, according to these activists, is that once a crime has occurred, the victim is relegated to a single role: being a witness against the suspect in court. Legally, he or she has no say in the prosecution of the offender, or even whether such a prosecution is to take place. Such powerlessness can be extremely frustrating, particularly in the wake of a traumatic, life-changing event.

substantive due process The constitutional requirement that laws used in accusing and convicting persons of crimes must be fair.

Figure 3.5 **Important United States Supreme Court Due Process Decisions**

YEAR	ISSUE	AMENDMENT INVOLVED	COURT CASE
1948	Right to a public trial	VI	*In re Oliver,* 333 U.S. 257
1952	Police searches cannot be so invasive as to "shock the conscience"	IV	*Rochin v. California,* 342 U.S. 165
1961	Exclusionary rule	IV	*Mapp v. Ohio,* 367 U.S. 643
1963	Right to a lawyer in all criminal felony cases	VI	*Gideon v. Wainwright,* 372 U.S. 335
1964	No compulsory self-incrimination	V	*Malloy v. Hogan,* 378 U.S. 1
1964	Right to have counsel when taken into police custody and subjected to questioning	VI	*Escobedo v. Illinois,* 378 U.S. 478
1965	Right to confront and cross-examine witnesses	VI	*Pointer v. Texas,* 380 U.S. 400
1966	Right to an impartial jury	VI	*Parker v. Gladden,* 385 U.S. 363
1966	Confessions of suspects not notified of due process rights ruled invalid	V	*Miranda v. Arizona,* 384 U.S. 436
1967	Right to a speedy trial	VI	*Klopfer v. North Carolina,* 386 U.S. 21
1967	Juveniles have due process rights	V	*In re Gault,* 387 U.S. 1
1968	Right to a jury trial ruled a fundamental right	VI	*Duncan v. Louisiana,* 391 U.S. 145
1969	No double jeopardy	V	*Benton v. Maryland,* 395 U.S. 784

Legislative Action To remedy this situation, all states have passed legislation creating certain rights for victims. On a federal level, such protections are encoded in the Crime Victims' Rights Act of 2004 (CVRA), which gives victims "the right to participate in the system."[63] This participation primarily focuses on three categories of rights:

Learning Objective

9 Describe the three ways that victims' rights legislation increases the ability of crime victims to participate in the criminal justice system.

1. The right to be *informed.* This includes receiving information about victims' rights in general, as well as specific information such as the dates and time of court proceedings relating to the relevant crime.
2. The right to be *present.* This includes the right to be present at those court hearings involving the case at hand, so long as the victim's presence does not interfere with the rights of the accused.
3. The right to be *heard.* This includes the ability to consult with prosecutorial officials before the criminal trial (addressed in Chapter 8), to speak during the sentencing phase of the trial (Chapter 9), and to offer an opinion when the offender is scheduled to be released from incarceration (Chapter 10).[64]

Some jurisdictions also provide victims with the right of law enforcement protection from the offender during the time period before a criminal trial. In addition, most states require *restitution,* or monetary payment, from offenders to help victims recoup any costs associated with the crime and rebuild their lives. In 2015, for instance, a district judge ordered a former volunteer firefighter who intentionally started a 440-acre fire near Boise, Idaho, to pay over $2 million to fifteen victims who suffered various injuries in the blaze.

Getting Linked in™

LinkedIn provides numerous opportunities for those interested in ensuring that crime victims are aware of their rights and have access to legal representation. By entering **"volunteer victim advocate"** into LinkedIn's search engine, you will get information on dozens of entry-level positions in this field.

Enforceability Although many victims have benefited from victims' rights legislation, advocates still find fault with the manner in which such legislation is applied. The main problem, they say, is that the federal and state laws do not contain sufficient enforcement mechanisms. That is, if a victim's rights are violated in some way, the victim has little recourse. Indeed, almost all victims' rights legislation gives criminal justice officials the discretion to deny the very protections they contain. Consequently, according to some, victims' rights are often more illusion than reality, a situation that can only be remedied by the proposed amendment to the Constitution mentioned above.[65]

Summary

For more information on these concepts, look back to the Learning Objective icons throughout the chapter.

1 **List the four written sources of American criminal law.** (a) The U.S. Constitution and state constitutions; (b) statutes passed by Congress and state legislatures (plus local ordinances); (c) administrative agency regulations; and (d) case law.

2 **Explain the two basic functions of criminal law.** The primary function is to protect citizens from harms to their safety and property and from harms to society's interest collectively. The second function is to maintain and teach social values as well as social boundaries—for example, speed limits and laws against bigamy.

3 **Discuss the primary goals of civil law and criminal law, and explain how these goals are realized.** Civil law is designed to resolve disputes between private individuals and between other entities, such as corporations. In these disputes, one party, called the plaintiff, tries to gain monetary damages by proving that the accused party, the defendant, is to blame for a tort, or wrongful act. In contrast, criminal law exists to protect society from criminal behavior. To that end, the government prosecutes defendants, or persons who have been charged with committing a crime.

4 **Explain how the doctrine of strict liability applies to criminal law.** Strict liability crimes do not allow the alleged wrongdoer to claim ignorance or mistake to avoid criminal responsibility—for example, exceeding the speed limit and statutory rape.

5 **List and briefly define the most important excuse defenses for crimes. Insanity**—different tests of insanity can be used, including (a) the *M'Naghten* rule (right-wrong test); (b) the ALI/MPC test, also known as the substantial-capacity test; and (c) the irresistible-impulse test. **Intoxication**—voluntary and involuntary, the latter being a possible criminal defense. **Mistake**—sometimes valid if the law was not published or reasonably known or if the alleged offender relied on an official statement of the law that was erroneous. Also, a mistake of fact may negate the mental state necessary to commit a crime.

6 **Discuss a common misperception concerning the insanity defense in the United States.** Contrary to popular opinion, the insanity defense is not an oft-used loophole that allows criminals to avoid responsibility for committing heinous crimes. Insanity defenses are difficult to mount and very rarely succeed. Even when a defendant is found not guilty by reason of insanity, she or he does not "go free." Instead, such defendants are sent to mental health care institutions.

7 **Describe the four most important justification criminal defenses. Duress**—requires that (a) the threat is of serious bodily harm or death; (b) the harm is greater than that caused by the crime; (c) the threat is immediate and inescapable; and (d) the defendant became involved in the situation through no fault of his or her own. **Justifiable use of force**—the defense of one's person, dwelling, or property, or the prevention of a crime. **Necessity**—justifiable if the harm sought to be avoided is greater than that sought to be prevented by the law defining the offense charged. **Entrapment**—the criminal action was induced by certain governmental persuasion or trickery.

8 **Explain the importance of the due process clause in the criminal justice system.** The due process clause acts to limit the power of government. In the criminal justice system, the due process clause requires that certain procedures be followed to ensure the fairness of criminal proceedings and that all criminal laws be reasonable and in the interest of the public good.

9 **Describe the three ways that victims' rights legislation increases the ability of crime victims to participate in the criminal justice system.** (a) The right to be informed of victims' rights in general and of specific information relating to the relevant criminal case; (b) the right to be present at court proceedings involving the victim; and (c) the right to be heard on matters involving the prosecution, punishment, and release of the offender.

Questions for Critical Analysis

1. Give an example of a criminal law whose main purpose seems to be teaching societal boundaries rather than protecting citizens from harm. Do you think this behavior should be illegal? Explain your answer.
2. Why is murder considered a *mala in se* crime? What argument can be made that murder is not a *mala in se* crime?
3. Keith lends his car to Jermaine, who drives with two other friends to the home of a marijuana dealer. The three men break into the home, intending to steal a safe full of cash. The drug dealer is unexpectedly at home, however, and in a struggle Jermaine winds up murdering him. What rule allows local prosecutors to charge Keith with first degree murder? Why?
4. Gerald, whose house has been burgled four times in previous weeks, sets a trap for future intruders by placing his wife's purse in clear view of a window in his garage. Then he leaves the garage door slightly open, and hides in the shadows with his shotgun. If Gerald shoots and kills a would-be burglar who takes the bait, would he be protected from murder charges by Florida's "stand your ground" law? Why or why not? What is your opinion of this result?
5. Suppose that Louisiana's legislature passes a law allowing law enforcement officers to forcibly remove residents from their homes in the face of an imminent hurricane. Why might a court uphold this law even though, in most circumstances, such forcible removal would violate the residents' due process rights? If you were a judge, would you uphold Louisiana's new law?

Key Terms

actus reus 77
administrative law 71
alibi 84
attempt 77
attendant circumstances 81
ballot initiative 70
beyond a reasonable doubt 75
Bill of Rights 92
case law 71
civil law 74
competency hearing 86
conspiracy 83
constitutional law 69
corpus delicti 76
defendant 74
due process clause 92
duress 88
duty to retreat 89
entrapment 90
felony 75
felony-murder 81
hate crime law 82
inchoate offenses 83
infancy 84
infraction 75
insanity 85
intoxication 86
involuntary manslaughter 79
irresistible-impulse test 86
liability 74
mala in se 76
mala prohibita 76
mens rea 77
misdemeanor 75
M'Naghten rule 85
necessity 90
negligence 78
plaintiff 74
precedent 71
preponderance of the evidence 75
procedural criminal law 91
procedural due process 92
recklessness 78
rule of law 69
self-defense 89
stare decisis 71
statutory law 70
statutory rape 80
strict liability crimes 80
substantial-capacity test (ALI/MPC test) 86
substantive criminal law 91
substantive due process 93
supremacy clause 70
voluntary manslaughter 79

Notes

1. John S. Baker, Jr., *Measuring the Explosive Growth of Federal Crime Legislation* (Washington, D.C.: The Federalist Society for Law and Public Policy Studies, 2008), 1.
2. Erik Eckholm, "Legal Conflicts on Medical Marijuana Ensnare Hundreds as Courts Debate a New Provision," *New York Times* (April 9, 2015), A14.
3. Quoted in "Judge: Federal Law Trumps Montana's Medical Pot Law," *Associated Press* (January 23, 2012).
4. *Texas v. Johnson*, 491 U.S. 397 (1989).
5. *States of Nebraska and Oklahoma v. State of Colorado* (December 2014), at **www.scribd.com/doc/250506006/Nebraska-Oklahoma-lawsuit**.
6. Clean Water Act Section 309, 33 U.S.C.A. Section 1319 (1987).
7. *Bowers v. Hardwick*, 478 U.S. 186 (1986)
8. *Lawrence v. Texas*, 539 U.S., 558, 578 (2003).
9. Joel Feinberg, *The Moral Limits of the Criminal Law: Harm to Others* (New York: Oxford University Press, 1984), 221–232.

10. "Bertino-Tarrant's Caffeine Powder Ban Signed into Law," (July 16, 2015), at **senatorbertinotarrant.com/news/17-news/press-releases/112-bertino-tarrant-s-caffeine-powder-ban-signed-into-law.**
11. Henry M. Hart, Jr., "The Aims of the Criminal Law," *Law & Contemporary Problems* 23 (1958), 405–406.
12. John L. Diamond, "The Myth of Morality and Fault in Criminal Law Doctrine," *American Criminal Law Review* 34 (Fall 1996), 111.
13. Kentucky Statutes Section 437.060; and New Hampshire Revised Statutes Section 207:61.
14. Robby Korth and Jessica Boehm, "Butt Out: State Legislatures Move to Nullify Federal Gun Laws," *NBCNews.com* (August 21, 2014), at **www.nbcnews.com/news/investigations/butt-out-state-legislatures-move-nullify-federal-gun-laws-n185326.**
15. Idaho Senate Bill 1332 (March 19, 2014), at **legislature.idaho.gov/legislation/2014/S1332.htm.**
16. *Federal Criminal Rules Handbook*, Section 2.1 (West 2008).
17. 625 Illinois Compiled Statutes Annotated Section 5/16-104 (West 2002).
18. Johannes Andenaes, "The Moral or Educative Influence of Criminal Law," *Journal of Social Issues* (Spring 1971), 17, 26.
19. Thomas A. Mullen, "Rule without Reason: Requiring Independent Proof of the *Corpus Delicti* as a Condition of Admitting Extrajudicial Confession," *University of San Francisco Law Review* 27 (1993), 385.
20. *Hawkins v. State*, 219 Ind. 116, 129, 37 N.E.2d 79 (1941).
21. David C. Biggs, "'The Good Samaritan Is Packing': An Overview of the Broadened Duty to Aid Your Fellowman, with the Modern Desire to Possess Concealed Weapons," *University of Dayton Law Review* 22 (Winter 1997), 225.
22. Terry Halbert and Elaine Ingulli, *Law and Ethics in the Business Environment*, 6th ed. (Mason, Ohio: South-Western Cengage Learning, 2009), 8.
23. Model Penal Code Section 2.02.
24. Model Penal Code Section 2.02(c).
25. *Black's Law Dictionary*, 1423.
26. *United States v. Dotterweich*, 320 U.S. 277 (1943).
27. *State v. Stiffler*, 763 P.2d 308, 311 (Idaho Ct.App. 1988).
28. *State v. Harrison*, 425 A.2d 111 (1979).
29. Richard G. Singer and John Q. LaFond, *Criminal Law: Examples and Explanations* (New York: Aspen Law & Business, 1997), 322.
30. *State v. Linscott*, 520 A.2d 1067 (1987).
31. Federal Bank Robbery Act, 18 U.S.C.A. Section 2113.
32. *In re Winship*, 397 U.S. 358, 364, 368–369 (1970).
33. Cindy George, "Texas Court Throws Out 'Upskirt' Photo Law," *Houston Chronicle* (September 18, 2014), 6A.
34. Massachusetts Statutes, Chapter 272, Section 105, at **www.womenslaw.org/statutes_detail.php?statute_id=7544#statute-top.**
35. *Wisconsin v. Mitchell*, 508 U.S. 476 (1993); and *Apprendi v. New Jersey*, 530 U.S. 466 (2000).
36. *United States v. Jiminez Recio*, 537 U.S. 270 (2003).
37. *M'Naghten's* Case, 10 Cl.&F. 200, Eng.Rep. 718 (1843). Note that the name is also spelled M'Naughten and McNaughten.
38. Model Penal Code Section 401 (1952).
39. Joshua Dressler, *Cases and Materials on Criminal Law*, 2d ed. (St. Paul, Minn.: West Group, 1999), 599.
40. Ronald Schouten, "The Insanity Defense: An Intersection of Morality, Public Policy, and Science," *Psychology Today* (August 16, 2012), at **www.psychologytoday.com/blog/almost-psychopath/201208/the-insanity-defense.**
41. Lawrence P. Tiffany and Mary Tiffany, "Nosologic Objections to the Criminal Defense of Pathological Intoxication: What Do the Doubters Doubt?" *International Journal of Law and Psychiatry* 13 (1990), 49.
42. Paul Walsh, "Rare Defense Wins Dismissal of Child Assault Case, but Jailed Falcon Heights Mom Lost Home, Job," *Star Tribune* (July 20, 2015), at **www.startribune.com/involuntary-intoxication-cited-child-assault-case-dropped-against-twin-cities-mom/317554121.**
43. 518 U.S. 37 (1996).
44. Quoted in Gary Fields and John R. Emshwiller, "As Criminal Laws Proliferate, More Are Ensnared," *Wall Street Journal* (July 23, 2011), at **online.wsj.com/article/SB10001424052748703749504576172714184601654.html.**
45. *Lambert v. California*, 335 U.S. 225 (1957).
46. Federal Bureau of Investigation, *Crime in the United States 2014* (Washington, D.C.: U.S. Department of Justice, 2014), at **www.fbi.gov/about-us/cjis/ucr/crime-in-the-u.s/2014/crime-in-the-u.s.-2014**, Expanded Homicide Table 14 and Expanded Homicide Table 15.
47. Craig L. Carr, "Duress and Criminal Responsibility," *Law and Philosophy* 10 (1990), 161.
48. Arnold N. Enker, "In Supporting the Distinction between Justification and Excuse," *Texas Tech Law Review* 42 (2009), 277.
49. *United States v. May*, 727 F.2d 764 (1984).
50. *United States v. Contento-Pachon*, 723 F.2d 691 (1984).
51. *People v. Murillo*, 587 N.E.2d 1199, 1204 (Ill. App.Ct. 1992).
52. Florida Statutes Section 776.03 (2005).
53. *Ibid.*
54. Michael Bloomberg, quoted in "A Lethal Right to Self-Defense," *The Week* (May 4, 2012), 13.
55. Kevin Schwaller, "Justifiable Homicides Rise in Texas," *KXAN.com* (January 8, 2015), at **kxan.com/2015/01/08/justifiable-homicides-rise-in-texas.**
56. "Man Acquitted of Concealed Weapon Charge on 'Necessity' Defense," *San Francisco Examiner* (July 10, 2011), 13A.
57. *Sorrells v. United States*, 287 U.S. 435 (1932).
58. Henry J. Abraham, *Freedom and the Court: Civil Liberties in the United States*, 7th ed. (New York: Oxford University Press, 1998), 38–41.
59. Emily Yoffe, "A Campus Rape Ruling, Reversed," *Slate.com* (September 15, 2015), at **www.slate.com/articles/double_x/doublex/2015/09/drew_sterrett_and_university_of_michigan_the_school_vacates_its_findings.html.**
60. *Skinner v. Oklahoma*, 316 U.S. 535, 546–547 (1942).
61. Jonathan Stempel, "Supreme Court Declines to Review Insanity Defense Appeal," *Reuters* (November 26, 2012).
62. National Victims' Constitutional Amendment Passage, "House Joint Resolution 40" (April 23, 2013), at **www.nvcap.org/legis/113/VRAtext.html.**
63. 18 U.S.C. Section 3771 (2006).
64. Victim Law Bulletin, *Fundamentals of Victims' Rights: A Summary of 12 Common Victims' Rights* (National Crime Victim Law Institute, Portland, Ore.: November 2011), 1-4.
65. Douglas E. Beloof, "The Third Wave of Crime Victims' Rights: Standing, Remedy, and Review," *Brigham Young University Law Review* 2 (2005), 258.

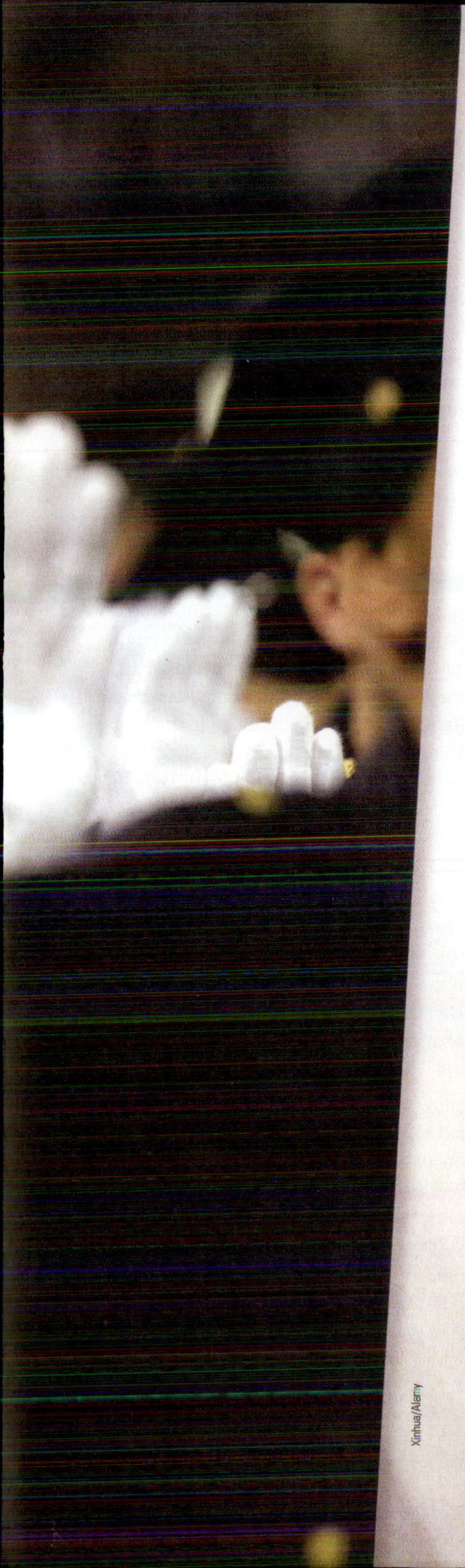

Xinhua/Alamy

4

Law Enforcement Today

Chapter Outline		Corresponding Learning Objectives
The Responsibilities of the Police	1	List the four basic responsibilities of the police.
A Short History of the American Police	2	Explain how intelligence-led policing works and how it benefits modern police departments.
Recruitment and Training: Becoming a Police Officer	3	Identify the differences between the police academy and field training as learning tools for recruits.
Women and Minorities in Policing Today	4	Describe some of the benefits that female police officers bring to law enforcement.
	5	Identify the main advantage of a racially and ethnically diverse police force.
Public and Private Law Enforcement	6	Indicate some of the most important law enforcement agencies under the control of the Department of Homeland Security.
	7	Summarize the duties of the FBI.
	8	Analyze the importance of private security today.

To target your study and review, look for these numbered Learning Objective icons throughout the chapter.

first Response

Lieutenant Mike Madden of the San Bernardino (California) Police Department was eating lunch on December 2, 2015, when an active-shooter call came across his radio. From the tone of the dispatcher's voice, Madden could tell that the situation at the nearby Inland Regional Center was serious. Still, he was unprepared for what followed. "As we entered the [government building], the situation was unreal," said Madden, who was one of the first law enforcement officers on the scene. "It was unspeakable the carnage we were seeing, the number of people who were injured, and, unfortunately, already dead."

Amid the chaos—ringing fire alarms, ceiling sprinklers spraying water, the smell of gunpowder in the air, "pure panic" from the survivors—Madden and his colleagues made a crucial decision. They chose to search for the shooter (or shooters) rather than provide the wounded with medical aid. As it turned out, Syed Rizwan Farook and Tashfeen Malik had already fled and would be killed hours later in a gun battle with law enforcement. Farook and Malik left fourteen people dead and twenty-two injured at the regional center, most of them county employees who were enjoying a holiday party.

A decade ago, Lt. Madden probably would not have rushed into the building without waiting for more heavily armed backup or a hostage negotiator. Because of a series of terrorist attacks in the United States and in other parts of the world, however, police tactics have changed. Today, the consensus is that immediate entry in such situations is the best way to save lives. This leaves patrol officers such as Madden, often armed with only a handgun, vulnerable. Just five days before the San Bernardino incident, a University of Colorado campus officer was killed as he rushed to confront a gunman at a Planned Parenthood clinic in Colorado Springs. In fact, according to a study conducted by the Police Executive Research Forum, about one-third of police officers who enter active shooting scenes by themselves wind up being shot.

Marcus Yam/Los Angeles Times/Getty Images

▲ Lieutenant Mike Madden of the San Bernardino Police Department and other first responders take questions from reporters a week after the domestic terrorist attack on a local government building.

1. Why do you think patrol officers such as Mike Madden are encouraged to immediately enter the scene of an active shooting instead of waiting for backup or a hostage negotiator? What is your opinion of this strategy?
2. What factors do you think went into the decision made by Madden and his colleagues to search for the shooters instead of aiding wounded victims? Do you agree with their decision? Why or why not?
3. Efforts to lessen police use of force during confrontations between officers and civilians are presently a priority for law enforcement authorities in the United States. How might strategies that support the use of deadly force by police in potential terrorist situations complicate these efforts? Explain your answer.

The Responsibilities of the Police

"My job was to go in there," said San Bernardino police lieutenant Mike Madden of his reaction to the mass shooting at the Inland Regional Center. "People don't call the police because they're having a great day. They call because there's a tragedy going on."[1] Often the first government employees to respond to tragedies and other emergency situations, police officers such as Madden are the most visible representatives of our criminal justice system. Indeed, they symbolize the system for many Americans who may never see the inside of a courtroom or a prison cell. Still, the general perception of a "cop's life" is often shaped by television dramas such as *Criminal Minds* and *Hawaii Five-O.* In reality, police spend a great deal of time on such mundane tasks as responding to noise complaints, confiscating firecrackers, and poring over paperwork.

Sociologist Egon Bittner warned against the tendency to see the police primarily as agents of law enforcement and crime control. A more inclusive accounting of "what the police do," Bittner believed, would recognize that they provide "situationally justified force in society."[2] In other words, the function of the police is to solve any problem that may *possibly,* though not *necessarily,* require the use of force.

Within Bittner's rather broad definition of "what the police do," we can pinpoint four basic responsibilities of the police:

1. To enforce laws.
2. To provide services.
3. To prevent crime.
4. To preserve the peace.

Learning Objective

1 List the four basic responsibilities of the police.

As will become evident over the next two chapters, there is a great deal of debate among legal and other scholars and law enforcement officers over which responsibilities deserve the most police attention and what methods should be employed in meeting those responsibilities.

Enforcing Laws

In the public mind, the primary role of the police is to enforce society's laws—hence, the term *law enforcement officer.* In their role as "crime fighters," police officers have a clear mandate to seek out and apprehend those who have violated the law. The crime-fighting responsibility is so dominant that all police activity—from the purchase of new automobiles to a plan to hire more minority officers—must often be justified in terms of its law enforcement value.[3]

Police officers also see themselves primarily as crime fighters, a perception that often leads people into what they believe will be an exciting career in law enforcement. Although the job certainly offers challenges unlike any other, police officers normally do not spend the majority of their time performing law enforcement duties. After surveying a year's worth of dispatch data from the Wilmington (Delaware) Police Department, researchers Jack Greene and Carl Klockars found that officers spent only about half of their time enforcing the law or dealing with crimes. The other half was spent on order maintenance, service provision, traffic patrol, and medical assistance.[4]

Furthermore, information provided by the Uniform Crime Report shows that most arrests are made for "crimes of disorder" or public annoyances rather than violent or property crimes.[5] In 2014, for example, police made about 9.2 million arrests for drunkenness, liquor law violations, disorderly conduct, vagrancy, loitering, and other minor offenses, but only about 500,000 arrests for violent crimes.[6]

Providing Services

The popular emphasis on crime fighting and law enforcement tends to overshadow the fact that a great deal of a police officer's time is spent providing services for the community. The motto "To Serve and Protect" has been adopted by thousands of local police departments, and the *Law Enforcement Code of Ethics* recognizes the duty "to serve the community" in its first sentence.[7] The services that police provide are numerous—a partial list would include directing traffic, performing emergency medical procedures, counseling those involved in domestic disputes, providing directions to tourists, and finding lost children.

As we will see in the next section, many police departments have adopted a strategy called *community policing*. This strategy requires officers to provide assistance in areas that are not, at first glance, directly related to law enforcement. Often, regardless of official policy, the police are forced into providing certain services. For example, in many instances, law enforcement officers are first on the scene when a person has been seriously injured. As a result, officers increasingly are becoming proficient in emergency medical procedures. Some cities even allow police officers to take injured persons to the hospital in a squad car rather than wait for an ambulance.[8]

Also, because of changes in American national health-service policy, law enforcement agents find themselves on the front lines when it comes to dealing with mental illness and substance abuse. The Tucson (Arizona) Police Department, for example, receives more calls about mental illness than about stolen cars or burglaries.[9] Police officers in numerous cities now carry naloxone, a drug that can instantly reverse the effects of a heroin overdose. Police in Quincy, Massachusetts, saved 211 lives using naloxone between 2011 and 2014.[10] (See the feature *Discretion in Action—Handle with Care* to consider the best course of action for police when confronted with a suspect suffering from mental illness.)

Preventing Crime

Perhaps the most controversial responsibility of the police is to *prevent* crime. According to Jerome Skolnick, co-director of the Center for Research in Crime and Justice at the New York University School of Law, there are two predictable public responses when crime rates begin to rise in a community. The first is to punish convicted criminals with stricter laws and more severe penalties. The second is to demand that the police "do something" to prevent crimes from occurring in the first place. Is it, in fact, possible for the police to "prevent" crimes? The strongest response that Professor Skolnick is willing to give to this question is "maybe."[11]

On a limited basis, police can certainly prevent some crimes. If a rapist is dissuaded from attacking a solitary woman because a patrol car is cruising the area, then the police officer behind the wheel has prevented a crime. Furthermore, exemplary police work can have a measurable effect. "Quite simply, cops count," says William Bratton, who has directed police departments in Boston, Los Angeles, and New York. "[T]he quickest way to impact crime is with a well-led, managed, and appropriately resourced police force."[12] In Chapter 5, we will study a number of policing strategies that have been credited, by some, for decreasing crime rates in the United States.

In general, however, the deterrent effects of law enforcement are unclear. One study found no relationship between the size of the police presence in a neighborhood and the residents' perceived risk of being arrested for wrongdoing.[13] Furthermore, Carl Klockars has written that the "war on crime" is a war that the police cannot win because

Discretion in ACTION

Handle with Care

Rachel Donahue/Shutterstock.com

The Situation Terri lives in a group home for people who suffer from mental illness. After Terri stops taking her medication, a social worker stops by to check on her well-being. She responds by threatening the social worker, yelling, "Get out of here! I have a knife, and I'll kill you if I have to!" The social worker contacts the police, and Officers Helton and Ramirez take the call. Using a master key to open Terri's locked door, the officers find her holding a five-inch kitchen knife and screaming, "I am going to kill you. I don't need help. Get out." Officers Helton and Ramirez, who did not have their weapons drawn, leave the room and now ponder their next move.

The Law Under the Fourth Amendment, as we will see in Chapter 6, law enforcement agents have the right to enter a home or dwelling without permission from a judge in emergency situations. The potential for injury to an occupant of that home or dwelling is recognized as being one such situation.

What Would You Do? On the one hand, Terri has threatened to kill three people, possesses a deadly weapon, and may harm herself. (Plus, if she escapes from her room, which is on the ground floor and has a window, she could harm others.) On the other hand, police officers should not assume that just because someone is suffering from mental illness, she necessarily poses a threat to herself or to society. Furthermore, the goal here is not to arrest Terri, but rather to move her to a mental health facility for involuntary treatment.

Officers Helton and Ramirez have several options. They can reenter Terri's room and try to subdue her themselves, or they can call for police backup. Another option would be to request the assistance of mental health experts, thereby lessening the chances that they will need to use force against Terri. Which is the best option? Why?

To see how two police officers in San Francisco reacted in similar circumstances, go to Example 4.1 in Appendix B.

they cannot control the factors—such as unemployment, poverty, immorality, inequality, political change, and lack of educational opportunities—that contribute to criminal behavior in the first place.[14]

Preserving the Peace

To a certain extent, the fourth responsibility of the police, that of preserving the peace, is related to preventing crime. Police have the legal authority to use the power of arrest, or even force, in situations in which no crime has yet occurred but might occur in the immediate future.

In the words of James Q. Wilson, the police's peacekeeping role (which Wilson believed to be the most important role of law enforcement officers) often takes on a pattern of simply "handling the situation."[15] For example, when police officers arrive on the scene of a loud, late-night house party, they may feel the need to disperse the party and even arrest some of the partygoers for disorderly conduct. By their actions, the officers have lessened the chances of serious and violent crimes taking place later in the evening. The same principle is often used when dealing with domestic disputes, which, if they escalate, can lead to homicide. Such situations are in need of, to use Wilson's terminology again, "fixing up," and police can use the power of arrest, or threat, or coercion, or sympathy, to do just that.

The basis of Wilson and George Kelling's zero-tolerance theory is similar: street disorder—such as public drunkenness, urination, and loitering—signals to both law-abiding citizens and criminals that the law is not being enforced and therefore leads to more violent crime. Hence, if police preserve the peace and "crack down" on the minor crimes that make up street disorder, they will in fact be preventing serious crimes that would otherwise occur in the future.[16]

Ethics Challenge

Do law enforcement agents have an ethical obligation to provide offenders with medical assistance? What if a police officer's partner has been killed by a suspect during a shootout, and the suspect—also shot—is bleeding profusely nearby? Ethically, must that officer do everything in his or her power to save the suspect's life? Why or why not?

A Short History of the American Police

Although modern society relies on law enforcement officers to control and prevent crime, in the early days of this country police services had little to do with crime control. The policing efforts in the first American cities were directed toward controlling certain groups of people (mostly slaves and Native Americans), delivering goods, regulating activities such as buying and selling in the town market, maintaining health and sanitation, controlling gambling and vice, and managing livestock and other animals.[17]

Furthermore, these police services were for the most part performed by volunteers, as a police force was an expensive proposition. Often, the volunteers were organized using the **night watch system**, brought over from England by colonists in the seventeenth century. Under this system, all physically fit males were required to offer their services to protect the community on a rotating nightly basis.[18]

night watch system An early form of American law enforcement in which volunteers patrolled their community from dusk to dawn to keep the peace.

The Evolution of American Law Enforcement

The night watch system did not ask much of its volunteers, who were often required to do little more than loudly announce the time and the state of the weather. Furthermore, many citizens avoided their duties by hiring others to "go on watch" in their place, and those who did serve frequently spent their time on watch sleeping and drinking.[19] Eventually, as the populations of American cities grew in the late eighteenth and early nineteenth centuries, so did the need for public order and the willingness to devote public resources to the establishment of formal police forces. The night watch system was insufficient to meet these new demands, and its demise was inevitable.

Early Police Departments In 1833, Philadelphia became the first city to employ both day and night watchmen. Five years later, working from a model established by British home secretary Sir Robert "Bobbie" Peel in London, England, Boston formed the first organized police department, consisting of six full-time officers. In 1844, New York City laid the foundation for the modern police department by combining its day and night watches under the control of a single police chief. By the onset of the Civil War in 1861, a number of American cities, including Baltimore, Boston, Chicago, Cincinnati, New Orleans, and Philadelphia, had similarly consolidated police departments, modeled on the Metropolitan Police of London.[20]

The Political Era Like their modern counterparts, many early police officers were hardworking, honest, and devoted to serving and protecting the public. On the whole, however, in the words of historian Samuel Walker, "The quality of American police service in the nineteenth century could hardly have been worse."[21] This poor quality can be attributed to the fact that the recruitment and promotion of police officers were intricately tied to the politics of the day. Police officers received their jobs as a result of political connections, not because of any particular skills or knowledge. Whichever political party was in power in a given city would hire its own cronies to run the police department. Consequently, the police were often more concerned with serving the interests of the political powers than with protecting the citizens.[22]

▲ A horse-drawn police wagon used by the New York City Police Department, circa 1886. **Why might this new form of transportation have represented a "revolution" for early American police forces?** Bettmann/Corbis

Corruption was rampant during this *political era* of policing, which lasted roughly from 1840 to 1930. Police salaries were relatively low, and many police officers saw their positions as opportunities to make extra income through any number of illegal activities. Bribery was common, as police would use their close proximity to the people to request "favors," which went into the police officers' own pockets or into the coffers of the local political party as "contributions."[23] This was known as the **patronage system**, or the "spoils system," because to the political victors went the spoils.

The Reform Era Led by August Vollmer, the police chief of Berkeley, California, from 1905 to 1932, advocates of dramatic changes to law enforcement in the United States initiated the *reform era* in American policing.[24] Along with his protégé O. W. Wilson, Vollmer promoted a style of policing known as the **professional model**. Under the professional model, police chiefs, who had been little more than figureheads during the political era, took more control over their departments. A key to these efforts was the reorganization of police departments in many major cities. To improve their control over operations, police chiefs began to add mid-level positions to the force. These new officers, known as majors or assistant chiefs, could develop and implement crime-fighting strategies and more closely supervise individual officers. Police chiefs also tried to consolidate their power by bringing large areas of a city under their control so that no local ward, neighborhood, or politician could easily influence a single police department.

The professionalism trend benefited law enforcement agents in a number of ways. Salaries and working conditions improved, and for the first time, women and members of minority groups were given opportunities—albeit limited ones—to serve.[25] At the same time, police administrators controlled officers to a much greater extent than in the past, expecting them to meet targets for arrests and other numerical indicators that were seen as barometers of effectiveness. Any contact with citizens that did not explicitly relate to law enforcement was considered "social work" and was discouraged.[26] As police expert Chris Braiden puts it, American police officers were expected to "park their brains at the door of the stationhouse" and simply "follow orders like a robot."[27]

The isolation of officers from the public was made complete by an overreliance on the patrol car, a relatively new technological innovation at the time. In the political era, officers walked their beats, interacting with citizens. In the reform era, they were expected to stay inside their "rolling fortresses," driving from one call to the next without wasting time or resources on public relations.[28]

patronage system A form of corruption in which the political party in power hires and promotes police officers and receives job-related "favors" in return.

professional model A style of policing advocated by August Vollmer and O. W. Wilson that emphasizes centralized police organizations, increased use of technology, and a limitation of police discretion through regulations and guidelines.

CJ & Technology

High-Tech Cops

Michael Hanson/*New York Times*/Redux

When patrol cars came into common use by police departments in the 1930s, they changed the face of American policing. Nine decades later, the technology associated with patrol cars continues to evolve. Today, approximately 80 percent of all police cars in the United States are equipped with on-board computers with which officers can immediately retrieve a suspect's criminal record or access neighborhood crime data. More than two-thirds of police departments also attach video cameras to their patrol automobiles, and many are able to "live stream" video content from these devices. Another mounted camera commonly found on police autos automatically reads the license plates of nearby vehicles and performs an instant background check on both car and driver.

In addition to their sophisticated transportation, today's police officers enjoy a multitude of other technological advantages. Using their smartphones and tablet computers, law enforcement agents are able to use a new generation of apps to locate the source of 911 calls and "tagged" tweets. As we saw in Chapter 1, mobile biometric technology provides officers with the ability to immediately identify a suspect using her or his fingerprints or facial features. Advances in through-the-wall sensor devices are increasingly allowing law enforcement agents to track people's movements within buildings.

Thinking about Police Technology

Google is in the process of developing Glass, an optical head-mounted display that essentially transforms the wearer's eyes into mobile, visual computers. At some point, Google Glass will enable users to immediately identify every object—or person—in his or her field of vision. How could this technology eventually benefit law enforcement?

The Community Era The drawbacks of the professional model became evident in the 1960s, one of the most turbulent decades in American history. Unrest associated with the civil rights movement and protests against the Vietnam War (1965–1975) led to a series of clashes—often violent—between police and certain segments of society. By the early 1970s, many observers believed that inadequate policing was contributing to the national turmoil. The National Advisory Commission on Civil Disorders stated bluntly that poor relations between the police and African American communities were partly to blame for the violence that plagued many of those communities.[29] In striving for professionalism, the police appeared to have lost touch with the citizens they were supposed to be serving. To repair their damaged relations with a large segment of the population, police would have to rediscover their community roots.

The result of this rediscovery was the *community era* of American policing. Starting in the 1970s, most large-city police departments established entire units devoted to community relations, implementing programs that ranged from summer recreation activities for inner-city youths to "officer-friendly" referral operations that encouraged citizens to come to the police with their crime concerns.

At the same time, the country was hit by a crime wave. Thus, police administrators were forced to combine efforts to improve community relations with aggressive and innovative crime-fighting strategies. As we will see in Chapter 5 when we discuss these strategies in more depth, the police began to focus on stopping crimes before they occur, rather than concentrating only on solving crimes that had already been committed. A dedication to such proactive strategies led to widespread acceptance of *community policing* in the 1980s and 1990s. Community policing is based on the notion that meaningful interaction

Figure 4.1 **The Three Historical Eras of American Policing**

George L. Kelling and Mark H. Moore have separated the history of policing in the United States from 1840 to 2000 into three distinct periods. Below is a brief summarization of these three eras.

1840 1850 1860 1870 1880 1890 1900 1910 1920 1930 1940 1950 1960 1970 1980 1990 2000

	The Political Era	The Reform Era	The Community Era
Time Period	1840 to 1930	1930 to 1980	1980 to 2000
Primary Function of Police	Provide range of social services to citizenry	Crime control	Continue to control crime while providing a broader range of social services
Organization	Decentralized	Centralized	Decentralized, with specialized units and task forces
Police/Community Relationship	Intimate	Professional and distant	Return to intimate
Tactics	Patrolling neighborhoods on foot	Patrolling neighborhoods in cars, rapid response to emergency calls for service (911 calls)	Foot patrol, problem solving, and public relations
Strategic Goal	Satisfy the needs of citizens and political bosses	Crime control	Improve the quality of life of citizens
Strategic Weakness	Widespread police corruption and brutality	Lack of communication with citizens fostered mistrust and community violence (riots)	An overreliance on police officers to solve all of society's problems

Sources: Adapted from George L. Kelling and Mark H. Moore, "From Political to Reform to Community: The Evolving Strategy of Police," in *Community Policing: Rhetoric or Reality*, eds. Jack R. Greene and Stephen D. Mastrofski (New York: Praeger Publisher, 1991), 14-15, 22-23; plus authors' updates. Reproduced with permission of Greenwood Publishing Group, Inc., Westoport, Connecticut.

between officers and citizens will lead to a partnership in preventing and fighting crime.[30] (See Figure 4.1 for an overview of the three eras of policing described in this section.)

Policing Today: Intelligence, Terrorism, and Technology

Many law enforcement experts believe that the events of September 11, 2001, effectively ended the community era of policing.[31] Though police departments have not, in general, abandoned the idea of partnering with the community, their emphasis has shifted toward developing new areas of expertise, including counterterrorism and surveillance through technology. In particular, the process of collecting, analyzing, and mapping crime data has become a hallmark of law enforcement in the twenty-first century.

Learning Objective

2 Explain how intelligence-led policing works and how it benefits modern police departments.

Intelligence-Led Policing Relying on hard-earned experience and criminological studies, law enforcement officials know that two strategies are particularly effective in reducing crime: focusing on repeat offenders and focusing on high-crime neighborhoods. Police departments across the nation are increasingly relying on technology to put this knowledge to good use.

Thanks to data gathered by its Real-Time Analysis Critical Response Division, for example, the Los Angeles Police Department (LAPD) recently was able to determine that its Newton division was a "hot spot" for drug crime and gang activity. In response, the LAPD launched Operation LASER, flooding the Newton area with additional patrol officers. Over a ten-month period, Operation LASER resulted in a dramatic decrease in gun-related murders and other crimes, including robbery and aggravated assault.[32]

The LAPD's approach to gun crime in Newton is known as predictive policing, or **intelligence-led policing** (ILP), because it relies on data—or intelligence—concerning past crime patterns to predict future crime patterns. In theory, ILP is relatively simple. Just as commercial fishers are most successful when they concentrate on the areas of the ocean where the fish are, law enforcement does well to focus its scarce resources on the areas where the most crime occurs. With strategies such as the LAPD's Operation LASER and other "hot spot" technologies that we will discuss in the next chapter, police administrators are able to deploy small forces to specific locations, rather than blanketing an entire city with random patrols. Doing "more with less" in this manner is a particularly important consideration as police budgets shrink around the country.

The Challenges of Counterterrorism When basic ILP principles are applied to the issue of terrorism, it quickly becomes clear that terrorists, like other criminals, are likely to choose targets close to their homes. At the same time, when terrorist attacks occur great distances from those homes, the attacks are more deadly. Consequently, counterterrorism provides three specific challenges for American law enforcement:

1. The need to focus scarce resources to prevent and fight crimes that are relatively uncommon,
2. The scrutiny that comes with crimes that sometimes have international implications, and
3. The difficult task of gathering information, or intelligence, about crimes before they happen.[33]

The only way to meet these challenges, clearly, is for a level of cooperation between federal and local law enforcement that was not required in previous eras of policing.

Hard Power On a federal level, American counterterrorism forces are focusing on "lone wolf," homegrown violent extremists who have been radicalized online. Federal agents generally move to apprehend these suspects in the early stages of plotting, a strategy discussed more fully in the next chapter. In 2015, federal authorities arrested nearly sixty domestic terrorism suspects before they could cause any serious harm.[34]

On a local level, police departments engage in a variety of anti-terrorism tactics. More than one hundred local and state police organizations now operate intelligence units, with at least one in each state. The New York City Police Department, in a class by itself, has a permanent counterterrorism force, known as the Critical Response Command, made up of nearly 500 members. This group of experienced officers engages in "hostile surveillance" of suspects, and its arsenal includes special cars mounted with semiautomatic assault rifles.[35]

Soft Power In other municipalities, law enforcement is partnering with local institutions to discourage homegrown radicalization. For example, prosecutors have charged more than thirty suspects from predominantly Somali-American neighborhoods in Minnesota with providing support to foreign terrorist groups such as al Shabaab (in Africa) and the Islamic State (in the Middle East).

To counter this trend, the U.S. Department of Justice has pledged $1 million to local mentoring groups in these neighborhoods, with a goal of "getting to" vulnerable young men before they fall under the influence of extremist ideologies. Similar community-based programs are underway in Boston and Los Angeles. Overall, the federal government annually awards more than $1 billion in grants to help support local organizations, including the police, in the continuing struggle against domestic terrorism.[36]

intelligence-led policing An approach that measures the risk of criminal behavior associated with certain individuals or locations so as to predict when and where such criminal behavior is most likely to occur in the future.

Law Enforcement 2.0 Fortunately, just as more intelligence has become crucial to police work, the means available to gather such intelligence have also increased greatly. Nearly every successful anti-terrorism investigation has relied on information gathered from the Internet. Just like the rest of society, criminals are active on social networking sites, providing police officers with a wealth of potential evidence, including messages, chat logs, tweets, photos, videos, tags, "likes," profiles, lists of friends, locations, and more.[37] At least 90 percent of American law enforcement agencies monitor social media to find leads on criminal activity.[38]

▲ Psychotherapist Hodan Hassan of Save the Children USA, left, and Minneapolis City Council member Abdi Warsame address the issue of youth radicalization in Minnesota at the White House's Countering Violent Extremism Summit. Given that the root causes of youth radicalization center on community-level social issues such as poverty and lack of education, what role can the police play in addressing this problem? AP Photo/Carolyn Kaster

Going Undercover Online Hundreds of federal, state, and local law enforcement agencies also allow their agents to create fake profiles online as part of criminal investigations. Federal drug agents have set up false Facebook pages using the identities of known drug dealers to "friend" their unwitting criminal associates. In New Jersey, authorities operated a fake Instagram account to fool a suspected burglar into sharing photos of stolen cash and jewelry, leading to his arrest. On at least three occasions, the FBI has taken clandestine control of a child pornography website in the hopes of uncovering users who would otherwise be protected by anonymity settings.[39]

Technology on the Beat As the leaders of the reform movement envisioned, technology also continues to improve the capabilities of officers in the field. In this section's *CJ & Technology* feature, we saw that law enforcement agents can use smartphones and tablets to access a wealth of crime information and have turned their patrol cars into command centers on wheels. Officers are also able to use less lethal weapons such as laser beams (discussed in Chapter 5), monitor suspects via satellite (discussed in Chapter 6), and incorporate dozens of other technological innovations into their day-to-day-duties.

Some law enforcement veterans are concerned that the "art" of policing is being lost in an era of intelligence-led policing and increased reliance on technology. "If it becomes all about the science," says Los Angeles Police Department deputy chief Michael Downing, "I worry we'll lose the important nuances."[40] As the remainder of this chapter and the two that follow show, however, the human element continues to dominate all aspects of policing in America.

EthicsChallenge

The user agreements of Facebook and Instagram both ban law enforcement agents from going "undercover" online by impersonating others or setting up fake accounts. As you saw earlier in this section, this has not stopped police officers from engaging in the practice. Is this an ethical means of conducting a criminal investigation? Why or why not? ■

Recruitment and Training: Becoming a Police Officer

In 1961, police expert James H. Chenoweth commented that the methods used to hire police officers had changed little since the days of the first American police forces.[41] The past six decades, however, have seen a number of improvements in the way that police administrators handle the task of **recruitment**, or the development of a pool of qualified applicants from which to select new officers. Efforts have been made to diversify police rolls, and recruits in most police departments undergo a substantial array of tests and screens—discussed next—to determine their aptitude. Furthermore, annual starting salaries that can exceed $70,000, along with the opportunities offered by an interesting profession in the public service field, have attracted a wide variety of applicants to police work.

Basic Requirements

The selection process involves a number of steps, and each police department has a different method of choosing candidates. Most agencies, however, require at a minimum that a police officer:

- Be a U.S. citizen.
- Not have been convicted of a felony.
- Have or be eligible to have a driver's license in the state where the department is located.
- Be at least twenty-one years of age.
- Meet weight and eyesight requirements.

In addition, few departments will accept candidates older than forty-five years of age.

Background Checks and Tests Beyond these minimum requirements, police departments usually engage in extensive background checks, including drug tests; a review of the applicant's educational, military, and driving records; credit checks; interviews with spouses, acquaintances, and previous employers; and a background search to determine whether the applicant has been convicted of any criminal acts. Police agencies generally require certain physical attributes in applicants: normally, they must be able to pass a physical agility or fitness test. (For an example of one such test, see Figure 4.2.)

In some departments, particularly those that serve large metropolitan areas, the applicant must take a psychological screening test to determine if he or she is suited to law enforcement work. Generally, such suitability tests measure the applicant's ability to handle stress, follow rules, use good judgment, and avoid off-duty behavior that would reflect negatively on the department.[42]

Along these same lines, many American police agencies now review an applicant's social media activity on sources such as Facebook, Instagram, and Twitter. "A single posting on Facebook in poor taste won't automatically eliminate someone from our hiring process," explains Miami Beach (Florida) deputy police chief Lauretta Hill. "But if we see a pattern of behavior or something that raises a red flag, it lets us know that we need to dig a little deeper during our background investigation."[43]

Educational Requirements One of the most dramatic differences between today's police recruits and those of several generations ago is their level of education. In the 1920s, when August Vollmer began promoting the need for higher education in

recruitment The process by which law enforcement agencies develop a pool of qualified applicants from which to select new employees.

Figure 4.2 Physical Agility Test for the Miami (Florida) Police Department

The physical agility test for all applicants to the Miami Police Department consists of the following four events, each of which must be successfully completed as described below.

1.5 Mile-Run, maximum time in minutes

Age	19–29	30–39	40–49
Male	13:08	13:48	14:33
Female	15:56	16:46	18:26

Push-Ups, minimum repetitions in 1 minute

Age	19–29	30–39	40–49
Male	26	20	15
Female	13	9	7

Sit-Ups, minimum repetitions in 1 minute

Age	19–29	30–39	40–49
Male	35	32	27
Female	30	22	17

300-Meter Run, maximum time in seconds

Age	19–29	30–39	40–49
Male	62.1	63	77
Female	75	82	106.7

Sources: Miami Police Department

police officers, few had attended college. Today, 84 percent of all local police departments require at least a high school diploma, and 10 percent require at least a degree from a two-year college.[44] Although a four-year degree is necessary for certain elite law enforcement positions such as Federal Bureau of Investigation special agent, only about 5 percent of large local police departments have such a requirement.[45] Those officers with four-year degrees do, however, generally enjoy an advantage in hiring and promotion, and often receive higher salaries than their less-educated co-employees.

probationary period A period of time at the beginning of a police officer's career during which she or he may be fired without cause.

Not all police observers believe that education is a necessity for police officers, however. In the words of one police officer, "Effective street cops learn their skills on the job, not in a classroom."[46] By emphasizing a college degree, say some, police departments discourage those who would make solid officers but lack the education necessary to apply for positions in law enforcement.

Training

Learning Objective

3 Identify the differences between the police academy and field training as learning tools for recruits.

If an applicant successfully navigates the application process, he or she will be hired on a *probationary* basis. During this **probationary period**, which can last from six to eighteen months depending on the department, the recruit is in jeopardy of being fired without cause if he or she proves inadequate to the challenges of police work. Almost every state requires that police recruits pass through a training period while on probation. During this time, they are taught the basics of police work and are under constant supervision by superiors. The training period usually has two components: the police academy and field training.

▲ A recruit goes through an exercise routine at a police academy for the U.S. Capitol Police in Cheltenham, Maryland. **Why are police academies an important part of the learning process for a potential police officer?**

Tom Williams/CQ Roll Call/Getty Images

Academy Training The *police academy*, run by either the state or a police agency, provides recruits with a controlled, militarized environment in which they receive their introduction to the world of the police officer. They are taught the laws of search, seizure, arrest, and interrogation; how and when to use weapons; the procedures of securing a crime scene and interviewing witnesses; first aid; self-defense; and other essentials of law enforcement work. Nine in ten police academies also provide terrorism-related training to teach recruits how to respond to terrorist incidents, including those involving weapons of mass destruction.[47] Academy instructors evaluate the recruits' performance and send intermittent progress reports to police administrators.

In the Field **Field training** takes place outside the confines of the police academy. A recruit is paired with an experienced police officer known as a field training officer (FTO). The goal of field training is to help rookies apply the concepts they have learned in the academy "to the streets," with the FTO playing a supervisory role to make sure that nothing goes awry. According to many, the academy introduces recruits to the formal rules of police work, but field training gives the rookies their first taste of the informal rules. In fact, the initial advice to recruits from some FTOs is often along the lines of "O.K., kid. Forget everything you learned in the classroom. You're in the real world now." Nonetheless, the academy is a critical component in the learning process, as it provides rookies with a road map to the job.

EthicsChallenge

How much impact do you think ethics training in a police academy will have on the future ethical behavior of recruits? Can ethics be taught, or is each person's concept of "right and wrong" permanently shaped in childhood? Explain your answers.

Women and Minorities in Policing Today

For most of this nation's history, the typical American police officer was white and male. As recently as 1968, African Americans represented only 5 percent of all sworn officers in the United States, and the percentage of "women in blue" was even lower.[48] Only within the past thirty years has this situation been addressed, with many police departments actively trying to recruit women, African Americans, Hispanics, Asian Americans, and members of other minority groups. The result, as you will see, has been a steady though not dramatic increase in the diversity of the nation's police forces. When it comes to issues of gender, race, and ethnicity, however, mere statistics rarely tell the entire story.

Antidiscrimination Law and Affirmative Action

To a certain point, external forces have driven law enforcement agencies to increase the number of female and minority recruits. The 1964 Civil Rights Act and its 1972

field training The segment of a police recruit's training in which he or she is removed from the classroom and placed on the beat, under the supervision of a senior officer.

amendments guaranteed members of minority groups and women equal access to jobs in law enforcement, partly by establishing the Equal Employment Opportunity Commission (EEOC) to ensure fairness in hiring practices. The United States Supreme Court has also ruled on several occasions that **discrimination** by law enforcement agencies violates federal law.[49] In legal terms, discrimination occurs when hiring and promotion decisions are based on individual characteristics such as gender or race, and not on job-related factors.

Since the early 1970s, numerous law enforcement agencies have instituted **affirmative action** programs to increase the diversity of their employees. These programs are designed to give women and members of minority groups certain advantages in hiring and promotion to remedy the effects of past discrimination and prevent future discrimination. Often, affirmative action programs are established voluntarily. Sometimes, however, they are the result of lawsuits brought by employees or potential employees who believe that the employer has discriminated against them.

In such instances, if the court finds that discrimination did occur, it will implement a *consent decree* to remedy the situation. Under a consent decree, the law enforcement agency often agrees to meet certain numerical goals in hiring women and members of minority groups. If it fails to meet these goals, it is punished with a fine or some other sanction.[50] (See the feature *CJ Controversy—Affirmative Action in Law Enforcement* to express your own views on policies aimed at diversifying American police departments.)

discrimination The illegal use of characteristics such as gender or race by employers when making hiring or promotion decisions.

affirmative action A hiring or promotion policy favoring those groups, such as women, African Americans, or Hispanics, who have suffered from discrimination in the past or continue to suffer from discrimination.

CJ Controversy
EQUAL JUSTICE UNDER LAW
M Dogan/Shutterstock.com

Affirmative Action in Law Enforcement

About a decade ago, in a case involving school desegregation, U.S. Supreme Court Chief Justice John Roberts, Jr., wrote, "The way to stop discriminating on the basis of race is to stop discriminating on the basis of race." Roberts's point, that affirmative action is itself an outdated form of racial discrimination, is disputed by those who feel that the historical wrongs of racism are still clearly evident in our society. As proof, these critics often point to the lack of diversity in many local police departments, particularly when compared to the racial and ethnic makeup of the communities they serve.

Affirmative Action in Law Enforcement Benefits Society Because . . .

- For most of the nation's history, women and minorities suffered from widespread discrimination in police hiring. Affirmative action remedies these past wrongs.
- It works. In Chicago, the African American share of new police hires rose from 10 percent to 40 percent in just two years after the implementation of a consent decree.

Affirmative Action in Law Enforcement Harms Society Because . . .

- A stigma is attached to persons perceived to have benefited from affirmative action. "I don't want to be in a department where I was hired because of my skin color," said one black police applicant in Dayton, Ohio. "I want it because I earned it."
- Public safety requires that all police officers be the most competent and skilled people available, regardless of their gender, race, or ethnicity.

Your Assignment

In March 2015, the **U.S. Department of Justice** released a report entitled **"Investigation of the Ferguson Police Department"** in response to the killing of an unarmed black man by a white police officer the previous year. After reading this report, which you can find online, do you think that an affirmative action program for hiring African American police officers would benefit the Ferguson, Missouri, community? Explain your answer in at least two full paragraphs.

Working Women: Gender and Law Enforcement

In 1987, about 7.6 percent of all local police officers were women. By 2013, that percentage had risen to 12.2 percent—17.6 percent in departments serving populations of more than one million people.[51] That increase seems less impressive, however, when one considers that women make up more than half of the population of the United States, meaning that they are severely underrepresented in law enforcement.

Added Scrutiny There are several reasons for the low levels of women serving as police officers. First, relatively few women hold positions of high rank in American police departments, and only about 3 percent of the police chiefs in the United States are women.[52] Consequently, female police officers have few superiors who might be able to mentor them in what can be a hostile work environment. In addition, women are more likely to fail entry-level physical ability tests—a problem that can be alleviated by providing female applicants with pretest training.[53]

In addition to the dangers and pressures facing all law enforcement agents, which we will discuss in the next chapter, women must deal with an added layer of scrutiny. Many male police officers feel that their female counterparts are mentally soft, physically weak, and generally unsuited for the rigors of the job. At the same time, male officers often try to protect female officers by keeping them out of hazardous situations, thereby denying the women the opportunity to prove themselves.[54]

Tokenism Women in law enforcement also face the problem of *tokenism,* or the belief that they have been hired or promoted to fulfill diversity requirements and have not earned their positions. Tokenism creates pressure to prove the stereotypes wrong. When comparing the arrest patterns of male and female officers over a twelve-month period in Cincinnati, Ohio, for example, researchers noted several interesting patterns. Although overall arrest rates were similar, female officers were much more likely than their male counterparts to arrest suspects who were "non-deferential" or hostile. Also, the presence of a supervisor greatly increased the likelihood that a female officer would make an arrest.

Such patterns, the researchers concluded, show that female officers feel pressure to demonstrate that they are "good cops" who cannot be intimidated because of their gender.[55] One officer said that her female colleagues "go into that physical-arrest mode quicker [because] you want to prove that you can do it."[56] Similarly, women who rise through the law enforcement ranks often face questions concerning their worthiness. According to former Tampa (Florida) police chief Jane Castor, "No matter how qualified you are or how much experience you have . . . people will say that you were promoted—in part, if not fully—because you're a woman."[57]

In fact, most of the negative attitudes toward women police officers are based on prejudice rather than actual experience. A number of studies have shown that there is very little difference between the performance of men and women in uniform.[58] (For more on this topic, see the feature *Myth vs Reality—Women Make Bad Cops.*)

Minority Report: Race and Ethnicity in Law Enforcement

As Figure 4.3 shows, like women, members of minority groups have been slowly increasing their presence in local police departments since the late 1980s. A closer look at the statistics shows that the percentage of African American police officers has remained relatively steady since 1993, while the number of Latinos and Asians on police rolls nearly doubled during that same period of time.[59]

Given that many police departments are striving to hire more African American personnel, these figures show several structural problems in the recruitment process. First, a disproportionate number of black candidates fail police background checks, credit checks, and mental-health checks, for reasons pertaining to poverty that we touched on in Chapter 2. Second, questions on written exams may be culturally biased in favor of white applicants.[60] Finally, a perception in the African American community that the profession is tainted by racial prejudice—discussed in the next chapter—may discourage potential black applicants.[61]

Myth vs Reality

Women Make Bad Cops

Learning Objective 4 Describe some of the benefits that female police officers bring to law enforcement.

The Myth The perception that women are not physically strong enough to be effective law enforcement officers prevails both in the public mind and within police forces themselves. Criminologist Susan Martin has found that policewomen are under "constant pressure to demonstrate their competence and effectiveness vis-à-vis their male counterparts." One female police officer describes her experience:

> I was the smallest person . . . . [The male officers] didn't feel I could do the job. They tried to get me into fighting situations to see if I would back down. They told me, "You know, if you aren't strong enough or are going to be a coward, we have to find out fast and get you out of here."

The Reality Female police officers are certainly capable of acts of bravery and physical prowess. In fact, a number of studies have shown that policewomen can be as effective as men in most situations, and often more so. Citizens appear to prefer dealing with a female police officer rather than a male during service calls—especially those that involve domestic violence. In general, policewomen are less aggressive and more likely to reduce the potential for a violent situation by relying on verbal skills rather than their authority as law enforcement agents. According to one large-scale study of local police departments in the southeast United States, women made up 12.4 percent of the sworn officer workforce and accounted for only 5.7 percent of misconduct allegations.

For Critical Analysis

Do you believe that female police officers can be just as effective as men in protecting citizens from criminal behavior? Why or why not?

Double Marginality According to Peter C. Moskos, a professor at the John Jay College of Criminal Justice in New York, "Black and white police officers remain two distinct shades of blue, with distinct attitudes toward each other and the communities they serve."[62] While that may be true, minority officers generally report that they have good relationships with their white fellow officers.[63] Often, though, members of minority groups in law enforcement—particularly African Americans and Hispanics—do face the problem of **double marginality.** This term refers to a situation in which minority officers are viewed with suspicion by both sides:

double marginality The double suspicion that minority law enforcement officers face from their white colleagues and from members of the minority community to which they belong.

1. White police officers believe that minority officers will give members of their own race or ethnicity better treatment on the streets.
2. Those same minority officers face hostility from members of their own community who are under the impression that black and Hispanic officers are traitors to their race or ethnicity.

In response, minority officers may feel the need to act more harshly toward minority offenders to prove that they are not biased in favor of their own racial or ethnic group.[64]

The Benefits of a Diverse Police Force In 1986, Supreme Court justice John Paul Stevens spoke for many in the criminal justice system when he observed that "an integrated police force could develop a better relationship [with a racially diverse citizenry] and therefore do a more effective job of maintaining law and order than a force composed of white officers."[65] Indeed, when practiced by a mostly white police force in

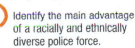

Learning Objective 5 Identify the main advantage of a racially and ethnically diverse police force.

Figure 4.3 Members of Minority Groups in Local Law Enforcement

	Percentage of Full-Time Sworn Personnel		
Year	African American	Hispanic/ Latino	Other*
2013	12.2	11.6	3.5
2007	11.9	10.3	3.0
2003	11.7	9.1	2.8
2000	11.7	8.3	2.7
1997	11.7	7.8	2.1
1993	11.3	6.2	1.5
1990	10.5	5.2	1.3
1987	9.0	4.5	0.8

*Includes Asians, Native Hawaiian or other Pacific Islanders, American Indians or Alaska Natives, and persons identifying two or more races.

Source: Bureau of Justice Statistics, *Local Police Departments, 2013: Personnel, Policies, and Practices* (Washington, D.C.: U.S. Department of Justice, May 2015), Figure 5, page5.

primarily African American neighborhoods, aggressive law enforcement tactics such as frequent stops of pedestrians and drivers for minor violations can lead to mistrust in the community. Given that many American cities in which blacks make up at least 35 percent of the population have disproportionately white police forces,[66] this mistrust can have explosive consequences. In recent years, Baltimore, Cleveland, and Philadelphia have experienced racially charged protests after white officers used force against black citizens that was perceived to be excessive and unfair.

Despite the effects of double marginality, African American officers may have more credibility in a predominantly black neighborhood than white police officers, leading to better community-police relations and a greater ability to solve and prevent crimes. Certainly, in the Mexican American communities common to border states such as Arizona, Texas, and California, many Hispanic officers are able to gather information that would be very difficult for non-Spanish-speaking officers to collect. Finally, however, the best argument for a diverse police force is that members of minority groups represent a broad source of talent in this country, and such talent can only enhance the overall effectiveness of American law enforcement.

Public and Private Law Enforcement

Americans are served by a multitude of police organizations. Overall, there are about 18,000 law enforcement agencies in the United States, employing about 880,000 officers.[67] For the most part, these agencies operate on three different levels: local, state, and federal. Each level has its own set of responsibilities, which we shall discuss starting with local police departments.

Municipal Law Enforcement Agencies

About three-quarters of all *sworn officers,* or those officers with arrest powers, work in police departments serving cities with populations of under 1 million residents.[68] While the New York City Police Department employs about 35,000 police personnel, about 90 percent of all local police departments have fifty or fewer law enforcement officers.[69]

Of the three levels of law enforcement, municipal agencies have the broadest authority to apprehend criminal suspects, maintain order, and provide services to the community. Whether the local officer is part of a large force or the only law enforcement officer in the community, he or she is usually responsible for a wide spectrum of duties, from responding to noise complaints to investigating homicides. Larger police departments will often assign officers to specialized task forces or units that deal with a particular crime or area of concern. For example, in Washington, D.C., the police department features a Lesbian, Gay, Bisexual and Transgender Liaison Unit that handles anti-homosexual crimes in the city. The Knoxville (Tennessee) Police Department has a squad devoted to combating Internet crimes against children, while the three hundred officers assigned to the New York City Police Department's Emergency Service Unit are trained in suicide rescue, hostage negotiation, and SCUBA operations.

sheriff The primary law enforcement officer in a county, usually elected to the post by a popular vote.

Sheriffs and County Law Enforcement

The **sheriff** is a very important figure in American law enforcement. Almost every one of the more than three thousand counties in the United States (except those in Alaska) has a sheriff. In every state except Rhode Island and Hawaii, sheriffs are elected by members of the community for two- or four-year terms and are paid a salary set by the state legislature or county board.

As elected officials who do not necessarily need a background in law enforcement, modern sheriffs resemble their counterparts from the political era of policing in many ways. Simply stated, the sheriff is also a politician. When a new sheriff is elected, she or he will sometimes repay political debts by appointing new deputies or promoting those who have given her or him support.

Size and Responsibility of Sheriffs' Departments Like municipal police forces, sheriffs' departments vary in size. The largest is the Los Angeles County Sheriff's Department, with more than 9,000 deputies. Of the 3,063 sheriffs' departments in the country, thirteen employ more than 1,000 officers, while forty-five have only one.[70]

Keep in mind that cities, which are served by municipal police departments, often exist within counties, which are served by sheriffs' departments. Therefore, police officers and sheriffs' deputies often find themselves policing the same geographical areas. Police departments, however, are generally governed by a local political entity such as a mayor's office, while most sheriffs' departments are assigned their duties by state law. About 80 percent of all sheriffs' departments are responsible for investigating violent crimes in their jurisdictions. Other common responsibilities of a sheriff's department include:

- Investigating drug crimes.
- Maintaining the county jail.
- Carrying out civil and criminal processes within county lines, such as serving eviction notices and court summonses.
- Keeping order in the county courthouse.
- Enforcing orders of the court, such as overseeing the isolation of a jury during a trial.[71]

It is easy to confuse sheriffs' departments and local police departments. Both law enforcement agencies are responsible for many of the same tasks, including crime investigation and routine patrol. There are differences, however. Sheriffs' departments are more likely to be involved in county court and jail operations and to perform certain services such as search

▲ Police Officer Todd Geist of Medicine Lodge, Kansas, diverts traffic from a road closed by a grass fire. **In what ways are local police departments and sheriffs' departments similar? In what ways do these two law enforcement agencies differ?** AP Photo/Travis Morisse/*The Hutchinson News*

and rescue. Local police departments, for their part, are more likely to perform traffic-related functions than are sheriffs' departments.[72]

The County Coroner Another elected official on the county level is the **coroner**, or medical examiner. Duties vary from county to county, but the coroner has a general mandate to investigate "all sudden, unexplained, unnatural, or suspicious deaths" reported to the office. The coroner is ultimately responsible for determining the cause of death in these cases. Coroners also perform autopsies and assist other law enforcement agencies in homicide investigations. For example, when a four-month-old baby died in August 2015 in an East Baton Rouge, Louisiana, hospital, the local coroner was required to determine her cause of death. By finding that the baby girl was killed by blunt force injuries of the head and neck, the coroner provided law enforcement authorities with enough evidence to charge her father with first degree murder.

State Police and Highway Patrols

The most visible state law enforcement agency is the state police or highway patrol agency. Historically, state police agencies were created for three reasons:

1. To assist local police agencies, which often did not have adequate resources or training to handle their law enforcement tasks.
2. To investigate criminal activities that crossed jurisdictional boundaries (such as when bank robbers committed a crime in one county and then fled to another part of the state).
3. To provide law enforcement in rural communities and other areas that did not have local or county police agencies.

Today, there are twenty-three state police agencies and twenty-six highway patrols in the United States. State police agencies have statewide jurisdiction and are authorized to perform a wide variety of law enforcement tasks. Thus, they provide the same services as city or county police departments and are restricted only by the boundaries of the state.

In contrast, highway patrols have limited authority. Their duties are generally defined either by their jurisdiction or by the specific types of offenses they have the authority to control. As their name suggests, most highway patrols concentrate primarily on regulating traffic. Specifically, they enforce traffic laws and investigate traffic accidents. Furthermore, they usually limit their activity to patrolling state and federal highways.

Federal Law Enforcement Agencies

Statistically, employees of federal agencies do not make up a large part of the nation's law enforcement force. In fact, the New York City Police Department has about one-fifth as many employees as all of the federal law enforcement agencies combined. Nevertheless, the influence of these federal agencies is substantial.

Unlike local police departments, which must deal with all forms of crime, federal agencies have been authorized, usually by Congress, to enforce specific laws or attend to specific situations. The U.S. Coast Guard, for example, patrols the nation's waterways, while U.S. Postal inspectors investigate and prosecute crimes perpetrated through the use of the U.S. Mail. In this section, you will learn the elements and duties of the most important federal law enforcement agencies, which are grouped according to the federal department or bureau to which they report. (See Figure 4.4 for the current federal law enforcement "lineup.")

coroner The medical examiner of a county, usually elected by popular vote.

Figure 4.4 Federal Law Enforcement Agencies

A number of federal agencies employ law enforcement officers who are authorized to carry firearms and make arrests. The most prominent ones are under the control of the U.S. Department of Homeland Security, the U.S. Department of Justice, and the U.S. Department of the Treasury.

DEPARTMENT OF HOMELAND SECURITY

DEPARTMENT NAME	APPROXIMATE NUMBER OF OFFICERS	MAIN RESPONSIBILITIES
U.S. Customs and Border Protection (CBP)	44,000	(1) Prevent the illegal flow of people and goods across America's international borders; (2) facilitate legal trade and travel
U.S. Immigration and Customs Enforcement (ICE)	12,000	Uphold public safety and homeland security by enforcing the nation's immigration and customs laws
U.S. Secret Service	4,500	(1) Protect the president, the president's family, former presidents and their families, and other high-ranking politicians; (2) combat currency counterfeiters

DEPARTMENT OF JUSTICE

DEPARTMENT NAME	APPROXIMATE NUMBER OF OFFICERS	MAIN RESPONSIBILITIES
Federal Bureau of Investigation (FBI)	14,000	(1) Protect national security by fighting international and domestic terrorism; (2) enforce federal criminal laws such as those dealing with cyber crime, public corruption, and civil rights violations
Drug Enforcement Administration (DEA)	5,200	Enforce the nation's laws regulating the sale and use of drugs
Bureau of Alcohol, Tobacco, Firearms and Explosives (ATF)	2,500	(1) Combat the illegal use and trafficking of firearms and explosives; (2) investigate the illegal diversion of alcohol and tobacco products
U.S. Marshals Service	4,300	(1) Provide security at federal courts; (2) protect government witnesses; (3) apprehend fugitives from the federal court or corrections system

DEPARTMENT OF THE TREASURY

DEPARTMENT NAME	APPROXIMATE NUMBER OF OFFICERS	MAIN RESPONSIBILITIES
Internal Revenue Service (IRS)	3,200	Investigate potential criminal violations of the nation's tax code

The Department of Homeland Security Comprising twenty-two federal agencies, the Department of Homeland Security (DHS) coordinates national efforts to protect the United States against international and domestic terrorism. While most of the agencies under DHS control are not specifically linked with the criminal justice system, the department does oversee three agencies that play an important role in counterterrorism and fighting crime: U.S. Customs and Border Protection, U.S. Immigration and Customs Enforcement, and the U.S. Secret Service.

Learning Objective

6 Indicate some of the most important law enforcement agencies under the control of the Department of Homeland Security.

U.S. Customs and Border Protection (CBP) The federal government spends about $19 billion annually to enforce immigration law.[73] A large chunk of these funds go to **U.S. Customs and Border Protection (CBP)**, which polices the flow of goods and people across the United States' international borders. In general terms, this means that the agency has two primary goals:

U.S. Customs and Border Protection (CBP) The federal agency responsible for protecting U.S. borders and facilitating legal trade and travel across those borders.

1. To keep undocumented immigrants, illegal drugs, and drug traffickers from crossing our borders; and
2. To facilitate the smooth flow of legal trade and travel.

Consequently, CBP officers are stationed at all 328 ports of entry and exit to the United States. The officers have widespread authority to investigate and search all international passengers, whether they arrive on airplanes, ships, or other forms of transportation.

To ensure that those coming into the United States from abroad have permission to do so, CBP officers check documents such as passports and *visas*. (A **visa** is a document issued by the U.S. State Department that indicates the conditions under which a holder can enter and travel within the United States.) The officers also have the responsibility of inspecting luggage and cargo to ensure compliance with immigration and trade laws.

The U.S. Border Patrol, a branch of CBP, has the burden of policing the Mexican and Canadian borders between official ports of entry. Every year, hundreds of thousands of non-U.S. citizens, unable to legally obtain visas, attempt to enter the country illegally by crossing these large, underpopulated regions, particularly in the southern part of the country. In 2014, Border Patrol agents apprehended about 337,000 illegal border crossers.[74]

CJ Policy—Your Take

California's Trust Act prohibits sheriffs' departments in the state from providing ICE with access to immigrants who have been jailed for non-serious crimes. Because almost every immigrant who is in the United States without permission is **eligible for removal** by ICE, this legislation, in practice, allows certain low-level, immigrant criminal offenders to remain in the country illegally. **Why would California take such steps to protect nonviolent immigration law violators? Do you think local law enforcement agencies favor this legislation? Why or why not? What is your opinion on the matter?**

U.S. Immigration and Customs Enforcement (ICE) CBP shares responsibility for locating and apprehending those persons illegally in the United States with special agents from **U.S. Immigration and Customs Enforcement (ICE)**. While CBP focuses almost exclusively on the nation's borders, ICE has a broader mandate to investigate and enforce our country's immigration and customs laws. Simply stated, CBP covers the borders, and ICE covers everything else. The latter agency's duties include detaining undocumented aliens and deporting (removing) them from the United States, ensuring that those without permission do not work or gain other benefits in this country. ICE also takes measures to disrupt human trafficking—a crime that has been on the rise of late.

Recently, ICE has been aggressively removing undocumented immigrants from the United States. In 2014, for example, the agency conducted about 315,000 removals, 56 percent of which involved those who had been convicted of a crime.[75] ICE also partners with Mexican law enforcement to disrupt drug-smuggling operations along the U.S.-Mexico border. In January 2016, as part of Operation Diablo Express, ICE agents helped Mexican authorities apprehend twenty-four members of the Sinaloa Cartel, one of Mexico's largest drug-trafficking organizations. (This chapter's *CJ Policy—Your Take* feature focuses on a controversial state law that limits ICE's ability to deport undocumented immigrants who have committed petty crimes.)

The U.S. Secret Service When it was created in 1865, the **U.S. Secret Service** was primarily responsible for combating currency counterfeiters. In 1901, the agency was given the added responsibility of protecting the president of the United States, the president's family, the vice president, the president-elect, and former presidents. These duties have remained the cornerstone of the agency, with several expansions. After a number of threats against presidential candidates in the 1960s and early 1970s, including the shootings of Robert Kennedy of New York and Governor George Wallace of Alabama, in 1976 Secret Service agents became responsible for protecting those political figures as well.

In addition to its special plainclothes agents, the agency also directs two uniformed groups of law enforcement officers. The Secret Service Uniformed Division protects the grounds of the White House and its inhabitants, and the Treasury Police Force polices the Treasury Building in Washington, D.C. To aid its battle against counterfeiters and

visa Official authorization allowing a person to travel to and within the issuing country.

U.S. Immigration and Customs Enforcement (ICE) The federal agency that enforces the nation's immigration and customs laws.

U.S. Secret Service A federal law enforcement organization with the primary responsibility of protecting the president, the president's family, the vice president, and other important political figures.

Careers in CJ

Courtesy of Arnold E. Bell

Arnold E. Bell
Federal Bureau of Investigation (FBI) Agent

I came to the FBI from the U.S. Army, where I worked as a crewman on a UH-1 helicopter and subsequently as a special agent with the U.S. Army Criminal Investigation Command. My work experience in the U.S. Army and degree from St. Leo College (now University) provided the educational foundation that allowed entry into the FBI. After graduating from the FBI Academy in Quantico, Virginia, I was assigned to our Los Angeles division, where I spent the next twelve years. It was a particularly interesting time to be working in Los Angeles, which was experiencing a boom in bank robberies. During the most intense stretches, we were averaging between five and seven bank robberies a day! When I wasn't chasing down a bank robber, I had my hands full with hunting down fugitives, working against organized crime, and dealing with public corruption.

fbi.gov

I am currently assigned to the FBI's cyber division as an assistant section chief. The primary mission of my division is to combat cyber-based terrorism and hostile-intelligence operations conducted via the Internet, and to address general cyber crime. Since September 11, 2001, our primary focus has shifted from criminal work to counterterrorism. This has been a difficult transformation for many of us "old-timers" because we grew up in the Bureau doing criminal work. We all recognize, however, the importance of this new challenge, and, despite the difficulties, I believe we have been successful in fulfilling both missions.

SOCIAL MEDIA CAREER TIP Be aware of your e-mail address/screen name/login name and what it represents. Stay away from nicknames. Use a professional and unique name to represent yourself consistently across social media platforms.

FASTFACTS

FBI agent

Job description:

- Primary role is to oversee intelligence and investigate crimes.
- Special agent careers are divided into five career paths: intelligence, counterintelligence, counterterrorism, criminal, and cyber.

What kind of training is required?

- Bachelor's and/or master's degree, plus three years of work experience. U.S. citizen, 23–36 years old.
- A written and oral examination, medical and physical examinations, a psychological assessment, and an exhaustive background investigation.

Annual salary range?

- $65,000–$74,000

forgers of government bonds, the agency has the use of a laboratory at the Bureau of Engraving and Printing in the nation's capital.

Additional DHS Agencies Besides the three already discussed—CBP, ICE, and the U.S. Secret Service—three other DHS agencies play a central role in preventing and responding to crime and terrorist-related activity:

- The *U.S. Coast Guard* defends the nation's coasts, ports, and inland waterways. It also combats illegal drug shipping and enforces immigration law at sea.
- The *Transportation Security Administration* is responsible for the safe operation of our airline, rail, bus, and ferry services. It also operates the Federal Air Marshals program that places undercover federal agents on commercial flights.
- The *Federal Emergency Management Agency* holds a position as the lead federal agency in preparing for and responding to disasters such as hurricanes, floods, terrorist attacks, and *infrastructure* concerns. Our national **infrastructure** includes all of the facilities and systems that provide the daily necessities of modern life, such as electric power, food, water, transportation, and telecommunications.

infrastructure The services and facilities that support the day-to-day needs of modern life, such as electricity, food, transportation, and water.

The Department of Justice The U.S. Department of Justice, created in 1870, is still the primary federal law enforcement agency in the country. With the responsibility of enforcing criminal law and supervising the federal prisons, the Justice Department plays a leading role in the American criminal justice system. To carry out its law enforcement responsibilities, the department incorporates a number of law enforcement agencies, including the Federal Bureau of Investigation; the federal Drug Enforcement Administration; the Bureau of Alcohol, Tobacco, Firearms and Explosives; and the U.S. Marshals Service.

Learning Objective 7

Summarize the duties of the FBI.

The Federal Bureau of Investigation (FBI) Initially created in 1908 as the Bureau of Investigation, this agency was renamed the **Federal Bureau of Investigation (FBI)** in 1935. One of the primary investigative agencies of the federal government, the FBI has jurisdiction over nearly two hundred federal crimes, including white-collar crimes, espionage (spying), kidnapping, extortion, interstate transportation of stolen property, bank robbery, interstate gambling, and civil rights violations. With its network of agents across the country and the globe, the FBI is also uniquely positioned to combat worldwide criminal activity such as terrorism and drug trafficking. In fact, since 2001, the agency has shifted its focus from traditional crime to national security. Between that year and 2009, the FBI doubled its roster of counterterrorism agents, while reducing its number of criminal investigations. At any time, the agency is engaged in 10,000 counterterrorism investigations.[76] The FBI recently even officially changed its primary function from "law enforcement" to "national security."[77]

The agency is also committed to providing valuable support for local and state law enforcement agencies. FBI agents provide homicide investigation assistance to local police departments in cities with unusually high violent crime rates such as Baltimore; Flint, Michigan; and Oakland. Its Identification Division maintains a large database of fingerprint information and offers assistance in finding missing persons and identifying the victims of fires, airplane crashes, and other disfiguring accidents. The services of the FBI Laboratory, the largest crime laboratory in the world, are available at no cost to other agencies.

In addition, the FBI's Next Generation Identification (NGI) program gathers data such as fingerprints, iris scans, photographs, and information collected through facial recognition software. Eventually, the agency hopes to able to use NGI to find criminal suspects using driver's license photos and images from surveillance cameras, and to share this information with local and state law enforcement agencies.

The Drug Enforcement Administration (DEA) The mission of the **Drug Enforcement Administration (DEA)** is to enforce domestic drug laws and regulations and to assist other federal and foreign agencies in combating illegal drug manufacture and trade on an international level. The agency also enforces the provisions of the Controlled Substances Act (CSA). The CSA specifies five categories for drugs and the penalties for the manufacture, sale, distribution, possession, or consumption of these drugs, based on the substances' medical use, potential for abuse, and addictive qualities.[78]

The DEA operates a network of six regional laboratories used to test and categorize seized drugs. Local law enforcement agencies have access to the DEA labs and often use them to ensure that information about particular drugs that will be presented in court is accurate and up to date. In recent years, Congress has given the FBI more authority to enforce drug laws, and the two agencies now share a number of administrative controls.

Federal Bureau of Investigation (FBI) The branch of the Department of Justice responsible for investigating violations of federal law.

Drug Enforcement Administration (DEA) The federal agency responsible for enforcing the nation's laws and regulations regarding narcotics and other controlled substances.

The Bureau of Alcohol, Tobacco, Firearms and Explosives (ATF) As its name suggests, the Bureau of Alcohol, Tobacco, Firearms and Explosives (ATF) is primarily concerned with the illegal sale, possession, and use of firearms and the control of untaxed tobacco and liquor products. The Firearms Division of the agency has the responsibility of enforcing the Gun Control Act of 1968, which sets the circumstances under which firearms may be sold and used in this country. The bureau also regulates all gun trade between the United States and foreign nations and collects taxes on all firearm importers, manufacturers, and dealers. In keeping with these duties, the ATF is also responsible for policing the illegal use and possession of explosives. Furthermore, the ATF is charged with enforcing federal gambling laws.

Getting Linked in

More than 30,000 employees either directly or indirectly associated with the **U.S. Department of Homeland Security** have posted their profiles on LinkedIn. You can connect with these individuals by accessing a link to the department's home page on the LinkedIn website.

The U.S. Marshals Service The oldest federal law enforcement agency is the U.S. Marshals Service. In 1789, President George Washington assigned thirteen U.S. Marshals to protect his attorney general. That same year, Congress created the office of the U.S. Marshals and Deputy Marshals. Originally, the U.S. Marshals acted as the main law enforcement officers in the western territories. Following the Civil War (1861–1865), when most of these territories had become states, these agents were assigned to work for the U.S. district courts, where federal crimes are tried. The relationship between the U.S. Marshals Service and the federal courts continues today and forms the basis for the officers' main duties, which include:

1. Providing security at federal courts for judges, jurors, and other courtroom participants.
2. Controlling property that has been ordered seized by federal courts.
3. Protecting government witnesses who put themselves in danger by testifying against the targets of federal criminal investigations. This protection is sometimes accomplished by relocating the witnesses and providing them with different identities.
4. Transporting federal prisoners to detention institutions.
5. Investigating violations of federal fugitive laws.[79]

The Department of the Treasury The Department of the Treasury, formed in 1789, is mainly responsible for all financial matters of the federal government. It pays all the federal government's bills, borrows funds, collects taxes, mints coins, and prints paper currency. The largest bureau of the Treasury Department, the Internal Revenue Service (IRS), is concerned with violations of tax laws and regulations. The bureau's criminal investigation division focuses on various forms of tax evasion and tax fraud, as well as prosecuting identity theft and public corruption. In 2015, the IRS's criminal investigation division gained about 3,200 convictions in cases involving these types of wrongdoing.[80]

Private Security

Learning Objective

8 Analyze the importance of private security today.

Even with increasing numbers of local, state, and federal law enforcement officers, the police do not have the ability to prevent every crime. Recognizing this, many businesses and citizens have decided to hire private guards for their properties and homes. In fact, according to a 2013 study released by ASIS International, an industry-research firm, demand for **private security** generates revenues of more than $300 billion a year.[81] More than 10,000 firms employing around 1.9 million people provide private security services in this country, compared with about 1.1 million public law enforcement employees.

private security The practice of private corporations or individuals offering services traditionally performed by police officers.

Privatizing Law Enforcement As there are no federal regulations regarding private security, each state has its own rules for this form of employment. In several states,

▲ A private security guard patrols the Manhattan Mall in New York City. **Why is being visible such an important aspect of many private security jobs?** Mario Tama/Getty Images

including California and Florida, prospective security guards must have at least forty hours of instruction. Ideally, a security guard—lacking the extensive training of a law enforcement agent—should only observe and report criminal activity, unless use of force is needed to prevent a felony.[82]

As a rule, private security is not designed to replace law enforcement. It is intended to deter crime rather than stop it. A uniformed security guard patrolling a shopping mall parking lot or a bank lobby has one primary function—to convince a potential criminal to search out a shopping mall or bank that does not have private security. For the same reason, many citizens hire security personnel to drive marked cars through their neighborhoods, making them a less attractive target for burglaries, robberies, vandalism, and other crimes.

Secondary Policing Although many states have minimum training requirements for private security officers, such training lags far behind the requirements to be a public officer. Consequently, there is a high demand for **secondary policing**, an umbrella term that covers the work that off-duty cops do when "moonlighting" for private companies or government agencies.

Generally speaking, police officers operate under the same rules whether they are off duty or on duty. In addition, 83 percent of local police departments in the United States have written policies for secondary policing.[83] For example, among other restrictions, Seattle police officers cannot work (on duty or off duty) longer than eighteen consecutive hours in a twenty-four-hour period and must clear all private employment with a superior.[84] Off-duty police officers commonly provide traffic control and pedestrian safety at road construction sites, or crowd control at large-scale functions such as music festivals or sporting events. They are also often hired to protect private properties and businesses, just like their nonpublic counterparts.[85]

Continued Health of the Industry Indicators point to continued growth for the private security industry. The *Hallcrest Report II,* a far-reaching overview of private security trends funded by the National Institute of Justice, identifies four factors driving this growth:

1. An increase in fear on the part of the public triggered by media coverage of crime.
2. The problem of crime in the workplace. According to the National Retail Security Survey, American retailers lose about $44 billion a year because of shoplifting and employee theft.[86]
3. Budget cuts in states and municipalities that have forced reductions in the number of public police, thereby raising the demand for private ones.
4. A rising awareness of private security products (such as home burglar alarms) and services as cost-effective protective measures.[87]

Another reason for the industry's continued health is terrorism. Private security is responsible for protecting more than three-fourths of the nation's likely terrorist targets such as power plants, financial centers, dams, malls, oil refineries, and transportation hubs.

secondary policing The situation in which a police officer accepts off-duty employment from a private company or government agency.

Summary

For more information on these concepts, look back to the Learning Objective icons throughout the chapter.

1 **List the four basic responsibilities of the police.** (a) To enforce laws, (b) to provide services, (c) to prevent crime, and (d) to preserve the peace.

2 **Explain how intelligence-led policing works and how it benefits modern police departments.** Intelligence-led policing uses past crime patterns to predict when and where crime will occur in the future. In theory, intelligence-led policing allows police administrators to use fewer resources because it removes costly and time-consuming "guesswork" from the law enforcement equation.

3 **Identify the differences between the police academy and field training as learning tools for recruits.** The police academy is a controlled environment where police recruits learn the basics of policing from instructors in classrooms. In contrast, field training takes place in the "real world": the recruit goes on patrol with an experienced police officer.

4 **Describe some of the benefits that female police officers bring to law enforcement.** Apart from bravery and prowess, female police officers seem to put citizens at ease and are therefore often more effective during service calls. Policewomen are also more likely to use verbal skills rather than force when placed in situations of potential violence, leading to fewer claims of brutality than is the case with their male counterparts.

5 **Identify the main advantage of a racially and ethnically diverse police force.** Particularly in communities that are themselves racially and ethnically diverse, police officers who are members of minority groups are often more easily able to communicate with citizens. This trust enables the officers to do a better job maintaining order, as well as solving and preventing crimes.

6 **Indicate some of the most important law enforcement agencies under the control of the Department of Homeland Security.** (a) U.S. Customs and Border Protection, which polices the flow of goods and people across the United States' international borders and oversees the U.S. Border Patrol; (b) U.S. Immigration and Customs Enforcement, which investigates and enforces our nation's immigration and customs laws; and (c) the U.S. Secret Service, which protects high-ranking federal government officials and federal property.

7 **Summarize the duties of the FBI.** The FBI has jurisdiction to investigate hundreds of federal crimes, including white-collar crime, kidnapping, bank robbery, and civil rights violations. The FBI is also heavily involved in combating terrorism and drug-trafficking operations in the United States and around the world. Finally, the agency provides support to state and local law enforcement agencies through its crime laboratories and databases.

8 **Analyze the importance of private security today.** In the United States, businesses and citizens spend billions of dollars each year on private security. Heightened fear of crime and increased crime in the workplace have fueled the growth in spending on private security.

Questions for Critical Analysis

1. Nationwide, a number of local police departments are offering "fight back" courses for citizens on how to best prepare for and respond to active-shooter attacks. Do you think such courses are appropriate? Why or why not?
2. Should law enforcement agencies have the same physical agility and fitness requirements for male and female applicants? Explain your answer.
3. Review the discussion of double marginality in this chapter. Why would members of a minority community think that police officers of the same race or ethnicity were "traitors"? What can police departments do to dispel this misperception?
4. One of the major differences between a local police chief and a sheriff is that the sheriff is elected, while the police chief is appointed. What are some of the possible problems with having a law enforcement official who, like any other politician, is responsible to voters? What are some of the possible benefits of this situation?
5. Twenty-nine states do not require any specific training for private security personnel. What are the arguments for and against requiring at least forty hours of training, as is the case in California and Florida?

Key Terms

Notes

1. Quoted in Rick Rojas, "An Officer Who Trained for the Worst and Faced It: 'This Was Actually Happening,'" *New York Times* (December 4, 2015), A24.
2. Egon Bittner, *The Functions of Police in a Modern Society,* Public Health Service Publication No. 2059 (Chevy Chase, Md.: National Institute of Mental Health, 1970), 38–44.
3. Carl Klockars, "The Rhetoric of Community Policing," in *Community Policing: Rhetoric or Reality,* eds. Jack Greene and Stephen Mastrofski (New York: Praeger Publishers, 1991), 244.
4. Jack R. Greene and Carl B. Klockars, "What Do Police Do?" in *Thinking about Police,* 2d ed., eds. Carl B. Klockars and Stephen D. Mastrofski (New York: McGraw-Hill, 1991), 273–284.
5. John S. Dempsey and Linda S. Forst, *An Introduction to Policing,* 6th ed. (Clifton Park, N.Y.: Delmar Cengage Learning, 2012), 380–381.
6. Federal Bureau of Investigation, *Crime in the United States 2014* (Washington, D.C.: U.S. Department of Justice, 2015), at **www.fbi.gov/about-us/cjis/ucr/crime-in-the-u.s/2014/crime-in-the-u.s.-2014**, Table 29.
7. Reprinted in *The Police Chief* (January 1990), 18.
8. Jason Busch, "Shots Fired: When a Police Car Becomes an Ambulance," *Law Enforcement Technology* (September 2013), 8–10.
9. Darren DaRonco and Carli Brosseau, "Hundreds in Mental Crisis Call Police," *Arizona Daily Star* (April 14, 2013), C1.
10. Donna L. Leger, "Police Armed with Heroin Antidote," *USA Today* (January 31, 2014), 3A.
11. Jerome H. Skolnick, "Police: The New Professionals," *New Society* (September 5, 1986), 9–11.
12. Quoted in Nancy Ritter, ed., "LAPD Chief Bratton Speaks Out: What's Wrong with Criminal Justice Research—and How to Make It Right," *National Institute of Justice Journal* 257 (2007), 29.
13. Gary Kleck and J. C. Barnes, "Do More Police Lead to More Crime Deterrence?" *Crime & Delinquency* (August 2014), 716–738.
14. Klockars, *op. cit.*, 250.
15. James Q. Wilson, *Varieties of Police Behavior: The Management of Law and Order in Eight Communities* (Cambridge, Mass.: Harvard University Press, 1968).
16. James Q. Wilson and George L. Kelling, "Broken Windows," *Atlantic Monthly* (March 1982), 29.
17. M. K. Nalla and G. R. Newman, "Is White-Collar Crime Policing, Policing?" *Policing and Society* 3 (1994), 304.
18. Mitchell P. Roth, *Crime and Punishment: A History of the Criminal Justice System,* 2d ed. (Belmont, Calif.: Wadsworth Cengage Learning, 2011), 65.
19. *Ibid.*
20. Mark H. Moore and George L. Kelling, "'To Serve and Protect': Learning from Police History," *Public Interest* 70 (1983), 53.
21. Samuel Walker, *The Police in America: An Introduction* (New York: McGraw-Hill, 1983), 7.
22. Moore and Kelling, *op. cit.*, 54.
23. Mark H. Haller, "Chicago Cops, 1890–1925," in *Thinking about Police,* eds. Carl Klockars and Stephen Mastrofski (New York: McGraw-Hill, 1990), 90.
24. Roger G. Dunham and Geoffrey P. Alpert, *Critical Issues in Policing: Contemporary Issues* (Prospect Heights, Ill.: Waveland Press, 1989).
25. Ken Peak and Emmanuel P. Barthe, "Community Policing and CompStat: Merged, or Mutually Exclusive?" *The Police Chief* (December 2009), 73.
26. *Ibid.*, 74.
27. Quoted in *ibid.*
28. Peter K. Manning, "The Police: Mandate, Strategies, and Appearances," in *Crime and Justice in American Society,* ed. Jack D. Douglas (Indianapolis, Ind.: Bobbs-Merrill, 1971), 149–163.
29. National Advisory Commission on Civil Disorder, *Report* (Washington, D.C.: U.S. Government Printing Office, 1968), 157–160.
30. Jayne Seagrave, "Defining Community Policing," *American Journal of Police* 1 (1996), 1–22.
31. Jason Vaughn Lee, "Policing after 9/11: Community Policing in an Age of Homeland Security," *Police Quarterly* (November 2010), 351–353.
32. Craig D. Uchida and Marc L. Swatt, "Operation LASER and the Effectiveness of Hotspot Patrol: A Panel Analysis," *Police Quarterly* (September 2013), 287–304.
33. Gary LaFree, *Policing Terrorism* (Washington, D.C.: The Police Foundation, 2012), 1.
34. Lorenzo Vidino and Seamus Hughes, *ISIS in America: From Retweets to Raqqa* (Washington, D.C.: The George Washington University's Program on Extremism, December 2015), ix.
35. J. David Goodman, "With Permanent Squad, New York Police Step Up Fight on Terrorism," *New York Times* (November 21, 2015), A1.
36. Department of Homeland Security, "DHS Announces Grant Allocations for Fiscal Year (FY) 2015 Preparedness Grants," (July 28, 2015), at **www.dhs.gov/news/2015/07/28/dhs-announces-grant-allocations-fiscal-year-fy-2015-preparedness-grants.**
37. Adrian Fontecilla, "The Ascendance of Social Media as Evidence," *Criminal Justice* (Spring 2013), 55.
38. *How Are Innovations in Technology Transforming Policing?* (Washington, D.C.: Police Executive Research Forum, January 2012), 2.
39. Brad Heath, "FBI Ran Website Sharing Thousands of Child Porn Images," *USA Today* (January 22–24, 2016), 1A.
40. Quoted in Joel Rubin, "Stopping Crime before It Starts," *Los Angeles Times* (August 21, 2010), A17.
41. James H. Chenoweth, "Situational Tests: A New Attempt at Assessing Police Candidates," *Journal of Criminal Law, Criminology and Police Science* 52 (1961), 232.
42. Yossef S. Ben-Porath et al., "Assessing the Psychological Suitability of Candidates for Law Enforcement Positions," *The Police Chief* (August 2011), 64–70.
43. Quoted in *How Are Innovations in Technology Transforming Policing?, op. cit.*, 10.

44. Bureau of Justice Statistics, *Local Police Departments: Personnel, Policies, and Practice, 2013* (Washington, D.C.: U.S. Department of Justice, May 2015), 7.

45. *Ibid.*, Table 7, page 5.

46. D. P. Hinkle, "College Degree: An Impractical Prerequisite for Police Work," *Law and Order* (July 1991), 105.

47. Bureau of Justice Statistics, *State and Local Law Enforcement Training Academies, 2006* (Washington, D.C.: U.S. Department of Justice, February 2009), 7.

48. National Advisory Commission on Civil Disorder, *Report* (Washington, D.C.: U.S. Government Printing Office, 1968), Chapter 11.

49. *Griggs v. Duke Power Co.*, 401 U.S. 424 (1971); and *Albermarle Paper Co. v. Moody*, 422 U.S. 405 (1975).

50. Gene L. Scaramella, Steven M. Cox, and William P. McCamey, *Introduction to Policing* (Thousand Oaks, Calif.: Sage Publications, 2011), 30–31.

51. *Local Police Departments, 2013: Personnel, Policies, and Practices, op. cit.* Table 4, page 4.

52. *Ibid.*, 5.

53. Cassie L. Fields, "Recruiting a Diverse Law Enforcement Workforce," *The Police Chief* (June 2015), 26–29.

54. Scaramella, Cox, and McCamey, *op. cit.*, 318.

55. Kenneth J. Novak, Robert A. Brown, and James Frank, *Women on Patrol: An Analysis of Differences in Officer Arrest Behavior* (Bingley, United Kingdom: Emerald Group Publishing Ltd., 2006), 21–27.

56. Quoted in Robin N. Haarr and Merry Morash, "The Effect of Rank on Police Women Coping with Discrimination and Harassment," *Police Quarterly* (December 2013), 403.

57. Quoted in Talk of the Nation, "What Changes as Women Rise through Law Enforcement's Ranks?" *NPR* (April 2, 2013), at **www.npr.org/2013/04/02/176037643/what-changes-as-women-rise-through-law-enforcements-ranks.**

58. Katherine Stuart van Wormer and Clemens Bartollas, *Women and the Criminal Justice System*, 3d ed. (Upper Saddle River, N.J.: Pearson Education, 2011), 318–319.

59. *Local Police Departments, 2013: Personnel, Policies, and Practices, op. cit.*, Figure 5, page 5.

60. Anne Li Kringen, "Examining the Relationship between Civil Service Commissions and Municipal Police Diversity," *Criminal Justice Policy Review* (October 25, 2016), at **cjp.sagepub.com/content/early/2015/10/23/0887403415612252.full.pdf+html.**

61. Ben Kesling and Cameron McWhirter, "Percentage of African Americans in U.S. Police Departments Remains Flat Since 2007," *Wall Street Journal* (May 15, 2015), at **www.wsj.com/articles/percentage-of-african-americans-in-u-s-police-departments-remains-flat-since-2007-1431628990.**

62. Peter C. Moskos, "Two Shades of Blue: Black and White in the Blue Brotherhood," *Law Enforcement Executive Forum* (2008), 57.

63. Scaramella, Cox, and McCamey, *op. cit.*, 324.

64. Dempsey and Forst, *op. cit.*, 183.

65. *Wygant v. Jackson Board of Education*, 476 U.S. 314 (1986).

66. Matt Apuzzo and Sarah Cohen, "Police Chiefs, Looking to Diversify Forces, Face Structural Hurdles," *New York Times* (November 8, 2015), A14.

67. Bureau of Justice Statistics, *Census of State and Local Law Enforcement Agencies, 2008* (Washington, D.C.: U.S. Department of Justice, July 2011), 1; and Bureau of Justice Statistics, *Federal Law Enforcement Officers, 2008* (Washington, D.C.: U.S. Department of Justice, June 2012), 1.

68. *Local Police Departments, 2013: Personnel, Policies, and Practices, op. cit.*, Table 3, page 3.

69. *Ibid.*, Table 2, page 3.

70. *Census of State and Local Law Enforcement Agencies, 2008, op. cit.*, Table 4, page 5.

71. Bureau of Justice Statistics, *Sheriffs' Offices, 2003* (Washington, D.C.: U.S. Department of Justice, May 2006), 15–18.

72. Bureau of Justice Statistics, *Sheriffs' Departments, 1997* (Washington, D.C.: U.S. Department of Justice, February 2000), 14.

73. U.S. Department of Homeland Security, "Budget-in-Brief: Fiscal Year 2016," at **www.dhs.gov/sites/default/files/publications/FY_2016_DHS_Budget_in_Brief.pdf.**

74. U.S. Customs and Border Protection, *Fiscal Year 2015: CBP Border Security Report* (Washington, D.C.: U.S. Department of Homeland Security, December 22, 2015), 1.

75. U.S. Immigration and Customs Enforcement, "FY 2014 ICE Immigration Removals," at **www.ice.gov/removal-statistics.**

76. Eric Schmitt, "ISIS Followers in U.S. Are Diverse and Young," *New York Times* (December 2, 2015), A3.

77. John Hudson, "FBI Drops Law Enforcement as 'Primary' Mission," *Foreign Policy* (January 5, 2014), at **foreignpolicy.com/2014/01/05/fbi-drops-law-enforcement-as-primary-mission.**

78. Uniform Controlled Substances Act (1994), Section 201(h).

79. United States Marshals Service, "Fact Sheet," at **https://www.usmarshals.gov/duties/factsheets/overview.pdf.**

80. *2015 Annual Report* (Washington, D.C.: Internal Revenue Service Criminal Investigation, 2015), 2.

81. *The United States Security Industry* (Alexandria, Va.: ASIS International, 2013), 1.

82. John B. Owens, "Westec Story: Gated Communities and the Fourth Amendment," *American Criminal Law Review* (Spring 1997), 1138.

83. Bureau of Justice Statistics, *Local Police Departments, 2007* (Washington, D.C.: U.S. Department of Justice, December 2010), Table 8, page 13.

84. Seattle Police Department, Seattle Police Manual, "5.120—Secondary Employment" (updated March 19, 2014), at **www.seattle.gov/police/publications/manual/05_120_Secondary_Employment.html.**

85. Michael J. Palmiotto, *Policing: Concepts, Strategies and Current Issues in American Police Forces*, 3d ed. (San Bernadino, Calif.: CreateSpace Independent, 2014), 76–77.

86. National Retail Federation, "National Retail Security Survey 2015," at **nrf.com/resources/retail-library/national-retail-security-survey-2015.**

87. William C. Cunningham, John J. Strauchs, and Clifford W. Van Meter, *The Hallcrest Report II: Private Security Trends, 1970 to 2000* (Boston: Butterworth-Heinemann, 1990), 236.

Tom Pennington/Getty Images

5

Problems and Solutions in Modern Policing

Chapter Outline		Corresponding Learning Objectives
Police Organization and Field Operations	1	List the three primary purposes of police patrol.
	2	Describe how forensic experts use DNA fingerprinting to solve crimes.
Police Strategies: What Works	3	Explain why differential response strategies enable police departments to respond more efficiently to 911 calls.
	4	Explain community policing and its contribution to the concept of problem-oriented policing.
"Us versus Them": Issues in Modern Policing	5	Describe the process of socialization in police subculture.
	6	Clarify the concepts of nondeadly force, deadly force, and reasonable force in the context of police use of force.
Police Misconduct and Ethics	7	Explain why police officers are allowed discretionary powers.
	8	Determine when police officers are justified in using deadly force.
	9	Explain what an ethical dilemma is, and name four categories of ethical dilemmas that a police officer typically may face.

To target your study and review, look for these numbered Learning Objective icons throughout the chapter.

first Impressions

"it's very shocking and it looks very bad," said Bexar County (Texas) Judge Nelson Wolff. The judge was referring to a cell phone video of two sheriff's deputies fatally shooting an apparently unarmed man named Gilbert Flores. On August 31, 2015, local television station KSAT showed the images of Flores's death, contributing to a national debate on police use of force fueled by similar incidents in places such as Cincinnati and North Charleston, South Carolina. "This is a very unique situation where we actually have the shooting on video," said Nicholas LaHood, the district attorney who would have to decide whether deputies Greg Vasquez and Robert Sanchez would be criminally charged for killing Flores. "That gives us a whole different perspective that we've never had before."

As it turned out, the perspective of the cell phone video was not entirely reliable. According to an emotional 911 call made by Flores himself earlier that night, he was distraught because he had harmed his wife and their young child and wanted to commit "suicide by cop." Furthermore, on the audio of a second video of the incident taken by neighbors, a man whispers, "[Flores has] a knife in his hand." In the first video, a utility pole obscures Flores's raised left arm, blocking the view of any weapon he might have been using to threaten the law enforcement agents. Because of this additional information, district attorney LaHood decided not to charge the deputies with any wrongdoing related to Flores's death.

In the midst of this controversy, local authorities approved nearly $1 million to equip Bexar County deputies with body-worn cameras. Today, thousands of police departments—including those in large cities such as Houston, New York, and Los Angeles—require their officers to wear these video cameras on their uniforms and record contact with civilians. This trend is, at least in part, a response to the proliferation of cell phone videos of police force, such as the one that showed Flores's death in Bexar County. Though such videos frequently expose police misconduct, they rarely, in the words of one expert, show "the whole story."

AP Photo/Eric Gay

▲ Bexar County Sheriff Susan Pamerleau holds a press conference to address the controversy surrounding the fatal shooting of Gilbert Flores by two sheriff's deputies.

1. How would body-worn cameras or cameras on the dashboards of police cars protect law enforcement officers against charges of excessive use of force and other forms of police misbehavior?
2. In the first year after Rialto, California, police officers began using body-worn cameras, citizen complaints against officers decreased by 88 percent. How might the cameras help explain this statistic?
3. What are some of the privacy issues raised by body-worn cameras? Consider, for example, a police video taken during a domestic violence arrest.

Police Organization and Field Operations

bureaucracy A hierarchically structured administrative organization that carries out specific functions.

delegation of authority The principles of command on which most police departments are based, in which personnel take orders from and are responsible to those in positions of power directly above them.

The Bexar County Sheriff's Office placed deputies Greg Vasquez and Robert Sanchez, the officers involved in the fatal shooting of Gilbert Flores, on *administrative leave* pending an investigation into the incident. In other words, the deputies were temporarily relieved of their duties, with pay. This step does not imply that officials thought Vasquez and Sanchez had behaved improperly. Most law enforcement agencies react similarly when a firearm is fired in the line of duty, both to allow for a full investigation of the event and to give the officer a chance to recover from what can be a traumatic experience.

Administrative leave is a *bureaucratic* response to an officer-involved shooting. In a **bureaucracy**, formal rules govern an individual's actions and relationships with co-employees. The ultimate goal of any bureaucracy is to reach its maximum efficiency—in the case of a police department, to provide the best service for the community within the confines of its limited resources such as staff and budget. Although some police departments are experimenting with alternative structures based on a partnership between management and the officers in the field, most continue to rely on the hierarchical structure described below.

The Structure of the Police Department

Each police department is organized according to its environment: the size of its jurisdiction, the type of crimes it must deal with, and the demographics of the population it must police. The Metropolitan Police Department of Washington, D.C., operates an Asian Liaison Unit that works within that city's Asian community, while the Evansville, Indiana, Police Department has set up a "No Meth" task force. Geographic location also influences police organization. The San Diego Police Department has a Harbor Patrol Unit, which would be unproductive in Grand Forks, North Dakota—as would be the Grand Forks Police Department's snowmobile patrol in Southern California.

Chain of Command Whatever the size or location of a police department, it needs a clear rank structure and strict accountability to function properly. One of the goals of the police reformers, especially beginning in the 1950s, was to lessen the corrupting influence of politicians. The result was a move toward a militaristic organization of police.[1] As you can see in Figure 5.1, a typical police department is based on a "top-down" chain of command that leads from the police chief down to detectives and patrol officers. In this formalized structure, all persons are aware of their place in the chain and of their duties and responsibilities within the organization.

Delegation of authority is a critical component of the chain of command, especially in larger departments. The chief of police delegates authority to division chiefs, who delegate authority to commanders, and on down through the organization. This structure creates a situation in which nearly every member of a police department is directly accountable to a superior. As was the original goal of police reformers, these links encourage discipline and control, and lessen the possibility that any individual police employee will have the unsupervised freedom to abuse her or his position.[2] Furthermore, experts suggest that no single supervisor should be responsible for too many employees. The ideal number of subordinates for a police sergeant, for example, is eight to ten patrol officers. This number is often referred to as the *span of control*. If the span of control rises above fifteen, then it is assumed that the superior officer will not be able to effectively manage his or her team.[3]

FIGURE 5.1 A Typical Police Department Chain of Command

Most American police departments follow this model of the chain of command, though smaller departments with fewer employees often eliminate several of these categories.

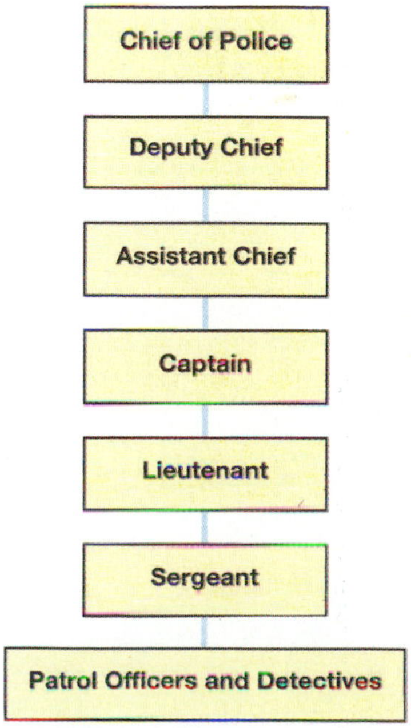

Chief of Police
Deputy Chief
Assistant Chief
Captain
Lieutenant
Sergeant
Patrol Officers and Detectives

▲ A lieutenant (in the white shirt) gives instructions to two sergeants. On his left, a patrol officer appears to be awaiting instructions. How do the delegation of authority and the chain of command contribute to police efficiency? Elyse Rieder/ScienceSource

Organizing by Area and Time In most metropolitan areas, police responsibilities are divided according to zones known as *beats* and *precincts.* A beat is the smallest stretch that a police officer or a group of police officers regularly patrol. A precinct—also known as a *district* or a *station*—is a collection of beats. A precinct commander, or captain, is held responsible by his or her superiors at police headquarters for the performance of the officers in that particular precinct.[4]

Police administrators must also organize their personnel by time. Most departments separate each twenty-four-hour day into three eight-hour *shifts,* also called *tours* or *platoons.* The night shift generally lasts from midnight to 8 A.M., the day shift from 8 A.M. to 4 P.M., and the evening shift from 4 P.M. to midnight. Officers either vary their hours by, say, working days one month and nights the next, or they have fixed tours in which they consistently take day, night, or evening shifts.[5] A number of police departments have implemented compressed workweeks, in which officers work longer shifts (ten or twelve hours) and fewer days. Such schedules are believed to improve the officers' quality of life by providing more substantial blocks of time off the job to recover from the stresses of police work.[6]

Law Enforcement in the Field To a large extent, the main goal of any police department is the most efficient organization of its *field services.* Also known as "operations" or "line services," field services include patrol activities, investigations, and special operations. According to Henry M. Wrobleski and Karen M. Hess, most police departments are "generalists." That is, police officers are assigned to general areas and perform all field service functions within the boundaries of their beats. Larger departments may be more specialized, with personnel assigned to specific types of crime, such as illegal drugs or white-collar crime, rather than geographic locations. Smaller departments, which make up the bulk of local law enforcement agencies, rely almost exclusively on general patrol.[7]

Police on Patrol: The Backbone of the Department

Every police department has a patrol unit, and patrol is usually the largest division in the department. More than two-thirds of the sworn officers, or those officers authorized to make arrests and use force, in local police departments in the United States have patrol duties.[8]

"Life on the street" is not easy. Patrol officers must be able to handle any number of difficult situations, and experience is often the best and, despite training programs, the only teacher. As one patrol officer commented:

> You never stop learning. You never get your street degree. The person who says . . . they've learned it all is the person that's going to wind up dead or in a very compromising position. They've closed their minds.[9]

It may take a patrol officer years to learn when a gang is "false flagging" (trying to trick rival gang members into the open) or what to look for in a suspect's eyes to sense if he or she is concealing a weapon. This learning process is the backdrop to a number of different general functions that a patrol officer must perform on a daily basis.

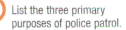

Learning Objective

1 List the three primary purposes of police patrol.

The Purpose of Patrol In general, patrol officers do not spend most of their shifts chasing, catching, and handcuffing suspected criminals. The vast majority of patrol shifts are completed without a single arrest.[10] Officers spend a great deal of time meeting with other officers, completing paperwork, and patrolling with the goal of preventing crime in general rather than focusing on any specific crime or criminal activity.

As police accountability expert Samuel Walker has noted, the basic purposes of the police patrol have changed very little since 1829, when Sir Robert Peel founded the modern police department. These purposes include:

1. The deterrence of crime by maintaining a visible police presence.
2. The maintenance of public order and a sense of security in the community.
3. The twenty-four-hour provision of services that are not crime related.[11]

The first two goals—deterring crime and keeping order—are generally accepted as legitimate police functions. The third, however, has been more controversial.

As noted in Chapter 4, the community era of policing saw a resurgence of the patrol officer as a provider of community services, many of which have little to do with crime. The extent to which noncrime incidents dominate patrol officers' time is evident in the Police Services Study, a survey of 26,000 calls to police in sixty different neighborhoods. The study found that only one out of every five calls involved the report of criminal activity.[12] (See Figure 5.2 for the results of another survey of crime calls.)

Figure 5.2 Calls for Service

Over a period of fifteen months, researchers at the University of New Mexico gathered information on approximately 700,000 calls for service received by the Albuquerque Police Department (APD). As the data below show, the APD deals with far more calls for service involving nonviolent incidents than violent incidents. Indeed, traffic-related calls occurred almost three times as often as the next most common type of call.

Call Type	Percent of Calls
Traffic	37
Suspicious persons	13
Public disorder (examples: drunk, disorderly, begging, prostitution)	13
Property crime	9
Violent crime	5
House alarm	5
Auto theft	2
Hang up call	1
Unknown/other	15

Source: Dan Cathey and Paul Guerin, *Analyzing Calls for Service to the Albuquerque Police Department* (Albuquerque, N.M.: Institute for Social Research, University of New Mexico, June 2009), Table 4, page 6.

Law Enforcement and Mental Illness Of particular concern is the frequency with which police officers on patrol find themselves acting as psychiatric social workers. According to various studies, between 7 percent and 10 percent of all police-public contacts involve people with mental illness.[13] If law enforcement officers are not properly trained or otherwise prepared for these encounters, the results can be disastrous. By one estimate, at least half of the people justifiably killed by the police each year are mentally ill.[14]

A number of law enforcement agencies have set up *crisis intervention teams,* designed to improve this situation. Although the programs vary, many of them include:

1. Specialized training for law enforcement officers in managing encounters with mentally ill members of the community,
2. Access to mental health professionals who are "on call" to respond to police requests for assistance, and
3. Drop-off locations, such as hospitals or mobile crisis vehicles, that provide mental health services beyond the expertise of law enforcement agencies.[15]

On the positive side, it appears that the crisis intervention model is favorably viewed by police officers and can result in reduced arrest rates of the mentally ill.[16] At the same time, such programs may be beyond the limited financial and personnel resources of small law enforcement agencies in rural areas.

Patrol Activities To recap, the purposes of police patrols are to prevent and deter crime and also to provide social services. How can the police best accomplish these goals? Of course, each department has its own methods and strategies, but William Gay, Theodore Schell, and Stephen Schack are able to divide routine patrol activity into four general categories:[17]

1. *Preventive patrol.* By maintaining a presence in a community, either in a car or on foot, patrol officers attempt to prevent crime from occurring. This strategy, which O. W. Wilson called "omnipresence," was a cornerstone of early policing philosophy and still takes up roughly 40 percent of patrol time.
2. *Calls for service.* Patrol officers spend nearly a quarter of their time responding to 911 calls for emergency service or other citizen problems and complaints.
3. *Administrative duties.* Paperwork takes up nearly 20 percent of patrol time.
4. *Officer-initiated activities.* Incidents in which the patrol officer initiates contact with citizens, such as stopping motorists and pedestrians and questioning them, account for 15 percent of patrol time.

The category estimates made by Gay, Schell, and Schack are not universally accepted. Professor of criminal justice Gary W. Cordner argues that administrative duties account for the largest percentage of patrol officers' time. According to Cordner, when officers are not consumed with paperwork and meetings, they are either answering calls for service (which takes up 67 percent of the officers' time on the street) or initiating activities themselves (the remaining 33 percent).[18]

Police Investigations

Investigation is the second main function of police, along with patrol. Whereas patrol is primarily preventive, investigation is reactive. After a crime has been committed and the patrol officer has gathered the preliminary information from the crime scene, the responsibility of finding "who dunnit" is delegated to the investigator, generally known as the **detective**. The most common way for someone to become a detective is to be promoted from patrol officer. Detectives have not been the focus of nearly as much reform attention as their patrol counterparts, mainly because the scope of the detective's job is limited to law enforcement, with less emphasis given to social services or order maintenance.

detective The primary police investigator of crimes.

The detective's job is not quite as glamorous as it is sometimes portrayed by the media. Detectives spend much of their time investigating common crimes such as burglaries and are more likely to be tracking down stolen property than a murderer. They must also prepare cases for trial, which involves a great deal of time-consuming paperwork. Furthermore, a landmark RAND Corporation study estimated that more than 97 percent of cases that are "solved" can be attributed to a patrol officer making an arrest at the scene, witnesses or victims identifying the perpetrator, or detectives undertaking routine investigative procedures that could easily be performed by clerical personnel.[19]

confidential informant (CI) A human source for police who provides information concerning illegal activity in which he or she is involved.

Aggressive Investigation Strategies

Detective bureaus also have the option of implementing aggressive strategies. For example, if detectives suspect that a person was involved in the robbery of a Mercedes-Benz parts warehouse, one of them might pose as a "fence"—or purchaser of stolen goods. In what is known as a "sting" operation, the suspect is deceived into thinking that the detective (fence) wants to buy stolen car parts. After the transaction takes place, the suspect can be arrested.

Undercover Operations Perhaps the most dangerous and controversial operation a law enforcement agent can undertake is to go *undercover,* or to assume a false identity in order to obtain information concerning illegal activities. Though each department has its own guidelines on when undercover operations are necessary, all that is generally required is the suspicion that illegal activity is taking place. Today, undercover officers are commonly used to infiltrate large-scale narcotics operations or those run by organized crime.

In some situations, a detective bureau may not want to take the risk of exposing an officer to undercover work or may believe that an outsider cannot infiltrate an organized crime network. When the police need access and information, they have the option of turning to a **confidential informant (CI)**. A CI is a person who is involved in criminal activity and gives information about that activity and those who engage in it to the police. As many as 80 percent of all illegal drug cases in the United States involve confidential informants. "They can get us into places we can't go," says one police administrator. "Without them, narcotics cases would practically cease to function."[20]

▼ American citizens Noelle Velentzas, left, and Asia Siddiqui conferred with a federal undercover agent for nearly two years before being arrested in 2015 for conspiring to use an explosive device as part of a planned terrorist attack in New York City. **Explain why such law enforcement tactics—known as preventive policing—are effective in countering domestic terrorism.** AP Photo/Jane Rosenberg

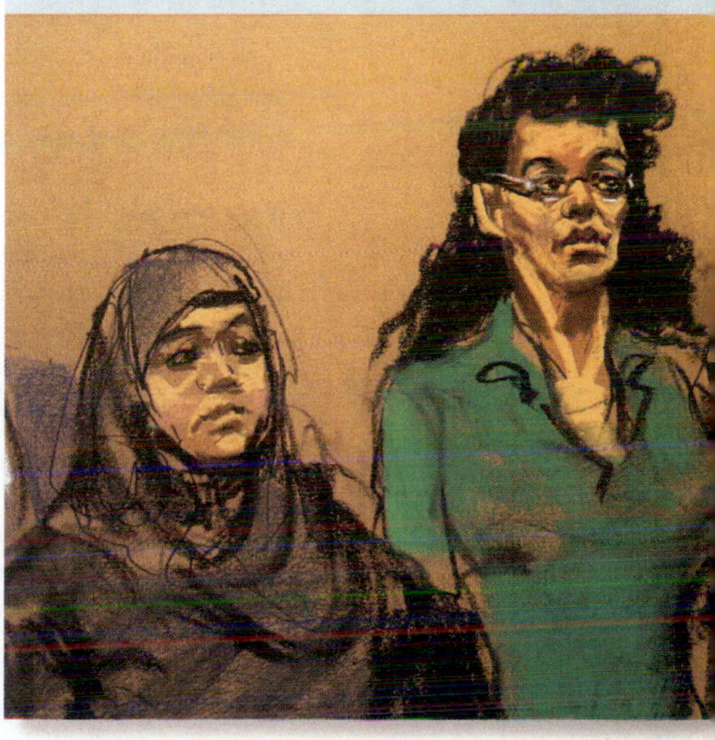

Preventive Policing and Domestic Terrorism Aggressive investigative strategies also play a crucial role in the federal government's efforts to combat domestic terrorism. Because would-be terrorists often need help to procure the weaponry necessary for their schemes, they are natural targets for well-placed informants and undercover agents. According to the Center on Law and Security at New York University, about two-thirds of the federal government's major terrorism prosecutions in the decade following September 11, 2001, relied on evidence provided by informants.[21]

The recent arrest of Christopher Cornell provides an example of *preventive policing*, a popular counterterrorism strategy employed by the federal government. Federal agents arrested Cornell in the parking lot of a Cincinnati gun shop where he had just purchased two semiautomatic rifles and six hundred rounds of ammunition. About a month earlier, Cornell had met with an FBI informant and discussed plans to attack "enemies" working in the U.S. Capitol Building.[22]

With preventive policing, then, the goal is not to solve the crime after it has happened. Rather, the goal is to prevent the crime from happening in the first place. Inevitably, such tactics raise the issue of entrapment. As you learned in Chapter 3, entrapment is a possible defense for criminal behavior when a government agent plants the idea of committing a crime in a defendant's mind. In the Cornell case, the suspect's father claimed that his son could not have afforded to purchase the weaponry he was caught with, and that the funds to do so must have been provided by the FBI.[23] Although the entrapment defense has been raised often in domestic terrorism cases involving informants and undercover agents, it has yet to succeed. The government has been uniformly successful in proving that these defendants were predisposed to commit the crime regardless of any outside influence.

Clearance Rates and Cold Cases

The ultimate goal of all law enforcement activity is to *clear* a crime, or secure the arrest and prosecution of the offender. Even a cursory glance at **clearance rates**, which show the percentage of reported crimes that have been cleared, reveals that investigations succeed only part of the time. In 2014, just 65 percent of homicides and 47 percent of total violent crimes were solved, while police cleared only 20 percent of property crimes.[24] For the most part, the different clearance rates for different crimes reflect the resources that a law enforcement agency expends on each type of crime. The police generally investigate a murder or a rape more vigorously than the theft of an automobile or a computer.

As a result of low clearance rates, police departments are saddled with an increasing number of **cold cases**, or criminal investigations that are not cleared after a certain amount of time. (The length of time before a case becomes "cold" varies from department to department. In general, a cold case must be "somewhat old" but not "so old that there can be no hope of ever solving it."[25]) Even using the various technologies we will explore in the next section, cold case investigations rarely succeed. A RAND study found that only about one in twenty cold cases eventually leads to an arrest, and only about one in a hundred results in a conviction.[26]

Forensic Investigations and DNA

Although the crime scene typically offers a wealth of evidence, some of it is incomprehensible to a patrol officer or detective without assistance. For that aid, law enforcement officers rely on experts in **forensics**, or the practice of using science and technology to investigate crimes. Forensic experts apply their knowledge to items found at the crime scene to determine crucial facts such as:

- The cause of death or injury.
- The time of death or injury.
- The type of weapon or weapons used.
- The identity of the crime victim, if that information is unavailable.
- The identity of the offender (in the best-case scenario).[27]

To assist forensic experts, many police departments operate or are affiliated with approximately 400 publicly funded crime laboratories in the United States. As we noted

clearance rate A comparison of the number of crimes cleared by arrest and prosecution with the number of crimes reported during any given time period.

cold case A criminal investigation that has not been solved after a certain amount of time.

forensics The application of science to establish facts and evidence during the investigation of crimes.

Careers in CJ

Photo Courtesy of Martha Blake

Martha Blake
Forensic Scientist

In high school, I was interested in science but didn't want to end up being a technician doing the same thing every day. I was looking in college catalogues and came across criminalistics at UC Berkeley. The coursework included such courses as microscopy, instrumental analysis, trace evidence, criminal law, and statistics, and it sounded fascinating. I decided in my senior year of high school to become a forensic scientist.

As quality assurance manager at the San Francisco Police Department's crime lab, I am often called to criminal court to testify about evidence that has passed through our lab. I am always nervous when I testify, and I think it is healthy to be a little nervous. As an expert witness, the most challenging part of my testimony is describing my findings to a jury of primarily nonscientists in a way that will make my testimony understandable and credible. I've found that juries tend to understand evidence that is part of their lives. Everyone can identify the writing of a family member or spouse, so describing how handwriting is identified is not too hard. Explaining how DNA analysis works is more difficult.

SOCIAL MEDIA CAREER TIP When people search for you online, they won't click past the first page. Check to see where material about you appears on a regular basis.

FASTFACTS

Forensic scientist

Job description:

- Examine, test, and analyze tissue samples, chemical substances, physical materials, and ballistics evidence collected at a crime scene.

What kind of training is required?

- Bachelor's degree in science, particularly chemistry, biology, biochemistry, or physics.
- Certification programs (usually two years' additional study) can help prospective applicants specialize as forensic consultants, fingerprint technicians, forensic investigators, laboratory technicians, and fingerprint examiners.

Annual salary range?

- $42,000–$75,000

in the previous chapter, the FBI also offers the services of its crime lab to agencies with limited resources. The FBI's aid in this area is crucial, given that the nation's crime labs are burdened with a crippling backlog of hundreds of thousands of requests for forensic services.

Crime Scene Forensics The first law enforcement agent to reach a crime scene has the important task of protecting any **trace evidence** from contamination. Trace evidence is generally very small—often invisible to the naked human eye—and often requires technological aid for detection. Hairs, fibers, blood, fingerprints, broken glass, and footprints are all examples of trace evidence. A study released by the National Institute of Justice confirmed that when police are able to link such evidence to a suspect, the likelihood of a conviction rises dramatically.[28] The forensic science of **toxicology** is similarly crucial, as it involves determining the presence of drugs or poison in the bodily fluids of persons connected with a crime, such as victims, suspects, or potential witnesses.

Police will also search a crime scene for bullets and spent cartridge casings. These items can provide clues as to how far the shooter was from the target. They can also be compared with information stored in national firearms databases to determine, under some circumstances, the gun used and its most recent owner. The study of firearms and its application to solving crimes goes under the general term **ballistics**. A new generation of ballistics technology allows technicians to create a 3-D image of a bullet and match that image to the gun from which the original was fired.

trace evidence Evidence such as a fingerprint, blood, or hair found in small amounts at a crime scene.

toxicology The branch of forensic science concerned with the effects and detection of foreign chemicals in the human body.

ballistics The study of firearms, including the firing of a weapon and the flight of a bullet.

DNA fingerprinting The identification of a person based on a sample of her or his DNA, the genetic material found in the cells of all living things.

cold hit The establishment of a connection between a suspect and a crime, often through the use of DNA evidence, in the absence of an ongoing criminal investigation.

For more than a century, the most important piece of trace evidence has been the human fingerprint. Because no two fingerprints are alike, they are considered reliable sources of identification. Forensic scientists compare a fingerprint lifted from a crime scene with that of a suspect and declare a match if there are between eight and sixteen "points of similarity." This method of identification, though highly reliable, is not infallible.[29] It is often difficult to lift a suitable print from a crime scene, and researchers have uncovered numerous cases in which innocent persons were convicted based on evidence obtained through faulty fingerprinting procedures.[30]

The DNA Revolution The technique of **DNA fingerprinting**, or using a suspect's DNA to match the suspect to a crime, emerged in the mid-1990s and has now all but replaced fingerprint evidence in many types of criminal investigations. The shift has been a boon to crime fighters: one law enforcement agent likened DNA fingerprinting to "the finger of God pointing down" at a guilty suspect.[31]

Learning Objective 2

Describe how forensic experts use DNA fingerprinting to solve crimes.

DNA, which is the same in each cell of a person's body, provides a "genetic blueprint" or "code" for every living organism. DNA fingerprinting is useful in criminal investigations because no two people, save for identical twins, have the same genetic code. Therefore, lab technicians can compare the DNA sample of a suspect to the evidence found at the crime scene. If the match is negative, it is certain that the two samples did not come from the same source. If the match is positive, the lab will determine the odds that the DNA sample could have come from someone other than the suspect. Those odds are so high—sometimes reaching 30 billion to one—that a match is practically conclusive.[32]

The process begins when forensic technicians gather blood, semen, skin, saliva, or hair from the scene of a crime. Blood cells and sperm are rich in DNA, making them particularly useful in murder and rape cases, but DNA has also been extracted from sweat on dirty laundry, skin cells on eyeglasses, and saliva on used envelope seals. Once a suspect is identified, her or his DNA can be used to determine whether she or he can be placed at the crime scene. In 2015, for instance, investigators connected Willie Guillory to the killings of a married couple in their Arlington, Texas, apartment by obtaining his DNA from a marijuana cigarette left at the site of the double murder.

Getting Linked in™

Although openings for **forensic scientists** at law enforcement agencies are scarce, LinkedIn consistently features postings for such positions at private laboratories. Such laboratories assist clients—such as doctors' offices, drug-testing facilities, and hospitals—that have a need for forensic laboratory services. A listing of available positions can be accessed by entering the search term "forensic scientist."

DNA in Action The ability to "dust" for genetic information on such a wide variety of evidence, as well as that evidence's longevity and accuracy, greatly increases the chances that a crime will be solved. Indeed, police no longer need a witness or even a suspect in custody to solve crimes. What they do need is a piece of evidence and a database.

In 1990, for example, Gloria Dickinson was found strangled to death in a downtown North Augusta, South Carolina, hotel room. The case remained open with no leads for twenty-four years, until Vincent Hampton was convicted of aggravated assault in Georgia and authorities took a sample of his DNA. This sample matched the DNA on evidence taken from the hotel room in which Dickinson was killed, and in December 2015 Hampton was charged with her murder.

Databases and Cold Hits The identification of Vincent Hampton is an example of what police call a **cold hit**, which occurs when law enforcement finds a suspect "out of nowhere" by comparing DNA evidence from a crime scene against the contents of a database. The largest and most important database is the National Combined DNA

Index System (CODIS). Operated by the FBI since 1998, CODIS gives local and state law enforcement agencies access to the DNA profiles of over 15 million people who have been connected to criminal activity. As of March 2016, the database had produced about 325,000 cold hits nationwide.[33]

New Developments DNA fingerprinting has been widely available for a relatively short time, and the scope of its investigative uses continues to expand. For example, a new rapid-testing device reduces the time needed to process DNA samples from at least two weeks to ninety minutes. This technology, which several states started using in late 2014, will aid law enforcement immensely by quickly matching suspects to crimes.[34] Other recent developments involving DNA fingerprinting technology include:

1. *Touch DNA*, which allows investigators to test for the presence of DNA by scraping items such as a piece of food or an article of clothing for microscopic cells left behind by the suspect.
2. *Familial searches*, based on the premise that parents, siblings, and other relatives have DNA similar to that of suspects whose identity might be unknown or who might be unavailable for testing.
3. The possible use of DNA as a genetic witness by providing law enforcement with a physical description of a suspect, including her or his age or eye, skin, and hair color. This developing branch of DNA fingerprinting, known as *phenotyping*, has the potential to eventually provide forensic scientists with enough genetic information to create a facial image of a criminal suspect.[35]

Furthermore, because of its cost, DNA fingerprinting has traditionally been used mostly in conjunction with "important" violent crime investigations. The National Institute of Justice has found, however, that not only was using DNA testing in property crimes cost effective, but it also dramatically increased the police's ability to identify burglary and theft suspects.[36] Because many property offenders commit violent crimes as well, it seems logical that apprehending "unimportant" burglars and thieves would prevent a significant amount of serious criminal activity.[37] (Another use of DNA to prevent crime is the subject of this chapter's feature *CJ Controversy—DNA Fingerprinting of Arrestees.*)

EthicsChallenge

In speaking with a domestic terrorism suspect, an undercover FBI agent says, "Allah has more work for you to do," adding, "Revelation is going to come in your dreams that you have to do this thing." The "thing" is to shoot down American military airplanes with handheld missiles. Is this ethical behavior on the part of the FBI agent? What should happen to the suspect if he goes on to purchase a handheld missile launcher on the black market?

Police Strategies: What Works

Phong Trang, a detective with the Oakland (California) Police Department, was searching for clues at the crime scene of the death of Karlton "Bam" McFay when a woman walked up to the yellow police tape. The killer was a man called "Quacky," the woman whispered. None of Trang's contacts knew of a Quacky, but one did recall a "Cracky."

CJ Controversy

M Dogan/Shutterstock.com

DNA Fingerprinting of Arrestees

All fifty states collect DNA from offenders convicted of felonies. Thirty states and the federal government go one step further by collecting DNA from those who have only been arrested for committing a violent crime. Maryland is one of those states, and police in Wicomico County took a DNA sample of Alonzo King after arresting him on assault charges. When the sample connected King to an unsolved rape case from six years earlier, King challenged Maryland's law before the U.S. Supreme Court. His lawyers argued that it is unfair to "punish" those not yet proven guilty of a committing any crime by extracting their DNA.

Police Should Take DNA from Arrestees Because . . .

- By increasing the number of DNA samples in law enforcement databases, we increase the likelihood of cold hits and of preventing future crimes by unidentified offenders who would otherwise remain free.
- Society's interest in combating violent crime is more important than the rights of people who have been arrested for violent, criminal behavior.

Police Should Not Take DNA from Arrestees Because . . .

- Our criminal justice system is based on the premise that a suspect is innocent until proven guilty. A person should not suffer the consequences of a guilty verdict until his or her guilt has been proven in court.
- DNA samples provide a wealth of personal information about suspects, including genetic conditions and predisposition to disease. The government should not have access to this information based on a mere arrest.

Your Assignment

In 2013, the Supreme Court upheld the government's right to take DNA samples from arrestees. You can learn the reasoning behind this decision by finding ***Maryland v. King*** online. Justice Antonin Scalia disagreed with the Court's ruling, stating that it would have the "beneficial effect of solving more crimes; then again, so would the taking of DNA samples from anyone who flies on an airplane, applies for a driver's license, or attends a public school." What point was Scalia trying to make? Do you agree with him? Your answer should include at least two full paragraphs.

Following this lead, Trang eventually tracked down Cracky, whose real name was James Watson-Dixon. After Watson-Dixon admitted to shooting McFay during an attempted robbery, he was charged with murder.[38]

Studies show that clearance rates are seven times higher when a suspect is identified early in an investigation.[39] Of course, police officers are rarely fortunate enough to have a mysterious stranger walk up and provide the actual wrongdoer's name at a crime scene. In this section, we will examine strategies being used by police departments to reduce and prevent crime in the absence of such a stroke of good luck.

Calls for Service

While law enforcement officers do not like to think of themselves as being at the "beck and call" of citizens, that is the operational basis of much police work. All police departments practice **incident-driven policing**, in which calls for service are the primary instigators of action. Ideally, about one-third of a patrol officer's time should be taken with responding to calls for service.[40] In practice, the percentage is often much greater. During a typical eight-hour shift, for example, a Philadelphia patrol police officer will answer eighty 911 calls for service.[41]

Response Time and Efficiency The speed with which the police respond to calls for service has traditionally been seen as a crucial aspect of crime fighting and crime prevention. In incident-driven policing, the ideal scenario is as follows: a citizen sees a person committing a crime, calls 911, and the police arrive quickly, catching the perpetrator in the

incident-driven policing A reactive approach to policing that emphasizes a speedy response to calls for service.

act. Alternatively, a citizen who is the victim of a crime, such as a robbery, calls 911 as soon as possible, and the police arrive to catch the robber before she or he can flee the immediate area of the crime. Although such scenarios are quite rare in real life, **response time**, or the time elapsed between the instant a call for service is received and the instant the police arrive on the scene, has become a benchmark for police efficiency.

Improving Response Time Efficiency Many police departments have come to realize that overall response time is not as critical as response time for the most important calls. For this reason, a number of metropolitan areas have introduced 311 nonemergency call systems to reduce the strain on 911 operations. The Miami Police Department deploys about fifty "public service aides" to answer nonemergency calls, freeing up sworn officers for more pressing matters. Another popular method of improving performance in this area is a **differential response** strategy, in which the police distinguish among different calls for service so that they can respond more quickly to the most serious incidents.

Suppose, for example, that a police department receives two calls for service at the same time. The first caller reports that a burglar is in her house, and the second says that he has returned home from work to find his automobile missing. If the department employs differential response, the burglary in progress—a "hot" crime—will receive immediate attention. The missing automobile—a "cold" crime that could have been committed several hours earlier—will receive attention "as time permits," and the caller may even be asked to make an appointment to come to the police station to formally report the theft. So, for example, officers from the Fort Worth, Texas, Police Department take an average of 7:06 minutes to respond to "top priority calls," compared to an average of 27:53 minutes for all calls.[42]

Learning Objective

3 Explain why differential response strategies enable police departments to respond more efficiently to 911 calls.

911 Technology Automatic differential response is an integral part of **computer-aided dispatch (CAD)** systems, used by nearly every police department in the country. With CAD, a 911 dispatcher enters the information from a caller into his or her computer, which prioritizes the emergency based on its nature. CAD also verifies the caller's address and phone number, and determines the closest patrol unit to the site of the emergency. In many jurisdictions, the details, including any previous 911 calls from the location, are then sent to a *mobile digital terminal* in the police officer's patrol car.

A growing number of 911 calls come from mobile phones rather than landlines. In fact, four in ten American homes now use these devices only, a figure that is sure to increase in the near future.[43] This trend has forced police departments across the country to adopt Next Generation 911 systems, which make it possible for officers to receive text messages, videos, photos, and location data about crime incidents.[44] Additionally, a number of local law enforcement agencies are offering free 911 apps that automatically upload video of possible criminal activity to a secure cloud-based server for police use. These apps also use GPS technology, discussed next chapter, to pinpoint the location of the person initiating the call for service.

Patrol Strategies

Many experts believe that, in the words of Grand Rapids (Michigan) police chief Kevin Belk, an overreliance on calls for service "tends to make you a reactive department," rather than a police force that prevents crimes from happening in the first place.[45] Similarly, another traditional police strategy, *random patrol*, is increasingly felt to be an inefficient use of law enforcement resources.[46]

response time The speed with which calls for service are answered.

differential response A strategy for answering calls for service in which response time is adapted to the seriousness of the call.

computer-aided dispatch (CAD) A method of dispatching police patrol units to the site of 911 emergencies with the assistance of a computer program.

▲ A City of Miami (Florida) police officer patrols the Little Haiti neighborhood. **What are some of the benefits of having two officers in a patrol car instead of one? Given these benefits, why do you think single-officer automobile patrols are so common?** Joe Raedle/Getty Images

Random patrol refers to police officers making the rounds of a specific area with the general goal of detecting and preventing crime. Every police department in the United States randomly patrols its jurisdiction using automobiles. In addition, 53 percent utilize foot patrols, 32 percent bicycle patrols, 16 percent motorcycle patrols, 4 percent boat patrols, and 1 percent horse patrols.[47]

Testing Random Patrol Police researchers have been questioning the effectiveness of random patrols since the influential Kansas City Preventive Patrol Experiment of the early 1970s. As part of this experiment, different neighborhoods in the city were subjected to three different levels of patrol: random patrol by a single police car, random patrol by multiple police cars, and no random patrol whatsoever. The results of the Kansas City experiment were somewhat shocking. Researchers found that increasing or decreasing preventive patrol had little or no impact on crimes, public opinion, the effectiveness of the police, police response time, traffic accidents, or reports of crime to police.[48]

For some, the Kansas City experiment and other similar data prove that patrol officers, after a certain threshold, are not effective in preventing crime and that scarce law enforcement resources should therefore be diverted to other areas. "It makes about as much sense to have police patrol routinely in cars to fight crime as it does to have firemen patrol routinely in fire trucks to fight fire," said University of Delaware professor Carl Klockars.[49] Still, random patrols are important for maintaining community relations, and they have been shown to reduce fear of crime in areas where police have an obvious presence.[50]

Directed Patrols In contrast to random patrols, **directed patrols** target specific areas of a city and often attempt to prevent a specific type of crime. Directed patrols have found favor among law enforcement experts as being a more efficient use of police resources than random patrols, as indicated by the Philadelphia Foot Patrol Experiment. As part of this evaluation, extra foot patrols were utilized in sixty Philadelphia locations plagued by high levels of violent crime. During three months of directed patrols, arrests increased by 13 percent in the targeted areas, and violent crime decreased by 23 percent. In addition, an estimated fifty-three violent crimes were prevented over the three-month period.[51]

Predictive Policing and Crime Mapping

In the previous chapter, we discussed how predictive, or intelligence-led, policing strategies help law enforcement agencies anticipate patterns of criminal activity, allowing them to respond to, or even prevent, crime more effectively. Predictive policing is increasingly attractive to police administrators because, in theory, it requires fewer resources than traditional policing.

Finding "Hot Spots" Predictive policing strategies are strongly linked with directed patrols, which seek to improve on random patrols by targeting specific high-crime areas already known to law enforcement. The target areas for directed patrols

random patrol A patrol strategy that relies on police officers monitoring a certain area with the goal of detecting crimes in progress or preventing crime due to their presence. Also known as *general* or *preventive patrol.*

directed patrol A patrol strategy that is designed to focus on a specific type of criminal activity in a specific geographic area.

are often called **hot spots** because they contain greater numbers of criminals and have higher-than-average levels of victimization. Needless to say, police administrators are no longer sticking pins in maps to determine where hot spots exist. Rather, police departments are using **crime mapping** technology to locate and identify hot spots and "cool" them down. Crime mapping uses geographic information systems (GIS) to track criminal acts as they occur in time and space. Once sufficient information has been gathered, it is analyzed to predict future crime patterns.

hot spots Concentrated areas of high criminal activity that draw a directed police response.

crime mapping Technology that allows crime analysts to identify trends and patterns of criminal behavior within a given area.

One review of "hot spot" policing tactics found that of twenty-five high-crime areas targeted with an increased police presence, all but five experienced significant reductions in criminal activity.[52] Why does this particular strategy seem to work so well? Criminologists Lawrence Sherman and David Weisburd provided a clue more than twenty years ago by observing the anticrime impact of patrol officers. Sherman and Weisburd noticed that after a police officer left a certain high-crime area, about fifteen minutes elapsed before criminal activity occurred at that spot.[53] Therefore, a police officer on patrol is most efficient when she or he spends a certain amount of time at a hot spot and then returns after fifteen minutes.

A 2011 experiment involving the Sacramento Police Department supports this hypothesis. Over a three-month period, twenty-one crime hot spots in the city received fifteen-minute randomized patrols, while another twenty-one crime hot spots received normal random patrols. Using calls for service as a measuring stick, the hot spots subject to fifteen-minute patrols were found to experience much less criminal activity.[54]

The Rise of CompStat Computerized crime mapping was popularized when the New York City Police Department launched CompStat in the mid-1990s. Still in use, CompStat starts with police officers reporting the exact location of crime and other crime-related information to department officials. These reports are then fed into a computer, which prepares grids of a particular city or neighborhood and highlights areas with a high incidence of serious offenses. (See Figure 5.3 for an example of a GIS crime map.)

Figure 5.3 A GIS Crime Map for a Neighborhood in New Orleans

This crime map shows the incidence of various crimes during a two-week period in a neighborhood near downtown New Orleans.

In New York and many other cities, the police department holds "Crime Control Strategy Meetings," during which precinct commanders are held accountable for CompStat's data-based reports in their districts. In theory, this system provides the police with accurate information about patterns of crime and gives them the ability to "flood" hot spots with officers at short notice. By 2014, police departments in forty-three of the nation's fifty largest cities were using CompStat,[55] and Wesley Skogan, a criminologist at Northwestern University, believes that CompStat and similar technologies are the most likely cause of recent declines in big-city crime.[56]

Arrest Strategies

Like patrol strategies, arrest strategies can be divided into two categories that reflect the intent of police administrators. **Reactive arrests** are those arrests made by police officers, usually on general patrol, who observe a criminal act or respond to a call for service. **Proactive arrests** occur when the police take the initiative to target a particular type of criminal or behavior. Proactive arrests are often associated with directed patrols of hot spots and thus are believed by many experts to have a greater influence on an area's crime rates.[57]

Quality-of-Life Crimes

The popularity of proactive theories was solidified by a magazine article that James Q. Wilson and George L. Kelling wrote in 1982.[58] In their piece, entitled "Broken Windows," Wilson and Kelling argued that reform-era policing strategies focused on violent crime to the detriment of the vital police role of promoting the quality of life in neighborhoods. As a result, many communities, particularly in large cities, had fallen into a state of disorder and disrepute, with two very important consequences.

First, these neighborhoods—with their broken windows, dilapidated buildings, and lawless behavior by residents—were sending out "signals" that criminal activity is tolerated. Second, this disorder was spreading fear among law-abiding citizens, dissuading them from leaving their homes or attempting to improve their surroundings. Thus, the **broken windows theory** is based on "order maintenance" of neighborhoods by cracking down on "quality-of-life" crimes such as panhandling, public drinking and urinating, loitering, and graffiti painting.

The Broken Windows Effect

Only by encouraging directed arrest strategies with regard to quality-of-life crime, Wilson and Kelling argued, could American cities be rescued from rising crime rates. Along with CompStat, the implementation of this theory has been given a great deal of credit for crime decreases in the United States (particularly New York City) over the past three decades.[59] It continues to influence police strategy: several years ago, the Cincinnati Police Department cracked down on traffic infractions in "micro" hot spots of criminal activity such as intersections and street corners. Within twelve months, the impacted areas had experienced a significant decrease in both traffic crashes and crime.[60]

Some experts question how much impact broken windows strategies actually have, pointing out that violent crime rates have also dropped in cities that do not implement this approach.[61] Critics also contend that instituting "zero-tolerance" arrest policies for lesser crimes in low-income neighborhoods not only discriminates against the poor and minority groups but also fosters a strong mistrust of police.[62] Such criticism was fueled by the July 2014 death of Eric Garner, a black man who was unintentionally killed by a New York

reactive arrests Arrests that come about as part of the ordinary routine of police patrol and responses to calls for service.

proactive arrests Arrests that occur because of concerted efforts by law enforcement agencies to respond to a particular type of criminal behavior.

broken windows theory Wilson and Kelling's theory that a neighborhood in disrepair signals that criminal activity is tolerated in the area. By cracking down on quality-of-life crimes, police can reclaim the neighborhood and encourage law-abiding citizens to live and work there.

City police officer while resisting arrest for selling seventy-five cent "loosies"—individual, untaxed cigarettes. In response, under pressure from the public, New York City police authorities moved to scale back aggressive enforcement of such "quality-of-life" crimes as littering, public alcohol consumption, public urination, and excessive noise.[63]

community policing A policing philosophy that emphasizes community support for and cooperation with the police in preventing crime.

Community Policing and Problem Solving

In "Broken Windows," Wilson and Kelling insisted that, to reduce fear and crime in high-risk neighborhoods, police had to rely on the cooperation of citizens. For all its drawbacks, the political era of policing (see Chapter 4) did have characteristics that observers such as Wilson and Kelling had come to see as advantageous. During the nineteenth century, the police were much more involved in the community than they were after the reforms. Officers performed many duties that today are associated with social services, such as operating soup kitchens and providing lodging for homeless people. They also played a more direct role in keeping public order by "running in" drunks and intervening in minor disturbances.[64] To a large degree, **community policing** advocates a return to this understanding of the police mission.

Learning Objective

4 Explain community policing and its contribution to the concept of problem-oriented policing.

Return to the Community Community policing can be defined as an approach that promotes community-police partnerships, proactive problem solving, and community engagement to address issues such as fear of crime and the causes of such fear in a particular area. Neighborhood watch programs, in which police officers and citizens work together to prevent local crime and disorder, are a popular version of a community policing initiative.

Under community policing, patrol officers have the freedom to improvise. They are expected to develop personal relationships with residents and to encourage those residents to become involved in making the community a safer place. For example, beset by incidents of excessive force and high levels of citizen mistrust, the Albuquerque Police Department recently created six "neighborhood policing teams" to improve community relations. Each of these teams—made up of a sergeant and six patrol officers—will work with residents to develop plans addressing specific problems in individual neighborhoods.[65]

▼ A Grant County (Washington) sheriff's deputy allows local children to sit on his motorcycle during the annual Mattawa Community Days celebration. **How can establishing friendly relations with citizens help law enforcement agencies reduce crime?** Jessica Rinaldi/*The Boston Globe*/Getty Images

Collaborative Reform About two-thirds of all American police departments mention community policing in their mission statements, and a majority of the departments in large cities offer community police training for employees.[66] At the same time, the federal government has shifted local grant funds to fighting terrorism, and many local police departments continue to use aggressive tactics against low-level criminal behavior. The result seems to be a growing lack of trust between law enforcement and the

problem-oriented policing A policing philosophy that requires police to identify potential criminal activity and develop strategies to prevent or respond to that activity.

public, particularly in minority communities. One resident of a mixed-race Cleveland, Ohio, neighborhood says that the police "don't make an effort to know us. They're trying to get a bust or a collar."[67]

To improve trust within their communities, a number of police departments have turned to *collaborative reform*. In this offshoot of community policing, law enforcement officials form partnerships with local leaders to address difficult issues such as police use of force and arrest policies. Policing experts call this strategy "putting good will in the bank" for use at times of crisis.[68] In South Los Angeles, for example, officers are in constant contact with community organizers and church leaders. These efforts were partially credited for the public reaction in August 2014 when Los Angeles police officers fatally shot an unarmed African American. Although local residents expressed concern, the response was relatively calm in comparison to other cities that had experienced similar incidents that year.

Problem-Oriented Policing

Several years ago, the city of Glendale, Arizona, was experiencing property crime levels that were 63 percent above the national average. Using crime mapping, the Glendale police found that a disproportionate amount of the city's property offenses were taking place at ten Circle K convenience stores. After analyzing the situation, the police determined that Circle K management practices such as inadequate staffing, failure to respond to panhandling, and poor lighting were making the stores breeding grounds of property crime.

By working with Circle K to resolve these issues, as well as putting a proactive arrest strategy into effect in the stores, the Glendale police reduced property crime at the stores by 42 percent in a single year.[69] These efforts are an example of **problem-oriented policing**, a strategy based on the premise that police departments devote too many of their resources to reacting to calls for service and too few to "acting on their own initiative to prevent or reduce community problems."[70] To rectify this situation, problem-oriented policing moves beyond simply responding to incidents and attempts instead to control or even solve the root causes of criminal behavior.

Problem-oriented policing encourages police officers to stop looking at their work as a day-to-day proposition. Rather, they should try to shift the patterns of criminal behavior in a positive direction. For example, instead of responding to a 911 call concerning illegal drug use by simply arresting the offender—a short-term response—the patrol officers should also look at the long-term implications of the situation. They should analyze the pattern of similar arrests in the area and interview the arrestee to determine the reasons, if any, that the site was selected for drug activity.[71] Then, additional police action should be taken to prevent further drug sales at the identified location. Research shows that, when properly implemented, problem-oriented policing can be even more effective than directed patrols in reducing "hot spot" crime.[72] (See Figure 5.4 for an example of problem-oriented policing in action.)

EthicsChallenge

Waze, a popular traffic navigation app, has a feature that allows users to pinpoint the location of patrol officers. Some law enforcement trade groups want Waze to disable this police-spotting function, claiming that it not only encourages lawbreaking but also acts as a "stalking app" for those who might want to harm an officer. Is Waze acting unethically by providing a police-tracking app? Why or why not?

Figure 5.4 The SARA Model of Problem-Oriented Policing

The reaction of the Boston Police Department (BPD) to a surge in violent crime in the early 2000s gives an example of the four-step SARA (scanning, analysis, response, assessment) model of problem-oriented policing.

Step 1: *Scanning (identifying the problem).* The number of shootings, fatal and nonfatal, in Boston increased 133 percent from 2000 to 2006.

Step 2: *Analysis (researching the problem).* Gun violence "hot spots" covered 5.1 percent of Boston's square mileage and accounted for 53 percent of shooting incidents.

Step 3: *Response (finding a solution to the problem).* The BPD created Safe Street Teams (SSTs) consisting of a sergeant and six patrol officers to work each gun violence hot spot. These SSTs sought to improve the appearance of the neighborhoods by removing graffiti and trash and repairing lighting systems. They also operated directed patrols and improved social services in the areas.

Step 4: *Assessment (determining whether the solution was effective).* Violent crimes declined by 17.3 percent over a three-year period in the targeted hot spots.

Source: Adapted from Bureau of Justice Assistance, *Boston, Massachusetts Smart Policing Initiative* (Washington, D.C.: U.S. Department of Justice, August 2012).

"Us versus Them": Issues in Modern Policing

"Nowadays, we're in a culture where everything's against the police, or at least in the areas I patrol," said Ernie Williams, an officer with the Philadelphia Police Department recently. "Social media, news outlets, they're really coming down on the police. And we still gotta come to work. I pray nobody's going to get shot or hurt, but the reality is, someone probably is. We still have a job to do. And at times it can be a very difficult job."[73]

Officer Williams was reacting to antipolice publicity that spread throughout the country following a number of high-profile encounters in which unarmed suspects were injured or killed by law enforcement agents. The negative force of these incidents—often captured on cell phone video recordings—was exacerbated by the fact that, in many of cases, the police officer was white and the suspect was a member of a minority group. "Any cop that uses his gun now has to worry about being indicted and losing his job and family," remarked a New York City police officer.[74] This frustration underscores the many on-the-job issues that bind police officers together while at the same time potentially alienating them from the society that they are sworn to protect and serve.

Police Subculture

As a rule, police officers do not appreciate being second-guessed about their decisions on when to use force against a civilian. "A majority of people don't understand what officers face on a daily basis," said one retired detective. "There were a lot of situations where I almost got killed."[75]

Feelings of frustration and mistrust toward civilians are hallmarks of **police subculture.** This broad term encompasses the basic assumptions and values that permeate law enforcement agencies and are taught to new members of a law enforcement agency as the proper way to think, perceive, and act. Every organization has a subculture, with values shaped by the particular aspects and pressures of that organization. In the police subculture, those values are formed in an environment characterized by danger, stress, boredom, and violence.

From the first day on duty, rookies begin the process of **socialization**, in which they are taught the values and rules of police work. This process is aided by a number

police subculture The values and perceptions that are shared by members of a police department and, to a certain extent, by all law enforcement agents.

socialization The process through which a police officer is taught the values and expected behavior of the police subculture.

Learning Objective

Describe the process of socialization in police subculture. **5**

of rituals that are common to the law enforcement experience. Police theorist Harry J. Mullins believes that the following rituals are critical to a police officer's acceptance, and even embrace, of police subculture:

- Attending a police academy.
- Working with a senior officer, who passes on the "lessons" of police work and life to the younger officer.
- Making the initial felony arrest.
- Using force to make an arrest for the first time.
- Using or witnessing deadly force for the first time.
- Witnessing major traumatic incidents for the first time.[76]

Each of these rituals makes it clear to the police officer that this is not a "normal" job. The only other people who can understand the stresses of police work are fellow officers, and consequently law enforcement officers tend to insulate themselves from civilians. Eventually, the insulation breeds mistrust, and the police officer develops an "us versus them" outlook toward those outside the force. In turn, this outlook creates what sociologist William Westly called the **blue curtain**, also known as the "blue wall of silence" or simply "the code."[77] This curtain separates the police from the civilians they are meant to protect.

The Physical and Mental Dangers of Police Work

Within a span of several hours on January 17, 2016, Officer Thomas Cottrell was fatally shot by a chronic violent offender in Danville, Ohio, and Officer Doug Barney was shot and killed by a fleeing suspect in Salt Lake City, Utah. Officers Cottrell and Barney were the first law enforcement officers to die in the line of duty in 2016, after 129 officers were killed during the previous year. Thirty-nine of those deaths were caused by hostile gunfire, with another forty-two officers losing their lives in traffic accidents.[78] In addition, about 50,000 assaults were committed against police officers in 2014, with about 28 percent of these assaults resulting in an injury.[79]

These numbers are hardly surprising. As police experts John S. Dempsey and Linda S. Forst point out, police "deal constantly with what may be the most dangerous species on this planet—the human being."[80] At the same time, Dempsey and Forst note that according to data compiled by the federal government, citizens and the police come into contact about 44 million times a year, mostly without incident.[81]

Police Stressors In addition to physical dangers, police work entails considerable mental pressure and stress. The conditions that cause stress—such as worries over finances or relationships—are known as **stressors**, Each profession has its own set of stressors, but police are particularly vulnerable to occupational pressures and stress factors such as the following:

- The constant fear of being a victim of violent crime.
- Exposure to violent crime and its victims.
- The need to comply with the law in nearly every job action.
- Lack of community support.
- Negative media coverage.

Police officers may face a number of internal pressures as well, including limited opportunities for career advancement, excessive paperwork, and low wages and benefits.[82]

blue curtain A metaphorical term used to refer to the value placed on secrecy and the general mistrust of the outside world shared by many police officers.

stressors The aspects of police work and life that lead to feelings of stress.

Both male and female law enforcement agents experience these stressors, as well as others such as lack of sleep and chaotic private lives. Some stressors are, however, unique to female police officers, for reasons we touched on last chapter. These challenges include sexism, sexual harassment, the constant demand to prove one's self, and lack of acceptance in the male-dominated police subculture.[83]

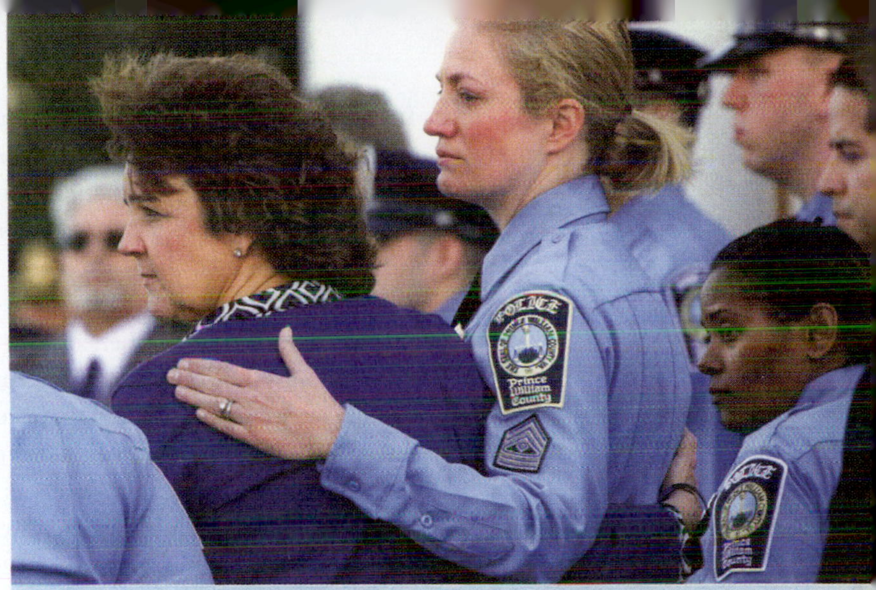

▲ Family and colleagues mourn at the funeral of Prince William County (Virginia) police officer Ashley Guindon, who was fatally shot by a suspect in February 2016. **How might violence against police officers contribute to the "blue curtain" between law enforcement and the public?** AP Photo/Cliff Owen

The Consequences of Police Stress

Police stress can manifest itself in different ways. A University at Buffalo study found that the stresses of law enforcement often lead to high blood pressure and heart problems.[84] Interviewing a random sample of 184 officers from eleven different law enforcement agencies, public health expert Elizabeth Mumford found that over half of both female and male police officers "screened positive for alcohol misuse."[85]

If stress becomes overwhelming, an officer may suffer from **burnout**, becoming listless and ineffective as a result of mental and physical exhaustion. Another problem related to stress is *post-traumatic stress disorder (PTSD).* Often recognized in war veterans and rape victims, PTSD is a reaction to a traumatic event that evokes significant stress. For police officers, such events might include the death of a co-worker or the shooting of a civilian. An officer suffering from PTSD will:

1. Re-experience the traumatic event through nightmares and flashbacks.
2. Become less and less involved in the outside world by withdrawing from others and refusing to participate in normal social interactions.
3. Experience "survival guilt," which may lead to loss of sleep and memory impairment.[86]

Several years ago, Columbia (South Carolina) police chief Randy Scott resigned after struggling with PTSD related to the fatal automobile crash of a fellow officer.

To put it bluntly, law enforcement officers are exposed to more disturbing images—of violent death, bloody crime scenes, horrible accidents, and human cruelty—in their first few years on the job than most people will see in a lifetime. Though some studies suggest that police officers have higher rates of suicide than the general population, it appears that most develop an extraordinary ability to handle the difficulties of the profession and persevere.[87]

Police Use of Force

After a cell phone video caught McKinney, Texas, police officer Eric Casebolt shoving a teenage girl to the ground outside a pool party in June 2015, the officer defended his actions by saying that he was under stress from handling two suicide calls earlier that day.[88] The incident contributed to an ongoing national debate over the use of force by law enforcement agents—a debate that often seems to set the realities of police work against the letter of the law.

burnout A mental state that occurs when a person suffers from exhaustion and has difficulty functioning normally as a result of overwork and stress.

Incidence of Force In general, the use of physical force by law enforcement personnel is very rare, occurring in only about 1.6 percent of the 44 million annual police-public encounters mentioned earlier. Still, the Department of Justice estimates that law enforcement officers threaten to use force or use force in encounters with 715,000 civilians a year.[89] Federal authorities also report that about 690 deaths occur in the process of an arrest on an annual basis.[90] Of course, police officers are often justified in using force to protect themselves and other citizens. As we noted previously, they are the targets of tens of thousands of assaults each year. Law enforcement agents are also usually justified in using force to make an arrest, to prevent suspects from escaping, to restrain suspects or other individuals for their own safety, or to protect property.[91]

At the same time, few observers would be naïve enough to believe that the police are *always* justified in the use of force. The *Washington Post* has determined that 986 police shooting deaths took place in 2015, with a quarter of those killed displaying signs of mental illness.[92] How, then, is "misuse" of force to be defined? To provide guidance for officers in this tricky area, nearly every law enforcement agency designs a *use of force matrix*. As the example in Figure 5.5 shows, such a matrix presents officers with the proper force options for different levels of contact with a civilian.

Figure 5.5 The Orlando (Florida) Police Department's Use of Force Matrix

Like most local law enforcement agencies, the Orlando Police Department has a policy to guide its officers' use of force. These policies instruct an officer on how to react to an escalating series of confrontations with a civilian and are often expressed visually, as shown here.

Source: Michael E. Miller, "Taser Use and the Use-of-Force Continuum," *Police Chief* (September 2010). 72. Photo credit: ©iStockphoto.com/Susan Chiang/kali9

Types of Force To comply with the various, and not always consistent, laws concerning the use of force, a police officer must understand that there are two kinds of force: *nondeadly force* and *deadly force*. Most force used by law enforcement is nondeadly force. In a majority of states, the use of nondeadly force is regulated by the concept of **reasonable force**, which allows the use of nondeadly force when a reasonable person would assume that such force was necessary for the officer to carry out her or his legal duties. So, for example, when New York City police officer James Frascatore threw ex-professional tennis player James Blake to the ground in November 2015, the officer was not stripped of his badge only because he used force on an innocent man. Frascatore was disciplined because his superiors felt that tackling an unarmed, compliant suspect as part of an investigation into a fraudulent credit-card operation was excessive and unreasonable.

In contrast with nondeadly force, **deadly force** is force that an objective police officer realizes will place the subject in direct threat of serious injury or death. A law enforcement agent is justified in using deadly force if she or he reasonably believes that such force is necessary to protect herself, himself, or another person from serious harm.[93] Generally speaking, the key question in use-of-force cases is: did the officer behave reasonably given the circumstances? (See the feature *CJ Policy—Your Take* to learn about a police culture with a dramatically different concept of what constitutes "reasonable" force.)

The United States Supreme Court and Use of Force The United States Supreme Court set the standards for the use of deadly force by law enforcement officers in *Tennessee v. Garner* (1985).[94] The case involved an incident in which Memphis police officer Elton Hymon shot and killed a suspect who was trying to climb over a fence after stealing ten dollars from a residence. Hymon testified that he had been trained to shoot to keep a suspect from escaping, and indeed Tennessee law at the time allowed police officers to apprehend fleeing suspects in this manner.

In reviewing the case, the Supreme Court focused not on Hymon's action but on the Tennessee statute itself, ultimately finding it unconstitutional:

> When the suspect poses no immediate threat to the officer and no threat to others, the use of deadly force is unjustified. . . . It is not better that all felony suspects die than that they escape.[95]

The Court's decision forced twenty-three states to change their fleeing felon rules, but it did not completely eliminate police discretion in such situations. Police officers still may use deadly force if they have probable cause to believe that the fleeing suspect poses a threat of serious injury or death to the officers or others. (We will discuss the concept of probable cause in the next chapter.)

In essence, the Court recognized that police officers must be able to make split-second decisions without worrying about the legal ramifications. Four years after the *Garner* case, the Court tried to clarify this concept in *Graham v. Connor* (1989), stating that the use of any force should be judged by the "reasonableness of the officer on the scene, rather than with the 20/20 vision of hindsight."[96] In 2004, the Court modified this rule by suggesting that an officer's use of force could be "reasonable" even if, by objective measures, the force was not needed to protect the officer or others in the area.[97]

Learning Objective

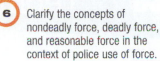

6 Clarify the concepts of nondeadly force, deadly force, and reasonable force in the context of police use of force.

CJ Policy—Your Take

In Scotland, the average patrol officer carries a baton, handcuffs, and pepper spray—but no gun. When confronting a violent suspect, Scottish officers practice a strategy called "tactical withdrawal" to de-escalate the situation. As a result, the last time a law enforcement agent was killed in the line of duty was 1994, and police have shot civilians only two times in the past decade. **To what extent would it be realistic for law enforcement in the United States to borrow from Scotland's "community-based policing by unarmed officers" policy to reduce the use of force by and against American police officers?**

reasonable force The degree of force that is appropriate to protect the police officer or other citizens and is not excessive.

deadly force Force applied by a police officer that is likely or intended to cause death.

CJ & Technology

Conducted Energy Devices (CEDs)

seanfboggs/iStock

Facing withering criticism following a series of fatal shootings by officers, in December 2015 Mayor Rahm Emanuel announced a "major overhaul" of the Chicago Police Department's approach to deadly force. By the following summer, Emanuel promised, all Chicago police officers who answer calls for service would be armed with Tasers. The Taser is a *conducted energy device (CED)* designed to incapacitate uncooperative suspects with an electrical shock. The device fires blunt darts up to twenty-one feet at speeds of 200 to 220 feet per second. These darts deliver 50,000 volts into the target for a span of about five seconds.

Nationwide, about 10,000 local police departments arm their officers with CEDs. When properly used, these devices enhance the safety of both officers and suspects—according to a study conducted at Wake Forest University, 99.7 percent of people shocked by Tasers had minor or no injuries. Researchers are also working on Active Denial Systems, which rely on "laser beams" of electromagnetic energy that deliver painful but harmless heat sensations directly to the skin of targeted suspects.

Thinking about CEDs

At least forty-eight people died in the United States in 2015 after being Tasered by police. Many of these deaths occurred because the target had a weakened heart or was in ill health because of drug use. What impact, if any, should these deaths have on a police department's decision to use CEDs?

Police Misconduct and Ethics

As the two deadly force cases highlighted at the end of the previous section show, American courts generally will uphold a police officer's freedom to decide "what law to enforce, how much to enforce it, against whom, and on what occasions."[98] This judicial support of police discretion is based on the following factors:

Learning Objective 7
Explain why police officers are allowed discretionary powers.

1. Police officers are generally considered trustworthy and are therefore assumed to make well-reasoned decisions, regardless of contradictory testimony by a suspect.
2. Experience and training give officers the ability to determine whether certain activity poses a threat to society and to take any reasonable action necessary to investigate or prevent such activity.
3. Due to the nature of their jobs, police officers are extremely knowledgeable about human—and, by extension criminal—behaviors.
4. Police officers may find themselves in danger of personal physical harm and must be allowed to take reasonable and necessary steps to protect themselves.[99]

Ben Kelly, a veteran officer with the Seattle Police Department (SPD), describes police work as being "very individualistic," adding, "There's one thousand ways to do things, and you have to find a style that meshes with your personality."[100] At the same time, when mixed with the temptations inherent in the law enforcement working environment, such an enormous amount of discretion can lead to excessive force and other forms of police misconduct addressed in this section. "We want to limit officers' discretion," says Lieutenant Scott Bachler of the SPD, rebutting Officer Kelly's earlier remark. "We are saying: 'We don't want twenty-five ways of doing things anymore. We want it to be uniform.'"[101]

Police Corruption

Police *corruption* has been a concern since the first organized American police departments. As you recall from Chapter 4, a desire to eradicate, or at least limit, corruption was one of the motivating factors behind the reform movement of policing. For general purposes, **police corruption** can be defined as the misuse of authority by a law enforcement officer "in a manner designed to produce personal gain." The Knapp Commission, set up to investigate the behavior of "dirty cops" in New York City in the 1970s, identified three basic, traditional types of police corruption:

1. *Bribery,* in which a police officer accepts money or other forms of payment in exchange for "favors," which may include allowing a certain criminal activity to continue or misplacing a key piece of evidence before a trial. Related to bribery are *payoffs,* in which an officer demands payment from an individual or a business in return for certain services.
2. *Shakedowns,* in which an officer attempts to coerce money or goods from a citizen or criminal.
3. *Mooching,* in which a police officer accepts free "gifts" such as cigarettes, liquor, or services in return for favorable treatment of the gift giver.[102]

Additionally, corrupt police officers have many opportunities to engage in theft or burglary by taking money or property in the course of their duties. Vice investigations, for example, often uncover temptingly large amounts of illegal drugs and cash. Several years ago, six Philadelphia police officers were arrested for improperly "confiscating" $500,000 in cash, drugs, and personal property such as Rolex watches from suspects.

police corruption The abuse of authority by a law enforcement officer for personal gain.

internal affairs unit (IAU) A division within a police department that receives and investigates complaints of wrongdoing by police officers.

Police Accountability

Even in a police department with excellent recruiting methods, state-of-the-art ethics and discretionary training programs, and a culturally diverse workforce that nearly matches the makeup of the community, the problems discussed in this chapter are bound to occur. The question then becomes—given the inevitability of excessive force, corruption, and other misconduct—*who shall police the police?*

Internal Disciplinary Measures When corruption or misbehavior is uncovered within a department, the first step is generally disciplinary. Such discipline includes the officer being placed on administrative leave, suspended, or fired. During this process, the officer is generally represented by her or his police union and provided the due process protections afforded all civil servants.[103]

The mechanism for investigations within a police department is the **internal affairs unit (IAU).** In many smaller police departments, the police chief conducts internal affairs investigations, while midsized and large departments have a team of internal affairs officers. The New York City Police Department's IAU has an annual budget of nearly $68 million and consists of about 650 officers.

Self-Surveillance Placing body-worn cameras on the uniforms of police officers, discussed at the opening of this chapter, is a management strategy designed to hold law enforcement officers accountable for their actions. Michael White, a professor of criminal justice at Arizona State University, estimated that, as of April 2015, up to 6,000 local police departments in the United States were using body-worn cameras in some

▲ A Washington, D.C., police officer models one of her department's body-worn cameras. **Should police officers have discretion to decide when the cameras are recording and when the devices are turned off? Explain your answer.** Win McNamee/Getty Images

capacity.[104] Generally speaking, this strategy is believed to enhance accountability by:

- Documenting circumstances in which police force is used;
- Documenting daily interactions between police and members of the community;
- Proving or disproving allegations of misconduct against police officers; and
- Recording statements made in the field by police officers, suspects, and witnesses.[105]

According to Denver (Colorado) police commander Magen Dodge, civilians generally respond positively to being recorded by body-worn cameras. In fact, a large-scale study in Denver found that officers using body-worn cameras were 35 percent less likely to be the subject of use-of-force complaints than those not wearing the devices.[106] At the same time, there are still a number of questions surrounding this emerging technology: How much discretion should police officers have to turn the cameras on and off? How long should recordings be stored? Should the recordings be made public? How can the privacy of people being filmed, such as crime victims, be protected?

Citizen Oversight Many communities also rely on an external procedure for handling citizen complaints against the police, known as **citizen oversight**. In this process, citizens—people who are not sworn officers and, by inference, not biased in favor of law enforcement officers—review allegations of police misconduct or brutality. According to data gathered by police accountability expert Samuel Walker, nearly one hundred cities now operate some kind of review procedure by an independent body.[107]

For the most part, citizen review boards can only recommend action to the police chief or other executive. They do not have the power to discipline officers directly. Police officers generally resent this intrusion by civilians, and most studies have shown that civilian review boards are not widely successful in their efforts to convince police chiefs to take action against their subordinate officers.[108]

External Punishments Officer Jason Van Dyke of the Chicago Police Department (CPD) seemed impervious to both internal and external disciplinary measures. Although Van Dyke, who is white, had eighteen civilian complaints filed against him, including allegations of using excessive force and racial slurs, neither the CPD's internal affairs division nor a civilian police oversight authority found evidence of any wrongdoing. Finally, a dashboard camera video showed Van Dyke firing sixteen shots into the body of African American teenager Laquan McDonald, who had been holding a knife. After the video was released to the public in November 2015, a grand jury charged the police officer with murder the following month.

As this example shows, law enforcement agents can be charged with criminal conduct. Gaining convictions is, however, another matter. By one measurement, from 2005 to 2011, only eleven of fifty-five police officers charged in shooting deaths were convicted.[109] Because of the dangerousness of their work, both the law and juries are

citizen oversight The process by which citizens review complaints brought against individual police officers or police departments.

Discretion in ACTION

Deadly Force

Rachel Donahue/Shutterstock.com

Learning Objective

8 Determine when police officers are justified in using deadly force.

The Situation On the day of his death, twelve-year-old Tamir was playing with a pellet gun in a park. Someone called 911 to report Tamir's behavior, saying that the gun was "probably fake" and the person pointing it at other people was "probably a juvenile." This information was not passed along to Officer Timothy Loehmann, who arrived at the park with his partner on the lookout for an armed, adult male. Grainy video, taken by a surveillance camera, shows Loehmann stepping out of the police car and immediately firing twice at Tamir, killing the boy. The video also shows that, just before he is shot, Tamir reaches into his waistband and pulls out the pellet gun, possibly either to show the officers that it is not a real gun or to give it to them.

The Law Police officers are authorized to use deadly force when they reasonably believe such force is necessary to protect themselves or third parties from serious bodily harm.

What Would You Do? Officer Loehmann claims that he believed the pellet gun to be real and that Tamir—large for his age—was going to shoot him or his partner. Lawyers for Tamir's family counter that Loehmann rushed into the situation and shot Tamir immediately, without first assessing whether the boy actually posed a threat. If you were the district attorney in this jurisdiction, would you recommend to a grand jury (described in Chapter 8) that Loehmann be charged with criminal homicide? Remember, your decision rests on whether you think the officer's actions were reasonable under the circumstances.

To see how a district attorney in Cleveland, Ohio, decided this case, go to Example 5.1 in Appendix B.

inclined to give police officers the benefit of the doubt when it comes to acting "reasonably" in use-of-force situations. (See the feature *Discretion in Action—Deadly Force* to better understand the mechanics of finding that law enforcement agents are criminally liable for their actions.)

Civil Liability Because the burden of proof is less difficult to meet in civil law than in criminal law (see Chapter 3), many disputes over excessive use of police force wind up in civil court. These lawsuits often prove costly for local taxpayers. The city of Chicago, for example, agreed to pay Laquan McDonald's family $5 million to avoid a civil wrongful death lawsuit claiming that CPD officer Van Dyke was *civilly liable* for McDonald's death. Overall, Chicago paid more than $500 million to settle civil lawsuits regarding the **civil liability** of its police officers between 2004 and 2015.[110]

Keep in mind that, because of the doctrine of **qualified immunity**, police officers generally cannot be sued because they used poor judgment in their discretionary decisions. Rather, they usually only face civil sanctions when their actions are extremely negligent or they have violated another person's legal or constitutional rights. In the words of the United States Supreme Court, qualified immunity gives police officers "breathing room to make reasonable but mistaken judgments."[111]

The Impact of Citizen Videos Increasingly, as noted earlier in the chapter, evidence of police misconduct is being provided by citizen videos. For instance, after North Charleston (South Carolina) police officer Michael Slager fatally shot Walter Scott, the officer claimed that he feared for his safety when Scott tried to grab his stun gun.

civil liability The potential responsibility of police officers, police departments, or municipalities to defend themselves against civil lawsuits.

qualified immunity A doctrine that shields law enforcement officers from damages for civil liability so long as they have not violated an individual's statutory or constitutional rights.

Footage taken with a bystander's camera phone, however, showed Slager firing eight times at Scott as the suspect tried to flee after a traffic stop. Without this video evidence, it is unlikely that, in June 2015, local authorities would have charged Slager with Scott's murder.

As long as she or he does not interfere with the police officer's work or place that police officer in danger, a civilian has a constitutional right to record the actions of law enforcement agents in public places.[112] With millions of Americans carrying camera-equipped cell phones, it seems likely that videos of police force will continue to pose challenges for law enforcement, not only in criminal and civil court, but also in the court of public opinion.

Issues of Race and Ethnicity

The death of African American Walter Scott, who was shot by police officer Michael Slager, who is white (described above), came in the midst of months of nationwide protests over similarly deadly episodes involving white law enforcement officers and black suspects. Such incidents contribute to the perception among minorities that they do not receive equal treatment from the criminal justice system. When polled, African Americans consistently express less confidence in the police than do whites (see Figure 5.6). Consequently, the legitimacy of the police is compromised for many minorities by the specter of bias.

Figure 5.6 Racial Attitudes toward the Police

As these polls conducted by the federal government show, members of minority groups are more likely than whites to have negative views of the police.

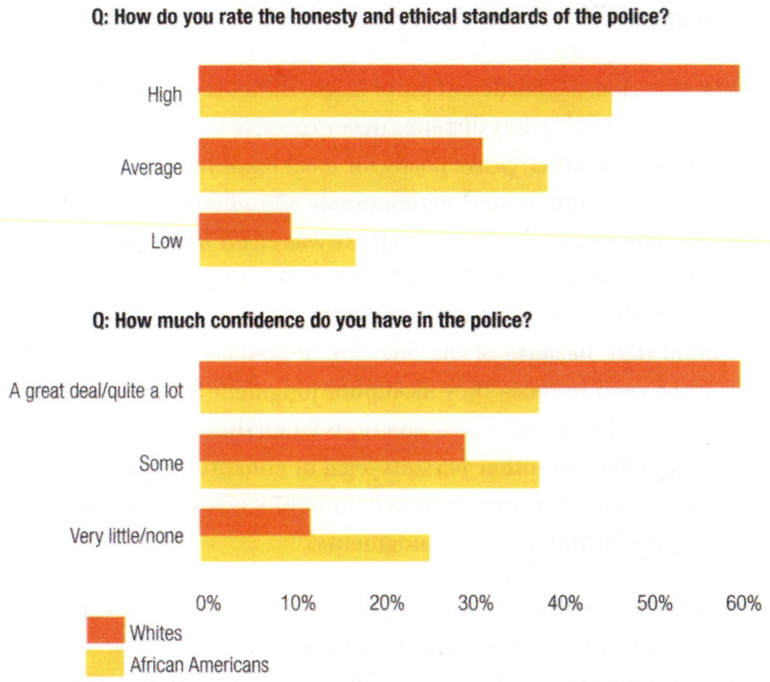

Source: Gallup, 2014.

Perceived Bias Residents of minority communities often feel that they are the targets of *over-policing* by law enforcement. In other words, they feel that police subject them to scrutiny mainly because of the neighborhood in which they live or the color of their skin.[113] Such suspicions can find support in certain data. A recent Justice Department study found that, although police pull over white, black, and Latino drivers at similar rates, blacks and Hispanics are three times more likely to be searched following the stop.[114]

On a local level, insensitivity on the part of police officers adds to the perception of bias. In 2015, for example, the city government of San Francisco released a series of offensive texts by a small group of white police officers. The texts—which contained racial slurs against African Americans and Hispanics and seemed to celebrate "white power"—confirmed the suspicions of those minority community members who feel that they are targets of harassment by police. Even though African Americans make up about 6 percent of San Francisco's population, they account for 45 percent of all citations in the city for resisting arrest.[115]

Police Presence Although there is little doubt that some individual officers may be influenced by prejudice, the greater police presence and arrest rates in minority neighborhoods should not be accepted as automatic evidence of law enforcement discrimination. As we learned earlier in the chapter, the primary operational tactic of all metropolitan police forces is responding to calls for service. According to research by law enforcement experts, the greater police presence in these communities is mainly the result of calls for service from residents, which, in turn, are caused by higher local crime rates. Indeed, Harvard law professor Randall Kennedy believes that such "selective law enforcement" should be, and for the most part is, welcomed by those who live in high-crime areas and benefit from the added protection.[116]

Civil Rights Violations In situations where a police officer does act with evident bias, he or she may be subject to federal prosecution. A **civil rights violation** is not protected by qualified immunity, discussed earlier, and involves the denial of the rights afford to all Americans by the United States Constitution. Because the Constitution prohibits government officials from discriminating against citizens on the basis of race or ethnicity, many prosecutions of law enforcement agents involve members of minority groups.

Also, the U.S. Department of Justice has the power to investigate city governments for law enforcement civil rights violations.[117] If, following the investigation, the federal government finds the pattern of such violations to be pervasive, it can enter into a consent decree (see previous chapter) with the city to improve the situation. In general, under these consent decrees, a local police department agrees to:

1. Implement policies and training that minimize the use of force,
2. Set up tracking systems to identify and discipline those officers most often involved in use-of-force incidents, and
3. Improve community relations, particularly by providing effective protocols for responding to citizen complaints.

Since 2009, the Justice Department has opened civil rights investigations in about twenty cities, including Albuquerque, Baltimore, Cleveland, Ferguson (Missouri), New Orleans, and Portland (Oregon).

civil rights violation Any interference with a citizen's constitutional rights by a civil servant, such as a police officer.

Ethics in Law Enforcement

Police misconduct is intricately connected with the ethics of law enforcement officers. As you saw in Chapter 1, ethics has to do with fundamental questions of the fairness, justice, rightness, or wrongness of any action. Given the significant power that police officers hold, society expects very high standards of ethical behavior from them.

Ethical Dilemmas Some police actions are obviously unethical, such as the behavior of the Philadelphia police officers who stole cash and jewelry from suspects, described in a previous section. The majority of ethical dilemmas that a police officer will face are not so clear cut. Criminologists Joycelyn M. Pollock and Ronald F. Becker define an ethical dilemma as a situation in which law enforcement officers:

Learning Objective 9

Explain what an ethical dilemma is, and name four categories of ethical dilemmas that a police officer typically may face.

- Do not know the right course of action;
- Have difficulty doing what they consider to be right; and/or
- Find the wrong choice very tempting.[118]

Because of the many rules that govern policing—the subject of the next chapter—police officers often find themselves tempted by a phenomenon called *noble cause corruption.* This type of corruption occurs when, in the words of John P. Crank and Michael A. Caldero, "officers do bad things because they believe the outcomes will be good."[119] Examples include planting evidence or lying in court to help convict someone the officer knows to be guilty.

Elements of Ethics Pollock and Becker, both of whom have extensive experience as ethics instructors for police departments, further identify four categories of ethical dilemmas, involving discretion, duty, honesty, and loyalty.[120]

- *Discretion.* The law provides rigid guidelines for how police officers must act and how they cannot act, but it does not offer guidelines for how officers *should act* in many circumstances. As mentioned at the beginning of this chapter, police officers often use discretion to determine how they should act, and ethics plays an important role in guiding discretionary actions.
- *Duty.* The concept of discretion is linked with **duty**, or the obligation to act in a certain manner. Society, by passing laws, can make a police officer's duty clearer and, in the process, help eliminate discretion from the decision-making process. But an officer's duty will not always be obvious, and ethical considerations can often supplement "the rules" of being a law enforcement agent.
- *Honesty.* Of course, honesty is a critical attribute for an ethical police officer. A law enforcement agent must make hundreds of decisions in a day, and most of them require him or her to be honest in order to do the job properly.
- *Loyalty.* What should a police officer do if he or she witnesses a partner using excessive force on a suspect? The choice often sets loyalty against ethics, especially if the officer does not condone the violence.

Although an individual's ethical makeup is determined by a multitude of personal factors, police departments can create an atmosphere that is conducive to professionalism. Brandon V. Zuidema and H. Wayne Duff, both captains with the Lynchburg (Virginia)

duty The moral sense of a police officer that she or he should behave in a certain manner.

▲ California attorney general Kamala Harris and governor Jerry Brown present a Medal of Valor to El Cajon police officer Jarred Slocum, who was shot and wounded by a suspect while entering a burning home. What role does the concept of duty play in a law enforcement agent's decision, regardless of her or his own safety, to protect the life of another person? oag.ca.gov

Police Department, believe that law enforcement administrators can encourage ethical policing by:

1. Incorporating ethics into the department's mission statement.
2. Conducting internal training sessions in ethics.
3. Accepting "honest mistakes" and helping the officer learn from those mistakes.
4. Adopting a zero-tolerance policy toward unethical decisions when the mistakes are not so honest.[121]

EthicsChallenge

Greg Suhr, San Francisco's police chief, decided to fire seven police officers who were responsible for sending or receiving racist e-mails, as described earlier in this section. Although such behavior is evidently unethical, should it result in termination of employment for law enforcement agents? Why or why not?

Summary

For more information on these concepts, look back to the Learning Objective icons throughout the chapter.

1 **List the three primary purposes of police patrol.** (a) The deterrence of crime, (b) the maintenance of public order, and (c) the provision of services that are not related to crime.

2 **Describe how forensic experts use DNA fingerprinting to solve crimes.** Law enforcement agents gather trace evidence such as blood, semen, skin, and hair from the crime scene. Because these items are rich in DNA, which provides a unique genetic blueprint for every living organism, crime labs can create a DNA profile of the suspect and test it against other such profiles stored in databases. If the profiles match, then law enforcement agents have found a strong suspect for the crime.

3 **Explain why differential response strategies enable police departments to respond more efficiently to 911 calls.** A differential response strategy allows a police department to distinguish among calls for service so that officers may respond to important calls more quickly. Therefore, a "hot" crime, such as a burglary in progress, will receive more immediate attention than a "cold" crime, such as a missing automobile that disappeared several days earlier.

4 **Explain community policing and its contribution to the concept of problem-oriented policing.** Community policing involves proactive problem solving and a community-police partnership in which the community engages itself along with the police to address crime and the fear of crime in a particular geographic area. By establishing a cooperative presence in a community, police officers are better able to recognize the root causes of criminal behavior there and apply problem-oriented policing methods when necessary.

5 **Describe the process of socialization in police subculture.** This process occurs as inexperienced police officers are taught the values and rituals of police subculture. Such lessons come as a rookie officer works with a senior officer, uses force in making an arrest for the first time, and witnesses traumatic on-the-job incidents. Eventually, the socialization process creates a strong bond with other officers and possibly leads to mistrust of the civilian population.

6 **Clarify the concepts of nondeadly force, deadly force, and reasonable force in the context of police use of force.** Nondeadly force is the amount of force that is required for police officers to carry out their duties. Deadly force refers to force that a police officer is aware will place a subject in direct threat of serious injury or death. In all cases of police use of force, such force is only legally justified if it is reasonable. That is, if a reasonable police officer in the given situation would find the degree of force necessary.

7 **Explain why police officers are allowed discretionary powers.** Police officers are considered trustworthy and able to make honest decisions. They have experience and training. They are knowledgeable in criminal behavior. Finally, they must have the discretion to take reasonable steps to protect themselves.

8 **Determine when police officers are justified in using deadly force.** A law enforcement agent is justified in using deadly force if she or he reasonably believes that such force is necessary to protect herself, himself, or a third party from serious harm or death. The key determination in such cases is whether the officer's use of deadly force was reasonable under the circumstances.

9 **Explain what an ethical dilemma is, and name four categories of ethical dilemmas that a police officer typically may face.** An ethical dilemma is a situation in which police officers (a) do not know the right course of action, (b) have difficulty doing what they consider to be right, and/or (c) find the wrong choice very tempting. The four types of ethical dilemmas involve (a) discretion, (b) duty, (c) honesty, and (d) loyalty.

Questions for Critical Analysis

1. Glenn voluntarily comes to the police station to answer questions about a rape case. When Glenn refuses to provide a DNA sample, police extract his DNA from a tissue he leaves behind on a chair. What arguments could you make to say that this form of DNA collection is unlawful?

2. Criminologists John and Emily Beck suggest that crime reduction strategies should treat crime as if it were a form of pollution. How does this comparison make sense in the context of predictive policing and crime mapping?

3. In many large cities, "hot spots" of crime are located in low-income, minority neighborhoods. Given this reality, how might such data-driven policing contribute to tensions between the police and members of minority groups?

4. Suppose a police officer is walking up a lightless stairway. Nervous, he points his gun into the darkness and puts his finger on the trigger, which goes against the training he received as a cadet. The officer accidentally fires his gun, and the bullet, after ricocheting off a wall, kills a man talking to his girlfriend. Apply the concepts of "reasonable force" and "qualified immunity" to this situation. Should the officer be held criminally liable for the shooting? Why or why not?

5. The International Association of Chiefs of Police's *Code of Conduct* states that law enforcement agents should "never allow personal feelings, animosities, or friendships to influence official conduct." Is this standard for police behavior realistic? Explain your answer.

Key Terms

ballistics 137
blue curtain 148
broken windows theory 144
bureaucracy 131
burnout 149
citizen oversight 154
civil liability 155
civil rights violation 157
clearance rate 136
cold case 136
cold hit 138
community policing 145
computer-aided dispatch (CAD) 141
confidential informant (CI) 135
crime mapping 143
deadly force 151
delegation of authority 131
detective 134
differential response 141
directed patrol 142
DNA fingerprinting 138
duty 158
forensics 136
hot spots 143
incident-driven policing 140
internal affairs unit (IAU) 153
police corruption 153
police subculture 147
proactive arrests 144
problem-oriented policing 146
qualified immunity 155
random patrol 142
reactive arrests 144
reasonable force 151
response time 141
socialization 147
stressors 148
toxicology 137
trace evidence 137

Notes

1. Samuel Walker, *The Police in America: An Introduction*, 2d ed. (New York: McGraw-Hill, 1992), 16.
2. George L. Kelling and Mark H. Moore, "From Political to Reform to Community: The Evolving Strategy of Police," in *Community Policing: Rhetoric or Reality*, ed., Jack Greene and Stephen Mastrofski (New York: Praeger Publishers, 1988), 13.
3. Michael White, *Controlling Officer Behavior in the Field* (New York: John Jay College of Criminal Justice, 2011), 19.
4. John S. Dempsey and Linda S. Forst, *An Introduction to Policing*, 7th ed. (Clifton Park, N.Y.: Delmar Cengage Learning, 2014), 91.
5. *Ibid.*, 93–95.
6. Karen L. Amendola, "Schedule Matters: The Movement to Compressed Work Weeks," *The Police Chief* (May 2012), 30–35.
7. Henry M. Wrobleski and Karen M. Hess, *Introduction to Law Enforcement and Criminal Justice*, 7th ed. (Belmont, Calif.: Wadsworth/Thomson Learning, 2003), 119.
8. Bureau of Justice Statistics, *Local Police Departments, 2013: Personnel, Policies, and Practices* (Washington, D.C.: U.S. Department of Justice, May 2015), 2.
9. Connie Fletcher, "What Cops Know," *On Patrol* (Summer 1996), 44–45.
10. David H. Bayley, *Police for the Future* (New York: Oxford University Press, 1994), 20.
11. Walker, *op. cit.*, 103.
12. Eric J. Scott, *Calls for Service: Citizens Demand an Initial Police Response* (Washington, D.C.: National Institute of Justice, 1981), 28–30.
13. Vivian B. Lord et al., "Factors Influencing the Response of Crisis Intervention Team-Certified Law Enforcement Officers," *Police Quarterly* (December 2011), 388.
14. E. Fuller Torrey, *Justifiable Homicides by Law Enforcement Officers: What Is the Role of Mental Illness?* (Arlington, Va.: Treatment Advocacy Center, September 2013), 3.
15. Lord et al., *op. cit.*, 390–391.
16. *Ibid.*, 391–392.
17. William G. Gay, Theodore H. Schell, and Stephen Schack, *Routine Patrol: Improving*

Patrol Productivity, Vol. 1 (Washington, D.C.: National Institute of Justice, 1977), 3–6.

18. Gary W. Cordner, "The Police on Patrol," in *Police and Policing: Contemporary Issues,* ed. Dennis Jay Kenney (New York: Praeger Publishers, 1989), 60–71.
19. Peter W. Greenwood and Joan Petersilia, *The Criminal Investigation Process: Summary and Policy Implications* (Santa Monica, Calif.: RAND Corporation, 1975).
20. Quoted in Sarah Stillman, "The Throwaways," *New Yorker* (September 3, 2012), 38–39.
21. Center on Law and Security, *Terrorist Trial Report Card: September 11, 2001–September 11, 2009* (New York: New York University School of Law, January 2010), 42–44.
22. Kimball Perry and Patrick Brennan, "Father: Terror Plot Suspect Was a 'Momma's Boy,'" *Cincinnati Enquirer* (January 24, 2015), A1.
23. "Dad Accuses FBI of Setting Up 'Mommy's Boy' Son in Bomb Plot," *ABC News* (January 15, 2015), at **abcnews.go.com/US/dad-accuses-fbi-setting-son-bomb-plot/story?id=28240751.**
24. Federal Bureau of Investigation, *Crime in the United States 2014* (Washington, D.C.: U.S. Department of Justice, 2015), at **www.fbi.gov/about-us/cjis/ucr/crime-in-the-u.s/2014/crime-in-the-u.s.-2014,** Table 25.
25. James M. Cronin, Gerard R. Murphy, Lisa L. Spahr, Jessica I. Toliver, and Richard E. Weger, *Promoting Effective Homicide Investigations* (Washington, D.C.: Police Executive Research Forum, August 2007), 102–103.
26. Robert C. Davis, Carl Jenses, and Karin E. Kitchens, *Cold Case Investigations: An Analysis of Current Practices and Factors Associated with Successful Outcomes* (Santa Monica, Calif.: RAND Corporation, 2011), xii.
27. Ronald F. Becker, *Criminal Investigations,* 2d ed. (Sudbury, Mass.: Jones & Bartlett, 2004), 7.
28. Joseph Peterson, Ira Sommers, Deborah Baskin, and Donald Johnson, *The Role and Impact of Forensic Evidence in the Criminal Justice Process* (Washington, D.C.: National Institute of Justice, September 2010), 8–9.
29. Igor Pacheco, Brian Cerchiai, and Stephanie Stoiloff, *Miami-Dade Research Study for the Reliability of ACE-V Process: Accuracy & Precision in Latent Fingerprint Examinations* (Miami, Fla.: Miami-Dade Police Department Forensic Services Bureau, December 2014), 5–12.
30. Simon A. Cole, "More than Zero: Accounting for Error in Latent Fingerprinting Identification," *Journal of Criminal Law and Criminology* (Spring 2005), 985–1078.
31. Quoted in "New DNA Database Helps Crack 1979 N.Y. Murder Case," *Miami Herald* (March 14, 2000), 18A.
32. Judith E. Lewter, "The Use of Forensic DNA in Criminal Cases in Kentucky as Compared with Other Selected States," *Kentucky Law Journal* (1997–1998), 223.
33. "CODIS—NDIS Statistics," at **www.fbi.gov/about-us/lab/biometric-analysis/codis/ndis-statistics.**
34. Annette Summers and Stephanie Yeung, "Speeding Up DNA Analysis," *Police* (February 6, 2014), at **www.policemag.com/channel/technology/articles/2014/02/speeding-up-dna-analysis.aspx.**
35. David J. Roberts, "A Kodak Moment for Law Enforcement: Using DNA Blueprints to Build Facial Composites," *The Police Chief* (March 2015), 78–79.
36. Nancy Ritter, "DNA Solves Property Crimes (But Are We Ready for That?)," *NIJ Journal* (October 2008), 2–12.
37. Phil Bulman, "DNA and Property Crimes," *The Police Chief* (April 2013), 16.
38. Zusha Elinson, "FBI Lends Local Police a Hand," *Wall Street Journal* (October 26, 2015), at **www.wsj.com/articles/fbi-lends-local-police-a-hand-1445902822.**
39. Apollo Kowalyk, "Past Predicted: How the Intelligence Paradox Undermines Our Ability to Solve Crimes," *The Police Chief* (September 2015), 26.
40. *Glendale Police Staffing Study* (Glendale, Ariz: City of Glendale, 2010), 19.
41. Karl Vick, "What It's Like Being a Cop Now," *Time* (August 24, 2015), 35.
42. Dan Cathey and Paul Guerin, *Analyzing Calls for Service to the Albuquerque Police Department* (Albuquerque, N.M.: Institute for Social Research, University of New Mexico, June 2009), Table 2, page 3.
43. Stephen J. Blumberg and Julian V. Luke, "Wireless Substitution: Early Release of Estimates from the National Health Interview Survey, July–December 2013," *National Health Interview Survey* (Centers for Disease Control and Prevention, July 2014), 1.
44. Police Executive Research Forum, *Future Trends in Policing* (Washington, D.C.: Office of Community Oriented Policing Services, 2014), 30–33.
45. Quoted in Carl Bialik, "Detroit Police Response Times No Guide to Effectiveness," *Wall Street Journal* (August 2, 2013), at **online.wsj.com/news/articles/SB10001424127887323997004578642250518125898.**
46. Cody W. Telep and David Weisburd, "What Is Known about the Effectiveness of Police Practices in Reducing Crime and Disorder?" *Police Quarterly* (December 2012), 344.
47. Bureau of Justice Statistics, *Local Police Departments, 2007* (Washington, D.C.: U.S. Department of Justice, December 2010), Table 12, page 15.
48. George L. Kelling, Tony Pate, Duane Dieckman, and Charles Brown, *The Kansas City Preventive Patrol Experiment: A Summary Report* (Washington, D.C.: The Police Foundation, 1974), 3–4.
49. Carl B. Klockars and Stephen D. Mastrofski, "The Police and Serious Crime," in *Thinking about Police,* eds. Carl B. Klockars and Stephen Mastrofski (New York: McGraw-Hill, 1990), 130.
50. Anthony M. Pate, "Experimenting with Foot Patrol: The Newark Experience," in *Community Crime Prevention: Does It Work?* ed. Dennis P. Rosenbaum (Newbury Park, Calif.: Sage, 1986).
51. Jerry H. Ratcliffe et al., "The Philadelphia Foot Patrol Experiment: A Randomized Controlled Trial of Police Patrol Effectiveness in Violent Crime Hotspots," *Criminology* (August 2011), 795–830.
52. Anthony Braga, Andrew Papachristos, and David M. Hureau, "Hot Spots Policing Effects on Crime," *Campbell Systematic Reviews* (2012), 8.
53. Lawrence W. Sherman and David Weisburd, "General Deterrent Effects of Police Patrol in Crime 'Hot Spots': A Randomized Controlled Trial," *Justice Quarterly* (December 1995), 625–648.
54. Renée J. Mitchell, "Hot-Spot Randomized Control Works for Sacramento," *The Police Chief* (February 2013), 12.
55. Oliver Roeder, Lauren Brooke-Eisen, and Julia Bowling, *What Caused the Crime Decline?* (New York: Brennan Center for Justice, 2015), 68.
56. Quoted in "New Model Police," *The Economist* (June 9, 2007), 29.
57. Lawrence W. Sherman, "Policing for Crime Prevention," in *Contemporary Policing: Controversies, Challenges, and Solutions,* eds. Quint C. Thurman and Jihong Zhao (Los Angeles: Roxbury Publishing Co., 2004), 63–66.
58. *Ibid.,* 65.
59. William Sousa and George L. Kelling, "Of 'Broken Windows,' Criminology, and Criminal Justice," in *Police Innovation: Contrasting Perspectives,* eds. David L. Weisburd and Anthony A. Braga (New York: Cambridge University Press, 2006), 77–97.
60. Daniel W. Gerard, "Cincinnati HAZARD: A Place-Based Traffic Enforcement and Violent Crime Strategy," *The Police Chief* (July 2013), 44–46.
61. Richard Rosenfeld, "Crime Decline in Context," *Contexts* (Spring 2002), 25–34.
62. Ralph B. Taylor, "Incivilities Reduction Policing, Zero Tolerance, and the Retreat from Coproduction: Weak Foundations and Strong Pressures," in *Police Innovation: Contrasting Perspectives,* eds. David L. Weisburd and Anthony A. Braga (New York: Cambridge University Press, 2006), 133–153.
63. J. David Goodman, "New York City Is Set to Adopt New Approach on Policing Minor Offenses," *New York Times* (January 21, 2016), A1.
64. Mark H. Moore and George L. Kelling, "'To Serve and Protect': Learning from Police History," *Public Interest* (Winter 1983), 54–57.
65. Dan McKay, "Overhaul at ADP Moves Cops into Neighborhoods," *Albuquerque Journal* (December 15, 2015), A1, A3.

66. *Local Police Departments, 2013: Personnel, Policies, and Practices, op. cit.,* 8, 9.

67. Quoted in Richard A. Oppel, Jr., "National Questions over Police Hit Home in Cleveland," *New York Times* (December 9, 2014), A16.

68. Dennis Rosenbaum, quoted in Jon Schuppe, "Can Smarter Police Work Prevent Another Ferguson?" *NBC News* (August 15, 2014), at **www.nbcnews.com/storyline/michael-brown-shooting/can-smarter-police-work-prevent-another-ferguson-n180841.**

69. Michael D. White and Charles M. Katz, "Policing Convenience Store Crime: Lessons from the Glendale, Arizona Smart Policing Initiative," *Police Quarterly* (September 2013), 305–322.

70. Herman Goldstein, "Improving Policing: A Problem-Oriented Approach," *Crime and Delinquency* 25 (1979), 236–258.

71. Bureau of Justice Assistance, *Problem-Oriented Drug Enforcement: A Community-Based Approach for Effective Policing* (Washington, D.C.: Office of Justice Programs, 1993), 5.

72. Christopher S. Koper, Bruce Taylor, and Jamie Roush, "What Works Best at Violent Crime Hot Spots? A Test of Directed Patrol and Problem-Solving Approaches in Jacksonville, Florida," *The Police Chief* (October 2013), 12–13.

73. Quoted in Vick, *op. cit.,* 34.

74. Quoted in Heather Mac Donald, "The New Nationwide Crime Wave," *Wall Street Journal* (May 29, 2015), at **www.wsj.com/articles/the-new-nationwide-crime-wave-1432938425?cb=logged0.5874846762133238.**

75. Quoted in Benjamin Mueller, "Outcome of Eric Garner Case Bares a Staten Island Divide," *New York Times* (December 5, 2014), A30.

76. Harry J. Mullins, "Myth, Tradition, and Ritual," *Law and Order* (September 1995), 197.

77. William Westly, *Violence and the Police: A Sociological Study of Law, Custom, and Morality* (Cambridge, Mass.: MIT Press, 1970).

78. Officer Down Memorial Page, at **www.odmp.org/search/year?year=2015.**

79. Federal Bureau of Investigation, *Law Enforcement Officers Killed & Assaulted, 2014* (Washington, D.C.: U.S. Department of Justice, 2015), at **www.fbi.gov/about-us/cjis/ucr/leoka/2014/officers-assaulted.**

80. Dempsey and Forst, *op. cit.,* 180.

81. Bureau of Justice Statistics, *Police Use of Nonfatal Force, 2002–11* (Washington, D.C.: U.S. Department of Justice, November 2015), 1.

82. Gail A. Goolsakian et al., *Coping with Police Stress* (Washington, D.C.: National Institute of Justice, 1985).

83. Kim S. Ménard and Michael L. Arter, "Stress, Coping, Alcohol Use, and Posttraumatic Stress Disorder among an International Sample of Police Officers: Does Gender Matter?" *Police Quarterly* (December 2014), 309–310.

84. University at Buffalo, "Impact of Stress on Police Officers' Physical and Mental Health," *Science Daily* (September 29, 2008), at **www.sciencedaily.com/releases/2008/09/080926105029.htm.**

85. Elizabeth A. Mumford, Bruce G. Taylor, and Bruce Kubu, "Law Enforcement Officer Safety and Wellness," *Police Quarterly* (June 2015), 122.

86. M. J. Horowitz, N. Wilner, N. B. Kaltreider, and W. Alvarez, "Signs and Symptoms of Post Traumatic Stress Disorder," *Archives of General Psychiatry* 37 (1980), 85–92.

87. L. M. Rouse et al., "Law Enforcement Suicide: Discerning Etiology through Psychological Autopsy," *Police Quarterly* (March 2015), 79–108.

88. Manny Fernandez, "Texas Officer Was under Stress When He Arrived at Pool Party, Lawyer Says," *New York Times* (June 11, 2015), A15.

89. *Police Use of Nonfatal Force, 2002–11, op. cit.,* 1.

90. Bureau of Justice Statistics, *Arrest-Related Deaths, 2003–2009, Statistical Tables* (Washington, D.C.: U.S. Department of Justice, November 2011), 1.

91. David J. Spotts, "Reviewing Use-of-Force Practices," *The Police Chief* (August 2012), 12.

92. Sandhya Somashekhar and Steven Rich, "Final Tally: Police Shot and Killed 986 People in 2015," *Washington Post* (January 6, 2015), at **www.washingtonpost.com/national/final-tally-police-shot-and-killed-984-people-in-2015/2016/01/05/3ec7a404-b3c5-11e5-a76a-0b5145e8679a_story.html.**

93. *Scott v. Harris,* 127 S.Ct. 1779 (2007).

94. 471 U.S. 1 (1985).

95. 471 U.S. 1, 11 (1985).

96. 490 U.S. 386 (1989).

97. *Brosseau v. Haugen,* 543 U.S. 194 (2004).

98. Kenneth Culp David, *Police Discretion* (St. Paul, Minn.: West Publishing Co., 1975).

99. C. E. Pratt, "Police Discretion," *Law and Order* (March 1992), 99–100.

100. Quoted in Timothy Williams, "Long Taught to Use Force, Police Warily Learn to De-Escalate," *New York Times* (June 28, 2015), A16.

101. *Ibid.*

102. Knapp Commission, *Report on Police Corruption* (New York: Brazilier, 1973).

103. Dempsey and Forst, *op. cit.,* 245.

104. Quoted in Dan Frosch and Zusha Elinson, "Police Cameras Bring Problems of Their Own," *Wall Street Journal* (April 9, 2015), at **www.wsj.com/articles/police-cameras-bring-problems-of-their-own-1428612804.**

105. Paul Figueroa, "Body-Worn Cameras: Using the Wealth of Data Effectively," *The Police Chief* (January 2016), 54–55.

106. Cole Zercoe, "Body Camera Study: Denver Police See Drop in Arrests, UOF Complaints," *PoliceOne.com* (September 4, 2015), at **www.policeone.com/police-products/body-cameras/articles/9485301-Body-camera-study-Denver-police-see-drop-in-arrests-UOF-complaints.**

107. "Roster of Civilian Oversight Agencies in the U.S.," National Association for Civilian Oversight of Law Enforcement, at **www.nacole.org.**

108. Hazel Glenn Beh, "Municipal Liability for Failure to Investigate Citizen Complaints against Police," *Fordham Urban Law Journal* 23 (Winter 1998), 209.

109. Kimberly Kindy and Kimbriell Kelly, "Thousands Dead, Few Prosecuted," *Washington Post* (April 11, 2015), at **www.washingtonpost.com/sf/investigative/2015/04/11/thousands-dead-few-prosecuted.**

110. Monica Davey and Timothy Williams, "Chicago Pays Millions but Punishes Few in Killings by Police," *New York Times* (December 18, 2015), A1.

111. *Ashcroft v. al-Kidd,* 563 U.S. ____ (2011).

112. *Glik v. Cunniffe,* 655 F.3d 78 (1st Cir. 2011).

113. Anthony A. Braga and Rod K. Brunson, *The Police and Public Discourse on "Black-on-Black" Violence* (Washington, D.C.: National Institute of Justice, 2015), 14.

114. Bureau of Justice Statistics, *Police Behavior during Traffic and Street Stops, 2011* (Washington, D.C.: U.S. Department of Justice, September 2013), Table 5, page 7, and Table 7, page 9.

115. Emily Green, "African Americans Cited for Resisting Arrest at a High Rate in S.F.," *San Francisco Chronicle* (April 29, 2015), at **www.sfgate.com/bayarea/article/African-Americans-cited-for-resisting-arrest-at-6229946.php.**

116. Randall L. Kennedy, "*McClesky v. Kemp,* Race, Capital Punishment, and the Supreme Court," *Harvard Law Review 101* (1988), 1436–1438.

117. 42 U.S.C. Section 14141 (2006).

118. Jocelyn M. Pollock and Ronald F. Becker, "Ethics Training Using Officers' Dilemmas," *FBI Law Enforcement Bulletin* (November 1996), 20–28.

119. Quoted in Thomas J. Martinelli, "Dodging the Pitfalls of Noble Cause Corruption and the Intelligence Unit," *The Police Chief* (October 2009), 124.

120. Pollock and Becker, *op. cit.,* 120–128.

121. Brandon V. Zuidema and H. Wayne Duff, "Organizational Ethics through Effective Leadership," *Law Enforcement Bulletin* (March 2009), 8–9.

POLICE
POLICE K-9

THE FREE LANCE-STAR/AP Photos

6

Police and the Constitution

The Rules of Law Enforcement

Chapter Outline		Corresponding Learning Objectives
The Fourth Amendment	1	Outline the four major sources that may provide probable cause.
	2	Explain the exclusionary rule and the exceptions to it.
Lawful Searches and Seizures	3	Explain when searches can be made without a warrant.
	4	Describe the plain view doctrine and indicate one of its limitations.
Stops and Frisks	5	Distinguish between a stop and a frisk, and indicate the importance of the case *Terry v. Ohio.*
Arrests	6	List the four elements that must be present for an arrest to take place.
The Interrogation Process and *Miranda*	7	Explain why the U.S. Supreme Court established the *Miranda* warnings.
	8	Indicate situations in which a *Miranda* warning is unnecessary.

To target your study and review, look for these numbered Learning Objective icons throughout the chapter.

eight **Long Minutes**

the use of dogs to find evidence that would otherwise stay hidden is a common and crucial aspect of American law enforcement. As with their human handlers, however, the actions of sniffer dogs are bound by the rules of police procedure. If these rules are not closely followed, a court has the option to undo an otherwise valid arrest. For example, just after midnight on March 27, 2012, police officer Morgan Struble observed a car driven by Dennys Rodriguez veer onto the shoulder of Nebraska State Highway 275. Struble proceeded to perform a routine traffic stop, questioning Rodriguez and running a records check. After issuing Rodriguez a written warning, the police officer asked for permission to walk Floyd, a drug-sniffing dog, around the vehicle.

Rodriguez refused this request. Struble then had the driver turn off the engine, exit the vehicle, and wait by the patrol car while Struble radioed for backup. When the second police officer arrived, eight minutes later, Struble led Floyd twice around the car. Midway through the second pass, the dog signaled the presence of drugs. A subsequent search of the vehicle uncovered a large bag of methamphetamine, and Rodriguez was arrested and charged with a drug crime. In court, Rodriguez's lawyers moved to suppress the bag of methamphetamine as evidence. They argued that Struble had no good reason to improperly prolong the traffic stop for the purpose of conducting a sniff search.

In 2015, the United States Supreme Court agreed. According to the Supreme Court, Struble erred when he waited eight minutes to search Rodriguez's vehicle absent any *reasonable suspicion* (a concept discussed later in the chapter) that the driver had committed a crime. "A police stop exceeding the time needed to handle the matter for which the stop was made violates the Constitution's shield against unreasonable seizures," explained Justice Ruth Bader Ginsberg. In other words, under the circumstances, the eight-minute interval between Struble's written warning and Floyd's sniff search was eight minutes too long.

Eduardo Munoz Alvarez/Getty Images

▲ The United States Supreme Court has ruled that sniff searches of automobiles by police dogs must be done in a reasonable time and a reasonable manner.

1. Do you agree with the Supreme Court's reasoning in this case? Why or why not?
2. What steps could Officer Morgan Struble have taken that would have allowed Floyd to sniff-search Dennys Rodriguez's car without prolonging the traffic stop by eight minutes?
3. When asked by Struble why he was driving so late at night, Rodriguez said that he was returning from Omaha, where he had been looking at a Ford Mustang for sale. Rodriguez also said he had veered to avoid a pothole. In addition, Struble noticed a strong smell of air freshener in the car and thought that the passenger appeared nervous. Taken together, are these factors reason enough to support Struble's "hunch" that drugs were in the vehicle? Explain your answer.

The Fourth Amendment

In *Rodriguez v. United States,* the United States Supreme Court did not address whether Dennys Rodriguez was guilty or innocent of the charges against him. That was for the trial court to decide. Rather, the Court ruled that the Nebraska K-9 officer had overstepped the boundaries of his authority by using a drug-sniffing dog to discover the bag of methamphetamine in Rodriguez's vehicle.[1] In the previous chapter, we discussed the importance of discretion for police officers. This discretion, as we noted, is not absolute. A law enforcement agent's actions are greatly determined by the rules for policing set down in the U.S. Constitution and enforced by the courts.

To understand these rules, law enforcement officers must understand the Fourth Amendment, which reads as follows:

> The right of the people to be secure in their persons, houses, papers, and effects, against unreasonable searches and seizures, shall not be violated, and no Warrants shall issue, but upon probable cause, supported by Oath or affirmation, and particularly describing the place to be searched, and the persons or things to be seized.

This amendment contains two critical legal concepts: a prohibition against *unreasonable* **searches and seizures** and the requirement of **probable cause** to issue a warrant. (A *warrant* is written permission from a judge to engage in a search or arrest and will be covered extensively later in the chapter.)

Reasonableness

Law enforcement personnel use searches and seizures to look for and collect the evidence prosecutors need to convict individuals suspected of crimes. As you have just read, when police are conducting a search or seizure, they must be *reasonable*. Though courts have spent innumerable hours scrutinizing the word, no specific meaning for *reasonable* exists. A thesaurus can provide useful synonyms—logical, practical, sensible, intelligent, plausible—but because each case is different, those terms are relative.

In the *Rodriguez* case, the Supreme Court accepted the argument that the search had been so unreasonable as to violate the Fourth Amendment's prohibition against unreasonable searches and seizures. That does not mean that the police officer's actions would have been unreasonable under any circumstances. Indeed, a decade before its *Rodriguez* ruling, the Court accepted a dog sniff search under similar circumstances. In that case, while an Illinois state trooper was writing the driver a speeding ticket, a K-9 officer walked a police dog around the vehicle. After a signal from the dog, the officer found a large amount of marijuana in the car's trunk. Because the sniff search took place *at the same time* as the "course of a routine traffic stop," the Court upheld the driver's conviction for narcotics trafficking.[2]

Probable Cause

The concept of reasonableness is linked to probable cause. The Supreme Court has ruled, for example, that any arrest or seizure is unreasonable unless it is supported by probable cause.[3] The burden of probable cause requires more than mere suspicion on a police officer's part. The officer must know of facts and circumstances that would reasonably lead to "the belief that an offense has been or is being committed."[4]

searches and seizures The legal term, as found in the Fourth Amendment to the U.S. Constitution, that generally refers to the searching for and the confiscating of evidence by law enforcement agents.

probable cause Reasonable grounds to believe the existence of facts warranting certain actions, such as the search or arrest of a person.

Careers in CJ

FASTFACTS

Police detective

Job description:

- Collect evidence and obtain facts pertaining to criminal cases.
- Conduct interviews, observe suspects, examine records, and help with raids and busts.

What kind of training is required?

- Two to five years' experience as a police patrol officer is required before testing to become a detective.
- Larger departments require 60 units of college credit or an associate's degree.

Annual salary range?

- $42,000–$110,000

William Howe
Police Detective

Courtesy William Howe

Each crime scene, each major accident, each time you are called to investigate, you are presented with a puzzle with various pieces missing. When you discover and interpret the interlocking missing pieces together in a successful prosecution, there is no better feeling. The payoff is when you get the opportunity to show off your completed "puzzle" to the jury, and they agree that the pieces fit. When I once thrilled at the chase of the bad guy through the alleys and neighborhoods, I now enjoy even more pursuing them with the mental skills I have developed—accident reconstruction, fingerprint identification, and the interpretation of crime scenes. This can be every bit as rewarding as the foot pursuit, not to mention ever so much easier on the body.

Having been in police work for thirty-five years, I have been assaulted only four times on the job (two of which were at gunpoint). This confirmed for me, once and for all, the importance of being able to use your mind rather than your size to, first, talk your way out of trouble and, second, talk the bad guys into going along with your plans for them.

SOCIAL MEDIA CAREER TIP For your profile photo, stick with a close-up, business-appropriate photo in which you are smiling and wearing something you would wear as a potential employee. Avoid symbols, party photos, long-distance shots, or baby pictures.

Sources of Probable Cause If no probable cause existed when a police officer took a certain action, it cannot be retroactively applied. If, for example, a police officer stops a person for jaywalking and then finds several ounces of marijuana in that person's pocket, the arrest for marijuana possession would probably be disallowed. Remember, suspicion does not equal probable cause. If, however, an informant had tipped the officer off that the person was a drug dealer, probable cause might exist and the arrest could be valid. Several sources that may provide probable cause include:

Learning Objective 1
Outline the four major sources that may provide probable cause.

1. *Personal observation.* Police officers may use their personal training, experience, and expertise to infer probable cause from situations that may not be obviously criminal. If, for example, a police officer observes several people in a car slowly circling a certain building in a high-crime area, that officer may infer that the people are "casing" the building in preparation for a burglary. Probable cause could be established for detaining the suspects.
2. *Information.* Law enforcement officers receive information from victims, eyewitnesses, informants, and official sources such as police bulletins or broadcasts. Such information, as long as it is believed to be reliable, is a basis for probable cause.
3. *Evidence.* In certain circumstances, which will be examined later in this chapter, police have probable cause for a search or seizure based on evidence—such as a shotgun—in plain view.
4. *Association.* In some circumstances, if the police see a person with a known criminal background in a place where criminal activity is openly taking place, they

have probable cause to stop that person. Generally, however, association is not adequate to establish probable cause.[5]

exclusionary rule A rule under which any evidence that is obtained in violation of the accused's rights, as well as any evidence derived from illegally obtained evidence, will not be admissible in criminal court.

fruit of the poisoned tree Evidence that is acquired through the use of illegally obtained evidence and is therefore inadmissible in court.

The Probable Cause Framework In a sense, the concept of probable cause allows police officers to do their job effectively. Most arrests are made without a warrant because most arrests are the result of quick police reaction to the commission of a crime. Indeed, it would not be practical to expect a police officer to obtain a warrant from a judge before making an arrest on the street. Thus, probable cause provides a framework that limits the situations in which police officers can make arrests, but also gives officers the freedom to act within that framework. In 2003, the Supreme Court reaffirmed this freedom by ruling that Baltimore (Maryland) police officers acted properly when they arrested all three passengers of a car in which cocaine had been hidden in the back seat. "A reasonable officer," wrote Chief Justice William H. Rehnquist, "could conclude that there was probable cause to believe" that the defendant, who had been sitting in the front seat, was in "possession" of the illicit drug despite his protestations to the contrary.[6]

Once an arrest is made, the arresting officer must prove to a judge that probable cause existed. In *County of Riverside v. McLaughlin* (1991),[7] the Supreme Court held that this judicial determination of probable cause must be made within forty-eight hours after the arrest, even if this two-day period includes a weekend or holiday.

The Exclusionary Rule

Historically, the courts have looked to the Fourth Amendment for guidance in regulating the activity of law enforcement officers, as the language of the Constitution does not expressly do so. The courts' most potent legal tool in this endeavor is the **exclusionary rule**, which prohibits the use of illegally seized evidence. According to this rule, any evidence obtained by an unreasonable search or seizure is inadmissible (may not be used) against a defendant in a criminal trial.[8] Even highly incriminating evidence, such as a knife stained with the victim's blood, usually cannot be introduced at a trial if illegally obtained.

Furthermore, any physical or verbal evidence police are able to acquire by using illegally obtained evidence is known as the **fruit of the poisoned tree** and is also inadmissible. For example, if the police use the existence of the bloodstained knife to get a confession out of a suspect, that confession will be excluded as well.

One of the implications of the exclusionary rule is that it forces police to gather evidence properly. If they follow appropriate procedures, they are more likely to be rewarded with a conviction. If they are careless or abuse the rights of the suspect, they are unlikely to get a conviction. A strict application of the exclusionary rule, therefore, will permit guilty people to go free because of police carelessness or honest errors. In practice, relatively few apparently guilty suspects benefit from the exclusionary rule. Research shows that about 3 percent of felony arrestees avoid incarceration because of improper police searches and seizures.[9]

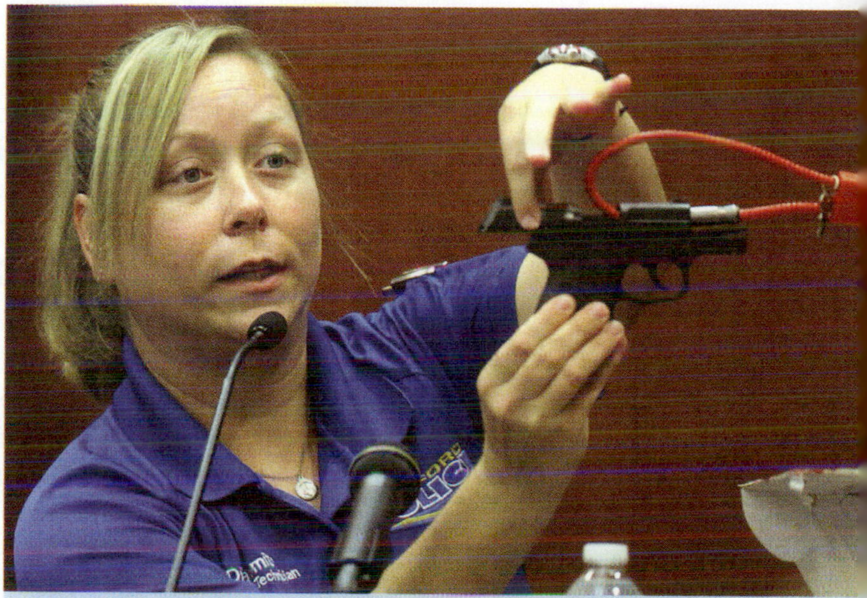

▲ Suppose that this gun—used by a defendant to murder a victim—was found as the result of an improper police search. **Why might the exclusionary rule keep evidence of this gun's existence out of the court? What is your opinion of the exclusionary rule?** Gary W. Green/*Orlando Sentinel*/Getty Images

Learning Objective

Explain the exclusionary rule and the exceptions to it. **2**

The "Inevitable Discovery" Exception

Critics of the exclusionary rule maintain that, regardless of statistics, the rule hampers the police's ability to gather evidence and causes prosecutors to release numerous suspects before their cases make it to court. Several Supreme Court decisions have mirrored this view and provided exceptions to the exclusionary rule.

The **"inevitable discovery" exception** was established in the wake of the disappearance of ten-year-old Pamela Powers of Des Moines, Iowa, on Christmas Eve, 1968. The primary suspect in the case, a religious fanatic named Robert Williams, was tricked by a detective into leading police to the site where he had buried Powers. The detective convinced Williams that if he did not lead police to the body, he would soon forget where it was buried. This would deny his victim a "Christian burial." Initially, in *Brewer v. Williams* (1977),[10] the Court ruled that the evidence (Powers's body) had been obtained illegally because Williams's attorney had not been present during the interrogation that led to his admission. Several years later, in *Nix v. Williams* (1984),[11] the Court reversed itself, ruling that the evidence was admissible because the body would have eventually ("inevitably") been found by lawful means.

The "Good Faith" Exception

The scope of the exclusionary rule has been further diminished by two cases involving faulty warrants. In the first, *United States v. Leon* (1984),[12] the police seized evidence on authority of a search warrant that had been improperly issued by a judge. In the second, *Arizona v. Evans* (1995),[13] due to a computer error, a police officer detained Isaac Evans on the mistaken belief that he was subject to an arrest warrant. As a result, the officer found a marijuana cigarette on Evans's person and, after a search of his car, discovered a bag of marijuana.

In both cases, the Court allowed the evidence to stand under a **"good faith" exception** to the exclusionary rule. Under this exception, evidence acquired by a police officer using a technically invalid warrant is admissible if the officer was unaware of the error. In these two cases, the Court said that the officers acted in "good faith." By the same token, if police officers use a search warrant that they know to be technically incorrect, the good faith exception does not apply, and the evidence can be suppressed.

EthicsChallenge

Explain the exclusionary rule in terms of its impact on the ethical behavior of law enforcement agents.

Lawful Searches and Seizures

How far can law enforcement agents go in searching and seizing private property? Consider the steps taken by Jenny Stracner, an investigator with the Laguna Beach (California) Police Department. After receiving information that a suspect, Greenwood, was engaged in drug trafficking, Stracner enlisted the aid of the local trash collector in procuring evidence. Instead of taking Greenwood's trash bags to be incinerated, the collector agreed to give them to Stracner. The officer found enough drug paraphernalia in the garbage to obtain a warrant to search the suspect's home. Subsequently, Greenwood was arrested and convicted on narcotics charges.[14]

Remember, the Fourth Amendment is quite specific in forbidding unreasonable searches and seizures. Were Stracner's search of Greenwood's garbage and her seizure of its contents "reasonable"? The Supreme Court thought so, holding that Greenwood's garbage was not protected by the Fourth Amendment.[15]

"inevitable discovery" exception The legal principle that illegally obtained evidence can be admissible in court if police using lawful means would have "inevitably" discovered it.

"good faith" exception The legal principle that evidence obtained with the use of a technically invalid search warrant is admissible during trial if the police acted in good faith when they sought the warrant from a judge.

The Role of Privacy in Searches

A crucial concept in understanding search and seizure law is *privacy*. By definition, a **search** is a governmental intrusion on a citizen's reasonable expectation of privacy. The recognized standard for a "reasonable expectation of privacy" was established in *Katz v. United States* (1967).[16] The case dealt with the question of whether the defendant was justified in his expectation of privacy in the calls he made from a public phone booth. The Supreme Court held that "the Fourth Amendment protects people, not places," and Katz prevailed.

search The process by which police examine a person or property to find evidence that will be used to prove guilt in a criminal trial.

In his concurring opinion, Justice John Harlan, Jr., set a two-pronged test for a person's expectation of privacy:

1. The individual must prove that she or he expected privacy, and
2. Society must recognize that expectation as reasonable.[17]

Accordingly, the Court agreed with Katz's claim that he had a reasonable right to privacy in a public phone booth. Even though the phone booth was a public place, accessible to anyone, Katz had taken clear steps to protect his privacy.

A Legitimate Privacy Interest Despite the *Katz* ruling, simply taking steps to protect one's privacy is not enough to protect against law enforcement intrusion. The steps must be reasonably certain to ensure privacy. If a person is unreasonable or mistaken in expecting privacy, he or she may forfeit that expectation. For instance, in *California v. Greenwood* (1988),[18] described at the beginning of this section, the Court did not believe that the suspect had a reasonable expectation of privacy when it came to his garbage bags. The Court noted that when we place our trash on a curb, we expose it to any number of intrusions by "animals, children, scavengers, snoops, and other members of the public."[19] In other words, if Greenwood had truly intended for the contents of his garbage bags to remain private, he would not have left them on the side of the road.

Privacy and Satellite Monitoring As you can see, a number of factors go into determining whether a reasonable expectation of privacy exists. In *United States v. Jones* (2012),[20] the United States Supreme Court emphasized the important roles that time and technology play in this equation. The Court's ruling invalidated the efforts of federal agents who had placed a GPS tracking device on the car of Antoine Jones, a Washington, D.C., nightclub owner suspected of drug trafficking. Using the device, which relies on satellite transmissions to determine location, the agents were able to follow Jones's movements for a month. This evidence helped bring about Jones's conviction for conspiring to distribute cocaine.

The Court found that the government had "physically occupied" private property—Jones's car—for an unreasonably long amount of time. As a result, all evidence gathered by the GPS device was ruled inadmissible. Several Supreme Court justices also pointed out that most citizens do not expect the police to be monitoring every drive they

▲ Should law enforcement be able to use police helicopters such as the one shown here to determine if people are carrying out illegal behavior in their fenced-in backyards? Why or why not? Ricky Carioti/*The Washington Post*/Getty Images

search warrant A written order, based on probable cause and issued by a judge or magistrate, commanding that police officers or criminal investigators search a specific person, place, or property to obtain evidence.

affidavit A written statement of facts, confirmed by the oath or affirmation of the party making it and made before a person having the authority to administer the oath or affirmation.

seizure The forcible taking of a person or property in response to a violation of the law.

make over the course of twenty-eight days.[21] As one commentator stated, the ruling seemed to acknowledge that just because technology now permits greater levels of surveillance, this "does not mean that society has decided there's no such thing as privacy anymore."[22]

Search and Seizure Warrants

The Supreme Court's ruling in the case of Antoine Jones does not mean that law enforcement officers can *never* track someone for a month using a GPS device or any other technology. Rather, it means that, to do so, they need to obtain a **search warrant**, a step that the federal agents failed to take before beginning their surveillance of Jones. A search warrant is a court order that authorizes police to search a certain area. Before a judge or magistrate will issue a search warrant, law enforcement officers must provide:

- Information showing probable cause that a crime has been or will be committed.
- Specific information on the premises to be searched, the suspects to be found and the illegal activities taking place at those premises, and the items to be seized.

The purpose of a search warrant is to establish, before the search takes place, that a *probable cause to search* justifies infringing on the suspect's reasonable expectation of privacy.

Particularity of Search Warrants

The members of the First Congress specifically did not want law enforcement officers to have the freedom to make "general, exploratory" searches through a person's belongings.[23] Consequently, the Fourth Amendment requires that a warrant describe with "particularity" the place to be searched and the things—either people or objects—to be seized.

This "particularity" requirement places a heavy burden on law enforcement officers. Before going to a judge to ask for a search warrant, they must prepare an **affidavit** in which they provide specific, written information on the property that they wish to search and seize. They must know the specific address of any place they wish to search. General addresses of apartment buildings or office complexes are not sufficient. Furthermore, courts generally frown on vague descriptions of goods to be seized. For example, several years ago, a federal court ruled that a warrant permitting police to search a home for "all handguns, shotguns and rifles" and "evidence showing street gang membership" was too broad. As a result, the seizure of a shotgun was disallowed for lack of a valid search warrant.[24]

A **seizure** is the act of taking possession of a person or property by the government because of a (suspected) violation of the law. In general, four categories of items can be seized by use of a search warrant:

1. Items resulting from a crime, such as stolen goods.
2. Items that are inherently illegal for anybody to possess (with certain exceptions), such as certain narcotics and counterfeit currency.
3. Items that can be called "evidence" of a crime, such as a bloodstained sneaker or a ski mask.
4. Items used in committing a crime, such as an ice pick or a printing press used to make counterfeit bills.[25]

See Figure 6.1 for an example of a search warrant.

Figure 6.1 Example of a Search Warrant

United States District Court

__________ DISTRICT OF __________

In the Matter of the Search of
(Name, address or brief description of person or property to be searched)

SEARCH WARRANT

CASE NUMBER:

TO: __________ and any Authorized Officer of the United States

Affidavit(s) having been made before me by __________ (Affiant) who has reason to believe that ☐ on the person of or ☐ on the premises known as (name, description and/or location)

in the __________ District of __________ there is now concealed a certain person or property, namely (describe the person or property)

I am satisfied that the affidavit(s) and any recorded testimony establish probable cause to believe that the person or property so described is now concealed on the person or premises above-described and establish grounds for the issuance of this warrant.

YOU ARE HEREBY COMMANDED to search on or before __________ (Date)

(not to exceed 10 days) the person or place named above for the person or property specified, serving this warrant and making the search (in the daytime — 6:00 A.M. to 10:00 P.M.) (at any time in the day or night as I find reasonable cause has been established) and if the person or property be found there to seize same, leaving a copy of this warrant and receipt for the person or property taken, and prepare a written inventory of the person or property seized and promptly return this warrant to __________ (U.S. Judge or Magistrate) as required by law.

__________ at __________
Date and Time Issued — City and State

__________ __________
Name and Title of Judicial Officer — Signature of Judicial Officer

Reasonableness during a Search and Seizure No matter how "particular" a warrant is, it cannot provide for all the conditions that are bound to come up during its service. Consequently, legal custom gives law enforcement officers the ability to act "reasonably" during a search and seizure in the event of unforeseeable circumstances. For example, if a police officer is searching an apartment for a stolen MacBook Pro laptop computer and notices a vial of crack cocaine sitting on the suspect's bed, that contraband is considered to be in "plain view" and can be seized.

Note that if law enforcement officers have a search warrant that authorizes them to search for a stolen laptop computer, they would not be justified in opening small drawers. Because a computer could not fit in a small drawer, an officer would not have a basis for reasonably searching one. Hence, officers are restricted in terms of where they can look according to the items they are searching for.

CJ & Technology

Electronic Search Warrants

For law enforcement officers in Butte County, California, the process of obtaining a search warrant was often time-consuming. First, the officer had to prepare the warrant itself. Then, the warrant had to be reviewed by a district attorney. Finally, the warrant had to be physically presented to a judge for review and a handwritten signature. If the process took place at night, the officers frequently had to visit the judge at home, which could add an hour or more to the procedure.

Several years ago, however, Butte County switched to electronic search warrants. Now, using smartphones or laptop computers, officers in the field upload digital warrants to a secure site where the documents are accessed by city attorneys and judges. Those parties then provide an e-signature to validate the warrant, completing the process in minutes. "[We are] constantly searching for new and innovative ways to increase public safety," says Butte County district attorney Mike Ramsey. "This is just another step on that path."

© iStockphoto.com/Jacom Stephens

Thinking about Electronic Search Warrants

When a law enforcement officer pulls over a drunk driving suspect, the officer often must wait for a search warrant to test the suspect's blood alcohol level. How would electronic search warrants help law enforcement gain a more accurate indication of a suspect's degree of impairment at the time of the stop?

Searches and Seizures without a Warrant

Learning Objective

3 Explain when searches can be made without a warrant.

Although the Supreme Court has established the principle that searches conducted without warrants are *per se* (by definition) unreasonable, it has set "specifically established" exceptions to the rule.[26] In fact, most searches take place in the absence of a judicial order. Warrantless searches and seizures can be lawful when police are in "hot pursuit" of a subject or when they search bags of trash left at the curb for regular collection. Because of the magnitude of smuggling activities in "border areas" such as airports, seaports, and international boundaries, a warrant normally is not needed to search property in those places.

Furthermore, in 2006 the Court held unanimously that police officers do not need a warrant to enter a private home in an emergency, such as when they reasonably fear for the safety of the inhabitants.[27] The two most important circumstances in which a warrant is not needed, though, are (1) searches incidental to an arrest and (2) consent searches.

Searches Incidental to an Arrest

The most frequent exception to the warrant requirement involves **searches incidental to arrests**, so called because nearly every time police officers make an arrest (a procedure discussed in detail later in the chapter), they also search the suspect. As long as the original arrest was based on probable cause, these searches are valid for two reasons, established by the Supreme Court in *United States v. Robinson* (1973):

1. The need for a police officer to find and confiscate any weapons a suspect may be carrying.
2. The need to protect any evidence on the suspect's person from being destroyed.[28]

Law enforcement officers are, however, limited in the searches they may make during an arrest. These limits were established by the Supreme Court in *Chimel v. California* (1969).[29] In that case, police arrived at Chimel's home with an arrest warrant but not a search warrant. Even though Chimel refused their request to "look around," the officers searched the entire three-bedroom house for nearly an hour, finding stolen coins in the process. Chimel was convicted of burglary and appealed, arguing that the evidence of the coins should have been suppressed.

The Supreme Court held that the search was unreasonable. In doing so, the Court established guidelines as to the acceptable extent of searches incidental to an arrest. Primarily, the Court ruled that police may search any area within the suspect's "immediate control" to confiscate any weapons or evidence that the suspect could destroy. The Court found, however, that there was no justification

> for routinely searching rooms other than that in which the arrest occurs—or, for that matter, for searching through all desk drawers or other closed or concealed areas in that room itself. Such searches, in the absence of well-recognized exceptions, may be made only under the authority of a search warrant.[30]

The exact interpretation of the "area within immediate control" has been left to individual courts, but in general it has been taken to mean the area within the reach of the arrested person. Thus, the Court is said to have established the "arm's reach doctrine" in its *Chimel* decision.

Searches with Consent

Consent searches, the second most common type of warrantless searches, take place when individuals voluntarily give law enforcement officers permission to search their persons, homes, or belongings. The most relevant factors in determining whether consent is voluntary are:

1. The age, intelligence, and physical condition of the consenting suspect;
2. Any coercive behavior by the police, such as the language used to request consent; and
3. The length of the questioning and its location.[31]

If a court finds that a person has been physically threatened or otherwise coerced into giving consent, the search is invalid.[32] Furthermore, the search consented to must be

searches incidental to arrests Searches for weapons and evidence that are conducted on persons who have just been arrested.

consent searches Searches by police that are made after the subject of the search has agreed to the action. In these situations, consent, if given of free will, validates a warrantless search.

reasonable. In 2007, the North Carolina Supreme Court invalidated a consent search that turned up a packet of cocaine. As part of this search, the police had pulled down the suspect's underwear and shone a flashlight on his groin. The court ruled that a reasonable person in the defendant's position would not consent to such an intrusive examination.[33]

The standard for consent searches was set in *Schneckcloth v. Bustamonte* (1973),[34] in which, after being asked, the defendant told police officers to "go ahead" and search his car. A packet of stolen checks found in the trunk was ruled valid evidence because the driver consented to the search. As the feature *Myth vs Reality—Consent to Search Automobiles* explains, as a general rule, drivers are not required to agree to such searches.[35]

Myth vs Reality

Consent to Search Automobiles

The Myth If a police officer pulls over a driver, issues a speeding ticket, and then asks to search the car, the driver must agree to the officer's request and submit to a vehicle search.

The Reality In fact, in this scenario, the driver is well within his or her rights to refuse an officer's request to search his or her car. So long as police officers do not improperly coerce a suspect to cooperate, however, they are not required to inform the person that he or she has a choice in the matter. In *Ohio v. Robinette* (1996), the United States Supreme Court held that police officers do not need to notify people that they are "free to go" after an initial stop when no arrest is involved. This lack of notification has significant consequences. In the two years leading up to the *Robinette* case, four hundred Ohio drivers were convicted of narcotics offenses that resulted directly from search requests that could have been denied but were not.

For Critical Analysis

Do you think police officers should be required to tell drivers that permission to search a vehicle can be denied? Why or why not?

Numerous court decisions have also supported the "knock and talk" strategy, in which the law enforcement agent simply walks up to the door of a residence, knocks, and asks to come in and talk to the resident.[36] The officer does not need reasonable suspicion or probable cause that a crime has taken place in this situation because the decision to cooperate rests with the civilian. (Figure 6.2 provides an overview of the circumstances under which warrantless searches have traditionally been allowed.)

Searches of Automobiles

In *Carroll v. United States* (1925),[37] the Supreme Court ruled that the law could distinguish among automobiles, homes, and persons that are subject to police searches. Since handing down its *Carroll* decision, the Court has established that the Fourth Amendment does not require police to obtain a warrant to search automobiles or other movable vehicles when they have probable cause to believe that a vehicle contains contraband or evidence of criminal activity.[38]

The reasoning behind such leniency is straightforward: requiring a warrant to search an automobile places too heavy a burden on police officers. By the time the officers could communicate with a judge and obtain the warrant, the suspects could have driven away and destroyed any evidence. Consequently, the Court has consistently held that someone in a vehicle does not have the same reasonable expectation of privacy as someone at home or even in a phone booth.

Warrantless Searches of Automobiles Until relatively recently, police officers believed that if they lawfully arrested the driver of a car, they could legally make a warrantless search of the car's entire front and back compartments.[39]

Figure 6.2 Exceptions to the Requirement that Officers Have a Search Warrant

In many instances, it would be impractical for police officers to leave a crime scene, go to a judge, and obtain a search warrant before conducting a search. Therefore, under the following circumstances, a search warrant is not required.

INCIDENT TO LAWFUL ARREST Police officers may search the area within immediate control of a person after they have arrested him or her.	**AUTOMOBILE EXCEPTION** If police officers have probable cause to believe that an automobile contains evidence of a crime, they may, in most instances, search the vehicle without a warrant.
CONSENT Police officers may search a person without a warrant if that person voluntarily agrees to be searched and has the legal authority to authorize the search.	**PLAIN VIEW** If police officers are legally engaged in police work and happen to see evidence of a crime in "plain view," they may seize it without a warrant.
STOP AND FRISK Police officers may frisk, or "pat down," a person if they suspect that the person may be involved in criminal activity or pose a danger to those in the immediate area.	**ABANDONED PROPERTY** Any abandoned property, such as a hotel room that has been vacated or contraband that has been discarded, may be searched and seized by police officers without a warrant.
HOT PURSUIT If police officers are in "hot pursuit" or chasing a person they have probable cause to believe committed a crime, and that person enters a building, the officers may search the building without a warrant.	**BORDER SEARCHES** Law enforcement officers on border patrol do not need a warrant to search vehicles crossing the border.

In *Arizona v. Gant* (2009), however, the Court announced that such warrantless searches are only allowed if

1. The person being arrested is close enough to the car to grab or destroy evidence or a weapon inside the car, or
2. The arresting officer reasonably believes that the car contains evidence pertinent to the same crime for which the arrest took place.[40]

So, for example, police are not able to search an automobile for contraband if the driver has been arrested for failing to pay previous speeding tickets—unless the officer reasonably believes the suspect has the ability to reach and destroy any such contraband.

As you can imagine, the law enforcement community reacted negatively to the restrictions outlined in the *Gant* decision.[41] Police officers, however, still can conduct a warrantless search of an automobile based on circumstances other than the incidental-to-an-arrest doctrine. These circumstances include probable cause of criminal activity, consent of the driver, and "protective searches" to search for weapons if police officers have a reasonable suspicion that such weapons exist.[42]

Pretextual Stops In 2015, a police officer in Starke, Florida, pulled over professional football player Letroy Guion for "failure to maintain a single lane." While writing Guion a ticket, the officer smelled marijuana, giving him legal justification to conduct a search that uncovered 357 grams of the drug, about $190,000 in cash, and an illegally owned firearm in Guion's truck.

It is important to understand that such automobile stops and searches are a valid part of police work. As long as an officer has probable cause to believe that a traffic law has been broken, her or his "true" motivation for making a stop is irrelevant.[43] So, even if the police officer does not have a legally sufficient reason to search for evidence of a crime such as drug trafficking, the officer can use a minor traffic violation to pull over the car and investigate his or her "hunch." (To learn more about such "pretextual stops," see the feature *Discretion in Action—A Valid Pretext?*)

Discretion in ACTION

A Valid Pretext?

Rachel Donahue/Shutterstock.com

The Situation You are a police officer patrolling an area of Washington, D.C., that is marked by extremely high rates of drug-related crime. You become suspicious of a truck with temporary plates being driven slowly by a young African American male. Although you do not consider yourself as being racially biased, you are well aware, from experience, that in this neighborhood many young black men in these types of cars with temporary plates are drug dealers. These suspicions do not, however, reach the level of probable cause needed to pull over the truck. Then, the driver fails to signal while making a right turn.

The Law As far as Fourth Amendment law is concerned, any subjective reasons that a police officer might have for stopping a suspect, including any motives based on racial stereotyping or bias, are irrelevant. As long as the officer has objective probable cause to believe a traffic violation or other wrongdoing has occurred, the stop is valid.

What Would You Do? You are convinced that the driver of the truck is selling illegal drugs, and you want to stop and search him. The "failure to signal" gives you a valid pretext to pull over the truck, even though your real reasons for the stop would be its slow pace, its temporary plates, the race of its driver, and the level of drug crime in the neighborhood. What do you do?

To see how the United States Supreme Court reacted to an officer's decision in a similar situation, go to Example 6.1 in Appendix B.

The Plain View Doctrine

Learning Objective

4 Describe the plain view doctrine and indicate one of its limitations.

As we have already seen several times in this chapter, the Constitution, as interpreted by our courts, provides very little protection to evidence *in plain view.* For example, suppose a traffic officer pulls over a person for speeding, looks in the driver's side window, and clearly sees what appears to be a bag of heroin resting on the passenger seat. In this instance, under the **plain view doctrine**, the officer would be justified in seizing the drugs without a warrant.

The plain view doctrine was first put forward by the Supreme Court in *Coolidge v. New Hampshire* (1971).[44] The Court ruled that law enforcement officers may make a warrantless seizure of an item if four criteria are met:

1. The item is positioned so as to be detected easily by an officer's sight or some other sense.
2. The officer is legally in a position to notice the item in question.
3. The discovery of the item is inadvertent. That is, the officer had not intended to find the item.
4. The officer immediately recognizes the illegal nature of the item. No interrogation or further investigation is allowed under the plain view doctrine.

In addition, police officers must have probable cause to believe that any item in plain view is potentially connected to criminal activity before that item can be searched or seized.

Advances in technology that allow law enforcement agents to "see" beyond normal human capabilities have raised new issues in regard to plain view principles. *Thermal imagers,* for example, measure otherwise invisible levels of infrared radiation. These devices are particularly effective in detecting marijuana plants grown indoors because of the heat thrown off by the "grow lights" that the plants need to survive. The

plain view doctrine The legal principle that objects in plain view of a law enforcement agent who has the right to be in a position to have that view may be seized without a warrant and introduced as evidence.

Getting **Linked in**™

In many jurisdictions, instead of a police officer, only a licensed **phlebotomist** is authorized to draw blood from a person who has been stopped for driving under the influence. You can learn more about the career paths in this field, and how such paths intersect with the criminal justice system, by going to LinkedIn and searching for "phlebotomist."

question for the courts has been whether a warrantless search of a dwelling through its walls by means of a thermal imager violates Fourth Amendment protections of privacy. According to the Supreme Court, an item is not in plain view if law enforcement agents need the aid of this technology to "see" it.[45] Thus, information from a thermal imager is not by itself justification for a warrantless search.

Electronic Surveillance

During the course of a criminal investigation, law enforcement officers may decide to use **electronic surveillance**, or electronic devices such as wiretaps or hidden microphones ("bugs"), to monitor and record conversations, observe movements, and trace or record telephone calls.

electronic surveillance The use of electronic equipment by law enforcement agents to record private conversations or observe conduct that is meant to be private.

Basic Rules: Consent and Probable Cause Given the invasiveness of electronic surveillance, the Supreme Court has generally held that the practice is prohibited by the Fourth Amendment. In *Burger v. New York* (1967),[46] however, the Court ruled that it was permissible under certain circumstances. That same year, *Katz v. United States* (discussed at the beginning of this section) established that recorded conversations are inadmissible as evidence unless certain procedures are followed.

In general, law enforcement officers can use electronic surveillance only if consent is given by one of the parties to be monitored, or, in the absence of such consent, with a warrant.[47] For the warrant to be valid, it must:

1. Detail with "particularity" the conversations that are to be overheard.
2. Name the suspects and the places that will be under surveillance.
3. Show probable cause to believe that a specific crime has been or will be committed.[48]

Once the relevant information has been gathered, the law enforcement officers must end the electronic surveillance immediately.[49] In any case, the surveillance cannot last more than thirty days without a judicial extension.

Force Multiplying Pervasive forms of electronic surveillance are allowed under the theory, generally upheld by American courts,[50] that people who are in public places have no reasonable expectation of privacy. This principle allows for operations such as the Fresno (California) Police Department's Real Time Crime Center. Besides taking about 1,200 calls for service a day, five operators at the center observe fifty-seven monitors that provide feeds from about two hundred closed-circuit television surveillance (CCTV) cameras located around the city. Another Fresno program, called Media Sonar, trawls social media for evidence of illegal activity such as school-violence threats and gang hashtags.[51]

Fresno's Crime Center operators also have access to computerized infrared cameras that take digital photos of license plates. Usually mounted on police cars or affixed on traffic lights, these *automatic license plate recognition (ALPR)* devices electronically match all photographed numbers against a national database that contains records of the license plates of stolen cars or other vehicles driven by criminal suspects. Such technological devices are known as *force multipliers,* because they allow law enforcement agencies to expand their capabilities without a significant increase in personnel. Today, more than 75 percent of all local police departments in the United States employ some form of electronic surveillance as a force multiplier.[52]

Tracking Cell Phones Given the pervasiveness of cell phones in everyday life and the amount of information stored on these "mobile computers," it should come as no surprise that a number of legal issues have arisen when it comes to police surveillance of these devices. For example, *cell site simulators* are small surveillance devices that mimic cell phone towers, providing police with location data on all cell-phone use in the area. In numerous instances, these devices have helped law enforcement find fugitives by tracking their cell phone usage.

If a law enforcement agency does not first obtain a search warrant before employing this technology, however, it leaves itself open to a legal challenge. Several years ago, Baltimore police relied on a cell site simulator called Hailstorm to locate a suspect in a drug-related shooting. A judge subsequently suppressed any evidence—including the suspect's gun—stemming from the use of Hailstorm. The judge held that, by failing to secure a search warrant in this instance, the Baltimore police had breached the suspect's rights under the Fourth Amendment.[53]

▲ In 2014, the Supreme Court required police officers to obtain a warrant before searching the contents of a cell phone confiscated during an arrest—except in the event of an emergency. **Name one "emergency" circumstance in which you think a police officer would be justified in searching the contents of an arrestee's cell phone without a warrant or without the owner's consent.** AP Images/Jose Luis Magana

Searching Cell Phones In 2014, the Supreme Court ruled, unanimously, that police officers do need a warrant to search the contents of cell phones belonging to suspects they have just arrested.[54] As we saw earlier in this section, law enforcement agents may, in many instances, carry out a warrantless search on an arrestee's body following an arrest. Because of the vast amounts of personal information on cell phones, the Court decided that these items were deserving of greater protections than items such as wallets or cigarette packets. Furthermore, once a cell phone has been secured by police, the arrestee will not be able to "delete incriminating data" and the "data on the phone can endanger no one"—the two primary justifications for warrantless searches incidental to an arrest.[55]

In his opinion, Chief Justice John G. Roberts acknowledged that the Court's decision would "have an impact on the ability of law enforcement to combat crime." But, he added, "Privacy comes at a cost."[56] Practically, the ruling does not mean the end of cell phone searches. Rather, it means that police will need to get a warrant before engaging in such searches. Or, they will need the consent of the cell phone owner. As we saw earlier in the chapter, such consent is often given despite it being against a suspect's best interests.

Ethics Challenge

Even though state law requires only a single working brake light, a police officer in North Carolina pulled over a car that had one broken brake light. Several years ago, the United States Supreme Court ruled that the officer's subsequent search of the vehicle, which uncovered cocaine, was valid because the officer was "reasonably mistaken" about the state's brake-light law. What ethical issues regarding traffic stops and automobile searches are raised by the Court's ruling in this case? ■

Stops and Frisks

When reasonable suspicion exists, police officers may *stop and frisk* a suspect. In a stop and frisk, law enforcement officers (1) briefly detain a person they reasonably believe to be suspicious, and (2) if they believe the person to be armed, proceed to pat down, or "frisk," that person's outer clothing.[57]

Defining Reasonable Suspicion

Learning Objective 5

Distinguish between a stop and a frisk, and indicate the importance of the case *Terry v. Ohio*.

The precedent for the ever-elusive definition of a "reasonable" suspicion in stop-and-frisk situations was established in *Terry v. Ohio* (1968).[58] In that case, a detective named McFadden observed two men (one of whom was Terry) acting strangely in downtown Cleveland. The men would walk past a certain store, peer into the window, and then stop at a street corner and confer. While they were talking, another man joined the conversation and then left quickly.

Several minutes later, the three men met again at another corner a few blocks away. Detective McFadden believed the trio was planning to break into the store. He approached them, told them who he was, and asked for identification. After receiving a mumbled response, the detective frisked the three men and found handguns on two of them, who were tried and convicted of carrying concealed weapons.

The Supreme Court upheld the conviction, ruling that Detective McFadden had reasonable cause to believe that the men were armed and dangerous and that swift action was necessary to protect himself and other citizens in the area.[59] The Court accepted McFadden's interpretation of the unfolding scene as based on objective facts and practical conclusions. It therefore concluded that his suspicion was reasonable.

Police Discretion For the most part, the judicial system has refrained from placing restrictions on police officers' ability to make stops. In the *Terry* case, the Supreme Court did say that an officer must have "specific and articulable facts" to support the decision to make a stop, but added that the facts may be "taken together with rational inferences."[60] The Court has consistently ruled that because of their practical experience, law enforcement agents are in a unique position to make such inferences and should be given a good deal of freedom in doing so.

The "Totality of the Circumstances" In the years since the *Terry* case was decided, the Court has settled on a "totality of the circumstances" test to determine whether a stop is based on reasonable suspicion.[61] In 2002, for example, the Court ruled that a U.S. Border Patrol agent's stop of a minivan in Arizona was reasonable.[62] On being approached by the Border Patrol car, the driver had stiffened, slowed down his van, and avoided making eye contact with the agent. Furthermore, the children in the van waved at the officer in a mechanical manner, as if ordered to do so. The agent pulled over the van and found 128 pounds of marijuana.

In his opinion, Chief Justice William Rehnquist pointed out that such conduct might have been unremarkable on a busy city highway, but on an unpaved road thirty miles from the Mexican border, it was enough to reasonably arouse the agent's suspicion.[63] The justices also made clear that the need to prevent terrorist attacks is part of the "totality of the circumstances," and, therefore, law enforcement agents will have more leeway to make stops near U.S. borders.

A Stop

The terms *stop* and *frisk* are often used in concert, but they describe two separate acts. A **stop** takes place when a law enforcement officer has reasonable suspicion that criminal activity has taken place or is about to take place. Because an investigatory stop is not an arrest, there are limits to the extent police can detain someone who has been stopped. For example, in one situation an airline traveler and his luggage were detained for ninety minutes while the police waited for a drug-sniffing dog to arrive. The Supreme Court ruled that the initial stop of the passenger was constitutional, but that the ninety-minute wait was excessive.[64]

stop A brief detention of a person by law enforcement agents for questioning.

frisk A pat-down or minimal search by police to discover weapons.

In 2004, the Court held that police officers could require suspects to identify themselves during a stop that is otherwise valid under the *Terry* ruling.[65] The case involved a Nevada rancher who was fined $250 for refusing to give his name to a police officer investigating a possible assault. The defendant argued that such requests force citizens to incriminate themselves against their will, which is prohibited by the Fifth Amendment, as we shall see later in the chapter. Justice Anthony Kennedy wrote, however, that "asking questions is an essential part of police investigations" that would be made much more difficult if officers could not determine the identity of a suspect.[66] The ruling validated "stop-and-identify" laws in twenty states and numerous cities and towns.

A Frisk

The Supreme Court has stated that a **frisk** should be a protective measure. Police officers cannot conduct a frisk as a "fishing expedition" simply to try to find items besides weapons, such as illegal narcotics, on a suspect.[67] A frisk does not necessarily follow a stop and in fact may occur only when the officer is justified in thinking that the safety of police officers or other citizens may be endangered.

As with stops, frisks must be supported by reasonable suspicion. In the *Terry* case, the Supreme Court accepted that Detective McFadden reasonably believed that the three suspects posed a threat. The suspects' refusal to answer McFadden's questions, though within their rights because they had not been arrested, provided him with sufficient motive for the frisk. In 2009, the Court extended the "stop-and-frisk" authority by ruling that a police officer could order a passenger in a car that had been pulled over for a traffic violation to submit to a pat-down.[68] To do so, the officer must have a reasonable suspicion that the suspect may be armed and dangerous.

▼ A police officer frisks a suspect in San Francisco, California. **What is the main purpose behind a frisk? When are police justified in frisking someone?** Mark Richards/PhotoEdit

Race and Reasonable Suspicion

By the letter of the law, a person's race or ethnicity alone cannot provide reasonable suspicion for stops and frisks.[69] Some statistical measures, however, seem to show that these factors do, at times, play a troubling role in this area of policing. In Florida, for example, a recent twelve-month research project found that African American drivers were stopped nearly twice as often as whites for failing to wear a seatbelt. Statewide, seatbelt use among black drivers is only slightly less common than among white drivers.[70] Furthermore, as you will recall from the last chapter, on a national level police officers are almost three times as likely to search members of minority groups than whites after a traffic stop.[71]

Racial Profiling Such statistics are often seen as proof that some police departments or officers use **racial profiling** in deciding which suspects to stop. Racial profiling occurs when a police action is based on the race, ethnicity, or national origin of the suspect rather than any reasonable suspicion that he or she has broken the law. As you may remember from our discussion of pretextual stops earlier in the chapter, as long as a police officer can provide a valid reason for a stop, any racial motivation on his or her part is often legally irrelevant.

When data show that a law enforcement agency is improperly focusing its attention on members of minority groups, the remedies include:

1. A civil lawsuit against the law enforcement agency for violating provisions of the U.S. Constitution that require all citizens to be treated fairly and equally by the government, and
2. Law enforcement agency policies designed to stop the practice.

In addition, thirty states have passed laws that restrict racial profiling, and another seventeen states ban "pretextual" traffic stops.[72]

Immigration Law and Profiling In 2010, the Arizona legislature passed a state law aimed at policing its large number of undocumented immigrants. The legislation, known as S.B. 1070, requires state and local police officers, "when practicable," to check the immigration status of someone they reasonably suspect to be in the country illegally.[73] Much to the disappointment of the law's many critics, in 2012 the United States Supreme Court upheld the so-called "papers, please" provision of S.B. 1070.[74] Thus, law enforcement agents in Arizona have been empowered to check the immigration status of suspects who have been detained for other valid reasons, such as questioning about a crime or receiving a speeding ticket.

In its decision, the Supreme Court seemed to hint that, if the implementation of S.B. 1070 were to result in blatant levels of racial profiling, the Court would revisit the constitutionality of the law.[75] Because of insufficient data, however, it has proven difficult to determine the exact impact of "papers, please" provisions in Arizona and the four other states that have passed similar legislation.[76] (To better understand this issue in the context of counterterrorism, see the feature *CJ Controversy—Ethnic Profiling and Airport Security*.)

Arrests

As happened in the *Terry* case discussed earlier, a stop and frisk may lead to an **arrest**. An arrest is the act of apprehending a suspect for the purpose of detaining him or her on a criminal charge. It is important to understand the difference between a stop and an arrest. In the eyes of the law, a stop is a relatively brief intrusion on a citizen's rights, whereas an arrest—which involves a deprivation of liberty—is deserving of a full range of constitutional protections (see this chapter's *Mastering Concepts—The Difference*

racial profiling The practice of targeting people for police action based solely on their race, ethnicity, or national origin.

arrest To deprive the liberty of a person suspected of criminal activity.

M Dogan/Shutterstock.com

Ethnic Profiling and Airport Security

Despite being located in one of the most dangerous regions in the world, Israel's Ben Gurion International Airport has not experienced a terrorist incident since 1972. Israeli counter-terrorism officials credit this accomplishment, in part, to ethnic profiling—the national airline El Al has a policy of singling out young Arabs for extensive search procedures. In contrast, the U.S. Transportation and Security Administration essentially treats all airline travelers the same by way of random screening. Has America's commitment to avoiding discrimination on the basis of race, nationality, and ethnicity led it to reject a potentially effective method of combating terrorism?

The U.S. Should Employ Ethnic Profiling at Airports Because . . .

- At present, most terrorist acts have been committed by men of Middle Eastern background. "We're at war with a terrorist network," says one commentator. "Are we really supposed to ignore the one identifiable fact that we know about them?"
- It is a waste of time and money to screen and rescreen all passengers, the vast majority of whom pose no threat to national security.

The U.S. Should Not Employ Ethnic Profiling at Airports Because . . .

- If terrorist groups know in advance that security agencies are focusing on certain ethnic groups, they will simply select individuals of different ethnic groups for future attacks. Random selection of passengers for screening protects against this ability to "beat the profile."
- Without statistical evidence that such profiling works in the United States, ethnic profiling would encourage racism and bigotry for no defensible reason.

Your Assignment

Until several years ago, the New York City Police Department (NYPD) operated a Demographics Unit devised to gather intelligence on potential terrorist plots in the city's Muslim communities. Search for **NYPD Demographics Unit** online and then write two full paragraphs in which you (1) describe the tactics of this surveillance unit and (2) give your opinion on whether the NYPD made the right decision by abandoning this strategy.

---

between a Stop and an Arrest). Consequently, while a stop can be made based on reasonable suspicion, a law enforcement officer needs probable cause, as defined earlier, to make an arrest.[77]

Elements of an Arrest

When is somebody under arrest? The easy—and incorrect—answer would be whenever the police officer says so. In fact, the state of being under arrest is dependent not only on the actions of the law enforcement officers, but also on the perception of the suspect. Suppose Mr. Smith is stopped by plainclothes detectives, driven to the police station, and detained for three hours for questioning. During this time, the police never tell Mr. Smith he is under arrest, and in fact, he is free to leave at any time. But if Mr. Smith or any other reasonable person *believes* he is not free to leave, then, according to the Supreme Court, that person is in fact under arrest and should receive the necessary constitutional protections.[78]

Criminal justice professor Rolando V. del Carmen of Sam Houston State University has identified four elements that must be present for an arrest to take place:

Learning Objective

6 List the four elements that must be present for an arrest to take place.

1. The *intent* to arrest. In a stop, though it may entail slight inconvenience and a short detention period, there is no intent on the part of the law enforcement officer to

Mastering**Concepts** The Difference between a Stop and an Arrest

Getty Images

Both stops and arrests are considered seizures because both police actions involve the restriction of an individual's freedom to "walk away." Both must be justified by a showing of reasonableness as well. You should be aware, however, of the differences between a stop and an arrest. **During a stop,** police can interrogate the person and make a limited search of his or her outer clothing. If anything occurs during the stop, such as the discovery of an illegal weapon, then officers may arrest the person. **If an arrest is made,** the suspect is now in police custody and is protected by the U.S. Constitution in a number of ways that will be discussed later in the chapter.

	Stop	Arrest
Justification	Reasonable suspicion only	Probable cause
Warrant	None	Required in some, but not all, situations
Intent of Officer	To investigate suspicious activity	To make a formal charge against the suspect
Search	May frisk, or "pat down," for weapons	May conduct a full search for weapons or evidence
Scope of Search	Outer clothing only	Area within the suspect's immediate control or "reach"

deprive the suspect of her or his freedom. Therefore, there is no arrest. As intent is a subjective term, it is sometimes difficult to determine whether the police officer intended to arrest. In situations when the intent is unclear, courts often rely—as in our hypothetical case of Mr. Smith—on the perception of the possible arrestee.[79]

2. The *authority* to arrest. State laws give police officers the authority to place citizens under custodial arrest, or take them into *custody,* a concept defined later in the chapter.
3. *Seizure or detention.* A necessary part of an arrest is the detention of the subject. Detention is considered to have occurred as soon as the arrested individual submits to the control of the officer, whether peacefully or under the threat or use of force.
4. The *understanding* of the person that she or he has been arrested. Through either words—such as "you are now under arrest"—or actions, the person taken into custody must understand that an arrest has taken place. When a suspect has been forcibly subdued by the police, handcuffed, and placed in a patrol car, he or she is believed to understand that an arrest has been made. This understanding may be lacking if the person is intoxicated, insane, or unconscious.[80]

Arrests with a Warrant

When law enforcement officers have established probable cause to arrest an individual who is not in police custody, they obtain an **arrest warrant** for that person. An arrest warrant, similar to a search warrant, contains information such as the name of the person suspected and the crime he or she is suspected of having committed. (See Figure 6.3 for an example of an arrest warrant.) Judges or magistrates issue arrest warrants after first determining that the law enforcement officers have indeed established probable cause.

arrest warrant A written order, based on probable cause and issued by a judge or magistrate, commanding that the person named on the warrant be arrested by the police.

Entering a Dwelling There is a perception that an arrest warrant gives law enforcement officers the authority to enter a dwelling without first announcing themselves. This is not accurate. In *Wilson v. Arkansas* (1995),[81] the Supreme Court reiterated the common law requirement that police officers must knock and announce their identity and purpose before entering a dwelling. Under certain conditions, known as **exigent circumstances**, law enforcement officers need not announce themselves. As determined by the courts, these circumstances include situations in which the officers have a reasonable belief of any of the following:

- The suspect is armed and poses a strong threat of violence to the officers or others inside the dwelling.
- Persons inside the dwelling are in the process of destroying evidence or escaping because of the presence of the police.
- A felony is being committed at the time the officers enter.[82]

Figure 6.3 Example of an Arrest Warrant

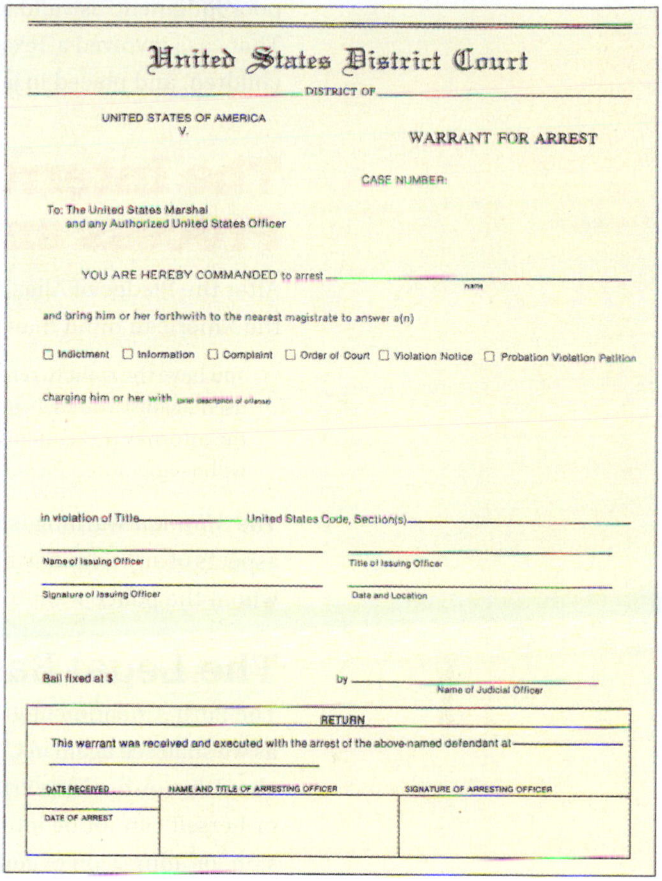

United States District Court

DISTRICT OF

UNITED STATES OF AMERICA
V.

WARRANT FOR ARREST

CASE NUMBER:

To: The United States Marshal
and any Authorized United States Officer

YOU ARE HEREBY COMMANDED to arrest ______ name

and bring him or her forthwith to the nearest magistrate to answer a(n)

☐ Indictment ☐ Information ☐ Complaint ☐ Order of Court ☐ Violation Notice ☐ Probation Violation Petition

charging him or her with (brief description of offense)

in violation of Title ______ United States Code, Section(s) ______

Name of Issuing Officer | Title of Issuing Officer

Signature of Issuing Officer | Date and Location

Bail fixed at $ ______ by ______ Name of Judicial Officer

RETURN

This warrant was received and executed with the arrest of the above-named defendant at ______

DATE RECEIVED	NAME AND TITLE OF ARRESTING OFFICER	SIGNATURE OF ARRESTING OFFICER
DATE OF ARREST		

The Waiting Period The Supreme Court severely weakened the practical impact of the "knock-and-announce" rule with its decision in *Hudson v. Michigan* (2006).[83] In that case, Detroit police did not knock before entering the defendant's home with a warrant. Instead, they announced themselves and then waited only three to five seconds before making their entrance, not the fifteen to twenty seconds suggested by a prior Court ruling.[84] Hudson argued that the drugs found during the subsequent search were inadmissible because the law enforcement agents did not follow proper procedure.

By a 5–4 margin, the Court disagreed. In his majority opinion, Justice Antonin Scalia stated that an improper "knock and announce" is not unreasonable enough to provide defendants with a "get-out-of-jail-free card" by disqualifying evidence uncovered on the basis of a valid search warrant.[85] Thus, the exclusionary rule, discussed earlier in this chapter, would no longer apply under such circumstances. Legal experts still advise, however, that police observe a reasonable waiting period after knocking and announcing to be certain that any evidence found during the subsequent search will stand up in court.[86]

Arrests without a Warrant

Arrest warrants are not always required, and in fact, most arrests are made on the scene without a warrant. A law enforcement officer may make a **warrantless arrest** if:

1. The offense is committed in the presence of the officer; or
2. The officer has probable cause to believe that the suspect has committed a particular crime; or
3. The time lost in obtaining a warrant would allow the suspect to escape or destroy evidence, and the officer has probable cause to make an arrest.[87]

The type of crime also comes to bear in questions of arrests without a warrant. As a general rule, officers can make a warrantless arrest for a crime they did not see if they have probable cause to believe that a felony has been committed. For misdemeanors, the crime must have been committed in the presence of the officer for a warrantless arrest to be valid. According to a 2001 Supreme Court ruling, even an arrest for a misdemeanor

exigent circumstances Situations that require extralegal or exceptional actions by the police.

warrantless arrest An arrest made without first seeking a warrant for the action.

that involves "gratuitous humiliations" imposed by a police officer "exercising extremely poor judgment" is valid as long as the officer can satisfy probable cause requirements.[88] That case involved a Texas mother who was handcuffed, taken away from her two young children, and placed in jail for failing to wear her seat belt.

The Interrogation Process and *Miranda*

After the Pledge of Allegiance, there is perhaps no recitation that comes more readily to the American mind than the *Miranda* warning:

> You have the right to remain silent. If you give up that right, anything you say can and will be used against you in a court of law. You have the right to speak with an attorney and to have the attorney present during questioning. If you so desire and cannot afford one, an attorney will be appointed for you without charge before questioning.

The *Miranda* warning is not a mere prop. It strongly affects one of the most important aspects of any criminal investigation—the **interrogation**, or questioning of a suspect from whom the police want to get information concerning a crime and perhaps a confession.

The Legal Basis for *Miranda*

The Fifth Amendment guarantees protection against self-incrimination. In other words, as we shall see again in Chapter 8, a defendant cannot be required to provide information about his or her own criminal activity. A defendant's choice *not* to incriminate himself or herself cannot be interpreted as a sign of guilt by a jury in a criminal trial. A confession, or admission of guilt, is by definition a statement of self-incrimination. How, then, to reconcile the Fifth Amendment with the critical need of law enforcement officers to gain confessions? The answer lies in the concept of **coercion**, or the use of physical or psychological duress to obtain a confession.

When a law enforcement official uses physical force during the interrogation process, it is relatively easy to determine that a suspect's confession has been improperly coerced and is therefore invalid. In handing down its *Miranda* decision,[89] which established the ***Miranda* rights**, the Supreme Court was more concerned with what Columbia University law professor H. Richard Uviller called *inherent coercion.* This term refers to the assumption that even if a police officer does not lay a hand on a suspect, the general atmosphere of an interrogation is in and of itself coercive.[90]

Though the *Miranda* case, decided in 1966, is best remembered for the procedural requirement it spurred, at the time the Supreme Court was more concerned about the treatment of suspects during interrogation. (See the feature *Landmark Cases*—Miranda v. Arizona.) The Court found that routine police interrogation strategies, such as leaving suspects alone in a room for several hours before questioning them, were inherently coercive. Therefore, the Court reasoned, every suspect needed protection from coercion, not just those who had been physically abused. The *Miranda* warning is a result of this need. In theory, if the warning is not given to a suspect before an interrogation, the fruits of that interrogation, including a confession, are invalid.

interrogation The direct questioning of a suspect to gather evidence of criminal activity and to try to gain a confession.

coercion The use of physical force or mental intimidation to compel a person to do something—such as confess to committing a crime—against her or his will.

***Miranda* rights** The constitutional rights of accused persons taken into custody by law enforcement officials, such as the right to remain silent and the right to counsel.

When a *Miranda* Warning Is Required

As we shall see, a *Miranda* warning is not necessary under several conditions, such as when no questions are asked of the suspect. Generally, *Miranda* requirements apply only when a suspect is in **custody**. In a series of rulings since *Miranda*, the Supreme Court has defined custody as an arrest or a situation in which a reasonable person would not feel free to leave.[91] Consequently, a **custodial interrogation** occurs when a suspect is under arrest or is deprived of her or his freedom in a significant manner.

Remember, a *Miranda* warning is only required before a custodial interrogation takes place. For example, if four police officers enter a suspect's bedroom at 4:00 A.M., wake him, and form a circle around him, then they must give him a *Miranda* warning before questioning. Even though the suspect has not been arrested, he will "not feel free to go where he please[s]."[92]

custody The forceful detention of a person, or the perception that a person is not free to leave the immediate vicinity.

custodial interrogation The questioning of a suspect after that person has been taken into custody. In this situation, the suspect must be read his or her *Miranda* rights before interrogation can begin.

Landmark Cases

Miranda v Arizona

Learning Objective

7 Explain why the U.S. Supreme Court established the *Miranda* warnings.

In 1963, a rape and kidnapping victim identified produce worker Ernesto Miranda as her assailant in a lineup. Phoenix detectives questioned Miranda for two hours concerning the crimes, at no time informing him that he had a right to have an attorney present. When the police emerged from the session, they had a signed statement by Miranda confessing to the crimes. He was subsequently convicted and sentenced to twenty to thirty years in prison. After the conviction was confirmed by the Arizona Supreme Court, Miranda appealed to the United States Supreme Court, claiming that he had not been warned that any statement he made could be used against him, and that he had a right to counsel during the interrogation.

Miranda v. Arizona
United States Supreme Court
384 U.S. 436 (1966)

In the Words of the Court . . .

Chief Justice Warren, Majority Opinion

* * * *

The cases before us raise questions which go to the roots of our concepts of American criminal jurisprudence: the restraints society must observe consistent with the Federal Constitution in prosecuting individuals for crime. More specifically, we deal with the admissibility of statements obtained from an individual who is subjected to custodial police interrogation and the necessity for procedures which assure that the individual is accorded his privilege under the Fifth Amendment to the Constitution not to be compelled to incriminate himself.

* * * *

It is obvious that such an interrogation environment is created for no purpose other than to subjugate the individual to the will of his examiner. This atmosphere carries its own badge of intimidation. To be sure, this is not physical intimidation, but it is equally destructive of human dignity. The current practice of incommunicado interrogation is at odds with one of our Nation's most cherished principles—that the individual may not be compelled to incriminate himself. Unless adequate protective devices are employed to dispel the compulsion inherent in custodial surroundings, no statement obtained from the defendant can truly be the product of his free choice.

Decision

The Court overturned Miranda's conviction, stating that police interrogations are, by their very nature, coercive and therefore deny suspects their constitutional right against self-incrimination by "forcing" them to confess. Consequently, any person who has been arrested and placed in custody must be informed of his or her right to be free from self-incrimination and to be represented by counsel during any interrogation. In other words, suspects must be told that they *do not have* to answer police questions. To accomplish this, the Court established the *Miranda* warning, which must be read prior to questioning a suspect in custody.

For Critical Analysis

What is meant by the sentence "Coercion can be mental as well as physical"? What role does the concept of "mental coercion" play in Chief Justice Warren's opinion?

When a *Miranda* Warning Is Not Required

A *Miranda* warning is not necessary in a number of situations:

Learning Objective

8 Indicate situations in which a *Miranda* warning is unnecessary.

1. When the police do not ask the suspect any questions that are *testimonial* in nature. Such questions are designed to elicit information that may be used against the suspect in court. Note that "routine booking questions," such as the suspect's name, address, height, and eye color, do not require a *Miranda* warning. Even though answering these questions may provide incriminating evidence (especially if the person answering is a prime suspect), the Supreme Court has held that they are absolutely necessary if the police are to do their jobs.[93] (Imagine the officer not being able to ask a suspect her or his name.)
2. When the police have not focused on a suspect and are questioning witnesses at the scene of a crime.
3. When a person volunteers information before the police have asked a question.
4. When the suspect has given a private statement to a friend or some other acquaintance. *Miranda* does not apply to these statements so long as the government did not orchestrate the situation.
5. During a stop and frisk, when no arrest has been made.
6. During a traffic stop.[94]

Public Safety In 1984, the Supreme Court also created a "public-safety exception" to the *Miranda* rule. The case involved a police officer who, after feeling an empty shoulder holster on a man he had just arrested, asked the suspect the location of the gun without informing him of his *Miranda* rights. The Court ruled that the gun was admissible as evidence because the police's duty to protect the public is more important than a suspect's *Miranda* rights.[95] In April 2013, federal law enforcement agents relied on this exception to question Boston Marathon bomber Dzhokhar Tsarnaev from a hospital bed without first "Mirandizing" him. Once the agents were satisfied that Tsarnaev knew of no other active plots or threats to public safety, they read the suspect his *Miranda* rights in the presence of a lawyer.[96]

▲ Study the details of this photo of an Aspen, Colorado, police officer and a suspect. **Why must the officer "Mirandize" the suspect before asking him any questions, even if the officer never formally places the suspect under arrest?** Chris Hondros/Getty Images

Waiving *Miranda* Suspects can *waive* their Fifth Amendment rights and speak to a police officer, but only if the waiver is made voluntarily. Silence on the part of a suspect does not mean that his or her *Miranda* protections have been relinquished. To waive their rights, suspects must state—either in writing or orally—that they understand those rights and that they will voluntarily answer questions without the presence of counsel.

To ensure that the suspect's rights are upheld, prosecutors are required to prove by a preponderance of the evidence that the suspect "knowingly and intelligently" waived his or her *Miranda* rights.[97] To make the waiver perfectly clear, police will ask suspects two questions in addition to giving the *Miranda* warning:

1. Do you understand your rights as I have read them to you?
2. Knowing your rights, are you willing to talk to another law enforcement officer or me?

If the suspect indicates that she or he does not want to speak to the officer, thereby invoking her or his right to silence, the officer must *immediately* stop any questioning.[98] Similarly, if the suspect requests a lawyer, the police can ask no further questions until an attorney is present.[99]

The Weakening of *Miranda*

Over the past several decades, a series of Supreme Court rulings have created numerous exceptions to the rules of interrogations set forth by the original *Miranda* decision. One such exception, created by the Supreme Court in 2004, is crucial to understanding the status of *Miranda* rights in current criminal law. The case involved a Colorado defendant who voluntarily told the police the location of his gun (which, being an ex-felon, he was not allowed to possess) without being read his rights.[100] The Court upheld the conviction, finding that the *Miranda* warning is merely *prophylactic*. In other words, it is only intended to prevent violations of the Fifth Amendment. Because only the gun, and not the defendant's testimony, was presented at trial, the police had not violated the defendant's constitutional rights.

In essence, the Court was ruling that the "fruit of the poisoned tree" doctrine, discussed earlier in this chapter, does not bar the admission of physical evidence that is discovered based on voluntary statements by a suspect who has not been "Mirandized." (See Figure 6.4 for a rundown of several other significant Court rulings that have weakened the *Miranda* requirements over the past decades.)

Figure 6.4 Supreme Court Decisions Eroding *Miranda* Rights

Moran v. Burbine (475 U.S. 412 [1986]). **This case established that police officers are not required to tell suspects undergoing custodial interrogation that their attorney is trying to reach them.** The Court ruled that events that the suspect could have no way of knowing about have no bearing on the ability to waive his or her *Miranda* rights.

Arizona v. Fulminante (499 U.S. 279 [1991]). **In this very important ruling, the Court held that a conviction is not automatically overturned if the suspect was coerced into making a confession.** If the other evidence introduced at the trial is strong enough to justify a conviction without the confession, then the fact that the confession was illegally gained can be, for all intents and purposes, ignored.

Texas v. Cobb (532 U.S. 162 [2001]). When a suspect refuses to waive his or her *Miranda* rights, a police officer cannot lawfully continue the interrogation until the suspect's attorney arrives on the scene. In this case, however, **the Court held that a suspect may be questioned without having a lawyer present if the interrogation does not focus on the crime for which he or she was arrested,** even though it does touch on another, closely related, offense.

Florida v. Powell (559 U.S. 50 [2010]). Florida's version of the *Miranda* warning informs suspects that they have a right "to talk with an attorney" but does not clearly inform them of the right to a lawyer during any police interrogation. The Court upheld Florida's warning, **ruling that different jurisdictions may use whatever version of the *Miranda* warning they please, as long as it reasonably conveys the essential information about a suspect's rights.**

Maryland v. Shatzer (559 U.S. 98 [2010]). **The Court announced a new rule that permits police to resume questioning of a suspect two weeks after that suspect has invoked her or his *Miranda* rights and been released from custody.** The Court reasoned that fourteen days "provides plenty of time for the suspect to get reacclimated to his normal life . . . and to shake off any residual coercive effect of his prior custody."

Berghuis v. Thompkins (560 U.S. 370 [2010]). The Court upheld the conviction of a suspect who implicated himself in a murder after remaining mostly silent during three hours of police questioning. The Court rejected the claim that the defendant invoked his *Miranda* rights by being uncommunicative, holding that **silence is not enough—the suspect must actually state that he or she wishes to cut off questioning for the *Miranda* protections to apply.**

False Confessions

While observing more than two hundred interrogations over a nine-month period in northern California, University of San Francisco law professor Richard Leo noted that more than 80 percent of the suspects waived their *Miranda* rights.[101] Apparently, the suspects wanted to appear cooperative, a "willingness to please" that contributes to the troubling phenomenon of *false confessions* in the American criminal justice system.

Coercion and False Confessions

A **false confession** occurs when a suspect admits to a crime that she or he did not actually commit. Given that juries tend to place a great deal of weight on admissions, sometimes to the exclusion of other evidence,

false confession An admission of guilt when the confessor did not, in fact, commit the crime.

false confessions can have disastrous consequences for a defendant in court. About one in four wrongful convictions overturned by DNA evidence are at least partially the result of a false confession.[102]

The Reid Technique One theory holds that this high incidence of false confessions is linked to the prevailing method of law enforcement interrogation in this country.[103] This method, called the Reid Technique, is premised on the assumption that all interrogation subjects are guilty. Police officers trained in this method reject any denials during the interrogation. They are also taught to minimize the moral seriousness of the crime, and to present the suspect's actions as the lesser of two evils. ("Was this your idea, or did your buddies talk you into it?") When the suspect finally does admit to the crime, he or she is to be congratulated and immediately asked for corroborating details.[104]

CJ Policy—Your Take

Every police officer in England receives training in the **PEACE method of interrogation.** Instead of relying on confrontation, this technique starts with a long series of open-ended questions to gather evidence and information. Then, the suspect is requestioned several times to determine whether there are any dubious discrepancies in his or her story. **How might the PEACE method reduce false confessions? Should it replace the Reid Technique in the United States? Why or why not?**

Pressure Points Critics believe that the Reid Technique creates feelings of helplessness in the suspect, and turns a confession into an "escape hatch" from the unpleasantness of the interrogation.[105] In 1983, for example, after five hours of questioning with no lawyer present, Henry Lee McCollum told police that he was involved in the rape and murder of an eleven-year-old girl. He was eventually sentenced to death for the crimes. "I had never been under this much pressure, with a person hollering at me and threatening me," McCollum said in 2014, when a North Carolina judge declared him innocent and released him from prison. "I just made up a story and gave it to them so they would let me go home."[106]

Another potential problem with the Reid Technique, noted earlier, is that it is predicated on the assumption that the suspect is guilty.[107] Because both guilty and innocent suspects show stress when being interrogated by police, the interrogator may be "fooled" by an innocent person's evasive and nervous behavior. An alternative method of police interrogation, which resembles a journalistic interview rather than psychological combat, is the subject of this chapter's *CJ Policy—Your Take* feature.

Recording Confessions As with body-worn cameras (discussed in the previous chapter), the mandatory videotaping of interrogations has been offered as a means to promote police accountability. About one thousand law enforcement agencies, including the Federal Bureau of Investigation and the Drug Enforcement Administration, now regularly record police interviews, particularly as part of felony investigations.[108]

In theory, such recordings will make clear any improper tactics used by law enforcement to gain a confession. In reality, this strategy might not live up to reformers' expectations. As Professor Jennifer Mnookin of the University of California, Los Angeles, points out, there is no guarantee that "judges or jurors can actually tell the difference between true and false confessions, even with the more complete record of interactions that recorded interrogations provide."[109]

Ethics Challenge

Police in Troy, New York, told a suspect that his son's life could be saved only if the suspect explained how the boy had injured his head. In fact, the child was already brain dead, which the suspect did not known when he admitted to slamming his son's head against a mattress. Law enforcement agents can use deception when interviewing suspects to gain a confession. Even so, did the Troy police behave ethically in this instance? Explain your answer.

Summary

For more information on these concepts, look back to the Learning Objective icons throughout the chapter.

1 Outline the four major sources that may provide probable cause. (a) Personal observation, usually due to an officer's personal training, experience, and expertise; (b) information, gathered from informants, eyewitnesses, victims, police bulletins, and other sources; (c) evidence, which often has to be in plain view; and (d) association, which generally must involve a person with a known criminal background who is seen in a place where criminal activity is openly taking place.

2 Explain the exclusionary rule and the exceptions to it. This rule prohibits illegally seized evidence, or evidence obtained by an unreasonable search and seizure in an inadmissible way, from being used against the accused in criminal court. Exceptions to the exclusionary rule are the "inevitable discovery" exception established in *Nix v. Williams* and the "good faith" exception established in *United States v. Leon* and *Arizona v. Evans.*

3 Explain when searches can be made without a warrant. Searches and seizures can be made without a warrant if they are incidental to an arrest (but they must be reasonable); when they are made with voluntary consent; when they involve the "movable vehicle" exception; when property has been abandoned; and when items are in plain view, under certain restricted circumstances (see *Coolidge v. New Hampshire*).

4 Describe the plain view doctrine and indicate one of its limitations. Under the plain view doctrine, police officers are justified in seizing an item if (a) the item is easily seen by an officer who is legally in a position to notice it; (b) the discovery of the item is unintended; and (c) the officer, without further investigation, immediately recognizes the illegal nature of the item. An item is not in plain view if the law enforcement agent needs to use technology such as a thermal imager to "see" it.

5 Distinguish between a stop and a frisk, and indicate the importance of the case *Terry v. Ohio*. Though the terms *stop* and *frisk* are often used in concert, a stop is the separate act of detaining a suspect when an officer reasonably believes that a criminal activity is about to take place. A frisk is the physical "pat-down" of a suspect. In *Terry v. Ohio,* the Supreme Court ruled that an officer must have "specific and articulable facts" before making a stop, but those facts may be "taken together with rational inferences."

6 List the four elements that must be present for an arrest to take place. (a) Intent, (b) authority, (c) seizure or detention, and (d) the understanding of the person that he or she has been arrested.

7 Explain why the U.S. Supreme Court established the *Miranda* warnings. The Supreme Court recognized that police interrogations are, by their nature, coercive. Consequently, to protect a suspect's constitutional rights during interrogation, the Court ruled that the suspect must be informed of those rights before being questioned.

8 Indicate situations in which a *Miranda* warning is unnecessary. (a) When no questions that are testimonial in nature are asked of the suspect; (b) when there is no suspect and witnesses in general are being questioned at the scene of a crime; (c) when a person volunteers information before the police ask anything; (d) when a suspect has given a private statement to a friend without the government orchestrating it; (e) during a stop and frisk when no arrests have been made; (f) during a traffic stop; and (g) when a threat to public safety exists.

Questions for Critical Analysis

1. What are the two most significant legal concepts contained in the Fourth Amendment, and why are they important?
2. The Washington State Court of Appeals compared text messages to voice mail messages that can be overheard by anybody in a room. Using this logic, the court upheld a conviction based on text messages seized by police. Do you agree that people do not have a reasonable expectation of privacy when it comes to their text messaging? Why or why not?
3. Suppose a suspect refuses to consent to a warrantless search of his home in connection with a robbery investigation. Police then arrest the suspect for abusing his domestic partner, who consents to a search of the home she shares with the suspect while he is in jail. Should such searches over the objection of an absent resident be allowed? Why or why not?
4. In Belgium, law enforcement agents are prohibited from entering private homes without consent from 9 P.M. to 5 A.M. What do you think is the reasoning behind this ban on nighttime raids? What might be some unintended consequences of the ban?
5. If, during questioning, a suspect says, "Maybe I should talk to a lawyer," should police immediately stop the interrogation? Why or why not? (To see how the Supreme Court ruled on this matter, search for ***Davis v. United States* [1994]** online.)

Key Terms

affidavit 172
arrest 182
arrest warrant 184
coercion 186
consent searches 174
custodial interrogation 187
custody 187
electronic surveillance 178
exclusionary rule 169
exigent circumstances 185
false confession 189
frisk 181
fruit of the poisoned tree 169
"good faith" exception 170
"inevitable discovery" exception 170
interrogation 186
Miranda rights 186
plain view doctrine 177
probable cause 167
racial profiling 182
search 171
searches and seizures 167
searches incidental to arrests 174
search warrant 172
seizure 172
stop 181
warrantless arrest 185

Notes

1. *Rodriguez v. United States,* 575 U.S. ____ (2015).
2. *Illinois v. Caballes,* 543 U.S. 407 (2005).
3. *Michigan v. Summers,* 452 U.S. 692 (1981).
4. *Brinegar v. United States,* 338 U.S. 160 (1949).
5. Rolando V. del Carmen, *Criminal Procedure for Law Enforcement Personnel* (Monterey, Calif.: Brooks/Cole Publishing Co., 1987), 63–64.
6. *Maryland v. Pringle,* 540 U.S. 366 (2003).
7. 500 U.S. 44 (1991).
8. *United States v. Leon,* 468 U.S. 897 (1984).
9. Thomas Y. Davis, "A Hard Look at What We Know (and Still Need to Learn) about the 'Costs' of the Exclusionary Rule: The NIJ Study and Other Studies of 'Lost' Arrests," *A.B.F. Research Journal* (1983), 680.
10. 430 U.S. 387 (1977).
11. 467 U.S. 431 (1984).
12. 468 U.S. 897 (1984).
13. 514 U.S. 1 (1995).
14. *California v. Greenwood,* 486 U.S. 35 (1988).
15. *Ibid.*
16. 389 U.S. 347 (1967).
17. *Ibid.,* 361.
18. 486 U.S. 35 (1988).
19. *Ibid.*
20. 565 U.S. _____ (2012).
21. *Ibid.*
22. Quoted in James Vicini, "Supreme Court Limits Police Use of GPS to Track Suspects," *Reuters* (January 23, 2012).
23. *Coolidge v. New Hampshire,* 403 U.S. 443, 467 (1971).
24. *Millender v. Messerschmidt,* 620 F.3d 1016 (9th Cir. 2010).
25. del Carmen, *op. cit.,* 158.
26. *Katz v. United States,* 389 U.S. 347, 357 (1967).
27. *Brigham City v. Stuart,* 547 U.S. 398 (2006).
28. 414 U.S. 234–235 (1973).
29. 395 U.S. 752 (1969).
30. *Ibid.,* 763.
31. Carl A. Benoit, "Questioning 'Authority': Fourth Amendment Consent Searches," *FBI Law Enforcement Bulletin* (July 2008), 24.
32. *Bumper v. North Carolina,* 391 U.S. 543 (1968).
33. *State v. Stone,* 362 N.C. 50, 653 S.E.2d 414 (2007).
34. 412 U.S. 218 (1973).
35. *Ohio v. Robinette,* 519 U.S. 33 (1996).
36. Jayme W. Holcomb, "Knock and Talks," *FBI Law Enforcement Bulletin* (August 2006), 22–32.
37. 267 U.S. 132 (1925).

38. *United States v. Ross,* 456 U.S. 798, 804–809 (1982); and *Chambers v. Maroney,* 399 U.S. 42, 44, 52 (1970).
39. 453 U.S. 454 (1981).
40. *Arizona v. Gant,* 556 U.S. 332 (2009).
41. Adam Liptak, "Justices Significantly Cut Back Officers' Searches of Cars of People They Arrest," *New York Times* (April 22, 2009), A12.
42. Dale Anderson and Dave Cole, "Search and Seizure after *Arizona v. Gant,*" *Arizona Attorney* (October 2009), 15.
43. *Whren v. United States,* 517 U.S. 806 (1996).
44. 403 U.S. 443 (1971).
45. *Kyollo v. United States,* 533 U.S. 27 (2001).
46. 388 U.S. 42 (1967).
47. 18 U.S.C. Sections 2510(7), 2518(1)(a), 2516 (1994).
48. Christopher K. Murphy, "Electronic Surveillance," in "Twenty-Sixth Annual Review of Criminal Procedure," *Georgetown Law Journal* (April 1997), 920.
49. *United States v. Nguyen,* 46 F.3d 781, 783 (8th Cir. 1995).
50. Joseph Siprut, "Privacy through Anonymity: An Economic Argument for Expanding the Right of Privacy in Public Places," *Pepperdine Law Review* 33 (2006), 311, 320.
51. Justin Jouvenal, "The New Way Police Are Surveilling You: Calculating Your Threat 'Score,'" *Washington Post* (January 10, 2016), at **www.washingtonpost.com/local/public-safety/the-new-way-police-are-surveilling-you-calculating-your-threat-score/2016/01/10/e42bccac-8e15-11e5-baf4-bdf37355da0c_story.html.**
52. Bureau of Justice Statistics, *Local Police Departments, 2013: Equipment and Technology* (Washington, D.C.: U.S. Department of Justice, July 2015), Table 3, page 4.
53. "The StingRay's Tale," *The Economist* (January 30, 2016), 24, 26.
54. *California v. Riley,* 134 S.Ct. 2473 (2014).
55. *Ibid.,* 2485.
56. *Ibid.,* 2473.
57. Karen M. Hess and Henry M. Wrobleski, *Police Operation: Theory and Practice* (St. Paul, Minn.: West Publishing Co., 1997), 122.
58. 392 U.S. 1 (1968).
59. *Ibid.,* 20.
60. *Ibid.,* 21.
61. See *United States v. Cortez,* 449 U.S. 411 (1981); and *United States v. Sokolow,* 490 U.S. 1 (1989).
62. *United States v. Arvizu,* 534 U.S. 266 (2002).
63. *Ibid.,* 270.
64. *United States v. Place,* 462 U.S. 696 (1983).
65. *Hibel v. Sixth Judicial District Court,* 542 U.S. 177 (2004).
66. *Ibid.,* 182.
67. *Minnesota v. Dickerson,* 508 U.S. 366 (1993).
68. *Arizona v. Johnson,* 555 U.S. 328 (2009).
69. *United States v. Avery,* 137 F.3d 343, 353 (6th Cir. 1997).
70. The American Civil Liberties Union Racial Justice Program and American Civil Liberties Union of Florida, *Racial Disparities in Florida Safety Belt Law Enforcement* (New York: American Civil Liberties Union, January 2016), 1, 3.
71. Lynn Langton and Matthew Durose, *Police Behavior during Traffic and Street Stops* (Washington, D.C.: U.S. Department of Justice, September 2013), Table 7, page 9.
72. *Born Suspect: Stop-and-Frisk Abuses & the Continued Fight to End Racial Profiling in America* (Baltimore, Md.: National Association for the Advancement of Colored People, September 2014), Appendix 1.
73. Arizona Revised Statutes Sections 11-1051(B), 13-1509, 13-2929(C).
74. *Arizona v. United States,* 567 U.S. ___ (2012).
75. Julia Preston, "Immigration Ruling Leaves Issues Unresolved," *New York Times* (June 27, 2012), A14.
76. *Local Perspectives on State Immigration Policies* (Washington, D.C.: Police Executive Research Forum, July 2014), 9–12.
77. Rolando V. del Carmen and Jeffrey T. Walker, *Briefs of Leading Cases in Law Enforcement,* 2d ed. (Cincinnati, Ohio: Anderson, 1995), 38–40.
78. *Florida v. Royer,* 460 U.S. 491 (1983).
79. See also *United States v. Mendenhall,* 446 U.S. 544 (1980).
80. del Carmen, *op. cit.,* 97–98.
81. 514 U.S. 927 (1995).
82. Linda J. Collier and Deborah D. Rosenbloom, *American Jurisprudence,* 2d ed. (Rochester, N.Y.: Lawyers Cooperative Publishing, 1995), 122.
83. 547 U.S. 586 (2006).
84. *United States v. Banks,* 540 U.S. 31, 41 (2003).
85. *Hudson v. Michigan,* 547 U.S. 586, 593 (2006).
86. Tom Van Dorn, "Violation of Knock-and-Announce Rule Does Not Require Suppression of All Evidence Found in Search," *The Police Chief* (October 2006), 10.
87. "Warrantless Searches and Seizures" in *Georgetown Law Journal Annual Review of Criminal Procedure, 2011* (Washington, D.C.: Georgetown Law Journal, 2011), 955.
88. *Atwater v. City of Lago Vista,* 532 U.S. 318, 346–347 (2001).
89. *Miranda v. Arizona,* 384 U.S. 436 (1966).
90. H. Richard Uviller, *Tempered Zeal* (Chicago: Contemporary Books, 1988), 188–198.
91. *Orozco v. Texas,* 394 U.S. 324 (1969); *Oregon v. Mathiason,* 429 U.S. 492 (1977); and *California v. Beheler,* 463 U.S. 1121 (1983).
92. *Orozco v. Texas, op. cit.,* 325.
93. *Pennsylvania v. Muniz,* 496 U.S. 582 (1990).
94. del Carmen, *op. cit.,* 267–268.
95. *New York v. Quarles,* 467 U.S. 649 (1984).
96. Ethan Bronner and Michael S. Schmidt, "In Questions at First, No *Miranda* for Suspect," *New York Times* (April 23, 2013), A13.
97. *Moran v. Burbine,* 475 U.S. 412 (1986).
98. *Michigan v. Mosley,* 423 U.S. 96 (1975).
99. *Fare v. Michael C.,* 442 U.S. 707, 723–724 (1979).
100. *United States v. Patane,* 542 U.S. 630 (2004).
101. Richard A. Leo, "Inside the Interrogation Room," *Journal of Criminal Law and Criminology* (1996), 266.
102. The Innocence Project, "False Confessions or Admissions," at **www.innocenceproject.org/causes-wrongful-conviction/false-confessions-or-admissions.**
103. Saul M. Kassin, "Internalized False Confessions," in *Handbook of Eyewitness Psychology, Vol. 1,* eds. Michael P. Toglia et al. (New York: Psychology Press, 2007), 171.
104. Douglas Starr, "The Interview: Do Police Interrogation Techniques Produce False Confessions?" *The New Yorker* (December 9, 2013), 43–44.
105. *Ibid.,* 44.
106. "Death Row Interview with Henry McCollum," *News and Observer* (Raleigh, N.C.) (August 30, 2014), at **www.youtube.com/watch?v=NxV6PWfa7i8.**
107. Gregg McCrary, quoted in Starr, *op. cit.,* 46.
108. The Innocence Project, "False Confessions & Recording of Custodial Interrogations," at **www.innocenceproject.org/free-innocent/improve-the-law/fact-sheets/false-confessions-recording-of-custodial-interrogations.**
109. Jennifer L. Mnookin, "Can a Jury Believe What It Sees?" *New York Times* (July 14, 2014), A19.

EQUAL JUSTICE UNDER LAW

Katherine Frey/The Washington Post/Getty Images

7

Courts and the Quest for Justice

Chapter Outline		Corresponding Learning Objectives
Functions of the Courts	1	Define and contrast the four functions of the courts.
The Basic Principles of the American Judicial System	2	Define *jurisdiction,* and contrast geographic and subject-matter jurisdiction.
	3	Explain the difference between trial and appellate courts.
State Court Systems	4	Outline the several levels of a typical state court system.
The Federal Court System	5	Outline the federal court system.
	6	Explain briefly how a case is brought to the United States Supreme Court.
Judges in the Court System	7	Explain the difference between the selection of judges at the state level and at the federal level.
The Courtroom Work Group	8	List the different names given to public prosecutors, and indicate the general powers that they have.
	9	Explain why defense attorneys must often defend clients they know to be guilty.

To target your study and review, look for these numbered Learning Objective icons throughout the chapter.

minor Threat?

after Anthony Elonis's wife Tara left him, taking their children with her, his online behavior became increasingly erratic. Elonis began posting violent rap lyrics on Facebook aimed at Tara, including "If I only knew then what I know now . . . I would have smothered your ass with a pillow. Dumped your body in the back seat. Dropped you off in Toad Creek and made it look like a rape and murder." He also wrote that he would like to see a Halloween costume of his wife's "head on a stick."

In due course, Elonis was arrested for breaking a federal law that makes it a crime to transmit "any communication containing . . . any threat to injure the person of another." At his trial, Elonis claimed that his remarks were nothing more than a form of therapy to help "deal with the pain" of separation from his family. "I would never hurt my wife," he told the jury. "I felt like I was being stalked," countered Tara during her testimony. "I felt extremely afraid for [my life] and my children's lives." The trial judge instructed the jurors to find Elonis guilty if a "reasonable person" would consider his statements "as a serious expression of an intention to inflict bodily injury or take the life of an individual." The jury did so, and he was sentenced to forty-four months in prison.

Elonis appealed his conviction, and the case eventually wound up before the United States Supreme Court. There, Elonis's attorneys argued that the prosecution should have been required to prove that he intended to harm his wife, *not* that she reasonably feared he would do so. In other words, the Court was asked to decide which point of view matters most in such cases—the speaker's or the listener's. In 2015, the justices decided in Elonis's favor by a 7–2 margin. Ordering a retrial, the Supreme Court ruled that the trial court had been wrong to convict Elonis without proving that he had intended for his violent online postings to be taken as threats by his wife. "Wrongdoing," explained Chief Justice John Roberts, Jr., "must be conscious to be criminal."

Win McNamee/Getty Images

▲ Explaining why the Supreme Court reversed the conviction of Anthony Elonis for threatening his estranged wife online, Chief Justice John Roberts, Jr. (shown here), said that a lower court should have taken the defendant's state of mind into consideration.

1. What is your opinion of the United States Supreme Court's ruling in this case?
2. In defending his actions, Anthony Elonis compared himself to well-known rap artists such as Eminem who routinely use violent imagery in their lyrics without facing criminal charges. If you were opposing Elonis in court, how would you counter this argument?
3. Justice Samuel Alito, Jr., proposed a new rule for such situations: a person is guilty of making a threat if the violent words were uttered recklessly. After reviewing the recklessness standard in Chapter 3, what do you think of Alito's suggestion? Would application of this standard have resulted in Elonis's conviction? Why or why not?

Functions of the Courts

The United States Supreme Court's decision in *Elonis v. United States* (2015)[1] poses a difficult challenge for American courts—to establish the true motives of defendants such as Anthony Elonis who make online threats. "How does one prove what's in somebody else's mind?" asked Supreme Court justice Ruth Bader Ginsburg.[2] Along those same lines, Cindy Southworth of the National Network to End Domestic Violence points out that, "Every abuser says, 'I didn't mean for her to think I would kill her.'"[3]

On the other side, free speech advocates worry that "words are slippery things" and argue that laws disregarding the speaker's intent run the risk of punishing comments simply because they are "crudely" expressed.[4] As this example shows, court cases—particularly those that reach the Supreme Court—can operate on two levels. First and foremost, the proceedings must determine the guilt or innocence of the individual defendant charged with a crime. At the same time, a court's ruling can express ideas of fairness and justice that pertain to society as a whole.

Courts have extensive powers in our criminal justice system: they can bring the authority of the state to seize property and to restrict individual liberty. Given that the rights to own property and to enjoy personal freedom are enshrined in the U.S. Constitution, a court's *legitimacy* in taking such measures must be unquestioned by society. This legitimacy is based on two factors: impartiality and independence.[5] In theory, each party involved in a courtroom dispute must have an equal chance to present its case and must be secure in the belief that no outside factors are going to influence the decision rendered by the court. In reality, as we shall see over the next three chapters, it does not always work that way.

Due Process and Crime Control in the Courts

Learning Objective

1 Define and contrast the four functions of the courts.

As mentioned in Chapter 1, the criminal justice system has two sets of underlying values: due process and crime control. Due process values focus on protecting the rights of the individual, whereas crime control values stress the punishment and repression of criminal conduct. The competing nature of these two value systems is often evident in the nation's courts.

The Due Process Function The primary concern of early American courts was to protect the rights of the individual against the power of the state. Memories of injustices suffered at the hands of the British monarchy were still strong, and most of the procedural rules that we have discussed in this textbook were created with the express purpose of giving the individual a "fair chance" against the government in any courtroom proceedings. Therefore, the due process function of the courts is to protect individuals from the unfair advantages that the government—with its immense resources—automatically enjoys in legal battles.

Seen in this light, constitutional guarantees such as the right to counsel, the right to a jury trial, and protection from self-incrimination are equalizers in the "contest" between the state and the individual. The idea that the two sides in a courtroom dispute are adversaries is, as we shall discuss in the next chapter, fundamental in American courts.

The Crime Control Function Advocates of crime control distinguish between the court's obligation to be fair to the accused and its obligation to be fair to society. The crime control function of the courts emphasizes punishment and retribution—criminals must suffer for the harm done to society, and it is the courts' responsibility to see that they do so.

▲ Why is it important that American criminal courtrooms, such as this one in Cape May, New Jersey, are places of impartiality and independence?
AP Images/*The Press of Atlantic City*, Dale Gerhard

Given this responsibility to protect the public, deter criminal behavior, and "get criminals off the streets," the courts should not be concerned solely with giving the accused a fair chance. Rather than using due process rules as "equalizers," the courts should use them as protection against blatantly unconstitutional acts. For example, a detective who beats a suspect with a tire iron to get a confession has obviously infringed on the suspect's constitutional rights. If, however, the detective uses trickery to gain a confession, the court should allow the confession to stand because it is not in society's interest that law enforcement agents be deterred from outwitting criminals.

The Rehabilitation Function

A third view of the court's responsibility is based on the "medical model" of the criminal justice system. In this model, criminals are analogous to patients, and the courts perform the role of physicians who dispense "treatment."[6] The criminal is seen as sick, not evil, and therefore treatment is morally justified. Of course, treatment varies from case to case, and some criminals require harsh penalties such as incarceration. In other cases, however, it may not be in society's best interest for the criminal to be punished according to the formal rules of the justice system. Perhaps the criminal can be rehabilitated to become a productive member of society and thus save taxpayers the costs of incarceration or other punishment.

The Bureaucratic Function

To a certain extent, the crime control, due process, and rehabilitation functions of a court are secondary to its bureaucratic function. In general, a court may have the goal of protecting society or protecting the rights of the individual, but on a day-to-day basis that court has the more pressing task of dealing with the cases brought before it. Like any bureaucracy, a court is concerned with speed and efficiency, and loftier concepts such as justice can be secondary to a judge's need to wrap up a particular case before six o'clock so that administrative deadlines can be met. Indeed, many observers feel that the primary adversarial relationship in the courts is not between the two parties involved but between the ideal of justice and the reality of bureaucratic limitations.[7]

The Basic Principles of the American Judicial System

One of the most often cited limitations of the American judicial system is its complex nature. In truth, the United States does not have a single judicial system, but fifty-two different systems—one for each state, the District of Columbia, and the federal government. As each state has its own unique judiciary with its own set of rules, some of which may be in conflict with the federal judiciary, it is helpful at this point to discuss some basics—jurisdiction, trial and appellate courts, and the dual court system.

Jurisdiction

Learning Objective

2 Define *jurisdiction*, and contrast geographic and subject-matter jurisdiction.

In Latin, *juris* means "law," and *diction* means "to speak." Thus, **jurisdiction** literally refers to the power "to speak the law." Before any court can hear a case, it must have jurisdiction over the persons involved in the case or its subject matter. The jurisdiction of every court, even the United States Supreme Court, is limited in some way.

Geographic Jurisdiction One limitation is geographic. Generally, a court can exercise its authority over residents of a certain area. A state trial court, for example, normally has jurisdictional authority over crimes committed in a particular area of the state, such as a county or a district. A state's highest court (often called the state supreme court) has jurisdictional authority over the entire state, and the United States Supreme Court has jurisdiction over the entire country. For the most part, criminal jurisdiction is determined by legislation. The U.S. Congress or a state legislature can determine what acts are illegal within the geographic boundaries it controls, thus giving federal or state courts jurisdiction over those crimes.

Federal versus State Jurisdiction Most criminal laws are state laws, so the majority of all criminal trials are heard in state courts. Many acts that are illegal under state law, however, are also illegal under federal law. What happens when more than one court system has jurisdiction over the same criminal act? As a general rule, when Congress "criminalizes" behavior that is already prohibited under a state criminal code, the federal and state courts both have jurisdiction over that crime unless Congress states otherwise in the initial legislation. Thus, **concurrent jurisdiction**, which occurs when two different court systems have simultaneous jurisdiction over the same case, is quite common.

For instance, both the federal courts and the South Carolina state court system have jurisdiction over Dylann Roof, who allegedly killed nine African American parishioners during Bible study at a Charleston church in June 2015. Given the location of the crime, there was little question that Roof would face capital murder charges in state court, with that trial set to start in the summer of 2016. South Carolina does not, however, have a hate crime law, and federal officials felt that the racial component of Roof's actions needed to be addressed. So, he also faces thirty-three charges in federal court for federal hate crimes, firearms violations, and obstructing his victims' religious freedom. (See this chapter's *CJ Policy—Your Take* feature to consider concurrent jurisdiction in a different context.)

CJ Policy—Your Take

All fifty states have legislation that makes cruelty to animals a crime. Nevertheless, in 2015, several members of Congress introduced the Preventing Animal Cruelty and Torture (PACT) Act. The PACT Act would give the federal government the ability to investigate and prosecute certain acts of animal abuse. **What are some of the benefits of giving federal courts concurrent jurisdiction over a seemingly local crime such as animal abuse? What are some of the drawbacks of this proposed legislation? Explain your answers.**

Tribal Jurisdiction The 310 Native American reservations in the United States operate under an interesting geographic jurisdictional framework. Because of treaties with the federal government, tribes enjoy a considerable amount of self-rule on reservation land. Leaders of the Yakama Nation in Washington, for example, will not adhere to the recent state law legalizing marijuana.[8] Furthermore, in 2013 federal legislation gave tribal courts jurisdiction to investigate and prosecute non-Native suspects for committing crimes of domestic violence or dating violence against tribal members on tribal property.[9] These courts cannot, however, sentence most convicted defendants to more than three years in prison. Consequently, tribal leaders often ask the U.S. Department of Justice to prosecute, in federal court, serious crimes such as murder and rape that take place on reservations.

International Jurisdiction Under international law, each country has the right to create and enact criminal law for its territory. Therefore, the notion that a nation has

jurisdiction The authority of a court to hear and decide cases within an area of the law or a geographic territory.

concurrent jurisdiction The situation that occurs when two or more courts have the authority to preside over the same criminal case.

▲ Several years ago, Honduras extradited drug dealer Carlos Lobo, shown here with members of the Honduran military police, to the United States. **Should the possibility that Lobo was shipping cocaine into this country give the American court system jurisdiction over him? Why or why not?**
Orlando Sierra/AFP/Getty Images

jurisdiction over any crimes committed within its borders is well established. The situation becomes more delicate when one nation feels the need to go outside its own territory to enforce its criminal law. International precedent does, however, provide several bases for expanding jurisdiction across international borders.

For example, through either treaty-based agreements or case-by-case negotiations, one country may decide to *extradite* a criminal suspect to another country. **Extradition** is the formal process by which one legal authority, such as a state or a nation, transfers a fugitive or a suspect to another state or nation that has a valid claim on that person. In 2016, Mexico extradited Joaquin "El Chapo" Guzman to the United States to face murder and drug trafficking charges. According to federal prosecutors, Guzman's criminal network has been responsible for exporting thousands of pounds of cocaine onto American streets.

Subject-Matter Jurisdiction Jurisdiction over subject matter also acts as a limitation on the types of cases a court can hear. State court systems include courts of *general* (unlimited) *jurisdiction* and courts of *limited jurisdiction*. Courts of general jurisdiction have no restrictions on the subject matter they may address and therefore deal with the most serious felonies and civil cases. Courts of limited jurisdiction, also known as lower courts, handle misdemeanors and civil matters under a certain amount, usually $1,000.

As we will discuss later in the chapter, many states have created special subject-matter courts that only dispose of cases involving a specific crime. For example, a number of jurisdictions have established drug courts to handle an overload of illicit narcotics arrests. Furthermore, under the Uniform Code of Military Justice, the U.S. military has jurisdiction over active personnel who commit crimes, even if those crimes occur outside the course of duty.[10] In such cases, military officials can either attempt to *court-martial* the suspect in military court or allow civilian prosecutors to handle the case in state or federal court.

Trial and Appellate Courts

Another distinction is between courts of original jurisdiction and courts of appellate, or review, jurisdiction. Courts having *original jurisdiction* are courts of the first instance, or **trial courts**. Almost every case begins in a trial court. It is in this court that a trial (or a guilty plea) takes place, and the judge imposes a sentence if the defendant is found guilty. Trial courts are primarily concerned with *questions of fact*. They are designed to determine exactly what events occurred that are relevant to questions of the defendant's guilt or innocence.

Courts having *appellate jurisdiction* act as reviewing courts, or **appellate courts**. In general, cases can be brought before appellate courts only on appeal by one of the parties in the trial court. (Note that because of constitutional protections against being tried twice for the same crime, prosecutors who lose in criminal trial court *cannot*

extradition The process by which one jurisdiction surrenders a person accused or convicted of violating another jurisdiction's criminal law to the second jurisdiction.

trial courts Courts in which most cases begin and in which questions of fact are examined.

appellate courts Courts that review decisions made by lower courts, such as trial courts; also known as *courts of appeals*.

appeal the verdict.) An appellate court does not use juries or witnesses to reach its decision. Instead, its judges make a decision on whether the case should be *reversed* and *remanded,* or sent back to the court of original jurisdiction for a new trial. (We saw this occur in the opening of the chapter, when the United States Supreme Court—the nation's highest appellate court—ordered a retrial of Anthony Elonis with a different standard in place for determining his guilt.) Appellate judges present written explanations for their decisions, and these **opinions** of the court are the basis for a great deal of the precedent in the criminal justice system.

It is important to understand that appellate courts do not determine the defendant's guilt or innocence—they only make judgments on questions of procedure. In other words, they are concerned with *questions of law* and normally accept the facts as established by the trial court. Only rarely will an appeals court question a jury's decision. Instead, the appellate judges will review the manner in which the facts and evidence were provided to the jury and rule on whether errors were made in the process.

Learning Objective

3 Explain the difference between trial and appellate courts.

The Dual Court System

As we saw in Chapter 1, America's system of federalism allows the federal government and the governments of the fifty states to hold authority in many areas. As a result, the federal government and each of the fifty states, as well as the District of Columbia, have their own separate court systems. Because of the split between the federal courts and the state courts, this is known as the **dual court system**. (See Figure 7.1 to get a better idea of how federal and state courts operate as distinct yet parallel entities.)

Federal and state courts both have limited jurisdiction. Generally, federal courts preside over cases involving violations of federal law, and state courts preside over cases involving violations of state law. The distinction is not always clear, however. Federal courts have jurisdiction over more than 4,500 crimes, many of which also can be found in state criminal codes. As we saw earlier in this section, when such *concurrent jurisdiction* exists, both sides can try the defendant under their own laws, or one side can step aside and let the other decide the fate of the defendant. Because the federal court system has greater resources than most state court systems, federal criminal charges often take precedence over state criminal charges for practical reasons.

opinions Written statements by appellate judges expressing the reasons for the court's decision in a case.

dual court system The separate but interrelated court system of the United States, made up of the courts on the national level and the courts on the state level.

Figure 7.1 **The Dual Court System**

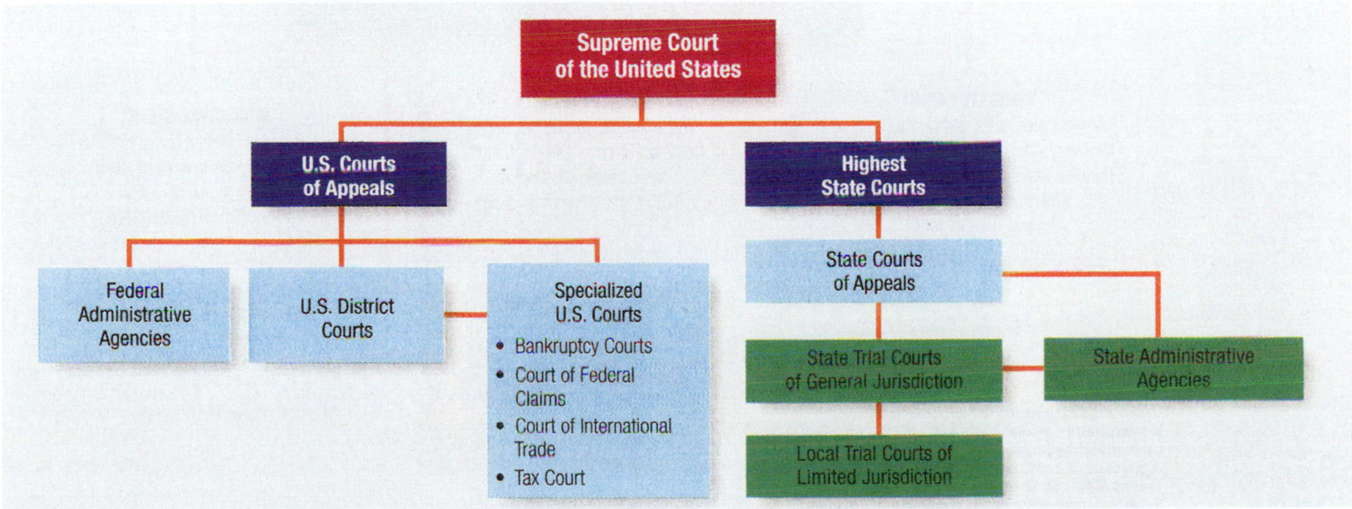

Ethics Challenge

The U.S. military opened fire on a hotel in Baghdad, Iraq, believing that enemy troops were hiding in the building. During the battle, a Spanish journalist named José Couso was killed in the hotel. Eight years later, a Spanish judge indicted three U.S. soldiers in connection with Couso's death. Would it have been ethical for the American government to send the soldiers to Spain for a criminal trial? Why or why not? ■

Learning Objective 4

Outline the several levels of a typical state court system.

State Court Systems

Typically, a state court system includes several levels, or tiers, of courts. State courts may include:

1. Lower courts, or courts of limited jurisdiction,
2. Trial courts of general jurisdiction,
3. Appellate courts, and
4. The state's highest court.

As previously mentioned, each state has a different judicial structure, in which different courts have different jurisdictions, but there are enough similarities to allow for a general discussion. Figure 7.2 shows a typical state court system.

Figure 7.2 A Typical State Court System

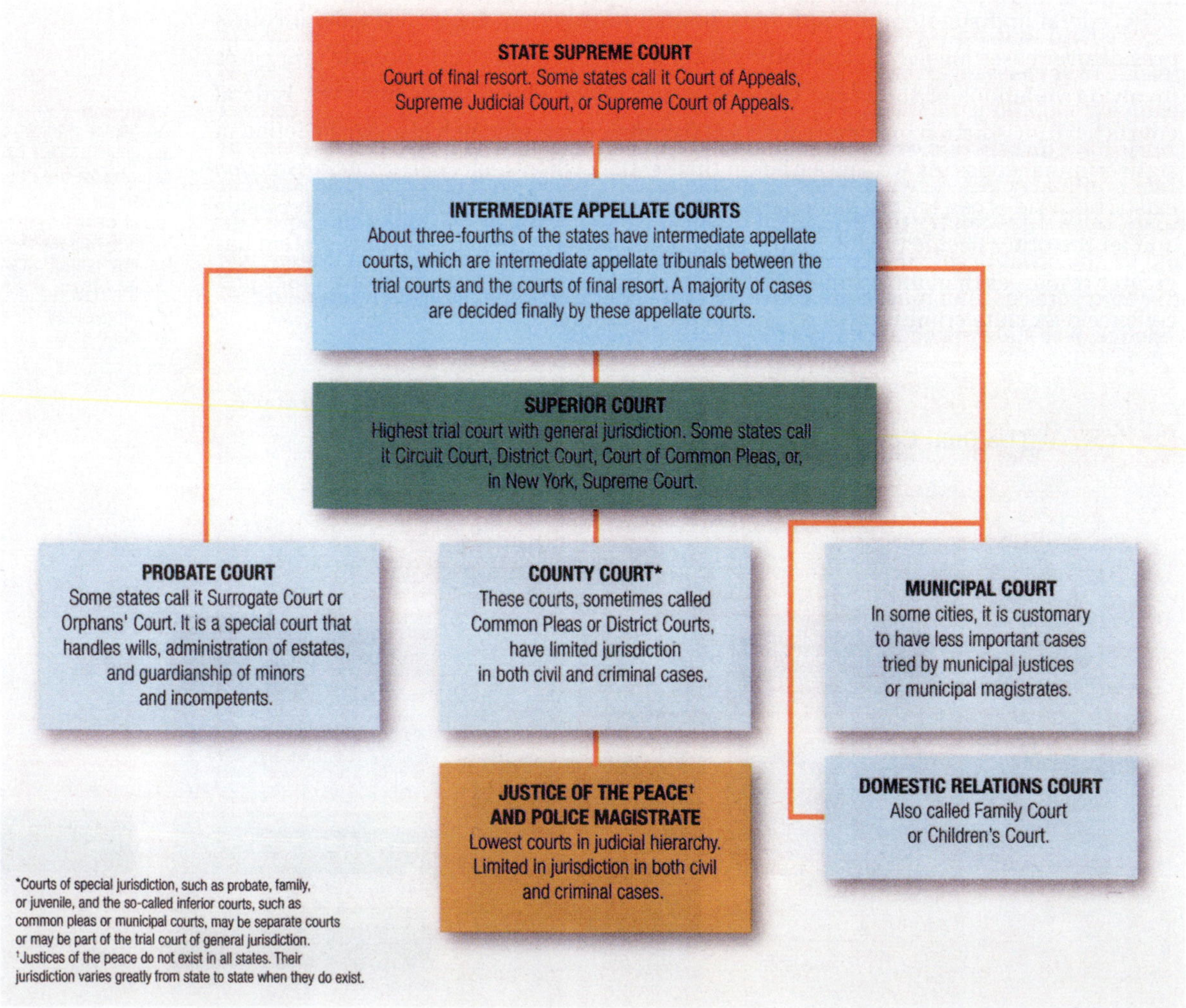

STATE SUPREME COURT
Court of final resort. Some states call it Court of Appeals, Supreme Judicial Court, or Supreme Court of Appeals.
INTERMEDIATE APPELLATE COURTS
About three-fourths of the states have intermediate appellate courts, which are intermediate appellate tribunals between the trial courts and the courts of final resort. A majority of cases are decided finally by these appellate courts.
SUPERIOR COURT
Highest trial court with general jurisdiction. Some states call it Circuit Court, District Court, Court of Common Pleas, or, in New York, Supreme Court.
PROBATE COURT
Some states call it Surrogate Court or Orphans' Court. It is a special court that handles wills, administration of estates, and guardianship of minors and incompetents.
COUNTY COURT*
These courts, sometimes called Common Pleas or District Courts, have limited jurisdiction in both civil and criminal cases.
MUNICIPAL COURT
In some cities, it is customary to have less important cases tried by municipal justices or municipal magistrates.
JUSTICE OF THE PEACE† AND POLICE MAGISTRATE
Lowest courts in judicial hierarchy. Limited in jurisdiction in both civil and criminal cases.
DOMESTIC RELATIONS COURT
Also called Family Court or Children's Court.
*Courts of special jurisdiction, such as probate, family, or juvenile, and the so-called inferior courts, such as common pleas or municipal courts, may be separate courts or may be part of the trial court of general jurisdiction.
†Justices of the peace do not exist in all states. Their jurisdiction varies greatly from state to state when they do exist.

Trial Courts of Limited Jurisdiction

Most states have local trial courts that are limited to trying cases involving minor criminal matters, such as traffic violations, prostitution, and drunk and disorderly conduct. Although these minor courts sometimes keep no written record of the trial proceedings and cases are decided by a judge rather than a jury, defendants have the same rights as those in other trial courts. The majority of all minor criminal cases are decided in these lower courts. Courts of limited jurisdiction can also be responsible for the preliminary stages of felony cases. Arraignments, bail hearings, and preliminary hearings often take place in these lower courts.

Magistrate Courts One of the earliest courts of limited jurisdiction was the justice court, presided over by a *justice of the peace*, or JP. In the early days of this nation, JPs were found everywhere in the country. Today, more than half the states have abolished justice courts, though JPs still serve a useful function in some cities and rural areas, notably in Texas.

The jurisdiction of justice courts is limited to minor disputes between private individuals and to crimes punishable by small fines or short jail terms. The equivalent of a county JP in a city is known as a **magistrate** or, in some states, a municipal court judge. Magistrate courts have the same limited jurisdiction as do justice courts in rural settings. In most jurisdictions, magistrates are responsible for providing law enforcement agents with search and seizure warrants, discussed in Chapter 6.

Specialty Courts As mentioned earlier, many states have created **problem-solving courts** that have jurisdiction over very narrowly defined areas of criminal justice. Not only do these courts remove many cases from the existing court systems, but they also allow court personnel to become experts in a particular subject. Problem-solving courts include:

1. Drug courts, which deal only with illegal substance crimes.
2. Gun courts, which have jurisdiction over crimes that involve the illegal use of firearms.
3. Juvenile courts, which specialize in crimes committed by minors. (We will discuss juvenile courts in more detail in Chapter 13.)
4. Domestic violence courts, which deal with crimes such as child and spousal abuse.
5. Mental health courts, which focus primarily on the treatment and rehabilitation of offenders with mental health problems.

As we will see in Chapter 10, many state and local governments are searching for cheaper alternatives to locking up nonviolent offenders in prison or jail. Because problem-solving courts offer a range of treatment options for wrongdoers, these courts are becoming increasingly popular in today's more budget-conscious criminal justice system. For example, about 3,000 drug courts are now operating in the United States, a number that is expected to increase as the financial benefits of diverting drug law violators from correctional facilities become more attractive to politicians.

Trial Courts of General Jurisdiction

State trial courts that have general jurisdiction may be called county courts, district courts, superior courts, or circuit courts. In Ohio, the name is the court of common pleas and in Massachusetts, the trial court. (The name sometimes does not correspond with the court's functions. For example, in New York the trial court is called the

magistrate A public civil officer or official with limited judicial authority within a particular geographic area, such as the authority to issue an arrest warrant.

problem-solving courts Lower courts that have jurisdiction over one specific area of criminal activity, such as illegal drugs or domestic violence.

supreme court, whereas in most states the supreme court is the state's highest court.) Courts of general jurisdiction have the authority to hear and decide cases involving many types of subject matter, and they are the setting for criminal trials (discussed in Chapter 8).

State Courts of Appeals

Every state has at least one court of appeals (known as an appellate, or reviewing, court), which may be an intermediate appellate court or the state's highest court. About three-fourths have intermediate appellate courts. The highest appellate court in a state is usually called the supreme court, but in both New York and Maryland, the highest state court is called the court of appeals. The decisions of each state's highest court on all questions of state law are final. Only when issues of federal law or constitutional procedure are involved can the United States Supreme Court overrule a decision made by a state's highest court.

The Federal Court System

Learning Objective 5
Outline the federal court system.

The federal court system is basically a three-tiered model consisting of (1) U.S. district courts (trial courts of general jurisdiction) and various courts of limited jurisdiction, (2) U.S. courts of appeals (intermediate courts of appeals), and (3) the United States Supreme Court.

Unlike state court judges, who are usually elected, federal court judges—including the justices of the Supreme Court—are appointed by the president of the United States, subject to the approval of the Senate. All federal judges receive lifetime appointments (because under Article III of the Constitution they "hold their offices during Good Behavior").

U.S. District Courts

On the lowest tier of the federal court system are the U.S. district courts, or federal trial courts. These are the courts in which cases involving federal laws begin, and a judge or jury decides the case (if it is a jury trial). Every state has at least one federal district court, and there is one in the District of Columbia. The number of judicial districts varies over time, primarily owing to population changes and corresponding caseloads. At the present time, there are ninety-four judicial districts. The federal system also includes other trial courts of limited jurisdiction, such as the Tax Court and the Court of International Trade.

U.S. Courts of Appeals

In the federal court system, there are thirteen U.S. courts of appeals—also referred to as U.S. circuit courts of appeals. The federal courts of appeals for twelve of the circuits hear appeals from the district courts located within their respective judicial circuits (see Figure 7.3). The Court of Appeals for the Thirteenth Circuit, called the Federal Circuit, has national appellate jurisdiction over certain types of cases, such as cases in which the U.S. government is a defendant. The decisions of the circuit courts of appeals are final unless a further appeal is pursued and granted. In that case, the matter is brought before the United States Supreme Court.

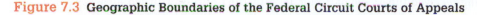

Figure 7.3 **Geographic Boundaries of the Federal Circuit Courts of Appeals**

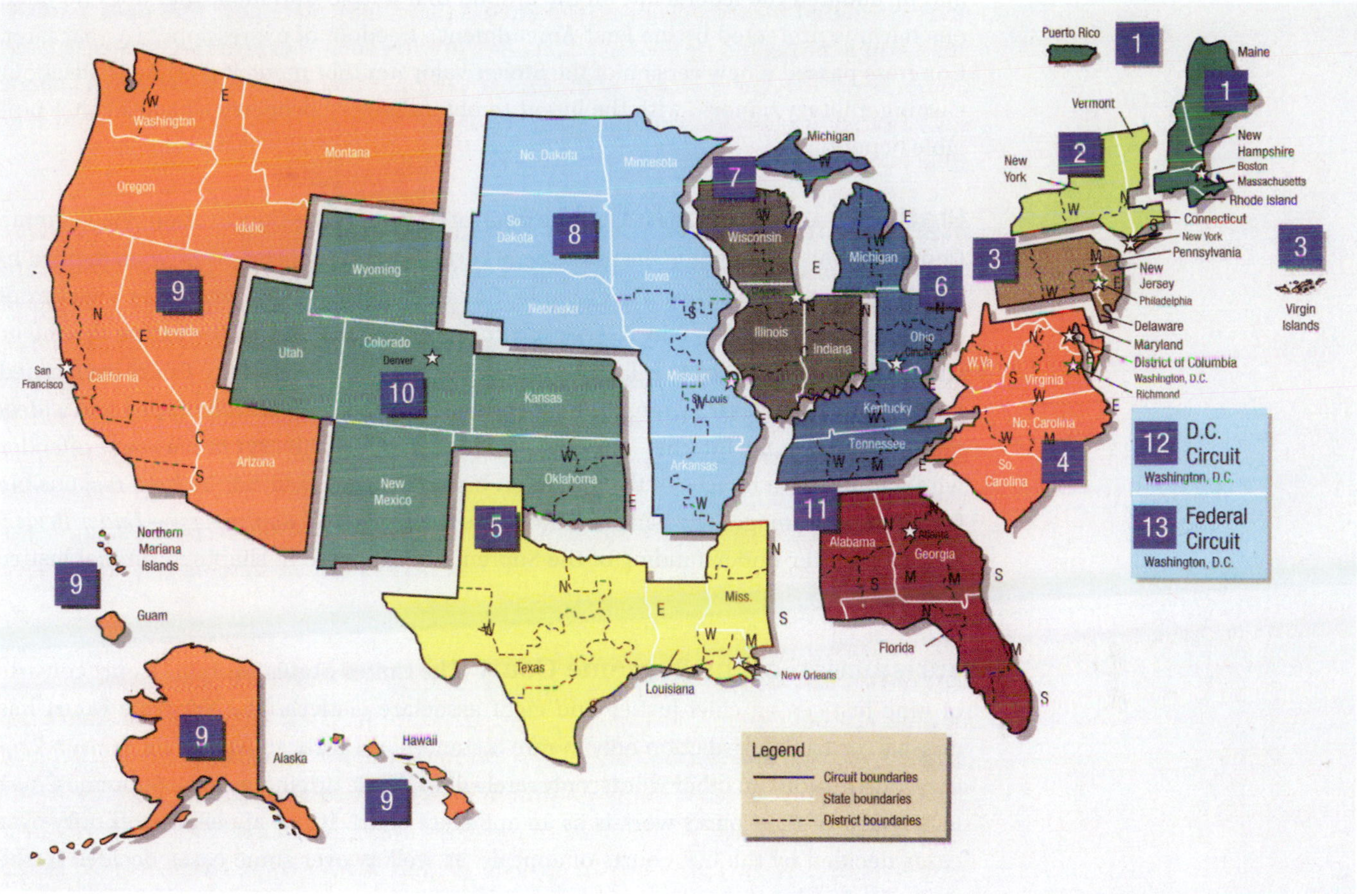

Source: Administrative Office of the United States Courts, January 1994.

The United States Supreme Court

Although the United States Supreme Court reviews a minuscule percentage of the cases decided in this country each year, its rulings profoundly affect American society. The impact of Court decisions on the criminal justice system is equally far reaching: *Gideon v. Wainwright* (1963)[11] established every American's right to be represented by counsel in a criminal trial; *Miranda v. Arizona* (1966)[12] transformed pretrial interrogations; *Furman v. Georgia* (1972)[13] ruled that the death penalty was unconstitutional; and *Gregg v. Georgia* (1976)[14] spelled out the conditions under which it could be allowed. As you have no doubt noticed from references in this textbook, the Court has addressed nearly every important facet of criminal law.

Judicial Review The Supreme Court "makes" criminal justice policy in two important ways: through *judicial review* and through its authority to interpret the law. **Judicial review** refers to the power of the Court to determine whether a law or action by the other branches of the government is constitutional.

In 2005, for example, Congress passed the Stolen Valor Act, which made it a crime punishable by up to six months in prison for someone to falsely claim that he or she had earned military honors or medals.[15] Several years after passage of this legislation, Xavier Alvarez was sentenced to three years' probation and given a $5,000 fine for lying about

judicial review The power of a court—particularly the United States Supreme Court—to review the actions of the executive and legislative branches and, if necessary, declare those actions unconstitutional.

having received the Medal of Honor. In 2012, the Court overturned Alvarez's conviction and invalidated the federal law on the ground that a false statement that does no obvious harm is protected by the First Amendment's freedom of expression.[16] (A year later, Congress passed a new version of the Stolen Valor Act that made it a crime to lie about earning military honors "with the intent to obtain money, property, or some other tangible benefit."[17])

Statutory Interpretation As the final interpreter of the Constitution, the Supreme Court must also determine the meaning of certain statutory provisions when applied to specific situations. In 1994, for example, Congress passed a law that gives a victim of child pornography the ability to seek restitution from offenders to the extent that he or she has been harmed by the illegal behavior.[18] Twenty years later, the Court overturned a $3.4 million award to a woman whose childhood rape had been videotaped and widely disseminated on the Internet. The Court ruled that, under the 1994 law, a single offender who had just two images of the victim on his computer could not be held responsible for all of the damages she had suffered.[19] (See the feature *CJ Controversy—Under Review* to gain a better understanding of the Supreme Court's role in shaping criminal justice policy.)

Jurisdiction of the Supreme Court The United States Supreme Court consists of nine justices—a chief justice and eight associate justices. The Supreme Court has original, or trial, jurisdiction only in rare instances (set forth in Article III, Section 2, of the Constitution). In other words, only rarely does a case originate at the Supreme Court level. Most of the Court's work is as an appellate court. It has appellate authority over cases decided by the U.S. courts of appeals, as well as over some cases decided in the state courts when federal questions are at issue.

Learning Objective 6
Explain briefly how a case is brought to the United States Supreme Court.

Which Cases Reach the Supreme Court? There is no absolute right to appeal to the United States Supreme Court. Although thousands of cases are filed with the Supreme Court each year, in 2014–2015 the Court heard only seventy-six. With a **writ of *certiorari*** (pronounced sur-shee-uh-*rah*-ree), the Supreme Court orders a lower court to send it the record of a case for review. A party can petition the Supreme Court to issue a writ of *certiorari*, but whether the Court will do so is entirely within its discretion. More than 90 percent of the petitions for writs of *certiorari* (or "certs," as they are popularly called) are denied. A denial is not a decision on the merits of a case, nor does it indicate agreement with the lower court's opinion. Therefore, the denial of the writ has no value as a precedent.

The Court will not issue a writ unless at least four justices approve of it. This is called the **rule of four**. Although the justices are not required to give their reasons for refusing to hear a case, most often the discretionary decision is based on whether the legal issue involves a "substantial federal question." Frequently, such questions arise when lower courts split on a particular issue. For example, different federal and state courts had produced varying opinions on the question of whether law enforcement agencies need to obtain a search warrant before tracking a suspect's location through her or his cell phone. In 2015, the American Civil Liberties Union asked the Supreme Court to clarify the law surrounding this crucial new police tactic, which we discussed last chapter.[20] Practical considerations aside, if the justices feel that a case does not address an important federal law or constitutional issue, they will vote to deny the writ of *certiorari.*

writ of *certiorari* A request from a higher court asking a lower court for the record of a case. In essence, the request signals the higher court's willingness to review the case.

rule of four A rule of the United States Supreme Court that the Court will not issue a writ of *certiorari* unless at least four justices approve of the decision to hear the case.

CJ Controversy

M Dogan/Shutterstock.com

Under Review

It seems likely that, at some point in this textbook, you have found yourself disagreeing with a United States Supreme Court decision regarding the criminal justice system. You are certainly not alone. Given the importance of the subjects on which it is asked to rule—from abortion to same-sex marriage to affirmative action—the Supreme Court is a lightning rod for controversy. Indeed, there are many who ask whether the Supreme Court should have the authority to overturn laws passed by politicians in this country.

Judicial Review by the Supreme Court Helps Society Because . . .

- Supreme Court justices are unelected and therefore insulated from the political process. Thus, they are in the best position to decide if legislation that may enjoy public support violates the Constitution.
- Without judicial review, the executive branch (the president) and the legislative branch (Congress) would have an easier time ignoring the protections of the Constitution.

Judicial Review by the Supreme Court Hurts Society Because . . .

- It is undemocratic, as it permits unelected judges to thwart the intent of members of Congress who have been elected by citizens to carry out the wishes of the majority.
- The morals and concerns of Supreme Court justices—wealthy, highly educated lawyers who until relatively recently were primarily white males—are not always in keeping with the morals and concerns of most Americans.

Your Assignment

In the late 1990s, Congress passed a law restricting the sale of videos showing graphic violence against animals. In 2010, the Supreme Court ruled that this law was unconstitutional. Learn more about the Court's decision by searching the Internet for the terms **crush videos** and ***United States v. Stevens.*** Do you agree with the Court's decision? Does this decision weaken or strengthen arguments in favor of judicial review? Your answers should include at least two full paragraphs.

Supreme Court Decisions Like all appellate courts, the Supreme Court normally does not hear any evidence. The Court's decision in a particular case is based on the written record of the case and the written arguments (briefs) that the attorneys submit. The attorneys also present **oral arguments**—arguments presented in person rather than on paper—to the Court, after which the justices discuss the case in *conference.* The conference is strictly private—only the justices are allowed in the room.

Majorities and Pluralities When the Court has reached a decision, the chief justice, if in the majority, assigns the task of writing the Court's opinion to one of the justices. When the chief justice is not in the majority, the most senior justice voting with the majority assigns the writing of the Court's opinion. The opinion outlines the reasons for the Court's decision, the rules of law that apply, and the decision.

From time to time, the justices agree on the outcome of a case, but no single reason for that outcome gains five votes. When this occurs, the rationale that gains the most votes is called the *plurality* opinion. Plurality opinions are problematic, because they do not provide a strong precedent for lower courts to follow.

Concurrence and Dissent Often, one or more justices who agree with the Court's decision may do so for different reasons than those outlined in the majority opinion. These justices may write **concurring opinions** setting forth their own legal reasoning on the issue. Frequently, one or more justices disagree with the Court's conclusion. These justices may write **dissenting opinions** outlining the reasons why they feel the majority erred.

oral arguments The verbal arguments presented in person by attorneys to an appellate court. Each attorney presents reasons why the court should rule in his or her client's favor.

concurring opinions Separate opinions prepared by judges who support the decision of the majority of the court but who want to make or clarify a particular point or to voice disapproval of the grounds on which the decision was made.

dissenting opinions Separate opinions in which judges disagree with the conclusion reached by the majority of the court and expand on their own views about the case.

For instance, in the case that opened this chapter, Supreme Court justice Clarence Thomas wrote a dissent that argued against overturning the conviction of Anthony Elonis for making threatening communications to his wife. Justice Thomas also criticized the majority opinion for failing to provide lower courts with the standard for an "appropriate mental state" that would indicate intent to threaten in such situations.[21] Although a dissenting opinion does not affect the outcome of the case before the Court, it may be important later. In a subsequent case concerning the same issue, a justice or attorney may use the legal reasoning in the dissenting opinion as the basis for an argument to reverse the previous decision and establish a new precedent.

Judges in the Court System

Supreme Court justices are the most visible and best-known American jurists, but in many ways they are unrepresentative of the profession as a whole. Few judges enjoy three-room office suites fitted with a fireplace and a private bath, as do the Supreme Court justices. Few judges have four clerks to assist them. Few judges get a yearly vacation that stretches from July through September. Most judges, in fact, work at the lowest level of the system, in criminal trial courts, where they are burdened with overflowing caseloads and must deal daily with the pettiest of criminals.

One attribute a Supreme Court justice and a criminal trial judge in any small American city do have in common is the expectation that they will be just. Of all the participants in the criminal justice system, no single person is held to the same high standards as the judge. From her or his lofty perch in the courtroom, the judge is counted on to be "above the fray" of the bickering defense attorneys and prosecutors. When the other courtroom contestants rise at the entrance of the judge, they are placing the burden of justice squarely on the judge's shoulders.

The Roles and Responsibilities of Trial Judges

One of the reasons that judicial integrity is considered so important is the amount of discretionary power a judge has over the court proceedings. Nearly every stage of the trial process includes a decision or action to be taken by the presiding judge.

Before the Trial A great deal of the work done by a judge takes place before the trial even starts, free from public scrutiny. These duties, some of which you have seen from a different point of view in the section on law enforcement agents, include determining the following:

1. Whether there is sufficient probable cause to issue a search or arrest warrant.
2. Whether there is sufficient probable cause to authorize electronic surveillance of a suspect.
3. Whether enough evidence exists to justify the temporary incarceration of a suspect.
4. Whether a defendant should be released on bail and, if so, the amount of the bail.
5. Whether to accept pretrial motions by prosecutors and defense attorneys.
6. Whether to accept a plea bargain.

During these pretrial activities, the judge takes on the role of the *negotiator*. As most cases are decided through plea bargains rather than through trial proceedings, the judge often offers his or her services as a negotiator to help the prosecution and the defense "make a deal." The amount at which bail is set is often negotiated as well. Throughout the trial process, the judge usually spends a great deal of time in his or her *chambers,* or office, negotiating with the prosecutors and defense attorneys.

During the Trial When the trial starts, the judge takes on the role of *referee.* In this role, she or he is responsible for seeing that the trial unfolds according to the dictates of the law and that the participants in the trial do not overstep any legal or ethical bounds. Furthermore, the judge is expected to be neutral, determining the admissibility of testimony and evidence on a completely objective basis.

The judge also acts as a *teacher* during the trial, explaining points of law to the jury. If the trial is not a jury trial, then the judge must also make decisions concerning the guilt or innocence of the defendant. At the close of the trial, if the defendant is found guilty, the judge must decide on the length of the sentence and the type of sentence. (Different types of sentences, such as incarceration, probation, and other forms of community-based corrections, will be discussed in Chapters 9 and 10.)

▲ Before the 2016 trial of alleged serial killer Lonnie Franklin, Jr., Los Angeles Superior Court judge Kathleen Kennedy ruled that Franklin's defense attorneys could not present DNA evidence showing that another person committed the murders in question. Judge Kennedy, shown here, criticized the defense's expert in this matter as "woefully" incompetent. **Why must judges ensure that every person participating in a criminal trial is qualified to do so?** Al Seib/*Los Angeles Times*/Getty Images

The Administrative Role Judges are also *administrators* and are responsible for the day-to-day functioning of their courts. A primary administrative task of a judge is scheduling. Each courtroom has a **docket**, or calendar of cases, and it is the judge's responsibility to keep the docket current. This entails not only scheduling the trial, but also setting pretrial motion dates and deciding whether to grant attorneys' requests for *continuances,* or additional time to prepare for the trial.

Judges must also keep track of the immense paperwork generated by each case and manage the various employees of the court. Some judges are even responsible for the budgets of their courtrooms. In 1939, Congress, recognizing the burden of such tasks, created the Administrative Office of the United States Courts to provide administrative assistance for federal court judges.[22] Most state court judges, however, do not have the luxury of similar aid, though they are supported by a court staff.

Selection of Judges

In the federal court system, all judges are appointed by the president and confirmed by the Senate. It is difficult to make a general statement about how judges are selected in state court systems, however, because the procedure varies widely from state to state. In some states, such as New Jersey, all judges are appointed by the governor and confirmed by the upper chamber of the state legislature. In other states, such as Alabama, **partisan elections** are used to choose judges. In these elections, a judicial candidate declares allegiance to a political party, usually the Democrats or the Republicans, before the election.

States such as Kentucky that conduct **nonpartisan elections** do not require a candidate to affiliate herself or himself with a political party in this manner. Today, all but

docket The list of cases entered on a court's calendar and thus scheduled to be heard by the court.

partisan elections Elections in which candidates are affiliated with and receive support from political parties.

nonpartisan elections Elections in which candidates are presented on the ballot without any party affiliation.

Comparative Criminal Justice

Pable631/Dreamstime.com

Central Intelligence Agency

Back to School

Elections for judges are extremely rare outside the United States. Indeed, only two nations—Japan and Switzerland—engage in the practice, and then only in very limited situations. To the rest of the world, according to one expert, "American adherence to judicial elections is as incomprehensible as our rejection of the metric system." Much more common, for example, is the French system, crafted to provide extensive training for potential judges.

French judicial candidates must pass two exams. The first, open to law school graduates only, combines oral and written sections and lasts at least four days. In some years, only 5 percent of the applicants overcome this hurdle. Not surprisingly, the pressure is intense. "It gives you nightmares for years afterwards," says Jean-Marc Baissus, a judge in Toulouse. "You come out of [the exam] completely shattered." Those who do survive the first test enter a two-year program at the École Nationale de la Magistrature, a judicial training academy. This school is similar to a police training academy in the United States, in that candidates spend half of their time in the classroom and the other half in the courtroom.

At the end of this program, judicial candidates are subject to a second examination. Only those who pass the exam may become judges. The result, in the words of Mitchel Lasser, a law professor at Cornell University, is that French judges "actually know what the hell they are doing. They've spent years in school taking practical and theoretical courses on how to be a judge." The French also pride themselves on creating judges who are free from the kind of political pressures faced by American judges who must go before the voters.

For Critical Analysis

Do you think that the French system of training judges is superior to the American system of electing them? Before explaining your answer, consider that French judges lack the practical courtroom experience of American judges, many of whom served as lawyers earlier in their careers.

Learning Objective 7

Explain the difference between the selection of judges at the state level and at the federal level.

eleven states choose at least some of their judges through elections.[23] Nearly 90 percent of all state judges face elections at some point in their judicial careers.[24]

Nineteen states and the District of Columbia combine appointment and election in a so-called merit selection process. Also known as the **Missouri Plan** for the state in which it originated, merit selection consists of three basic steps:

- When a vacancy on the bench arises, candidates are nominated by a nonpartisan committee of citizens.
- The names of the three most qualified candidates are sent to the governor or executive of the state judicial system, and that person chooses who will be the judge.
- A year after the new judge has been installed, a "retention election" is held so that voters can decide whether the judge deserves to keep the post.[25]

The goal of the Missouri Plan is to eliminate partisan politics from the selection procedure, while at the same time giving the citizens a voice in the process. (See the feature *Comparative Criminal Justice—Back to School* to learn about the French alternative to choosing judges through elections.)

Diversity on the Bench

One of the supposed benefits of judicial elections is that they make judges more representative of the communities in which they serve. According to the Brennan Center for Justice in New York City, however, "Americans who enter the courtroom often face a predictable presence on the bench: a white male."[26] Overall, about two-thirds of all state appellate judges are white males, and women in particular are notably absent from the highest courts of most states.[27] In many states, members of minority groups

Missouri Plan A method of selecting judges that combines appointment and election.

are underrepresented in comparison to the demographics of the general population. California, for example, is 39 percent Hispanic and 14 percent Asian American. The state judiciary, however, is only 9.8 percent Hispanic and 6.5 percent Asian American.[28] New York is 67 percent white and 52 percent female, and its judiciary is 81 percent white and 35 percent female.[29]

Federal Diversity Members of minority groups are also underrepresented in the federal judiciary. Of the approximately 1,700 federal judges in this country, about 13 percent are African American, 8 percent are Hispanic, and less than 3 percent are Asian American. Furthermore, about one-quarter are women.[30] Of the 111 justices who have served on the United States Supreme Court, two have been African American: Thurgood Marshall (1967–1991) and Clarence Thomas (1991–present). In 2009, Sonia Sotomayor became the first Hispanic appointed to the Court and the third woman, following Sandra Day O'Connor (1981–2006) and Ruth Bader Ginsburg (1993–present). A year later, Elena Kagan became the fourth woman appointed to the Court.

The Benefits of Judicial Diversity There is a sense among criminal justice professionals that citizens are more likely to recognize the legitimacy of a diverse judiciary. That is, people tend to trust judges that resemble themselves.[31] Along those lines, Sherrilyn A. Ifill of the University of Maryland School of Law believes that "diversity on the bench" enriches our judiciary by introducing a variety of voices and perspectives into positions of power. By the same token, Ifill credits the lack of diversity in many trial and appeals courts with a number of harmful consequences, such as more severe sentences for minority youths than for white youths who have committed similar crimes, disproportionate denial of bail to minority defendants, and the disproportionate imposition of the death penalty on minority defendants accused of killing white victims.[32]

EthicsChallenge

In every state that has judicial elections, judges are allowed to receive campaign contributions from lawyers that appear before them in court. What ethical issues arise from this situation? Some states ban judges from making personal requests for funds, though such requests can still be made by the judges' campaign committees. Does this strategy remove—or at least lessen—the risk of corruption? Why or why not?

The Courtroom Work Group

Television dramas often depict the courtroom as a battlefield, with prosecutors and defense attorneys spitting fire at each other over the loud and insistent protestations of a frustrated judge. Consequently, many people are somewhat disappointed when they witness a real courtroom at work. Rarely does anyone raise his or her voice, and the courtroom professionals appear—to a great extent—to be cooperating with each other. In Chapter 5, we discussed the existence of a police subculture, based on the shared values of law enforcement agents. A courtroom subculture exists as well, centered on the **courtroom work group.**

The most important feature of any work group is that it is a *cooperative* unit whose members establish shared values and methods that help the group efficiently reach its goals. Though cooperation is not a concept usually associated with criminal courts, it is in fact crucial to the adjudication process.

courtroom work group The social organization consisting of the judge, prosecutor, defense attorney, and other court workers.

Members of the Courtroom Work Group

The courtroom work group is made up of those individuals who are involved with the defendant from the time she or he is arrested until sentencing. The most prominent members are the judge, the prosecutor, and the defense attorney. (You will be introduced to the latter two shortly.) Three other court participants complete the work group:

1. The *bailiff of the court* is responsible for maintaining security and order in the judge's chambers and the courtroom. Bailiffs lead the defendant in and out of the courtroom and attend to the needs of the jurors during the trial. A bailiff, often a member of the local sheriff's department but sometimes an employee of the court, also delivers summonses in some jurisdictions.
2. The *clerk of the court* has an exhausting list of responsibilities. Any plea, motion, or other matter to be acted on by the judge must go through the clerk. The large amount of paperwork generated during a trial, including transcripts, photographs, evidence, and any other records, is maintained by the clerk. The clerk also issues subpoenas for jury duty and coordinates the jury selection process. In the federal court system, judges select clerks, while state clerks are either appointed or, in nearly a third of the states, elected.
3. *Court reporters* record every word that is said during the course of the trial. They also record any *depositions,* or pretrial question-and-answer sessions in which a party or a witness answers an attorney's questions under oath.

The Judge in the Courtroom Work Group

The judge is the dominant figure in the courtroom and therefore exerts the most influence over the values and norms of the work group. A judge who runs a "tight ship" follows procedure and restricts the freedom of attorneys to deviate from regulations, while a *"laissez-faire"* judge allows more leeway to members of the work group. A judge's personal philosophy also affects the court proceedings. If a judge has a reputation for being "tough on crime," both prosecutors and defense attorneys will alter their strategies accordingly.

▼ Two trial lawyers confer as the judge waits at the Sedgwick County Courthouse in Wichita, Kansas. **How is working in a courtroom similar to working in a corporate office? How is it different?** Al Hartmann-Pool/Getty Images

Although preeminent in the work group, a judge must still rely on other members of the group. To a certain degree, the judge is the least informed member of the trio. Like a juror, the judge learns the facts of the case as they are presented by the attorneys. If the attorneys do not properly present the facts, then the judge is hampered in making rulings. Judges also have the power to discipline other members of the courtroom work group. In 2015, for example, Superior Court judge Thomas Goethals removed several Orange County (California) prosecutors from a high-profile murder case the judge called "a comedy of errors." Along with other misdeeds, the prosecutors had apparently lied to the court about conspiring with the local sheriff's department to place the defendant in a jail cell next to an inmate acting as a government informant.[33]

The Prosecution

If the judge is, as we suggested earlier, the referee of the courtroom, then the prosecutor and the defense attorney are its two main combatants. On the side of the government, acting in the name of "the people," the **public prosecutor** tries cases against criminal defendants. The public prosecutor in federal criminal cases is called a U.S. attorney. In cases tried in state or local courts, the public prosecutor may be referred to as a *prosecuting attorney, state attorney, district attorney, county attorney*, or *city attorney*. Given their great autonomy, prosecutors are generally considered the most dominant figures in the American criminal justice system.

Learning Objective

8 List the different names given to public prosecutors and indicate the general powers that they have.

A Duty of Fairness In some jurisdictions, the district attorney is the chief law enforcement officer, with broad powers over police operations. Prosecutors have the power to bring the resources of the state against the individual and hold the legal keys to meting out or withholding punishment. Ideally, this power is balanced by a duty of fairness and a recognition that the prosecutor's ultimate goal is not to win cases, but to see that justice is done. In *Berger v. United States* (1935), Justice George Sutherland said of the prosecutor, "It is as much his duty to refrain from improper methods calculated to produce a wrongful conviction as it is to use every legitimate means to bring about a just one."[34]

The *Brady* Rule To lessen the opportunity for improper behavior by prosecutors, the United States Supreme Court established the *Brady rule* more than half a century ago. This rule holds that prosecutors are not permitted to keep evidence from the defendant and her or his attorneys that may be useful in showing innocence.[35]

For example, in 1990 Debra Milke was convicted of helping two men kill her four-year-old son in the desert near Phoenix, Arizona. Milke's conviction was based solely on a confession she supposedly gave to a detective who had a history of misconduct and lying under oath. In 2015, Maricopa County Superior Court judge Rosa Mroz dismissed the case against Milke, ruling that prosecutors violated the *Brady* rule by deliberately withholding from the defense evidence of the detective's previous wrongdoing. Obviously, Milke's attorneys could have used this information to create a reasonable doubt concerning their client's guilt in court. Milke was subsequently set free after spending more than twenty years on death row.[36]

The Office of the Prosecutor When he or she is acting as an *officer of the law* during a criminal trial, there are limits on the prosecutor's conduct, as we shall see in the next chapter. During the pretrial process, however, prosecutors hold a great deal of discretion in deciding the following:

1. Whether an individual who has been arrested by the police will be charged with a crime.
2. The level of the charges to be brought against the suspect.
3. If and when to stop the prosecution.

There are more than eight thousand prosecutors' offices around the country, serving state, county, and municipal jurisdictions. Even though the **attorney general** is the chief

public prosecutors Individuals, acting as trial lawyers, who initiate and conduct cases in the government's name and on behalf of the people.

attorney general The chief law officer of a state; also, the chief law officer of the nation.

law enforcement officer in any state, she or he has limited (and in some states, no) control over prosecutors within the state's boundaries.

Each jurisdiction has a chief prosecutor, who is sometimes appointed but more often elected. As an elected official, he or she typically serves a four-year term, though in some states, such as Alabama, the term is six years. In smaller jurisdictions, the chief prosecutor has several assistants, and they work closely together. In larger ones, the chief prosecutor may have numerous *assistant prosecutors,* many of whom he or she rarely meets. Assistant prosecutors—for the most part, young attorneys recently graduated from law school—may be assigned to particular sections of the organization, such as criminal prosecutions in general or areas of *special prosecution,* such as narcotics or gang crimes. (See Figure 7.4 for the structure of a typical prosecutor's office.)

The Prosecutor as Elected Official The chief prosecutor's autonomy is not absolute. As an elected official, she or he must answer to the voters. (There are exceptions: U.S. attorneys are nominated by the president and approved by the Senate, and chief prosecutors in Alaska, Connecticut, New Jersey, Rhode Island, and the District of Columbia are either appointed or hired as members of the attorney general's office.) The prosecutor may be part of the political machine. In many jurisdictions, the prosecutor must declare a party affiliation and is expected to reward fellow party members with positions in the district attorney's office if elected.

The post of prosecutor is also considered a "stepping-stone" to higher political office, and many prosecutors have gone on to serve in legislatures or as judges. Sonia Sotomayor, the first Hispanic member of the United States Supreme Court, started

Figure 7.4 **The Baltimore City State's Attorney's Office**

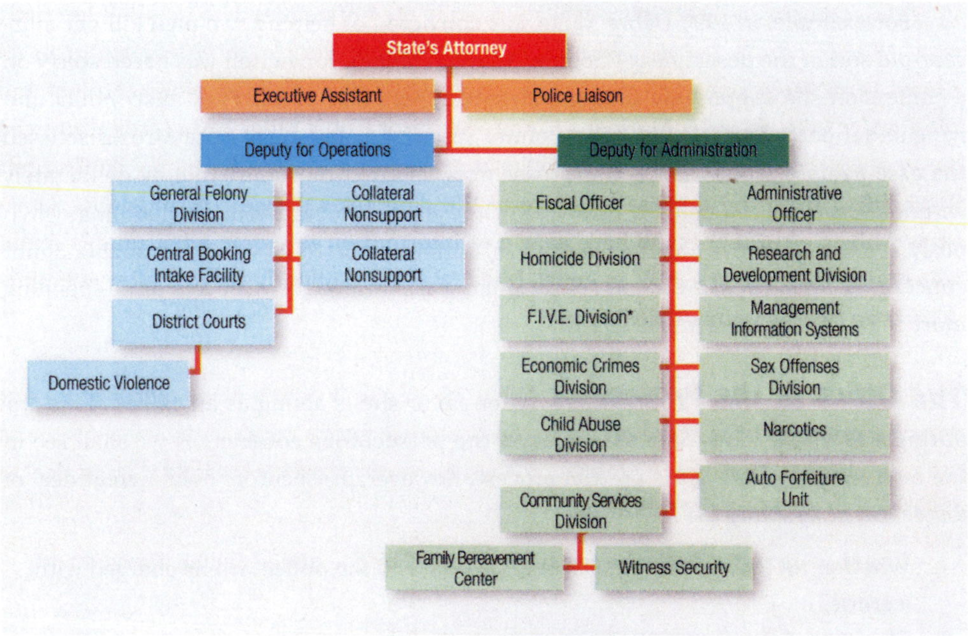

*F.I.V.E. is an acronym for "Firearms Investigation Violence Enforcement."

Source: Baltimore City State's Attorney's Office.

her legal career in 1979 as an assistant district attorney in New York City. While at that job, she first came to public attention by helping to prosecute the "Tarzan Murderer," an athletic criminal responsible for at least twenty burglaries and four killings.

▲ About 80 percent of elected state and local prosecutors in the United States are white men, making Baltimore City state attorney Marilyn Mosby, left, an exception to the rule. **Given the responsibilities of public prosecutors within the criminal justice system, how might society benefit from more diversity in the profession?** Mark Wilson/Getty Images

Community Pressures A prosecutor's electability is often influenced by her or his involvement in high-profile cases. Such cases can be challenging for prosecutors to navigate, as Marilyn Mosby, Baltimore's chief prosecutor, recently discovered. On April 19, 2015, soon after Mosby was elected to her post, a twenty-five-year-old African American man named Freddie Gray died of spinal injuries he suffered while in police custody. Daily protests by the city's black community followed, with many expressing outrage at what they saw as a trend of improper police use of force against members of minority groups.

Only eighteen days after Gray's death, Mosby announced that six Baltimore police officers would face charges ranging from false imprisonment to second degree murder. To justify the charges, Mosby argued that Gray had been wrongly arrested for carrying a legal folding knife, and that he had not received proper medical attention for a spinal injury he suffered in a police van during transfer to the local police station. Not surprisingly, Mosby was criticized by law enforcement officials for bowing to public pressure. "I have never seen such a hurried rush to deliver criminal charges," said a lawyer for the Baltimore police union.[37]

Prosecutors and Victims Because prosecutors have the responsibility of trying and convicting offenders, crime victims often see themselves as being on "the same side" as the prosecution. This perception is only strengthened when prosecutors publicly align themselves with victims. In fact, prosecutors do not represent crime victims. Understandably, most victims are focused primarily on the fate of the defendant who caused them harm. Prosecutors, in contrast, must balance the rights of the victims with those of the accused and the best interests of the public at large. Indeed, if a prosecutor becomes too involved in the personal tragedies of crime victims, he or she runs the risk of losing the neutrality that is the hallmark of the office.[38]

A prosecutor's duty of neutrality does not mean that he or she should ignore crime victims or their wishes. Practically, prosecutors rely on victims as sources of information and valuable witnesses. Believable victims are also quite helpful if a case goes to trial, as they may be able to elicit a sympathetic response from the jury. Furthermore, as we saw in Chapter 3, federal and state victims' rights legislation requires the prosecutor to confer with victims at various stages of the criminal justice process.

CJ & Technology

Untested Rape Kits

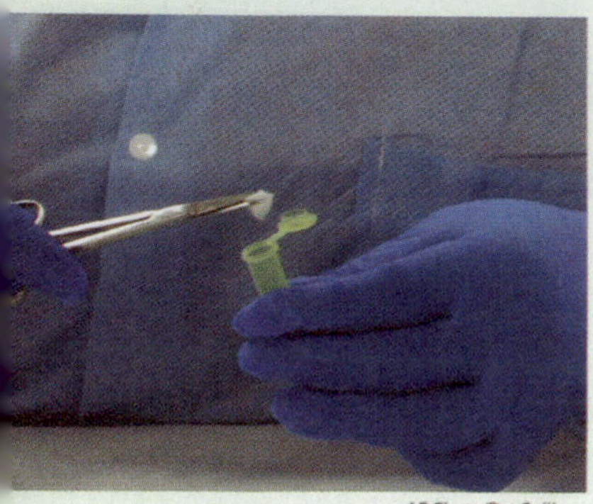

AP Photo/Pat Sullivan

In 2010, the Wayne County Prosecutor's Office found 11,000 untested rape kits in a Detroit police storage unit. These kits are prepared by forensic medical experts in the hours following a sexual assault and often contain DNA left by the offender. In the six years following this discovery, prosecutor Kym Worthy arranged for more than 10,000 of the kits to be tested, gathering evidence of nearly 500 serial rapists and obtaining twenty-one convictions in the process. Though the pace of Worthy's efforts may seem slow, it isn't. A crime lab can take weeks to extract usable DNA evidence from a rape kit, at a cost of up to $1,500 per kit.

Nationwide, there is a backlog of about 400,000 untested rape kits, meaning that innumerable sexual assault offenders have escaped arrest and conviction. Given that most crime labs in the country are already overwhelmed with requests to test evidence, it seems that technology offers the best hope of reducing this backlog. Presently, lab technicians must laboriously separate the DNA of the victim from the DNA of the offender by slicing the cells of material in the rape kit such as blood, semen, skin, or saliva. A new process called *pressure cycling* immediately identifies the offender's semen, which significantly lessens the amount of time needed to get a usable DNA sample for database-matching purposes.

Thinking about Untested Rape Kits

How might the massive backlog of untested rape kits in this country discourage victims of sexual assault from reporting the crime to police?

The Defense Attorney

The media provide most people's perception of defense counsel: the idealistic public defender who nobly serves the poor, the "ambulance chaser," or the celebrity attorney in the $3,000 suit. These stereotypes, though not entirely fictional, tend to obscure the crucial role that the **defense attorney** plays in the criminal justice system.

Most persons charged with crimes have little or no knowledge of criminal procedure. Without assistance, they would be helpless in court. By acting as a staunch advocate for her or his client, the defense attorney (ideally) ensures that the government proves every point against that client beyond a reasonable doubt, even for cases that do not go to trial. In sum, the defense attorney provides a counterweight against the state in our adversary system.

The Responsibilities of the Defense Attorney The Sixth Amendment right to counsel is not limited to the actual criminal trial. In a number of instances, the United States Supreme Court has held that defendants are entitled to representation as soon as their rights may be denied, which, as we have seen, includes the custodial interrogation and lineup identification procedures.[39] Therefore, an important responsibility of the defense attorney is to represent the defendant at the various stages of the custodial process, such as arrest, interrogation, lineup, and arraignment. Other responsibilities include:

defense attorney The lawyer representing the defendant.

- Investigating the incident for which the defendant has been charged.
- Communicating with the prosecutor, which includes negotiating plea bargains.

- Preparing the case for trial.
- Submitting defense motions, including motions to suppress evidence.
- Representing the defendant at trial.
- Negotiating a sentence, if the client has been convicted.
- Determining whether to appeal a guilty verdict.[40]

Defending the Guilty At one time or another in their careers, all defense attorneys will face a difficult question: Must I defend a client whom I know to be guilty? According to the American Bar Association's code of legal ethics, the answer is almost always "yes."[41] The most important responsibility of the criminal defense attorney is to be an advocate for her or his client. As such, the attorney is obligated to use all ethical and legal means to achieve the client's desired goal, which is usually to avoid or lessen punishment for the charged crime.

As Supreme Court justice Byron White once noted, defense counsel has no "obligation to ascertain or present the truth." Rather, our adversary system insists that the defense attorney "defend the client whether he is innocent or guilty."[42] Indeed, if defense attorneys refused to represent clients whom they believed to be guilty, the Sixth Amendment guarantee of a criminal trial for all accused persons would be rendered meaningless. (To learn more about the difficult situations that can arise with a guilty defendant, see the feature *Discretion in Action—The Repugnant Client.*)

Getting Linked in

Though not lawyers themselves, **paralegals** offer invaluable assistance to lawyers, helping them prepare for trial, research legal documents, draft contracts, and investigate cases. The high demand for these legal assistants will be evident if you enter the term "paralegal" into LinkedIn's search engine.

The Public Defender Generally speaking, there are two different types of defense attorneys: (1) private attorneys, who are hired by individuals, and (2) **public defenders**, who work for the government. The distinction is not absolute, as many private attorneys accept employment as public defenders, too. The modern role of the public defender was established by the Supreme Court's interpretation of the Sixth Amendment in *Gideon v. Wainwright* (1963).[43]

In that case, the Court ruled that no defendant can be "assured a fair trial unless counsel is provided for him," and therefore the state must provide a public defender to those who cannot afford to hire one for themselves. Subsequently, the Court extended this protection to juveniles in *In re Gault* (1967)[44] and those faced with imprisonment for committing misdemeanors in *Argersinger v. Hamlin* (1972).[45] The impact of these decisions has been substantial: about 90 percent of all criminal defendants in the United States are represented by public defenders or other appointed counsel.[46]

Defense Counsel Programs In most areas, the county government is responsible for providing indigent defendants with attorneys. Three basic types of programs are used to allocate defense counsel:

1. *Assigned counsel programs,* in which local private attorneys are assigned clients on a case-by-case basis by the county.
2. *Contracting attorney programs,* in which a particular law firm or group of attorneys is hired to regularly assume the representative and administrative tasks of indigent defense.
3. *Public defender programs,* in which the county assembles a salaried staff of full-time or part-time attorneys and creates a public (taxpayer-funded) agency to provide services.[47]

public defenders Court-appointed attorneys who are paid by the state to represent defendants who cannot afford private counsel.

Discretion in ACTION

The Repugnant Client

Rachel Donahue/Shutterstock.com

Learning Objective

9 Explain why defense attorneys must often defend clients they know to be guilty.

The Situation Gerard Marrone is the defense attorney for Levi Aron, charged with kidnapping, murdering, and dismembering eight-year-old Leiby Kletzky in Brooklyn, New York. There is little question of Aron's guilt, as he provided the police with a signed confession and has no alibi for his whereabouts at the time of the crime. Marrone is uncertain about whether he wants to continue representing this "horrific" client. "You can't look at your kids and then look at yourself in the mirror, knowing that a little boy, who's close in age to my eldest son, was murdered so brutally," Marrone said about his conflicted feelings.

The Law The Sixth Amendment requires that all criminal defendants are entitled to the right to assistance of counsel. Nonetheless, no state or federal law requires defense attorneys to represent clients they know to be guilty of committing a crime. The American Bar Association (ABA) Model Rules of Professional Conduct, which provide informal guidance to the nation's lawyers, do not mandate representation of a client that an attorney finds "repugnant."

What Would You Do? Despite the ABA's advice about "repugnant" clients, the criminal justice system would not be able to function if lawyers refused to represent guilty defendants. Many believe that attorneys are ethically obligated to take on unpopular cases and clients to ensure the integrity of the American judicial system. At the same time, a lawyer must be guided by his or her own conscience. If a client is so repugnant to the lawyer as to impair the quality of representation, then perhaps the lawyer should drop the case. Given these opposing viewpoints, would you continue to represent Levi Aron if you were in Gerard Marrone's position?

To see Gerard Marrone's eventual decision, go to Example 7.1 in Appendix B.

Under the U.S. Constitution, a defendant who is paying for her or his defense attorney has a right to choose that attorney without interference from the court.[48] This right of choice does not extend to indigent defendants. According to the United States Supreme Court, "[A] defendant may not insist on an attorney he cannot afford."[49] In other words, an indigent defendant must accept the public defender provided by the court system. (Note that, unless the presiding judge rules otherwise, a person can waive her or his Sixth Amendment rights and act as her or his own defense attorney.)

The *Strickland* Standard In one Louisiana murder trial, not only did the court-appointed defense attorney spend only eleven minutes preparing for trial on a charge that carries a mandatory life sentence, but she also represented the victim's father and had been representing the victim at the time of his death. Not surprisingly, her defendant was found guilty. Such behavior raises a critical question: When a lawyer does such a poor job, has the client essentially been denied his or her Sixth Amendment right to assistance of counsel? In *Strickland v. Washington* (1984),[50] the Supreme Court set up a two-pronged test to determine whether constitutional requirements have been met. To prove that prior counsel was not sufficient, a defendant must show that:

1. The attorney's performance was deficient, *and*
2. This deficiency *more likely than not* caused the defendant to lose the case.

In practice, it has been very difficult to prove the second prong of this test. A prosecutor can always argue that the defendant would have lost the case even if his or her lawyer had not been inept. Sometimes, however, such ineptness is so intolerable that it

Careers in CJ

Annika Carlsten
Public Defender

My very first day on the job, I watched another attorney conduct *voir dire* (see Chapter 8) on a domestic violence assault. I wondered if I would ever be that comfortable and confident in court. Many years later, the cases have started to blur in my memory. That said, I will always remember my very first "not guilty" verdict. I was utterly convinced of my client's innocence, and very emotionally invested in winning the case for him. At the other end of the spectrum, I will never forget having to explain court proceedings to a man only hours after he accidentally shot and killed his child. Nothing in law school prepares you for that conversation. Nothing in life prepares you for that conversation.

Most of all, I believe passionately in the idea of what I do, in the principle of equal justice for everyone, regardless of money or circumstance. On a good day, I see that ideal fulfilled. On a great day, I feel like I personally have done something to make it so.

SOCIAL MEDIA CAREER TIP You need to differentiate yourself from everyone else on line by providing unique, relevant, high-quality content on a regular basis. You should network with a purpose, not just to share fun things.

FASTFACTS

Public defender

Job description:

- Interview low-income applicants for legal services; advise and counsel individuals and groups regarding their legal rights; handle a reasonable caseload; and, where necessary, engage in the negotiation, trial, and/or appeal of legal issues that have a substantial impact on the rights of eligible clients.

What kind of training is required?

- A law degree and membership in the relevant state bar association.

Annual salary range?

- $46,000–$100,000.

meets the *Strickland* standard and a new trial is required. Several years ago, the Kansas Supreme Court overturned the capital conviction of Phillip Cheatham, Jr., for the shooting deaths of two Topeka women a decade earlier. Most crucially, Cheatham's defense attorney had failed to present evidence that his client was driving to Chicago at the time of the shootings. The lawyer also spent only sixty hours preparing for the trial (being busy running for governor at the time) and referred to Cheatham as a "professional drug dealer" and "shooter of people" in court.[51]

Attorney-Client Privilege To defend a client effectively, a defense attorney must have access to all the facts concerning the case, even those that may be harmful to the defendant. To promote the unrestrained flow of information between the two parties, legislatures and lawyers themselves have constructed rules of **attorney-client privilege**. These rules require that communications between a client and his or her attorney be kept confidential, unless the client consents to the disclosure.

The Privilege and Confessions Attorney-client privilege does not stop short of confessions. Indeed, if, on hearing any statement that points toward guilt, the defense attorney could alert the prosecution or try to resign from the case, attorney-client privilege would be rendered meaningless. Even if the client says, "I have just killed seventeen women. I selected only pregnant women so I could torture them and kill two people at

attorney-client privilege A rule of evidence requiring that communications between a client and his or her attorney be kept confidential, unless the client consents to disclosure.

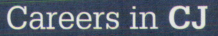

▲ Defense attorney Jill Corey appears in Quincy, Massachusetts, District Court with her client, Andrew Fanguiaire, who was charged with possession of child pornography. **Why are the rules of attorney-client privilege necessary for a defense attorney to properly do his or her job?** Pat Greenhouse/*Boston Globe*/Getty Images

once. I did it. I liked it. I enjoyed it," the defense attorney must continue to do his or her utmost to serve that client.[52]

Without attorney-client privilege protections, observes legal expert John Kaplan, lawyers would be forced to give their clients the equivalent of the *Miranda* warning before representing them.[53] In other words, lawyers would have to make clear what clients could or could not say in the course of preparing for trial, because any incriminating statement might be used against the client in court. Such a development would have serious ramifications for the criminal justice system.

The Exception to the Privilege The scope of attorney-client privilege is not all-encompassing. In *United States v. Zolin* (1989),[54] the Supreme Court ruled that lawyers may disclose the contents of a conversation with a client if the client has provided information concerning a crime that has yet to be committed. This exception applies only to communications involving a crime that is ongoing or will occur in the future. If the client reveals a past crime, the privilege is still in effect, and the attorney may not reveal any details of that particular criminal act.

EthicsChallenge

It has become common practice for federal prosecutors to read e-mails sent from prison inmates to their lawyers. Defense attorneys argue that such behavior violates the spirit of attorney-client privilege, while prosecutors contend that any e-mail sent from prison is government property and therefore subject to monitoring. What is your opinion of the ethics of this practice?

Summary

For more information on these concepts, look back to the Learning Objective icons throughout the chapter.

1 Define and contrast the four functions of the courts. The four functions are (a) due process, (b) crime control, (c) rehabilitation, and (d) bureaucratic. The most obvious contrast is between the due process and crime control functions. The former is mainly concerned with the procedural rules that allow each accused individual to have a "fair chance" against the government in a criminal proceeding. For crime control, the courts are supposed to impose enough "pain" on convicted criminals to deter criminal behavior. For the rehabilitation function, the courts serve as "doctors" who dispense "treatment." In their bureaucratic function, courts are more concerned with speed and efficiency.

2 Define *jurisdiction*, and contrast geographic and subject-matter jurisdiction. Jurisdiction relates to the power of a court to hear a particular case. Courts are typically limited in geographic jurisdiction—for example, to a particular state. Some courts are restricted in subject matter, such as a small claims court, which can hear only cases involving civil matters under a certain monetary limit.

3 Explain the difference between trial and appellate courts. Trial courts are courts of the first instance, where a case is first heard. Appellate courts review the proceedings of a lower court. Appellate courts do not have juries.

4 Outline the several levels of a typical state court system. (a) At the lowest level are courts of limited jurisdiction, (b) next are trial courts of general jurisdiction, (c) then appellate courts, and (d) finally, the state's highest court.

5 Outline the federal court system. (a) At the lowest level are the U.S. district courts in which trials are held, as well as various minor federal courts of limited jurisdiction; (b) next are the U.S. courts of appeals, otherwise known as circuit courts of appeals; and (c) finally, the United States Supreme Court.

6 Explain briefly how a case is brought to the United States Supreme Court. Cases decided in U.S. courts of appeals, as well as cases decided in the highest state courts (when federal questions arise), can be appealed to the Supreme Court. If at least four justices approve of a case filed with the Supreme Court, the Court will issue a writ of *certiorari,* ordering the lower court to send the Supreme Court the record of the case for review.

7 Explain the difference between the selection of judges at the state level and at the federal level. The president nominates all judges at the federal level, and the Senate must approve the nominations. A similar procedure is used in some states. In other states, all judges are elected on a partisan ballot or on a nonpartisan ballot. Some states use merit selection, or the Missouri Plan, in which a citizen committee nominates judicial candidates, the governor or executive of the state judicial system chooses among the top three nominees, and a year later a "retention election" is held.

8 List the different names given to public prosecutors and indicate the general powers that they have. At the federal level, the prosecutor is called the U.S. attorney. In state and local courts, the prosecutor may be referred to as the prosecuting attorney, state attorney, district attorney, county attorney, or city attorney. Prosecutors in general have the power to decide when and how the state will pursue an individual suspected of criminal wrongdoing. In some jurisdictions, the district attorney is also the chief law enforcement officer, holding broad powers over police operations.

9 Explain why defense attorneys must often defend clients they know to be guilty. In our criminal justice system, the most important responsibility of a defense attorney is to be an advocate for her or his client. This means ensuring that the client's constitutional rights are protected during criminal justice proceedings, regardless of whether the client is guilty or innocent.

Questions for Critical Analysis

1. In 2012, the United States Supreme Court "denied cert" in the case of Joel Tenenbaum, who had been ordered to pay a recording company $675,000 in fines for illegally downloading thirty-one songs using a file-sharing website. Tenenbaum claimed that the fine was excessive and unfair. What does it mean for the Court to "deny cert"? In this instance, what might have been some reasons for the Court's refusal to consider Tenenbaum's case?
2. The United States Supreme Court does not allow its proceedings to be televised. Do you think that doing so would increase or diminish public confidence in the Court? Why?
3. Do you think that politicians should make a concerted effort to appoint greater numbers of minorities and women as judges? Why or why not?
4. Prosecutors cannot face civil lawsuits for misconduct, even if they have deliberately sent an innocent person to prison. In practical terms, why do you think prosecutors are protected in this manner? Do you agree with a policy of blanket immunity for prosecutors? Explain your answers.
5. Government agencies can charge fees for "free" legal counsel when the fees will not impose a "significant legal hardship" on the defendant. Why might this practice go against the Supreme Court's ruling in *Gideon v. Wainwright*?

Key Terms

appellate courts 200
attorney-client privilege 219
attorney general 213
concurrent jurisdiction 199
concurring opinions 207
courtroom work group 211
defense attorney 216
dissenting opinions 207
docket 209
dual court system 201
extradition 200
judicial review 205
jurisdiction 199
magistrate 203
Missouri Plan 210
nonpartisan elections 209
opinions 201
oral arguments 207
partisan elections 209
problem-solving courts 203
public defender 217
public prosecutor 213
rule of four 206
trial courts 200
writ of *certiorari* 206

Notes

1. 575 U.S. ____ (2015).
2. Quoted in Adam Liptak, "Chief Justice Samples Eminem in Online Threats Case," *New York Times* (December 2, 2014), A14.
3. Quoted in Emily Bazelon, "Do Online Death Threats Count as Free Speech?" *New York Times* (November 30, 2014), MM11.
4. American Civil Liberties Union, "*Elonis v. United States*—Amicus Brief," 5, at **www.aclu.org/legal-document/elonis-v-united-states-amicus-brief.**
5. Russell Wheeler and Howard Whitcomb, *Judicial Administration: Text and Readings* (Englewood Cliffs, N.J.: Prentice Hall, 1977), 3.
6. Larry J. Siegel, *Criminology: Instructor's Manual*, 6th ed. (Belmont, Calif.: West/Wadsworth Publishing Co., 1998), 440.
7. Gerald F. Velman, "Federal Sentencing Guidelines: A Cure Worse than the Disease," *American Criminal Law Review* 29 (Spring 1992), 904.
8. Katy Steinmetz, "Legal Marijuana Raises Issues for Indian Tribes," *Time* (February 6, 2014), at **time.com/5301/legal-marijuana-indian-tribes-colorado-washington.**
9. U.S. Department of Justice, "Violence Against Women Act (VAWA) Reauthorization 2013," at **www.justice.gov/tribal/violence-against-women-act-vawa-reauthorization-2013-0.**
10. 18 U.S.C. Section 3231; and *Solorio v. United States*, 483 U.S. 435 (1987).
11. 372 U.S. 335 (1963).
12. 384 U.S. 436 (1966).
13. 408 U.S. 238 (1972).
14. 428 U.S. 153 (1976).
15. 18 U.S.C.A. Section 704.
16. *U.S. v. Alvarez*, 132 S.Ct. 2537 (2012).
17. 18 U.S.C.A. Section 704(a).
18. Public Law Number 103-322, Section 16001, 108 Statute 2036 (1994); codified as amended at 18 U.S.C. Section 2259.
19. *Paroline v. United States*, 134 S.Ct. 1710 (2014).
20. Steve Nelson, "Supreme Court Asked to End Warrantless Phone Tracking," *U.S. News & World Report* (July 31, 2015), at **www.usnews.com/news/articles/2015/07/31/supreme-court-asked-to-end-warrantless-phone-tracking.**
21. *Elonis v. United States*, 575 U.S. ____ (2015).
22. Pub. L. No. 76-299, 53 Stat. 1223, codified as amended at 28 U.S.C. Sections 601–610 (1988 & Supp. V 1993).

23. American Judicature Society, "Methods of Judicial Selection," at **www.judicialselection.us/judicial_selection/methods/selection_of_judges.cfm?state=.**

24. David K. Scott, "Zero-Sum Judicial Elections: Balancing Free Speech and Impartiality through Recusal Reform," *Brigham Young University Law Review* (2009), 481, 485.

25. James E. Lozier, "The Missouri Plan a.k.a. Merit Selection Is the Best Solution for Selecting Michigan's Judges," *Michigan Bar Journal* 75 (September 1996), 918.

26. Ciara Torres-Spelliscy, Monique Chase, and Emma Greenman, *Improving Judicial Diversity*, 2d ed. (New York: Brennan Center for Justice, 2010), 1.

27. *Ibid.*

28. California Courts, "Demographic Data Provided by Justice and Judges Relative to Gender, Race/Ethnicity, and Gender Identity/Sexual Orientation (Gov. Code, Section 12011.5(n)) as of December 31, 2015," at **www.courts.ca.gov/documents/2016-Demographic-Report.pdf.**

29. New York State Bar Association Executive Committee, *Judicial Diversity: A Work in Progress* (Albany, N.Y.: New York State Bar Association, September 2014), Table 1, page 5.

30. Federal Judicial Center, "Diversity on the Bench," at **www.fjc.gov/history/home.nsf/page/judges_diversity.html.**

31. Torres-Spelliscy, Chase, and Greenman, *op. cit.*, 36–42.

32. Sherrilyn A. Ifill, "Racial Diversity on the Bench: Beyond Role Models and Public Confidence," *Washington and Lee Law Review* (Spring 2000), 405.

33. Christopher Goffard, "D.A. Is Removed from Scott Dekraai Murder Trial," *Los Angeles Times* (March 12, 2015), at **www.latimes.com/local/orangecounty/la-me-jailhouse-snitch-20150313-story.html.**

34. 295 U.S. 78 (1935).

35. *Brady v. Maryland*, 373 U.S. 83 (1963).

36. Jennifer Soules, "Freed Woman Speaks Out after 23 Years on Death Row," *Arizona Republic* (March 24, 2015), at **www.usatoday.com/story/news/nation/2015/03/24/freed-woman-speaks-years-death-row/70393110.**

37. Quoted in Scott Calvert, Kris Maher, and Joe Palazzolo, "Six Baltimore Police Officers Charged in Freddie Gray Death," *Wall Street Journal* (May 1, 2015), at **www.wsj.com/articles/baltimore-prosecutor-probable-cause-to-charge-police-in-freddie-gray-death-1430492304.**

38. Bennett L. Gershman, "Prosecutorial Ethics and Victims' Rights: The Prosecutor's Duty of Neutrality," *Lewis & Clark Law Review* 9 (2005), 561.

39. *Gideon v. Wainwright*, 372 U.S. 335 (1963); *Massiah v. United States*, 377 U.S. 201 (1964); *United States v. Wade*, 388 U.S. 218 (1967); *Argersinger v. Hamlin*, 407 U.S. 25 (1972); and *Brewer v. Williams*, 430 U.S. 387 (1977).

40. Larry Siegel, *Criminology*, 6th ed. (Belmont, Calif.: West/Wadsworth Publishing Co., 1998), 487–488.

41. Center for Professional Responsibility, *Model Rules of Professional Conduct* (Washington, D.C.: American Bar Association, 2003), Rules 1.6 and 3.1.

42. *United States v. Wade*, 388 U.S. 218, 256–258 (1967).

43. 372 U.S. 335 (1963).

44. 387 U.S. 1 (1967).

45. 407 U.S. 25 (1972).

46. Laurence A. Benner, "Eliminating Excessive Public Defender Workloads," *Criminal Justice* (Summer 2011), 25.

47. Bureau of Justice Statistics, *County-Based and Local Public Defender Offices, 2007* (Washington, D.C.: U.S. Department of Justice, September 2010), 3.

48. *United States v. Gonzalez-Lopez*, 548 U.S. 140 (2006).

49. *Wheat v. United States*, 486 U.S. 153, 159 (1988).

50. 466 U.S. 668 (1984).

51. Sherman Smith, "Cheatham 'Elated' by Court's Decision to Give Him New Trial," *Topeka Capital Journal (Kansas)* (January 26, 2013), A1.

52. Randolph Braccialarghe, "Why Were Perry Mason's Clients Always Innocent?" *Valparaiso University Law Review* (Fall 2004), 65.

53. John Kaplan, "Defending Guilty People," *University of Bridgeport Law Review* (1986), 223.

54. 491 U.S. 554 (1989).

8

Pretrial Procedures and the Criminal Trial

Chapter Outline		Corresponding Learning Objectives
Pretrial Detention	1	Identify the steps involved in the pretrial criminal process.
Establishing Probable Cause	2	Summarize the main difference between an indictment and an information.
The Prosecutorial Screening Process	3	Explain how a prosecutor screens potential cases.
Pleading Guilty	4	Indicate why prosecutors, defense attorneys, and defendants often agree to plea bargains.
Special Features of Criminal Trials	5	Identify the basic protections enjoyed by criminal defendants in the United States.
Jury Selection	6	Contrast challenges for cause and peremptory challenges during *voir dire*.
The Trial	7	Describe the difference between direct and circumstantial evidence, and explain why evidence of a defendant's "evil character" is often excluded from trial.
	8	Identify the primary method that defense attorneys use in most trials to weaken the prosecution's case against their client.
	9	Delineate the circumstances in which a criminal defendant may be tried a second time for the same act.

To target your study and review, look for these numbered Learning Objective icons throughout the chapter.

when Uta von Schwedler's body was found in an overflowing bathtub by her boyfriend, there were plenty of clues as to the cause of her death. A small knife was stuck underneath her body. High doses of the antidepressant Xanax were in her system, and various pills had been spilled throughout the house. She had cuts on her left wrist and an injury to her throat, and there was blood splattered on the wall of her bedroom and on the edge of the bathroom sink. The question for a Salt Lake City, Utah, jury was: Did these clues add up to murder, an accident, or suicide?

According to prosecutors, the evidence showed that von Schwedler had been knifed by her pediatrician ex-husband Johnny Wall, who then dosed her with Xanax and drowned her in the bathtub to make the death look a suicide. Wall's defense attorneys countered that von Schwedler could have committed suicide, or she could have died by accident. The wounds on her wrist were "more likely self-inflicted than defensive," testified a forensic expert hired by the defense team. Law enforcement was unable to prove that Wall had visited his ex-wife's home the night of her death, leaving prosecutors with, in the words of a defense attorney, nothing but "a whole bunch of theories."

The prosecution's theories did, however, include a motive. The former husband and wife had spent years fighting for custody of their four children, leaving Wall full of anger toward von Schwedler. Prosecutors also pointed to a number of coincidences surrounding the case. Von Schwedler was not a known Xanax user, but Wall did fill a large prescription for the drug just before his ex-wife's death. The night von Schwedler drowned, Wall's children remembered their father coming home and asking them if he was a "monster." The next morning, Wall had the interior of his car washed and explained an eye injury by saying that the family dog had scratched him while he slept. By the end of the trial, these inferences provided jurors with enough proof to find Wall guilty of first degree murder, and, in 2015, a judge sentenced him to fifteen years to life in prison.

AP Photo/Rick Bowmer, Pool

▲ Prosecutors used circumstantial evidence to convince a Salt Lake City jury that Johnny Wall, left, drowned his ex-wife in a bathtub as part of an effort to make her death look like a suicide.

1. Consider four pieces of evidence used by the prosecution against Johnny Wall: his Xanax prescription, his calling himself a "monster," his morning visit to a car wash, and his "dog-scratched" eye. How might these combined circumstances have convinced a jury of his guilt?
2. Wall's defense attorneys argued that Uta von Schwedler, disoriented from an overdose of Xanax, stumbled around her home, slashed herself with a knife, and climbed into the bathtub, where she passed out and either accidentally or purposefully drowned. Given the other circumstances of this case, is this theory credible enough to create doubt in your mind that Wall killed his ex-wife? Why or why not?
3. Pelle Wall, the former couple's oldest son, told a number of media outlets that he was certain his father killed his mother. What are the arguments for and against allowing him to state these beliefs at court in front of a jury?

Pretrial Detention

Because of the defendant's social status, the sordid nature of Uta von Schwedler's death, and Pelle Wall's outspokenness regarding his father's guilt, Johnny Wall's trial drew nationwide attention. According to the "wedding cake" model of criminal trials, those who followed the proceedings may have gotten a skewed version of how the criminal justice system works. This model suggests that only the top, and smallest, "layer" of trials comes close to meeting our idealized standards of how the courtroom process should play out.[1]

In high-profile trials such as Wall's, committed attorneys argue minute technicalities for days, and numerous expert witnesses take the stand for both sides. On the bottom, largest layer of the wedding cake, the vast majority of defendants are dealt with informally, and the end goal seems to be speed rather than justice. Indeed, as you will learn in this chapter, trial by jury is quite rare. The fate of most criminal suspects in this country is decided during pretrial procedures, which start almost as soon as the police have identified a suspect.

The Initial Appearance

Learning Objective

1 Identify the steps involved in the pretrial criminal process.

After an arrest has been made, the first step toward determining the suspect's guilt or innocence is the **initial appearance** (for an overview of the entire process, see Figure 8.1). During this brief proceeding, a magistrate (see Chapter 7) informs the defendant of the charges that have been brought against him or her and explains his or her constitutional rights—particularly, the right to remain silent (under the Fifth Amendment) and the right to be represented by counsel (under the Sixth Amendment).

At this point, if the defendant cannot afford to hire a private attorney, a public defender may be appointed, or private counsel may be hired by the state to represent the defendant. As the U.S. Constitution does not specify how soon a defendant must be brought before a magistrate after arrest, it has been left to the judicial branch to determine the timing of the initial appearance. The Supreme Court has held that the initial appearance must occur "promptly," which in most cases means within forty-eight hours of booking.[2]

In misdemeanor cases, a defendant may decide to plead guilty and be sentenced during the initial appearance. Otherwise, the magistrate will usually release those charged with misdemeanors on their promise to return at a later date for further proceedings. For felony cases, however, the defendant is not permitted to make a plea at the initial appearance because a magistrate's court does not have jurisdiction to decide felonies.

Bail

At the initial appearance, in most cases the defendant will be released only if she or he posts **bail**—an amount paid by the defendant to the court and retained by the court until the defendant returns for further proceedings. Defendants who cannot afford bail are generally kept in a local jail or lockup until the date of their trial, though many jurisdictions are searching for alternatives to this practice because of overcrowded incarceration facilities. Just under two-thirds of felony defendants in state courts are released before their trials. Not surprisingly, release is more likely for defendants charged with property, public order, or drug crimes than for defendants charged with violent crimes.

initial appearance An accused's first appearance before a judge or magistrate following arrest.

bail The dollar amount or conditions set by the court to ensure that an individual accused of a crime will appear for further criminal proceedings.

Figure 8.1 The Steps Leading to a Trial

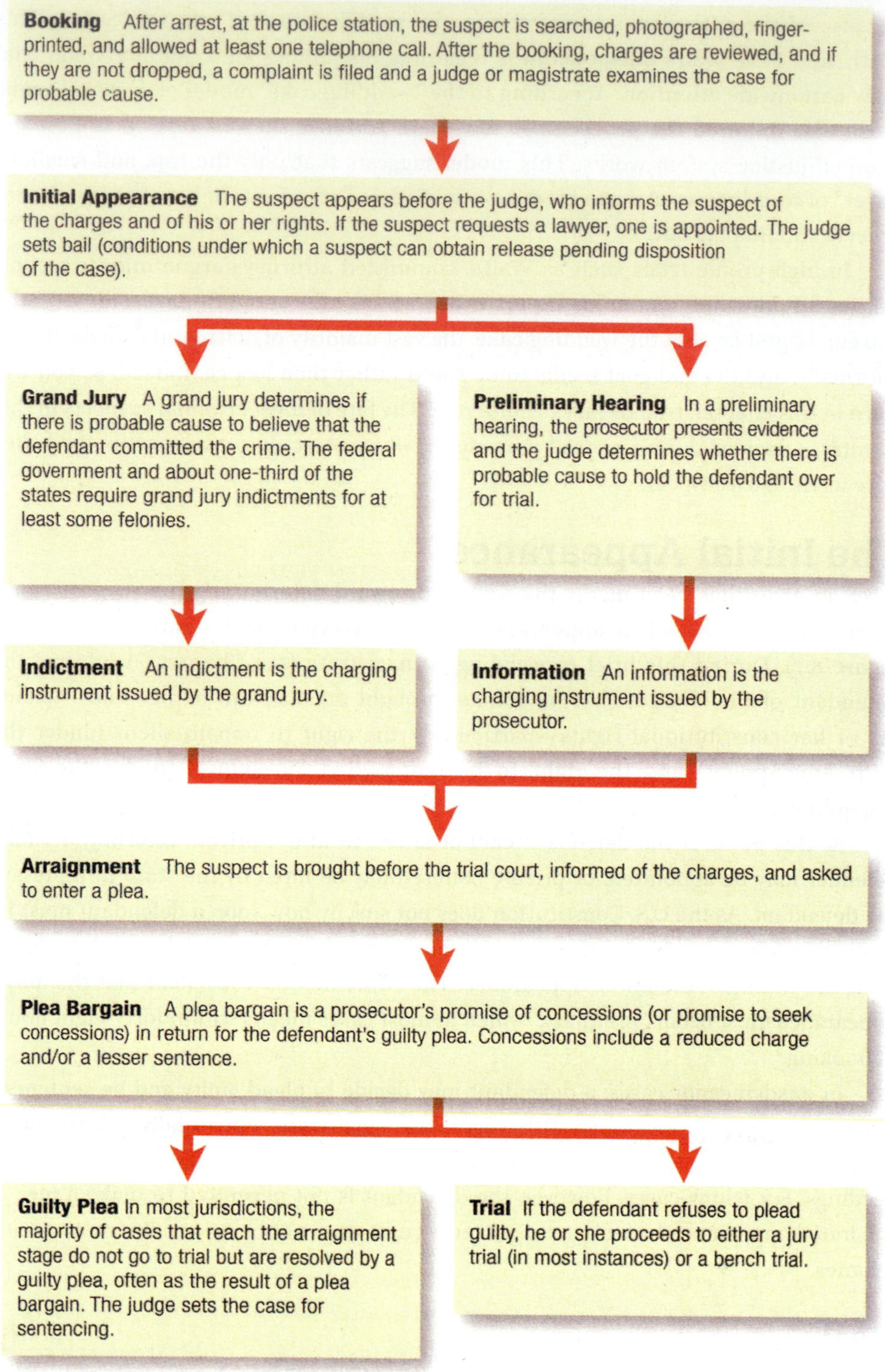
Booking After arrest, at the police station, the suspect is searched, photographed, fingerprinted, and allowed at least one telephone call. After the booking, charges are reviewed, and if they are not dropped, a complaint is filed and a judge or magistrate examines the case for probable cause.
Initial Appearance The suspect appears before the judge, who informs the suspect of the charges and of his or her rights. If the suspect requests a lawyer, one is appointed. The judge sets bail (conditions under which a suspect can obtain release pending disposition of the case).
Grand Jury A grand jury determines if there is probable cause to believe that the defendant committed the crime. The federal government and about one-third of the states require grand jury indictments for at least some felonies.
Preliminary Hearing In a preliminary hearing, the prosecutor presents evidence and the judge determines whether there is probable cause to hold the defendant over for trial.
Indictment An indictment is the charging instrument issued by the grand jury.
Information An information is the charging instrument issued by the prosecutor.
Arraignment The suspect is brought before the trial court, informed of the charges, and asked to enter a plea.
Plea Bargain A plea bargain is a prosecutor's promise of concessions (or promise to seek concessions) in return for the defendant's guilty plea. Concessions include a reduced charge and/or a lesser sentence.
Guilty Plea In most jurisdictions, the majority of cases that reach the arraignment stage do not go to trial but are resolved by a guilty plea, often as the result of a plea bargain. The judge sets the case for sentencing.
Trial If the defendant refuses to plead guilty, he or she proceeds to either a jury trial (in most instances) or a bench trial.

The Purpose of Bail Bail is provided for under the Eighth Amendment. The amendment does not, however, guarantee the right to bail. Instead, it states that "excessive bail shall not be required." This has come to mean that the bail amount must be reasonable compared with the seriousness of the wrongdoing. It does *not* mean that the amount of bail must be within the defendant's ability to pay. At the same time, in theory, bail is not intended be a punitive measure. That is, bail is not meant to be a sort of fine that a defendant must pay to avoid waiting for her or his trial in jail. Rather, bail is designed to provide an incentive for the accused to return to court and participate in her or his legal proceedings.

Setting Bail There is no uniform system for pretrial detention. Each jurisdiction has its own *bail tariffs,* or general guidelines concerning the proper amount of bail. For misdemeanors, the police usually follow a preapproved bail schedule created by local judicial authorities. In felony cases, the primary responsibility to set bail lies with the judge. As might be expected, bail amounts generally rise according to the seriousness of the underlying offense, with murder suspects facing the highest cost of pretrial freedom.[3]

Bail guidelines can be quite extensive. In Illinois, for example, a judge is required to take thirty-eight different factors into account when setting bail: fourteen involve the crime itself, two refer to the evidence gathered, four to the defendant's record, nine to the defendant's flight risk and immigration status, and nine to the defendant's general character.[4] For the most part, however, judges are free to use such tariffs as loose guidelines, and they have a great deal of discretion in setting bail according to the circumstances in each case.

Preventive Detention The vagueness of the Eighth Amendment has encouraged judges to use bail to serve another purpose: the protection of the community. That is, if a judge feels that the defendant poses a threat should he or she be released before trial, the judge will set bail at a level the suspect cannot possibly afford. For example, in the case that opened this chapter, district judge Denise Lindberg refused to lower Johnny Wall's $1.5 million bail, in part because she found that his children credibly feared for their safety should he be set free before trial.[5]

Alternatively, more than thirty states and the federal government have passed **preventive detention** legislation to the same effect. These laws allow judges to act "in the best interests of the community" by denying bail to arrestees with prior records of violence, thus keeping them in custody prior to trial.[6] In fact, about 17 percent of released defendants are rearrested before their trials begin, most of them for missing a scheduled court appearance. Only about 8 percent are rearrested for committing a felony while free on bail.[7]

Posting Bail To gain pretrial release, defendants must pay the full amount of the bail in cash to the court. The money, called a *cash bond,* will be returned when the suspect appears for trial. Given the large amount of funds required, and the relative lack of wealth of many criminal defendants, relatively few defendants are able to post bail in cash. Another option is to use real property, such as a house, instead of cash as collateral. These **property bonds** are also rare because most courts require property valued at double the bail amount. Thus, if bail is set at $5,000, the defendant (or the defendant's family and friends) will have to produce property valued at $10,000.

Bail Bond Agents If unable to post bail with cash or property, a defendant may arrange for a **bail bond agent** to post a bail bond on the defendant's behalf. The bond agent, in effect, promises the court that he or she will turn over to the court the full amount of bail if the defendant fails to return for further proceedings. The defendant usually must give the bond agent a certain percentage of the bail (frequently 10 percent)

preventive detention The retention of an accused person in custody due to fears that she or he will commit a crime if released before trial.

property bond An alternative to posting bail in cash, in which the defendant gains pretrial release by providing the court with property as assurance that he or she will return for trial.

bail bond agent A businessperson who agrees, for a fee, to pay the bail amount if the accused fails to appear in court as ordered.

release on recognizance (ROR) A judge's order that releases an accused from jail with the understanding that he or she will return of his or her own will for further proceedings.

in cash. This amount, which is often not returned to the defendant later, is considered payment for the bond agent's assistance and assumption of risk. Depending on the amount of the bail bond, the defendant may also be required to sign over to the bond agent rights to certain property (such as a car, a valuable watch, or other asset) as security for the bond.

Four states—Illinois, Kentucky, Oregon, and Wisconsin—have abolished bail bonding for profit. As an alternative, these jurisdictions offer defendants an option known as *ten percent cash bail.* This process requires the court, in effect, to take the place of the bond agent. An officer of the court will accept a deposit of 10 percent of the bail amount, refundable when the defendant appears at the assigned time. A number of jurisdictions allow for both bail bond agents and ten percent cash bail, with the judge deciding whether a defendant is eligible for the latter.

Alternatives to Bail One of the most consistent criticisms of bail is that the system is biased against low-income defendants who may not have the financial means to "buy" their temporary freedom. Numerous studies show that defendants detained in jail have worse trial outcomes than those who are able to gain pretrial release.[8] Furthermore, higher bail bond amounts make it more likely that members of minority groups will be kept in jail prior to their trials.[9]

To remedy this situation, bail reformers want to increase the use of **release on recognizance (ROR)**, in which the defendant is set free at no cost with the understanding that he or she will return at the time of the trial. Many jurisdictions are turning to *pretrial risk assessment tools* to determine which defendants should be eligible for ROR. For example, several local court systems in Colorado rely on the twelve factors listed in Figure 8.2 to measure the risk that a defendant will "jump" bail or be arrested on new charges while awaiting trial.

A study of nearly 2,000 defendants in Colorado found that ROR is just as effective as traditional bail bonds in protecting the public and ensuring appearance at trial, with significantly lower costs.[10] Some courts have also had success with automated notification systems, in which defendants released on recognizance are reminded of court dates via phone calls, text messages, or e-mails. In Multnomah County, Oregon,

Figure 8.2 The Colorado Pretrial Assessment Tool (CPAT) Risk Factors

In Colorado, defendants in certain jurisdictions are given a score based on the twelve CPAT factors listed below. Based on this score, the defendant is assigned to one of four risk categories, and those deemed low risk have a much greater chance of being released on their own recognizance before trial.

1. Having a home phone or a cell phone
2. Owning or renting a residence
3. Contributing to residential payments
4. Past or current problems with alcohol
5. Past or current mental health treatment
6. Age at first arrest*
7. Past jail sentence
8. Past prison sentence
9. Having active warrants
10. Having other pending cases in court
11. Currently on probation or parole
12. History of bail "jumping"

*The lower the age of first arrest, the more likely the defendant is at risk to skip trial or reoffend.

Sourece: *The Colorado Bail Book: A Defense Practitioner's Guide to Adult Pretrial Release* (Denver: Colorado Criminal Defense Institue, September 2015), 7.

for example, failure to appear for trial rates dropped 45 percent two years after such a system was put in place.[11]

preliminary hearing An initial hearing in which a magistrate decides if there is probable cause to believe that the defendant committed the crime with which he or she is charged.

discovery Formal investigation by each side prior to trial.

grand jury The group of citizens called to decide whether probable cause exists to believe that a suspect committed the crime with which she or he has been charged.

information The formal charge against the accused issued by the prosecutor after a preliminary hearing has found probable cause.

EthicsChallenge

Critique the following sentence: "The for-profit bail industry ignores public safety in making bail decisions and exploits low-income communities." Do you agree or disagree with this premise? What other ethical issues are raised by the American bail system?

Establishing Probable Cause

Once the initial appearance has been completed and bail has been set, the prosecutor must establish *probable cause*. In other words, the prosecutor must show that a crime was committed and link the defendant to that crime. There are two formal procedures for establishing probable cause at this stage of the pretrial process: preliminary hearings and grand juries.

The Preliminary Hearing

During the **preliminary hearing**, the defendant appears before a judge or magistrate who decides whether the evidence presented is sufficient for the case to proceed to trial. Normally, every person arrested has a right to this hearing within a reasonable amount of time after his or her initial arrest—usually, no later than ten days if the defendant is in custody or within thirty days if he or she has gained pretrial release.

The Preliminary Hearing Process The preliminary hearing is conducted in the manner of a mini-trial. Typically, a police report of the arrest is presented by a law enforcement officer, supplemented with evidence provided by the prosecutor. Because the burden of proving probable cause is relatively light (compared with proving guilt beyond a reasonable doubt), prosecutors rarely call witnesses during the preliminary hearing, saving them for the trial.

During this hearing, the defendant has a right to be represented by counsel, who may cross-examine witnesses and challenge any evidence offered by the prosecutor. In most states, defense attorneys can take advantage of the preliminary hearing to begin the process of **discovery**, in which they are entitled to have access to any evidence in the possession of the prosecution relating to the case. Discovery is considered a keystone in the adversary process, as it allows the defense to see the evidence against the defendant prior to making a plea.

Waiving the Hearing The preliminary hearing often seems rather perfunctory. It usually lasts no longer than five minutes, and the judge or magistrate rarely finds that probable cause does not exist. For this reason, defense attorneys commonly advise their clients to waive their right to a preliminary hearing. Once a judge has ruled affirmatively, in many jurisdictions the defendant is bound over to the **grand jury**, a group of citizens called to decide whether probable cause exists. In other jurisdictions, the prosecutor issues an **information**, which replaces the police complaint as the formal charge against the defendant for the purposes of a trial.

Learning Objective

2 Summarize the main difference between an indictment and an information.

▲ In 2013, a federal grand jury indicted Jordan Linn Graham, center, on murder charges for pushing her husband off a cliff to his death in Montana's Glacier National Park. **Practically, why does the prosecution hold a major advantage during grand jury proceedings?** AP Images/*The Missoulian*/Michael Gallacher

The Grand Jury

The federal government and about one-third of the states require a grand jury to make the decision as to whether a case should go to trial. Grand juries are *impaneled*, or created, for a period of time usually not exceeding three months. During that time, the grand jury sits in closed (secret) session and hears only evidence presented by the prosecutor—the defendant cannot offer evidence at this hearing. The prosecutor shows the grand jury whatever evidence the state has against the defendant, including photographs, documents, tangible objects, the testimony of witnesses, and other items.

If the grand jury finds that probable cause exists, it issues an **indictment** (pronounced in-*dyte*-ment) against the defendant. Like an information in a preliminary hearing, the indictment becomes the formal charge against the defendant. Some states require a grand jury to indict for certain crimes, while in other states a grand jury indictment is optional.

The Prosecutorial Screening Process

Some see the high government success rates in pretrial proceedings as proof that prosecutors successfully screen out weak cases before they get to a grand jury or preliminary hearing. Others, however, point out that procedural rules at this stage favor the prosecution and grand juries rarely, if ever, fail to indict defendants set before them. That being the case, what is to keep prosecutors from using their charging powers indiscriminately?

Nothing, say many observers. Once the police have initially charged a defendant with committing a crime, the prosecutor can prosecute the case as it stands, reduce or increase the initial charge, file additional charges, or dismiss the case. In a system of government and law that relies on checks and balances, asked legal expert Kenneth Culp Davis, why should the prosecutor be "immune to review by other officials and immune to review by the courts?"[12] Though American prosecutors have far-ranging discretionary charging powers, it is not entirely correct to say that they are unrestricted. Controls are indirect and informal, but they do exist.

Case Attrition

Prosecutorial discretion includes the power *not* to prosecute cases. Figure 8.3 depicts the average outcomes of one hundred felony arrests in the United States. As you can see, of the sixty-five adult arrestees brought before the district attorney, only thirty-five are prosecuted, and only eighteen of these prosecutions lead to incarceration. Consequently, fewer than one in three adults arrested for a felony sees the inside of a prison or jail cell. This phenomenon is known as **case attrition**, and it is explained in part by prosecutorial discretion.

indictment A charge or written accusation, issued by a grand jury, that probable cause exists to believe that a named person has committed a crime.

case attrition The process through which prosecutors, by deciding whether to prosecute each person arrested, effect an overall reduction in the number of persons prosecuted.

Figure 8.3 **Following One Hundred Felony Arrests: The Criminal Justice Funnel**

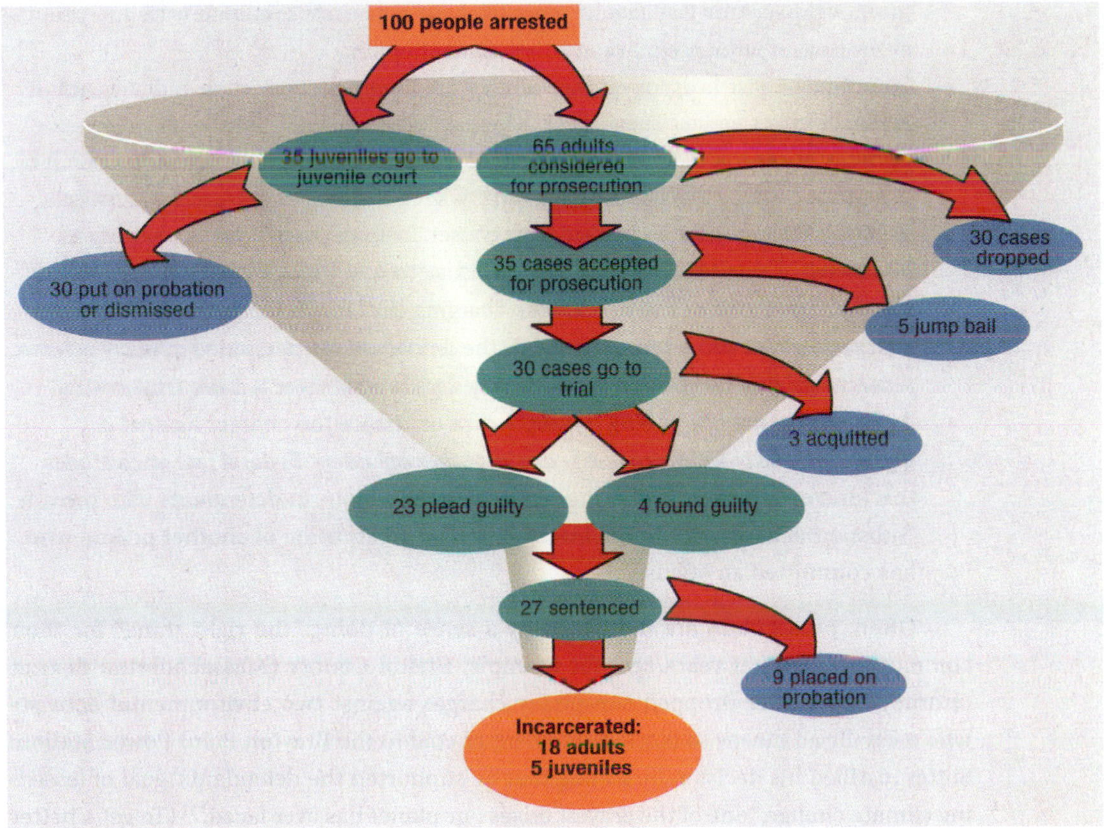

Source: Adapted from Todd R. Clear, George F. Cole, and Michael D. Reisig, *American Corrections,* 11th ed. (Belmont, CA: Wadsworth, 2016), 131.

About half of those adult felony cases brought to prosecutors by police are dismissed through a *nolle prosequi* (Latin for "unwilling to pursue"). Why are these cases "nolled," or not prosecuted by the district attorney? In the section on law enforcement, you learned that the police do not have the resources to arrest every lawbreaker in the nation. Similarly, district attorneys do not have the resources to prosecute every arrest. They must choose how to distribute their scarce resources.

In some cases, the decision is made for prosecutors, such as when police break procedural law and negate important evidence. This happens rarely—less than 3 percent of felony arrests are dropped because of the exclusionary rule, and almost all of these are the result of illegal drug searches.[13]

Screening Factors

Most prosecutors have a *screening* process for deciding when to prosecute and when to "noll." This process varies a bit from jurisdiction to jurisdiction, but most prosecutors consider several factors in making the decision:[14]

Learning Objective

3 Explain how a prosecutor screens potential cases.

- The most important factor in deciding whether to prosecute is not the prosecutor's belief in the guilt of the suspect, but whether there is *sufficient evidence for conviction.* If prosecutors have strong physical evidence and a number of reliable and believable witnesses, they are quite likely to prosecute.
- Prosecutors also rely heavily on *offense seriousness* to guide their priorities, preferring to take on felony offenses rather than misdemeanors. In other words, everything else being equal, a district attorney will prosecute a rapist instead of

a jaywalker because the former presents a greater threat to society than does the latter. A prosecutor will also be more likely to prosecute someone with an extensive record of wrongdoing than a first-time offender.

- Sometimes a case is dropped even when it involves a serious crime and a wealth of evidence exists against the suspect. These situations usually involve *uncooperative victims*. As you saw in Chapter 2, domestic violence cases are particularly difficult to prosecute because the victims may want to keep the matter private, fear reprisals, or have a strong desire to protect their abuser. In some jurisdictions, as many as 80 percent of domestic violence victims refuse to cooperate with the prosecution.[15]
- *Unreliability of victims* can also affect a charging decision. If the victim in a rape case is a crack addict and a prostitute, while the defendant is a decorated military veteran, prosecutors may be hesitant to have a jury decide which one is more trustworthy.
- A prosecutor may be willing to drop a case or reduce the charges against *a defendant who is willing to testify against other offenders*. Federal law encourages this kind of behavior by offering sentencing reductions to defendants who provide "substantial assistance in the investigation or prosecution of another person who has committed an offense."[16]

Often, prosecutors are motivated by a sense of doing "the right thing" for their communities. Several years ago, for example, Bristol County (Massachusetts) district attorney Sam Sutter dropped conspiracy charges against two environmental activists who used illegal means to block a shipment of coal to the Brayton Point Power Station. Sutter justified his decision by stating that he supported the defendants' goal of lessening climate change, "one of the gravest crises our planet has ever faced."[17] (To get a better idea of the difficulty of some charging decisions, see the feature *Discretion in Action—A Battered Woman.*)

Discretion in ACTION

A Battered Woman

Rachel Donahue/Shutterstock.com

The Situation For more than twenty years, John regularly beat his wife, Judy. He even put out cigarettes on her skin and slashed her face with glass. John was often unemployed and forced Judy into prostitution to earn a living. He regularly denied her food and threatened to maim or kill her. Judy left home several times, but John always managed to find her, bring her home, and punish her. Finally, Judy took steps to get John put in a psychiatric hospital. He told her that if anybody came for him, he would "see them coming" and cut her throat before they arrived. That night, Judy shot John three times in the back of the head while he was asleep, killing him. You are the prosecutor with authority over Judy.

The Law In your jurisdiction, a person can use deadly force in self-defense if it is necessary to kill an unlawful aggressor to save himself or herself from imminent death. (See Chapter 3 for a review of self-defense.) Voluntary manslaughter is the intentional killing of another human being without malice. It covers crimes of passion. First degree murder is premeditated killing, with malice. (Also, see Chapter 3 for a review of the different degrees of murder.)

What Would You Do? Will you charge Judy with voluntary manslaughter or first degree murder? Alternatively, do you believe she was acting in self-defense, in which case you will not charge her with any crime? Explain your choice.

To see how a Rutherford County, North Carolina, prosecutor decided a case with similar facts, go to Example 8.1 in Appendix B.

Pleading Guilty

Based on the information (delivered during the preliminary hearing) or indictment (handed down by the grand jury), the prosecutor submits a motion to the court to order the defendant to appear before the trial court for an **arraignment**. Due process of law, as guaranteed by the Fifth Amendment, requires that a criminal defendant be informed of the charges brought against her or him and be offered an opportunity to respond to those charges. The arraignment is one of the ways in which due process requirements are satisfied by criminal procedure law.

At the arraignment, the defendant is informed of the charges and must respond by pleading not guilty or guilty. In some but not all states, the defendant may also enter a plea of ***nolo contendere***, which is Latin for "I will not contest it." The plea of *nolo contendere* is neither an admission nor a denial of guilt. (The consequences for someone who pleads guilty and for someone who pleads *nolo contendere* are the same in a criminal trial, but the latter plea cannot be used in a subsequent civil trial as an admission of guilt.) Most frequently, the defendant pleads guilty to the initial charge or to a lesser charge that has been agreed on through *plea bargaining* between the prosecutor and the defendant. If the defendant pleads guilty, no trial is necessary, and the defendant is sentenced based on the crime he or she has admitted committing.

arraignment A court proceeding in which the suspect is formally charged with the criminal offense stated in the indictment.

nolo contendere Latin for "I will not contest it." A criminal defendant's plea, in which he or she chooses not to challenge, or contest, the charges brought by the government.

plea bargaining The process by which the accused and the prosecutor work out a mutually satisfactory conclusion to the case, subject to court approval.

Plea Bargaining in the Criminal Justice System

Plea bargaining most often takes place after the arraignment and before the beginning of the trial. In its simplest terms, it is a process by which the accused, represented by the defense counsel, and the prosecutor work out a mutually satisfactory disposition of the case, subject to court approval.

Usually, plea bargaining involves the defendant pleading guilty to the charges against her or him in return for a lighter sentence, but other variations are possible as well. The defendant can agree to plead guilty in exchange for having the charge against her or him reduced from, say, felony burglary to the lesser offense of breaking and entering. Or a person charged with multiple counts may agree to plead guilty if the prosecutor agrees to drop one or more of the counts. Whatever the particulars, the results of a plea bargain are generally the same: the prosecutor gets a conviction, and the defendant a lesser punishment.

In *Santobello v. New York* (1971),[18] the United States Supreme Court held that plea bargaining "is not only an essential part of the process but a highly desirable part for many reasons." Some observers would agree, but with ambivalence. They understand that plea bargaining offers the practical benefit of saving court resources, but question whether it is the best way to achieve justice.[19]

Motivations for Plea Bargaining

Given the high rate of plea bargaining—accounting for 97 percent of criminal convictions in state courts[20]—it follows that the prosecutor, defense attorney, and defendant each have strong reasons to engage in the practice.

Learning Objective

4 Indicate why prosecutors, defense attorneys, and defendants often agree to plea bargains.

Prosecutors and Plea Bargaining In most cases, a prosecutor has a single goal after charging a defendant with a crime: conviction. If a case goes to trial, no matter how certain a prosecutor may be that the defendant is guilty, there is always a

▲ For more than a decade, defense attorney Allan Karlin, left, argued that his client Joseph Buffey (not pictured) should be allowed to withdraw a guilty plea made after prosecutors withheld DNA evidence suggesting that Buffey was innocent. In 2015, the West Virginia Supreme Court agreed. **Do you think that defendants should be given access to DNA evidence during plea bargain negotiations? Why or why not?** AP Photo/The Exponent Telegram, Matt Harvey

chance that a jury or judge will disagree. Plea bargaining removes this risk. Furthermore, the prosecutorial screening process described earlier in the chapter is not infallible. Sometimes, a prosecutor will find that the evidence against the accused is weaker than first thought or will uncover new information that changes the complexion of the case. In these situations, the prosecutor may decide to drop the charges or, if he or she still feels that the defendant is guilty, turn to plea bargaining to "save" a questionable case.

The prosecutor's role as an administrator also comes into play. She or he may be interested in the quickest, most efficient manner to dispose of caseloads, and plea bargains reduce the time and money spent on each case. Personal philosophy can affect the proceedings as well. A prosecutor who feels that a mandatory minimum sentence for a particular crime, such as marijuana possession, is too strict may plea bargain in order to lessen the penalty. Similarly, some prosecutors will consider plea bargaining only in certain instances—for burglary and theft, for example, but not for more serious felonies such as rape and murder.

Defense Attorneys and Plea Bargaining Political scientist Milton Heumann has said that a defense attorney's most important lesson is that "most of his [or her] clients are guilty."[21] Given this stark reality, favorable plea bargains are often the best a defense attorney can do for clients, aside from helping them to gain acquittals. Some have suggested that defense attorneys have other, less savory motives for convincing a client to plead guilty, such as a desire to increase profit margins by quickly disposing of cases[22] or a wish to ingratiate themselves with the other members of the courtroom work group by showing their "reasonableness."[23]

Defendants and Plea Bargaining A plea bargain allows the defendant a measure of control over his or her fate. In May 2014, for example, Jeffrey Basil killed William Sager by pushing him down a flight of stairs in a Buffalo, New York, bar. Even though Basil maintained Sager's death was accidental, he risked facing life in prison if found guilty of second degree murder at trial. So, in July 2015, Basil pleaded guilty to first degree manslaughter, and a judge sentenced him to eighteen years behind bars. "It's not easy but you have to be practical and you have to be realistic," said Basil's defense attorney of his client's decision.[24]

Critics of plea bargaining claim that prosecutors use the threat of lengthy trial sentences to pressure defendants into pleading guilty. A recent study found that, in federal drug cases, offenders convicted at trial receive sentences that are three times longer than those who plead guilty.[25] Figure 8.4 shows that that defendants who plea bargain receive significantly lesser sentences on average than those found guilty in state courts, as well.

Figure 8.4 Sentencing Outcomes for Guilty Pleas

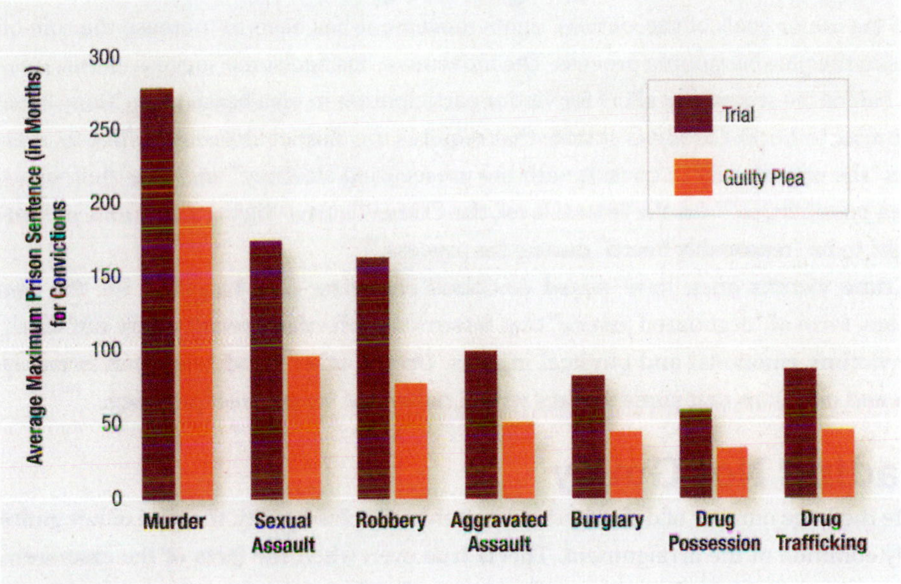

Source: Bureau of Justice Statistic, *Felony Sentences in State Courts, 2006 - Statistical Tables* (Washington, D.C.: U.S. Department of Justice, December 2009), Table 4.3.

Protecting the Defendant Often, the defendant plays only a minor role in the plea bargaining process, which is dominated by a give-and-take between the prosecutor and the defense attorney. The United States Supreme Court is aware of the potential for taking advantage of the defendant in plea bargaining and has therefore created safeguards to protect the accused. Until *Boykin v. Alabama* (1969),[26] judges would often accept the defense counsel's word that the defendant wanted to plead guilty. In that case, the Court held that the defendant must make a clear statement that he or she accepts the plea bargain. As a result, many jurisdictions now ask the accused to sign a ***Boykin* form** waiving his or her right to a trial.

Faulty Advice In 2012, the Supreme Court dramatically affected plea bargaining law by ruling that defendants have a constitutional right to effective representation during plea negotiations.[27] That year, the Court considered the plight of Anthony Cooper, who had shot a woman in Detroit. Based on faulty legal advice from his attorney, Cooper rejected a plea bargain that called for a sentence of four to seven years behind bars. Instead, he lost at trial and was sentenced to fifteen to thirty years. After hearing Cooper's appeal, the Court found that, in essence, defendants have a constitutional right to effective counsel during plea bargaining, just as they do during a trial.

A Second Chance to Plead Because of the Supreme Court's ruling, defendants like Anthony Cooper now have the opportunity to argue that had they received proper legal advice, they would have accepted the plea bargain rather than risk a trial. If a defendant successfully proves ineffective counsel during plea bargaining, he or she will be given another chance to make a favorable plea.[28] The four members of the Court who dissented from this decision warned that it would give defendants who lose at trial an unfair opportunity to revisit a rejected plea bargain. "It's going to be tricky," agrees Stephanos Bibas, a law professor at the University of Pennsylvania. "There are going to be a lot of defendants who say after they're convicted that they really would have taken the plea."[29]

***Boykin* form** A form that must be completed by a defendant who pleads guilty. The defendant states that she or he has done so voluntarily and with full comprehension of the consequences.

Victims and Plea Bargaining

One of the major goals of the victims' rights movement has been to increase the role of victims in the plea bargaining process. The movement has had some success in this area. About half of the states now allow for victim participation in plea bargaining. Many have laws similar to North Carolina's statute that requires the district attorney's office to offer victims "the opportunity to consult with the prosecuting attorney" and give their views on "plea possibilities."[30] On the federal level, the Crime Victims' Rights Act grants victims the right to be "reasonably heard" during the process.[31]

Crime victims often have mixed emotions regarding plea bargains. On the one hand, any form of "negotiated justice" that lessens the offender's penalty may add insult to the victim's emotional and physical injuries. On the other hand, trials can bring up events and emotions that some victims would rather not have to reexperience.

Pleading Not Guilty

Despite the large number of defendants who eventually plead guilty, the plea of not guilty is fairly common at the arraignment. This is true even when the facts of the case seem stacked against the defendant. Generally, a not guilty plea in the face of strong evidence is part of a strategy to:

1. Gain a more favorable plea bargain,
2. Challenge a crucial part of the evidence on constitutional grounds, or
3. Submit one of the affirmative defenses that we discussed in Chapter 3.

Of course, if either side is confident in the strength of its arguments and evidence, it will obviously be less likely to accept a plea bargain. Both prosecutors and defense attorneys may favor a trial to gain publicity, and sometimes public pressure after an extremely violent or high-profile crime will force a chief prosecutor (who is, remember, normally an elected official) to take a weak case to trial. Also, some defendants may insist on their right to a trial, regardless of their attorneys' advice. In the remainder of this chapter, we will examine what happens to the roughly 3 percent of indictments that do lead to the courtroom.

Special Features of Criminal Trials

Criminal trial procedures reflect the need to protect criminal defendants against the power of the state by providing them with a number of rights. Many of the significant rights of the accused are spelled out in the Sixth Amendment, which reads, in part, as follows:

Learning Objective 5

Identify the basic protections enjoyed by criminal defendants in the United States.

> In all criminal prosecutions, the accused shall enjoy the right to a speedy and public trial, by an impartial jury of the State and the district wherein the crime shall have been committed, . . . and to be informed of the nature and cause of the accusation; to be confronted with the witnesses against him; to have compulsory process for obtaining witnesses in his favor; and to have the Assistance of Counsel for his defense.

In the last chapter, we discussed the Sixth Amendment's guarantee of the right to counsel. In this section, we will examine the other important aspects of the criminal trial, beginning with two protections explicitly stated in the Sixth Amendment: the right to a speedy trial by an impartial jury.

A "Speedy" Trial

As you have just read, the Sixth Amendment requires a speedy trial for those accused of a criminal act. The reason for this requirement is obvious: depending on various factors, the defendant may lose his or her right to move freely and may be incarcerated prior to trial. Also, the accusation that a person has committed a crime jeopardizes that person's reputation in the community. If the defendant is innocent, the sooner the trial is held, the sooner his or her innocence can be established in the eyes of the court and the public.

The Definition of a Speedy Trial The Sixth Amendment does not specify what is meant by the term *speedy.* The United States Supreme Court has refused to quantify "speedy" as well, ruling instead in *Barker v. Wingo* (1972)[32] that only in situations in which the delay is unwarranted and proved to be prejudicial can the accused claim a violation of Sixth Amendment rights.

Speedy-Trial Laws To meet constitutional requirements, all fifty states have their own speedy-trial statutes. For example, the Illinois Speedy Trial Act holds that a defendant must be tried within 120 days of arrest unless both the prosecution and the defense agree otherwise.[33] Keep in mind, however, that a defendant does not automatically go free if her or his trial is not "speedy" enough. There must be judicial action, which is rare but does occur from time to time. Several years ago, for example, the Indiana Supreme Court overturned a child molestation conviction because the defendant's trial was not held until 1,291 days after his arrest. The court called the delay, "considerable, unfortunate and inexcusable."[34] Nearly half of all criminal trials in state courts are settled within three months of the defendant's arrest. About 15 percent take more than a year to adjudicate.[35]

At the national level, the Speedy Trial Act of 1974[36] (amended in 1979) specifies the following time limits for those in the federal court system:

1. No more than thirty days between arrest and indictment.
2. No more than ten days between indictment and arraignment.
3. No more than sixty days between arraignment and trial.

Both federal and state law allow extra time for hearings on pretrial motions, mental competency examinations, and other procedural actions. The resulting intervals can be considerable, particularly when it comes to high-profile trials. For example, in the case that opened this chapter, Johnny Wall's murder trial started three and a half years after the death of Uta von Schwedler.

Statutes of Limitations The Sixth Amendment's guarantee of a speedy trial does not apply until a person has been accused of a crime. Citizens are protected against unreasonable delays before accusation by **statutes of limitations**, which are legislative time limits that require prosecutors to charge a defendant with a crime within a certain amount of time after the illegal act took place. If the statute of limitations on a particular crime is ten years, and the police do not identify a suspect until ten years and one day after the criminal act occurred, then that suspect cannot be charged with that particular offense.

In general, prosecutions for murder and other offenses that carry the death penalty do not have a statute of limitations. This exception provides police with the ability

statute of limitations A law limiting the amount of time prosecutors have to bring criminal charges against a suspect after the crime has occurred.

▲ On December 30, 2015, authorities in Montgomery County, Pennsylvania, charged comedian Bill Cosby, center, with three counts of aggravated sexual assault for an incident that allegedly took place on January 15, 2004. Had prosecutors waited several more weeks, Cosby would have been immune from these charges because of the state's twelve-year statute of limitations pertaining to such crimes. **What are the arguments for and against statutes of limitations in rape and sexual assault cases?** Michael Bryant-Pool/Getty Images

to conduct cold case investigations that last for decades. In 2015, for example, authorities arrested Jose Ferreira, Jr., after he admitted to killing thirteen-year-old Carrie Ann Jopek and burying her body under a porch in Milwaukee, Wisconsin, thirty-three years earlier. The problem with prosecuting such cases, of course, is that so much time has passed since the criminal act that witnesses may be missing or dead, memories may be unreliable, and key evidence may have been lost.

The Role of the Jury

The Sixth Amendment also states that anyone accused of a crime shall be judged by "an impartial jury." In *Duncan v. Louisiana* (1968),[37] the Supreme Court solidified this right by ruling that in all felony cases, the defendant is entitled to a **jury trial**. The Court has, however, left it to the individual states to decide whether juries are required for misdemeanor cases.[38] If the defendant waives her or his right to trial by jury, a **bench trial** takes place in which a judge decides questions of legality and fact, and no jury is involved.

The typical American jury consists of twelve persons. About half the states allow fewer than twelve persons on criminal juries, though rarely for serious felony cases. In federal courts, defendants are entitled to have the case heard by a twelve-member jury unless both parties agree in writing to a smaller jury.

In most jurisdictions, jury verdicts in criminal cases must be *unanimous* for **acquittal** or conviction. As will be explained in more detail later, if the jury cannot reach unanimous agreement on whether to acquit or convict the defendant, the result is a *hung jury,* and the judge may order a new trial. The Supreme Court has held that unanimity is not a rigid requirement. It declared that jury verdicts must be unanimous in federal criminal trials but has given states leeway to set their own rules.[39] As a result, Louisiana and Oregon continue to require only ten votes for conviction in criminal cases.

The Privilege against Self-Incrimination

In addition to the Sixth Amendment, which specifies the protections we have just discussed, the Fifth Amendment to the Constitution also provides important safeguards for the defendant. The Fifth Amendment states that no person "shall be compelled in any criminal case to be a witness against himself." Therefore, a defendant has the right not to testify at his or her own trial—in popular parlance, to "take the Fifth." Because defense attorneys often are wary of exposing their clients to a prosecutor's questions in court, defendants rarely take the witness stand.

Prejudicing the Jury

It is important to note that not only does the defendant have the right to "take the Fifth," but also that the decision to do so should not prejudice the jury in the prosecution's favor. The Supreme Court came to this controversial decision while reviewing *Adamson v. California* (1947),[40] a case involving the convictions of two

jury trial A trial before a judge and a jury.

bench trial A trial conducted without a jury, in which a judge makes the determination of the defendant's guilt or innocence.

acquittal A declaration following a trial that the individual accused of the crime is innocent in the eyes of the law and thus is absolved from the charges.

defendants who had declined to testify in their own defense against charges of robbery, kidnapping, and murder. The prosecutor in the *Adamson* proceedings frequently and insistently brought this silence to the notice of the jury in his closing argument, insinuating that if the pair had been innocent, they would not have been afraid to testify.

The Court ruled that such tactics effectively invalidated the Fifth Amendment by using the defendants' refusal to testify as a ploy to insinuate guilt. Now judges are required to inform the jury that an accused's decision to remain silent cannot be held against him or her. This protection covers only post-arrest and trial silence, however. In 2013, the Supreme Court ruled that prosecutors can inform a jury that a defendant refused to answer police questions *before* being arrested, a process detailed in Chapter 5.[41]

Witnesses in Court Witnesses are also protected by the Fifth Amendment and may refuse to testify on the ground that such testimony would reveal their own criminal wrongdoing. In practice, however, witnesses are sometimes granted *immunity* before testifying, meaning that no information they disclose can be used to bring criminal charges against them. Witnesses who have been granted immunity cannot refuse to answer questions in court on the basis of self-incrimination.

The Presumption of a Defendant's Innocence

The presumption in criminal law is that a defendant is innocent until proved guilty. The burden of proving guilt falls on the state (the public prosecutor). Even if a defendant did in fact commit the crime, she or he will be "innocent" in the eyes of the law unless the prosecutor can substantiate the charge with sufficient evidence to persuade a jury (or judge in a bench trial) that the defendant is guilty.

Sometimes, especially when a case involves a high-profile violent crime, pretrial publicity may have convinced many members of the community—including potential jurors—that a defendant is guilty. In these instances, a judge has the authority to change the venue of the trial to increase the likelihood of an unbiased jury. In 2015, for example, Dzokhar Tsarnaev's defense attorneys unsuccessfully requested a change of venue from Boston for their client's trial on charges relating to the 2013 Boston Marathon bombings. They argued that most Boston residents—and potential jurors—had "six degrees of connections" with a victim of the attacks and therefore would be unable to remain impartial during a trial.[42]

A Strict Standard of Proof

In a criminal trial, the defendant is not required to prove his or her innocence. As mentioned earlier, the burden of proving the defendant's guilt lies entirely with the state. Furthermore, the state must prove the defendant's guilt *beyond a reasonable doubt.* In other words, the prosecution must show that, based on all the evidence, the defendant's guilt is clear and unquestionable. In *In re Winship* (1970),[43] a case involving the due process rights of juveniles, the Supreme Court ruled that the Constitution requires the reasonable doubt standard because it reduces the risk of convicting innocent people and therefore reassures Americans of the law's moral force and legitimacy.

This high standard of proof in criminal cases reflects a fundamental social value—the belief that it is worse to convict an innocent individual than to let a guilty one go free. The consequences to the life, liberty, and reputation of an accused person from an erroneous conviction for a crime are substantial, and this has been factored into the process. Placing a high standard of proof on the prosecutor reduces the margin of error in criminal cases (at least in one direction).

master jury list The list of citizens in a court's district from which a jury can be selected; compiled from voter-registration lists, driver's license lists, and other sources.

venire The group of citizens from which the jury is selected.

voir dire The preliminary questions that the trial attorneys ask prospective jurors to determine whether they are biased or have any connection with the defendant or a witness.

Jury Selection

The initial step in a criminal trial involves choosing the jury. The main goal of jury selection is to produce a representative cross section of the population of the jurisdiction where the crime was committed. Besides the need to live in the jurisdiction where the case is being tried, there are very few restrictions on eligibility to serve on a jury. State legislatures generally set the requirements, and they are similar in most states. For the most part, jurors must be:

1. Citizens of the United States.
2. Eighteen years of age or over.
3. Free of felony convictions.
4. Healthy enough to function in a jury setting.
5. Sufficiently intelligent to understand the issues of a trial.
6. Able to read, write, and comprehend the English language (with one exception—New Mexico does not allow non-English-speaking citizens to be eliminated from jury lists simply because of their lack of English-language skills).

The **master jury list**, sometimes called the *jury pool*, is made up of all the eligible jurors in a community. This list is usually drawn from voter-registration lists or driver's license rolls, which have the benefit of being easily available and timely.

The next step in gathering a jury is to draw together the ***venire*** (Latin for "to come"). The *venire* is composed of all those people who are notified by the clerk of the court that they have been selected for jury duty. Those selected to be part of the *venire* are ordered to report to the courthouse on the date specified by the notice.

Voir Dire

At the courthouse, prospective jurors are gathered, and the process of selecting those who will actually hear the case begins. This selection process is not haphazard. The court ultimately seeks jurors who are free of any biases that may affect their willingness to listen to the facts of the case impartially. To this end, both the prosecutor and the defense attorney have some input into the ultimate makeup of the jury. Each attorney questions prospective jurors in a proceeding known as ***voir dire*** (French for "to speak the truth"). During *voir dire*, jurors are required to provide the court with a significant amount of personal information, including home address, marital status, employment status, arrest record, and life experiences.

▼ A Boston jury waits to be dismissed after finding Christian K. Gerhartsreiter guilty of kidnapping his seven-year-old daughter during a supervised visit. **Why is it important for a defendant to be tried by a jury of her or his "peers"?** AP Images/CJ Gunther, Pool

Questioning Potential Jurors The *voir dire* process involves both written and oral questioning of potential jurors. Attorneys fashion their inquiries in such a manner as to uncover any biases on the parts of prospective jurors and to find persons who might identify with the plights of their respective sides. As one attorney noted, though a lawyer will have many chances to talk to a jury as a whole, *voir dire* is his or her only chance to talk with the individual jurors. (To better understand the specific kinds of questions asked during this process, see Figure 8.5.)

A potential juror's failure to be forthcoming and honest during *voir dire* can have serious consequences. In June 2015, five months after Cory Batey and Brandon Vandenburg were convicted of sexually assaulting a woman on the campus of Vanderbilt University in Nashville, Tennessee, a judge nullified the results of the trial. One of the jurors, it turned out, had failed to disclose that he had been a victim of sex crimes as a teenager. Judge Monte D. Watkins decided that this omission raised the "presumption of bias" on the juror's part and ordered that both defendants be retried.[44]

Figure 8.5 Sample Juror Questionnaire

In 2015, Aaron Hernandez went on trial for murdering Odin Lloyd in North Attleborough, Massachusetts, two years earlier. As the following excerpt from the juror questionnaire shows, lawyers in the case were interested in determining whether potential jurors had any biases that could keep them from objectively deciding the defendant's fate.

30. Do you believe that Mr. Hernandez is more likely to be guilty of the charges in this case because he has tattoos than an individual without tattoos would be?

31. Mr. Hernandez, the defendant, is Hispanic and the decedent, Odin Lloyd, was African American. Is there anything about those facts that would interfere with your ability to render a fair and just verdict?

37. Are you a fan of the New England Patriots?

39. In this case, you will hear evidence that the defendant was a professional football player for the New England Patriots. Is there anything about that fact that would impair your ability to be fair and impartial?

Source: Eric L. Muller, "Solving the Batson Paradox: Harmless Error, Jury Reprsentation, and the Sixth Amendment," *Yale Law Journal 106 (October 1996)*, 93

Challenging Potential Jurors During *voir dire*, the attorney for each side may exercise a certain number of challenges to prevent particular persons from serving on the jury. Both sides can exercise two types of challenges: challenges "for cause" and peremptory challenges.

Challenges for Cause If a defense attorney or prosecutor concludes that a prospective juror is unfit to serve, the attorney may exercise a **challenge for cause** and request that that person not be included on the jury. Attorneys must provide the court with a sound, legally justifiable reason for why potential jurors are "unfit" to serve. For example, jurors can be challenged for cause if they are mentally incompetent, do not understand English, or are proved to have a prior link—be it personal or financial—with the defendant or victim.

Peremptory Challenges Each attorney may also exercise a limited number of **peremptory challenges**. These challenges are based solely on an attorney's subjective reasoning, and the attorney usually is not required to give any legally justifiable reason for wanting to exclude a particular person from the jury. Because of the rather random nature of peremptory challenges, each state limits the number that an attorney may utilize: between five and ten for felony trials (depending on the state) and between ten and twenty for trials that could possibly result in the death penalty (also depending on the state). Once an attorney's peremptory challenges are used up, he or she must accept forthcoming jurors, unless a challenge for cause can be used.

Learning Objective

6 Contrast challenges for cause and peremptory challenges during *voir dire*.

Race and Gender Issues in Jury Selection

For many years, prosecutors used their peremptory challenges as an instrument of segregation in jury selection. Prosecutors were able to keep African Americans off juries in cases in which an African American was the defendant. The argument that African Americans—or members of any other minority group—would be partial toward one of

challenge for cause A *voir dire* challenge for which an attorney states the reason why a prospective juror should not be included on the jury.

peremptory challenges *Voir dire* challenges to exclude potential jurors from serving on the jury without any supporting reason or cause.

Careers in CJ

FASTFACTS

Trial court administrator

Job description:

- Oversees court operations, budget and accounting, technology, emergency management, and human resources.

What kind of training is required?

- A B.A. in court administration, management, or a related area, and five years of professional experience in court administration or government administration, plus five years in a supervisory capacity.

Annual salary range?

- $30,000–$90,000

Collins E. Ijoma
Trial Court Administrator

Courtesy of Collins E. Ijoma

As the trial court administrator, I serve principally as the chief administrative officer for the largest trial and municipal court system in New Jersey. We provide technical and managerial support to the court (more than sixty superior court judges and thirty-six municipal court judges) on such matters as personnel, program development, case flow, resources, and facilities management. This description may sound "highfalutin" considering that most people can only describe a court in terms of a judge, one or two courtroom staff, and a few other employees associated with the visible activities in the courthouse. Obviously, there is a lot more going on behind the scenes of which the average citizen is not aware.

One thing that keeps me going and enthused about this profession is the resolve and dedication of our judges and staff. The family division embraces a host of issues, and in some cases those who seek help are hurting and desperate. The court may be their only hope.

SOCIAL MEDIA CAREER TIP Many businesses and organizations have their own career websites for potential employees. Some have even set up *talent communities* to interact with applicants. Explore these options if you have a specific job in mind.

their own was tacitly supported by the Supreme Court. Despite its own assertion, made in *Swain v. Alabama* (1965),[45] that blacks have the same right to appear on a jury as whites, the Court mirrored the apparent racism of society as a whole by protecting the questionable actions of many prosecutors.

The *Batson* Reversal The Supreme Court reversed this policy in 1986 with *Batson v. Kentucky*.[46] In that case, the Court declared that the Constitution prohibits prosecutors from using peremptory challenges to strike possible jurors on the basis of race. Under the *Batson* ruling, the defendant must prove that the prosecution's use of a peremptory challenge was racially motivated. Doing so requires a number of legal steps:[47]

1. First, the defendant must make a *prima facie* case that there has been discrimination during *venire*. (*Prima facie* is Latin for "at first sight." Legally, it refers to a fact that is presumed to be true unless contradicted by evidence.)
2. To do so, the defendant must show that he or she is a member of a recognizable racial group and that the prosecutor has used peremptory challenges to remove members of this group from the jury pool.
3. Then, the defendant must show that these facts and other relevant circumstances raise the possibility that the prosecutor removed the prospective jurors solely because of their race.
4. If the court accepts the defendant's charges, the burden shifts to the prosecution to prove that its peremptory challenges were race neutral. If the court finds against the prosecution, it rules that a *Batson* violation has occurred.

The Court has revisited the issue of race a number of times in the years since its *Batson* decision. In *Powers v. Ohio* (1991),[48] it ruled that a defendant may contest race-based peremptory challenges even if the defendant is not of the same race as the excluded jurors. In *Georgia v. McCollum* (1992),[49] the Court placed defense attorneys under the same restrictions as prosecutors when making race-based peremptory challenges. Finally, in 2008, the Court, reaffirming its *Batson* decision of twenty-two years earlier, overturned the conviction of an African American death row inmate because a Louisiana prosecutor improperly picked an all-white jury for his murder trial.[50]

These rulings do not mean that a black defendant can never be judged by a jury made up entirely of whites. Rather, they indicate that attorneys cannot use peremptory challenges to reject a prospective juror because of her or his race.

Women on the Jury In *J.E.B. v. Alabama ex rel. T.B.* (1994),[51] the Supreme Court extended the principles of the *Batson* ruling to cover gender bias in jury selection. The case was a civil suit for paternity and child support brought by the state of Alabama. Prosecutors used nine of their ten challenges to remove men from the jury, while the defense made similar efforts to remove women. When challenged, the state defended its actions by referring to what it called the rational belief that men and women might have different views on the issues of paternity and child support. The Court disagreed and held this approach to be unconstitutional.

Getting Linked in

Trial lawyers often hire **jury consultants** to research jurors' backgrounds, assist with juror selection, create favorable potential juror profiles, develop *voir dire* questions, and organize mock trials. You can learn more about this specialized career by searching LinkedIn for "jury consultation."

Alternate Jurors

Because unforeseeable circumstances or illness may necessitate that one or more of the sitting jurors be dismissed, the court may also seat several *alternate jurors* who will hear the entire trial. Depending on the rules of the particular jurisdiction, two or three alternate jurors may be present throughout the trial. If a juror has to be excused in the middle of the trial, an alternate may take his or her place without disrupting the proceedings.

Ethics Challenge

During *voir dire* for a 2014 trial featuring a white defendant who allegedly fatally shot a black victim in Wayne County (Michigan), each of the defense attorney's five peremptory challenges removed a potential African American juror. The defense attorney claimed to have race-neutral reasons for dismissing all five, including that one had relatives killed in gunfire and another had slept during jury selection. Even if these reasons are valid, how does this situation underscore the potential for unethical behavior by lawyers in their use of peremptory challenges?

The Trial

Once the jury members have been selected, the judge swears them in and the trial itself can begin. A rather pessimistic truism among attorneys is that every case "has been won or lost when the jury is sworn." This reflects the belief that a juror's values are the major, if not dominant, factor in the decision of guilt or innocence.[52]

In actuality, it is difficult to predict how a jury will go about reaching a decision. Despite a number of studies on the question, researchers have not been able to identify any definitive consistent patterns of jury behavior. Sometimes, jurors in a criminal trial will follow instructions to find a defendant guilty unless there is a reasonable doubt,

opening statements The attorneys' statements to the jury at the beginning of the trial.

evidence Anything that is used to prove the existence or nonexistence of a fact.

testimony Verbal evidence given by witnesses under oath.

real evidence Evidence that is brought into court and seen by the jury, as opposed to evidence that is described for a jury.

lay witness A witness who can truthfully and accurately testify on a fact in question without having specialized training or knowledge.

and sometimes they seem to follow instinct or prejudice and apply the law any way they choose.

Opening Statements

Attorneys may choose to open the trial with a statement to the jury, though they are not required to do so. In these **opening statements**, the attorneys give a brief version of the facts and the supporting evidence that they will present during the trial. Because some trials can drag on for weeks or even months, it is extremely helpful for jurors to hear a summary of what will unfold. In short, the opening statement is a kind of "road map" that describes the destination that each attorney hopes to reach and outlines how she or he plans to reach it. (For an example of an opening statement, see Figure 8.6.)

The Role of Evidence

Once the opening statements have been made, the prosecutor begins the trial proceedings by presenting the state's *evidence* against the defendant. **Evidence** is anything that is used to prove the existence or nonexistence of a fact. Courts have complex rules about what types of evidence may be presented and how the evidence may be brought out during the trial. For the most part, evidence can be broken down into two categories: testimony and real evidence. **Testimony** consists of statements by competent witnesses. **Real evidence**, presented to the court in the form of exhibits, includes any physical items—such as the murder weapon or a bloodstained piece of clothing—that affect the case.

Rules of evidence are designed to ensure that testimony and exhibits presented to the jury are relevant, reliable, and not unfairly prejudicial against the defendant. One of the tasks of the defense attorney is to challenge evidence presented by the prosecution by establishing that the evidence is not reliable. Of course, the prosecutor also tries to demonstrate the irrelevance or unreliability of evidence presented by the defense. The final decision on whether evidence is allowed before the jury rests with the judge, in keeping with his or her role as the "referee" of the adversary system.

Testimonial Evidence

A person who is called to testify on factual matters that would be understood by the average citizen is referred to as a **lay witness**. If asked about the condition of a victim of an assault, for example, a lay witness could relate certain

Figure 8.6 The Opening Statement

Several years ago, Gigi Jordan (pictured here) went on trial in New York City for killing her eight-year-old son, an act she defended as necessary to save the boy from being abused by his father. In their opening statements, prosecutor Matt Bogdanos and defense attorney Allan Brenner attempted to place the defendant's actions in the worst (or best) possible light. (The jury found Jordan guilty of manslaughter rather than murder.)

Jefferson Siegel/NY Daily News/Getty Images

Bogdanos: Two fresh bruises on [the victim's] nose, fresh bruises on his chin and chest suggest [Jordan] got on top of him and, hopefully while he was asleep, filled a syringe with the poisonous concoction and pressed that plunger into his body. His fate was sealed. He didn't die fast. One by one, his vital organs shut down. It didn't take minutes. It took hours to die.

Brenner: [Jordan had] no malice. No murderous intent, only the firm love and devotion that everyone who came into contact with [Jordan and her son] will swear to. She protected him from the animals she couldn't keep from the door.

facts, such as "she was bleeding from her forehead" or "she was unconscious on the ground for several minutes." A lay witness could not, however, give information about the medical extent of the victim's injuries, such as whether she suffered from a fractured skull or internal bleeding. Coming from a lay witness, such testimony would be inadmissible.

When the matter in question requires scientific, medical, or technical skill beyond the scope of the average person, prosecutors and defense attorneys may call an **expert witness** to the stand. The expert witness is an individual who has professional training, advanced knowledge, or substantial experience in a specialized area, such as medicine, computer technology, or ballistics. The rules of evidence state that expert witnesses may base their opinions on three types of information:

1. Facts or data of which they have personal knowledge.
2. Material presented at trial.
3. Secondhand information given to the expert outside the courtroom.[53]

Expert witnesses are considered somewhat problematic for two reasons. First, they may be chosen for their "court presence"—whether they speak well or will appear sympathetic to the jury—rather than their expertise. Second, attorneys pay expert witnesses for their services. Given human nature, the attorneys expect a certain measure of cooperation from an expert they have hired, and an expert witness has an interest in satisfying the attorneys so that he or she will be hired again.[54] Under these circumstances, some have questioned whether the courts can rely on the professional nonpartisanship of expert witnesses.[55]

Direct versus Circumstantial Evidence Two types of testimonial evidence may be brought into court: direct evidence and circumstantial evidence. **Direct evidence** is evidence that has been witnessed by the person giving testimony. "I saw Bill shoot Chris" is an example of direct evidence. **Circumstantial evidence** is indirect evidence that, even if believed, does not establish the fact in question but only the degree of likelihood of the fact. In other words, circumstantial evidence can create an inference that a fact exists.

Learning Objective

7 Describe the difference between direct and circumstantial evidence, and explain why evidence of a defendant's "evil character" is often excluded from trial.

Suppose, for example, that the defendant owns a gun that shoots bullets of the type found in the victim's body. This circumstantial evidence, by itself, does not establish that the defendant committed the crime. Combined with other circumstantial evidence, however, it may do just that. For instance, if other circumstantial evidence indicates that the defendant had a motive for harming the victim and was at the scene of the crime when the shooting occurred, the jury might conclude that the defendant committed the crime. (As you may recall, the prosecution's successful case against Johnny Wall, described at the opening of this chapter, was based entirely on circumstantial evidence.)

The "CSI Effect" When possible, defense attorneys will almost always make the argument that the state has failed to present any evidence other than circumstantial evidence against their client. Recently, this tactic has been aided by a phenomenon known as the "CSI effect," taking its name from the popular television series *CSI: Crime Scene Investigation* and its spin-offs. According to many prosecutors, these shows have fostered unrealistic notions among jurors as to what high-tech forensic science can accomplish as part of a criminal investigation.

In reality, the kind of physical evidence used to solve crimes on *CSI* is often not available to the prosecution, which must rely instead on witnesses and circumstantial evidence. To test the CSI effect, researchers surveyed more than one thousand jurors in

expert witness A witness with professional training or substantial experience qualifying her or him to testify on a certain subject.

direct evidence Evidence that establishes the existence of a fact that is in question without relying on inference.

circumstantial evidence Indirect evidence that is offered to establish, by inference, the likelihood of a fact that is in question.

Washtenaw County, Michigan, and found that nearly half "expected the prosecutor to present scientific evidence in every criminal case." This expectation was particularly strong in rape trials and trials lacking direct evidence of a crime.[56]

▲ In 2015, Aaron Hernandez—shown here in a Bristol County, Massachusetts, courtroom—was found guilty of fatally shooting Odin Lloyd and sentenced to life in prison without parole. During his trial, Judge Susan Garsh ruled that a photograph from the celebrity gossip website TMZ that depicted Hernandez holding a gun was inadmissible as evidence. **Why do you think the judge made this decision?** John Tlumacki/*The Boston Globe*/Getty Images

Relevance Evidence will not be admitted in court unless it is *relevant* to the case being considered. **Relevant evidence** is evidence that tends to prove or disprove a fact in question. Forensic proof that the bullets found in a victim's body were fired from a gun discovered in the suspect's pocket at the time of arrest, for example, is certainly relevant. The suspect's prior record, showing a conviction for armed robbery ten years earlier, is, as we shall soon see, irrelevant to the case at hand and in most instances will be ruled inadmissible by the judge.

Prejudicial Evidence Evidence may be excluded if it would tend to distract the jury from the main issues of the case, mislead the jury, or cause jurors to decide the issue on an emotional basis. For example, during the murder trial of former professional football player Aaron Hernandez, first referenced in Figure 8.5, Judge Susan Garsh ruled that texts sent by Odin Lloyd, the victim, to his sister on the night of his death were inadmissible. The texts read, "U saw who I'm with," and "NFL [National Football League]," referring to Hernandez. Judge Garsh kept this evidence from the jury because the texts suggested, without proof, that Lloyd was warning his sister that Hernandez was responsible for any harm that might befall him that night.[57]

Prosecutors are also generally prohibited from using prior purported criminal activities or actual convictions to show that the defendant has criminal propensities or an "evil character." Also during Hernandez's trial, the prosecution was denied the opportunity to tell the jury that the defendant faced a civil lawsuit for shooting another friend following an argument in a South Florida nightclub two years earlier. "This case is about Odin Lloyd and no one else," said Hernandez's defense attorney, while arguing against the introduction of this evidence.[58]

Although this legal concept has come under a great deal of criticism, it is consistent with the presumption-of-innocence standards discussed earlier. Arguably, if a prosecutor is allowed to establish that the defendant has shown antisocial or even violent traits in the past, this will prejudice the jury against the defendant in the present trial. Even if the judge instructs jurors that this prior evidence is irrelevant, human nature dictates that it will probably have a "warping influence" on the jurors' perception of the defendant.[59] Therefore, whenever possible, defense attorneys will keep such evidence from the jury.

The Prosecution's Case

Because the burden of proof is on the state, the prosecution is generally considered to have a more difficult task than the defense. The prosecutor attempts to establish guilt beyond a reasonable doubt by presenting the *corpus delicti* ("body of the offense" in Latin) of the crime to the jury. The *corpus delicti* is simply a legal term that refers to the substantial facts that show a crime has been committed. By establishing such facts through the presentation of relevant and nonprejudicial evidence, the prosecutor hopes to convince the jury of the defendant's guilt.

relevant evidence Evidence tending to make a fact in question more or less probable than it would be without the evidence. Only relevant evidence is admissible in court.

Direct Examination of Witnesses Witnesses are crucial to establishing the prosecutor's case against the defendant. The prosecutor will call witnesses to the stand and ask them questions pertaining to the sequence of events that the trial is addressing. This form of questioning is known as **direct examination**. During direct examination, the prosecutor will usually not be allowed to ask *leading questions*—questions that might suggest to the witness a particular desired response.

A leading question might be something like "So, Mrs. Williams, you noticed the defendant threatening the victim with a broken beer bottle?" If Mrs. Williams answers "yes" to this question, she has, in effect, been "led" to the conclusion that the defendant was, in fact, threatening the victim with a broken beer bottle. The fundamental purpose behind testimony is to establish what actually happened, not what the trial attorneys would like the jury to believe happened. (A properly worded query would be, "Mrs. Williams, please describe the defendant's manner toward the victim during the incident.")

direct examination The examination of a witness by the attorney who calls the witness to the stand to testify.

confrontation clause The part of the Sixth Amendment that guarantees all defendants the right to confront witnesses testifying against them during the criminal trial.

cross-examination The questioning of an opposing witness during trial.

Competence and Reliability of Witnesses The rules of evidence include certain restrictions and qualifications pertaining to witnesses. Witnesses must have sufficient mental competence to understand the significance of testifying under oath. They must also be reliable in the sense that they are able to give a clear and reliable description of the events in question. If not, the prosecutor or defense attorney will make sure that the jury is aware of these shortcomings through *cross-examination.*

Cross-Examination

After the prosecutor has directly examined her or his witnesses, the defense attorney is given the chance to question the same witnesses. The Sixth Amendment states, "In all criminal prosecutions, the accused shall enjoy the right . . . to be confronted with witnesses against him." This **confrontation clause** gives the accused, through his or her attorneys, the right to cross-examine witnesses. **Cross-examination** refers to the questioning of an opposing witness during trial, and both sides of a case are allowed to do so.

Questioning Witnesses Cross-examination allows the attorneys to test the truthfulness of opposing witnesses and usually entails efforts to create doubt in the jurors' minds that the witness is reliable (see Figure 8.7). After the defense has cross-examined

Figure 8.7 The Cross-Examination

During Michael Dunn's 2014 trial for the murder of Jordan Davis outside a convenience store in Jacksonville, Florida, the defendant claimed he fatally shot Davis in self-defense. Crucially, Dunn insisted that Davis had pointed a shotgun at him, though no such weapon was found at the crime scene. When Dunn took the stand, the prosecution cross-examined him about what he said to his fiancée, Rhonda Rouer, following the shooting.

Prosecutor: How did you describe the weapon [to her]? Did you say [Davis and his friends] had a sword? Did you say they had a machete?

Dunn: Gun.

Prosecutor: A gun. You used the word "gun"?

Dunn: Multiple times.

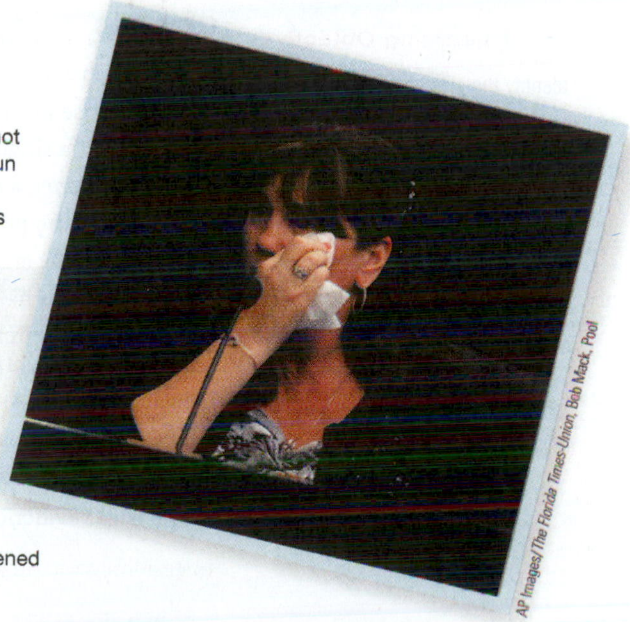

AP Images/The Florida Times-Union, Bob Mack, Pool

Later in the trial, the prosecution called Rouer (pictured here) as a witness. In her testimony, she stated that Dunn never mentioned that he had been threatened with a shotgun, or any other kind of weapon, during the confrontation.

hearsay An oral or written statement made by an out-of-court speaker that is later offered in court by a witness (not the speaker) concerning a matter before the court.

a prosecution witness, the prosecutor may want to reestablish any reliability that might have been lost. The prosecutor can do so by again questioning the witness, a process known as *redirect examination*. Following the redirect examination, the defense attorney will be given the opportunity to ask further questions of prosecution witnesses, or recross-examination. Thus, each side has two opportunities to question a witness. The attorneys need not do so, but only after each side has been offered the opportunity will the trial move on to the next witness or the next stage.

Hearsay Cross-examination is also linked to problems presented by *hearsay* evidence. **Hearsay** can be defined as any testimony given about a statement made by someone else. An example of hearsay would be: "Jenny told me that Bill told her that he was the killer." Literally, it is what someone heard someone else say. For the most part, hearsay is not admissible as evidence. When a witness offers hearsay, the person making the original remarks is not in court and therefore cannot be cross-examined. If such testimony were allowed, the defendant's Sixth Amendment right to confront witnesses against him or her would be violated.

There are a number of exceptions to the hearsay rule, and as a result a good deal of hearsay evidence finds its way into criminal trials. For example, a hearsay statement is usually admissible if there seems to be little risk of a lie. Therefore, a statement made by someone who believes that his or her death is imminent—a "dying declaration" or a suicide note—is often allowed in court even though it is hearsay.[60] Similarly, the rules of most states allow hearsay when the statement contains an admission of wrongdoing *and* the speaker is not available to testify in court. The logic behind this exception is that a person generally does not make a statement against her or his own best interests unless it is true.[61]

The Defendant's Case

After the prosecution has finished presenting its evidence, the defense attorney may offer the defendant's case. Because the burden is on the state to prove the accused's guilt, the defense is not required to offer any case at all. It can simply "rest" without calling any witnesses or producing any real evidence, and ask the jury to decide the merits of the case on what it has seen and heard from the prosecution.

Learning Objective 8

Identify the primary method that defense attorneys use in most trials to weaken the prosecution's case against their client.

Creating a Reasonable Doubt Defense lawyers most commonly defend their clients by attempting to expose weaknesses in the prosecutor's case. Remember that if the defense attorney can create reasonable doubt concerning the client's guilt in the mind of just a single juror, the defendant has a good chance of gaining an acquittal or at least a *hung jury*, a circumstance explained later in the chapter.

Even if the prosecution can present seemingly strong evidence, a defense attorney may succeed by creating reasonable doubt. In an illustrative case, Jason Korey bragged to his friends that he had shot and killed Joseph Brucker in Pittsburgh, Pennsylvania, and a great deal of circumstantial evidence linked Korey to the killing. The police, however, could find no direct evidence: they could not link Korey to the murder weapon, nor could they match his footprints to those found at the crime scene. Michael Foglia, Korey's defense attorney, explained his client's bragging as an attempt to gain attention, not a true statement. Though this explanation may strike some as unlikely, in the absence of physical evidence it did create doubt in the jurors' minds, and Korey was acquitted.

CJ Controversy

M Dogan/Shutterstock.com

Rape Shield Laws

Historically, the courtroom has been a hostile environment for victims of sexual assault. Because of a pervasive attitude labeled the "chastity requirement" by some experts, rape victims who were perceived to be sexually virtuous were much more likely to be believed by jurors than those who had been sexually active. If a woman had consented to sex before, so the line of thought went, she was more likely to do so again. To protect against this type of prejudicial thinking, almost every jurisdiction in the United States has passed a *rape shield law* to keep specific evidence, including most evidence about the victim's reputation and previous sexual conduct, out of the courtroom.

Rape Shield Laws Are Just Because . . .

- Without them, defense attorneys may subject victims of sexual assault to humiliating and degrading cross-examinations concerning their personal lives. This discourages many rape victims from reporting the rape to law enforcement.
- They ensure that defendants are convicted or acquitted based on the relevant evidence, not the prejudices of jurors more focused on the sexual history of the accuser than on the facts of the case.

Rape Shield Laws Are Unjust Because . . .

- The Sixth Amendment gives all defendants the right to question their accusers. By limiting this right, rape shield laws leave defendants in sexual-assault cases at the mercy of juries who do not know all the facts.
- In some instances, the victim's prior sexual history is relevant to the issue of whether she or he consented to the incident in question and should not be kept from the jury.

Your Assignment

Rape shield laws do contain certain exceptions that allow the defense to use evidence of the accuser's prior sexual conduct in court. To see two examples, search online for **Federal Rule of Evidence 412** and read **Exceptions (1)(A) and (1)(B)**. Do you feel that either or both of these exceptions are necessary to help balance the rights of the accuser and the accused? Explain your answer in two full paragraphs.

(Creating reasonable doubt concerning the victim's reliability can be very effective in sexual-assault cases, as explained in the feature *CJ Controversy—Rape Shield Laws.*)

Other Defense Strategies The defense can choose among a number of strategies to generate reasonable doubt in the jurors' minds. It can present an *alibi defense,* by submitting evidence that the accused was not at or near the scene of the crime at the time the crime was committed.

Another option is to attempt an *affirmative defense,* by presenting additional facts to the ones offered by the prosecution. Possible affirmative defenses, which we discussed in detail in Chapter 3, include (1) self-defense, (2) insanity, (3) duress, and (4) entrapment. With an affirmative defense strategy, the defense attempts to prove that the defendant should be found not guilty because of certain circumstances surrounding the crime. An affirmative strategy can be difficult to carry out because it forces the defense to prove the reliability of its own evidence, not simply disprove the evidence offered by the prosecution.

The defense is often willing to admit that a certain criminal act took place, especially if the defendant has already confessed. In this case, the primary question of the trial becomes not whether the defendant is guilty, but what the defendant is guilty of. In these situations, the defense strategy focuses on obtaining the lightest possible penalty for the defendant. As we saw earlier, this strategy is partially responsible for the high percentage of proceedings that end in plea bargains.

Rebuttal and Surrebuttal

After the defense closes its case, the prosecution is permitted to bring new evidence forward that was not used during its initial presentation to the jury. This is called the **rebuttal** stage of the trial. When the rebuttal stage is finished, the defense is given the opportunity to cross-examine the prosecution's new witnesses and introduce new witnesses of its own. This final act is part of the *surrebuttal.* After these stages have been completed, the defense may file a request called a *motion for a directed verdict,* asking the judge to find in the defendant's favor. If this motion is rejected, and it almost always is, the case is closed, and the opposing sides offer the closing arguments.

Closing Arguments

In their **closing arguments**, the attorneys summarize their presentations and argue one final time for their respective cases. In most states, the defense attorney goes first, and then the prosecutor. (In Colorado, Kentucky, and Missouri, the order is reversed.) An effective closing argument includes all of the major points that support the government's or the defense's case. It also emphasizes the shortcomings of the opposing party's case. Once both attorneys have completed their remarks, the case is submitted to the jury, and the attorneys' role in the trial is, for the moment, complete.

The Final Steps of the Trial

After closing arguments, the outcome of the trial is in the hands of the jury. Before the jurors begin discussing what they have heard and seen, the judge gives them a **charge**, summing up the case and instructing the jurors on the rules of law that apply to the issues in the case. These charges, also called jury instructions, are usually prepared during a special *charging conference* involving the judge and the trial attorneys. In this conference, the attorneys suggest the instructions they would like to see be sent to the jurors, but the judge makes the final decision as to the charges submitted. If the defense attorney disagrees with the charges sent to the jury, he or she can enter an objection, thereby setting the stage for a possible appeal.

Jury Deliberation After receiving the charge, the jury begins its deliberations. Jury deliberation is a somewhat mysterious process, as it takes place in complete seclusion. Most of what is known about how a jury deliberates comes from mock trials or interviews with jurors after the verdict has been reached. A general picture of the deliberation process constructed from this research shows that jurors are not necessarily predisposed to argue with one another over the fate of the defendant. In approximately three out of every ten cases, the initial vote by the jury led to a unanimous decision. In 90 percent of the remaining cases, the majority eventually dictated the decision.[62]

One of the most important instructions that a judge normally gives the jurors is that they should seek no outside information during deliberation. The idea is that jurors should base their verdict *only* on the evidence that the judge has deemed admissible. In extreme cases, the judge will order that the jury be *sequestered,* or isolated from the public, during the trial and deliberation stages of the proceedings. **Sequestration** is used when deliberations are expected to be lengthy, or if the trial is attracting a high amount of interest and the judge wants to keep the jury from being unduly influenced by external factors.

rebuttal Evidence given to counteract or disprove evidence presented by the opposing party.

closing arguments Arguments made by each side's attorney after the cases for the plaintiff and defendant have been presented.

charge The judge's instructions to the jury following the attorneys' closing arguments.

sequestration The isolation of jury members during a trial to ensure that their judgment is not tainted by information other than what is provided in the courtroom.

CJ & Technology

Wireless Devices in the Courtroom

One former juror, fresh from trial, complained that the members of the courtroom work group had not provided the jury with enough information to render a fair verdict. "We felt deeply frustrated at our inability to fill those gaps in our knowledge," he added. Until recently, frustrated jury members have lacked the means to carry out their own investigations in court. Today, however, jurors with smartphones and tablet computers can easily access news stories and online research tools. With these wireless devices, they can look up legal terms, blog and tweet about their experiences, and sometimes even try to contact other participants in the trial through "friend" requests on social media websites.

This access can cause serious problems for judges, whose responsibility it is to ensure that no outside information taints the jury's decision. Over the past several years, jurors have used smartphones to pull up images of a crime scene on Google Earth, measure the distance between a defendant's home and the crime scene on MapQuest, and look up the definitions of technical terms such as "reasonable doubt" and "retinal detachment." In many of these cases, the presiding judge felt obligated to call a mistrial, as these various forms of juror misconduct could have improperly influenced the final verdict.

iStockphoto.com/Alina555

Thinking about Wireless Devices in the Courtroom

The Sixth Amendment guarantees the accused the right to trial by an "impartial jury." How does the use of wireless devices in the courtroom threaten this right?

The Verdict Once it has reached a decision, the jury issues a **verdict**. The most common verdicts are guilty and not guilty, though, as we have seen, juries may signify different degrees of guilt if instructed to do so. Following the announcement of a guilty or not guilty verdict, the jurors are discharged, and the jury trial proceedings are finished.

When a jury in a criminal trial is unable to agree on a unanimous verdict—or a majority in certain states—it returns with no decision. This is known as a **hung jury**. Following a hung jury, the judge will declare a mistrial, and the case will be tried again in front of a different jury if the prosecution decides to pursue the matter a second time. A judge can do little to reverse a hung jury, considering that "no decision" is just as legitimate a verdict as guilty or not guilty.

In some states, if there are only a few dissenters to the majority view, a judge can send the jury back to the jury room under a set of rules put forth more than a century ago by the Supreme Court in *Allen v. United States* (1896).[63] The ***Allen* charge,** as this instruction is called, asks the jurors in the minority to reconsider the majority opinion. Many jurisdictions do not allow *Allen* charges on the ground that they improperly coerce jurors with the minority opinion to change their minds.[64] For all of the attention they receive, hung juries are relatively rare. Juries are unable to come to a decision in only about 6 percent of all cases.[65]

verdict A formal decision made by the jury.

hung jury A jury whose members are so irreconcilably divided in their opinions that they cannot reach a verdict.

***Allen* charge** An instruction by a judge to a deadlocked jury with only a few dissenters that asks the jurors in the minority to reconsider the majority opinion.

appeal The process of seeking a higher court's review of a lower court's decision for the purpose of correcting or changing this decision.

Appeals

Even if a defendant is found guilty, the trial process is not necessarily over. In our criminal justice system, a person convicted of a crime has a right to appeal. An **appeal** is the process of seeking a higher court's review of a lower court's decision for the purpose of

double jeopardy To twice place at risk (jeopardize) a person's life or liberty. Constitutional law prohibits a second prosecution in the same court for the same criminal offense.

correcting or changing the lower court's judgment. A defendant who loses a case in a trial court cannot automatically appeal the conviction. The defendant normally must first be able to show that the trial court acted improperly on a question of law. Common reasons for appeals include the introduction of tainted evidence by the prosecution or faulty jury instructions delivered by the trial judge. On the state level, an appellate court upholds the decision of the trial court in 52 percent of all appeals.[66]

Double Jeopardy The appeals process is available only to the defense. If a jury finds the accused not guilty, the prosecution cannot appeal to have the decision reversed. To do so would infringe on the defendant's Fifth Amendment rights against multiple trials for the same offense. This guarantee against being tried a second time for the same crime is known as protection from **double jeopardy**. The prohibition against double jeopardy means that once a criminal defendant is found not guilty of a particular crime, the government may not reindict the person and retry him or her for the same crime. (Some nations allow for such retrials, as explained in the feature *Comparative Criminal Justice—Double Trouble.*)

Comparative Criminal Justice

Pable631/Dreamstime.com

Central Intelligence Agency

Double Trouble

American college student Amanda Knox's long Italian nightmare began in Perugia on November 6, 2007. That day, she was arrested, along with her boyfriend, for killing her British roommate, Meredith Kercher. In 2009, Knox (pictured at right) was convicted of murder, on the theory that Kercher's death was the result of a drug-fed orgy gone wrong. In 2011, an Italian appellate court overturned this conviction. The court based its ruling on shoddy investigative techniques by Italian law enforcement, which misread DNA evidence at the crime scene that pointed to a drug dealer named Rudy Guede as the obvious wrongdoer. After serving four years of a twenty-six-year prison sentence, Knox was freed and returned home to continue her education at the University of Washington in Seattle.

In March 2013, however, Italy's Court of Cassation reversed Knox's 2011 acquittal and ordered that her case be reviewed. This created the possibility that she would face a new trial and be convicted, again, for the same crime. In Italy, prosecutors routinely appeal acquittals. In the United States, because of constitutional protections against double jeopardy, defendants almost never face a second trial for the same crime. On January 30, 2014, an Italian appellate court convicted Knox for a second time of murdering Kercher and sentenced her to twenty-eight and a half years in prison. Following this verdict, Knox vowed that she would "never go willingly back" to Italy.

AP Images/Mark Lennihan

For Critical Analysis

In March 2015, nearly eight years after the initial crime, Italy's highest court annulled Knox's murder conviction, thus ending her involvement with the Italian legal system. How does Knox's ordeal bolster the theory behind America's prohibition of double jeopardy?

The American prohibition against double jeopardy is not, however, absolute. There are several circumstances in which, for practical purposes, a defendant can find herself or himself back in court after a jury has failed to find her or him guilty of committing a particular crime:

1. One state's prosecution will not prevent a different state or the federal government from prosecuting the same crime.
2. Acquitted defendants can be sued in *civil court* for circumstances arising from the alleged wrongdoing on the theory that they are not being tried for the same *crime* twice.
3. A hung jury is not an acquittal for purposes of double jeopardy. So, if a jury is deadlocked, the government is free to seek a new trial.

habeas corpus An order that requires corrections officials to bring an inmate before a court or a judge and explain why he or she is being held in prison.

wrongful conviction The conviction, either by verdict or by guilty plea, of a person who is factually innocent of the charges.

As a consequence of the final listed exception to double jeopardy, Michael Dunn found himself back in court only seven months after a hung jury in his murder trial for fatally shooting Jordan Davis outside a Jacksonville, Florida, convenience store. At Dunn's first trial, referenced earlier in Figure 8.7, the jury could not decide whether he acted in self-defense. In November 2014, however, a second jury rejected his self-defense claim and convicted Dunn of first degree murder, sending to him prison for the remainder of his life.

Learning Objective

9 Delineate the circumstances in which a criminal defendant may be tried a second time for the same act.

The Appeals Process There are two basic reasons for the appeals process. The first is to correct an error made during the initial trial. The second is to review policy. Because of this second function, the appellate courts are an important part of the flexible nature of the criminal justice system. When existing law has ceased to be effective or no longer reflects the values of society, an appellate court can effectively change the law through its decisions and the precedents that it sets.[67] A classic example was the *Miranda v. Arizona* decision (see Chapter 6), which, although it failed to change the fate of the defendant (he was found guilty on retrial), had a far-reaching impact on the custodial interrogation of suspects.

It is also important to understand that once the appeals process begins, the defendant is no longer presumed innocent. The burden of proof has shifted, and the defendant is obligated to prove that her or his conviction should be overturned. The method of filing an appeal differs slightly among the fifty states and the federal government, but the five basic steps are similar enough for summarization in Figure 8.8. For the most part, defendants are not required to exercise their right to appeal. The one exception involves the death sentence. Given the seriousness of capital punishment, the defendant is required to appeal the case, regardless of his or her wishes.

Figure 8.8 The Steps of an Appeal

1. The defendant, or *appellant,* files a **notice of appeal**—a short written statement outlining the basis of the appeal.
2. The appellant transfers the trial court record to the appellate court. This record contains items such as evidence and a transcript of the testimony.
3. Both parties file **briefs.** A brief is a written document that presents the party's legal arguments.
4. Attorneys from both sides present **oral arguments** before the appellate court.
5. Having heard from both sides, the judges of the appellate court retire to deliberate the case and make their decision. As described in Chapter 7, this decision is issued as a **written opinion.** Appellate courts generally do one of the following:
   - **Uphold** the decision of the lower court.
   - **Modify** the lower court's decision by changing only a part of it.
   - **Reverse** the decision of the lower court.
   - **Reverse and remand** the case, meaning that the matter is sent back to the lower court for further proceedings.

Habeas Corpus Even after the appeal process is exhausted, a convict may have access to one final procedure, known as ***habeas corpus*** (Latin for "you have the body"). *Habeas corpus* is a judicial order that commands a corrections official to bring a prisoner before a federal court so that the court can hear the convict's claim that he or she is being held illegally. A writ of *habeas corpus* differs from an appeal in that it can be filed only by someone who is imprisoned.

Wrongful Convictions

The appeals process is primarily concerned with "legal innocence." That is, appeals courts focus on how the law was applied in a case, rather than on the facts of the case. But what if a defendant who is factually innocent has been found guilty at trial? For the most part, such **wrongful convictions** can be righted only with the aid of new evidence suggesting that the defendant was not, in fact, guilty. When such new evidence is uncovered, a prosecutor's office can choose to reopen the case and redress the initial injustice.

DNA Exoneration In Chapter 5, we saw how DNA fingerprinting has been a boon for law enforcement. According to the Innocence Project, a New York–based legal group, as of March 2016, this procedure has also led to the exoneration of 337 convicts in the United States.[68] For example, in 1994 Angel Gonzalez was wrongly found guilty of sexual assault and kidnapping after being misidentified by a rape victim in Waukegan, Illinois. Gonzalez spent twenty years behind bars before testing on multiple pieces of evidence, including the original rape kit and the victim's clothing, showed conclusively that he was innocent. In March 2015, Gonzalez's conviction was vacated and he was released from prison.

The Causes of Wrongful Convictions Angel Gonzalez was the subject of two misidentifications. First, the victim's boyfriend erroneously pointed out Gonzalez's car as being similar to the one driven by the rapist. Then, the victim identified Gonzalez while looking out at him, at night, from the back seat of police car. Furthermore, after being awake for twenty-six hours, Gonzalez signed a confession written in English, though he barely spoke the language.

Gonzalez's case highlights two of the five most common reasons[69] for wrongful convictions later overturned by DNA evidence:

1. *Eyewitness misidentification,* which research shows to be a factor in nearly three-fourths of all cases in which a falsely convicted person has been exonerated by DNA evidence.[70]
2. *False confessions,* which are often the result of overly coercive police interrogation techniques (see Chapter 6) or a suspect's mental illness.
3. *Faulty forensic evidence* produced by crime labs, which analyze evidence of everything from bite marks to handwriting samples to ballistics.
4. *False informant testimony,* provided by "jailhouse snitches" and other offenders who are motivated to lessen their own punishment by incriminating other suspects.
5. *Law enforcement misconduct* by overzealous or corrupt police officers and prosecutors.

Numerous jurisdictions are taking steps to lessen the probability that these factors will result in wrongful convictions. In particular, eyewitness misidentification has been targeted for reform. For example, Texas law enforcement agencies are increasingly replacing traditional simultaneous police lineups, in which an eyewitness is asked to choose the culprit from among six lineup members concurrently, with *sequential lineups,* in which the eyewitness is shown only one lineup member at a time.

Studies show that the traditional method is flawed because it encourages eyewitnesses to choose the lineup member who most closely resembles the offender, not necessarily the offender himself or herself.[71] Between 2008 and 2011, the use of sequential lineups in Austin significantly reduced the number of mistaken identifications without having any impact on the number of accurate identifications.[72] (See this chapter's *CJ Policy—Your Take* feature to consider how this process could be further reformed.)

CJ Policy—Your Take

Two policy changes have been suggested nationwide to reduce the incidence of eyewitness misidentification. The first is that police officers should be required to inform eyewitnesses that the actual suspect might not be in the lineup or photo array before them. The second is that lineup procedures should be "blind." That is, they should be conducted by a law enforcement official who does not know the identity of the suspect. **How might these two reforms reduce the possibility of eyewitness misidentification?**

EthicsChallenge

As you learned in this section, expert witnesses are paid for their testimony by either the prosecution or the defense. In your opinion, what ethical problems, if any, does this common practice raise? What role does cross-examination play in limiting any potential problems with partisan expert witnesses?

Summary

For more information on these concepts, look back to the Learning Objective icons throughout the chapter.

1 Identify the steps involved in the pretrial criminal process. (a) Suspect taken into custody or arrested; (b) initial appearance before a magistrate, at which time the defendant is informed of his or her constitutional rights and a public defender may be appointed or private counsel may be hired by the state to represent the defendant; (c) the posting of bail or release on recognizance; (d) preventive detention, if deemed necessary to ensure the safety of other persons or the community, or regular detention, if the defendant is unable to post bail; (e) preliminary hearing (mini-trial), at which the judge rules on whether there is probable cause and the prosecutor issues an information; or in the alternative (f) grand jury hearings, after which an indictment is issued against the defendant if the grand jury finds probable cause; (g) arraignment, in which the defendant is informed of the charges and must respond by pleading not guilty or guilty (or, in some cases, *nolo contendere*); and (h) plea bargaining.

2 Summarize the main difference between an indictment and an information. An indictment is the grand jury's declaration that probable cause exists to charge a defendant with a specific crime. In jurisdictions that do not use grand juries, the prosecution issues an information as the formal charge of a crime.

3 Explain how a prosecutor screens potential cases. (a) Is there sufficient evidence for conviction? (b) What is the priority of the case? The more serious the alleged crime, the higher the priority. The more extensive the defendant's criminal record, the higher the priority. (c) Are the victims cooperative? Violence against family members often yields uncooperative victims, so these cases are rarely prosecuted. (d) Are the victims reliable? (e) Might the defendant be willing to testify against other offenders?

4 Indicate why prosecutors, defense attorneys, and defendants often agree to plea bargains. For prosecutors, a plea bargain removes the risk of losing the case at trial, particularly if the evidence against the defendant is weak. For defense attorneys, the plea bargain may be the best deal possible for a potentially guilty client. For defendants, plea bargains give a measure of control over a highly uncertain future.

5 Identify the basic protections enjoyed by criminal defendants in the United States. According to the Sixth Amendment, a criminal defendant has the right to a speedy and public trial by an impartial jury in the physical location where the crime was committed. Additionally, a person accused of a crime must be informed of the nature of the crime and be confronted with the witnesses against him or her. Further, the accused must be able to summon witnesses in her or his favor and have the assistance of counsel.

6 Contrast challenges for cause and peremptory challenges during *voir dire*. A challenge for cause occurs when an attorney provides the court with a legally justifiable reason why a potential juror should be excluded—for example, the juror does not understand English. In contrast, peremptory challenges do not require any justification by the attorney and are usually limited to a small number. They cannot, however, be based, even implicitly, on race or gender.

7 Describe the difference between direct and circumstantial evidence, and explain why evidence of a defendant's "evil character" is often excluded from trial. Direct evidence is evidence presented by witnesses as opposed to circumstantial evidence, which can create an inference that a fact exists but does not directly establish the fact. "Evil character" evidence, which often refers to prior criminal acts by the defendant, is excluded because such evidence tends to prejudice the jury against the defendant in the case at hand.

8 Identify the primary method that defense attorneys use in most trials to weaken the prosecution's case against their client. To find a defendant guilty, a jury must believe beyond a reasonable doubt that he or she committed the crime. Therefore, defense attorneys will often present arguments and evidence designed to raise a reasonable doubt of guilt in the jurors' minds.

9 Delineate the circumstances in which a criminal defendant may be tried a second time for the same act. A defendant who is acquitted in a criminal trial may be sued in a civil case for essentially the same act. When an act is a crime under both state and federal law, a defendant who is acquitted in state court may be tried in federal court for the same act, and vice versa.

Questions for Critical Analysis

1. Preventive detention laws raise the troubling issue of *false positives*, or erroneous predictions that defendants, if released before trial, would commit a crime when in fact they would not. Why do you think that legislators, judges, and citizens are willing to accept the possibility of false positives when denying pretrial release to certain defendants?

2. Review the United States Supreme Court's ruling, discussed earlier in the chapter, that defendants have a constitutional right to effective representation during plea negotiations. Do you think the Court made the proper ruling? Why or why not?

3. Why is it important for the judge to tell jurors that a defendant's decision to remain silent during the trial cannot be taken as a sign of guilt?

4. Police find a critically wounded man lying in the parking lot of a gas station. When they ask him what happened, he indicates that Mr. X shot him. Then, the man dies. Should the dead man's identification of Mr. X be allowed in court? Or is it inadmissible hearsay? Explain your answer. (To see how the United States Supreme Court ruled in a similar case, go to **www.scotusblog.com/case-files/cases/michigan-v-bryant**.)

5. Texas has a law called the Timothy Cole Compensation Act, under which people who are wrongfully convicted of crimes may collect $80,000 from the state for each year of unwarranted imprisonment. Do you think this is fair? Why or why not? What are the goals of this kind of legislation?

Key Terms

acquittal 240
Allen charge 253
appeal 253
arraignment 235
bail 227
bail bond agent 229
bench trial 240
Boykin form 237
case attrition 232
challenge for cause 243
charge 252
circumstantial evidence 247
closing arguments 252
confrontation clause 249
cross-examination 249
direct evidence 247
direct examination 249
discovery 231
double jeopardy 254
evidence 246
expert witness 247
grand jury 231
habeas corpus 255
hearsay 250
hung jury 253
indictment 232
information 231
initial appearance 227
jury trial 240
lay witness 246
master jury list 242
nolo contendere 235
opening statements 246
peremptory challenges 243
plea bargaining 235
preliminary hearing 231
preventive detention 229
property bond 229
real evidence 246
rebuttal 252
release on recognizance (ROR) 230
relevant evidence 248
sequestration 252
statute of limitations 239
testimony 246
venire 242
verdict 253
voir dire 242
wrongful conviction 255

Notes

1. Lawrence M. Friedman and Robert V. Percival, *The Roots of Justice* (Chapel Hill, N.C.: University of North Carolina Press, 1981).
2. *County of Riverside v. McLaughlin*, 500 U.S. 44 (1991).
3. Bureau of Justice Statistics, *Felony Defendants in Large Urban Counties, 2009—Statistical Tables* (Washington, D.C.: U.S. Department of Justice, December 2013), Table 16, page 19.
4. Illinois Annotated Statutes Chapter 725 Paragraph 5/110-5.
5. Brooke Adams, "Judge Refuses to Lower Bail for Utah Doctor Accused of Killing Ex-Wife," *Salt Lake City Tribune* (June 22, 2013), at **archive.sltrib.com/story.php?ref=/sltrib/news/56490536-78/wall-pelle-schwedler-von.html.csp**.
6. *Bail Fail: Why the U.S. Should End the Practice of Using Money for Bail* (Washington, D.C.: Justice Policy Institute, September 2012), 7.
7. *Felony Defendants in Large Urban Counties, 2009—Statistical Tables, op. cit.*, Table 18, page 21; and Table 19, page 21.
8. *Bail Fail: Why the U.S. Should End the Practice of Using Money for Bail, op. cit.*, 13.
9. Jeremy Ball and Lisa Bostaph, "He Versus She: A Gender-Specific Analysis of Legal and Extralegal Effects on Pretrial Release for Felony Defendants," *Women & Criminal Justice* 19 (2009), 95–119.
10. Michael R. Jones, *Unsecured Bonds: The As Effective and Most Efficient Pretrial Release Option* (Washington, D.C.: Pretrial Justice Institute, October 2013).

11. *Bail Fail: Why the U.S. Should End the Practice of Using Money for Bail, op. cit.*, 35.

12. Kenneth C. Davis, *Discretionary Justice: A Preliminary Inquiry* (Baton Rouge, La.: Louisiana State University Press, 1969), 189.

13. Milton Hirsh and David Oscar Markus, "Fourth Amendment Forum," *Champion* (December 2002), 42.

14. Bruce Frederick and Don Stemen, *The Anatomy of Discretion: An Analysis of Prosecutorial Decision Making—Summary Report* (New York: Vera Institute of Justice, December 2012), 4–16.

15. Tom Lininger, "Evidentiary Issues in Federal Prosecutions of Violence against Women," *Indiana Law Review* 36 (2003), 709.

16. 18 U.S.C. Section 3553(e) (2006).

17. Quoted in David Abel, "Bristol DA Drops Charges, Says Protesters Were Right," *Boston Globe* (September 9, 2014), A8.

18. 404 U.S. 257 (1971).

19. Fred C. Zacharias, "Justice in Plea Bargaining," *William and Mary Law Review* 39 (March 1998), 1121.

20. Bureau of Justice Statistics, *Prosecutors in State Courts, 2007—Statistical Tables* (Washington, D.C.: U.S. Department of Justice, December 2011), 2.

21. Milton Heumann, *Plea Bargaining: The Experiences of Prosecutors, Judges, and Defense Attorneys* (Chicago: University of Chicago Press, 1978), 58.

22. Albert W. Alschuler, "The Defense Attorney's Role in Plea Bargaining," *Yale Law Journal* 84 (1975), 1200.

23. Stephen J. Schulhofer, "Plea Bargaining as Disaster," *Yale Law Journal* 101 (1992), 1987.

24. Quoted in Kate Alexander, "Jeffrey Basil Pleaded Guilty to 1st Degree Manslaughter," *WIVB4.com* (June 9, 2015), at **wivb.com/2015/06/09/source-jeffrey-basil-to-take-plea-deal.**

25. Human Rights Watch, "An Offer You Can't Refuse" (December 5, 2013), at **www.hrw.org/report/2013/12/05/offer-you-cant-refuse/how-us-federal-prosecutors-force-drug-defendants-plead.**

26. 395 U.S. 238 (1969).

27. *Lafler v. Cooper*, 132 S.Ct. 1376 (2012); and *Missouri v. Frye*, 132 S.Ct. 1399 (2012).

28. Laurence Benner, "Expanding the Right to Effective Counsel at Plea Bargaining," *Criminal Justice* (Fall 2012), 4–11.

29. Quoted in Adam Liptak, "Justices' Ruling Expands Rights of Accused in Plea Bargains," *New York Times* (March 22, 2012), A1.

30. North Carolina General Statutes Section 15A-832(f) (2003).

31. 18 U.S.C. Section 3771 (2004).

32. 407 U.S. 514 (1972).

33. 725 Illinois Compiled Statutes Section 5/103-5 (1992).

34. Jeff Parrott, "Indiana Supreme Court Overturns Elkhart Man's Child Molestation Conviction Because of Speedy Trial Violation," *The Elkhart (IN) Truth* (September 26, 2014).

35. *Felony Defendants in Large Urban Counties, 2009—Statistical Tables, op. cit.*, Table 20, page 23.

36. 18 U.S.C. Section 3161.

37. 391 U.S. 145 (1968).

38. *Blanton v. Las Vegas*, 489 U.S. 538 (1989).

39. *Apodaca v. Oregon*, 406 U.S. 404 (1972); and *Lee v. Louisiana*, No. 07-1523 (2008).

40. 332 U.S. 46 (1947).

41. *Salinas v. Texas*, 570 U.S. ______ (2013).

42. Quoted in Katharine Q. Seelye, "Defendant's Lawyers in Boston Bombing Trial Ask for Change of Venue," *New York Times* (February 20, 2015), A14.

43. 397 U.S. 358 (1970).

44. Quoted in Alan Binder, "Vanderbilt Rape Case Is Declared a Mistrial," *New York Times* (June 24, 2015), A12.

45. 380 U.S. 224 (1965).

46. 476 U.S. 79 (1986).

47. Eric L. Muller, "Solving the *Batson* Paradox: Harmless Error, Jury Representation, and the Sixth Amendment," *Yale Law Journal* 106 (October 1996), 93.

48. 499 U.S. 400 (1991).

49. 502 U.S. 1056 (1992).

50. *Snyder v. Louisiana*, 552 U.S. 472 (2008).

51. 511 U.S. 127 (1994).

52. Harry Kalven and Hans Zeisel, *The American Jury* (Boston: Little, Brown, 1966), 163–167.

53. Federal Rule of Evidence 703.

54. Richard A. Epstein, "Judicial Control over Expert Testimony: Of Deference and Education," *Northwestern University Law Review* 87 (1993), 1156.

55. L. Timothy Perrin, "Expert Witnesses under Rules 703 and 803(4) of the Federal Rules of Evidence: Separating the Wheat from the Chaff," *Indiana Law Journal* 72 (Fall 1997), 939.

56. Donald E. Shelton, "Juror Expectations for Scientific Evidence in Criminal Cases: Perceptions and Reality about the 'CSI Effect' Myth," *Thomas M. Cooley Law Review* 27 (2010), at **www.npr.org/documents/2011/feb/shelton-CSI-study.pdf.**

57. Maria Cramer, "Victim's Text Messages Tossed in Aaron Hernandez Case," *Boston Globe* (December 12, 2014), at **www.bostonglobe.com/metro/2014/12/12/aaron-hernandez-face-pretrial-hearing/eysaITd4n2nfWZHv1pU6QK/story.html.**

58. Quoted in Dan Wetzel, "Aaron Hernandez Avoids Major Defeat," *Yahoo Sports* (March 4, 2015), at **sports.yahoo.com/news/aaron-hernandez-avoids-major-defeat-172238118.html.**

59. *People v. Zackowitz*, 254 N.Y. 192 (1930).

60. Federal Rules of Procedure, Rule 804(b)(2).

61. Arthur Best, *Evidence: Examples and Explanations*, 4th ed. (New York: Aspen Law & Business, 2001), 89–90.

62. David W. Broeder, "The University of Chicago Jury Project," *Nebraska Law Review* 38 (1959), 744–760.

63. 164 U.S. 492 (1896).

64. *United States v. Fioravanti*, 412 F.2d 407 (3d Cir. 1969).

65. William S. Neilson and Harold Winter, "The Elimination of Hung Juries: Retrials and Nonunanimous Verdicts," *International Review of Law and Economics* (March 2005), 2.

66. Bureau of Justice Statistics, *Criminal Appeals in State Courts* (Washington, D.C.: U.S. Department of Justice, September 2015), 1.

67. David W. Neubauer, *America's Courts and the Criminal Justice System*, 5th ed. (Belmont, Calif.: Wadsworth Publishing Co. 1996), 254.

68. Innocence Project, "The Cases: DNA Exoneree Profiles," at **http://www.innocenceproject.org/cases/.**

69. Michigan Law School & Northwestern Law School, "The National Registry of Exonerations," at **www.law.umich.edu/special/exoneration/Pages/browse.aspx.**

70. Innocence Project, "The Causes of Wrongful Convictions," at **www.innocenceproject.org/causes-wrongful-conviction.**

71. Nancy K. Steblay, "Reduction of False Convictions through Improved Identification Procedures: Further Refinements for Street Practice and Public Policy" (January 2, 2012), at **www.ncjrs.gov/pdffiles1/nij/grants/249006.pdf.**

72. Paul Kix, "Recognition," *The New Yorker* (January 18, 2016), 41.

AP Photo/Atlanta Journal-Constitution, Kent D. Johnson

9

Punishment and Sentencing

Chapter Outline		Corresponding Learning Objectives
The Purpose of Sentencing	1	List and contrast the four basic philosophical reasons for sentencing criminals.
The Structure of Sentencing	2	Contrast indeterminate with determinate sentencing.
	3	State who has input into the sentencing decision, and list the factors that determine a sentence.
Inconsistencies in Sentencing	4	Explain some of the reasons why sentencing reform has occurred.
Sentencing Reform	5	Describe the goal of mandatory minimum sentencing guidelines, and explain why these laws have become unpopular in recent years.
	6	Identify the arguments for and against the use of victim impact statements during sentencing hearings.
Capital Punishment	7	Identify the two stages that make up the bifurcated process of death penalty sentencing.
	8	Explain why the U.S. Supreme Court abolished the death penalty for juvenile offenders.

To target your study and review, look for these numbered Learning Objective icons throughout the chapter.

a long Time Gone

In 1991, Timothy Tyler was arrested for selling five grams of the hallucinogenic drug LSD to a friend who was working as an informant for the federal government. In 1996, Scott Walker was arrested for being a low-level pusher of LSD, cocaine, marijuana, and methamphetamine. If their arrests for these nonviolent offenses had happened today, Tyler and Walker—lacking criminal records—would have been punished with relatively short prison sentences. Instead, both of them are still behind bars and might spend the rest of their lives there.

"Over the years, the absolute nature of his sentence has often weighed on my mind," wrote John Gilbert, the judge who sentenced Walker, in 2012. Gilbert did not, however, have any choice in the matter. Under a formula adopted by the United States government in 1987, federal judges could not deviate from strict sentencing guidelines for nonviolent crimes. This discretion was returned to them by the United States Supreme Court in 2005, but the consequences of harsh federal and state sentencing laws are still evident in our corrections system. According to the American Civil Liberties Union, more than 3,200 inmates presently are serving life prison sentences without the possibility of parole for nonviolent drug and property crimes.

For these offenders, the best hope of freedom is clemency, a process through which the president of the United States or a state governor essentially forgives an inmate's wrongdoing and sets her or him free from prison. In 2014, recognizing the unfair nature of many life prison sentences, the federal government announced changes to its clemency criteria. The new regulations offer federal prisoners a chance at freedom if they are low-level, nonviolent offenders who have served at least ten years of their sentences, with no history of violence before or during their prison terms. As of March 2016, eighty-nine of these offenders have been released under new guidelines. Scott Walker hopes that he, too, can benefit from the updated clemency standards. "I believe in my right to liberty," he says, "and I continue to wait for the moment when I receive the call."

bivdone/Shutterstock.com

▲ In an effort to reduce the federal prison population, the U.S. Department of Justice recently started an initiative designed to grant clemency to certain inmates serving time for nonviolent federal drug offenses.

1. Are there any circumstances under which you think a nonviolent criminal deserves to spend his or her life in prison? Explain your answer.
2. What is your opinion of a North Dakota law that gives judges discretion to sentence an offender to life in prison for selling at least two grams of cocaine in a designated "school zone"?
3. Do you think a judge should be able to overrule a sentencing law—created by elected politicians—that he or she feels is too harsh or too lenient? Why or why not?

The Purpose of Sentencing

Professor Herbert Packer has said that punishing criminals serves two ultimate purposes: the "deserved infliction of suffering on evil doers" and "the prevention of crime."[1] Even this straightforward assessment raises several questions. How does one determine the sort of punishment that is "deserved"? How can we be sure that certain penalties "prevent" crime? Should criminals be punished solely for the good of society, or should their well-being also be taken into consideration? Why are Timothy Tyler and Scott Walker spending their lives in prison for nonviolent drug offenses committed in the 1990s, when those same crimes committed in the 2010s would be punished much less harshly?

Sentencing laws indicate how any given group of people has answered these questions but do not tell us why they were answered in that manner. To understand why, we must first consider the four basic philosophical reasons for sentencing—retribution, deterrence, incapacitation, and rehabilitation.

Retribution

Learning Objective

1 List and contrast the four basic philosophical reasons for sentencing criminals.

The oldest and most common justification for punishing someone is that he or she "deserved it"—as the Old Testament states, "an eye for an eye and a tooth for a tooth." Under a system of justice that favors **retribution**, a wrongdoer who has freely chosen to violate society's rules must be punished for the infraction. Retribution relies on the principle of **just deserts**, which holds that the severity of the punishment must be in proportion to the severity of the crime. Retributive justice is not the same as *revenge*. Whereas revenge implies that the wrongdoer is punished only with the aim of satisfying a victim or victims, retribution is more concerned with the needs of society as a whole.

One problem with retributive ideas of justice lies in proportionality. Whether or not one agrees with the death penalty, the principle behind it is easy to fathom: the punishment (death) often fits the crime (murder). But what about the theft of an automobile? How does one fairly determine the amount of time the thief must spend in prison for that crime? Should the type of car or the wealth of the car owner matter? Theories of retribution often have a difficult time providing answers to such questions.

Deterrence

The concept of **deterrence** (as well as incapacitation and rehabilitation) takes a different approach than does retribution. That is, rather than seeking only to punish the wrongdoer, the goal of sentencing should be to prevent future crimes. By "setting an example," society is sending a message to potential criminals that certain actions will not be tolerated.

Deterrence can take two forms: general and specific. The basic idea of *general deterrence* is that by punishing one person, others will be discouraged from committing a similar crime. *Specific deterrence* assumes that an individual, after being punished once for a certain act, will be less likely to repeat that act because she or he does not want to be punished again. Proponents of harsh sentences for nonviolent drug crimes, addressed in the opening of this chapter, often rely on general deterrence principles to argue that such punishments discourage illegal drug possession and distribution by others.[2]

Both forms of deterrence have proved problematic in practice. General deterrence assumes that a person commits a crime only after a rational decision-making process, in which he or she implicitly weighs the benefits of the crime against the possible costs of the punishment. This is not necessarily the case, especially for young offenders who tend to value the immediate rewards of crime over the possible future consequences.

retribution The philosophy that those who commit criminal acts should be punished for breaking society's rules to the extent required by just deserts.

just deserts A sanctioning philosophy based on the assertion that criminal punishment should be proportionate to the severity of the crime.

deterrence The strategy of preventing crime through the threat of punishment.

▲ Several years ago, former Florida A&M University band member Jessie Baskin, right, pleaded guilty to manslaughter and was sentenced to nearly a year in jail for his role in the hazing death of drum major Robert Champion. **How does the theory of deterrence justify Baskin's punishment?** AP Images/ *Orlando Sentinel*, George Skene, Pool

The argument for specific deterrence is somewhat weakened by the fact that a relatively small number of habitual offenders are responsible for the majority of certain criminal acts.

Incapacitation

"Wicked people exist," said James Q. Wilson. "Nothing avails except to set them apart from innocent people."[3] Wilson's blunt statement summarizes the justification for **incapacitation** as a form of punishment. As a purely practical matter, incarcerating criminals guarantees that they will not be a danger to society, at least for the length of their prison terms. Such reasoning is partially responsible for the dramatic increase of life sentences without the possibility of parole in the criminal justice system. Since 1984, the inmate population serving life without parole has quadrupled, to nearly 160,000, encompassing one of every nine individuals behind bars in the United States.[4] (See the feature *Comparative Criminal Justice—Whole-Life Tariffs* to learn about Europe's philosophy regarding the incapacitation of violent offenders for life.)

Several studies do support incapacitation's efficacy as a crime-fighting tool. Criminologist Isaac Ehrlich of the University at Buffalo estimated that a 1 percent increase in sentence length will produce a 1 percent decrease in the crime rate.[5] More recently, Avinash Singh Bhati of the Urban Institute in Washington, D.C., found that higher levels of incarceration lead to fewer violent crimes but have little impact on property crime rates.[6]

Incapacitation as a theory of punishment does suffer from several weaknesses. Unlike retribution, it offers no proportionality with regard to a particular crime. Giving a burglar a life sentence would certainly ensure that she or he would not commit another burglary. Does that justify such a severe penalty? Furthermore, incarceration protects society only until the criminal is freed. Many studies have shown that, on release, offenders may actually be more likely to commit crimes than before they were imprisoned.[7] In that case, incapacitation may increase likelihood of crime, rather than diminish it.

Rehabilitation

For many, **rehabilitation** is the most "humane" goal of punishment. This line of thinking reflects the view that crime is a "social phenomenon" caused not by the inherent criminality of a person, but by factors in that person's surroundings. By removing wrongdoers from their environment and intervening to change their values and personalities, the rehabilitative model suggests that criminals can be "treated" and possibly even "cured" of their proclivities toward crime. Although studies of the effectiveness of rehabilitation are too varied to be easily summarized, it does appear that, in most instances, criminals who receive treatment are less likely to reoffend than those who do not.[8]

For the better part of the past three decades, the American criminal justice system has been characterized by a notable rejection of many of the precepts of rehabilitation in favor of retributive, deterrent, and incapacitating sentencing strategies that

incapacitation A strategy for preventing crime by detaining wrongdoers in prison, thereby separating them from the community and reducing criminal opportunities.

rehabilitation The philosophy that society is best served when wrongdoers are provided the resources needed to eliminate criminality from their behavioral pattern.

Comparative Criminal Justice

Pable631/Dreamstime.com

Central Intelligence Agency

Whole-Life Tariffs

In England, life prison sentences, called "whole-life tariffs," are reserved for "exceptionally" serious crimes. In fact, the country has only fifty-two offenders presently serving whole-life tariffs. Recently, three of these English "lifers" challenged their punishments in the European Court of Human Rights (ECHR), which oversees the provisions of a human rights treaty signed by most countries in Europe. At the ECHR, located in Strasbourg, France, the lawyer representing these offenders argued that a whole-life tariff "crushes human dignity from the outset" and leaves the inmate in a "position of hopelessness whereby he cannot progress whatever occurs."

The three inmates involved in this case are hardly sympathetic figures. One killed his wife and a work colleague, another murdered five members of his family, and the third is a serial killer of homosexual men. Nonetheless, the ECHR judges ruled sixteen to one in their favor. The Court found that England's whole-life tariffs amount to inhuman and degrading treatment because such sentences offer no hope of release or rehabilitation. Initially, the ECHR ordered England to provide those serving life terms a "right to review" after twenty-five years to determine whether their continued imprisonment is still justified. In 2015, however, the Court relented to withering public pressure from Britain, holding that whole-life tariffs are acceptable provided that release may be granted under "exceptional circumstances," such as a prisoner having only a few weeks to live.

For Critical Analysis

In the opening of this chapter, we discussed life sentences for nonviolent offenders. In Europe, as this feature highlights, such punishments for even the most violent offenders are considered "inhuman and degrading." What is your opinion of the European philosophy regarding life sentences?

"get tough on crime." Recently, however, more jurisdictions are turning to rehabilitation as a cost-effective (and, possibly, crime-reducing) alternative to punishment, a topic that we will explore more fully in the next few chapters. (See this chapter's first *Mastering Concepts* feature for an overview of the four main sentencing philosophies discussed in this section.)

Restorative Justice

On many reservations across the United States, Native Americans practice a "peacemaking" approach to criminal justice. Unlike the adversary system of the mainstream court system, peacemaking focuses on dispute resolution and the needs of the community rather than the rights of individual offenders. In a Navajo peacemaking session, members of the community, including the victim, describe the harm suffered because of the act in question. Then, the participants as a group decide on the proper *nalyeeh,* loosely translated as "payment," that the offender (or the offender's family) owes the community.[9]

The goal of *nalyeeh,* which may or may not include money, is to make the injured party and the community "feel better," in the words of one judge from a Navajo tribe.[10] In Native American jurisdictions, these principles have been applied to resolve criminal issues from domestic violence to gang activity to driving while intoxicated. They are also spreading to the nontribal criminal justice system as part of the **restorative justice** movement in this country.

A Different Approach Restorative justice strategies attempt to repair the damage that a crime does to the victim, the victim's family, and society as a whole. This outlook relies on the efforts of the offender to "undo" the harm caused by the criminal act through an apology and **restitution**, or monetary compensation for losses suffered by the

restorative justice An approach to punishment designed to repair the harm done to the victim and the community by the offender's criminal act.

restitution Monetary compensation for damages done to the victim by the offender's criminal act.

Mastering Concepts Sentencing Philosophies

In December 2015, Judge John Baricevic sentenced Thomas Kelley to seven years behind bars for cooking methamphetamine in a house where a one-year-old child was present. Even though Kelley was a nonviolent drug offender—a class of criminal that is increasingly being diverted from prison—the judge's decision was in keeping with the four main philosophies of sentencing.

Philosophy	Basic Principle	Explanation
Retribution	Punishment is society's means of expressing condemnation of illegal acts such as drug crimes.	According to a prosecutor, Thomas Kelley was not punished "for being an addict" but rather "for making a decision that put people at risk."
Deterrence	Harsh sentences for drug crimes may convince others not to engage in that illegal behavior.	Prosecutors said that Kelley's example would prevent others from making drugs in the presence of children, which constitutes a threat to "public safety."
Incapacitation	Incarcerated criminals are not a threat to the general society for the duration of their time behind bars.	Kelley will be unable to commit any drug-related crimes while incarcerated.
Rehabilitation	Prison programs can help inmates change their behavior so that they no longer pose a threat to themselves or others.	In prison, Kelley will be able to receive vocational training and substance abuse treatment. "You can come out better or you can come out worse," Judge Baricevic told the defendant. "That's your choice."

Source: Beth Hundsdorfer, "Belleville Man Admits Addiction, Receives Seven-Year Prison Sentence," *Belleville News-Democrat* (December 25, 2015), at **www.bnd.com/news/local/article51602055.html.**

victim(s). Restorative justice has five separate components that differentiate it from the mainstream criminal justice system:

1. *Offender involvement.* Offenders are given the opportunity to take responsibility for and address the reasons behind their behavior in ways that do not involve the corrections system.
2. *Victim involvement.* Victims have a voice in determining how the offender should atone for her or his crime.
3. *Victim-offender interaction.* On a voluntary basis, victims and offenders meet to discuss and better understand the circumstances of the crime. This meeting allows the victim to express her or his feelings related to the offense.
4. *Community involvement.* Community members also affected by the crime can participate in the process and request an apology and restitution from the offender.
5. *Problem-solving practices.* Participants in the process—including victims, offenders, and community members—can develop strategies for solving the problems that led to the crime in question.[11]

Although restorative justice is theoretically available for all types of criminal behavior, it almost always involves property crime, public order crime, and, particularly, offenses committed by juveniles. Rarely, if ever, will restorative justice principles be applied to violent crime.

Getting Linked in

LinkedIn offers a wellspring of information about careers in the field of **restorative justice**. Enter the term into the website's search engine for information concerning mediation, youth services, and other practices that attempt to repair the relationships damaged by crime.

Restorative Justice Legislation Nearly forty states have passed legislation that relies on restorative justice principles and uses the language of the movement. For the most part, these laws involve alternatives to the state juvenile justice system, victim participation in the justice process, and the requirement that offenders pay restitution directly to victims or into a victims' fund.[12] On the federal level, the Victims of Crime Act of 1984 established the Crime Victims Fund to provide financial aid for crime victims.[13] This program—financed by fines and penalties assessed on convicted federal offenders—distributes grants to state governments, which in turn pass the funds on to victims. In 2014, the fund contained nearly $12 billion and distributed almost $2.4 billion to crime victims to help cover expenses such as medical costs and lost wages.[14]

EthicsChallenge

In Iran, convicted criminals can buy their freedom from their victims. Several years ago, for example, a man found guilty of murdering a rival during a knife fight had the charges against him dropped after he paid the victim's family $50,000. Does this practice have any ethical benefits for society? How does it differ from the American practice of restitution, described in this section? Explain your answers.

The Structure of Sentencing

Philosophy not only is integral to explaining *why* we punish criminals, but also influences *how* we do so. The history of criminal sentencing in the United States has been characterized by shifts in institutional power among the three branches of the government. When public opinion moves toward more severe strategies of retribution, deterrence, and incapacitation, *legislatures* have responded by asserting their power with determining sentencing guidelines. In contrast, periods of rehabilitation are marked by a transfer of this power to the *judicial* branch.

Legislative Sentencing Authority

Because legislatures are responsible for making laws, these bodies are also initially responsible for passing the criminal codes that determine the length of sentences.

Learning Objective

2 Contrast indeterminate with determinate sentencing.

Indeterminate Sentencing Penal codes with **indeterminate sentencing** policies set a minimum and maximum amount of time that a person must spend in prison. For example, the indeterminate sentence for aggravated assault could be three to nine years, or six to twelve years, or twenty years to life. Within these parameters, a judge can prescribe a particular term, after which an administrative body known as the *parole board* decides at what point the offender is to be released. A prisoner is aware that he or she is eligible for *parole* as soon as the minimum time has been served and that good behavior can further shorten the sentence.

Determinate Sentencing Disillusionment with the somewhat vague nature of indeterminate sentencing often leads politicians to support **determinate sentencing**, or fixed sentencing. As the name implies, in determinate sentencing an offender serves exactly the amount of time to which she or he is sentenced (minus "good time," described below). For example, if the legislature deems that the punishment for a first-time armed robber is ten years, then the judge has no choice but to impose a sentence of ten years, and the criminal will serve ten years minus good time before being freed.

indeterminate sentencing Imposition of a sentence that prescribes a range of years rather than a definite period of years to be served.

determinate sentencing Imposition of a sentence that is fixed by a sentencing authority and cannot be reduced by judges or other corrections officials.

"Good Time" and Truth in Sentencing Often, the amount of time prescribed by a judge bears little relation to the amount of time the offender actually spends behind bars. In states with indeterminate sentencing, parole boards have broad powers to release prisoners once they have served the minimum portion of their sentence.

Figure 9.1 **Average Sentence Length and Estimated Time to Be Served in State Prison**

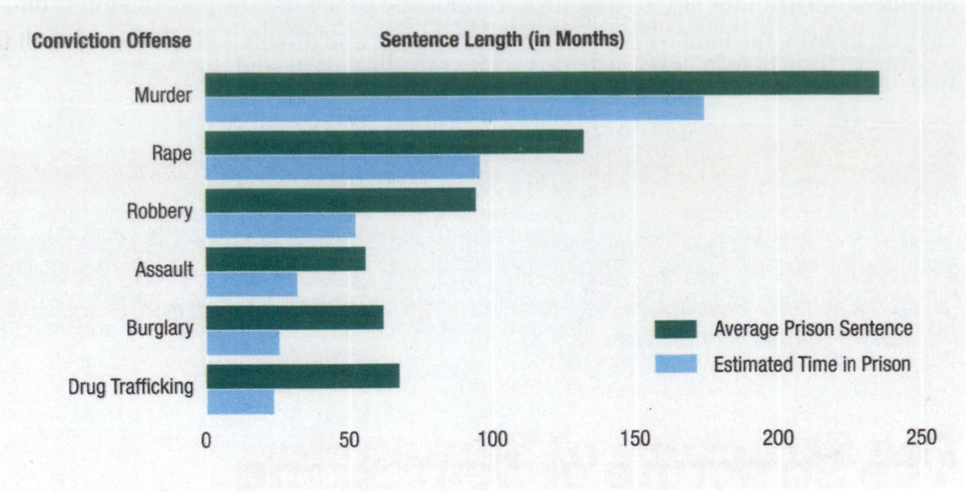

Source: Bureau of Justice Statistics, *National Corrections Reporting Program: Sentence Length of State Prisoners, by Offense, Admission Type, Sex, And Race* (May 5, 2011), "Table 9: First Releases from State Prison, 2009," at **www.bjs.gov/index.cfm?ty=pbdetail&iid=2056.**

Furthermore, most states offer prisoners the opportunity to reduce their sentences by doing **"good time"**—or behaving well—as determined by prison administrators. (See Figure 9.1 for an idea of the effects of good-time regulations and other early-release programs on state prison sentences.)

Sentence-reduction programs promote discipline within a correctional institution and reduce overcrowding, so many prison officials welcome them. The public, however, may react negatively to news that a violent criminal has served a shorter term than ordered by a judge and pressure elected officials to "do something." In Illinois, for example, some inmates were serving less than half their sentences by receiving a one-day reduction in their term for each day of "good time." Under pressure from victims' groups, the state legislature passed a **truth-in-sentencing law** in 1995 that requires murderers and others convicted of serious crimes to complete at least 85 percent of their sentences with no time off for good behavior.[15]

As their name suggests, the primary goal of these laws is to provide the public with more accurate information about the actual amount of time an offender will spend behind bars. The laws also keep convicts incapacitated for longer periods of time. Fifteen years after Illinois passed its truth-in-sentencing law, those murderers subject to the legislation were spending an average of seventeen months more in prison than those not subject to the legislation. For sex offenders in the state, the difference was 3.5 years.[16] Today, forty states have instituted some form of truth-in-sentencing laws, though the continued popularity of such statutes is being undermined by the pressures of overflowing prisons.

Judicial Sentencing Authority

During the pretrial procedures and the trial itself, the judge's role is somewhat passive and reactive. She or he is primarily a "procedural watchdog," ensuring that the rights of the defendant are not violated while the prosecutor and defense attorney dictate the course of action. At a traditional sentencing hearing, however, the judge is no longer an arbiter between the parties. She or he is now called on to exercise the ultimate authority of the state in determining the defendant's fate.

"good time" A reduction in time served by prisoners based on good behavior, conformity to rules, and other positive behavior.

truth-in-sentencing laws Legislative attempts to ensure that convicts will serve approximately the terms to which they were initially sentenced.

From the 1930s to the 1970s, when theories of rehabilitation held sway over the criminal justice system, indeterminate sentencing practices were guided by the theory of "individualized justice." Just as a physician gives specific treatment to individual patients depending on their particular health needs, the premise goes, a judge needs to consider the specific circumstances of each individual offender in choosing the best form of punishment. Taking the analogy one step further, just as the diagnosis of a qualified physician should not be questioned, a qualified judge should have absolute discretion in making the sentencing decision. *Judicial discretion* rests on the assumption that a judge should be given ample leeway in determining punishments that fit both the crime and the criminal.[17] As we shall see later in the chapter, the growth of determinate sentencing has severely restricted judicial discretion in many jurisdictions.

Judicial Dispositions Within whatever legislative restrictions apply, the sentencing judge has a number of options when it comes to choosing the proper form of punishment. These sentences, or *dispositions*, include:

1. *Capital punishment.* Reserved normally for those who commit first degree murder—that is, a premeditated killing—capital punishment is a sentencing option in thirty-one states. It is also an option in federal court, where a defendant can be put to death for murder, as well as for trafficking in a large amount of illegal drugs, *espionage* (spying), and *treason* (betraying the United States).
2. *Imprisonment.* Whether for the purpose of retribution, deterrence, incapacitation, or rehabilitation, a common form of punishment in American history has been imprisonment. In fact, it is used so commonly today that judges—and legislators—are having to take factors such as prison overcrowding into consideration when making sentencing decisions. The issues surrounding imprisonment will be discussed in Chapters 11 and 12.
3. *Probation.* The most common disposition is probation, in which an offender is permitted to live in the community under supervision and is not incarcerated. (Probation is covered in Chapter 10.) *Alternative sanctions* (also discussed in Chapter 10) combine probation with other dispositions such as electronic monitoring, house arrest, boot camps, and shock incarceration.
4. *Fines.* Fines can be levied by judges in addition to incarceration and probation or independently of other forms of punishment. Fines are generally considered a form of judicial leniency for nonviolent offenders. This disposition has, however, come under criticism recently for its often stark alternatives: pay or go to jail.[18] Although technically unconstitutional,[19] the widespread practice of incarcerating those who cannot pay their fines unavoidably discriminates against indigent defendants.

Whereas fines are payable to the government, *restitution* and *community service* are seen as reparations to the injured party or to the community. As noted earlier, restitution is a direct payment to the victim or victims of a crime. Community service consists of "good works"—such as cleaning up highway litter or tutoring disadvantaged youths—that benefit the entire community.

Along with restitution, *apologies* play an important role in restorative justice, also discussed previously in this chapter. An apology is seen as an effort by the offender to recognize the wrongness of her or his conduct and acknowledge the impact that it has had on the victim and the community. (See the feature *Discretion in Action—Cheating the System* to learn more about a judge's sentencing decision.)

Discretion in ACTION

Cheating the System

Rachel Donahue/Shutterstock.com

The Situation Following a lengthy investigation, about 180 employees of the Atlanta Public Schools were found to be complicit in a conspiracy to artificially inflate students' standardized test scores. Much of the blame for this scheme was directed toward school administrators who "created a culture of fear, intimidation and retaliation" that pressured teachers to cheat. Eventually, three of these administrators were found guilty of racketeering.

The Law Designed to combat drug trafficking and organized crime, racketeering statutes can also be used against government officials accused of using their offices for personal gain. Under Georgia law, the maximum penalty for this form of wrongdoing is twenty years in prison.

What Would You Do? On the one hand, the three defendants have no criminal records and have spent most of their careers working with the city's most vulnerable students. Also, it seems the primary motivation for their wrongdoing was to ensure that Atlanta schools not be closed for poor performance. On the other hand, the tainted test scores kept these students from getting the help they desperately needed. The prosecution recommends sentencing each of the defendants to three years in prison. If you were the judge, what sentence would you hand down in this case? Besides imprisonment, your options include probation, fines, and community service, or any combination of these sanctions.

To see what punishment a Fulton County, Georgia, judge handed down in this instance, go to Example 9.1 in Appendix B.

Creative Punishments In some jurisdictions, judges have a great deal of discretionary power and can impose sentences that do not fall into any of these categories. This "creative sentencing," as it is sometimes called, has produced some interesting results. A judge in South Euclid, Ohio, ordered a man who had harassed his neighbor for fifteen years to stand at a local intersection carrying a sign that said, "I AM A BULLY! I pick on children that are disabled, and I am intolerant of those that are different from myself."[20] In Broward County, Florida, a man who shoved his wife was sentenced to "take her to Red Lobster," go bowling with her, and then undergo marriage counseling.[21] Though these types of punishments are often ridiculed, many judges see them as a viable alternative to incarceration for less dangerous offenders.

The Sentencing Process

Learning Objective 3 State who has input into the sentencing decision, and list the factors that determine a sentence.

The decision of how to punish a wrongdoer is the end result of what Yale Law School professor Kate Stith and federal appeals court judge José A. Cabranes call the "sentencing ritual."[22] The two main participants in this ritual are the judge and the defendant, but prosecutors, defense attorneys, and probation officers also play a role in the proceedings. Individualized justice requires that the judge consider all the relevant circumstances in making sentencing decisions. Therefore, judicial discretion is often tantamount to *informed* discretion—without the aid of the other members of the courtroom work group, the judge would not have sufficient information to make the proper sentencing choice.

presentence investigative report An investigative report on an offender's background that assists a judge in determining the proper sentence.

The Presentence Investigative Report For judges operating under various states' indeterminate sentencing guidelines, information in the **presentence investigative report** is a valuable component of the sentencing ritual. Compiled by a probation officer, the report describes the crime in question, notes the suffering of any victims, and lists the defendant's prior offenses (as well as any alleged but uncharged criminal activity). The report also contains a range of personal data such as family background, work history, education, and community activities—information that is not admissible as evidence during trial. In putting together the presentence investigative report, the probation officer is supposed to gain a "feel" for the defendant and communicate these impressions of the offender to the judge.

The report also includes a sentencing recommendation. This aspect has been criticized as giving probation officers too much power in the sentencing process, because less diligent judges would simply rely on the recommendation in determining punishment.[23] For the most part, however, judges do not act as if they were bound by the presentence investigative report.

The Prosecutor and Defense Attorney To a certain extent, the adversary process does not end when the guilt of the defendant has been established. Both the prosecutor and the defense attorney are interviewed in the process of preparing the presentence investigative report, and both will try to present a version of the facts consistent with their own sentencing goals. The defense attorney in particular has a duty to make sure that the information contained in the report is accurate and not prejudicial toward his or her client. Depending on the norms of any particular courtroom work group, prosecutors and defense attorneys may petition the judge directly for certain sentences.

Sentencing and the Jury Juries also play an important role in the sentencing process. As we will see later in the chapter, it is the jury, and not the judge, who generally decides whether a convict eligible for the death penalty will in fact be executed. Additionally, six states—Arkansas, Kentucky, Missouri, Oklahoma, Texas, and Virginia—allow juries, rather than judges, to make the sentencing decision even when the death penalty is not an option. In these states, the judge gives the jury instructions on the range of penalties available, and then the jury makes the final decision.[24]

Juries have traditionally been assigned a relatively small role in felony sentencing, largely out of concern that jurors' lack of experience and legal expertise leaves them unprepared for the task. When sentencing by juries is allowed, the practice is popular with prosecutors because jurors are more likely than judges to give harsh sentences, particularly for drug crimes, sexual assault, and theft.[25]

Factors of Sentencing

The sentencing ritual strongly lends itself to the concept of individualized justice. With inputs—sometimes conflicting—from the prosecutor, attorney, and probation officer, the judge can be reasonably sure of getting the "full picture" of the crime and the criminal. In making the final decision, however, most judges consider two factors above all others: the seriousness of the crime and any mitigating or aggravating circumstances.

The Seriousness of the Crime As would be expected, the seriousness of the crime is the primary factor in a judge's sentencing decision. The more serious the crime, the harsher the punishment, for society demands no less. Each judge has his or her own methods of determining the seriousness of the offense. Many judges simply consider the "conviction offense," basing their sentence on the crime for which the defendant was convicted.

Other judges—some mandated by statute—focus instead on the **"real offense"** in determining the punishment. The "real offense" is based on the actual behavior of the defendant, regardless of the official conviction. For example, through a plea bargain, a defendant may plead guilty to simple assault when in fact he hit his victim in the face with a baseball bat. A judge, after reading the presentence investigative report, could decide

"real offense" The actual offense committed, as opposed to the charge levied by a prosecutor as the result of a plea bargain.

Careers in CJ

FASTFACTS

Judge

Job description:

- Preside over trials and hearings in federal, state, and local courts.

What kind of training is required?

- A law degree and several years of legal experience.
- Judges are either appointed or elected.

Annual salary range?

- $152,000–$174,000

Courtesy Ellen Kalama Clark

Ellen Kalama Clark
Superior Court Judge

My favorite thing about my work is making a difference in people's lives. This is especially true in juvenile court, which is my favorite assignment. For example, early one morning I was walking to the juvenile court building when I saw a group of teenage boys heading toward me. Some of them I recognized from being in court, and they recognized me. A couple avoided eye contact, one looked me straight in the eye rather defiantly, and the last one kind of smirked. As we got closer to each other, the last boy—a tall, stocky kid—stopped, and the group just about blocked the sidewalk. It made me nervous.

The boy then leaned forward toward me and said, not in an intimidating manner but certainly meaning to get my attention, "Hey, Judge." I said good morning. He then broke into a big smile and said, "I got my GED [general equivalency diploma]! And I'm staying out of trouble." I didn't remember his name or his offense, but I was absolutely thrilled that he had accomplished those things, that he would want me to know that, and that he was bragging about it in front of his friends. I consider this a great success story.

SOCIAL MEDIA CAREER TIP Think about your online presence as your online personal brand. You create this online personal brand through the sum of all the posts you make on different websites and social media tools.

to sentence the defendant as if he had committed aggravated assault, which is the "real offense." Though many prosecutors and defense attorneys are opposed to "real offense" procedures, which can render a plea bargain meaningless, there is considerable belief in criminal justice circles that they bring a measure of fairness to the sentencing decision.[26]

Mitigating and Aggravating Circumstances When deciding the severity of punishment, judges and juries are often required to evaluate the *mitigating* and *aggravating circumstances* surrounding the case. **Mitigating circumstances** are those circumstances, such as the fact that the defendant was coerced into committing the crime, that allow a lighter sentence to be handed down. In contrast, **aggravating circumstances**, such as a prior record, blatant disregard for the safety of others, or the use of a weapon, can lead a judge or jury to inflict a harsher penalty than might otherwise be warranted (see Figure 9.2).

Aggravating circumstances play an important role in a prosecutor's decision to charge a suspect with capital murder. The criminal code of every state that employs the death penalty contains a list of aggravating circumstances that make an offender eligible for execution. Most of these codes require that the murder take place during the commission of a felony, or create a grave risk of death for multiple victims, or interfere with the duties of law enforcement. (For a comprehensive rundown, go to **www.deathpenaltyinfo.org/aggravating-factors-capital-punishment-state**.) As you will see later in the chapter, mitigating factors such as mental illness and youth can spare an otherwise death-eligible offender from capital punishment.

mitigating circumstances Any circumstances accompanying the commission of a crime that may justify a lighter sentence.

aggravating circumstances Any circumstances accompanying the commission of a crime that may justify a harsher sentence.

Figure 9.2 Aggravating and Mitigating Circumstances

Aggravating Circumstances	Mitigating Circumstances
• An offense involved multiple participants, and the offender was the leader of the group. • A victim was particularly vulnerable. • A victim was treated with particular cruelty for which an offender should be held responsible. • The offense involved injury or threatened violence to others and was committed to gratify an offender's desire for pleasure or excitement. • The degree of bodily harm caused, attempted, threatened, or foreseen by an offender was substantially greater than average for the given offense. • The degree of economic harm caused, attempted, threatened, or foreseen by an offender was substantially greater than average for the given offense. • The amount of contraband materials possessed by the offender or under the offender's control was substantially greater than average for the given offense.	• An offender acted under strong provocation, or other circumstances in the relationship between the offender and the victim make the offender's behavior less serious and therefore less deserving of punishment. • An offender played a minor or passive role in the offense or participated under circumstances of coercion or duress. • An offender, because of youth or physical impairment, lacked substantial capacity for judgment when the offense was committed.

iStockphoto.com/mactrunk

Source: American Bar Association.

Judicial Philosophy Most states and the federal government spell out mitigating and aggravating circumstances in statutes, but there is room for judicial discretion in applying the law to particular cases. Judges are not uniform, or even consistent, in their opinions of which circumstances are mitigating or aggravating. One judge may believe that a fourteen-year-old is not fully responsible for his or her actions, while another may believe that teenagers should be treated as adults by criminal courts. A recent study of sentencing practices in Florida suggests that defendants who look less "trustworthy" are subjected to harsher sentences from the state's judges.[27]

Often, a judge's personal philosophy will place her or him at odds with the law. In February 2016, for example, a defendant who goes by the initials R.V. pleaded guilty to downloading about two dozen photos and videos depicting child pornography. Federal sentencing guidelines, which we will discuss shortly, called for a punishment of six-and-a-half to eight years in prison. Instead, U.S. district judge Jack Weinstein sentenced the defendant to five days behind bars. "Removing R.V. from his family will not further the interests of justice," the judge said. "It will cause serious harm to his young children by depriving them of a loving father and role model and will strip R.V. of the opportunity to heal through continued sustained treatment and the support of his close family."[28]

EthicsChallenge

In 2015, the Southern Poverty Law Center filed an ethics complaint against a judge in rural Alabama for giving defendants who could not pay fines the option of donating blood instead. If the defendant could not afford the fine and did not want to give blood, she or he faced jail time. Do you agree with one ethics expert who said that this practice "is wrong in about 3,000 ways?" Why or why not?

Inconsistencies in Sentencing

For some, the natural differences in judicial philosophies, when combined with a lack of institutional control, raise important questions. Why should a bank robber in South Carolina and a bank robber in Michigan receive different sentences? Even federal indeterminate sentencing guidelines seem overly vague: a bank robber can receive a prison term from one day to twenty years, depending almost entirely on the judge.[29] Furthermore, if judges have freedom to use their discretion, do they not also have the freedom to misuse it?

Learning Objective

Explain some of the reasons why sentencing reform has occurred. **4**

Purported improper judicial discretion is often the first reason given for two phenomena that plague the criminal justice system: *sentencing disparity* and *sentencing discrimination.* Though the two terms are often used interchangeably, they describe different statistical occurrences—the causes of which are open to debate.

Sentencing Disparity

Justice would seem to demand that those who commit similar crimes should receive similar punishments. **Sentencing disparity** occurs when this expectation is not met in one of three ways:

1. Criminals receive similar sentences for different crimes of unequal seriousness.
2. Criminals receive different sentences for similar crimes.
3. Mitigating or aggravating circumstances have a disproportionate effect on sentences.

Most of the blame for sentencing disparities is placed at the feet of the judicial profession. Even with the restrictive presence of the sentencing reforms we will discuss shortly, judges have a great deal of influence over the sentencing decision, whether they are making that decision themselves or instructing the jury on how to do so. Like other members of the criminal justice system, judges are individuals, and their discretionary sentencing decisions reflect that individuality. Besides judicial discretion, several other causes have been offered as explanations for sentencing disparity, including differences between geographic jurisdictions and between federal and state courts.

For offenders, the amount of time spent in prison often depends as much on where the crime was committed as on the crime itself. A comparison of the sentences for a firearms violation reveals that someone convicted of the crime in Colorado faces an average of 51 months in prison, whereas a similar offender in eastern Virginia can expect an average of 175 months.[30] The average sentences imposed in the Fourth Circuit, which includes North Carolina, South Carolina, Virginia, and West Virginia, are consistently harsher than those in the Ninth Circuit, comprising most of the western states: 36 months longer for convictions related to drug trafficking and 41 months longer for all offenses.[31] Such disparities can be attributed to a number of different factors, including local attitudes toward crime and available financial resources to cover the expenses of incarceration.

Also, because of different sentencing guidelines, which we will discuss later in the chapter, the punishment for the same crime in federal and state courts can be dramatically different. Figure 9.3 shows the sentencing disparities for certain crimes in the two systems.

sentencing disparity A situation in which those convicted of similar crimes do not receive similar sentences.

sentencing discrimination A situation in which the length of a sentence appears to be influenced by a defendant's race, gender, economic status, or other factor not directly related to the crime he or she committed.

Sentencing Discrimination

Sentencing discrimination occurs when disparities can be attributed to extralegal variables such as the defendant's gender, race, or economic standing.

Figure 9.3 Average Maximum Sentences for Selected Crimes in State and Federal Courts

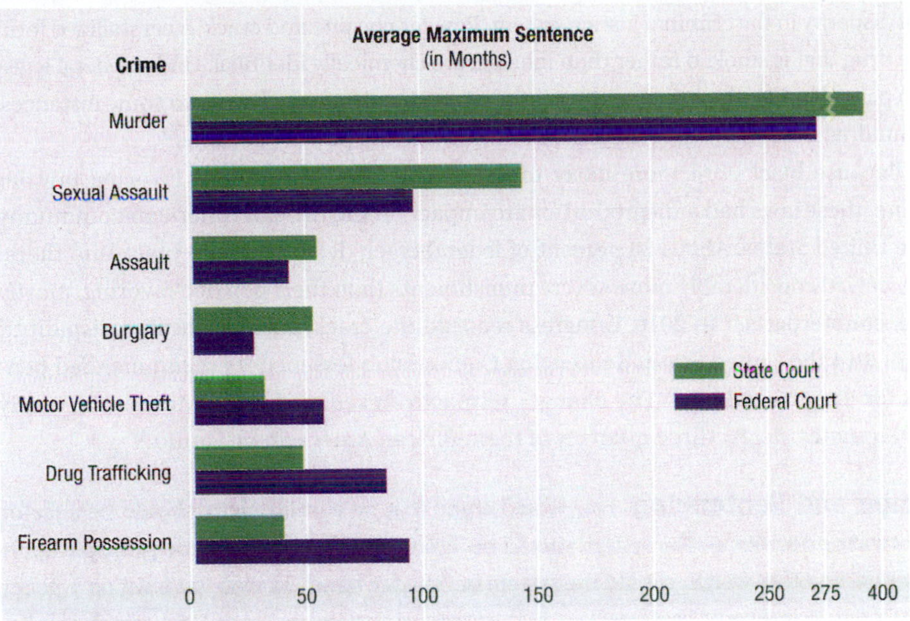

Source: Bureau of Justice Statistics, *Felony Defendants in Large Urban Counties, 2009 - Statistical Tables* (Washington, D.C.: U.S. Department of Justice, December 2013), Table 25, page 30; and U.S. Sentencing Commission, "Statistical Information Packet, Fiscal Year 2009, First Circuit," Table 7, at **www.ussc.gov/Data_and_Statistis/Federal_Sentencing_Statistics/State_District_Circuit/2009/1c09.pdf.**

Race and Sentencing At first glance, racial discrimination would seem to be rampant in sentencing practices. Research by Cassia Spohn of Arizona State University and David Holleran of the College of New Jersey suggests that minorities pay a "punishment penalty" when it comes to sentencing.[32] In Chicago, Spohn and Holleran found that convicted African Americans were 12.1 percent more likely and convicted Hispanics were 15.3 percent more likely to go to prison than convicted whites.

Nationwide, sentences imposed on African American males are about 20 percent greater than those imposed on white males for similar crimes.[33] Black and Latino defendants are also significantly more likely to be incarcerated than white defendants for comparable wrongdoing.[34] Furthermore, race seems to play an important role in determining which capital crimes are punished by death sentences.[35]

Sentencing Bias? Such numbers, while drastic, may not be the result of blatant sentencing bias. Spohn and Holleran found that the rate of imprisonment rose significantly for minorities who were young and unemployed. This led them to conclude that the disparities between races were not the result of "conscious" discrimination on the part of the sentencing judges. Rather, faced with limited time to make decisions and limited information about the offenders, the judges would resort to stereotypes, considering not just race, but age and unemployment as well.[36]

Another study, published in 2006, found that older judges and judges who were members of minority groups in Pennsylvania were less likely to send offenders to prison, regardless of their race.[37] Such research findings support the argument in favor of diversity among judges, discussed in Chapter 7. (This chapter's *CJ Policy—Your Take* examines an innovative strategy that several state governments have put in place to reduce bias in their sentencing processes.)

Length of Sentence Further evidence suggests that race has an impact on length of sentences. About 65 percent of those inmates serving life sentences without parole for nonvio-

CJ Policy—Your Take

Three states—Connecticut, Iowa, and Oregon—require **racial impact statements** for all new sentencing laws. These statements are designed to highlight the intended and unintended racial impacts of any such legislation, including how it might disproportionately impact members of minority groups. Suppose one of these states is considering a new law that increases penalties for any crime that prosecutors could prove was "gang-related." **What factors would a racial impact statement look at to determine whether the proposed statute unfairly targets minorities?**

lent offenses are African American. In Louisiana, that number is 91 percent.[38] Over the past decade, the issue of crack cocaine sentencing has placed a particularly harsh spotlight on racial disparity in the criminal justice system. Powder cocaine and crack, a crystallized form of the drug that is smoked rather than inhaled, are chemically identical. Under federal legislation passed in 1986, however, sentences for crimes involving crack were, in some instances, one hundred times more severe than for crimes involving powder cocaine.[39]

Because blacks are more likely to use crack, with white users favoring powder cocaine, these laws had a disproportionate impact on the African American community in the United States. About 80 percent of federal crack defendants are black and therefore received considerably more severe punishments than their powder-favoring, mostly white, counterparts.[40] In 2010, Congress reduced the crack/powder cocaine disparity,[41] and in 2014 the United States Sentencing Commission lessened its recommended penalties for drug trafficking.[42] The changes retroactively reduced the sentences for nearly 10,000 inmates, nearly three-quarters of them African American or Latino.[43]

Women and Sentencing Few would argue that race or ethnicity should be a factor in sentencing decisions—the system should be "color-blind." Does the same principle apply to women? In other words, should the system be "gender-blind" as well—at least on a policy level? Congress answered that question in the Sentencing Reform Act of 1984, which emphasized the ideal of gender-neutral sentencing.[44] In practice, however, this has not occurred. Women who are convicted of crimes are less likely to go to prison than men, and those who are incarcerated tend to serve shorter sentences. According to government data, on average, a woman receives a sentence that is twenty-nine months shorter than that of a man for a violent crime and nine months shorter for a property crime.[45]

When adjusting for comparable arrest offenses, criminal histories, and other presentencing factors, Sonja B. Starr of the University of Michigan Law School found that male convicts receive sentences that are 60 percent more severe than those for women.[46] One study attributes these differences to the elements of female criminality: in property crimes, women are usually accessories, and in violent crimes, women are usually reacting to physical abuse. In both situations, the mitigating circumstances lead to lesser punishment.[47]

▼ In 2015, a Los Angeles judge sentenced Dr. Hsui-Ying Tseng to thirty years to life in prison for improperly prescribing drugs to three of her patients who fatally overdosed. Tseng is the first doctor to be convicted of murder in the United States for overprescribing medication. **Do you think Tseng's gender could have played a role in her harsh punishment? Do you think her punishment was justified? Explain your answers.** Irfan Khan/Getty Images

Sentencing Reform

Judicial discretion, then, has both positive and negative aspects. Although it allows judges to impose a wide variety of sentences to fit specific criminal situations, it appears to fail to rein in a judge's subjective biases, which can lead to disparity and perhaps discrimination. Critics of judicial discretion believe that its costs (the lack of equality) outweigh its benefits (providing individualized justice). As Columbia law professor John C. Coffee noted:

> If we wish the sentencing judge to treat "like cases alike," a more inappropriate technique for the presentation could hardly be found than one that stresses a novelistic portrayal of each offender and thereby overloads the decisionmaker in a welter of detail.[48]

In other words, Professor Coffee feels that judges are given too much information in the sentencing process, making it impossible for them to be consistent in their decisions. It follows that limiting judicial discretion would not only simplify the process, but also lessen the opportunity for disparity or discrimination. This attitude has spread through state and federal legislatures, causing extensive changes in sentencing procedures within the American criminal justice system.

sentencing guidelines Legislatively determined guidelines that judges are required to follow when sentencing those convicted of specific crimes.

Sentencing Guidelines

In an effort to eliminate the inequities of disparity by removing judicial bias from the sentencing process, many states and the federal government have turned to **sentencing guidelines**. These instructions require judges to dispense legislatively determined sentences based on factors such as the seriousness of the crime and the offender's prior record.

State Sentencing Guidelines In 1978, Minnesota became the first state to create a Sentencing Guidelines Commission with a mandate to construct and monitor the use of a determinate sentencing structure. The Minnesota Commission left no doubt as to the philosophical justification for the new sentencing statutes, stating unconditionally that retribution was its primary goal.[49] Today, about twenty states employ some form of sentencing guidelines with similar goals.

In general, these guidelines remove discretionary power from state judges by turning sentencing into a mathematical exercise. Members of the courtroom work group are guided by a *grid*, which helps them determine the proper sentence. Figure 9.4 shows the grid established by the Massachusetts Sentencing Commission. As in the grids used by most states, one axis ranks the type of crime, while the other refers to the offender's criminal history. In the grid for Massachusetts, the red boxes indicate the "incarceration zone." A prison sentence is required for crimes in this zone. The yellow boxes delineate a "discretionary zone," in which the judge can decide between incarceration or

Figure 9.4 **Massachusetts's Sentencing Guidelines**

Sentencing Guidelines Grid

Level	Illustrative Offenses	Sentence Range				
6	Manslaughter (Involuntary) Armed Robbery A&B DW* (Significant Injury)	40–60 Months	45–67 Months	50–75 Months	60–90 Months	80–120 Months
5	Unarmed Robbery Unarmed Burglary Stalking in Violation of Order Larceny ($50,000 and over)	12–36 Months IS-IV IS-III IS-II	24–36 Months IS-IV IS-III IS-II	36–54 Months	48–72 Months	60–90 Months
	Criminal History Scale	A No/Minor Record	B Moderate Record	C Serious Record	D Violent/Repetitive	E Serious Violent

Intermediate Sanction Levels

IS-IV	24-Hour Restriction
IS-III	Daily Accountability
IS-II	Standard Supervision

*A&B DW = Assault and Battery, Dangerous Weapon

The numbers in each cell represent the range from which the judge selects the maximum sentence (Not More Than);

The minimum sentence (Not Less Than) is two-thirds of the maximum sentence and constitutes the initial parole eligibility date.

Source: **http://www.mass.gov/courts/court-info/trial-court/sent-commission/ma-sentencing-grid-gen.html.**

departure A stipulation in many federal and state sentencing guidelines that allows a judge to adjust his or her sentencing decision based on the special circumstances of a particular case.

mandatory sentencing guidelines Statutorily determined punishments that must be applied to those who are convicted of specific crimes.

intermediate sanctions, which you will learn about in the next chapter. In many state grids, certain crimes are "staircased," meaning that the same crime can result in different punishments based on other factors such as the seriousness of the victim's injury.

Federal Sentencing Guidelines In 1984, Congress passed the Sentencing Reform Act (SRA),[50] paving the way for federal sentencing guidelines that went into effect three years later. Similar in many respects to the state guidelines, the SRA also eliminated parole for federal prisoners and severely limited early release from prison due to good behavior.[51] The impact of the SRA and the state guidelines has been dramatic. Sentences have become harsher—by 2004, the average federal prison sentence was fifty months, more than twice as long as in 1984.[52]

Much to the disappointment of supporters of sentencing reform, a series of United States Supreme Court decisions handed down midway though the first decade of the 2000s held that federal sentencing guidelines were advisory only.[53] Five years after these Court decisions, according to the U.S. Sentencing Commission, African American male defendants were receiving sentences about 20 percent longer than white males who were convicted of similar crimes.[54] Similarly, a study released in 2015 shows that judicial leniency for white males and all women has increased significantly in federal courts, with sentence lengths moving in the opposite direction for black males.[55]

Judicial Departures In essence, the Supreme Court decisions just mentioned returned to federal judges the ability to "depart" from federal sentencing guidelines. Federal judges are taking advantage of this discretion, deviating from sentencing guidelines in just over half of all cases before them.[56] This "escape hatch" of judicial discretion is called a **departure**, and it is available to state judges as well as their federal counterparts. Judges in Massachusetts, for example, can depart from the grid in Figure 9.4 if a case involves mitigating or aggravating circumstances.[57]

Mandatory Sentencing Guidelines

In an attempt to close even the limited loophole of judicial discretion offered by departures, politicians (often urged on by their constituents) have passed sentencing laws even more contrary to the idea of individualized justice. These **mandatory** (minimum) **sentencing guidelines** further limit a judge's power to deviate from determinate sentencing laws by setting firm standards for certain crimes.

Learning Objective 5

Describe the goal of mandatory minimum sentencing guidelines, and explain why these laws have become unpopular in recent years.

State and Federal Mandatory Minimums The mandatory minimum "movement" started in the early 1970s in New York state, which was experiencing a wave of heroin-related crime. Governor Nelson Rockefeller pushed through a series of mandatory drug sentences, the most draconian being a fifteen-years-to-life punishment for anyone convicted of possessing four ounces of any illegal narcotic other than marijuana.[58] Today, nearly every state has mandatory sentencing laws, most related to crimes involving the sale or possession of illegal drugs.

The federal government passed its Anti-Drug Abuse Act[59] in the mid-1980s, in response to the cocaine overdose death of a well-known basketball player named Len Bias. Federal mandatory minimums are guided by a set of "triggers" based on the amount of drugs involved, the offender's criminal history, and many other attendant circumstances (see Chapter 3). These triggers include selling drugs to someone under twenty-one years of age, using a minor as part of "drug operations," and carrying a firearm during the drug-related crime.[60] This legislation has given a great deal of power to federal prosecutors, who, by using their discretion to add penalty enhancements, are able to coerce defendants into plea bargaining rather than risking a lengthy prison sentence.[61]

habitual offender laws Statutes that require lengthy prison sentences for those who are convicted of multiple felonies.

"Three-Strikes" Legislation

Habitual offender laws are a form of mandatory sentencing found in twenty-six states and used by the federal government. Also known as "three-strikes-and-you're-out" laws, these statutes require that any person convicted of a third felony must serve a lengthy prison sentence. In many cases, the crime does not have to be of a violent or dangerous nature. Under Washington's habitual offender law, for example, a "persistent offender" is automatically sentenced to life even if the third felony offense happens to be "vehicular assault" (an automobile accident that causes injury), unarmed robbery, or attempted arson, among other lesser felonies.[62] Consequently, two-thirds of all inmates serving life without parole in that state had been sentenced for a third strike.[63] In California, convicts have been sent to prison for life for third offenses that include shoplifting a pair of tube socks, stealing a slice of pizza, and possessing .14 grams of methamphetamine.[64]

The Supreme Court validated the most punitive aspects of habitual offender laws with its decision in *Lockyer v. Andrade* (2003).[65] That case involved the sentencing under California's "three-strikes" law of Leandro Andrade to fifty years in prison for stealing $153 worth of videotapes. Writing for the majority in a bitterly divided 5–4 decision, Justice Sandra Day O'Connor concluded that Andrade's punishment was not so "objectively" unreasonable that it violated the Constitution.[66] Basically, the justices who upheld the law said that if the California legislature—and by extension the California voters—felt that the law was reasonable, then the judicial branch was in no position to disagree.

Reforming Mandatory Minimums

Somewhat ironically, in 2012 California voters decided that the state's three-strikes law was indeed unreasonable. That year, by a two-thirds vote, Californians passed a ballot initiative revising the law. Now, a life sentence will be imposed only when the third felony conviction is for a serious or violent crime. Furthermore, the measure has authorized judges to resentence about 3,000 inmates who were serving life prison terms in California prisons because of a nonviolent "third strike." As of February 2015, just over 2,000 of these inmates had been released from prison.[67]

The California ballot initiative reflects nationwide discontent with mandatory minimum sentencing statutes. As we saw with the judge who was forced to sentence Scott Walker to life in prison at the beginning of the chapter, these laws are often unpopular with judges. They are also seen as contributing heavily to the explosive, and costly, growth of the U.S. prison population since the 1980s, which we will discuss in Chapter 11. In addition, the country's minority population seems to have borne the brunt of harsh sentencing legislation—nearly 70 percent of all convicts subject to mandatory minimum sentences are African American or Hispanic.[68]

▲ Through a ballot initiative, California voters decided to revise the state's "three strikes" law so that only a violent or serious third felony will trigger the automatic life sentence. **Do you think that the new version of California's habitual offender law is fairer than the old one? Why or why not?** Jim West/Alamy

In response to these issues, nearly thirty states have reformed their mandatory sentencing laws since 2000. In general, these reforms take one of three approaches:[69]

1. *Expanding judicial discretion.* In Connecticut, judges can depart from mandatory minimum sentences for certain drug crimes when no violence or threat of violence was present.[70]
2. *Limiting habitual offender "triggers."* In Nevada, misdemeanor convictions no longer count toward a five-year mandatory minimum sentence for a third conviction.[71]
3. *Repealing or revising mandatory minimum sentences.* In 2009, New York repealed the "Rockefeller drug laws," eliminating mandatory minimum sentences for low-level drug offenders.[72]

On the federal level, the U.S. Congress is considering several bills that would allow federal judges to depart from mandatory minimum sentences for nonviolent drug offenses.[73] Absent legislative reform, the U.S. Department of Justice has asked federal prosecutors to avoid charging nonviolent drug offenders with the penalty enhancements that lead to long prison terms.[74]

Victim Impact Evidence

The final piece of the sentencing puzzle involves victims and victims' families. As mentioned in Chapter 3, crime victims traditionally were banished to the peripheries of the criminal justice system. This situation has changed dramatically with the emergence of the victims' rights movement over the past few decades. Victims are now given the opportunity to testify—in person or through written testimony—during sentencing hearings about the suffering they experienced as a result of the crime. These **victim impact statements (VISs)** have proved extremely controversial, however, and legal experts have had a difficult time determining whether they cause more harm than good.

Learning Objective 6

Identify the arguments for and against the use of victim impact statements during sentencing hearings.

Balancing the Process The Crime Victims' Rights Act provides victims the right to be reasonably heard during the sentencing process,[75] and many state victims' rights laws contain similar provisions.[76] In general, these laws allow a victim (or victims) to tell his or her "side of the story" to the sentencing body, be it a judge, jury, or parole officer. In nonmurder cases, the victim can personally describe the physical, financial, and emotional impact of the crime. When the charge is murder or manslaughter, relatives or friends can give personal details about the victim and describe the effects of her or his death. In almost all instances, the goal of the VIS is to increase the harshness of the sentence.

Most of the debate surrounding VISs centers on their use in the sentencing phases of death penalty cases. Supporters point out that the defendant has always been allowed to present character evidence in the hopes of dissuading a judge or jury from capital punishment. According to some, a VIS balances the equation by giving survivors a voice in the process. Presenting a VIS is also said to have psychological benefits for victims, who are no longer forced to sit in silence as decisions that affect their lives are made by others.[77] Finally, on a purely practical level, a VIS may help judges and juries make informed sentencing decisions by providing them with an understanding of all of the consequences of the crime. (For an example of a victim impact statement from a recent death penalty case, see Figure 9.5.)

victim impact statement (VIS) A statement to the sentencing body (judge, jury, or parole board) in which the victim is given the opportunity to describe how the crime has affected her or him.

Figure 9.5 Victim Impact Statement (VIS)

In July 2015, a Colorado jury found James Holmes (see photo) guilty on twenty-four counts of first degree murder, two for each of the twelve victims he fatally shot inside an Aurora movie theater three years earlier. At least one hundred victims and witnesses testified at his sentencing hearing, including Kristian Cowden, whose father Gordon Cowden was killed by Holmes. A portion of her VIS is reprinted here.

RJ Sangosti/Getty Images

> The following victim impact statement is a testament to the gross inadequacy of words, as there is no human language that can convey the pain that I have witnessed seize ahold of my family or the pain I have personally experienced and continue to experience every day of my life as a result of the pointless tragedy that is homicide. Over the last three years since my father was murdered I have learned a lot of unsolicited information about the depths of anguish and the nature of grief.

The Risks of Victim Evidence Opponents of the use of VISs claim that they interject dangerously prejudicial evidence into the sentencing process, which should be governed by reason, not emotion. The inflammatory nature of VISs, they say, may distract judges and juries from the facts of the case, which should be the only basis for a sentence.[78] In fact, research has shown that hearing victim impact evidence makes jurors more likely to impose the death penalty.[79] The Supreme Court, however, has given its approval to the use of VISs, allowing judges to decide whether the statements are admissible on a case-by-case basis, just as they do with any other type of evidence.[80]

EthicsChallenge

Critics contend that victim impact statements unethically introduce the idea of a victim's "social value" into the courtroom. That is, judges and juries may feel compelled to base the punishment on the worthiness of the victim (his or her standing in the community, role as a family member, and the like) rather than the circumstances of the crime. What is your opinion of this argument?

Capital Punishment

Few topics in the criminal justice system inspire such heated debate as **capital punishment**, or the use of the death penalty. Opponents such as legal expert Stephen Bright wonder whether "there comes a time when a society gets beyond some of the more primitive forms of punishment."[81] They point out that the United States is the sole

capital punishment The use of the death penalty to punish wrongdoers for certain crimes.

Western democracy that continues that practice, putting it among China, Iran, Iraq, and Saudi Arabia on the list of nations that carry out the most executions.[82] Critics also claim that a process whose subjects are chosen by "luck and money and race" cannot serve the interests of justice.[83] Proponents believe that the death penalty serves as the ultimate deterrent for violent criminal behavior and that the criminals who are put to death are the "worst of the worst" and deserve their fate.

Today, about 3,000 convicts are living on "death row" in American prisons, meaning they have been sentenced to death and are awaiting execution. In the 1940s, as many as two hundred people were put to death in the United States in one year. As Figure 9.6 shows, the most recent high-water mark was ninety-eight in 1999. Despite declines since then, certain states and the federal government still regularly seek the death penalty for those offenders convicted of capital crimes. Consequently, the questions that surround the death penalty—Is it fair? Is it humane? Does it deter crime?—will continue to mobilize both its supporters and its detractors.

Methods of Execution

In its early years, when the United States adopted the practice of capital punishment from England, it also adopted English methods, which included drawing and quartering and boiling the convict alive. By the nineteenth century, these techniques had been deemed "barbaric" and were replaced by hanging. Indeed, the history of capital punishment in America is marked by attempts to make the act more humane. The late nineteenth century saw the introduction of electrocution as a less painful method of execution than hanging, and in 1890 in Auburn Prison, New York, William Kemmler became the first American to die in an electric chair.

The "chair" remained the primary form of execution until 1977, when Oklahoma became the first state to adopt lethal injection. Today, this method dominates executions in all thirty-one states that employ the death penalty. Fifteen states authorize at least two different methods of execution, meaning that electrocution (eight states), lethal gas (three states), hanging (three states), and the firing squad (two states) are still used on very rare occasions.[84]

Figure 9.6 Executions in the United States, 1976 to 2015

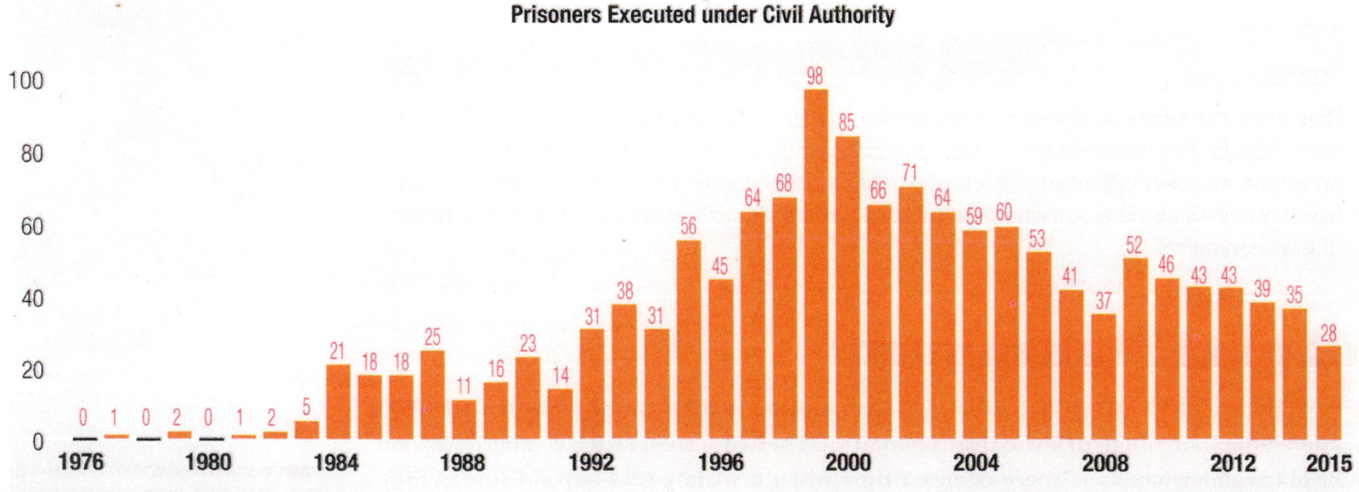

Source : Death Penalty Information Center.

For most of the past three decades, states have used a similar three-drug process to carry out lethal injections. The process—which involves a sedative, a paralyzing agent, and a drug that induces heart failure—was designed to be as painless as possible for the condemned convict. Over the past five years, however, the companies that manufacture these three drugs have increasingly refused to sell them for execution purposes. This has forced state officials to experiment with untested replacement drugs, a development that—as we shall soon see—has added an element of uncertainty to capital punishment in the United States.

The Death Penalty and the Supreme Court

The United States Supreme Court's attitude toward the death penalty has been shaped by two decisions made more than a century ago. In 1890, the Supreme Court established that so long as they are not carried out in an "inhuman" or "barbarous" fashion, executions are not forbidden by the Eighth Amendment.[85] Since then, the Court has never ruled that any *method* of execution is unconstitutionally "cruel and unusual."

The Weems Standard In *Weems v. United States* (1910),[86] the Court made a ruling that further clarified the meaning of "cruel and unusual" as defined by the Eighth Amendment, though the case did not involve capital punishment. The defendant had been sentenced to fifteen years of hard labor, a heavy fine, and a number of other penalties for the relatively minor crime of falsifying official records. The Court overturned the sentence, ruling that the penalty was too harsh considering the nature of the offense. Ultimately, in the *Weems* decision, the Court set three important precedents concerning sentencing:

1. Cruel and unusual punishment is defined by the changing norms and standards of society and therefore is not based on historical interpretations.
2. Courts may decide whether a punishment is unnecessarily cruel with regard to physical pain.
3. Courts may decide whether a punishment is unnecessarily cruel with regard to psychological pain.[87]

"Cruel and Unusual" Concerns In *Baze v. Rees* (2008),[88] the Supreme Court ruled that the mere possibility of pain "does not establish the sort of 'objectively intolerable risk of harm' that qualifies as cruel and unusual" punishment. That ruling, however, applied to the three-drug process described earlier. For a variety of reasons, manufacturers in America and Europe now refuse to sell those drugs to the states. Consequently, state corrections systems have been forced to try new lethal injection protocols, with controversial results. In April 2014, Oklahoma officials appeared to botch the execution of Clayton Lockett, who writhed in evident discomfort for forty-three minutes before dying. Similarly lengthy ordeals by condemned convicts in Arizona and Ohio brought attention to midazolam, a replacement anesthetic used in all three executions.

Some medical experts claim that midazolam cannot be relied upon to mask the pain suffered by convicts during executions.[89] Nevertheless, in 2015 the Supreme Court approved use of the drug, once again holding that methods of capital punishment are not cruel and unusual.[90] Writing for the Court's 5–4 majority, Justice Samuel Alito pointed out that rejecting all available means for executions would be the same as ending the practice, which remains constitutional. In her dissent, Justice Sonia Sotomayor accused her colleagues of sanctioning "the chemical equivalent of being burned alive."[91]

Death Penalty Sentencing

In the 1960s, the Supreme Court became increasingly concerned about what it saw as serious flaws in the way the states administered capital punishment. Finally, in 1967, the Court put a moratorium on executions until it could "clean up" the process. The chance to do so came with the *Furman v. Georgia* case, decided in 1972.[92]

Learning Objective 7

Identify the two stages that make up the bifurcated process of death penalty sentencing.

The Bifurcated Process In its *Furman* decision, by a 5–4 margin, the Supreme Court essentially held that the death penalty, as administered by the states, violated the Eighth Amendment. Justice Potter Stewart was particularly eloquent in his concurring opinion, stating that the sentence of death was so arbitrary as to be comparable to "being struck by lightning."[93] Although the *Furman* ruling invalidated the death penalty for more than six hundred offenders on death row at the time, it also provided the states with a window to make the process less arbitrary, therefore bringing their death penalty statutes up to constitutional standards.

The result was a two-stage, or *bifurcated,* procedure for capital cases. In the first stage, a jury determines the guilt or innocence of the defendant for a crime that has, by state statute, been determined to be punishable by death. If the defendant is found guilty, the jury reconvenes in the second stage and considers all aggravating and mitigating factors to decide whether the death sentence is in fact warranted. (See this chapter's second *Mastering Concepts* feature to get a better idea of how these two stages work.) Therefore, even if a jury finds the defendant guilty of a crime, such as first degree murder, that *may be* punishable by death, in the second stage it can decide that the circumstances surrounding the crime justify only a punishment of life in prison.

Today, thirty-one states and the federal government have capital punishment laws based on the bifurcated process. State governments are responsible for almost all executions in this country. The federal government has carried out only three death sentences since 1963. It usually seeks capital punishment only for high-profile defendants such as Dzokhar Tsarnaev, sentenced to die in May 2015 for his role in the Boston Marathon bombings that killed three spectators and wounded 260 others two years earlier.

▼ This photo shows the death chamber at the Southern Ohio Correctional Facility in Lucasville, Ohio—site of convicted murderer Dennis McGuire's January 2014 execution. During the lethal injection process, which took twenty-six minutes, McGuire choked several times and appeared to clench his fists in discomfort. **Do you think that offenders convicted of capital crimes are entitled to a pain-free execution? Why or why not?** AP Images/Kiichiro Sato

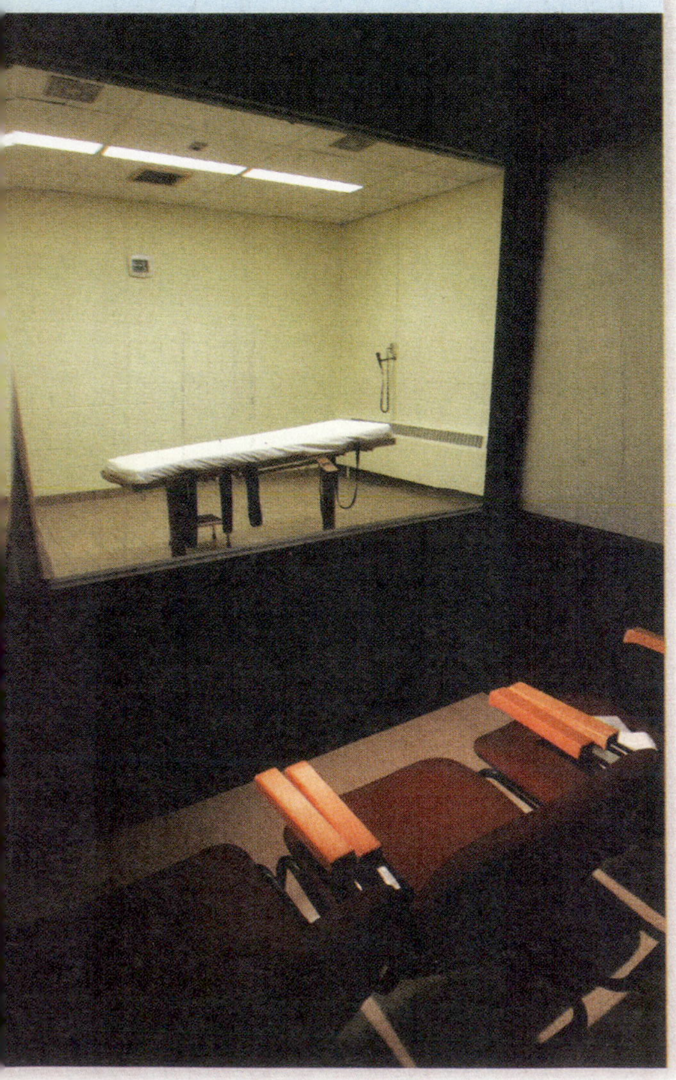

The Jury's Role The Supreme Court reaffirmed the important role of the jury in death penalties in *Ring v. Arizona* (2002).[94] The case involved Arizona's bifurcated process: after the jury determined a defendant's guilt or innocence, it would be dismissed, and the judge alone would decide whether execution was warranted. The Court found that this procedure violated the defendant's Sixth Amendment right to a jury trial, ruling that juries must be involved in *both* stages of the bifurcated process. The decision invalidated death penalty laws in Arizona, Colorado, Idaho, Montana, and Nebraska, forcing legislatures in those states to hastily revamp their procedures.

In most circumstances, a jury's decision to execute a defendant must be unanimous. For example, James Holmes, discussed in Figure 9.5, avoided the death penalty because a single juror felt that, due to his mental illness, Holmes deserved life in prison.[95] Only three states—Alabama, Delaware, and Florida—do not require unanimity of the jury to sentence a defendant to death. In 2016, the United States Supreme Court struck down the part of Florida's execution procedure that seemed to give judges rather than juries the final say in death penalty decisions.[96] Given that in Alabama jurors only *recommend* a sentence or life in prison, with a judge making the final ruling, observers expect the Court to address the states' inconsistencies involving jury unanimity and judicial overreach in the near future.[97]

Mitigating Circumstances Several mitigating circumstances will prevent a defendant found guilty of first degree murder from receiving the death penalty. These circumstances include:

1. *Insanity.* In 1986, the United States Supreme Court held that the Constitution prohibits the execution of "those who are unaware of the punishment they are about to suffer and why they are to suffer it."[98]
2. *Mental retardation.* In *Atkins v. Virginia* (2002),[99] the Court noted that eighteen states had barred the execution of mentally handicapped persons. Thus, applying the *Weems* test, it decided that the "changing norms of society" prohibited the execution of defendants with I.Q. scores of under "approximately 70."
3. *Age.* In 2005, the Court effectively ended the execution of those who had committed their capital crimes as juveniles.[100] (See the feature *Landmark Cases—Roper v. Simmons* for an explanation of the Court's reasoning.)

Mastering**Concepts**

The Bifurcated Death Penalty Process

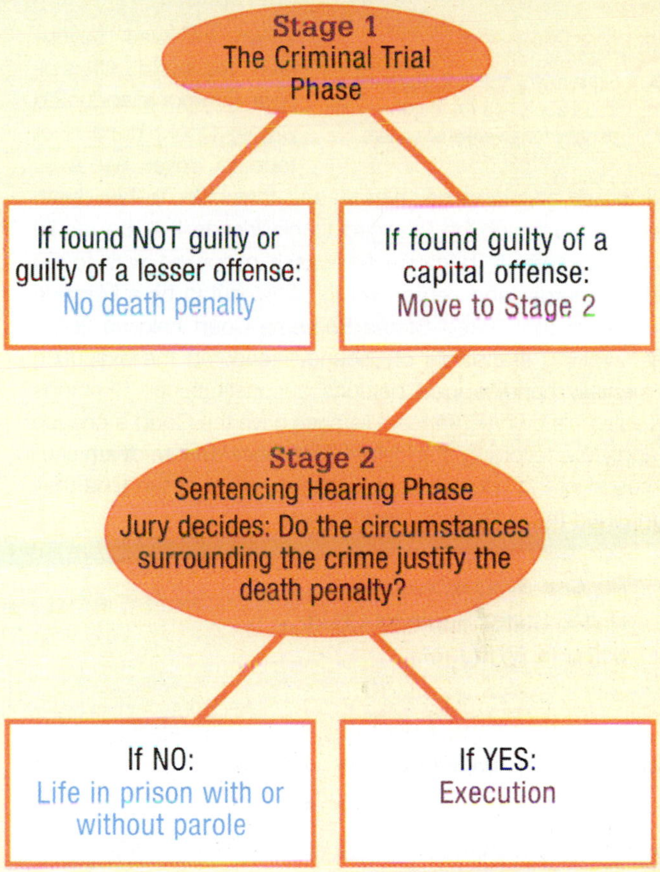
Stage 1
The Criminal Trial Phase
If found NOT guilty or guilty of a lesser offense:
No death penalty
If found guilty of a capital offense:
Move to Stage 2
Stage 2
Sentencing Hearing Phase
Jury decides: Do the circumstances surrounding the crime justify the death penalty?
If NO:
Life in prison with or without parole
If YES:
Execution

In 2014, the Court clarified one contentious area of the death penalty process—how to determine if a defendant is "mentally retarded" under the *Atkins* guidelines. The Court rejected Florida's use of a rigid I.Q. standard of 71 to make such a determination, criticized by opponents as an unfairly subjective cutoff point.[101]

Debating the Sentence of Death

Of the topics covered in this textbook, few inspire such passionate argument as the death penalty. Many advocates believe that execution is "just deserts" for those who commit heinous crimes. In the words of sociologist Ernest van den Haag, death is the "only fitting retribution for murder that I can think of."[102] Opponents worry that retribution is simply another word for vengeance and that "the use of the death penalty by the state will increase the acceptance of revenge in our society and will give official sanction to a climate of violence."[103] As the debate over capital punishment continues, it tends to focus on several key issues: deterrence, fallibility, arbitrariness, and discrimination.

Deterrence Those advocates of the death penalty who wish to show that the practice benefits society often turn to the idea of deterrence. In other words, they believe that by executing

Landmark Cases

Roper v Simmons

Learning Objective

8 Explain why the U.S. Supreme Court abolished the death penalty for juvenile offenders.

When he was seventeen years old, Christopher Simmons abducted Shirley Cook, used duct tape to cover her eyes and mouth and bind her hands, and threw her to her death in a river. Although he bragged to his friends that he would "get away with it" because he was a minor, he was found guilty of murder and sentenced to be executed by a Missouri court. After the United States Supreme Court held, in 2002, that "evolving standards of decency" rendered the execution of mentally handicapped persons unconstitutional, Simmons appealed his own sentence. His case gave the Court a chance to apply the "evolving standards of decency" test to death sentences involving offenders who were juveniles at the time they committed the underlying capital crime.

Roper v. Simmons
United States Supreme Court
543 U.S. 551 (2005)

In the Words of the Court . . .

Justice Kennedy, Majority Opinion

* * * *

The evidence of national consensus against the death penalty for juveniles is similar, and in some respects parallel, to the evidence *Atkins* held sufficient to demonstrate a national consensus against the death penalty for the mentally retarded.

* * * *

Three general differences between juveniles under 18 and adults demonstrate that juvenile offenders cannot with reliability be classified among the worst offenders. First, as any parent knows and as the scientific and sociological studies * * * tend to confirm, "[a] lack of maturity and an underdeveloped sense of responsibility are found in youth more often than in adults and are more understandable among the young. These qualities often result in impetuous and ill-considered actions and decisions." * * * In recognition of the comparative immaturity and irresponsibility of juveniles, almost every State prohibits those under 18 years of age from voting, serving on juries, or marrying without parental consent.

The second area of difference is that juveniles are more vulnerable or susceptible to negative influences and outside pressures, including peer pressure. * * * The third broad difference is that the character of a juvenile is not as well formed as that of an adult. The personality traits of juveniles are more transitory, less fixed.

These differences render suspect any conclusion that a juvenile falls among the worst offenders. * * * Retribution is not proportional if the law's most severe penalty is imposed on one whose culpability or blameworthiness is diminished, to a substantial degree, by reason of youth and immaturity.

Decision

The Court found that, applying the Eighth Amendment in light of "evolving standards of decency," the execution of offenders who were under the age of eighteen when their crimes were committed was cruel and unusual punishment and therefore unconstitutional.

For Critical Analysis

In his majority opinion, Justice Kennedy noted that a number of countries, including China, Iran, and Pakistan, had recently ended the practice of executing juveniles, leaving the United States "alone in a world that has turned its face against the practice." What impact, if any, should international customs have on American criminal law?

convicted criminals, the criminal justice system discourages potential criminals from committing similar violent acts. Several reports released in the first decade of the 2000s claim that each convict executed deters between three and eighteen future homicides.[104] More recent research suggests that if the death penalty does have a deterrent effect, it is small and relatively short-lived, influencing behavior only for about a month after an execution takes place.[105]

The main problem with studies that support the death penalty, say its critics, is that there are too few executions carried out in the United States each year to adequately determine their impact.[106] Furthermore, each study that "proves" the deterrent effect of the death penalty seems be matched by one that "disproves" the same premise.[107] In the end, the deterrence debate follows a familiar pattern. Opponents of the death penalty claim that murderers rarely consider the consequences of their act, and therefore it makes no difference whether capital punishment exists or not. Proponents counter that this proves the death penalty's deterrent value, because if the murderers *had* considered the possibility of execution, they would not have committed their crimes.

Fallibility In a sense, capital punishment acts as the ultimate deterrent by rendering those executed incapable of committing further crimes. Incapacitation as a justification for the death penalty, though, rests on two questionable assumptions: (1) every convicted murderer is likely to recidivate, and (2) the criminal justice system is *infallible*. In other words, the system never convicts someone who is actually not guilty.

Although several executions from the 1980s and 1990s are coming under increased scrutiny,[108] no court has ever found that an innocent person has been executed in the United States. According to the Death Penalty Information Center, however, between 1973, when the Supreme Court had temporarily suspended capital punishment, and March 2016, 156 American men and women who had been convicted of capital crimes and sentenced to death—though not executed—were later found to be innocent. Over that same time period, 1,430 executions took place, meaning that for about every nine convicts put to death during that period, about one death row inmate has been found innocent.[109]

Arbitrariness As noted earlier, one of the reasons it is so difficult to determine the deterrent effect of the death penalty is that it is rarely meted out. Despite the bifurcated process required by the Supreme Court's *Furman* ruling (discussed earlier in the chapter), a significant amount of arbitrariness appears to remain in the system. Only 2 percent of all defendants convicted of murder are sentenced to death, and relatively few of those on death row are ever executed.[110]

The chances of a defendant in a capital trial being sentenced to death seem to depend heavily on the jurisdiction where the crime was committed. As Figure 9.7 shows, a convict's likelihood of being executed is strongly influenced by geography. Five states

Figure 9.7 Executions by State, 1976–2015

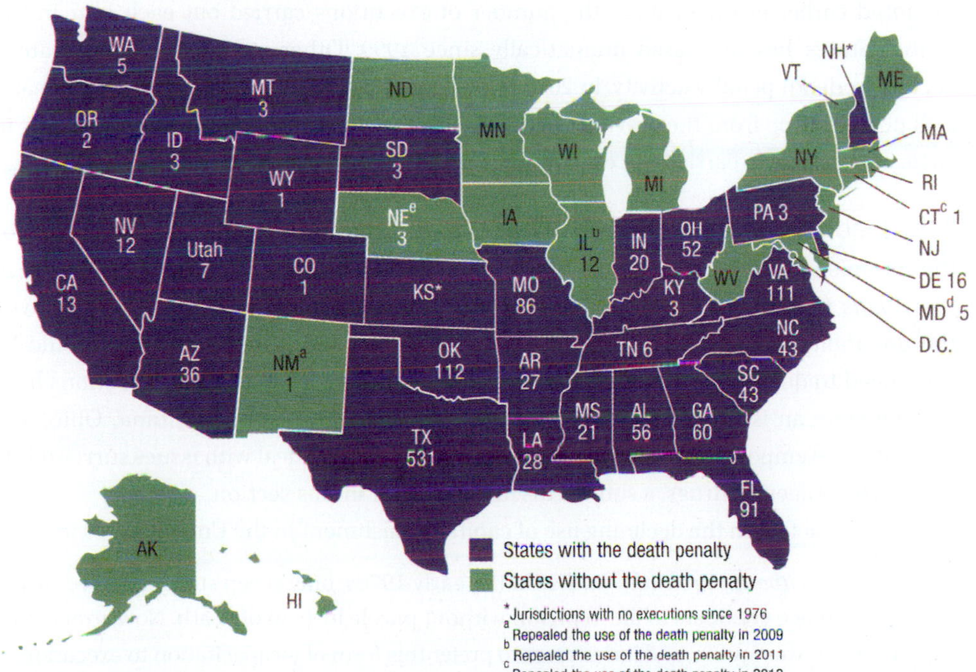

Source: Death Penalty Information Center.

(Florida, Missouri, Oklahoma, Texas, and Virginia) account for more than two-thirds of all executions, while nineteen states and the District of Columbia do not provide for capital punishment within their borders. In addition, because the decision to seek the death penalty is made on a local level by local prosecutors, the practice is not consistent within states that allow it. According to the Death Penalty Information Center, the jurisdiction of Riverside County, California, imposed eight death sentences in 2015, more than any state except for Florida, accounting for 16 percent of the national total that year.[111]

Discriminatory Effect Whether or not capital punishment is imposed arbitrarily, some observers claim that it is not done without bias. A disproportionate number of those executed since 1976—just over one-third—have been African American, and today 42 percent of all inmates on death row are black.[112] Another set of statistics also continues to be problematic: in 296 cases involving interracial murders in which the defendant was executed between 1976 and March 2016, the defendant was African American and the victim was white. Over that same time period, only 31 cases involved a white defendant and a black victim.[113] In fact, although slightly less than half of murder victims are white, three out of every four executions involve white victims.[114]

In *McCleskey v. Kemp* (1987),[115] the defense attorney for an African American sentenced to death for killing a white police officer used similar statistics to challenge Georgia's death penalty law. A study of two thousand Georgia murder cases showed that although African Americans were the victims of six out of every ten murders in the state, more than 80 percent of the cases in which death was imposed involved murders of whites.[116] In a 5–4 decision, the United States Supreme Court rejected the defense's claims, ruling that statistical evidence did not prove discriminatory intent on the part of Georgia's lawmakers. (For a discussion of the moral component of the death penalty debate, see the feature *CJ Controversy—The Morality of the Death Penalty*.)

The Future of the Death Penalty

As noted earlier in the chapter, the number of executions carried out each year in the United States has decreased dramatically since 1999. Other statistics also indicate a decline in death penalty activity. In 2015, only forty-nine people were sentenced to death, a 33 percent drop from the previous year's already historically low tally.[117] Furthermore, in 2015, only six states carried out executions, the fewest number since 1992.[118]

The Decline in Executions We have already addressed some of the reasons for the diminishing use of executions in the criminal justice system. With its decisions in the *Atkins* (2002) and *Roper* (2005) cases, the United States Supreme Court removed the possibility that hundreds of mentally handicapped and juvenile offenders could be sentenced to death. The availability and reliability of drugs used in lethal injections have also become an issue. In 2015, five states—Arkansas, Mississippi, Montana, Ohio, and Oklahoma—temporarily shut down their death chambers to deal with issues surrounding their lethal injection drugs, a subject discussed earlier in this section.

Other factors in the declining use of capital punishment in the United States include:

1. *The life-without-parole alternative.* In the early 1970s, only seven states allowed juries to sentence offenders to life in prison without parole instead of death. Now, every state provides this option, and juries seem to prefer this form of incapacitation to execution.[119]
2. *Plummeting murder rates.* The number of murders committed in this country is currently half what it was in the early 1990s.[120] As murder is the most common

M Dogan/Shutterstock.com

The Morality of the Death Penalty

When, on May 27, 2015, the Nebraska legislature voted 30–19 to abolish the death penalty, state senator Ernie Chambers called it a victory for "human dignity." Such sentiments angered JoAnn Brandon, the mother of twenty-one-year-old Teena, who was murdered in Richardson County twenty-three years earlier. (One of Teena's killers remains on Nebraska's death row.) "I ask [the politicians] how they would feel if it was one of their family members, especially a child who was that young," she said of the legislature's move. For Brandon and many others, the death penalty is not a question of "changing norms and standards," but rather an expression of moral judgment on those who commit murder.

The Execution of Murderers Is a Moral Act Because . . .

- If the death penalty can prevent even a single future murder, then it is morally justifiable and perhaps even required by the government.
- The victim's family members often say that a murderer's execution brings them a sense of "closure" by helping them come to terms with their grief.

The Execution of Murderers Is an Immoral Act Because . . .

- The death penalty is an inherently cruel and barbaric act, and it is improper for the government of a civilized nation to kill its own citizens.
- Problems of arbitrariness, discrimination, and wrongful convictions rob the death penalty of any moral weight or justification.

Your Assignment

How do arguments concerning the morality of the death penalty apply when the punishment extends to other crimes besides murder? In general, do you think an argument can be made that someone who rapes a child should be executed? To see how the United States Supreme Court views this issue, research the case ***Kennedy v. Louisiana*** online. Then, write two full paragraphs describing your own opinion of the matter.

capital crime, this reduction has led to a decline in the number of offenders eligible for the death penalty.

3. *High costs.* Because of the costs of intensive law enforcement investigations, extensive *voir dire* (see Chapter 8), and appellate reviews that average about sixteen years, pursuing capital punishment can be very expensive for states. Nevada recently determined that its death penalty cases cost twice as much as similar cases without the death penalty, resulting in a $76 million price tag for state taxpayers since 1976.[121]

Changing "Norms and Standards"? In the spring of 2015, Nebraska became the seventh state to abolish the death penalty since 2004, along with Connecticut, Illinois, Maryland, New Jersey, New Mexico, and New York. The majority of states that do carry out executions have not done so this decade. According to the Pew Research Center, 56 percent of Americans now favor the death penalty for those convicted of murder, down from 78 percent in 1996.[122] As already noted, executions and death sentences are at historically low levels. Under the circumstances, is it possible the "norms and standards" of our society are turning against capital punishment, as the *Weems* test requires?

In fact, there is some evidence that the United States Supreme Court is wavering on the issue. As part of the Court's *Glossip v. Gross* (2015) 5–4 ruling upholding lethal injection, two justices (Stephen Breyer and Ruth Bader Ginsburg) openly questioned the legality of executions.[123] Just before his death in February 2016, Justice Antonin Scalia, a supporter of capital punishment, said he "wouldn't be surprised" if his colleagues eventually found the death penalty to be unconstitutional.[124]

Summary

For more information on these concepts, look back to the Learning Objective icons throughout the chapter.

1 List and contrast the four basic philosophical reasons for sentencing criminals. (a) Retribution, (b) deterrence, (c) incapacitation, and (d) rehabilitation. Under the principle of retributive justice, the severity of the punishment is in proportion to the severity of the crime. Punishment is an end in itself. In contrast, the deterrence approach seeks to prevent future crimes by setting an example. Such punishment is based on its deterrent value and not necessarily on the severity of the crime. The incapacitation theory of punishment simply argues that a criminal in prison cannot inflict further harm on society. In contrast, the rehabilitation theory asserts that criminals can be rehabilitated in the appropriate prison environment.

2 Contrast indeterminate with determinate sentencing. Indeterminate sentencing follows from legislative penal codes that set minimum and maximum amounts of incarceration time. Determinate sentencing carries a fixed amount of time, although this may be reduced for "good time."

3 State who has input into the sentencing decision, and list the factors that determine a sentence. The prosecutor, defense attorney, probation officer, and judge provide inputs. The factors considered in sentencing are (a) the seriousness of the crime, (b) mitigating circumstances, (c) aggravating circumstances, and (d) judicial philosophy.

4 Explain some of the reasons why sentencing reform has occurred. One reason is sentencing disparity, which is indicative of a situation in which those convicted of similar crimes receive dissimilar sentences (often due to a particular judge's sentencing philosophy). Sentencing discrimination has also occurred on the basis of defendants' gender, race, or economic standing. An additional reason for sentencing reform has been a general desire to "get tough on crime."

5 Describe the goal of mandatory minimum sentencing guidelines, and explain why these laws have become unpopular in recent years. Mandatory minimum sentencing guidelines are designed to set a fixed punishment for certain crimes that is, for the most part, immune to judicial discretion. For that reason, they are unpopular with judges, who feel the laws do not recognize the individual aspects of each case. Others also believe that the guidelines contribute to America's immense prison census and the racial imbalance within the population behind bars.

6 Identify the arguments for and against the use of victim impact statements during sentencing hearings. Proponents of victim impact statements believe that they allow victims to provide character evidence in the same manner as defendants have always been allowed to do and that they give victims a therapeutic "voice" in the sentencing process. Opponents argue that the statements bring unacceptable levels of emotion into the courtroom and encourage judges and juries to make sentencing decisions based on the "social value" of the victim rather than the facts of the case.

7 Identify the two stages that make up the bifurcated process of death penalty sentencing. The first stage of the bifurcated process requires a jury to find the defendant guilty or not guilty of a crime that is punishable by execution. If the defendant is found guilty, then, in the second stage, the jury reconvenes to decide whether the death sentence is warranted.

8 Explain why the U.S. Supreme Court abolished the death penalty for juvenile offenders. In its *Roper v. Simmons* decision, the Supreme Court ruled that national "evolving standards of decency" no longer justified the execution of juvenile offenders. Such offenders are understood to be less blameworthy than adults because of various issues relating to immaturity and irresponsibility.

Questions for Critical Analysis

1. Suppose that the U.S. Congress passed a new law that punished shoplifting with a mandatory eighty-five-year prison term. What would be the impact of the new law on shoplifting nationwide? Would such a harsh law be justified by its deterrent effect? What about imposing a similarly extreme punishment on a more serious crime—a mandatory sentence of life in prison for, say, drunk driving? Would such a law be in society's best interest? Why or why not?

2. Why are truth-in-sentencing laws generally popular among victims' rights advocates? Why might these laws not be so popular with prison administrators or government officials charged with balancing a state budget?

3. After a trial in Boston, Massachusetts, Harold is convicted of unarmed burglary. He has no prior convictions. According to the grid in Figure 9.4, what punishment do the state guidelines require? What would his punishment be if he had a previous conviction for armed robbery, which means that he has a "serious" criminal record?

4. Defense attorneys are increasingly likely to submit expensive biographical videos of their clients during sentencing in hopes of gaining a more lenient punishment. Lawyers say that such videos give judges and juries a sense of the "totality of the defendant." What might be some of the criticisms of this practice, particularly among public defenders?

5. Supporters of the death penalty often use the principles of retribution and deterrence to argue in favor of the practice. How are these arguments affected by the long period of time (an average of sixteen years) from conviction to execution for many death row inmates in this country?

Key Terms

Notes

1. Herbert L. Packer, "Justification for Criminal Punishment," in *The Limits of Criminal Sanction* (Palo Alto, Calif.: Stanford University Press, 1968), 36–37.
2. Frank O. Bowman III, "Playing '21' with Narcotics Enforcement: A Response to Professor Carrington," *Washington and Lee Law Review* 52 (1995), 972.
3. James Q. Wilson, *Thinking about Crime* (New York: Basic Books, 1975), 235.
4. Ashley Nellis, *Life Goes On: The Historic Rise of Life Sentences in America* (Washington, D.C.: The Sentencing Project, September 2013), 1.
5. Isaac Ehrlich, "Participation in Illegitimate Activities: A Theoretical and Empirical Investigation," *Journal of Political Economy* 81 (May/June 1973), 521–564.
6. Avinash Singh Bhati, *An Information Theoretic Method for Estimating the Number of Crimes Averted by Incapacitation* (Washington, D.C.: Urban Institute, July 2007), 18–33.
7. Todd Clear, *Harm in Punishment* (Boston: Northeastern University Press, 1980).
8. Patricia M. Clark, "An Evidence-Based Intervention for Offenders," *Corrections Today* (February/March 2011), 62–64.
9. Robert V. Wolf, *Widening the Circle: Can Peacemaking Work Outside of Tribal Communities?* (New York: Center for Court Innovation, 2012), 2–8.
10. Quoted in *ibid.*, 8.
11. Kimberly S. Burke, *An Inventory and Examination of Restorative Justice Practices for Youth in Illinois* (Chicago: Illinois Criminal Justice Information Authority, April 2013), 6–7.
12. Shannon M. Silva and Carolyn G. Lambert, "Restorative Justice Legislation in the American States: A Statutory Analysis of Emerging Legal Doctrine," *Journal of Policy Practice* (April 2015), 77–95.
13. 42 U.S.C. Section 10601 (2006).
14. Devlin Barrett, "Budget Pact Raids Victims Fund," *Wall Street Journal* (November 1, 2015), at **www.wsj.com/articles/budget-pact-raids-victims-fund-1446424611**.
15. Gregory W. O'Reilly, "Truth-in-Sentencing: Illinois Adds Yet Another Layer of 'Reform' to Its Complicated Code of Corrections," *Loyola University of Chicago Law Journal* (Summer 1996), 986, 999–1000.
16. David E. Olson et al., *Final Report: The Impact of Illinois' Truth-in-Sentencing Law on Sentence Lengths, Time to Serve and Disciplinary Incidents of Convicted Murderers and Sex Offenders* (Chicago: Illinois Criminal Justice Information Authority, June 2009), 4–5.
17. Paul W. Keve, *Crime Control and Justice in America: Searching for Facts and Answers*

(Chicago: American Library Association, 1995), 77.

18. *Debtors' Prisons in New Hampshire* (Concord, N.H.: American Civil Liberties Union of New Hampshire, September 23, 2015).

19. *Bearden v. Georgia*, 462 U.S. 660 (1983).

20. Adam Ferrise, "Man Ordered by Judge to Hold Sign Saying He Bullied Disabled Children Starts His Five-Hour Shift," *Cleveland .com* (April 13, 2014), at **www.cleveland.com/metro/index.ssf/2014/04/man_ordered_by_judge_to_hold_s.html.**

21. Danielle A. Alvarez, "Flowers, Dinner, Bowling—and Counseling—Ordered by Broward Judge in Domestic Case," *Sunsentinel .com* (February 7, 2012), at **articles.sun-sentinel.com/2012-02-07/news/fl-flowers-food-bowling-20120207_1_red-lobster-broward-judge-judge-john-jay-hurley.**

22. Kate Stith and José A. Cabranes, "Judging under the Federal Sentencing Guidelines," *Northwestern University Law Review* 91 (Summer 1997), 1247.

23. Mark M. Lanier and Claud H. Miller III, "Attitudes and Practices of Federal Probation Officers towards Pre-Plea/Trial Investigative Report Policy," *Crime & Delinquency* 41 (July 1995), 365–366.

24. Nancy J. King and Rosevelt L. Noble, "Felony Jury Sentencing in Practice: A Three-State Study," *Vanderbilt Law Review* (2004), 1986.

25. Jena Iontcheva, "Jury Sentencing as Democratic Practice," *Virginia Law Review* (April 2003), 325.

26. Julie R. O'Sullivan, "In Defense of the U.S. Sentencing Guidelines Modified Real-Offense System," *Northwestern University Law Review* 91 (1997), 1342.

27. John Paul Wilson and Nicholas O. Rule, "Facial Trustworthiness Predicts Extreme Criminal-Sentencing Outcomes," *Psychological Science* (August 2015), 1325–1331.

28. Quoted in Tracy Connor, "Judge Gives Man 5 Days for Child Porn, Rails against Harsh Sentences," *NBCNews.com* (February 1, 2016), at **www.nbcnews.com/news/us-news/judge-gives-man-5-days-child-porn-rails-against-harsh-n507406.**

29. 18 U.S.C. Section 2113(a) (1994).

30. U.S. Sentencing Commission, "Statistical Information Packet, Fiscal Year 2014, Colorado," Table 7, at **www.ussc.gov/sites/default/files/pdf/research-and-publications/federal-sentencing-statistics/state-district-circuit/2014/co14.pdf**; and "Statistical Information Packet, Fiscal Year 2014, Eastern District of Virginia," Table 7, at **www.ussc.gov/sites/default/files/pdf/research-and-publications/federal-sentencing-statistics/state-district-circuit/2014/vae14.pdf.**

31. U.S. Sentencing Commission, "Statistical Information Packet, Fiscal Year 2014, Fourth Circuit," Table 7, at **www.ussc.gov/sites/default/files/pdf/research-and-publications/federal-sentencing-statistics/state-district-circuit/2014/4c14.pdf**; and "Statistical Information Packet, Fiscal Year 2014, Ninth Circuit," Table 7, at **www.ussc.gov/sites/default/files/pdf/research-and-publications/federal-sentencing-statistics/state-district-circuit/2014/9c14.pdf.**

32. Cassia Spohn and David Holleran, "The Imprisonment Penalty Paid by Young, Unemployed Black and Hispanic Male Offenders," *Criminology* 35 (2000), 281.

33. U.S. Sentencing Commission, "Report on the Continued Impact of *United States v. Booker* on Federal Sentencing (December 2012), at **www.ussc.gov/news/congressional-testimony-and-reports/booker-reports/report-continuing-impact-united-states-v-booker-federal-sentencing.**

34. Xia Wang et al., "Assessing the Differential Effects of Race and Ethnicity on Sentence Outcomes under Different Sentencing Systems," *Crime and Delinquency* (February 2013), 87–114.

35. David C. Baldus and George Woodworth, "Race Discrimination and the Legitimacy of Capital Punishment: Reflections on the Interaction of Fact and Perception," *DePaul Law Review* (2004), 1411.

36. Spohn and Holleran, *op. cit.*, 301.

37. Brian Johnson, "The Multilevel Context of Criminal Sentencing: Integrating Judge- and County-Level Influences," *Criminology* (May 2006), 259–298.

38. *A Living Death: Life without Parole for Nonviolent Offenses* (New York: American Civil Liberties Union, November 2013), Table 10, page 28.

39. Anti-Drug Abuse Act of 1986, Pub. L. No. 99-570, 100 Stat. 3207 (1986).

40. Solomon Moore, "Justice Department Seeks Equity in Sentences for Cocaine," *New York Times* (April 30, 2009), A17.

41. Pub. L. No. 111-220, Section 2, 124 Stat. 2372.

42. United States Sentencing Commission, "Materials on 2014 Drug Guidelines Amendment," at **www.ussc.gov/amendment-process/materials-2014-drug-guidelines-amendment.**

43. Julie H. Davis and Gardiner Harris, "Obama Issues Reductions of Sentences in Drug Cases," *New York Times* (July 14, 2015), A11.

44. 28 U.S.C. Section 991 (1994).

45. Bureau of Justice Statistics, *Felony Sentences in State Courts, 2006—Statistical Tables* (Washington, D.C.: U.S. Department of Justice, December 2009), Table 3.5, page 20.

46. Sonja B. Starr, "Estimating Gender Disparities in Federal Criminal Cases," *University of Michigan Law and Economics Research Paper* (August 29, 2012), at **papers.ssrn.com/sol3/papers.cfm?abstract_id=2144002.**

47. Clarice Feinman, *Women in the Criminal Justice System*, 3d ed. (Westport, Conn.: Praeger, 1994), 35.

48. John C. Coffee, "Repressed Issues of Sentencing," *Georgetown Law Journal* 66 (1978), 987.

49. J. S. Bainbridge, Jr., "The Return of Retribution," *ABA Journal* (May 1985), 63.

50. Pub. L. No. 98-473, 98 Stat. 1987, codified as amended at 18 U.S.C. Sections 3551–3742 and 28 U.S.C. Sections 991–998 (1988).

51. Julia L. Black, "The Constitutionality of Federal Sentences Imposed under the Sentencing Reform Act of 1984 after *Mistretta v. United States*," *Iowa Law Review* 75 (March 1990), 767.

52. *Fifteen Years of Guidelines Sentencing: An Assessment of How Well the Federal Criminal Justice System Is Achieving the Goals of Sentencing Reform* (Washington, D.C.: U.S. Sentencing Commission, November 2004), 46.

53. *Blakely v. Washington*, 542 U.S. 296 (2004); *United States v. Booker*, 543 U.S. 220 (2005); and *Gall v. United States*, 552 U.S. 38 (2007).

54. *Demographic Differences in Federal Sentencing Practices: An Update of the Booker Report's Multivariate Regression Analysis* (Washington, D.C.: U.S. Sentencing Commission, March 2010), C-3.

55. William Rhodes et al., *Federal Sentencing Disparity: 2005–2012* (Washington, D.C.: Bureau of Justice Statistics, October 22, 2015), 38–43.

56. U.S. Sentencing Commission, "Table N: National Comparison of Sentence Imposed and Position Relative to the Guideline Range, Fiscal Year 2014," *FY 2014 Sourcebook*, at **www.ussc.gov/sites/default/files/pdf/research-and-publications/annual-reports-and-sourcebooks/2014/TableN.pdf.**

57. Neal B. Kauder and Brian J. Ostrom, *State Sentencing Guidelines: Profiles and Continuum* (Williamsburg, Va.: National Center for State Courts, 2008), 15.

58. N.Y. Penal Law Sections 220.21, 60.5, 70.0(3) (1973).

59. Public Law Number 99-570 (1986).

60. 21 U.S.C. Section 859(b) (1986); 21 U.S.C. Section 861(a) (1986); and 18 U.S.C. Section 924(c)(1)(A)(i) (1998).

61. Todd R. Clear, George F. Cole, and Michael D. Reisig, *American Corrections*, 7th ed. (Belmont, Calif.: Thomson Wadsworth, 2006), 68–69.

62. Washington Revised Code Annotated Section 9.94A.030.

63. Nellis, *op. cit.*, 16.

64. Matt Taibbi, "Cruel and Unusual Punishment: The Shame of Three Strikes Laws," *Rolling Stone* (March 27, 2013), at **www.rollingstone.com/politics/news/cruel-and-unusual-punishment-the-shame-of-three-strikes-laws-20130327.**

65. *Lockyer v. Andrade*, 270 F.3d 743 (9th Cir. 2001).

66. *Ibid.*, 76.

67. Erik Eckholm, "Out of Prison, and Staying Out, after 3rd Strike in California," *New York Times* (February 27, 2015), A1.

68. *United States Sentencing Commission, Report to Congress: Mandatory Minimum Penalties in the Federal Criminal Justice System* (Washington, D.C.: United States Sentencing Commission, October 2011), xxviii.

69. Ram Subramanian and Ruth Delaney, *Playbook for Change? States Reconsider Mandatory Sentences* (New York: Vera Institute of Justice, February 2014), 8–12.

70. Connecticut Senate Bill Number 1160 (2001).

71. Nevada House Bill Number 239 (2009).

72. Jim Parsons et al., *End of an Era? The Impact of Drug Reform in New York City* (New York: Vera Institute of Justice, 2015).

73. Carl Hulse and Jennifer Steinhauer, "Sentencing Overhaul Proposed in Senate with Bipartisan Backing," *New York Times* (October 2, 2015), A19.

74. Erik Eckholm, "Prosecutors Draw Fire for Sentences Called Harsh," *New York Times* (December 6, 2013), A19.

75. Justice for All Act of 2004, Pub. L. No. 108-405, 118 Stat. 2260.

76. Paul G. Cassell, "In Defense of Victim Impact Statements," *Ohio State Journal of Criminal Law* (Spring 2009), 614.

77. Edna Erez, "Victim Voice, Impact Statements, and Sentencing: Integrating Restorative Justice and Therapeutic Jurisprudence Principles in Adversarial Proceedings," *Criminal Law Bulletin* (September/October 2004), 495.

78. Bryan Myers and Edith Greene, "Prejudicial Nature of Impact Statements," *Psychology, Public Policy, and Law* (December 2004), 493.

79. Bryan Myers and Jack Arbuthnot, "The Effects of Victim Impact Evidence on the Verdicts and Sentencing Judgments of Mock Jurors," *Journal of Offender Rehabilitation* (1999), 95–112.

80. *Payne v. Tennessee,* 501 U.S. 808 (1991).

81. Comments made at the Georgetown Law Center, "The Modern View of Capital Punishment," *American Criminal Law Review* 34 (Summer 1997), 1353.

82. "America and Its Fellow Executioners," *New York Times* (January 10, 2016), SR10.

83. David Bruck, quoted in Bill Rankin, "Fairness of the Death Penalty Is Still on Trial," *Atlanta Journal-Constitution* (July 29, 1997), A13.

84. Bureau of Justice Statistics, *Capital Punishment, 2013—Statistical Tables* (Washington, D.C.: U.S. Department of Justice, December 2014), 4.

85. *In re Kemmler,* 136 U.S. 447 (1890).

86. 217 U.S. 349 (1910).

87. Pamela S. Nagy, "Hang by the Neck until Dead: The Resurgence of Cruel and Unusual Punishment in the 1990s," *Pacific Law Journal* 26 (October 1994), 85.

88. 553 U.S. 35 (2008).

89. Erik Eckholm, "Justice to Hear Challenge That Argues Lethal-Injection Drug Causes Agony," *New York Times* (April 27, 2015), A10.

90. *Glossip v. Gross,* 576 U.S. ______ (2015).

91. Justia, "*Glossip v. Gross,*" at **supreme.justia.com/cases/federal/us/576/14-7955/dissent7.html**.

92. 408 U.S. 238 (1972).

93. 408 U.S. 309 (1972) (Stewart, concurring).

94. 536 U.S. 584 (2002).

95. Jack Healy, "Life Sentence for James Holmes, Aurora Theater Gunman," *New York Times* (August 8, 2015), A1.

96. *Hurst v. Florida,* 577 U.S. ____ (2016).

97. Lyle Denniston, "Opinion Analysis: Juries Control the Death Penalty," *SCOTUSBlog* (January 12, 2016), at **www.scotusblog.com/2016/01/opinion-analysis-juries-control-the-death-penalty**.

98. *Ford v. Wainwright,* 477 U.S. 399 (1986).

99. 536 U.S. 304 (2002).

100. 543 U.S. 551 (2005).

101. *Hall v. Florida,* 134 S.Ct. 1986, 2001 (2014).

102. Ernest van den Haag, "The Ultimate Punishment: A Defense," *Harvard Law Review* 99 (1986), 1669.

103. *The Death Penalty: The Religious Community Calls for Abolition* (pamphlet published by the National Coalition to Abolish the Death Penalty and the National Interreligious Task Force on Criminal Justice, 1988), 48.

104. Hashem Dezhbakhsh, Paul H. Rubin, and Joanna M. Shepherd, "Does Capital Punishment Have a Deterrent Effect? New Evidence from Postmoratorium Panel Data," *American Law and Economics Review* 5 (2003), 344–376; H. Naci Mocan and R. Kaj Gittings, "Getting Off Death Row: Commuted Sentences and the Deterrent Effect of Capital Punishment," *Journal of Law and Economics* 46 (2003), 453–478; Joanna M. Shepherd, "Deterrence versus Brutalization: Capital Punishment's Differing Impact among States," *Michigan Law Review* 104 (2005), 203–255; and Paul R. Zimmerman, "State Executions, Deterrence, and the Incidence of Murder," *Journal of Applied Economics* 7 (2005), 163–193.

105. Kenneth C. Land, Raymond H. C. Teske, Jr., and Hui Zheng, "Overview of 'The Differential Short-Term Impacts of Executions on Felony and Non-Felony Homicides,'" *Criminology & Public Policy* (August 2012), 539–563.

106. Richard Berk, "Can't Tell: Comments on 'Does the Death Penalty Save Lives?'" *Criminology and Public Policy* (November 2009), 845–851.

107. Aaron Chalfin, Amelia M. Haviland, and Steven Raphael, "What Do Panel Studies Tell Us about a Deterrent Effect of Capital Punishment? A Critique of the Literature," *Journal of Quantitative Criminology* (March 2013), 5–43.

108. Roger C. Barnes, "Death Penalty Undermines Justice," *San Antonio Express-News* (July 12, 202), 6B.

109. Death Penalty Information Center, "Innocence and the Death Penalty," at **www.deathpenaltyinfo.org/innocence-and-death-penalty.**

110. Adam Liptak, "Geography and the Machinery of Death," *New York Times* (February 5, 2007), A10.

111. *The Death Penalty in 2015: Year End Report* (Washington, D.C.: Death Penalty Information Center, 2015), 3.

112. Deborah Fins, *Death Row U.S.A.* (New York: NAACP Legal Defense and Educational Fund, Winter 2016), 1.

113. Death Penalty Information Center, "National Statistics on the Death Penalty and Race," at **www.deathpenaltyinfo.org/race-death-row-inmates-executed-1976#defend.**

114. *Ibid.*

115. 481 U.S. 279 (1987).

116. David C. Baldus, George Woodworth, and Charles A. Pulaski, *Equal Justice and the Death Penalty: A Legal and Empirical Analysis* (Boston: Northeastern University Press, 1990), 140–197, 306.

117. *Death Penalty in 2015: Year End Report, op. cit.*, 1.

118. *Ibid.*, 15.

119. "The Slow Death of the Death Penalty," *The Economist* (April 26, 2014), 27.

120. Federal Bureau of Investigation, *Crime in the United States 2013* (Washington, D.C.: U.S. Department of Justice, 2014), at **www.fbi.gov/about-us/cjis/ucr/crime-in-the-u.s/2013/crime-in-the-u.s.-2013,** Table 1.

121. Legislative Auditor, *Performance Audit: Fiscal Costs of the Death Penalty* (Carson City, Nev.: State of Nevada, 2014), 1.

122. Pew Research Center, "Less Support for Death Penalty, Especially among Democrats" (April 16, 2015), at **www.people-press.org/2015/04/16/less-support-for-death-penalty-especially-among-democrats.**

123. Death Penalty Information Center, "Two Supreme Court Justices Chronicle Death Penalty Flaws in *Glossip* Dissent," at **www.deathpenaltyinfo.org/node/6184.**

124. Quoted in Scott Martelle, "Justice Antonin Scalia 'Wouldn't Be Surprised' if Supreme Court Ends the Death Penalty," *Los Angeles Times* (September 25, 2015), at **www.latimes.com/opinion/opinion-la/la-ol-scalia-death-penalty-pope-francis-xi-jinpeng-trump-boehner-20150925-story.html.**

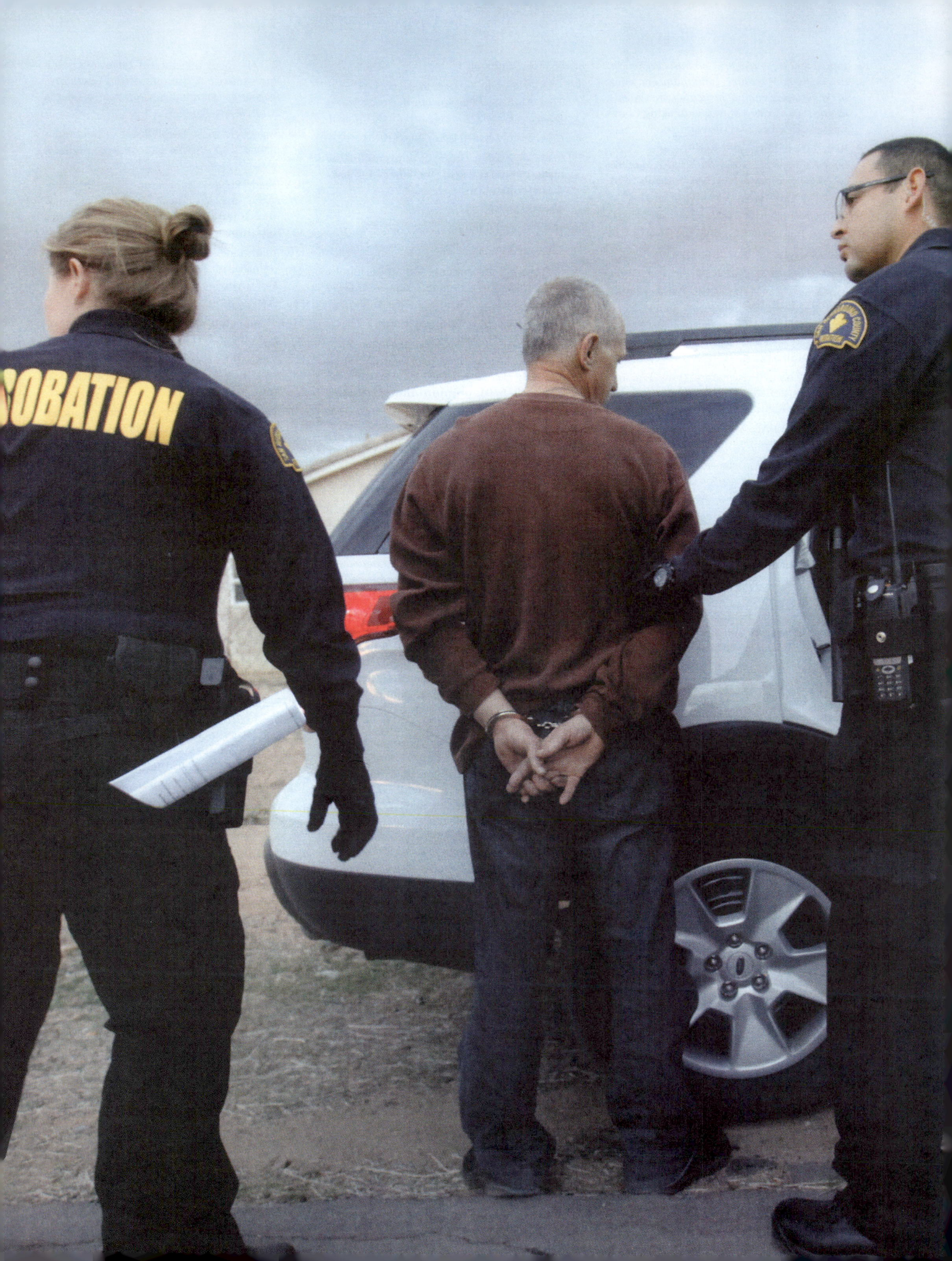
OBATION

AP Photo/Damian Dovarganes

10

Probation, Parole, and Intermediate Sanctions

Chapter Outline		Corresponding Learning Objectives
The Justifications for Community Corrections	1	Explain the justifications for community-based corrections programs.
Probation: Doing Time in the Community	2	Explain several alternative sentencing arrangements that combine probation with incarceration.
	3	Specify the conditions under which an offender is most likely to be denied probation.
	4	Describe the three general categories of conditions placed on a probationer.
The Parole Picture	5	Identify the main differences between probation and parole.
	6	Explain which factors influence the decision to grant parole.
Intermediate Sanctions	7	Contrast day reporting centers with intensive supervision probation.
	8	List the three levels of home monitoring.

To target your study and review, look for these numbered Learning Objective icons throughout the chapter.

family Ties

returning home from a barbecue at 3 A.M. in rural Philo, Illinois, twenty-four-year-old Katie Daly skidded on wet gravel and lost control of the all-terrain vehicle she was driving. Her nineteen-year-old cousin, Annie Daly, was thrown from the passenger seat and died in a hospital four hours later. At the time of the accident, Katie's blood alcohol level was well over the state's legal limit, and she was charged with felony aggravated driving under the influence (DUI). Given her family connection to the victim, local prosecutors agreed to a plea deal in which Katie would be spared prison, instead receiving a punishment of probation for her crime.

Champaign County judge Richard Klaus had other ideas. Despite impassioned calls for leniency from Annie's parents and brother, Klaus rejected the plea bargain and sentenced Katie to three and a half years in prison for reckless homicide. "Under the law, it is not a mitigating factor that a family member died. The loss to society is the same whether Annie was killed by a family member or a stranger," Klaus explained. "This is absolutely a deterrable crime and it must be deterred. It is the duty of the court to see that it is deterred."

Prosecutors and Katie's defense attorneys joined forces to appeal Klaus's decision. Noting Katie's youth, her lack of a criminal record, and the effect of the incarceration on her family, including her infant son, the appeals brief stated, "A prison sentence in this case would not be of any benefit to society, the defendant, or to our system of justice." Several years ago, an Illinois appellate court agreed, ruling that Klaus had abused his discretion by putting the defendant behind bars. After six months in prison, Katie was freed and resentenced to thirty months of probation. According to state's attorney Julia Reitz, the intent of the appellate court "was not to minimize the seriousness of the DUI aspect but more to focus on Katie's rehabilitative potential."

iStockphoto.com/Gaffizone

▲ Katie Daly was eventually sentenced to probation for killing her cousin Annie in an alcohol-related accident involving an all-terrain vehicle such as the one shown here.

1. What is your opinion of Judge Richard Klaus's justification for sentencing Katie Daly to prison rather than probation?
2. "We need to have Katie here to help us heal," Annie Daly's mother told the court. Should a victim's wishes influence the judge's sentencing decision? Why or why not?
3. What do you think prosecutor Julia Reitz meant when she referred to Katie's "rehabilitative potential"?

The Justifications for Community Corrections

In overturning Judge Richard Klaus's sentence of Katie Daly, the Fourth District Appellate Court of Illinois scolded the judge for focusing on incarceration and ignoring the "range of sentencing possibilities" called for by the facts of the case.[1] As this chapter will make clear, the range of sentencing possibilities for American judges includes numerous options that keep offenders out of prison and jail. For instance, about 3.8 million offenders such as Daly are serving their sentences in the community on *probation* rather than behind bars. In addition, approximately 850,000 convicts in the United States have been *paroled,* meaning that they are finishing their prison sentences "on the outside" under the supervision of correctional officers.[2]

America, says University of Minnesota law professor Michael Tonry, is preoccupied with the "absolute severity of punishment" and the "widespread view that only imprisonment counts."[3] Consequently, **community corrections** such as probation and parole are often considered less severe, and therefore less worthy, alternatives to imprisonment. In reality, community corrections are crucial to our criminal justice system. One in fifty adults in this country is living under community supervision,[4] and few criminal justice matters are more pressing than the need to successfully reintegrate these offenders into society.

Reintegration

Learning Objective

1 Explain the justifications for community-based corrections programs.

A very small percentage of all convicted offenders have committed crimes that warrant life imprisonment or capital punishment. Most, at some point, will return to the community. Consequently, according to one group of experts, the task of the corrections system

> includes building or rebuilding solid ties between the offender and the community, integrating or reintegrating the offender into community life—restoring family ties, obtaining employment and an education, securing in the larger sense a place for the offender in the routine functioning of society.[5]

Considering that some studies have shown higher recidivism rates for offenders who are subjected to prison culture, a frequent justification of community-based corrections is that they help to reintegrate the offender into society.

Reintegration has a strong theoretical basis in rehabilitative theories of punishment. An offender is generally considered to be "rehabilitated" when he or she no longer represents a threat to other members of the community and therefore is believed to be fit to live in that community. In the context of this chapter and the two that follow, it will also be helpful to see reintegration as a process through which criminal justice officials such as probation and parole officers provide the offender with incentives to follow the rules of society.

These incentives can be positive, such as enrolling the offender in a drug treatment program. They can also be negative—in particular, the threat of return to prison or jail for failure to comply. In all instances, criminal justice professionals must carefully balance the needs of the individual offender against the rights of law-abiding members of the community.

Diversion

Another justification for community-based corrections, based on practical considerations, is **diversion**. As you are already aware, many criminal offenses fall into the

community corrections The correctional supervision of offenders in the community as an alternative to sending them to prison or jail.

reintegration A goal of corrections that focuses on preparing the offender for a return to the community unmarred by further criminal behavior.

diversion In the context of corrections, a strategy to divert those offenders who qualify away from prison and jail and toward community-based and intermediate sanctions.

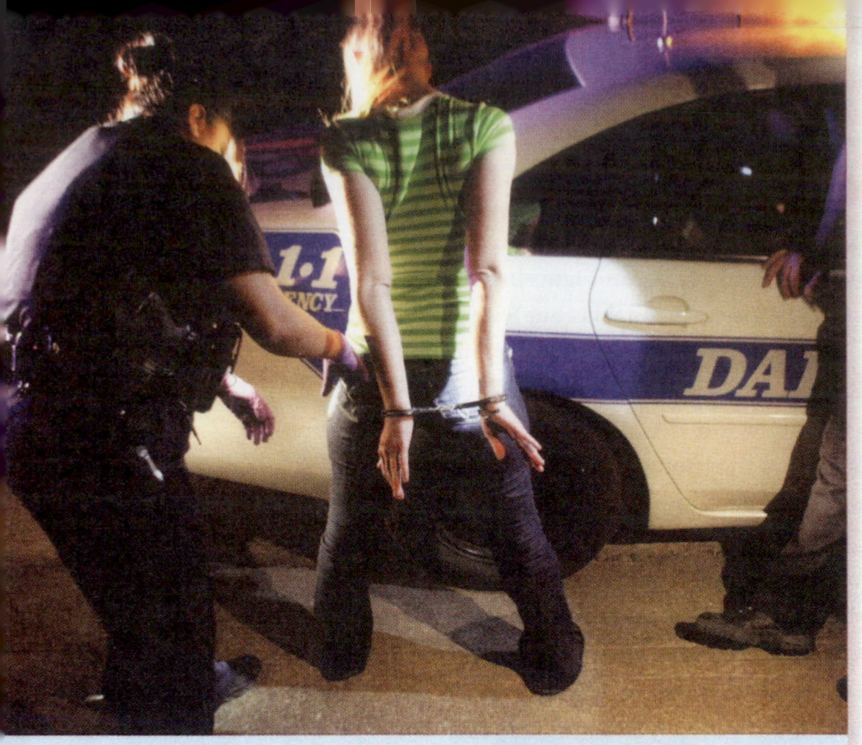

▲ In Dallas, street prostitutes such as the one shown here are often treated as crime victims and offered access to treatment and rehabilitation programs. **How might society benefit if such offenders are kept out of jail or prison through diversion programs?** AP Images/LM Otero

category of "petty," and it is well-nigh impossible, as well as unnecessary, to imprison every offender for every offense. Community-based corrections are an important means of diverting criminals to alternative modes of punishment so that scarce incarceration resources are consumed by only the most dangerous criminals.

In his "strainer" analogy, corrections expert Paul H. Hahn likens this process to the workings of a kitchen strainer. With each "shake" of the corrections "strainer," the less serious offenders are diverted from incarceration. At the end, only the most serious convicts remain in prison.[6] The diversionary role of community-based punishments has become more pronounced as prisons and jails have filled up over the past three decades. In fact, probationers and parolees now account for about 70 percent of all adults in the American corrections system.[7]

The "Low-Cost Alternative"

Not all of the recent expansion of community corrections can be attributed to acceptance of its theoretical underpinnings. Many politicians and criminal justice officials who do not look favorably on ideas such as reintegration and diversion have embraced programs to keep nonviolent offenders out of prison. The reason is simple: economics. The cost of constructing and maintaining prisons and jails, as well as housing and caring for inmates, has placed a great deal of pressure on corrections budgets across the country. States spend an estimated $72 billion a year on their corrections systems, most of which goes to prison operating costs.[8]

Community corrections offer an enticing financial alternative to imprisonment. The Bureau of Prisons estimates that the federal government saves about $25,600 annually by shifting a nonviolent offender from incarceration to supervised release.[9] The average yearly cost of housing an inmate in Nebraska is $35,169, compared to $3,760 for community corrections.[10] From 2014 to 2015, Pennsylvania experienced the largest one-year decline of its prison population in four decades, as state corrections officials moved nonviolent offenders to probation and parole. In the process, the state's annual corrections budget shrank by $34 million.[11]

EthicsChallenge

In 2016, an Indiana judge sentenced Jeremy Schwer to twelve years of probation for repeatedly molesting his six-year-old daughter. This judicial leniency was the direct result of a request by Schwer's estranged wife, who asked that he be kept out of prison so that he could work to financially support his children (including the victim). Do you think that this is a valid justification for community corrections? Are there any ethical problems with the judge's decision in this case? Explain your answers. ■

Probation: Doing Time in the Community

As Figure 10.1 shows, **probation** is the most common form of punishment in the United States. Although it is administered differently in various jurisdictions, probation can be generally defined as

> the legal status of an offender who, after being convicted of a crime, has been directed by the sentencing court to remain in the community under the supervision of a probation service for a designated period of time and subject to certain conditions imposed by the court or by law.[12]

The theory behind probation is that certain offenders can be treated more economically and humanely by putting them under controls while still allowing them to live in the community. One of the advantages of probation has been that it provides for the rehabilitation of the offender while saving society the costs of incarceration. Despite probation's widespread use, certain participants in the criminal justice system question its ability to reach its rehabilitative goals. Critics point to the immense number of probationers and the fact that many of them are violent felons as evidence that the system is "out of control." Supporters contend that nothing is wrong with probation in principle, but admit that its execution must be adjusted to meet the goals of modern corrections.[13]

Figure 10.1 Probation in American Corrections

As you can see, the majority of convicts under the control of the American corrections system are on probation.

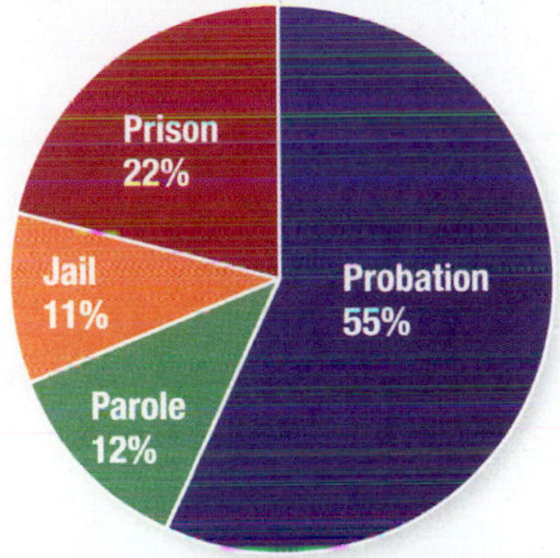

Source: Bureau of Justice Statistics, *Correctional Populations in the United States, 2014* (Washington, D.C.: U.S. Department of Justice, December 2015), Table 1, page 2.

Sentencing and Probation

Probation is basically an arrangement between sentencing authorities and the offender. In traditional probation, the offender agrees to comply with certain terms for a specified amount of time in return for serving the sentence in the community. One of the primary benefits for the offender, besides not getting sent to a correctional facility, is that the length of the probationary period is usually considerably shorter than the length of a prison term (see Figure 10.2).

The traditional form of probation is not the only arrangement that can be made. A judge can hand down a **suspended sentence**, under which a defendant who has been convicted and sentenced to be incarcerated is not required to serve the sentence. Instead, the judge puts the offender on notice, keeping open the option of reinstating the original sentence and sending the offender to prison or jail if he or she reoffends. In practice, suspended sentences are quite similar to probation.

Learning Objective

2 Explain several alternative sentencing arrangements that combine probation with incarceration.

Alternative Sentencing Arrangements

Judges can also combine probation with incarceration. Such sentencing arrangements include:

- *Split sentences.* In **split sentence probation**, also known as *shock probation,* the offender is sentenced to a specific amount of time in prison or jail, to be followed by a period of probation.
- *Shock incarceration.* In this arrangement, an offender is sentenced to prison or jail with the understanding that after a period of time, she or he may petition the court to be released on probation. Shock incarceration is discussed more fully later in the chapter.
- *Intermittent incarceration.* With intermittent incarceration, the offender spends a certain amount of time each week, usually during the weekend, in a jail, workhouse, or other government institution.

probation A criminal sanction in which a convict is allowed to remain in the community rather than be imprisoned.

suspended sentence A judicially imposed condition in which an offender is sentenced after being convicted of a crime, but is not required to begin serving the sentence immediately.

split sentence probation A sentence that consists of incarceration in a prison or jail, followed by a probationary period in the community.

Figure 10.2 Average Length of Sentence: Prison versus Probation

As you can see, the average probation sentence is much shorter than the average prison sentence for most crimes.

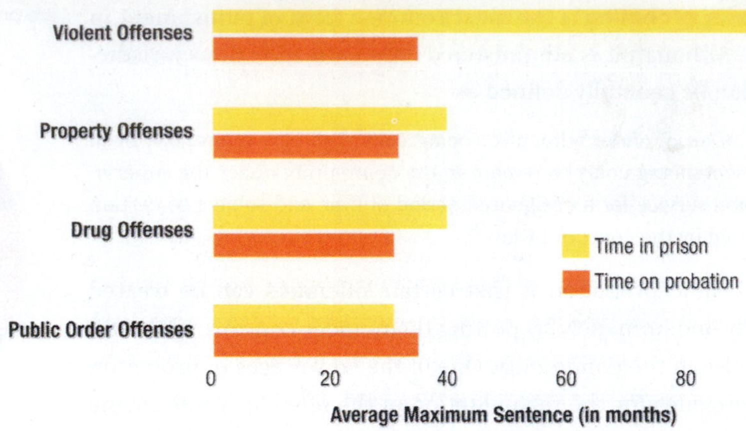

Source: Bureau of Justice Statistics, *Felony Defendants in Large Urban Counties, 2009 – Statistical Tables* (Washington, D.C.: U.S. Department of Justice, December 2013), Table 25, page 30; and Table 27, page 31.

Split sentences are popular with judges, as they combine the "treatment" aspects of probation with the "punishment" aspects of incarceration. According to the United States Sentencing Commission, about 3 percent of all sentences handed down by federal judges are split sentences.[14]

Learning Objective 3

Specify the conditions under which an offender is most likely to be denied probation.

Choosing Probation Generally, research has shown that offenders are most likely to be denied probation if they:

- Are convicted on multiple charges.
- Were on probation or parole at the time of the arrest.
- Have two or more prior convictions.
- Are addicted to narcotics.
- Seriously injured the victim of the crime.
- Used a weapon during the commission of the crime.[15]

As might be expected, the chances of a felon being sentenced to probation are highly dependent on the seriousness of his or her crime. Only 19 percent of probationers in the United States have committed a violent crime, including domestic violence and sex offenses. The majority of probationers have been convicted of property crimes, drug offenses, or public order crimes such as drunk driving.[16]

Probation Demographics As in other areas of the criminal justice system, African Americans make up a higher percentage of the national probation population (30 percent) than the general population (13 percent). Fifty-four percent of probationers are white, and 13 percent are Hispanic.[17] The percentage of female probationers is significantly higher than female prison inmates (25 percent to 7 percent),[18] which is in keeping with the gender sentencing trends we discussed in the previous chapter. More detailed surveys of probationers reveal that they tend to be between the ages of twenty-one and thirty-nine, single, high school graduates, and have annual incomes of less than $20,000.[19]

Conditions of Probation

A judge may decide to impose certain conditions as part of a probation sentence. These conditions represent a "contract" between the judge and the offender, in which the latter agrees that if she or he does not follow certain rules, probation may be *revoked* (see Figure 10.3). **Revocation** is the formal process by which probation is ended and a probationer is punished for his or her wrongdoing, often by being sent to jail or prison for the original term decided by the court.

revocation The formal process that follows the failure of a probationer or parolee to comply with the terms of his or her probation or parole, often resulting in the probationer's or parolee's incarceration.

Judges have a great deal of discretion to impose any terms of probation that they feel are necessary. In the case that opened this chapter, for example, Champaign County (Illinois) judge Tom Difanis ordered Katie Daly not to use any alcohol or illegal drugs during her thirty-month probationary period. He also prohibited her from entering an establishment whose primary purpose is selling alcohol and required her to wear an alcohol-monitoring device for the first year of her supervised sentence.

Principles of Probation

A judge's personal philosophy is often reflected in the probation conditions that she or he creates for probationers. In *In re Quirk* (1997),[20] for example, the Louisiana Supreme Court upheld the ability of a trial judge to impose church attendance as a condition of probation. Though judges may have discretion in setting the conditions of probation, they do operate under several guiding principles. First, the conditions must be related to the dual purposes of probation, which most federal and state courts define as (1) the rehabilitation of the probationer and (2) the protection of the community. Second, the conditions must not violate the U.S. Constitution, as probationers are generally entitled to the same constitutional rights as other prisoners.[21]

Of course, probationers do give up certain constitutional rights when they consent to the terms of probation. Most probationers, for example, agree to spot checks of their homes for contraband such as drugs or weapons, and they therefore have a diminished expectation of privacy.

In *United States v. Knights* (2001),[22] the United States Supreme Court upheld the actions of deputy sheriffs in Napa County, California, who searched a probationer's home without a warrant or probable cause. The unanimous decision was based on the premise that because those on probation are more likely to commit

Figure 10.3 Conditions of Probation

UNITED STATES DISTRICT COURT
FOR THE
DISTRICT OF COLUMBIA

To: ______________________ No. 84-417

Address: 1440 N St., N.W., #10, Wash., D.C.

In accordance with authority conferred by the United States Probation Law, you have been placed on probation this date, January 25, 2017 for a period of one year by the Hon. Thomas F. Hogan United States District Judge, sitting in and for this District Court at Washington, D.C.

CONDITIONS OF PROBATION

It is the order of the Court that you shall comply with the following conditions of probation:

(1)-You shall refrain from violation of any law (federal, state, and local). You shall get in touch immediately with your probation officer if arrested or questioned by a law enforcement officer.

(2)-You shall associate only with law-abiding persons and maintain reasonable hours.

(3)-You shall work regularly at a lawful occupation and support your legal dependents, if any, to the best of your ability. When out of work you shall notify your probation officer at once. You shall consult him prior to job changes.

(4)-You shall not leave the judicial district without permission of the probation officer.

(5)-You shall notify your probation officer immediately of any change in your place of residence.

(6)-You shall follow the probation officer's instructions.

(7)-You shall report to the probation officer as directed.

(8)-You shall not possess a firearm (handgun or rifle) for any reason.

The special conditions ordered by the Court are as follows:
Imposition of sentence suspended, one year probation, Fine of $75 on each count.

I understand that the Court may change the conditions of probation, reduce or extend the period of probation, and at any time during the probation period or within the maximum probation period of 5 years permitted by law, may issue a warrant and revoke probation for a violation occurring during the probation period.

I have read or had read to me the above conditions of probation. I fully understand them and I will abide by them.

______________________ Date __________
Probationer

You will report as follows: ______________ as directed by your Probation Officer

______________________ Date __________
U.S. Probation Officer

crimes, law enforcement agents "may therefore justifiably focus on probationers in a way that [they do] not on the ordinary citizen."[23]

Learning Objective

Describe the three general categories of conditions placed on a probationer. **4**

Types of Conditions Obviously, probationers who break the law are very likely to have their probation revoked. Other, less serious infractions may also result in revocation. The conditions placed on a probationer fall into three general categories:

- *Standard conditions,* which are imposed on all probationers. These include reporting regularly to the probation officer, notifying the agency of any change of address, not leaving the jurisdiction without permission, and remaining employed.
- *Punitive conditions,* which usually reflect the seriousness of the offense and are intended to increase the punishment of the offender. Such conditions include fines, community service, restitution, drug testing, and home confinement (discussed later).
- *Treatment conditions,* which are imposed to reverse patterns of self-destructive behavior. Such treatment generally includes counseling for drug and alcohol abuse, anger management, and mental health issues, and is a component of approximately 27 percent of probation sentences in this country.[24]

CJ Policy—Your Take

In Georgia, standard conditions for probation require probationers to "be of general good behavior" and "avoid injurious and vicious habits." In Rhode Island, "keeping the peace and remaining on good behavior" are two standard conditions of probation. **Why do you think these kinds of conditions have come under criticism as being too broad? Do you agree with such criticisms? Why or why not?**

Some observers feel that judges have too much discretion in imposing overly restrictive conditions that no person, much less one who has exhibited antisocial tendencies, could fulfill. Citing prohibitions on drinking liquor, gambling, and associating with "undesirables," as well as requirements such as meeting early curfews, the late University of Delaware professor Carl B. Klockars claimed that if probation rules were taken seriously, "very few probationers would complete their terms without violation."[25]

As the majority of probationers do complete their terms successfully,[26] Klockars's statement suggests that either probation officers are unable to determine that violations are taking place, or that many of them are exercising a great deal of discretion in reporting minor probation violations. Perhaps the officers realize that violating probationers for every single "slip-up" is unrealistic and would add to the already significant problem of jail and prison overcrowding. (To critique standard conditions of probation that provide probation officers with wide-reaching discretion, see this chapter's *CJ Policy—Your Take* feature.)

The Supervisory Role of the Probation Officer

The probation officer has two basic roles. The first is investigative and consists of conducting the presentence investigation (PSI), which was discussed in Chapter 9. The second is supervisory and begins as soon as the offender has been sentenced to probation. In smaller probation agencies, individual officers perform both tasks. In larger jurisdictions, the trend has been toward separating the responsibilities, with *investigating officers* handling the PSI and *line officers* concentrating on supervision.

One of the most difficult aspects of a probation officer's supervisory duties is an unavoidable *role conflict* in the work. On the one hand, the probation officer has the task of guiding the probationer to a successful completion of the probationary term. On the other hand, the probation officer must protect the community from the probationer, who has already shown that he or she is capable of breaking the law. Operating under vague institutional guidelines, probation officers mostly must rely on their own discretion to navigate the complexities of their profession.[27]

The Use of Authority Not surprisingly, research shows that the ideal officer-offender relationship is based on mutual respect, honesty, and trust.[28] In reality, these

Careers in CJ

Photo courtesy of Peggy McCarthy

Peggy McCarthy
Lead Probation Officer

The best thing about my job is that every day is different. I may be in court first thing in the morning, and then in my office meeting with defendants or developing case plans. In the afternoon, I may be at the jail taking statements for court reports or out in the field seeing my defendants. If I work a late shift, I may be visiting counseling agencies or talking to collateral sources or doing surveillance. I may be organizing a search on a defendant's home or making an arrest. I may be working with the police to solve crimes or locate absconders. Or I may simply be completing administrative duties like filing or returning phone calls to defendants and/or their family members. Anything can happen at any time, and I have to be ready to respond. If a probation officer gets bored, something is wrong.

I take a great deal of pride in assisting defendants with the difficult task of making positive change in their lives. The rewards may be few and far between, but when a defendant with a history of substance abuse stays clean and sober for a year, when a gang-affiliated defendant secures a job and no longer associates with negative peers, or when a defendant who admittedly never liked school obtains a GED or diploma, that is when I realize that what I'm doing day in and day out is 100 percent worthwhile.

SOCIAL MEDIA CAREER TIP Manage your online reputation—or someone else will do it for you. Monitor your profile using tools such as iSearch, Pipl, and ZabaSearch. Check BoardReader and Omgili for information on what people are saying about you on message boards and discussion threads.

FASTFACTS

Lead probation officer

Job description:

- Work with offenders or clients who have been sentenced to probation.
- Work with the courts. Investigate backgrounds, write presentence reports, and recommend sentences.

What kind of training is required?

- Bachelor's degree in criminal justice, social work/psychology, or related field.
- Must be at least 21 years of age, have no felony convictions, and have strong writing and interview skills. Experience in multicultural outreach a plus.

Annual salary range?

- $30,000–$80,000

qualities are often hard to maintain between probation officers and their clients. Any incentive an offender might have to be completely truthful with a line officer is marred by one simple fact: self-reported wrongdoing can be used to revoke probation. Even probation officers whose primary mission is to rehabilitate are under institutional pressure to punish their clients for violating conditions of probation. One officer deals with this situation by telling his clients

> that I'm here to help them, to get them a job, and whatever else I can do. But I tell them too that I have a family to support and that if they get too far off track, I can't afford to put my job on the line for them. I'm going to have to violate them.[29]

In the absence of trust, most probation officers rely on their **authority** to guide an offender successfully through the sentence. An officer's authority, or ability to influence a person's actions without resorting to force, is based partially on her or his power to revoke probation. It also reflects her or his ability to impose a number of lesser sanctions. For example, if a probationer fails to attend a required alcohol treatment program, the officer can send him or her to a "lockup," or detention center, overnight. To be successful, a probation officer must establish this authority early in the relationship because it is the primary tool for persuading the probationer to behave in an acceptable manner.

authority The power designated to an agent of the law over a person who has broken the law.

The Caseload Dilemma Even the most balanced, "firm but fair" approach to probation can be defeated by the problem of excessive *caseloads.* A **caseload** is the number of clients a probation officer is responsible for at any one time. Heavy probation caseloads seem inevitable: unlike a prison cell, a probation officer can always take "just one more" client. Furthermore, the ideal caseload size is very difficult to determine because different offenders require different levels of supervision.[30]

The consequences of disproportionate probation officer–probationer ratios are self-evident, however. When burdened with large caseloads, probation officers find it practically impossible to rigorously enforce the conditions imposed on their clients. Lack of surveillance leads to lack of control, which can undermine the very basis of a probationary system. In Williston, North Dakota, for example, where each probation officer is responsible for about 130 clients, there has been a rise in violent crimes committed by unsupervised probationers.[31]

Getting **Linked in**™

As you will learn in more detail in Chapter 13, **juvenile probation officers** play a crucial role in this nation's juvenile justice system. To get more information about this specialized profession from practitioners, and to see the many career opportunities for someone who wants to work with juvenile offenders, search the LinkedIn website for "juvenile probation."

Revocation of Probation

The probation period can end in one of two ways. Either the probationer successfully fulfills the conditions of the sentence, or the probationer misbehaves and probation is revoked, resulting in a prison or jail term. The decision of whether to revoke after a **technical violation**—such as failing to report a change of address or testing positive for drug use—is often made at the discretion of the probation officer and therefore the focus of controversy.

As we have seen, probationers do not always enjoy the same protections under the U.S. Constitution as other members of society. The United States Supreme Court has not stripped these offenders of all rights, however. In *Mempa v. Rhay* (1967),[32] the Court ruled that probationers were entitled to an attorney during the revocation process. Then, in *Morrissey v. Brewer* (1972) and *Gagnon v. Scarpelli* (1973),[33] the Court established a three-stage procedure by which the "limited" due process rights of probationers must be protected in potential revocation situations:

- *Preliminary hearing.* In this appearance before a "disinterested person" (often a judge), the facts of the violation or arrest are presented, and it is determined whether probable cause for revoking probation exists. This hearing can be waived by the probationer.
- *Revocation hearing.* During this hearing, the probation agency presents evidence to support its claim of violation, and the probationer can attempt to refute this evidence. The probationer has the right to know the charges being brought against him or her. Furthermore, probationers can testify on their own behalf and present witnesses in their favor, as well as confront and cross-examine adverse witnesses. A "neutral and detached" body must hear the evidence and rule on the validity of the proposed revocation.
- *Revocation sentencing.* If the presiding body rules against the probationer, then the judge must decide whether to impose incarceration and for what length of time. In a revocation hearing dealing with technical violations, the judge will often reimpose probation with stricter terms or intermediate sanctions.

In effect, this is a "bare-bones" approach to due process. Most of the rules of evidence that govern regular trials do not apply to revocation hearings. Probation officers are not, for example, required to read offenders their *Miranda* rights before questioning them about crimes they may have committed during probation. In *Minnesota v. Murphy* (1984),[34] the Supreme Court ruled that a meeting between probation officer and client does not equal

caseload The number of individual probationers or parolees under the supervision of a probation or parole officer.

technical violation An action taken by a probationer or parolee that, although not criminal, breaks the terms of probation or parole as designated by the court.

custody and, therefore, the Fifth Amendment protection against self-incrimination does not apply, either.

Does Probation Work?

On February 13, 2015, police in Little Rock, Arkansas, arrested Jeramye Hobbs for killing Frank Steinsiek after the two men met to discuss the sale of Steinsiek's motorcycle. At the time of the murder, Hobbs was on probation for a previous felony theft charge. Indeed, probationers are responsible for a significant amount of crime. According to the most recent data, 11 percent of all suspects arrested for violent crimes (and 13 percent of those arrested for murder) were on probation at the time of their apprehension.[35] Such statistics raise a critical question—is probation worthwhile?

▲ In Rutherford County (Tennessee), probation violators such as Rachael Hamm, shown here, must pay about $60 a day in fees for the costs of their own incarceration. If the probationer is unable to pay these fees, she or he is considered to have further violated the terms of probation and faces additional imprisonment. **Do you think that nonpayment of fees should be treated as a probation violation? Why or why not?** AP Photo/Mark Zaleski

To measure the effectiveness of probation, one must first establish its purpose. Generally, as we saw earlier, the goal of probation is to reintegrate and divert as many offenders as possible while at the same time protecting the public. Specifically, probation and other community corrections programs are evaluated by their success in preventing *recidivism*—the eventual rearrest of the probationer.[36] Given that most probationers are first-time, nonviolent offenders, the system is not designed to prevent relatively rare outbursts of violence, such as the murder allegedly committed by Jeramye Hobbs.

Risk Factors for Recidivism About 8 percent of all probationers exit probation by being sent to prison or jail.[37] There are several risk factors that make a probationer more likely to recidivate, including:

1. *Antisocial personality patterns,* meaning that the probationer is impulsive, pleasure seeking, restlessly aggressive, or irritable.
2. *Procriminal attitudes* such as negative opinions of authority and the law, as well as a tendency to rationalize one's prior criminal behavior.
3. *Social supports for crime,* including friends who are offenders and a living environment lacking in positive role models.[38]

Other important risk factors for recidivism include substance abuse and unemployment. By concentrating resources on those probationers who exhibit these risk factors, probation departments can succeed in lowering caseloads and overall recidivism rates.

Jurisdictions are increasingly using crime-prediction software to determine which probationers are at the greatest risk of recidivating and therefore need greater levels of supervision. Before implementing a risk-prediction tool called "Random Forest Modeling," for example, Philadelphia's Adult Probation and Parole Department (APPD) had each offender meet with his or her probation officer for about half an hour once each month. Using factors such as the probationer's criminal history, number of years since the last serious offense, and ZIP code, the APPD now assigns each offender to one of three risk categories. Its high-risk probationers are thirteen times more likely to recidivate than low-risk probationers and are supervised accordingly.[39]

parole The conditional release of an inmate before his or her sentence has expired.

"Swift and Certain" One of the problems with traditional methods of sanctioning probation violations is the length of the proceedings. If, for example, a probationer fails a drug test, it may take months before a penalty is enforced, weakening the link between wrongdoing and punishment. As criminologist James Q. Wilson pointed out, one does not discipline a child by saying, "Because [you've misbehaved], you have a 50-50 chance nine months from now of being grounded."[40]

A number of probation departments have implemented strategies that operate on the principle of providing "swift and certain" sanctions for probation violations. Perhaps the most successful of these strategies is Hawaii's Opportunity Probation with Enforcement (HOPE) program. The rules of HOPE are simple. Each substance abuse probationer must call the courthouse every day to learn if she or he is required to come in for a urine test for drugs, or *urinalysis*. If drugs are found in the probationer's system during one of these frequent tests, a short jail term—one to two weeks—is automatically served.[41] HOPE has resulted in large reductions in positive drug tests by probationers, and its 1,500 participants are significantly less likely to be rearrested than those not in the program.[42]

EthicsChallenge

You may have noticed that one of the factors used in Philadelphia to determine a probationer's risk category is his or her residential ZIP code. Why have some observers criticized this tactic as a form of racial and ethnic discrimination? Should the use of ZIP codes in offender risk assessment strategies be prohibited because it is unethical? Explain your answer.

The Parole Picture

At any given time, about 850,000 Americans are living in the community on **parole**, or the *conditional* release of a prisoner after a portion of his or her sentence has been served behind bars. Parole allows the corrections system to continue to supervise an offender who is no longer incarcerated. As long as parolees follow the conditions of their parole, they are allowed to finish their terms outside the prison. If parolees break the terms of their early release, however, they face the risk of being returned to a penal institution.

Parole is based on three concepts:[43]

1. *Grace.* The prisoner has no right to be given an early release, but the government has granted her or him that privilege.
2. *Contract of consent.* The government and the parolee enter into an arrangement whereby the latter agrees to abide by certain conditions in return for continued freedom.
3. *Custody.* Technically, though no longer incarcerated, the parolee is still the responsibility of the state. Parole is an extension of corrections.

Because of good-time credits and parole, most prisoners do not serve their entire sentence in prison. In fact, the average felon serves only about half of the term handed down by the court.

Comparing Probation and Parole

Learning Objective 5

Identify the main differences between probation and parole.

Both probation and parole operate under the basic assumption that the offender serves her or his time in the community rather than in a prison or jail. The main differences between the two concepts—which sound confusingly similar—involve their circumstances. Probation is a sentence handed down by a judge following conviction and usually does not include incarceration. Parole is a conditional release from prison and occurs after an offender has already served some time in a correctional facility. (See *Mastering Concepts—Probation versus Parole* for clarification.)

parole contract An agreement between the state and the offender that establishes the conditions of parole.

Conditions of Parole In many ways, parole supervision is similar to probation supervision. Like probationers, offenders who are granted parole are placed under the supervision of community corrections officers and required to follow certain conditions. Parole conditions often mirror probation conditions. All parolees, for example, must comply with the law, and they are generally responsible for reporting to their parole officer at certain intervals.

The frequency of these visits, along with the other terms of parole, is spelled out in the **parole contract**, which sets out the agreement between the state and the paroled offender. Under the terms of the contract, the state agrees to conditionally release the inmate, and the future parolee agrees that her or his conditional release will last only as long as she or he abides by the contract. (See Figure 10.4 for a list of standard parole conditions.)

Parole Revocation About a quarter of parolees return to prison before the end of their parole period, most because they were convicted of a new offense or had their parole revoked.[44] Property crimes are the most common reason that both male and female parolees return to incarceration, and men on parole are twice as likely as their

Mastering**Concepts** Probation versus Parole

Probation and parole have many aspects in common. In fact, probation and parole are so similar that many jurisdictions combine them into a single agency. There are, however, some important distinctions between the two systems, as noted below.

	Probation	Parole
Basic Definition	An **alternative to imprisonment** in which a person who has been convicted of a crime is allowed to serve his or her sentence in the community subject to certain conditions and supervision by a probation officer.	An **early release** from a correctional facility, in which the convicted offender is given the chance to spend the remainder of her or his sentence under supervision in the community.
Timing	The offender is sentenced to a probationary term in place of a prison or jail term. If the offender breaks the conditions of probation, he or she is sent to prison or jail. Therefore, **probation generally occurs *before* imprisonment.**	Parole is a form of early release. Therefore, **parole occurs *after* an offender has spent time behind bars.**
Authority	**Probation is under the domain of the judiciary.** A judge decides whether to sentence a convict to probation, and a judge determines whether a probation violation warrants revocation and incarceration.	**Parole often falls under the domain of the parole board.** This administrative body determines whether the prisoner qualifies for early release and the conditions under which the parole must be served.
Characteristics of Offenders	As a number of studies have shown, probationers are normally less involved in the criminal lifestyle. Most of them are **first-time offenders who have committed nonviolent crimes.**	Many parolees have **spent months or even years in prison** and, besides abiding by conditions of parole, must make the difficult transition to "life on the outside."

FIGURE 10.4 Standard Conditions of Parole

The parolee must do the following:

- Stay within a certain area.
- Obtain permission before changing residence or employment.
- Obtain and maintain employment.
- Maintain acceptable, nonthreatening behavior.
- Not possess firearms or weapons.
- Report any arrest within twenty-four hours.
- Not use illegal drugs or alcohol or enter drinking establishments.
- Not break any state or local laws.
- Allow contacts by parole officers at home or employment without obstruction.
- Submit to search of person, residence, or motor vehicle at any time by parole officers.

female counterparts to have their parole revoked for a violent crime.[45] Parole revocation is similar in many aspects to probation revocation. If the parolee commits a new crime, then a return to prison is very likely. If, however, the individual commits a technical violation by breaking a condition of parole, then parole authorities have discretion as to whether revocation proceedings should be initiated. A number of states, including Michigan, Missouri, and New York, have taken steps to avoid reincarcerating parolees for technical violations as part of their continuing efforts to reduce prison populations.[46]

When authorities do attempt to revoke parole for a technical violation, they must provide the parolee with a revocation hearing.[47] Although this hearing does not provide the same due process protections as a criminal trial, the parolee does have the right to be notified of the charges, to present witnesses, to speak in his or her defense, and to question any hostile witnesses (so long as such questioning would not place these witnesses in danger). In the first stage of the hearing, the parole authorities determine whether there is probable cause that a violation occurred. Then, they decide whether to return the parolee to prison.

Discretionary Release

As you may recall from Chapter 9, corrections systems are classified by sentencing procedure—indeterminate or determinate. Indeterminate sentencing occurs when the legislature sets a range of punishments for particular crimes, and the judge and the parole board exercise discretion in determining the actual length of the prison term. For that reason, states with indeterminate sentencing are said to have systems of **discretionary release**.

Eligibility for Parole Under indeterminate sentencing, parole is not a right but a privilege. This is a crucial point, as it establishes the terms of the relationship between the inmate and the corrections authorities during the parole process. In *Greenholtz v. Inmates of the Nebraska Penal and Correctional Complex* (1979),[48] the Supreme Court ruled that inmates do not have a constitutionally protected right to expect parole, thereby giving states the freedom to set their own standards for determining parole eligibility. In most states that have retained indeterminate sentencing, a prisoner is eligible to be considered for parole release after serving a legislatively determined percentage of the minimum sentence less any good time or other credits.

Not all convicts are eligible for parole. As we saw in Chapter 9, offenders who have committed the most serious crimes often receive life sentences without the possibility of early release. In general, life without parole is reserved for those who have committed first degree murder or are defined by statute as habitual offenders. As was also discussed in Chapter 9, however, about 3,300 inmates convicted of nonviolent drug and property crimes have also received this sentence.[49] Today, about one-third of convicts serving life sentences have no possibility of parole.[50]

discretionary release The release of an inmate into a community supervision program at the discretion of the parole board within limits set by state or federal law.

Parole Procedures A convict does not apply for parole. Rather, different jurisdictions have different procedures for determining discretionary release dates. In many states, the offender is eligible for discretionary release at the end of his or her minimum sentence minus good-time credits (see Chapter 9). In 2016, for example, Patrick Durocher was sentenced to three to five years in prison for sexually assaulting a woman on the campus of the University of Massachusetts Amherst. This means that Durocher will become eligible for parole after serving three years, less good time. In other states, parole eligibility is measured at either one-third or one-half of the maximum sentence, or it is a matter of discretion for the parole authorities.

In most, but not all, states, the responsibility for making the parole decision falls to the **parole board**, whose members are generally appointed by the governor. According to the American Correctional Association, the parole board has four basic roles:

1. To decide which offenders should be placed on parole.
2. To determine the conditions of parole and aid in the continuing supervision of the parolee.
3. To discharge the offender when the conditions of parole have been met.
4. If a violation occurs, to determine whether parole privileges should be revoked.[51]

Most parole boards are small, made up of three to seven members. In many jurisdictions, board members' terms are limited to between four and six years. The requirements for board members vary. Nearly half the states have no prerequisites, while others require a bachelor's degree or some expertise in the field of criminal justice.

The Parole Decision Parole boards use a number of criteria to determine whether a convict should be given discretionary release. These criteria include:

1. The nature and circumstances of the underlying offense and the offender's current attitude toward it.
2. The offender's prior criminal record.
3. The offender's attitude toward the victim and the victim's family members.
4. The offender's physical, mental, and emotional health.
5. The offender's behavior behind bars, including his or her participation in programs for self-improvement.[52]

In a system that uses discretionary parole, the actual release decision is made at a **parole grant hearing**. During this hearing, the entire board or a subcommittee reviews relevant information on the convict. Sometimes, but not always, the offender is interviewed.

Because the board members have only limited knowledge of each offender, key players in the case are often notified in advance of the parole hearing and asked to provide comments and recommendations. These participants include the sentencing judge, the attorneys at the trial, the victims, and any law enforcement officers who may be involved. After these preparations, the typical parole hearing itself is very short—usually lasting just a few minutes.

Parole Denial When parole is denied, the reasons usually involve poor prison behavior by the offender and/or the severity of the underlying crime.[53] After a parole denial, the entire process will generally be replayed at the next "action date," which depends on the nature of the offender's crimes and all relevant laws. In February 2016, for example, seventy-two-year-old Sirhan Sirhan was denied parole for the fifteenth time. Nearly five decades earlier, Sirhan had been convicted of murdering New York senator Robert F. Kennedy at the Ambassador Hotel in Los Angeles and sentenced to life in prison.

At his most recent parole hearing, Sirhan claimed that he did not remember shooting Kennedy, leading the California parole board to conclude that he did not show

parole board A body of appointed civilians that decides whether a convict should be granted conditional release before the end of his or her sentence.

parole grant hearing A hearing in which the entire parole board or a subcommittee reviews information, meets the offender, and hears testimony from relevant witnesses to determine whether to grant parole.

Discretion in ACTION

Cause for Compassion?

Rachel Donahue/Shutterstock.com

The Situation Thirty-seven years ago, Susan was convicted of first degree murder and sentenced to life in prison for taking part in a grisly killing spree in Los Angeles. Over the course of two days, Susan and her accomplices killed seven people. Susan stabbed one of the victims—a pregnant woman—sixteen times and wrote the word "PIG" on a door using another victim's blood. During her trial, Susan testified that she "was stoned, man, stoned on acid" at the time of her crimes. Now sixty-one years old, Susan is before your parole board, requesting release from prison. For most of her time behind bars, she has been a model prisoner, and she has apologized numerous times for her wrongdoing. Furthermore, her left leg has been amputated, the left side of her body is paralyzed, and she has been diagnosed with terminal brain cancer.

The Law You have a great deal of discretion in determining whether a prisoner should be paroled. Some of the factors you should consider are the threat the prisoner would pose to the community if released, the nature of the offense, and the level of remorse. In addition, California allows for "compassionate release" when an inmate is "terminally ill."

Learning Objective 6

Explain which factors influence the decision to grant parole.

What Would You Do? Susan obviously poses no threat to the community and is a viable candidate for compassionate release. Should she be set free on parole? Or are some crimes so horrific that the convict should never be given parole, no matter what the circumstances? Explain your vote.

To see how a California parole board voted in a similar situation, go to Example 10.1 in Appendix B.

adequate remorse or understand the enormity of his crime.[54] (See the feature *Discretion in Action—Cause for Compassion?* to learn more about the process of discretionary release.)

Parole Guidelines

Nearly twenty states have moved away from discretionary release systems to procedures that provide for **mandatory release**. Under mandatory release, offenders leave prison only when their prison terms have expired, minus adjustments for good time. No parole board is involved in this type of release, which is designed to eliminate discretion from the process.

Instead, in mandatory release, corrections officials rely on **parole guidelines** to determine the early release date. Similar to sentencing guidelines (see Chapter 9), parole guidelines determine a potential parolee's risk of recidivism using a mathematical equation. Under this system, inmates and corrections authorities know the *presumptive parole date* soon after the inmate enters prison. So long as the offender does not experience any disciplinary or other problems while incarcerated, he or she can be fairly sure of the time of release.

Note that a number of states and the federal government claim to have officially "abolished" parole through truth-in-sentencing laws. (As described in Chapter 9, this form of legislation requires certain statutorily determined offenders to serve at least 85 percent of their prison terms.) For the most part, however, these laws simply emphasize prison terms that are "truthful," not necessarily "longer." Mechanisms for parole, by whatever name, are crucial to the criminal justice system for several reasons. First, they provide inmates with an incentive to behave properly in the hope of an early release. Second, they reduce the costs related to incarceration by holding down the inmate population, a critical concern for prison administrators.[55]

mandatory release Release from prison that occurs when an offender has served the full length of his or her sentence, minus any adjustments for good time.

parole guidelines Standards that are used in the parole process to measure the risk that a potential parolee will recidivate.

Victims' Rights and Parole

Over the past several decades, the community corrections system has expanded to better encompass the wants and needs of victims. Many probation and parole departments now have employees responsible for assisting victims in areas such as collecting restitution or compensation, and providing information about the status and location of offenders.[56]

The federal Crime Victims' Rights Act provides victims with the right to be reasonably notified of any parole proceedings and the right to attend and be reasonably heard at such proceedings.[57] A number of states offer similar assurances of victim participation in the parole process. Generally, victim testimony before a parole board focuses on the emotional, physical, and financial hardship experienced by the victim or the victim's family because of the offender's criminal act. Given the moral power of such testimony, it is somewhat surprising to learn that victim input appears to have little effect on the parole decision. Instead, parole boards prefer to rely on the traditional criteria for determining parole, described earlier in this section.[58]

▲ Paul Schrade reacts with frustration during the 2016 parole hearings for Sirhan Sirhan in San Diego. Even though Schrade was wounded when Sirhan assassinated Senator Robert F. Kennedy nearly fifty years earlier, as described in the text, Schrade has forgiven Sirhan and argued that he should be granted parole. **How much weight should parole boards place on the wishes of victims when making the decision to grant or deny parole?** AP Photo/ Gregory Bull

Intermediate Sanctions

Many observers feel that the most widely used sentencing options—imprisonment and probation—fail to reflect the immense diversity of crimes and criminals. **Intermediate sanctions** provide a number of additional sentencing options for those wrongdoers who require stricter supervision than that supplied by probation, but for whom imprisonment would be unduly harsh and counterproductive. The intermediate sanctions discussed in this section are designed to match the specific punishment and treatment of an individual offender with a corrections program that reflects that offender's situation.

Dozens of different variations of intermediate sanctions are handed down each year. To cover the spectrum succinctly, two general categories of such sanctions will be discussed in this section: those administered primarily by the courts and those administered primarily by corrections departments, including day reporting centers, intensive supervision probation, shock incarceration, and home confinement. Remember that none of these sanctions are exclusive. They are often combined with imprisonment and probation and parole, and with each other.

Judicially Administered Sanctions

The lack of sentencing options is most frustrating for the person who, in the majority of cases, does the sentencing—the judge. Consequently, when judges are given the discretion to "color" a punishment with intermediate sanctions, they will often do so. In addition to imprisonment and probation, a judge has five sentencing options:

intermediate sanctions
Sanctions that are more restrictive than probation and less restrictive than imprisonment.

pretrial diversion program An alternative to trial offered by a judge or prosecutor, in which the offender agrees to participate in a specified counseling or treatment program in return for withdrawal of the charges.

1. Fines.
2. Community service.
3. Restitution.
4. Pretrial diversion programs.
5. Forfeiture.

Fines, community service, and restitution were discussed in Chapter 9. In the context of intermediate sanctions, it is important to remember that these punishments are generally combined with incarceration or probation. For that reason, some critics feel the retributive or deterrent impact of such punishments is severely limited. Many European countries, in contrast, rely heavily on fines as the sole sanctions for a variety of crimes. (See the feature *Comparative Criminal Justice—Swedish Day-Fines.*)

Pretrial Diversion Programs Not every criminal violation requires the courtroom process. Consequently, some judges have the discretion to order an offender into a **pretrial diversion program** during the preliminary hearing. (Prosecutors can also offer an offender the opportunity to join such a program in return for reducing or dropping the initial

Comparative Criminal Justice

Pable631/Dreamstime.com

Central Intelligence Agency

Swedish Day-Fines

Few ideals are cherished as highly in our criminal justice system as equality. Most Americans take it for granted that individuals guilty of identical crimes should face identical punishments. From an economic perspective, however, this emphasis on equality renders our system decidedly unequal. Take two citizens, one a millionaire investment banker and the other a checkout clerk earning the minimum wage. Driving home from work one afternoon, each is caught by a traffic officer doing 80 miles per hour in a 55-mile-per-hour zone. The fine for this offense is $150. This amount, though equal for both, has different consequences: it represents mere pocket change for the investment banker, but a significant chunk out of the checkout clerk's weekly paycheck.

Restricted by a "tariff system" that sets specific amounts for specific crimes, regardless of the financial situation of the convict, American judges often refrain from using fines as a primary sanction. They either assume that poor offenders cannot pay the fine or worry that a fine will allow wealthier offenders to "buy" their way out of a punishment.

Paying for Crime

In searching for a way to make fines more effective sanctions, many reformers have seized on the concept of the "day-fine," as practiced in Sweden and several other European countries. In this system, which was established in the 1920s and 1930s, the fine amount is linked to the monetary value of the offender's daily income. Depending on the seriousness of the crime, a Swedish offender will be sentenced to 1 to 120 day-fines or, as combined punishment for multiple crimes, up to 200 day-fines.

For each day-fine unit assessed, the offender is required to pay one-thousandth of her or his annual gross income (minus a deduction for basic living expenses, as determined by the Prosecutor General's Office) to the court. Consequently, the day-fine system not only reflects the degree of the crime, but also ensures that the economic burden will be equal for those with different incomes. (For example, in neighboring Finland, which has a similar system, a millionaire was recently fined 54,024 euros [about $58,000] for driving 64 miles per hour in a 50-mph zone.)

Swedish police and prosecutors can levy day-fines without court involvement. As a result, plea bargaining is nonexistent, and more than 80 percent of all offenders are sentenced to intermediate sanctions without a trial. The remaining cases receive full trials, with a nonconviction rate of only 6 percent, compared with 26 percent in the United States.

For Critical Analysis

Do you think a "day-fine" system would be feasible in the United States? Why might it be difficult to implement in this country?

charges.) These programs represent an "interruption" of the criminal proceedings and are generally reserved for young or first-time offenders who have been arrested on charges of illegal drug use, child or spousal abuse, or sexual misconduct. Pretrial diversion programs usually include extensive counseling, often in a treatment center. If the offender successfully follows the conditions of the program, the criminal charges are dropped.

Problem-Solving Courts Many judges have found opportunities to divert low-level offenders by presiding over problem-solving courts. In these comparatively informal courtrooms, judges attempt to address problems such as drug addiction, mental illness, and homelessness that often lead to the eventual rearrest of the offender. About three thousand problem-solving courts are operating in the United States. Although these specialized courts cover a wide variety of subjects, from domestic violence to juvenile crime to mental illness, the most common problem-solving courts are drug courts.

Although the specific procedures of drug courts vary widely, most follow a general pattern. Either after arrest or on conviction, the offender is given the option of entering a drug court program or continuing through the standard courtroom process. Those who choose the former come under the supervision of a judge who will oversee a mixture of treatment and sanctions designed to cure their addiction. When offenders successfully complete the program, the drug court rewards them by dropping all charges. Drug courts operate on the assumption that when a criminal addict's drug use is reduced, his or her drug-fueled criminal activity will also decline.

Forfeiture In 1970, Congress passed the Racketeer Influenced and Corrupt Organizations Act (RICO) in an attempt to prevent the use of legitimate business enterprises as shields for organized crime.[59] As amended, RICO and other statutes give judges the ability to implement *forfeiture* proceedings in certain criminal cases. **Forfeiture** is a process by which the government seizes property gained from or used in criminal activity.

For example, if a person is convicted for smuggling cocaine into the United States from South America, a judge can order the seizure of not only the narcotics, but also the speedboat the offender used to deliver the drugs to a pickup point off the coast of South Florida. In *Bennis v. Michigan* (1996),[60] the Supreme Court ruled that a person's home or car could be forfeited even though the owner was unaware that the property was connected to illegal activity.

Once property is forfeited, the government has several options. It can sell the property, with the proceeds going to the state and/or federal law enforcement agencies involved in the seizure. Alternatively, the government agency can use the property directly in further crime-fighting efforts or award it to a third party, such as an informant. In Harris County, Texas, for example, law enforcement officials purchased about eight hundred body-worn cameras for local police officers (discussed in Chapter 5) using funds from civil forfeitures.

Forfeiture is financially rewarding for both federal and local law enforcement agencies. The U.S. Marshals Service manages about $3.1 billion worth of contraband and property impounded from criminals and criminal suspects. In 2015, the agency shared about $365 million of these funds with state and local law enforcement agencies, with an additional $605 million going to crime victims.[61] (In the feature *CJ Controversy—Civil Forfeiture*, we examine the question of whether the government should be able to confiscate property in the absence of criminal guilt.)

forfeiture The process by which the government seizes private property attached to criminal activity.

Day Reporting Centers

Day reporting centers (DRCs) are mainly tools to reduce jail and prison overcrowding. Although the offenders are allowed to live in the community rather than jail or prison, they

day reporting center (DRC) A community-based corrections center to which offenders report on a daily basis for treatment, education, and rehabilitation.

M Dogan/Shutterstock.com

Civil Forfeiture

With criminal forfeiture, as described in the text, a defendant must be convicted of committing a crime before her or his property is confiscated. Under *civil forfeiture*, as implemented by the federal government and almost every state government, law enforcement agencies can confiscate property without the criminal conviction of its owner and can keep that property, even if the owner is ultimately found to be innocent of the crime. In general, the government need only prove a "substantial connection" between the property and underlying crime for civil forfeiture to apply.

Civil Forfeiture Is Acceptable Because . . .

- It gives law enforcement a powerful tool to fight drug dealers and white-collar criminals by allowing the police to more easily confiscate the illegal gains of these criminal activities.
- Each year, it raises hundreds of millions of dollars that can be used to better equip and train local police departments and provide restitution for crime victims.

Civil Forfeiture Is Unacceptable Because . . .

- Due process (see Chapter 3) requires that a person be found guilty of committing a crime before he or she can be punished for that crime.
- It introduces the concept of "profit motive" to policing and thus provides law enforcement agents with an incentive to improperly seize property even if no underlying crime has been committed.

Your Assignment

In 2015, lawmakers in Montana and New Mexico took steps to end civil forfeiture in those states. Should civil forfeiture be banned throughout the entire United States? As part of your answer, go online and find an example of **civil forfeiture seizure** that supports your argument either for or against this widespread practice. Your response should include at least two full paragraphs.

---

intensive supervision probation (ISP) A punishment-oriented form of probation in which the offender is placed under stricter and more frequent surveillance and control than in conventional probation.

must spend all or part of each day at a reporting center. In general, being sentenced to a DRC is an extreme form of supervision. With offenders under a single roof, they are much more easily monitored and controlled. (According to critics of DRCs, they are also more easily able to "network" with other individuals who have criminal histories and drug and alcohol abuse issues.[62])

DRCs are instruments of rehabilitation as well. They often feature treatment programs for drug and alcohol abusers and provide counseling for a number of psychological problems, such as depression and anger management. Many of those found guilty in the Roanoke (Virginia) Drug Court, for example, are ordered to participate in a yearlong day reporting program. At the center, offenders meet with probation officers, submit to urine tests, and attend counseling and education programs, such as parenting and life-skills classes. After the year has passed, if the offender has completed the program to the satisfaction of the judge and has found employment, the charges will be dropped.[63]

Learning Objective 7

Contrast day reporting centers with intensive supervision probation.

Intensive Supervision Probation

Over the past several decades, a number of jurisdictions have turned to **intensive supervision probation (ISP)** to solve the problems associated with the burdensome caseloads we discussed earlier in the chapter. ISP offers a more restrictive alternative to regular probation, with higher levels of face-to-face contact between offenders and officers and frequent modes of control such as urine tests for drugs. In New Jersey, for example, ISP officers have caseloads of only 20 offenders (compared with 115 for other probation officers in the state) and are provided with additional resources to help them keep tabs on their charges.[64] Different jurisdictions have different methods of determining who is eligible for ISP, but a majority of states limit ISP to offenders who do not have prior probation violations.

The main goal of ISP is to provide prisonlike control of offenders while keeping them out of prison. Critics of ISP believe that it "causes" high failure rates, as more supervision increases the chances that an offender will be caught breaking conditions of probation.[65] One comparison of ISP with DRCs, however, found the intensive supervision of ISP to be more effective. In the six months following termination of the program, DRC participants were more likely to be convicted of a new offense and to test positive for drugs than their ISP counterparts. The study suggests that when combined with services such as outpatient drug treatment and educational training, ISP can be effective in producing low rates of recidivism.[66]

shock incarceration A short period of incarceration that is designed to deter further criminal activity by "shocking" the offender with the hardships of imprisonment.

Shock Incarceration

As the name suggests, **shock incarceration** is designed to "shock" criminals into compliance with the law. Following conviction, the offender is first sentenced to a prison or jail term. Then, usually within ninety days, he or she is released and resentenced to probation. The theory behind shock incarceration is that by getting a taste of the brutalities of the daily prison grind, the offender will be shocked into a crime-free existence.

In the past, shock incarceration was targeted primarily toward youthful, first-time offenders, who were thought to be more likely to be "scared straight" by a short stint behind bars. Data show, however, that fully 20 percent of all adults sentenced to probation spend some time in jail or prison before being released into the community to complete their probation.[67] Critics of shock incarceration are dismayed by this trend. They argue that the practice needlessly disrupts the lives of low-level offenders who would not otherwise be eligible for incarceration and exposes them to the mental and physical hardships of prison life (which we will discuss in Chapter 12).[68] Furthermore, there is little evidence that shock probationers fare any better than regular probationers when it comes to recidivism rates.[69]

Impact incarceration programs, or *boot camps,* are a variation on traditional shock incarceration. Instead of spending the "shock" period of incarceration in prison or jail, offenders are sent to a boot camp. Modeled on military basic training, these camps are generally located within prisons and jails, though some can be found in the community. The programs emphasize strict discipline, manual labor, and physical training. They are designed to instill self-responsibility and self-respect in participants, thereby lessening the chances that they will return to a life of crime. More recently, boot camps have also emphasized rehabilitation, incorporating such components as drug and alcohol treatment programs, anger-management courses, and vocational training.

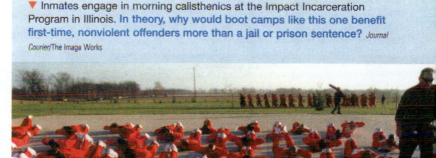

▼ Inmates engage in morning calisthenics at the Impact Incarceration Program in Illinois. **In theory, why would boot camps like this one benefit first-time, nonviolent offenders more than a jail or prison sentence?** *Journal Courier/The Image Works*

home confinement A community-based sanction in which offenders serve their terms of incarceration in their homes.

electronic monitoring A supervision technique in which the offender's whereabouts are kept under surveillance by an electronic device.

Home Confinement and Electronic Monitoring

Various forms of **home confinement**—in which offenders serve their sentences not in a government institution but at home—have existed for centuries. It has often served, and continues to do so, as a method of political control, used by totalitarian regimes to isolate and silence dissidents. For purposes of American law enforcement, home confinement was impractical until relatively recently. After all, one could not expect offenders to keep their promises to stay at home, and the personnel costs of guarding them were prohibitive.

In the 1980s, however, with the advent of **electronic monitoring**, or using technology to guard the prisoner, home confinement became more viable. Today, all fifty states and the federal government have home monitoring programs with about 200,000 offenders, including probationers and parolees, participating at any one time.[70]

Learning Objective 8 List the three levels of home monitoring.

The Levels of Home Monitoring

Home monitoring has three general levels of restriction:

1. *Curfew,* which requires offenders to be in their homes at specific hours each day, usually at night.
2. *Home detention,* which requires that offenders remain home at all times, with exceptions being made for education, employment, counseling, and other specified activities such as the purchase of food or, in some instances, attendance at religious services.
3. *Home incarceration,* which requires the offender to remain home at all times, save for medical emergencies.

Under ideal circumstances, home confinement serves many of the goals of intermediate sanctions. It protects the community. It saves public funds and space in correctional facilities by keeping convicts out of institutional incarceration. It meets public expectations of punishment for criminals. Uniquely, home confinement also recognizes that convicts, despite their crimes, play important roles in the community, and allows them to continue in those roles. An offender, for example, may be given permission to leave confinement to care for elderly parents.

▼ How might being required to wear an electronic ankle bracelet (such as the one shown here) negatively affect an offender's ability to find and keep a job? **Should such difficulties influence a judge's decision to impose this particular intermediate sanction? Why or why not?** AP Images/Wilfredo Lee

Home confinement is also lauded for giving sentencing officials the freedom to match the punishment with the needs of the offender. In 2016, for example, Rajat Gupta was allowed to serve the final six months of a two-year prison sentence for stock market fraud at his New York City apartment. Wearing an electronic ankle bracelet, Gupta could leave home to work, visit the doctor, or attend religious services. Indeed, home confinement is a popular punishment for white-collar criminals, who often need to earn funds to pay off significant court-ordered fines—nearly $20 million in Gupta's case.[71]

Types of Electronic Monitoring

According to some reports, the inspiration for electronic monitoring was a *Spider-Man* comic book in which the hero was tracked by the use of an electronic device on his arm. In 1979, a New Mexico judge named Jack Love, having read the comic, convinced an executive at Honeywell, Inc., to begin developing similar technology to supervise convicts.[72]

Two major types of electronic monitoring have grown out of Love's initial concept. The first is a "programmed contact" system, in which the offender is contacted periodically by voice or text to verify his or her whereabouts. Verification is obtained via a computer that uses voice or visual identification techniques or by requiring the offender to enter a code in an electronic box when called. The second is a "continuously signaling" device, worn around the convict's wrist, ankle, or neck. A transmitter in the device sends out a continuous signal to a "receiver-dialer" device located in the offender's dwelling. If the receiver device does not detect a signal from the transmitter, it informs a central computer, and the police are notified.

CJ & Technology

Global Positioning System (GPS)

Global positioning system (GPS) technology is a form of tracking technology that relies on twenty-four military satellites orbiting thousands of miles above the earth. The satellites transmit signals to each other and to a receiver on the ground, allowing a monitoring station to determine the location of a receiving device to within a few feet. GPS provides a much more precise level of supervision than regular electronic monitoring. The offender wears a transmitter, similar to a traditional electronic monitor, around his or her ankle or wrist. This transmitter communicates with a portable tracking device, a small box that uses military satellites to determine the probationer's movements.

GPS technology can be used either "actively" to constantly monitor the subject's whereabouts, or "passively" to ensure that the offender remains within the confines of a limited area determined by a judge or probation officer. Inclusion and exclusion zones are also important to GPS supervision. Inclusion zones are areas such as a home or workplace where the offender is expected to be at certain times. Exclusion zones are areas such as parks, playgrounds, and schools where the offender is not permitted to go. GPS-linked computers can alert officials immediately when an exclusion zone has been breached and create a computerized record of the probationer's movements for review at a later time. Despite the benefits of this technology, it is rarely implemented. According to the Bureau of Justice Statistics, only about eight thousand probationers are currently being tracked by GPS.

AP Images/Jeff T. Green

Thinking about GPS

How might GPS monitoring be used to improve and overhaul the American bail system, covered in Chapter 8?

Widening the Net

As we have seen, most of the convicts chosen for intermediate sanctions are low-risk offenders. From the point of view of the corrections official doing the choosing, this makes sense. Such offenders are less likely to commit crimes and attract negative publicity. This selection strategy, however, appears to invalidate one of the primary reasons

▲ Explain the possible connection between higher levels of surveillance by probation and parole officers and greater numbers of probationers and parolees being incarcerated.
AP Photo/Rich Pedroncelli

widen the net The criticism that intermediate sanctions designed to divert offenders from prison actually increase the number of citizens who are under the control and surveillance of the American corrections system.

intermediate sanctions exist: to reduce prison and jail populations. If most of the offenders in intermediate sanctions programs would otherwise have received probation, then the effect on these populations is nullified. Indeed, studies have shown this to be the case.[73]

At the same time, intermediate sanctions broaden the reach of the corrections system. In other words, they increase rather than decrease the amount of control the state exerts over the individual. Suppose a person is arrested for a misdemeanor such as shoplifting and, under normal circumstances, would receive probation. With access to intermediate sanctions, the judge may add a period of home confinement to the sentence. Critics contend that such practices **widen the net** of the corrections system by augmenting the number of citizens who are under the control and surveillance of the state and also *strengthen the net* by increasing the government's power to intervene in the lives of its citizens.[74] Technological advances such as the GPS devices mentioned in this chapter will only accelerate the trend.

EthicsChallenge

One concern about home confinement is that offenders are often required to defray its costs, which can be over $200 a month. What are some of the ethical implications of this policy? ■

Summary

For more information on these concepts, look back to the Learning Objective icons throughout the chapter.

1 **Explain the justifications for community-based corrections programs.** One justification involves reintegration of the offender into society. Reintegration restores family ties, encourages employment and education, and secures a place for the offender in the routine functioning of society. Other justifications involve diversion and cost savings. By diverting criminals to alternative modes of punishment, further overcrowding of jail and prison facilities can be avoided, as can the costs of incarcerating the offenders.

2 **Explain several alternative sentencing arrangements that combine probation with incarceration.** With a suspended sentence, a convicted offender is not required to serve the sentence, but the judge has the option of reinstating the sentence if the person reoffends. In addition, there are three other general types of sentencing arrangements: (a) split sentence probation, in which the judge specifies a certain time in jail or prison followed by a certain time on probation; (b) shock incarceration, in which a judge sentences an offender to be incarcerated, but allows that person to petition the court to be released on probation; and (c) intermittent incarceration, in which an offender spends a certain amount of time each week in jail or in a halfway house or another government institution.

3 **Specify the conditions under which an offender is most likely to be denied probation.** The offender (a) has been convicted of multiple charges, (b) was on probation or parole when arrested, (c) has two or more prior convictions, (d) is addicted to narcotics, (e) seriously injured the victim of the crime, or (f) used a weapon while committing the crime.

4 **Describe the three general categories of conditions placed on a probationer.** (a) Standard conditions, such as requiring that the probationer notify the agency of a change of address, not leave the jurisdiction without permission, and remain employed; (b) punitive conditions, such as restitution, community service, and home confinement; and (c) treatment conditions, such as required drug or alcohol treatment.

5 **Identify the main differences between probation and parole.** Probation is a sentence handed down by a judge that generally acts as an alternative to incarceration. Parole is a form of early release from prison determined by a parole authority, often a parole board. Probationers are usually first-time offenders who have committed nonviolent crimes, while parolees have often spent significant time in prison.

6 **Explain which factors influence the decision to grant parole.** In deciding whether to grant parole, parole board members primarily consider the severity of the underlying crime and the threat the offender will pose to the community if released. Other factors include the offender's level of remorse and his or her behavior while incarcerated.

7 **Contrast day reporting centers with intensive supervision probation.** In a day reporting center, the offender is allowed to remain in the community, but must spend all or part of each day at the reporting center. While at the center, offenders meet with probation officers, submit to drug tests, and attend counseling and education programs. With intensive supervision probation (ISP), more restrictions are imposed, and there is more face-to-face contact between offenders and probation officers. ISP may also include electronic surveillance.

8 **List the three levels of home monitoring.** (a) Curfew, which requires that the offender be at home during specified hours; (b) home detention, which requires that the offender be at home except for education, employment, and counseling; and (c) home incarceration, which requires that the offender be at home at all times except for medical emergencies.

Questions for Critical Analysis

1. In 2013, an eighty-six-year-old man was found guilty of fatally shooting his eighty-one-year-old wife. The victim was suffering from a painful health condition and had begged her husband to end her life. An Arizona judge sentenced the defendant to two years' probation. Do you agree with this punishment? Why or why not?
2. Why might probationers and parolees want to limit their social media activity? Give an example of a circumstance in which a Facebook posting could cause probation or parole to be revoked.
3. Review our discussion of Hawaii's Opportunity Probation with Enforcement (HOPE) from earlier in the chapter. What might be some of the reasons participants in the program are less likely to fail a second urinalysis test?
4. A number of courts have held that GPS monitoring, described in this chapter's *CJ & Technology* feature, is a form of regulation rather than punishment, and therefore is not subject to constitutional safeguards. Do you agree that GPS monitoring is not a punitive measure? Why or why not?
5. In your own words, explain what the phrase "widening the net" means. What might be some of the unintended consequences of increasing the number of offenders who are supervised by corrections officers in the community?

Key Terms

authority 303
caseload 304
community corrections 297
day reporting center (DRC) 313
discretionary release 308
diversion 297
electronic monitoring 316
forfeiture 313
home confinement 316
intensive supervision probation (ISP) 314
intermediate sanctions 311
mandatory release 310
parole 306
parole board 309
parole contract 307
parole grant hearing 309
parole guidelines 310
pretrial diversion program 312
probation 299
reintegration 297
revocation 301
shock incarceration 315
split sentence probation 299
suspended sentence 299
technical violation 304
widen the net 318

Notes

1. Mary Schenk and Michael Howie, "Reckless Homicide Sentence Reduced to Probation," *The News-Gazette* (Champaign, Ill.) (December 2, 2014), at **www.news-gazette.com/news/local/2014-12-02/reckless-homicide-sentence-reduced-probation.html.**
2. Bureau of Justice Statistics, *Correctional Populations in the United States, 2014* (Washington, D.C.: U.S. Department of Justice, December 2015), Table 1, page 2.
3. Michael Tonry, *Sentencing Matters* (New York: Oxford Press, 1996), 28.
4. *Correctional Populations in the United States, 2014, op. cit.*, 1.
5. Corrections Task Force of the President's Commission on Law Enforcement and Administration of Justice (1967).
6. Paul H. Hahn, *Emerging Criminal Justice: Three Pillars for a Proactive Justice System* (Thousand Oaks, Calif.: Sage Publications, 1998), 106–108.
7. *Correctional Populations in the United States, 2014, op. cit.*, Table 1, page 2.
8. Melissa S. Kearney et al., *Ten Economic Facts about Crime and Incarceration in the United States* (Washington, D.C.: The Brookings Institution, May 2014), 2, 13.
9. "Supervision Costs Significantly Less than Incarceration in Federal System," *United States Courts* (July 18, 2013), at **news.uscourts.gov/supervision-costs-significantly-less-incarceration-federal-system.**
10. Ram Subramanian and Rebecca Tublitz, *Realigning Justice Resources: A Review of Population Spending Shifts in Prison and Community Corrections* (New York: Vera Institute of Justice, 2012), 32, 33.
11. J. J. Abbott, "Pennsylvania Prison Population Sees Biggest Drop in 40 Years," *PA.gov* (January 20, 2016), at **www.governor.pa.gov/blog-pennsylvania-prison-population-sees-biggest-drop-in-40-years.**
12. Paul W. Keve, *Crime Control and Justice in America* (Chicago: American Library Association, 1995), 183.
13. Gerald Bayens and John Ortiz Smykla, *Probation, Parole, & Community-Based Corrections* (New York: McGraw-Hill, 2013), 186–217.
14. *Alternative Sentencing in the Federal Criminal Justice System* (Washington, D.C.: United States Sentencing Commission, May 2015), 4.
15. Joan Petersilia and Susan Turner, *Prison versus Probation in California: Implications for Crime and Offender Recidivism* (Santa Monica, Calif.: RAND Corporation, 1986).
16. Bureau of Justice Statistics, *Probation and Parole in the United States, 2014* (Washington, D.C.: U.S. Department of Justice, November 2015), Table 4, page 5.
17. *Ibid.*
18. *Ibid.;* and Bureau of Justice Statistics, *Prisoners in 2014* (Washington, D.C.: U.S. Department of Justice, September 2015), Table 1, page 2.
19. Sharyn Adams, Lindsay Bostwick, and Rebecca Campbell, *Examining Illinois Probationer Characteristics and Outcomes* (Chicago: Illinois Criminal Justice Information Authority, September 2011), Table 1, pages 16–17.
20. 705 So.2d 172 (La. 1997).
21. Neil P. Cohen and James J. Gobert, *The Law of Probation and Parole* (Colorado Springs, Colo.: Shepard's/McGraw-Hill, 1983), Section 5.01, 183–184; Section 5.03, 191–192.

22. 534 U.S. 112 (2001).
23. *Ibid.*, 113.
24. Bureau of Justice Statistics, *Felony Defendants in Large Urban Counties, 2009—Statistical Tables* (Washington, D.C.: U.S. Department of Justice, December 2013), Table 28, page 32.
25. Carl B. Klockars, Jr., "A Theory of Probation Supervision," *Journal of Criminal Law, Criminology, and Police Science* 63 (1972), 550–557.
26. *Probation and Parole in the United States, 2014, op. cit.*, Table 3, page 4.
27. Todd R. Clear, George F. Cole, and Michael D. Reisig, *American Corrections*, 11th ed. (Belmont, Calif.: Wadsworth Cengage Learning, 2016), 206.
28. Gwen Robinson, "What Works in Offender Management?" *The Howard Journal of Criminal Justice* 44 (2005), 307–318.
29. Klockars, *op. cit.*, 551.
30. Matthew T. DeMichele, *Probation and Parole's Growing Caseloads and Workload Allocation: Strategies for Managerial Decision Making* (Lexington, Ky.: American Probation and Parole Association, May 2007).
31. James MacPherson, "North Dakota Parole, Probation Offices Seeing Surge in Cases," *Associated Press* (May 18, 2015).
32. 389 U.S. 128 (1967).
33. *Morrissey v. Brewer,* 408 U.S. 471 (1972); and *Gagnon v. Scarpelli,* 411 U.S. 778 (1973).
34. 465 U.S. 420 (1984).
35. *Felony Defendants in Large Urban Counties, 2009—Statistical Tables, op. cit.*, Table 6, page 10.
36. Jennifer L. Skeem and Sarah Manchak, "Back to the Future: From Klockars' Model of Effective Supervision to Evidence-Based Practice in Probation," *Journal of Offender Rehabilitation* 47 (2008), 231.
37. *Probation and Parole, 2014, op. cit.*, Table 3, page 4.
38. Pamela M. Casey, Roger K. Warren, and Jennifer K. Elek, *Using Offender Risk and Needs Assessment Information at Sentencing* (Williamsburg, Va.: National Center for State Courts, 2011), Table 1, page 5.
39. Nancy Ritter, "Predicting Recidivism Risk: New Tool in Philadelphia Shows Great Promise," *NIJ Journal* (February 2013), 4–13.
40. James Q. Wilson, "Making Justice Swifter," *City Journal* 7 (1997), 4.
41. Graeme Wood, "Prison without Walls," *The Atlantic* (September 2010), 92–93.
42. Angela Hawken and Mark Kleiman, *Managing Drug Involved Probationers and Swift and Certain Sanctions: Evaluating Hawaii's HOPE* (Washington, D.C.: U.S. Department of Justice, December 2009), 4.
43. Clear, Cole, and Reisig, *op. cit.*, 386.
44. *Probation and Parole in the United States, 2014, op. cit.*, Appendix table 7, page 20.
45. Bureau of Justice Statistics, *Probation and Parole in the United States, 2012* (Washington, D.C.: U.S. Department of Justice, December 2013), Table 7, page 9.
46. Joseph Walker, "Rules May Help Parolees Avoid Jail for Small Errors," *New York Times* (January 5, 2012), at **cityroom.blogs.nytimes.com/2012/01/05/rating-a-parolees-risk-before-a-return-to-prison.**
47. *Morrissey v. Brewer,* 408 U.S. 471 (1972).
48. 442 U.S. 1 (1979).
49. American Civil Liberties Union, *A Living Death: Life without Parole for Nonviolent Offenses* (November 2013), 2.
50. Marie Gottschalk, "Days without End: Life Sentences and Penal Reform," *Prison Legal News* (April 11, 2013), at **https://www.prisonlegalnews.org/news/2012/jan/15/days-without-end-life-sentences-and-penal-reform/.**
51. William Parker, *Parole: Origins, Development, Current Practices, and Statutes* (College Park, Md.: American Correctional Association, 1972), 26.
52. Clear, Cole, and Reisig, *op. cit.*, 393.
53. *Ibid.*, 395.
54. "Sirhan Sirhan, Assassin of Robert Kennedy, Denied Parole for 15th Time," *Associated Press* (February 10, 2016).
55. Mark P. Rankin, Mark H. Allenbaugh, and Carlton Fields, "Parole's Essential Role in Bailing Out Our Nation's Criminal Justice Systems," *Champion* (January 2009), 47–48.
56. Council of State Government/American Probation and Parole Association, "Fact Sheet 1: The Role of Community Corrections in Victim Services" (2012), at **www.appa-net.org/eWeb/docs/APPA/pubs/PVRPPP-FACTSHEET-1.pdf.**
57. 18 U.S.C. Section 3771(a)(4) (2006).
58. Joel M. Caplan, "Parole Release Decisions: Impact of Victim Input on a Representative Sample of Inmates," *Journal of Criminal Justice* (May–June 2010), 291–300.
59. 18 U.S.C. Sections 1961–1968.
60. 516 U.S. 442 (1996).
61. U.S. Marshals Service, "Fact Sheet: Asset Forfeiture 2016" (March 11, 2016), at **www.usmarshals.gov/duties/factsheets/asset_forfeiture.pdf.**
62. Douglas J. Boyle et al., "Overview of: 'An Evaluation of Day Reporting Centers for Parolees: Outcomes of a Randomized Trial,'" *Criminology & Public Policy* (February 2013), 136.
63. Model State Drug Court Legislation Committee, *Model State Drug Court Legislation: Model Drug Offender Accountability and Treatment Act* (Alexandria, Va.: National Drug Court Institute, May 2004), 42.
64. *ISP Fact Sheet: Intensive Supervision Program* (Trenton, N.J.: Administrative Office of the Courts, February 2015), 1–2.
65. Joan Petersilia and Susan Turner, "Intensive Probation and Parole," *Crime and Justice* 17 (1993), 281–335.
66. Douglas J. Boyle et al., *Outcomes of a Randomized Trial of an Intensive Community Corrections Program—Day Reporting Center—for Parolees, Final Report for the National Institute of Justice* (Washington, D.C.: U.S. Department of Justice, October 2011), 3–4.
67. Bureau of Justice Statistics, *Probation and Parole in the United States, 2010* (Washington, D.C.: U.S. Department of Justice, December 2011), Appendix table 3, page 31.
68. Clear, Cole, and Reisig, *op. cit.*, 238.
69. Paul Stageberg and Bonnie Wilson, *Recidivism among Iowa Probationers* (Des Moines, Iowa: The Iowa Division of Criminal and Juvenile Justice Planning, July 2005); and Paul Koniceck, *Five Year Recidivism Follow-Up Offender Releases* (Columbus, Ohio: Ohio Department of Rehabilitation and Correction, August 1996).
70. Todd R. Clear et al., *American Corrections in Brief,* 2nd ed. (Belmont, Calif.: Wadsworth Cengage Learning, 2014), 102.
71. Anita Raghavanjan, "Rajat Gupta to Finish Insider Trading Sentence at His Home," *New York Times* (January 21, 2016), B3.
72. Josh Kurtz, "New Growth in a Captive Market," *New York Times* (December 31, 1989), 12.
73. Michael Tonry and Mary Lynch, "Intermediate Sanctions," in *Crime and Justice,* vol. 20, ed. Michael Tonry (Chicago: University of Chicago Press, 1996), 99.
74. Dennis Palumbo, Mary Clifford, and Zoann K. Snyder-Joy, "From Net Widening to Intermediate Sanctions: The Transformation of Alternatives to Incarceration from Benevolence to Malevolence," in *Smart Sentencing: The Emergence of Intermediate Sanctions,* eds. James M. Byrne, Arthur Lurigio, and Joan Petersilia (Newbury Park, Calif.: Sage, 1992), 231.

josefkubes/Shutterstock.com

11

Prisons and Jails

Chapter Outline		Corresponding Learning Objectives
A Short History of American Prisons	1	Contrast the Pennsylvania and the New York penitentiary theories of the 1800s.
Prison Organization and Management	2	Describe the formal prison management system, and indicate the three most important aspects of prison governance.
	3	List and briefly explain the four types of prisons.
Inmate Population Trends	4	List the factors that have caused the prison population to grow dramatically in the last several decades.
	5	Indicate some of the consequences of our high rates of incarceration.
The Emergence of Private Prisons	6	Describe the arguments for and against private prisons.
Jails	7	Summarize the distinctions between jails and prisons, and indicate the importance of jails in the American corrections system.
	8	Explain the four characteristics of many jail inmates that make the management of jails difficult for sheriffs' departments.

To target your study and review, look for these numbered Learning Objective icons throughout the chapter.

a trend Indeed?

according to John Chisholm, the district attorney of Milwaukee County, Wisconsin, criminals fall into two categories. There are those "who scare us," and those "who irritate the hell out of us." The first group includes violent criminals, and, Chisholm says, "The most important thing we can do with these people is incapacitate them, so they can't do any more harm." As for the second, much larger group of nonviolent arrestees, Chisholm's office has devised an "early intervention" strategy. These "irritating" defendants must agree to complete a drug-treatment course or other educational curriculum while on probation. If they do so, the charges against them will likely be dismissed.

"The whole program is designed to reduce the number of people we are putting in jail or prison, but to do it in a smart, accountable way," says one of Chisholm's associates. The strategy seems to be working. Between 2007 and 2015, the prison population in Wisconsin dropped from about 24,500 to 22,000, with most of the reduction occurring in Milwaukee County. Chisholm's efforts are not unique, or even uncommon. Since 2014, thirty states—including large ones such as California, New York, and Texas—have passed legislation designed to lower incarceration rates, often by steering nonviolent offenders to community supervision. These policy choices reflect a small but significant trend in American corrections: fewer inmates. In 2014, the U.S. prison population decreased by 1 percent, the second largest decline in more than thirty-five years. Between 2009 and 2014, the national tally of prison inmates dropped more than 3 percent.

To be sure, such modest decreases do little to threaten our nation's title as "the globe's leading incarcerator." About 2.2 million Americans are in prison and jail. The United States locks up six times as many of its citizens as Canada does, and eight times as many as a number of European democracies. Still, the fact that criminal justice professionals and politicians are willing to accept policies that reduce the number of inmates represents a sea change in the country's corrections strategies. "We're talking about using a scarce resource—beds in jails and prisons—in the most effective way. I would say to people, 'Who would you rather have [incarcerated]—a bank robber or an addict who is aggressively panhandling downtown?'" says Benjamin David, a district attorney from North Carolina. "This is not a political issue, it is a moral issue."

AP Photo/David Goldman

▲ About 630,000 inmates are admitted into American prisons each year, including these prisoners being processed for intake by the Georgia Department of Corrections

1. Do you agree with the assertion that reducing the number of inmates in the United States is a moral issue instead of a political issue? Why or why not?
2. David A. Clark, Jr., sheriff of Milwaukee County, Wisconsin, says, "My soft-on-crime opponents emerge from Candy Land to propose second chances, third chances, and fourth chances, in the process endangering our homes, neighborhoods, and schools." What is your opinion of this criticism of John Chisholm's "early intervention" program?
3. How do you think declining national crime rates over the past two decades, as discussed in Chapter 2, have contributed to an atmosphere in which politicians are less worried about being depicted as "soft on crime"?

A Short History of American Prisons

Today's high rates of imprisonment—often referred to as evidence of "mass incarceration" in the United States—are the result of many criminal justice strategies that we have discussed in this textbook. These include truth-in-sentencing guidelines, relatively long sentences for gun and drug crimes, "three-strikes" habitual offender laws, and judicial freedom to incarcerate convicts for relatively minor criminal behavior. At the base of all these policies is a philosophy that sees prisons primarily as instruments of punishment. The loss of freedom imposed on inmates is the penalty for the crimes they have committed. Punishment has not, however, always been the main reason for incarceration in this country.

English Roots

The prisons of eighteenth-century England, known as "bridewells" after London's Bridewell Palace, had little to do with punishment. These facilities were mainly used to hold debtors or those awaiting trial, execution, or banishment from the community. (In many ways, as will be made clear, these facilities resembled the modern jail.) English courts generally imposed one of two sanctions on convicted felons: they turned them loose, or they executed them.[1] To be sure, most felons were released, pardoned by either the court or the clergy after receiving a whipping or a branding.

The correctional system in the American colonies differed very little from that of their motherland. If anything, colonial administrators were more likely to use corporal punishment than their English counterparts, and the death penalty was not uncommon in early America. The one dissenter was William Penn, who adopted the "Great Law" in Pennsylvania in 1682. Based on Quaker ideals of humanity and rehabilitation, this criminal code forbade the use of torture and mutilation as forms of punishment. Instead, felons were ordered to pay restitution of property or goods to their victims. If the offenders did not have sufficient property to make restitution, they were placed in a prison, which was primarily a "workhouse."[2] The death penalty was still allowed under the "Great Law," but only in cases of premeditated murder. Penn proved to be an exception, however, and the path to reform was much slower in the colonies than in England.

Walnut Street Prison: The First Penitentiary

On William Penn's death in 1718, the "Great Law" was rescinded in favor of a harsher criminal code, similar to those of the other colonies. At the time of the American Revolution, however, the Quakers were instrumental in the first broad swing of the incarceration pendulum from punishment to rehabilitation. In 1776, Pennsylvania passed legislation ordering that offenders be reformed through treatment and discipline rather than simply beaten or executed.[3] Several states, including Massachusetts and New York, quickly followed Pennsylvania's example.

Pennsylvania continued its reformist ways by opening the country's first **penitentiary** in a wing of Philadelphia's Walnut Street Jail in 1790. The penitentiary operated on the assumption that silence and labor provided the best hope of rehabilitating the criminal spirit. Remaining silent would force the prisoners to think about their crimes, and eventually the weight of conscience would lead to repentance. At the same time, enforced labor would attack the problem of idleness—regarded as the main cause of crime by penologists of the time.[4] Consequently, inmates at Walnut Street were isolated from one another in solitary rooms and kept busy with constant menial chores.

penitentiary An early form of correctional facility that emphasized separating inmates from society and from each other.

separate confinement A nineteenth-century penitentiary system developed in Pennsylvania in which inmates were kept separate from each other at all times, with daily activities taking place in individual cells.

congregate system A nineteenth-century penitentiary system developed in New York in which inmates were kept in separate cells during the night but worked together in the daytime under a code of enforced silence.

Eventually, the penitentiary at Walnut Street succumbed to the same problems that continue to plague institutions of confinement: overcrowding and excessive costs. As an influx of inmates forced more than one person to be housed in a room, maintaining silence became nearly impossible. By the early 1800s, officials could not find work for all of the convicts, so many were left idle.

The Great Penitentiary Rivalry: Pennsylvania versus New York

Learning Objective

1 Contrast the Pennsylvania and the New York penitentiary theories of the 1800s.

The apparent lack of success at Walnut Street did little to dampen enthusiasm for the penitentiary concept. Throughout the first half of the nineteenth century, a number of states reacted to prison overcrowding by constructing new penitentiaries. Each state tended to have its own peculiar twist on the roles of silence and labor, and two such systems—those of Pennsylvania and New York—emerged to shape the debate over the most effective way to run a prison.

The Pennsylvania System After the failure of Walnut Street, Pennsylvania constructed two new prisons: the Western Penitentiary near Pittsburgh (opened in 1826) and the Eastern Penitentiary in Cherry Hill, near Philadelphia (1829). The Pennsylvania system took the concept of silence as a virtue to new extremes. Based on the idea of **separate confinement**, these penitentiaries were constructed with back-to-back cells facing outward from the center. (See Figure 11.1 for the layout of the original Eastern Penitentiary.) To protect each inmate from the corrupting influence of the others, prisoners worked, slept, and ate alone in their cells. Their only contact with other human beings came in the form of religious instruction from a visiting clergyman or prison official.[5]

The New York System If Pennsylvania's prisons were designed to transform wrongdoers into honest citizens, those in New York focused on obedience. When New York's Newgate Prison (built in 1791) became overcrowded, the state authorized the construction of Auburn Prison, which opened in 1816. Auburn initially operated under many of the same assumptions that guided the penitentiary at Walnut Street. Solitary confinement, however, seemed to lead to an inordinate amount of sickness, insanity, and even suicide among inmates, and it was abandoned in 1822. Nine years later, Elam Lynds became warden at Auburn and instilled the **congregate system**, also known as the Auburn system. Like Pennsylvania's separate confinement system, the congregate system was based on silence and labor. At Auburn, however, inmates worked and ate together, with silence enforced by prison guards.[6]

Figure 11.1 The Eastern Penitentiary

As you can see, the Eastern Penitentiary was designed in the form of a "wagon wheel," known today as the radial style. The back-to-back cells in each "spoke" of the wheel faced outward from the center to limit contact between inmates.

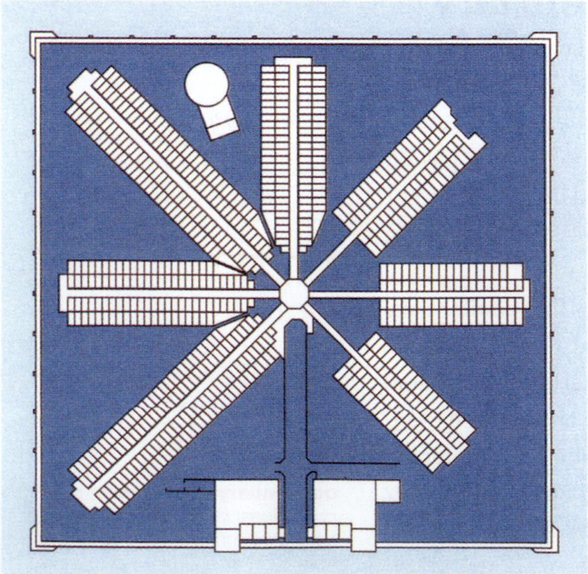

If either state can be said to have "won" the debate, it was New York. The Auburn system proved more popular, and a majority of the new prisons built during the first half of the nineteenth century followed New York's lead, though mainly for economic reasons rather than philosophical ones. New York's penitentiaries were cheaper to build because they did not require so much space. Furthermore, inmates in New York were employed in workshops, whereas those in Pennsylvania toiled alone in their cells. Consequently, the Auburn system was better positioned to exploit prison labor in the early years of widespread factory production.

The Reformers and the Progressives

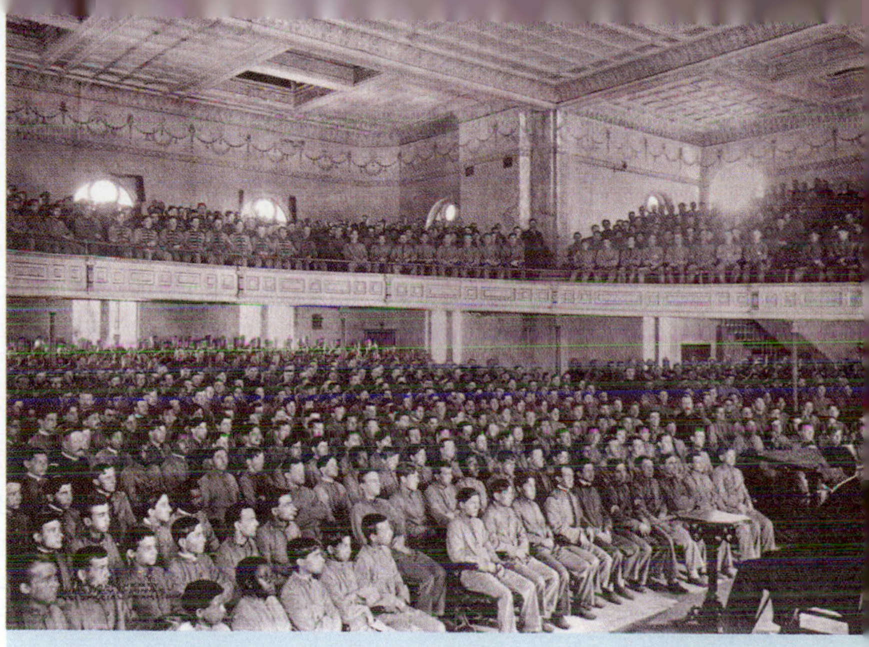

▲ Inmates of the Elmira Reformatory in New York attend a presentation at the prison auditorium. To what extent do you believe that treatment and rehabilitation should be provided to incarcerated criminals? Historical/Corbis

The Auburn system did not go unchallenged. In the 1870s, a group of reformers argued that fixed sentences, imposed silence, and isolation did nothing to improve prisoners. These critics proposed that penal institutions should offer the promise of early release as a prime tool for rehabilitation. Echoing the views of the Quakers a century earlier, the reformers presented an ideology that would heavily influence American corrections for the next century.

This "new penology" was put into practice at New York's Elmira Reformatory in 1876. At Elmira, good behavior was rewarded by early release, and misbehavior was punished with extended time under a three-grade system of classification. On entering the institution, the offender was assigned a grade of 2. If the inmate followed the rules and completed work and school assignments, after six months he was moved up to grade 1, the necessary grade for release. If, however, the inmate broke institutional rules, he was lowered to grade 3. A grade 3 inmate needed to behave properly for three months before he could return to grade 2 and begin to work back toward grade 1 and eventual release.[7]

Although other penal institutions did not adopt the Elmira model, its theories came into prominence in the first two decades of the twentieth century, thanks to the Progressive movement in criminal justice. The Progressives believed that criminal behavior was caused by social, economic, and biological factors and, therefore, a corrections system should have a goal of treatment, not punishment. Consequently, they trumpeted a **medical model** for prisons, which held that institutions should offer a variety of programs and therapies to cure inmates of their "ills," whatever the root causes. The Progressives were largely responsible for the spread of indeterminate sentences (Chapter 9), probation (Chapter 10), intermediate sanctions (Chapter 10), and parole (Chapter 10) in the first half of the twentieth century.

The Reassertion of Punishment

Even though the Progressives had a great influence on the corrections system as a whole, their theories had little impact on the prisons themselves. Many of these facilities had been constructed in the nineteenth century and were impervious to change. More important, prison administrators usually did not agree with the Progressives and their followers, so the day-to-day lives of most inmates varied little from the congregate system of Auburn Prison.

Academic attitudes began to shift away from the Progressives in the mid-1960s. Then, in 1974, the publication of Robert Martinson's famous "What Works?" essay provided opponents of the medical model with statistical evidence that rehabilitation efforts did nothing to lower recidivism rates.[8] This is not to say that Martinson's findings went unchallenged. A number of critics argued that rehabilitative programs could be successful.[9] In fact, Martinson himself retracted most of his claims in a little-noticed article published five years after his initial report.[10] Attempts by Martinson and others

medical model A model of corrections in which the psychological and biological roots of an inmate's criminal behavior are identified and treated.

to "set the record straight" went largely unnoticed, however, as crime rose sharply in the early 1970s. This trend led many criminologists and politicians to champion "get tough" measures to deal with criminals they now considered "incurable." By the end of the 1980s, the legislative, judicial, and administrative strategies that we have discussed throughout this text had positioned the United States for an explosion in inmate populations and prison construction unparalleled in the nation's history.

Prison Organization and Management

At present, the United States has a dual prison system that parallels its dual court system, which we discussed in Chapter 7. The Federal Bureau of Prisons (BOP) currently operates about one hundred confinement facilities, ranging from prisons to immigration detention centers to community corrections institutions.[11] In the federal corrections system, a national director, appointed by the president, oversees six regional directors and a staff of nearly 40,000 employees. All fifty states also operate state prisons, which number about 1,700 and make up more than 90 percent of the country's correctional facilities.[12] Governors are responsible for the organization and operation of state corrections systems, which vary widely based on each state's geography, *demographics* (population characteristics), and political culture.

Generally, those offenders sentenced in federal court for breaking federal law serve their time in federal prisons, and those offenders sentenced in state court for breaking state law serve their time in state prisons. As you can see in Figure 11.2, federal prisons hold relatively few violent felons, because relatively few federal laws involve violent crime. At the same time, federal prisons are much more likely to hold public order offenders, a group that includes violators of federal immigration law.

FIGURE 11.2 Types of Offenses of Federal and State Prison Inmates

As the comparison below shows, state prisoners are most likely to have been convicted of violent crimes, while federal prisoners are most likely to have been convicted of drug and public order offenses.

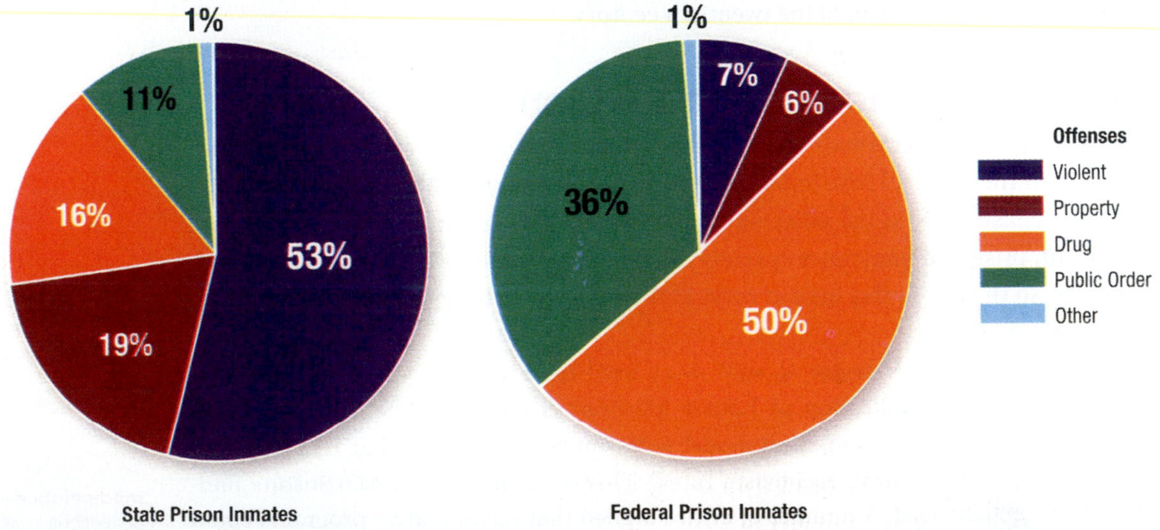

Source: Bureau of Justice Statistics, *Prisoners in 2014* (Washington, D.C.: U.S. Department of Justice, September 2015), Table 11, page 16; and Table 12, page 17.

Prison Administration

Whether the federal government or a state government operates a prison, its administrators have the same general goals, summarized by Charles Logan as follows:

> The mission of a prison is to keep prisoners—to keep them in, keep them safe, keep them in line, keep them healthy, and keep them busy—and to do it with fairness, without undue suffering and as efficiently as possible.[13]

Considering the environment of a prison—an enclosed world inhabited by people who are generally violent and angry and would rather be anywhere else—Logan's mission statement is somewhat unrealistic. A prison staff must supervise the daily routines of hundreds or thousands of inmates, a duty that includes providing them with meals, education, vocational programs, and different forms of leisure. The smooth operation of this supervision is made more difficult—if not, at times, impossible—by budgetary restrictions, overcrowding, and continual inmate turnover.

warden The prison official who is ultimately responsible for the organization and performance of a correctional facility.

Formal Prison Management In some respects, the management structure of a prison is similar to that of a police department, as discussed in Chapter 5. Both systems rely on a hierarchical (top-down) *chain of command* to increase personal responsibility. Both assign different employees to specific tasks, though prison managers have much more direct control over their subordinates than do police managers. The main difference is that police departments have a *continuity of purpose* that is sometimes lacking in prison organizations. All members of a police force are, at least theoretically, working to reduce crime and apprehend criminals. In a prison, this continuity is less evident. An employee in the prison laundry service and one who works in the visiting center have little in common. In some instances, employees may even have cross-purposes: a prison guard may want to punish an inmate, while a counselor in the treatment center may want to rehabilitate her or him.

Learning Objective

2 Describe the formal prison management system, and indicate the three most important aspects of prison governance.

Consequently, a strong hierarchy is crucial for any prison management team that hopes to meet Charles Logan's expectations. As Figure 11.3 shows, the **warden** (also known as a superintendent) is ultimately responsible for the operation of a prison. He or she oversees deputy wardens, who in turn manage the various organizational lines of the institution. The custodial employees, who deal directly with the inmates and make

FIGURE 11.3 **Organizational Chart for a Typical Correctional Facility**

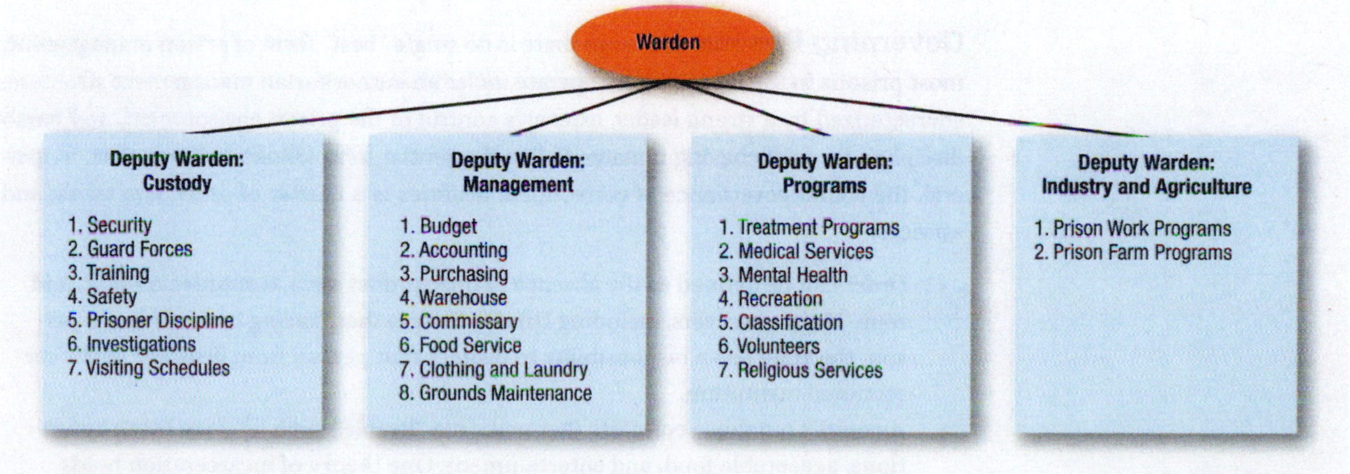

Careers in CJ

FASTFACTS

Prison warden

Job description:

- A prison warden is the chief managing officer of an adult correctional institution.

What kind of training is required?

- Bachelor's degree in criminal justice, corrections, law enforcement, or a related field.
- One or more years of work experience in the management of a major division of a correctional institution.

Annual salary range?

- $38,000–$100,000 (depending on size of institution and geographic region)

Photo courtesy of Berry Larson

Berry Larson
Prison Warden

Before I began my career as a correctional officer for the Arizona Department of Corrections, I had several people question my desire to work inside a prison. Why would I want to stick myself somewhere so unpleasant and stressful? While at the training academy, however, we were taught that "approach determines response." I found that to be very true during my time as a correctional officer. It is all about the way you carry yourself and the way you relate to the inmates. An inmate can tell if you are trying to be someone you are not. They can also tell if you are afraid. I never had to use physical force once in all the time I was a correctional officer—officer presence and nonverbal/verbal communication are usually sufficient to handle any situation, as long as you keep control of your emotions.

As warden of the Arizona State Prison Complex–Lewis, my duties include touring the units; attending special events such as inmate graduations for GED and vocational programs; managing emergency situations such as power outages, fights and assaults, and staff injuries; and eradicating all criminal activity from the facility. Many, if not most, of our inmates came to us in pretty bad shape—little or no education, a substance abuse history, or mental health or behavioral issues. These young men have spent their lives watching television and playing video games and simply do not have the skills to be successful in life. We try to remedy the situation by providing them with educational and vocational programs and "life-skills" classes that promote civil and productive behavior.

SOCIAL MEDIA CAREER TIP Regularly reevaluate your social media tools and the methods you use to keep up to date in your fields of interest. If you are still using the same tools as a year ago, you probably aren't keeping up with the latest developments in Internet technology.

up more than half of a prison's staff, operate under a militaristic hierarchy, with a line of command passing from the deputy warden to the captain to the correctional officer.

Governing Prisons Although there is no single "best" form of prison management, most prisons in the United States operate under an authoritarian management structure, characterized by a strong leader, extensive control of the prison environment, and harsh discipline for misbehaving inmates. Political scientist John DiIulio believes that, in general, the sound governance of correctional facilities is a matter of order, amenities, and services:

- *Order* can be defined as the absence of misconduct such as murder, assault, and rape. Many observers, including DiIulio, believe that, having incarcerated a person, the state has a responsibility to protect that person from disorder in the correctional institution.
- *Amenities* are those comforts that make life "livable," such as clean living conditions, acceptable food, and entertainment. One theory of incarceration holds that inmates should not enjoy a quality of life comparable to life outside prison.

Without the basic amenities, however, prison life becomes unbearable, and inmates are more likely to lapse into disorder.

- *Services* include programs designed to improve an inmate's prospects on release, such as vocational training, remedial education, and drug treatment. Again, many feel that a person convicted of a crime does not deserve to participate in these kinds of programs, but they have two clear benefits. First, they keep the inmate occupied and focused during her or his sentence. Second, they reduce the chances that the inmate will go back to a life of crime after she or he returns to the community.[14]

According to DiIulio, in the absence of order, amenities, and services, inmates will come to see their imprisonment as not only unpleasant but unfair, and they will become much more difficult to control.[15] Furthermore, weak governance encourages inmates to come up with their own methods of regulating their lives. As we shall see in the next chapter, the result is usually high levels of violence and the expansion of prison gangs and other unsanctioned forms of authority.

classification The process through which prison officials screen each incoming inmate to best determine that inmate's security and treatment needs.

maximum-security prison A correctional institution designed and organized to control and discipline dangerous felons, as well as prevent escape.

Types of Prisons

One of the most important aspects of prison administration occurs soon after a defendant has been convicted of a crime. In the **classification** process, administrators determine what sort of correctional facility provides the best "fit" for each individual convict. In general, prison administrators rely on three criteria for classification purposes:

1. The seriousness of the crime committed.
2. The risk of future criminal or violent conduct.
3. The need for treatment and rehabilitation programs.[16]

In the federal prison system, this need to classify—and separate—different kinds of offenders has led to six different levels of correctional facilities. Inmates in level 1 facilities are usually nonviolent and require the least amount of security, while inmates in level 6 facilities are the most dangerous and require the harshest security measures. Many states use a similar six-level system, and in both federal and state prisons, a committee headed by a deputy warden usually makes the classification decisions.

Learning Objective

3 List and briefly explain the four types of prisons.

Different facilities have different means of separating and classifying inmates. To simplify matters, most correctional facilities are designated as being one of three security levels—minimum, medium, or maximum. A fourth level—the supermaximum-security prison, known as the "supermax"—is relatively rare and extremely controversial due to its hyperharsh methods of punishing and controlling the most dangerous prisoners.

Maximum-Security Prisons In a certain sense, the classification of prisoners today owes a debt to the three-grade system developed at the Elmira Reformatory, discussed earlier in the chapter. Once wrongdoers enter a corrections facility, they are constantly graded on behavior. Those who serve "good time," as we have seen, are often rewarded with early release. Those who compile extensive misconduct records are usually housed, along with violent and repeat offenders, in **maximum-security prisons**.

The names of these institutions—Folsom, San Quentin, Sing Sing, Attica—conjure up foreboding images of concrete and steel jungles, with good reason. Maximum-security prisons are designed with full attention to security and surveillance. In these institutions, inmates' lives are programmed in a militaristic fashion to keep them from escaping or from harming themselves or the prison staff. About a quarter of the prisons in the United States are classified as maximum security, and these institutions house about a third of the country's prisoners.

supermax prison A highly secure, freestanding correctional facility—or such a unit within a correctional facility—that manages offenders who would pose a threat to the security and safety of other inmates and staff members if housed in the general inmate population.

The Design Maximum-security prisons tend to be large—holding more than a thousand inmates—and they have similar features. The entire operation is usually surrounded by concrete walls that stand twenty to thirty feet high and have also been sunk deep into the ground to deter tunnel escapes. Fences reinforced with razor-ribbon barbed wire that can be electrically charged may supplement these barriers. The prison walls are studded with watchtowers, from which guards armed with shotguns and rifles survey the movement of prisoners below. Inmates live in cells, most of them with similar dimensions to those found in the Topeka Correctional Facility, a maximum-security prison in Topeka, Kansas: eight feet by fourteen feet with cinder block walls. The space contains bunks, a toilet, a sink, and possibly a cabinet or closet. Cells are located in rows of *cell blocks,* each of which forms its own security unit, set off by a series of gates and bars. A maximum-security institution is essentially a collection of numerous cell blocks, each constituting its own prison within a prison.

Most prisons have cell blocks that open into sprawling prison yards, where the inmates commingle daily. The "prison of the future," however, rejects this layout. Instead, it relies on a podular design, as evident at the Two Rivers Correctional Institution in Umatilla, Oregon. At Two Rivers, which opened in 2007, fourteen housing pods contain ninety-six inmates each. Each unit has its own yard, so inmates rarely, if ever, interact with members of other pods. This design gives administrators the flexibility to, for example, place violent criminals in pod A and white-collar criminals in pod B without worrying about mixing the two different security levels.[17]

Security Measures Within maximum-security prisons, inmates' lives are dominated by security measures. Whenever they move from one area of the prison to another, they do so in groups and under the watchful eye of armed correctional officers. Television surveillance cameras may be used to monitor their every move, even when sleeping, showering, or using the toilet. They are subject to frequent pat-downs or strip searches at the guards' discretion. Constant "head counts" ensure that every inmate is where he or she should be. Tower guards—many of whom have orders to shoot to kill in the case of a disturbance or escape attempt—constantly look down on the inmates as they move around outdoor areas of the facility.

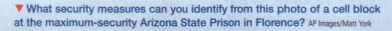

▼ What security measures can you identify from this photo of a cell block at the maximum-security Arizona State Prison in Florence? AP Images/Matt York

Supermax Prisons About thirty states and the Federal Bureau of Prisons (BOP) operate **supermax prisons** (short for supermaximum security), which are supposedly reserved for the "worst of the worst" of America's corrections population. Many of the inmates in these facilities are deemed high risks to commit murder behind bars—about a quarter of the occupants of the BOP's U.S. Penitentiary Administrative Maximum (ADX) in Florence, Colorado, have killed other prisoners or assaulted correctional officers elsewhere. Supermax prisons are also used as punishment for offenders who commit serious disciplinary infractions in maximum-security prisons, or for those inmates who become involved with prison gangs. In addition, a growing number of supermax occupants are either high-profile individuals who would be at constant risk of attack in a general prison population or convicted terrorists.

The main purpose of a supermax prison is to strictly control the inmates' movement, thereby limiting (or eliminating) situations that could lead to breakdowns in discipline. The conditions at California's Security Housing Unit (SHU) at Pelican Bay State Prison are representative of most supermax institutions. Prisoners are confined to their one-person cells for twenty-three hours each day under video camera surveillance. They receive meals through a slot in the door. The cells measure eight by ten feet in size and are windowless. Fluorescent lights are continuously on, day and night, making it difficult for inmates to enjoy any type of privacy or sleep.[18] For the most part, supermax prisons operate in a state of perpetual **lockdown**, in which all inmates are confined to their cells, and social activities such as meals, recreational sports, and treatment programs are nonexistent. (As the feature *CJ Controversy—Senseless Suffering?* shows, the lockdown experience is not confined to supermax inmates.)

lockdown A disciplinary action taken by prison officials in which all inmates are ordered to their quarters, and nonessential prison activities are suspended.

medium-security prison A correctional institution that houses less dangerous inmates and therefore uses less restrictive measures to prevent violence and escapes.

Medium- and Minimum-Security Prisons Medium-security prisons hold about 45 percent of the prison population and minimum-security prisons 20 percent. Inmates at **medium-security prisons** have for the most part committed less serious crimes than those housed in maximum-security prisons and are not considered high

CJ Controversy
EQUAL·JUSTICE·UNDER·LAW
M Dogan/Shutterstock.com

Senseless Suffering?

Solitary confinement refers to the disciplinary practice of confining inmates by themselves in small cells for more than twenty-two hours each day over the course of weeks, months, or even years. At any given time, about 81,000 prisoners are "in solitary" in the United States. These inmates are not sentenced to solitary confinement by a judge, and for most of them, the assignment has no connection with their original offense. Rather, solitary confinement is most commonly used as punishment for disciplinary infractions such as failure to obey an order given by a prison official.

Solitary Confinement Is Necessarily Harsh Because . . .

- It is a vital tool in maintaining order and discipline. As human contact is one of the few privileges that inmates enjoy, they have a strong incentive to conform to the rules of the institution rather than risk losing that privilege.
- The practice protects prison staff and inmates alike by removing violent convicts from the general inmate population.

Solitary Confinement Is Unnecessarily Harsh Because . . .

- It causes severe damage to the mental health of prisoners. Researchers have identified a number of resulting symptoms, including intense anxiety, hallucinations, violent fantasies, and reduced impulse control.
- The majority of inmates who suffer these psychological harms will eventually be returned to society, which will have to bear the burden of their mental illnesses.

Your Assignment

Most states have no legislation that controls the use of solitary confinement. If you were to draft such a law, what elements would it contain? Would you give prison officials a "free hand" in this area of prison discipline? Or, would you restrict their discretion in determining who is placed in solitary, the length of the punishment, and the infractions to which it applies? Before answering, research the terms **California** and **solitary confinement guidelines** online to see how one state recently addressed these issues in response to a lawsuit. Your response should include at least two full paragraphs.

minimum-security prison A correctional institution designed to allow inmates, most of whom pose low security risks, a great deal of freedom of movement and contact with the outside world.

risks for escaping or causing harm. Consequently, medium-security institutions are not designed for control to the same extent as maximum-security prisons and have a more relaxed atmosphere. These facilities also offer more educational and treatment programs and allow for more contact between inmates. Medium-security prisons are rarely walled, relying instead on high fences. Prisoners have more freedom of movement within the structures, and the levels of surveillance are much lower. Living quarters are less restrictive as well—many of the newer medium-security prisons provide dormitory housing.

A **minimum-security prison** seems at first glance to be more like a college campus than an incarceration facility. Most of the inmates at these institutions are first-time offenders who are nonviolent and well behaved. A high percentage are white-collar criminals. Indeed, inmates are often transferred to minimum-security prisons as a reward for good behavior in other facilities. Therefore, security measures are lax compared with even medium-security prisons. Unlike medium-security institutions, minimum-security prisons do not have armed guards. Prisoners are provided with amenities such as televisions and computers in their rooms. They also enjoy freedom of movement and are allowed off prison grounds for educational or employment purposes to a much greater degree than those held in more restrictive facilities.

Some critics have likened minimum-security prisons to "country clubs," but in the corrections system, everything is relative. A minimum-security prison may seem like a vacation spot when compared with the horrors of Sing Sing, but it still represents a restriction of personal freedom and separates the inmate from the outside world. (The feature *Comparative Criminal Justice—Prison Lite* provides a look at Norway's approach to incarceration, in which even the worst offenders are afforded the minimum-security experience.)

Comparative Criminal Justice

Pable631/Dreamstime.com

Central Intelligence Agency

Prison Lite

In Norway, incarceration is based on the premise that loss of liberty is punishment enough for offenders. Consequently, the prisons themselves are made as pleasant as possible. For example, Halden prison, which houses murderers and rapists, provides amenities such as a recording studio, a "kitchen laboratory" for cooking classes, and a two-bedroom house where inmates can house their families for overnight visits. An inmate at the Skien maximum-security island prison compares his incarceration to "living in a village." He adds, "Everybody has to work. But we have free time so we can do some fishing, or in summer we can swim off the beach. We know we are prisoners but here we feel like people."

Norway's methods have, it appears, created certain expectations among its inmates. After spending several months behind bars following a conviction on multiple counts of murder, one Norwegian prisoner wrote a letter to authorities protesting the conditions of his imprisonment. Among the complaints: not enough butter for his bread, cold coffee, and no skin moisturizer. By at least one measurement, however, Norway's "prison lite" strategy is effective, as the country has a five-year recidivism rate of only 20 percent—one of the lowest such rates in the world.

For Critical Analysis

In the United States, life behind bars has long been predicated on the *principle of least eligibility,* which holds that the least advantaged members of society outside prison should lead a better existence than any prison or jail inmate. Do you favor the American or the Norwegian approach to prison conditions? Why?

EthicsChallenge

The federal government pays inmates wages as low as twenty-five cents an hour to make goods for the U.S. military and other federal agencies. Should inmates be paid a reasonable minimum wage for any work that they do? Why or why not? Why might competing private companies think that prison labor at such low wages is unethical?

Inmate Population Trends

As Figure 11.4 shows, the number of Americans in prison or jail has increased dramatically in the past three decades. A number of different factors, described below, have been given as reasons for this long-term trend, which has only recently begun to level off.

Factors in Prison Population Growth

John Pfaff, an expert on sentencing from Fordham University's School of Law, attributes much of the growth in the U.S. prison population to a greater willingness on the part of prosecutors to bring felony—rather than misdemeanor—charges against arrestees.[19] (We saw the power of prosecutors to influence incarceration rates in Wisconsin at the beginning of the chapter.)

Other experts point to the enhancement and stricter enforcement of the nation's illegal drug laws. In 1980, about 19,000 drug offenders were incarcerated in state prisons and 4,800 drug offenders were in federal prisons. Thirty-four years later, state prisons held about 208,000 inmates who had been arrested for drug offenses, and the number of drug offenders in federal prisons had risen to approximately 96,500 (representing about half of all inmates in federal facilities).[20]

Learning Objective

4 List the factors that have caused the prison population to grow dramatically in the last several decades.

Increased Probability of Incarceration The growth of America's inmate population also reflects the reality that the chance of an arrestee going to prison today is much greater than it was thirty years ago. Most of this growth took place in the 1980s,

FIGURE 11.4 The Inmate Population of the United States

The total number of inmates in the United States has risen from 744,208 in 1985 to about 2.2 million in 2014.

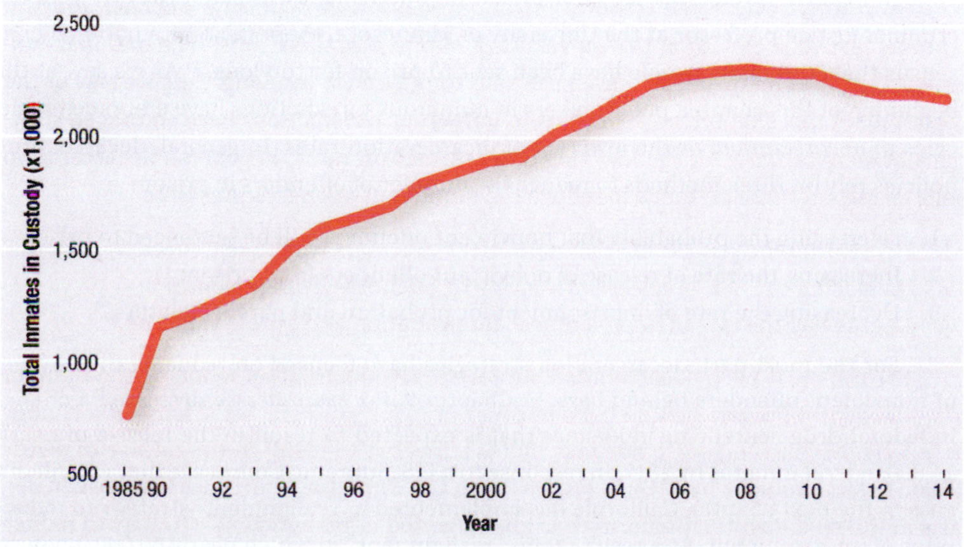

Source: U.S. Department of Justice.

when the likelihood of incarceration in a state prison after arrest increased fivefold for drug offenses, threefold for weapons offenses, and twofold for crimes such as sexual assault, burglary, auto theft, and larceny.[21] For federal crimes, the proportion of convicted defendants being sent to prison rose from 54 percent in 1988 to 89 percent in 2014.[22]

Inmates Serving More Time In Chapter 9, we discussed a number of "get tough" sentencing laws passed in reaction to the crime wave of the 1970s and 1980s. These measures, including sentencing guidelines, mandatory minimum sentences, and truth-in-sentencing laws, have significantly increased the length of prison terms in the United States.[23] Overall, inmates released from state prison in 2009 spent an average of nine months—about 36 percent—longer behind bars than those inmates released in 1990.[24] On the federal level, in the fifteen years after the passage of the Sentencing Reform Act of 1984, the average time served in federal prison increased more than 50 percent.[25]

Federal Prison Growth The number of inmates in the federal prison population declined by 34 percent (or 5,300 prisoners) in 2014.[26] This decrease was too small, however, to offset the recent expansion of the federal corrections system. Between 1990 and 2014, the federal prison population grew almost 300 percent, from about 65,000 to just over 191,000.[27]

As already mentioned, an increase in federal drug offenders is largely responsible for the growth of the federal prison population. Because of mandatory minimum sentencing laws, federal drug traffickers spend an average of seventy-four months behind bars, considerably longer than those sentenced to state prisons.[28] Other factors driving federal prison population growth include:

1. Starting in 1987, Congress *abolished parole* in the federal corrections system, meaning that federal inmates must serve their entire sentences, minus good time credits.[29]
2. The number of federal inmates sentenced for *immigration violations* (covered by federal law rather than state law) increased by 70 percent from 1999 to 2014.[30]
3. In 2016, approximately 13,000 *female offenders* were behind bars in federal prison, about double their numbers in 1995.[31] Indeed, there were about the same number of women in federal prison for drug offenses in 2015 as there were for all offenses in 1995.[32]

Decarceration

To significantly reverse the trend of prison population growth, says Michael Tonry, a criminal justice professor at the University of Minnesota, there must be a national consensus that "too many people have been sent to prison for too long."[33] As we saw at the beginning of this chapter, policymakers in numerous jurisdictions have embraced strategies of *decarceration,* or the lowering of incarceration rates. In general, decarceration policies rely on three methods to reduce the number of offenders in prison:

1. Decreasing the probability that nonviolent offenders will be sentenced to prison.
2. Increasing the rate of release of nonviolent offenders from prison.
3. Decreasing the rate of imprisonment for probation and parole violators.[34]

For the most part, decarceration strategies have focused on reducing the number of nonviolent offenders behind bars. In Chapter 9, for example, we discussed a change in federal drug-sentencing guidelines that is expected to result in the release of nearly 15,000 federal inmates by 2017. In response to a U.S. Supreme Court case that we will discuss in the next chapter, California has implemented a "realignment" strategy to reduce rates of imprisonment. As a result of this "realignment," in which nearly 60,000 low-level offenders were released into some form of community corrections, the state's prison inmate population declined by 51 percent from 2006 to 2015.[35]

In general, states are relying on *evidence-based practices*, or those strategies supported by statistical research, to decarcerate. Besides California, three other states (New Jersey, New York, and Rhode Island) have decreased their prison populations by over 20 percent in the twenty-first century, and thirty-nine states in total have experienced some decline since 2000.[36] At the same time, experts caution that decarceration policies that focus only on nonviolent offenders have their limits. "If you released every person in prison on a drug charge today," said criminologist John Pfaff, "[the United States would] still be the world's largest incarcerating country."[37] To truly reverse America's incarceration trends, decarceration policies in the future will need to concentrate on freeing violent criminals from prison—an unlikely possibility, given national attitudes regarding crime and punishment.

Myth vs Reality

Does Putting Criminals in Prison Reduce Crime?

The Myth Since the early 1990s, crime rates in the United States have been stable or declining. During most of that same period, as seen in Figure 11.4 earlier in the chapter, the number of imprisoned Americans climbed precipitously. Thus, it seems clear that crime falls when the prison population rises.

This perception is supported by the theories of deterrence and incapacitation, which we covered in Chapter 9. First, the threat of prison deters would-be criminals from committing crimes. Second, a prison inmate is incapable of committing crimes against the public because he or she has been separated from the community.

The Reality Numerous statistical examples discredit a direct, sustained link between decreased crime rates and increased prison populations. From 2000 to 2013, five states (California, Maryland, New Jersey, New York, and Texas) saw imprisonment and crime rates both decrease by at least 15 percent. By the same token, eight of the ten states that experienced increases in violent crime during that time period also saw increases in incarceration.

According to one theory, massive incarceration accounted for about a quarter of the crime drop of the 1990s, as many of the most violent offenders were removed from society and remain behind bars. Since then, however, a large percentage of new prison admissions have been drug law offenders and probation/parole violators. The data tell us that removing these sorts of criminals from the community has a relatively limited effect on violent and property crime rates. In fact, their absence from their homes may even contribute to criminal activity. As we discussed in Chapter 2, many criminologists believe that widespread family disruption greatly increases the incidence of crime in a community.

For Critical Analysis

Some experts believe that prisons are "schools of crime" that "teach" low-level offenders to be habitual criminals. If true, how would this circumstance influence the relationship between incarceration rates and crime rates?

Public Safety Issues Many observers believe that America's high rate of incarceration has contributed significantly to the drop in the nation's crime rates,[38] an assertion discussed in the feature *Myth vs. Reality—Does Putting Criminals in Prison Reduce Crime?* Similarly, there is concern that the decarceration movement just discussed will reverse the nation's positive crime trends. "People come out of prison hardened and angry and more likely to offend," says Ronald Teachman, formerly the police chief in South Bend, Indiana.[39]

Learning Objective

5 Indicate some of the consequences of our high rates of incarceration.

Initial studies do not support the argument that releasing low-level offenders necessarily leads to an increase in crime rates. In November 2014, California voters passed Proposition 47, which downgraded a number of nonviolent felonies involving less than $950—including grand theft, shoplifting, writing bad checks, receiving stolen property, and drug possession—to misdemeanors. Because this change to state law was applied retroactively, inmates serving time for these crimes were eligible for immediate release from prison. By March 2015, about 4,500 prisoners who committed crimes covered by Proposition 47 had been freed from incarceration.

Research conducted by Mike Males of the Center on Juvenile and Criminal Justice shows that it is unlikely these ex-inmates had any appreciable impact on local crime rates in California.[40] Similarly, drug offenders who were diverted to treatment programs in New York City following statewide drug law reform in 2009 have had a two-year recidivism rate of 36 percent. Prior to the reforms, similar offenders sentenced to prison, jail, or probation had a two-year recidivism rate of 54 percent.[41]

The Negative Consequences of Incarceration Proponents of decarceration also point out that mass incarceration can have severe social repercussions for communities and the families that make up those communities. About 2.7 million minors in this country—one in twenty-eight—have a parent in prison.[42] These children are at an increased risk of suffering from poverty, depression, and academic problems, as well as higher levels of juvenile delinquency and eventual arrest themselves.[43] Incarceration also has a harmful impact on the offenders. After being released from prison or jail, these men and women suffer from a higher rate of physical and mental health problems than the rest of the population, and are more likely to struggle with addiction, unemployment, and homelessness.[44]

Because of the demographics of the U.S. prison population, these problems have a disproportionate impact on members of minority groups. African American males are incarcerated at a rate more than six times that of white males and about two and a half times that of Hispanic males.[45] With more black men behind bars than enrolled in the nation's colleges and universities, Marc Mauer of the Sentencing Project, a nonprofit research group in Washington, D.C., believes that the "ripple effect on their communities and on the next generation of kids, growing up with their fathers in prison, will certainly be with us for at least a generation."[46] (This chapter's *CJ Policy—Your Take* feature highlights another hardship faced by America's offender population: loss of the right to vote.)

CJ Policy—Your Take

A felony conviction denies one of the basic rights of our democracy—**the right to vote**—to about 5.8 million Americans with criminal records. Florida, Iowa, and Virginia permanently take away the ability to vote, or *disenfranchise*, those convicted of felonies. Other states have various requirements, such as a waiting period, before the right to vote is reinstated. These laws have a significant impact on African American men, about one in thirteen of whom are disenfranchised at present. **What is your opinion of the fairness of policies that deny ex-inmates the right to vote?**

The Emergence of Private Prisons

As the prison population soared at the end of the twentieth century, state corrections officials faced a serious problem: too many inmates, not enough prisons. "States couldn't build space fast enough," explains corrections expert Martin Horn. "And so they had to turn to the private sector."[47] With corrections exhibiting every appearance of "a recession-proof industry," American businesses eagerly entered the market.

Today, **private prisons**, or prisons run by private firms to make a profit, are an important part of the criminal justice system. About two dozen private companies operate more than two hundred facilities across the United States. The two largest corrections firms, Corrections Corporation of America (CCA) and the GEO Group, Inc., manage approximately 160 correctional facilities and generate about $3.3 billion in annual revenue combined.[48] By 2014, private penal institutions housed about 131,000 inmates, representing 8.4 percent of all prisoners in the state and federal corrections systems.[49]

Why Privatize?

It would be a mistake to automatically assume that private prisons are less expensive to run than public ones. Nevertheless, the incentive to privatize is primarily financial.

Cost Efficiency In the 1980s and 1990s, a number of states and cities reduced operating costs by transferring government-run services such as garbage collection and road maintenance to the private sector. Similarly, private prisons can often be run more cheaply and efficiently than public ones for the following reasons:

- *Labor costs.* The wages of public employees account for nearly two-thirds of a prison's operating expenses. Although private corrections firms pay base salaries

private prisons Correctional facilities operated by private corporations instead of the government and, therefore, reliant on profits for survival.

comparable to those enjoyed by public prison employees, their nonunionized staffs receive lower levels of overtime pay, workers' compensation claims, sick leave, and health-care insurance.

- *Competitive bidding.* Because of the profit motive, private corrections firms have an incentive to buy goods and services at the lowest possible price.
- *Less red tape.* Private corrections firms are not part of the government bureaucracy and therefore do not have to contend with the massive amount of paperwork that can clog government organizations.[50]

Learning Objective

6 Describe the arguments for and against private prisons.

In 2005, the National Institute of Justice released the results of a five-year study comparing low-security public and private prisons in California. The government agency found that private facilities cost taxpayers between 6 and 10 percent less than public ones.[51] More recent research conducted at Temple University found that, by replacing public correctional facilities with private ones, states could save up to 45 percent in operating costs per prison.[52]

Overcrowding and Outsourcing Private prisons are becoming increasingly attractive to state governments faced with the competing pressures of tight budgets and overcrowded corrections facilities. Lacking the funds to alleviate overcrowding by building more prisons, state officials are turning to the private institutions for help. In 2015, for example, the Oklahoma Corrections Department spent $2 million to purchase beds at private institutions to handle a prison population that was at 112 percent of capacity.[53] Often, the private prison is out of state, which leads to the "outsourcing" of inmates. Washington State has alleviated its overcrowding problems by sending about 1,000 inmates to private institutions in Michigan.[54]

The Argument against Private Prisons

The assertion that private prisons offer economic benefits is not universally accepted. A number of studies have found that private prisons are no more cost-effective than public ones.[55] Furthermore, opponents of private prisons worry that, despite the assurances of corporate executives, private corrections companies will "cut corners" to save costs, denying inmates important security guarantees in the process.

Safety Concerns Criticism of private prisons is somewhat supported by the anecdotal evidence. Certainly, these institutions have been the setting for a number of violent incidents over the past several years. In 2014, the federal government launched an investigation into management practices at the Idaho Correctional Center (ICC), a CCA facility. Understaffing had created such a violent atmosphere in the ICC that inmates had nicknamed it "Gladiator School."[56] In 2015, the Arizona State Prison in Kingman—operated by Management and Training Corp.—experienced a riot that required the evacuation of 1,200 inmates. According to prisoners, the disturbance was the result of pent-up frustration caused by constant use of pepper spray by correctional officers.[57]

Apart from anecdotal evidence, various studies have also uncovered disturbing patterns of misbehavior at private prisons. For example, in the year after CCA took over operations of Ohio's Lake Erie Correctional Institution from the state corrections department, the number of assaults against correctional officers and inmates increased by over 40 percent.[58] In addition, research conducted by Curtis R. Blakely of the University of South Alabama and Vic W. Bumphus of the University of Tennessee at Chattanooga found that a prisoner in a private correctional facility was twice as likely to be assaulted by a fellow inmate as a prisoner in a public one.[59]

CJ & Technology

Video Visits

Mikael Karlsson/Alamy

Thousands of prisons and jails in the United States now offer "video visitation" to inmates. Instead of face-to-face contact, these communications take place via closed-circuit video systems located within the corrections facility. Administrators favor video visits because they promote safety and require less work for correctional staffers, who do not need to accompany an inmate to a visiting area. There is also a profit motive. For example, Securus Technologies, which provides these services to thousands of jails, typically charges inmates or their visitors a dollar a minute for such teleconferences. Twenty percent of this fee goes back to the correctional facility.

Opponents of visual visitation condemn the burden that these costs place on the often low-income families of inmates, who still must pay for transportation to the prison or jail. In addition, critics point out that the practice tends to displace face-to-face visits, which have a number of benefits. Research shows that seeing friends and family members "in person" creates social bonds, lessens stress, and even reduces recidivism among inmates.

Thinking about Video Visits

In some instances, Securus has required that, before using its services, a jail must ban all in-person visitation, forcing inmates to rely on the video feeds to contact loved ones. What is your opinion of this situation, in which a private company is essentially dictating correctional policy?

Philosophical Concerns Other critics see private prisons as inherently unjust, even if they do save tax dollars or provide enhanced services. These observers believe that corrections is not simply another industry, like garbage collection or road maintenance, and that only the government has the authority to punish wrongdoers. In the words of John DiIulio:

> It is precisely because corrections involves the deprivation of liberty, precisely because it involves the legally sanctioned exercise of coercion by some citizens over others, that it must remain wholly within public hands.[60]

Furthermore, some observers note, if a private corrections firm receives a fee from the state for each inmate housed in its facility, does that not give management an incentive to increase the amount of time each prisoner serves? Though government parole boards make the final decision on an inmate's release from private prisons, the company could manipulate misconduct and good behavior reports to maximize time served and, by extension, higher profits.[61] "You can put a dollar figure on each inmate that is held at a private prison," says Alex Friedmann of *Prison Legal News*. "They are treated as commodities. And that's very dangerous and troubling, when a company sees the people it incarcerates as nothing more than a money stream."[62]

Getting Linked in

At any given time, Corrections Corporation of America and the GEO Group, Inc., post hundreds of employment opportunities, from youth development specialists to accounting clerks to registered nurses. To learn more about the multiple careers available in **private corrections**, enter the names of these corporations into the LinkedIn search engine.

The Future of Private Prisons

The number of inmates in private prisons declined by 1.6 percent from 2013 to 2014,[63] largely as a result of a reduction in the number of federal prisoners noted earlier in the chapter. Still, the private prison industry will continue to play an important role in American corrections, for two reasons. First, states experiencing shrinking corrections budgets and congested prisons rely on private correctional institutions to handle their inmate population overflow. Second, federal law requires that at least

34,000 immigration law violators be housed in detention facilities daily, and private corporations operate nine of the nation's ten largest "Criminal Alien Requirement" correctional facilities.[64]

jail A facility, usually operated by the county government, used to hold persons awaiting trial or those who have been found guilty of less serious felonies or misdemeanors.

EthicsChallenge

Several private prisons have been criticized for accepting only inmates who are in relatively good health. If true, why would this strategy make financial sense? What ethical questions does it raise concerning private prisons?

Jails

Learning Objective

7 Summarize the distinctions between jails and prisons, and indicate the importance of jails in the American corrections system.

Although prisons and prison issues dominate the public discourse on corrections, there is an argument to be made that jails are the dominant penal institutions in the United States. In general, a prison is a facility designed to house people convicted of felonies for lengthy periods of time, while a **jail** is authorized to hold pretrial detainees and offenders who have committed misdemeanors. On any given day, about 745,000 inmates are in jail in this country, and jails admit approximately 11.4 million persons over the course of an entire year.[65] Nevertheless, jail funding is often the lowest priority for the cash-strapped local governments, leading to severe overcrowding, less-than-acceptable medical facilities, and other dismal conditions.

Many observers see this negligence as having far-reaching consequences for criminal justice. Jail is often the first contact that citizens have with the corrections system. It is at this point that treatment and counseling have the best chance to deter future criminal behavior.[66] By failing to take advantage of this opportunity, says Professor Franklin Zimring of the University of California at Berkeley School of Law, corrections officials have created a situation in which "today's jail folk are tomorrow's prisoners."[67] (To better understand the role that these two correctional institutions play in the criminal justice system, see *Mastering Concepts—The Main Differences between Public Prisons and Jails*.)

MasteringConcepts The Main Differences between Public Prisons and Jails

	Prisons	Jails
1.	. . . are operated by the federal and state governments.	. . . are operated by county and city governments.
2.	. . . hold inmates who may have lived quite far away before being arrested.	. . . hold mostly inmates from the local community.
3.	. . . house only those who have been convicted of a crime.	. . . house those who are awaiting trial or have recently been arrested, in addition to convicts.
4.	. . . generally hold inmates who have been found guilty of serious crimes and received sentences of longer than one year.	. . . generally hold inmates who have been found guilty of minor crimes and are serving sentences of less than a year.
5.	. . . often offer a wide variety of rehabilitation and educational programs for long-term prisoners.	. . . due to smaller budgets, tend to focus only on the necessities of safety, food, and clothing.

pretrial detainees Individuals who cannot post bail after arrest and are therefore forced to spend the time prior to their trial incarcerated in jail.

time served The period of time a person denied bail (or unable to pay it) has spent in jail prior to his or her trial.

The Jail Population

Like their counterparts in state prisons, jail inmates are overwhelmingly young male adults. About 47 percent of jail inmates are white, 35 percent are African American, and 15 percent are Hispanic.[68] The main difference between state prison and jail inmates involves their criminal activity. As Figure 11.5 shows, jail inmates are more likely to have been convicted of nonviolent crimes than their counterparts in state prison.

Pretrial Detainees A significant number of those held in jail on any given day—about 470,000 inmates[69]—technically are not prisoners. They are **pretrial detainees** who have been arrested by the police and, for a variety of reasons that we discussed in Chapter 8, are unable to post bail. Pretrial detainees are, in many ways, walking legal contradictions. According to the U.S. Constitution, they are innocent until proved guilty. At the same time, by being incarcerated while awaiting trial, they are denied a number of personal freedoms and are subjected to the poor conditions of many jails.

In *Bell v. Wolfish* (1979), the Supreme Court rejected the notion that this situation is inherently unfair by refusing to give pretrial detainees greater legal protections than sentenced jail inmates have.[70] In essence, the Court recognized that treating pretrial detainees differently than convicted jail inmates would place too much of a burden on corrections officials and was therefore impractical.

Sentenced Jail Inmates According to the U.S. Department of Justice, 37 percent of those in jail have been convicted of their current charges.[71] In other words, they have been found guilty of a crime, usually a misdemeanor, and sentenced to time in jail. The typical jail term lasts between thirty and ninety days, and rarely does a prisoner spend more than one year in jail for any single crime. Often, a judge will credit the length of time the convict has spent in detention waiting for trial—known as **time served**—toward his or her sentence. This practice acknowledges two realities of jails:

1. Terms are generally too short to allow the prisoner to gain any benefit (that is, rehabilitation) from the jail's often limited or nonexistent treatment facilities.

FIGURE 11.5 Types of Offenses of Prison and Jail Inmates

As the comparison below shows, jail inmates are more likely than state prisoners to have been convicted of nonviolent crimes. This underscores the main function of jails: to house less serious offenders for relatively short periods of time.

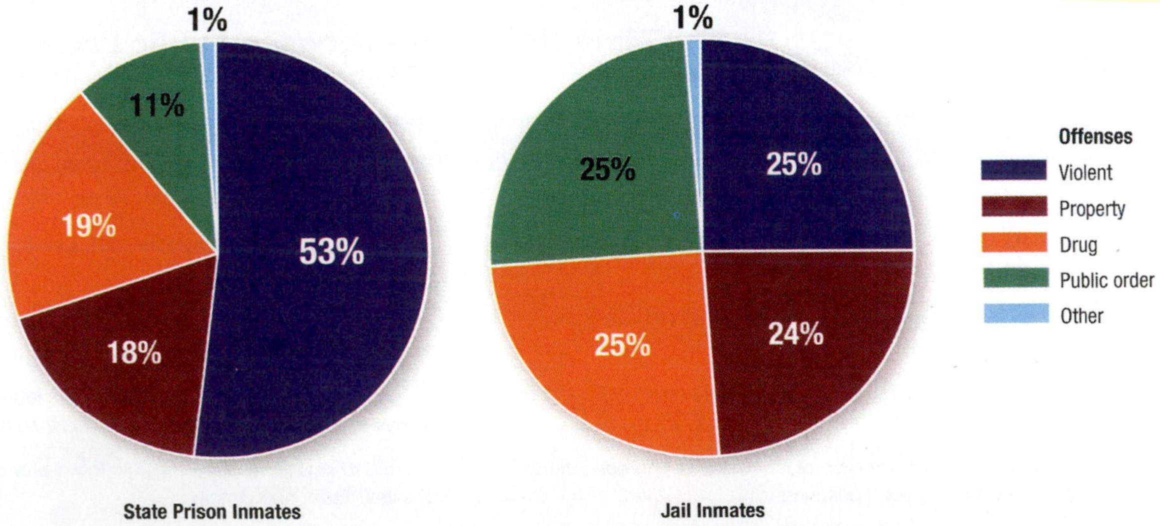

1%
11%
19%
53%
18%
State Prison Inmates
1%
25%
25%
25%
24%
Jail Inmates
Offenses
Violent
Property
Drug
Public order
Other

Source: Bureau of Justice Statistics, *Prisoners in 2014* (Washington, D.C.: U.S. Department of Justice, September 2015) Table 11, page 16; and Bureau of Justice Statistics, *Profile of Jail Inmates, 2002* (Washington, D.C.: U.S. Department of Justice, July 2004, 1.

Therefore, the jail term can serve no purpose except to punish the wrongdoer. (Judges who believe jail time can serve purposes of deterrence and incapacitation may not agree with this line of reasoning.)
2. Jails are chronically overcrowded, and judges need to clear space for new offenders.

fee system A system in which the sheriff's department is reimbursed by a government agency for the costs of housing jail inmates.

Other Jail Inmates Pretrial detainees and those convicted of misdemeanors make up the majority of the jail population. Jail inmates also include probation and parole violators, the mentally ill, juveniles awaiting transfer to juvenile authorities, and immigration law violators being held for the federal government. Increasingly, in states such as California, Minnesota, and Ohio, jails are also called on to handle the overflow of inmates from state prisons.

Jail Administration

About 2,800 jails are in operation in the United States. The vast majority of these are managed on a county level by an elected sheriff. Most of the remainder are under the control of the federal government or local municipalities, and six state governments (Alaska, Connecticut, Delaware, Hawaii, Rhode Island, and Vermont) also manage jails. The capacity of jails varies widely. The Los Angeles County Men's Central Jail holds nearly seven thousand people, but jails that large are the exception rather than the rule. Forty percent of all jails in this country house fewer than fifty inmates.[72]

Many jails operate on the principle of a **fee system**, in which a government agency reimburses the sheriff's department for the daily cost of housing and feeding each inmate. This practice is often problematic, because once the daily fee per inmate has been established (at, say $8), the sheriff is free to divert some of those funds to other areas of need in her or his department. Also, it is not uncommon for sheriffs' departments to charge inmates "pay-to-stay" fees for aspects of their incarceration such as food, clothing, and medical and dental care.

Problems of Jail Inmates Jails are often more difficult to manage than prisons, primarily because of their volatile and diverse inmate populations. According to sociologist John Irwin, the unofficial purpose of jails is to control society's "rabble," or those who are unable to integrate themselves into mainstream society.[73] Certainly, jail inmates have a number of problems, including the following:

Learning Objective

8 Explain the four characteristics of many jail inmates that make the management of jails difficult for sheriffs' departments.

1. *Mental illness.* About 60 percent of jail inmates have a history of mental illness, including symptoms of schizophrenia, depression, hallucinations, and suicidal tendencies.[74]
2. *Physical health problems.* More than one-third of jail inmates report having a current medical problem such as an injury or ailments such as arthritis, asthma, or sexually transmitted diseases.[75] Furthermore, 40 percent have disabilities in areas such as hearing, vision, and cognitive ability.[76]
3. *Substance abuse and dependency.* About two-thirds of jail inmates are dependent on alcohol or other drugs, and half of all convicted jail inmates were under the influence of drugs or alcohol at the time of their arrest.[77]

Given that most jails lack the resources and facilities to properly deal with these problems, the task of managing jail inmate populations falls disproportionately on untrained prison staff. Speaking of mentally ill inmates at Rikers Island, New York City's main jail complex, one corrections official said, "They need medication, treatment, psychological help. They don't need a corrections officer.[78] In response to these challenges, jails in cities

Figure 11.6 Miami-Dade County's Criminal Mental Health Project

On any given day, the Miami-Dade County Jail houses about 1,200 inmates who suffer from a *serious mental illness* (or SMI, which includes schizophrenia, bipolar disorder, and major depression), making it the largest psychiatric facility in the state of Florida. To combat this problem, local criminal justice officials have established the following two strategies to divert nonviolent offenders with an SMI from the jail.

Strategy #1: Pre-Booking Diversion	Strategy #2: Post-Booking Diversion
• Provide local police officers with forty hours of Crisis Intervention Team (CIT) training, which helps them recognize SMI symptoms and de-escalate crises involving offenders with mental illnesses. • When appropriate, offenders suffering from an SMI will be taken to a local psychiatric treatment center rather than being arrested and put in jail.	• All defendants booked into the jail are screened for possible SMI symptoms and, if necessary, referred to the corrections health services psychiatric staff for a more thorough evaluation. • Those defendants who meet the criteria (nonviolent offender convicted of a misdemeanor, SMI diagnosis) are transferred from the jail to a community-based crisis stabilization facility. • With the consent of the defendant, she or he will receive community-based treatment and help in finding housing.

Source: **www.jud11.flcourts.org/scsingle.aspx?pid=285.**

such as Chicago, Miami (see Figure 11.6), New York, and Los Angeles recently have taken dramatic steps to improve living conditions for at-need inmate populations.

The Challenges of Overcrowding Overcrowding exacerbates the difficulties involved in jail management. Cells intended to hold one or two people are packed with up to six. Inmates are forced to sleep in hallways. Treatment facilities, when they exist, are overwhelmed. In such stressful situations, tempers flare, leading to violent, aggressive behavior. The jails most likely to suffer from such issues are those in heavily populated metropolitan areas with large numbers of "pass through" pretrial detainees.[79]

Given the emphasis on reducing prison populations discussed throughout this chapter, there are concerns that jails will be forced to house more low-level offenders in the future than they have in the past. As most jurisdictions do not have the resources to build new jails, administrators will have to come up with creative ways to alleviate possible overcrowding. Two possible solutions involve pretrial procedures we discussed in Chapter 8:

1. Increasing options for pretrial release, and
2. Speeding up trials so that detainees do not need to spend as much time waiting in jail for court proceedings to begin.[80]

Also, community corrections—the subject of the previous chapter—can be useful in reducing jail inmate populations. In 2014, about 63,500 offenders sentenced to jail terms were supervised in the community, with nearly a quarter subjected to electronic monitoring.[81]

New-Generation Jails

For most of the nation's history, the architecture of a jail was secondary to its purpose of keeping inmates safely locked away. Consequently, most jails in the United States continue to resemble those from the days of the Walnut Street Jail in Philadelphia. In this *traditional,* or *linear design*, jail cells are located along a corridor. To supervise the inmates while they are in their cells, custodial officers must walk up and down the corridor, so the number of prisoners they can see at any one time is severely limited. With this limited supervision, inmates can more easily break institutional rules.

new-generation jail A type of jail that is distinguished architecturally from its predecessors by a design that encourages interaction between inmates and jailers and that offers greater opportunities for treatment.

direct supervision approach A process of prison and jail administration in which correctional officers are in continuous visual contact with inmates during the day.

Podular Design In the 1970s, planners at the Bureau of Federal Prisons decided to upgrade the traditional jail design with the goal of improving conditions for both the staff and the inmates. The result was the **new-generation jail**, which differs significantly from its predecessors.[82] The layout of the new facilities makes it easier for the staff to monitor cell-confined inmates. The basic structure of the new-generation jail is based on a podular design. Each "pod" contains "living units" for individual prisoners. These units, instead of lining up along a straight corridor, are often situated in a triangle so that a staff member in the center of the triangle has visual access to nearly all the cells.

Daily activities such as eating and showering take place in the pod, which also has an outdoor exercise area. Treatment facilities are also located in the pod, allowing greater access for the inmates. During the day, inmates stay out in the open and are allowed back in their cells only when given permission. The officer locks the door to the cells from his or her control terminal.

Direct Supervision Approach The podular design also enables a new-generation jail to be managed using a **direct supervision approach**.[83] One or more jail officers are stationed in the living area of the pod and are therefore in constant interaction with all prisoners in that particular pod. Some new-generation jails even provide a

▲ How does the layout of this direct supervision jail differ from that of the maximum-security prison pictured earlier in the chapter? What do these differences tell you about the security precautions needed for jail inmates as opposed to prison inmates? Photo courtesy Bergen County Sheriff's Office, Bergen, NJ desk in the center of the living area, which sends a very different message to the prisoners than the traditional control booth. Theoretically, jail officials who have constant contact with inmates will be able to stem misconduct quickly and efficiently, and will also be able to recognize "danger signs" from individual inmates and stop outbursts before they occur. (As noted earlier in the chapter, corrections officials are using aspects of podular design when building new prisons, for many of the same reasons that the trend has been popular in jails.)

One problem that consistently plagues jails is the inability to live up to the American Correctional Association's requirement that they "operate effectively as self-contained communities in which all necessary goods are provided in a safe, secure and controlled manner."[84] Given the challenges already mentioned in this section, many jails need expensive upgrades to (1) add bed space for increased inmate populations and (2) provide better health and psychiatric care. So, for example, the new Muskegon (Michigan) County Jail, which opened in 2015, has six hundred inmate beds (up from 370 in the old jail) and a "medical triage" center to better determine the health needs of inmates during the intake process.[85]

EthicsChallenge

Local officials recently started charging inmates at the Elko County (Nevada) Jail about $7 a day for their meals, to be paid when the inmate is released. In this section, you learned that many jail inmates are awaiting trial. Is it ethical for the county to require these inmates to pay for meals when they have not yet been found guilty of any crime? Why or why not? What should Elko County do with the meal funds collected from an inmate who is eventually found not guilty?

Summary

For more information on these concepts, look back to the Learning Objective icons throughout the chapter.

1 **Contrast the Pennsylvania and the New York penitentiary theories of the 1800s.** Basically, the Pennsylvania system imposed total silence on its prisoners. Based on the concept of separate confinement, penitentiaries were constructed with back-to-back cells facing both outward and inward. Prisoners worked, slept, and ate alone in their cells. In contrast, New York used the congregate system: silence was imposed, but inmates worked and ate together.

2 **Describe the formal prison management system, and indicate the three most important aspects of prison governance.** A formal system is militaristic with a hierarchical (top-down) chain of command; the warden (or superintendent) is on top, then deputy wardens, and last, custodial employees. Sound governance of a correctional facility requires officials to provide inmates with a sense of order, amenities such as clean living conditions and acceptable food, and services such as vocational training and remedial education programs.

3 **List and briefly explain the four types of prisons.** (a) Maximum-security prisons, which are designed mainly with security and surveillance in mind. Such prisons are usually large and consist of cell blocks, each of which is set off by a series of gates and bars. (b) Medium-security prisons, which offer considerably more educational and treatment programs and allow more contact between inmates. Such prisons are usually surrounded by high fences rather than by walls. (c) Minimum-security prisons, which permit prisoners to have televisions and computers and often allow them to leave the grounds for educational and employment purposes. (d) Supermaximum-security (supermax) prisons, in which prisoners are confined to one-person cells for up to twenty-three hours per day under constant video camera surveillance.

4 **List the factors that have caused the prison population to grow dramatically in the last several decades.** (a) Willingness of prosecutors to charge arrestees with felonies rather than misdemeanors; (b) the enhancement and stricter enforcement of the nation's drug laws; (c) increased probability of incarceration; (d) inmates serving more time for each crime; (e) federal prison growth; and (f) rising incarceration rates for women.

5 **Indicate some of the consequences of our high rates of incarceration.** Some people believe that the reduction in the country's crime rate is a direct result of increased incarceration rates. Others believe that high incarceration rates are having increasingly negative social consequences, such as financial hardships, reduced supervision and discipline of children, and a general deterioration of the family structure when one parent is in prison.

6 **Describe the arguments for and against private prisons.** Proponents of private prisons contend that they can be run more cheaply and efficiently than public ones. Opponents of prison privatization dispute such claims and argue that private prisons are financially motivated to deny inmates the same protections and rights they receive in public correctional facilities.

7 **Summarize the distinctions between jails and prisons, and indicate the importance of jails in the American corrections system.** Generally, a prison is for those convicted of felonies who will serve lengthy periods of incarceration, whereas a jail is for those who have been convicted of misdemeanors and will serve less than a year of incarceration. Jails also hold individuals awaiting trial, juveniles awaiting transfer to juvenile authorities, probation and parole violators, and the mentally ill. In any given year, approximately 11.4 million people are admitted to jails, and therefore jails often provide the best chance for treatment or counseling that may deter future criminal behavior by these low-level offenders.

8 **Explain the four characteristics of many jail inmates that make the management of jails difficult for sheriffs' departments.** More than half of jail inmates suffer from mental illness. Many of these inmates also exhibit a wide range of medical problems and have physical disabilities. In addition, the majority of jail inmates are dependent on alcohol or other drugs.

Questions for Critical Analysis

1. By most measures, the United States imprisons more of its citizens than any other country in the world. Economic considerations aside, what is your opinion of our dramatically high incarceration rates?
2. Following the implementation of Proposition 47 (described earlier in the chapter), California experienced a small increase in the occurrence of auto theft. Why might this be the case? Does this increase in property crime provide a compelling argument against decarceration strategies that require the release of nonviolent offenders from prison and jail? Why or why not?
3. Do you agree with the argument that private prisons are inherently unjust, no matter what costs they may save taxpayers? Why or why not?
4. Why have pretrial detainees been called "walking legal contradictions"? What are the practical reasons why pretrial detainees will continue to be housed in jails prior to trial, regardless of whether their incarceration presents any constitutional irregularities?
5. Experience shows that building new jails does little or nothing to alleviate jail overcrowding. Why might this be the case?

Key Terms

classification 331
congregate system 326
direct supervision approach 345
fee system 343
jail 341
lockdown 333
maximum-security prison 331
medical model 327
medium-security prison 333
minimum-security prison 334
new-generation jail 345
penitentiary 325
pretrial detainees 342
private prisons 338
separate confinement 326
supermax prison 332
time served 342
warden 329

Notes

1. James M. Beattie, *Crime and the Courts in England, 1660–1800* (Princeton, N.J.: Princeton University Press, 1986), 506–507.
2. Samuel Walker, *Popular Justice* (New York: Oxford University Press, 1980), 11.
3. Michael Meranze, *Laboratories of Virtue: Punishment, Revolution, and Authority in Philadelphia, 1760–1835* (Chapel Hill, N.C.: University of North Carolina Press, 1996), 55.
4. Negley K. Teeters, *The Cradle of the Penitentiary: The Walnut Street Jail at Philadelphia, 1773–1835* (Philadelphia: Pennsylvania Prison Society, 1955), 30.
5. Negley K. Teeters and John D. Shearer, *The Prison at Philadelphia's Cherry Hill* (New York: Columbia University Press, 1957), 142–143.
6. Henry Calvin Mohler, "Convict Labor Policies," *Journal of the American Institute of Criminal Law and Criminology* 15 (1925), 556–557.
7. Zebulon Brockway, *Fifty Years of Prison Service* (Montclair, N.J.: Patterson Smith, 1969), 400–401.
8. Robert Martinson, "What Works? Questions and Answers about Prison Reform," *Public Interest* 35 (Spring 1974), 22.
9. See Ted Palmer, "Martinson Revisited," *Journal of Research on Crime and Delinquency* (1975), 133; and Paul Gendreau and Bob Ross, "Effective Correctional Treatment: Bibliotherapy for Cynics," *Crime & Delinquency* 25 (1979), 499.
10. Robert Martinson, "New Findings, New Views: A Note of Caution Regarding Sentencing Reform," *Hofstra Law Review* 7 (1979), 243.
11. Bureau of Justice Statistics, *Census of State and Federal Correctional Facilities, 2005* (Washington, D.C.: U.S. Department of Justice, October 2008), 2.
12. *Ibid.*
13. Charles H. Logan, "Well Kept: Comparing Quality of Confinement in a Public and Private Prison," *Journal of Criminal Law and Criminology* 83 (1992), 580.
14. John J. DiIulio, *Governing Prisons* (New York: Free Press, 1987), 12.
15. *Ibid.*
16. Todd R. Clear, George F. Cole, and Michael D. Reisig, *American Corrections*, 11th ed. (Belmont, Calif.: Wadsworth Cengage Learning, 2016), 157.
17. Douglas Page, "The Prison of the Future," *Law Enforcement Technology* (January 2012), 11–13.
18. Keramet Reiter, *Parole, Snitch, or Die: California's Supermax Prisons and Prisoners, 1987–2007* (Berkeley, Calif.: University of California Institute for the Study of Social Change, 2010), 1.
19. Quoted in David Brooks, "The Prison Problem," *New York Times* (September 29, 2015), A27.
20. Bureau of Justice Statistics, *Prisoners in 2014* (Washington, D.C.: U.S. Department of Justice, September 2015), Appendix table 4, page 30; and Appendix table 5, page 30.
21. Allen J. Beck, "Growth, Change, and Stability in the U.S. Prison Population, 1980–1995," *Corrections Management Quarterly* (Spring 1997), 9–10.
22. U.S. District Courts, "Criminal Defendants Sentenced after Conviction, by Offense, during the 12-Month Period Ending September 30, 2015," at **www.uscourts.gov/statistics/table/d-5/judicial-business/2015/09/30.**
23. Joan Petersilia, "Beyond the Prison Bubble," *Wilson Quarterly* (Winter 2011), 27.
24. *Time Served: The High Cost, Low Return of Longer Prison Terms* (Washington, D.C.: The Pew Center on the States, June 2012), 2.
25. *Fifteen Years of Guidelines Sentencing: An Assessment of How Well the Federal Criminal Justice System Is Achieving the Goals of Sentencing Reform* (Washington, D.C.: U.S. Sentencing Commission, November 2004), 46.
26. *Prisoners in 2014, op. cit.*, 2.
27. Bureau of Justice Statistics, *Prisoners in 2000* (Washington, D.C.: U.S. Department of Justice, August 2001), 1; and *Ibid.*, Table 3, page 5.
28. Julie Samuels, Nancy La Vigne, and Samuel Taxy, *Stemming the Tide: Strategies to Reduce the Growth and Cut the Cost of the Federal*

Prison System (Washington, D.C.: Urban Institute, November 2013), 1.

29. Comprehensive Crime Control Act of 1984, Public Law Number 98-473.

30. *Prisoners* in 2000, *op. cit.*, Table 19, page 12; and *Prisoners in 2014, op. cit.*, Appendix table 5, page 30.

31. Federal Bureau of Prisons, "Inmate Gender" (February 27, 2016), at **www.bop.gov/about/statistics/statistics_inmate_gender.jsp.**

32. *Prisoners in 2014, op. cit.*, Appendix table 5, page 30.

33. Quoted in Jeremy Travis, "Assessing the State of Mass Incarceration: Tipping Point or the New Normal?" *Criminology & Public Policy* (November 2014), 571.

34. Rosemary Gartner, Anthony N. Doob, and Franklin E. Zimring, "The Past as Prologue? Decarceration in California Then and Now," *Criminology & Public Policy* (May 2011), 294–296.

35. "The Right Choices," *The Economist* (June 20, 2015), 26.

36. The Sentencing Project, "Prison Population Trends 1999–2014: Broad Variation among States in Recent Years" (February 16, 2016), at **sentencingproject.org/doc/publications/inc_US_Prison_Population_Trends_1999-2014.pdf.**

37. Quoted in Leon Neyfakh, "Why Are So Many Americans in Prison?" *Slate.com* (February 6, 2015), at **www.slate.com/articles/news_and_politics/crime/2015/02/mass_incarceration_a_provocative_new_theory_for_why_so_many_americans_are.html.**

38. Dan Seligman, "Lock 'Em Up," *Forbes* (May 23, 2005), 216–217.

39. Quoted in Michael S. Schmidt, "U.S. to Begin Freeing 6,000 from Prisons," *New York Times* (October 7, 2015), A1.

40. Mike Males, *Is Proposition 47 to Blame for California's 2015 Increase in Urban Crime?* (San Francisco: Center on Juvenile and Criminal Justice, March 2016).

41. Jim Parsons et al., *End of an Era? The Impact of Drug Law Reform in New York City* (New York; Vera Institute of Justice, January 2015), 18.

42. Bruce Western and Becky Pettit, *Collateral Costs: Incarceration's Effect on Economic Mobility* (Washington, D.C.: The Pew Charitable Trusts, 2010), 4.

43. John Tierney, "Prison and the Poverty Trap," *New York Times* (February 19, 2013), D1.

44. *Rethinking the Blues: How We Police in the U.S. and at What Cost* (Washington, D.C.: Justice Policy Institute, May 2012), 34.

45. *Prisoners in 2014, op. cit.*, Table 5, page 15.

46. Quoted in Fox Butterfield, "Study Finds 2.6% Increase in U.S. Prison Population," *New York Times* (July 28, 2003), A8.

47. Quoted in Scott Cohn, "Private Prison Industry Grows Despite Critics," *cnbc.com* (October 18, 2011), at **www.nbcnews.com/id/44936562/ns/business-cnbc_tv/t/private-prison-industry-grows-despite-critics/#.UW6vC7_zdzU.**

48. Michael Cohen, "How For-Profit Prisons Have Become the Biggest Lobby No One Is Talking About," *Washington Post* (April 28, 2015), at **www.washingtonpost.com/posteverything/wp/2015/04/28/how-for-profit-prisons-have-become-the-biggest-lobby-no-one-is-talking-about/?.**

49. *Prisoners in 2014, op. cit.*, Table 9, page 14.

50. "A Tale of Two Systems: Cost, Quality, and Accountability in Private Prisons," *Harvard Law Review* (May 2002), 1872.

51. Douglas C. McDonald and Kenneth Carlson, *Contracting for Imprisonment in the Federal Prison System: Cost and Performance of the Privately Operated Taft Correctional Institution* (Cambridge, Mass.: Abt Associates, Inc., October 2005), vii.

52. Simon Hakin and Erwin A. Blackstone, *Prison Break: A New Approach to Public Cost and Safety* (Oakland, Calif.: The Independent Institute, June 2014), 4.

53. Jennifer Palmer, "Adding Beds Isn't Enough to Address Oklahoma Prison Overcrowding, Experts Say," *The Oklahoman* (October 25, 2015), at **newsok.com/article/5455820.**

54. Jennifer Sullivan, "Overcrowding to Force State to Export Prisoners to Michigan," *Seattle Times* (June 2, 2015), at **www.seattletimes.com/seattle-news/overcrowding-to-force-state-to-send-prisoners-to-michigan-facility.**

55. Gerald G. Gaes, "The Current Status of Prison Privatization Research on American Prisons" (2012), at **works.bepress.com/gerald_gaes/1/.**

56. "FBI Investigates Company Running 'Gladiator School' Prison," *Associated Press* (March 7, 2014).

57. "Prisoners, Sheriffs Say Abuse Led to Prison Riot in Kingman," *Associated Press* (August 13, 2015).

58. Gregory Geisler, *CIIC: Lake Erie Correctional Institution* (Columbus, Ohio: Correctional Institution Inspection Committee, January 2013), 16.

59. Curtis R. Blakely and Vic W. Bumphus, "Private and Public Sector Prisons," *Federal Probation* (June 2004), 27.

60. John DiIulio, "Prisons, Profits, and the Public Good: The Privatization of Corrections," in *Criminal Justice Center Bulletin* (Huntsville, Tex.: Sam Houston State University, 1986).

61. Richard L. Lippke, "Thinking about Private Prisons," *Criminal Justice Ethics* (Winter/Spring 1997), 32.

62. Quoted in Cohn, *op. cit.*

63. *Prisoners in 2014, op. cit.*, Table 9, page 14.

64. Bethany Carson and Eleana Diaz, "Payoff: How Congress Ensures Private Prison Profit with an Immigrant Detention Quota," *Grassroots Leadership* (April 2015), at **grassrootsleadership.org/reports/payoff-how-congress-ensures-private-prison-profit-immigrant-detention-quota#1.**

65. Bureau of Justice Statistics, *Jail Inmates at Midyear 2014—Statistical Tables* (Washington, D.C.: U.S. Department of Justice, June 2015), 1.

66. Arthur Wallenstein, "Jail Crowding: Bringing the Issue to the Corrections Center Stage," *Corrections Today* (December 1996), 76–81.

67. Quoted in Fox Butterfield, "'Defying Gravity,' Inmate Population Climbs," *New York Times* (January 19, 1998), A10.

68. *Jail Inmates at Midyear 2014—Statistical Tables, op. cit.*, Table 2, page 3.

69. *Ibid.*

70. 441 U.S. 520 (1979).

71. *Jail Inmates at Midyear 2014—Statistical Tables, op. cit.*, 1.

72. Bureau of Justice Statistics, *Census of Jail Facilities, 2006* (Washington, D.C.: U.S. Department of Justice, December 2011), 14.

73. John Irwin, *The Jail: Managing the Underclass in American Society* (Berkeley, Calif.: University of California Press, 1985), 2.

74. Doris J. James and Lauren E. Glaze, *Bureau of Justice Statistics Special Report: Mental Health Problems of Prison and Jail Inmates* (Washington, D.C.: U.S. Department of Justice, September 2006), 1.

75. Laura M. Maruschak, *Bureau of Justice Statistics Special Report: Medical Problems of Jail Inmates* (Washington, D.C.: U.S. Department of Justice, November 2006), 1.

76. Bureau of Justice Statistics, *Disabilities among Prison and Jail Inmates*, 2011–12 (Washington, D.C.: U.S. Department of Justice, December 2015), 1.

77. Jennifer C. Karberg and Doris J. James, *Bureau of Justice Statistics Special Report: Substance Dependence, Abuse, and Treatment of Jail Inmates, 2002* (Washington, D.C.: U.S. Department of Justice, July 2005), 1.

78. Quoted in Michael Schwirtz, "Rikers Island Struggles with a Surge in Violence and Mental Illness," *New York Times* (March 19, 2014), A1.

79. Clear, Cole, and Reisig, *op. cit.*, 183.

80. Mark Cuniff, *Jail Crowding: Understanding Jail Population Dynamics* (Washington, D.C.: National Institute of Corrections, January 2002), 36.

81. *Jail Inmates at Midyear 2014—Statistical Tables, op. cit.*, Table 9, page 9.

82. R. L. Miller, "New Generation Justice Facilities: The Case for Direct Supervision," *Architectural Technology* 12 (1985), 6–7.

83. David Bogard, Virginia A. Hutchinson, and Vicci Persons, *Direct Supervision Jails: The Role of the Administrator* (Washington, D.C.: National Institute of Corrections, February 2010), 1–2.

84. Quoted in Sara Scullin, "Building to a Better Blueprint," *Law Enforcement Technology* (June 2015), 21.

85. *Ibid.*; and Heather L. Peters, "Tour of New Muskegon County Jail Brings Out Hundreds of Curious Citizens," *MLive.com* (August 22, 2015), at **www.mlive.com/news/muskegon/index.ssf/2015/08/hundreds_of_citizens_check_out.html.**

New Punisher/Shutterstock.com

12

The Prison Experience and Prisoner Reentry

Chapter Outline		Corresponding Learning Objectives
Prison Culture	1	Explain the concept of prison as a total institution.
	2	Describe a risk run by corrections officials who fail to provide adequate medical care to the inmates under their control.
Prison Violence	3	Indicate some of the reasons for violent behavior in prisons.
Correctional Officers and Discipline	4	List the circumstances in which courts have found that the "legitimate security interests" of a jail or prison justify the use of force by correctional officers.
	5	Describe the hands-off doctrine of prisoner law and indicate two standards used to determine if prisoners' rights have been violated.
Inside a Women's Prison	6	Explain the aspects of imprisonment that prove challenging for incarcerated mothers and their children.
Return to Society	7	Contrast parole, expiration release, pardon, and furlough.
	8	Explain the goal of prisoner reentry programs.

To target your study and review, look for these numbered Learning Objective icons throughout the chapter.

a history **of Violence**

the Attica Correctional Facility, a maximum-security correctional institution located in a small upstate New York village, is a prison with a past. In September 1971, as part of one of the bloodiest battles between Americans since the Civil War, eleven prison employees and thirty-two prisoners were killed when inmates used group violence to protest harsh living conditions. "Attica has a unique personality, in part because of the riot," says Brian Fischer, who spent thirty-five years working in the New York prison system. "There's a historical negativity . . . that doesn't go away."

George Williams would certainly agree. On the evening of August 9, 2011, Williams was sitting in his cell in Attica, serving a maximum four-year sentence for robbing a pair of Manhattan jewelry stores. Three correctional officers entered, telling Williams that he was about to be subjected to a surprise urine test for drugs. Instead, according to what inmates in nearby cells told investigators, the officers took Williams to an empty room and kicked him at least fifty times and struck him at least a dozen times with wooden batons. As a result, Williams suffered a broken shoulder, several cracked ribs, two broken legs, and severe fractures of the bones surrounding his left eye.

Officially, the staffers claimed that Williams had been armed with a razor blade and an ice pick. Unofficially, it appears the beating was retaliation for Williams having earlier cursed at a prison employee, an act Williams denies. In March 2015, each of the officers pleaded guilty to a misdemeanor charge of misconduct that cost them their jobs but spared them any time behind bars. For his part, with the help of an online fund-raising campaign started by Attica residents that raised $5,800, Williams attended barber school after his release and hoped to open his own shop. Back in Attica, inmates were disappointed that Williams's case did little to change the violent disciplinary measures used against them. "We feel [the state government] doesn't give a damn," explained one prisoner. "Guys say: 'We need a riot. It's the only way to stop it.'"

Philip Scalia/Alamy

▲ The Attica Correctional Facility in upstate New York has experienced violent clashes between correctional officers and inmates at various times throughout its history.

1. During a search of the Attica Correctional Facility shortly after the incident involving George Williams, prison officials found sixty homemade weapons in prison cells. How might this help explain a readiness among correctional officers to use force against inmates?
2. Do you agree with the punishment handed down against the three correctional officers in this case? Why or why not?
3. Under New York law, a person convicted of a crime, such as Williams, can be denied a barber's license if state officials decide the applicant lacks "moral character." What might be some of the goals of this legislation? What is your opinion of it?

Prison Culture

In this chapter, we will look at the life of the imprisoned convict, starting with the realities of an existence behind bars and finishing with the challenges of returning to free society. Along the way, we will discuss violence in prison, correctional officers, women's prisons, different types of release, and several other issues that are at the forefront of American corrections today. To start, we must understand the forces that shape prison culture and how those forces affect the overall operation of the correctional facility.

total institution An institution, such as a prison, that provides all of the necessities for existence to those who live within its boundaries.

Any institution, whether a school, a bank, or a police department, has an organizational culture—a set of values that help the people in the organization understand what actions are acceptable and what actions are unacceptable. According to a theory put forth by the influential sociologist Erving Goffman, prison cultures are unique because prisons are **total institutions** that encompass every aspect of an inmate's life. Unlike a student or a bank teller, a prisoner cannot leave the institution or have any meaningful interaction with outside communities. Others arrange every aspect of daily life, and all prisoners are required to follow this schedule in the same manner.[1]

Learning Objective

1 Explain the concept of prison as a total institution.

Inmates develop their own argot, or language, and ways of expressing themselves through body art (see Figure 12.1). They create their own economy, which, in the absence of currency, is based on the barter of valued commodities such as food, contraband, and sexual favors. They establish methods of determining power, many of which, as we shall see, involve violence. Isolated and heavily regulated, prisoners create a social existence that is, out of both necessity and design, separate from the outside world.

Figure 12.1 Prison Tattoos

Using makeshift needles and ink from contraband pens or melted plastic, many inmates are proficient at the art of tattooing. These tattoos help establish the inmate's place in prison culture by symbolizing concepts such as toughness, racism, or the length of time spent behind bars.

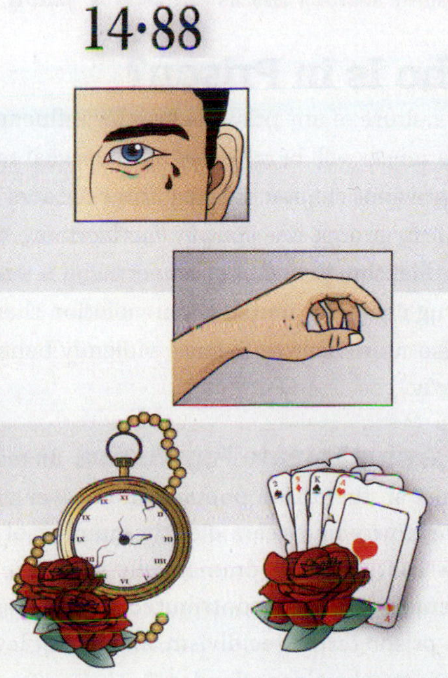

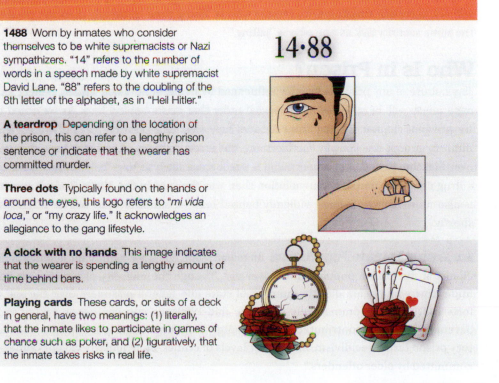

1488 Worn by inmates who consider themselves to be white supremacists or Nazi sympathizers. "14" refers to the number of words in a speech made by white supremacist David Lane. "88" refers to the doubling of the 8th letter of the alphabet, as in "Heil Hitler."

A teardrop Depending on the location of the prison, this can refer to a lengthy prison sentence or indicate that the wearer has committed murder.

Three dots Typically found on the hands or around the eyes, this logo refers to "*mi vida loca*," or "my crazy life." It acknowledges an allegiance to the gang lifestyle.

A clock with no hands This image indicates that the wearer is spending a lengthy amount of time behind bars.

Playing cards These cards, or suits of a deck in general, have two meanings: (1) literally, that the inmate likes to participate in games of chance such as poker, and (2) figuratively, that the inmate takes risks in real life.

Adapting to Prison Society

On arriving at prison, each convict attends an orientation session and receives a "Resident's Handbook." The handbook provides information such as meal and official count times, disciplinary regulations, and visitation guidelines. The norms and values of the prison society, however, cannot be communicated by the staff or learned from a handbook. As first described by Donald Clemmer in his classic 1940 work, *The Prison Community*, the process of **prisonization**—or adaptation to the prison culture—advances as the inmate gradually understands what constitutes acceptable behavior in the institution, as defined not by the prison officials but by other inmates.[2]

In studying prisonization, criminologists have focused on two areas: how prisoners change their behavior to adapt to life behind bars, and how life behind bars has changed because of inmate behavior. Sociologist John Irwin has identified several patterns of inmate conduct, each one driven by the inmate's personality and values:

1. Professional criminals adapt to prison by "doing time." In other words, they follow the rules and generally do whatever is necessary to speed up their release and return to freedom.
2. Some convicts, mostly state-raised youths or those frequently incarcerated in juvenile detention centers, are more comfortable inside prison than outside. These inmates serve time by "jailing," or establishing themselves in the power structure of prison culture.
3. Other inmates take advantage of prison resources such as libraries or drug treatment programs by "gleaning," or working to improve themselves to prepare for a return to society.
4. Finally, "disorganized" criminals exist on the fringes of prison society. These inmates may have mental impairments or low levels of intelligence, and find it impossible to adapt to prison culture on any level.[3]

The process of categorizing prisoners has a theoretical basis, but it serves a practical purpose as well, allowing administrators to reasonably predict how different inmates will act in certain situations. An inmate who is "doing time" generally does not present the same security risk as one who is "jailing."

Who Is in Prison?

The culture of any prison is heavily influenced by its inmates. Their values, beliefs, and experiences will be reflected in the social order that exists behind bars. As we noted in the previous chapter, the past three decades have seen incarceration rates of women and minority groups rise sharply. Furthermore, the arrest patterns of inmates have changed over that time period. A prisoner today is much more likely to have been incarcerated on a drug charge or immigration violation than was the case in the 1980s. Today's inmate is also more likely to behave violently behind bars—a situation that will be addressed shortly.

An Aging Inmate Population

In recent years, the most significant demographic change in the prison population involves age. Though the majority of inmates are still under thirty-four years old, the number of state and federal prisoners over the age of forty has increased dramatically since the mid-1990s, as you can see in Figure 12.2. Several factors have contributed to this upsurge, including longer prison terms, mandatory prison terms, recidivism, and higher levels of crimes—particularly violent crimes—committed by older offenders.[4]

prisonization The socialization process through which a new inmate learns the accepted norms and values of the prison culture.

An Ailing Inmate Population Overall, about half of those incarcerated in the United States (including federal and state prisoners and jail inmates) report having a chronic medical condition such as cancer, high blood pressure, diabetes, or asthma.[5] Furthermore, given the frailties of older inmates, prisons and jails are now holding more people with medical issues than in the past. Poor health is the cause of nine of ten inmate deaths in state prisons, with heart disease and cancer accounting for just over half of these fatalities.[6] Not surprisingly, the mortality rates of inmates fifty-five and older from heart disease and cancer are significantly higher than those of any other age group.[7]

Corrections budgets are straining under the financial pressures caused by the health-care needs of aging inmates. Nationwide, an inmate aged fifty years or older is three times more expensive to incarcerate than a younger prisoner.[8] In Virginia, inmates fifty years or older have average annual medical expenses of about $5,372, compared with an average annual medical expense of $795 for those prisoners under fifty.[9] Given the burden of inmate medical costs, state corrections officials may be tempted to cut such services whenever possible. As the feature *Landmark Cases—Brown v. Plata* shows, however, prisoners have a constitutional right to adequate health care.

Figure 12.2 The Aging Prison Population

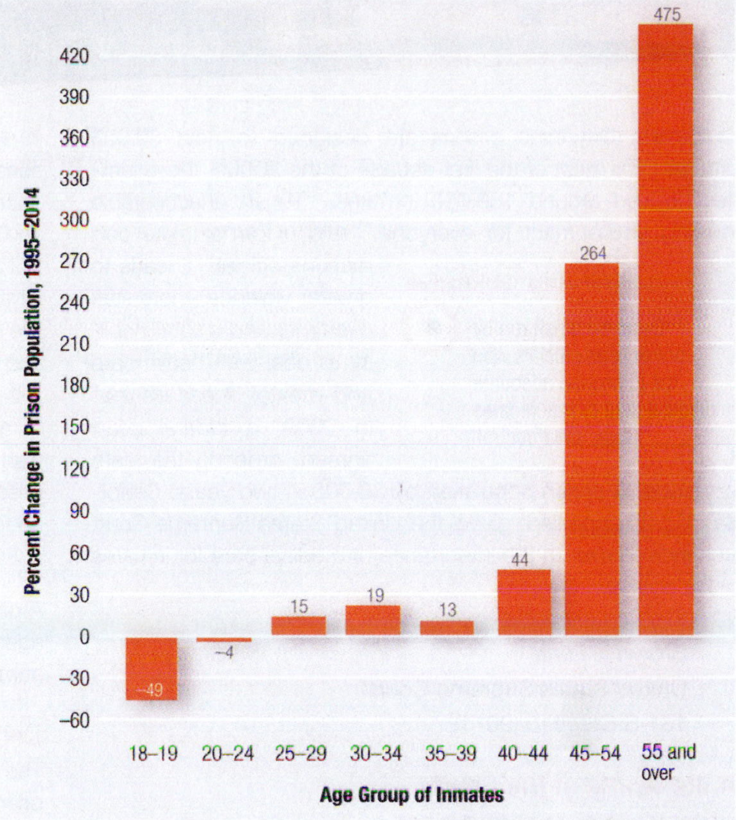

Sources: Bureau of Justice Statistics, *Prisoners in 2003* (Washington, D.C.: U.S. Department of Justice, November 2004), Table 10, page 8; Bureau of Justice Statistics, *Prisoners in 2014* (Washington, D.C.: U.S. Department of Justice, September 2015), Appendix table 3, page 29.

Mental Illness behind Bars As noted in the previous chapter, jails and prisons have also become, in the words of criminal justice experts Katherine Stuart van Wormer and Clemens Bartollas, "the dumping grounds for people whose bizarre behavior lands them behind bars."[10] On any given day, for example, Los Angeles County jails hold 4,000 inmates who have been diagnosed with a mental illness.[11] Nearly 10 percent of all federal inmates receive medications to treat illnesses such as depression and bipolar disorder.[12]

As with aging and ailing prisoners, correctional facilities are required by law to provide treatment to mentally ill inmates, thus driving the costs associated with their confinement well above the average. For reasons that should become clear over the course of this chapter, correctional facilities are not designed to foster mental well-being, and indeed inmates with mental illnesses often find that their problems are exacerbated by the prison environment.[13]

Rehabilitation and Prison Programs

In Chapter 9, we saw that rehabilitation is one of the basic theoretical justifications for punishment. **Prison programs**, which include any organized activities designed to foster rehabilitation, benefit inmates in several ways. On a basic level, these programs get prisoners out of their cells and alleviate the boredom that marks prison and jail life. The programs also help inmates improve their health and skills, giving them a better chance of reintegration into society after release. Consequently, nearly every federal and state prison in the United States offers some form of rehabilitation.[14]

prison programs Organized activities for inmates that are designed to improve their physical and mental health, provide them with vocational skills, or simply keep them busy while incarcerated.

Landmark Cases

Brown v Plata

California's thirty-three prisons are designed to hold 80,000 inmates. For most of the first decade of the 2000s, these facilities housed around 160,000 inmates. "It's an unacceptable working environment for everyone," said a former state corrections official. "It leads to greater violence, more staff overtime, and a total inability to deal with health care and mental illness issues." In 2009, a federal court agreed, ordering the state to reduce its prison population by 30,000 in two years. California officials appealed, giving the United States Supreme Court a chance to rule on the importance of medical care for inmates in this country.

Learning Objective 2
Describe a risk run by corrections officials who fail to provide adequate medical care to the inmates under their control.

Brown v. Plata
United States Supreme Court
131 S.Ct. 1910 (2011)

In the Words of the Court . . .

Justice Kennedy, Majority Opinion

* * * *

For years the medical and mental health care provided by California's prisons has fallen short of minimum constitutional requirements and has failed to meet prisoners' basic health needs. Needless suffering and death have been the well documented result.

* * * *

Prisoners are crammed into spaces neither designed nor intended to house inmates. As many as 200 prisoners may live in a gymnasium, monitored by as few as two or three correctional officers. * * * The consequences of overcrowding include "increased, substantial risk for transmission of infectious illness" and a suicide rate "approaching an average of one per week." * * * A correctional officer testified that, in one prison, up to 50 sick inmates may be held together in a 12- by 20-foot cage for up to five hours awaiting treatment. The number of staff is inadequate, and prisoners face significant delays in access to care. A prisoner with severe abdominal pain died after a 5-week delay in referral to a specialist; a prisoner with "constant and extreme" chest pain died after an 8-hour delay in evaluation by a doctor; and a prisoner died of testicular cancer after a "failure of MDs to work up for cancer in a young man with 17 months of testicular pain."

* * * *

A prison that deprives prisoners of basic sustenance, including adequate medical care, is incompatible with the concept of human dignity and has no place in civilized society.

Decision

The Court found that severe overcrowding in California state prisons denied inmates satisfactory levels of mental and physical health care and therefore amounted to unconstitutional cruel and unusual punishment. It ordered the state to reduce the prison population to 137.5 percent of capacity—about 110,000 inmates—by June 2013. (As of April 2016, California's prison population stood at nearly 123,000.)

For Critical Analysis

In his dissent, Justice Alito wrote, "I fear that today's decision will lead to a grim roster of victims." What might be some of the reasons behind this fear? What steps could California corrections officials take to alleviate Alito's worries?

The primary goal of rehabilitation programs, from an administrative standpoint, is to reduce recidivism. Research demonstrates that offenders who earn a college education behind bars are more likely to find employment after release and therefore are less likely to be rearrested.[15] Prison drug treatment programs can also be beneficial, reducing the probability of relapse in the "real world."[16] Given their budget constraints, however, prison systems are often forced to limit their vocational, educational, and treatment programs. Many inmates suffering from mental illness would benefit from medication and twenty-four-hour psychiatric care. Yet these services are often unavailable behind bars, mostly due to their high costs.[17]

Ethics Challenge

Do you feel that corrections officials are ethically obligated to provide all necessary health care to inmates? Consider the case of Prisoner X, who is serving life in prison for murder. He has fallen ill, and only a $1 million heart transplant will save his life. Should taxpayers pay for the heart transplant? Should Prisoner X receive the transplant instead of other, law-abiding citizens who also need a new heart? Explain your answers.

deprivation model A theory that inmate aggression is the result of the frustration inmates feel at being deprived of freedom, consumer goods, sex, and other staples of life outside the institution.

Prison Violence

Prisons and jails are dangerous places to live. Prison culture is predicated on violence—one observer calls the modern institution an "unstable and violent jungle."[18] Correctional officers use the threat of violence (and, at times, actual violence) to control the inmate population. Sometimes, the inmates strike back. In 2011, the year of the incident involving George Williams described in the chapter opening, there were 563 inmate assaults on New York state prison employees. In 2014, that number rose to 747.[19]

Among prisoners, violence is often used to establish power and dominance. On occasion, this violence leads to death. About eighty inmates in state prisons and twenty inmates in local jails are murdered by fellow inmates each year.[20] (Note, though, that this homicide rate is lower than the national average.) With nothing but time on their hands, prisoners have been known to fashion deadly weapons out of everyday items such as toothbrushes and mop handles. Many inmates also bring the "code of the street," with its fixation on "respect, toughness, and retribution," into prison, making them likely both to engage in violent acts behind bars and to be victims of such violence.[21]

Violence in Prison Culture

Learning Objective

3 Indicate some of the reasons for violent behavior in prisons.

Violence behind bars is primarily used to establish the prisoner hierarchy by separating the powerful from the weak. For example, inmates subjected to sexual assault are often near the bottom of the prison power structure and, in some instances, may accept rape by one particularly powerful inmate in return for protection from others.[22] According to the federal government, about 4 percent of state and federal prisoners report being victims of sexual assault, with a prison staff member slightly more likely to be the perpetrator than another inmate.[23]

Humboldt State University's Lee H. Bowker has identified several other reasons for violent behavior:

- It provides a deterrent against being victimized, as a reputation for violence may eliminate an inmate as a target of assault.
- It enhances self-image in an environment that does not respect other attributes, such as intelligence.
- In the case of rape, it gives sexual relief.
- It serves as a means of acquiring material goods through extortion or outright robbery.[24]

The **deprivation model** also can be used to explain the high level of prison violence. According to this model, the stressful and oppressive conditions of prison life, including a lack of basic human comforts such as freedom, entertainment, and companionship, lead to aggressive behavior on the part of inmates. Prison researcher Stephen C. Light found that when conditions such as overcrowding worsen, inmate misconduct often increases.[25] In these circumstances, the violent behavior may not have any express purpose. That is, it may just be a means of relieving tension.

▼ A correctional official displays a set of homemade knives, also known as *shivs,* made by inmates at Attica Correctional Facility in Attica, New York. **What are some of the reasons that violence flourishes behind bars?** AP Images/David Duprey

Prison Riots Researchers use a variation of the deprivation model to explain prison *riots*, or the outbreak of group violence behind bars. The concept of **relative deprivation** focuses on the gap between what is expected in a certain situation and what is achieved. Criminologist Peter C. Kratcoski has argued that because prisoners enjoy such meager privileges to begin with, any further deprivation can spark disorder.[26] A number of prison experts have noted that collective violence occurs in response to heightened measures of security at corrections facilities.[27] Thus, the violence is primarily a reaction to additional reductions in freedom for inmates, who enjoy very little freedom to begin with.

Riots, which have been defined as situations in which a number of prisoners are beyond institutional control for a significant amount of time, are relatively rare. These incidents are marked by extreme levels of inmate-on-inmate violence and can often be attributed, at least in part, to poor living conditions and inadequate prison administration. For example, a riot at the Adams County Correctional Center in Natchez, Mississippi, that left one correctional officer dead and twenty others injured was sparked by inmate protests over poor food and lack of medical care. Afterward, a prisoner said, "The guard that died yesterday was a sad tragedy, but the situation is simple: if you treat a human as an animal for over two years, the response will be as an animal."[28]

Issues of Race and Ethnicity As prison populations have changed over the past three decades, with African Americans and Hispanics becoming the majority in many penal institutions, issues of race and ethnicity have become increasingly important to prison administrators and researchers. These characteristics play a major role in prison life, and prison violence is often an outlet for racial and ethnic tension. Leo Carroll, professor of sociology at the University of Rhode Island, has written extensively about how today's prisoners are divided into hostile groups, with race determining nearly every aspect of an inmate's life, including friends, job assignments, and cell location.[29]

More than four decades ago, the United States Supreme Court put an end to the widespread practice of **prison segregation**, under which correctional officials would place inmates in cells or blocks with those of a similar race or ethnicity.[30] According to the Supreme Court, prison segregation was unconstitutional because government officials were discriminating against individuals based on their skin color.

Years after this ruling, however, the California Department of Corrections began implementing an unwritten policy of putting all new and transferred male inmates in cells with inmates of the same race or ethnicity for the first sixty days of incarceration. The goal of this policy was to determine if an inmate was a member of a race-based gang before allowing him to live in integrated quarters. In 2005, the Supreme Court struck down California's version of prison segregation.[31] The Court did, however, leave prison officials with an "out": they can still segregate prisoners in an "emergency situation."[32]

Prison Gangs and Security Threat Groups (STGs)

In 2014, in response to legal action, the California Department of Corrections agreed to refrain from segregating inmates by race, even during an "emergency situation."[33] The lawsuit was brought by inmates claiming that state corrections officials unfairly used race to determine which of them was involved in *prison gang* activity. In reality, corrections officials routinely rely on racial and ethnic identification as a shortcut to identify members of **prison gangs**, or cliques of inmates who join together in an organizational structure to engage in illegal activity. Gang affiliation is often the cause of inmate-on-inmate violence.

relative deprivation The theory that inmate aggression is created when freedoms and services that the inmate has come to accept as normal are decreased or eliminated.

prison segregation The practice of separating inmates based on a certain characteristic, such as ethnicity or race.

prison gang A group of inmates who band together within the corrections system to engage in social and criminal activities.

For decades, the California prison system has been plagued by feuds involving various gangs such as the Mexican Mafia, composed of U.S.-born inmates of Mexican descent; their enemies, a spin-off organization called La Nuestra Familia; the Black Guerilla Family; and the Aryan Brotherhood.

In part, the prison gang is a natural result of life in the modern prison. As one expert says of these gangs:

> Their members have done in prison what many people do elsewhere when they feel personally powerless, threatened, and vulnerable. They align themselves with others, organize to fight back, and enhance their own status and control through their connection to a more powerful group.[34]

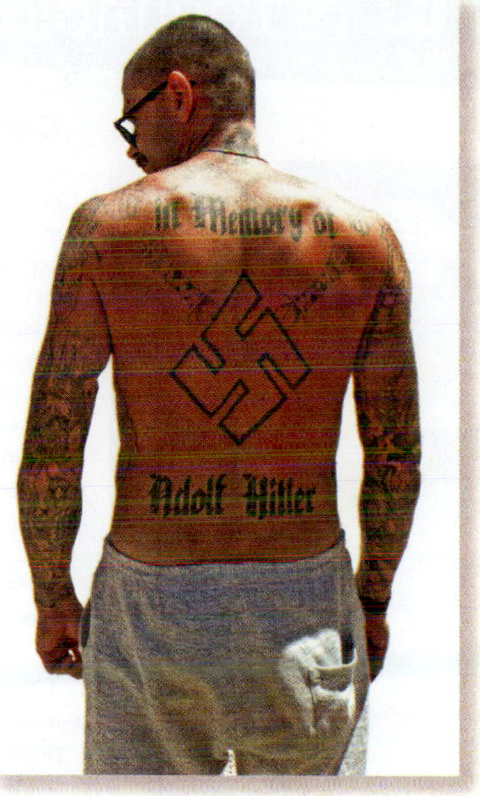

▲ A member of the Aryan Brotherhood in California's Calipatria State Prison. This particular prison gang espouses white supremacy, but for the most part its leadership focuses on illegal activities such as extortion and drug trafficking. **Why might an inmate join a prison gang?**

Mark Allen Johnson/Zumapress/Newscom

In addition to their important role in the social structure of correctional facilities, prison gangs participate in a wide range of illegal economic activities within these institutions, including prostitution, drug selling, gambling, and loan sharking. A study released in 2011 by Alan J. Drury and Matt DeLisi of Iowa State University found that gang members were more likely to be involved in prison misconduct than those inmates who had been convicted of murder.[35]

The Prevalence of Prison Gangs There is little question that the nation's correctional institutions are hotbeds of gang activity. The most recent research conducted by the National Gang Crime Research Center places the rate of gang members in state prisons and local jails at 30 percent of male inmates and 9 percent of female inmates. In the same survey, 87 percent of corrections officials answered "yes" to the question, "Do you believe that some inmates may have voluntarily joined or may have been recruited into a gang while incarcerated?"[36]

In many instances, prison gangs are extensions of street gangs. In fact, with the help of corrupt correctional officers and using contraband cell phones, gang members "at sea" (behind bars) often are able to coordinate criminal activities with gang members "on land" (on the streets). This relationship can serve a mixture of practical and economic motivations. Those gang members incarcerated with lengthy sentences will offer protection to other gang members serving shorter terms. On release, the latter will provide financial support to the families of their still-incarcerated counterparts.[37]

Combating Prison Gangs In their efforts to combat the influence of prison gangs, correctional officials have increasingly turned to the **security threat group (STG)** model for guidance. Generally speaking, an STG is an identifiable group with three or more individuals and a leadership structure that poses a threat to the safety of other inmates or members of the corrections community. About two-thirds of all prisons have a correctional officer who acts as an STG coordinator.[38] This official is responsible for the classification of individuals who are likely to be involved in STG (though not necessarily prison gang) activity and for taking measures to protect the prison community from these individuals.

In many instances, these measures are punitive. Prison officials, for example, have reduced overall levels of violence significantly by putting gang members in solitary confinement, away from the general prison population. Other punitive measures include restrictions on privileges such as family visits and prison program participation, as well as delays of parole eligibility.[39] Treatment philosophies also have a place in these strategies. New York prison administrators have increased group therapy and anger-management classes for STGs, a decision they credit for low murder rates in their state prisons.[40]

security threat group (STG)
A group of three or more inmates who engage in activity that poses a threat to the safety of other inmates or the prison staff.

CJ & Technology

Contraband Cell Phones

AP Photo/Mel Evans

One piece of technology has made the task of controlling prison gangs extremely difficult: the cell phone. Although inmates are prohibited from possessing these devices, cell phones are routinely used to arrange attacks, plan escapes, and operate illegal money-making schemes from behind bars. The phones are usually smuggled in by visitors, who hide them in locations as varied as babies' diapers, food packages, soda cans, and body cavities. Each year, Florida corrections staff confiscate more than 4,000 cell phones from prisoners and, as one state official points out, "We know that's not all of them."

Several years ago, forty-four inmates and correctional officers at the Baltimore City Detention Center were arrested for helping to operate the Black Guerrilla Family gang from within the prison using cell phones. In response, the state of Maryland started a managed access program to deal with the problem. This "cellular umbrella" antenna technology is designed to analyze all calls made from the prison and instantly block any that originate from a contraband phone. Between 2010 and 2015, authorities at the Mississippi State Penitentiary in Parchman estimate that their managed access system, while not 100 percent effective, captured more than six million illicit transmissions.

Thinking about Contraband Cell Phones

It would be much easier—and cheaper—for corrections officials to combat contraband cell phones by disrupting *all* cell phone activity in a prison or jail. However, this practice—called "jamming"—is illegal under federal law. What do you think is the reasoning behind this blanket prohibition of "jamming"?

Correctional Officers and Discipline

Ideally, the presence of correctional officers—the standard term used to describe prison guards—has the effect of lessening violence in American correctional institutions. Practically speaking, this is indeed the case. Without correctional officers, the prison would be a place of anarchy. But in the highly regulated, oppressive environment of the prison, correctional officers must use the threat of violence, if not actual violence, to instill discipline and keep order. Thus, the relationship between prison staff and inmates is marked by mutual distrust. Consider the two following statements, the first made by a correctional officer and the second by a prisoner:

> [My job is to] protect, feed, and try to educate scum who raped and brutalized women and children . . . who, if I turn my back, will go into their cell, wrap a blanket around their cellmate's legs, and threaten to beat or rape him if he doesn't give sex, carry contraband, or fork over radios, money, or other goods willingly. And they'll stick a shank in me tomorrow if they think they can get away with it.[41]

> The pigs in the state and federal prisons . . . treat me so violently, I cannot possibly imagine a time I could ever have anything but the deepest, aching, searing hatred for them. I can't begin to tell you what they do to me. If I were weaker by a hair, they would destroy me.[42]

It may be difficult for an outsider to understand the emotions that fuel such sentiments. French philosopher Michel Foucault points out that discipline, both in prison and in the general community, is a means of social organization as well as punishment.[43] Discipline is imposed when a person behaves in a manner that is contrary to the values of the dominant social group. Correctional officers and inmates have different concepts of the ideal structure of prison society, and, as the two quotations just cited demonstrate, this conflict generates intense feelings of fear and hatred, which often lead to violence.

Prison Employment

Despite negative coverage of the profession that comes with controversies such as the one involving the Attica Correctional Facility discussed at the beginning of the chapter, there are numerous benefits to a career as a correctional officer. Because the position is a civil service (government) job, it offers steady benefits and employment security. In some states, such as California and New York, salaries can reach $70,000. Furthermore, because of a professionalism movement in hiring, the standards of correctional officers have risen dramatically in the past few decades.[44]

Getting Linked in™

Hundreds of correctional facilities across the United States are posting job advertisements for **correctional officers** at any given time. To better understand the wide variety of opportunities in this profession, enter the term "correctional officer" into LinkedIn's search engine.

Becoming a Correctional Officer Most prospective correctional officers are required to pass the civil service exam in their state of employment. Furthermore, as with police cadets (see Chapter 4), correctional officers usually go through a military-style training program prior to deployment in a prison. This program incorporates classwork and physical training, including instruction in areas such as self-defense, inmate control, and protection against communicable disease. Like police cadets, correctional officer trainees also go through a period of supervision with an experienced co-worker, in which they learn not only the job's specific techniques and procedures, but also about the prison environment and subculture.[45]

Rank and Duties The custodial staff at most prisons is organized according to four general ranks—captain, lieutenant, sergeant, and officer. In keeping with the militaristic model, captains are primarily administrators who deal directly with the warden on custodial issues. Lieutenants are the disciplinarians of the prison, responsible for policing and transporting the inmates. Sergeants oversee platoons of officers in specific parts of the prison, such as various cell blocks or work spaces.

Lucien X. Lombardo, professor of sociology and criminal justice at Old Dominion University, has identified six general job categories among correctional officers:[46]

1. *Block officers.* These employees supervise cell blocks containing as many as four hundred inmates, as well as the correctional officers on block guard duty. In general, the block officer is responsible for the well-being of the inmates. He or she tries to ensure that the inmates do not harm themselves or other prisoners and also acts as something of a camp counselor, dispensing advice and seeing that inmates understand and follow the rules of the facility.
2. *Work detail supervisors.* In many penal institutions, the inmates work in the cafeteria, the prison store, the laundry, and other areas. Work detail supervisors oversee small groups of inmates as they perform their tasks.
3. *Industrial shop and school officers.* These officers perform maintenance and security functions in workshop and educational programs. Their primary responsibility is to make sure that inmates are on time for these programs and do not cause any disturbances during the sessions.
4. *Yard officers.* Officers who work the prison yard usually have the least seniority, befitting the assignment's reputation as dangerous and stressful. These officers must be constantly on alert for breaches in prison discipline or regulations in the relatively unstructured environment of the prison yard.
5. *Tower guards.* These officers spend their entire shifts, which usually last eight hours, in isolated, silent posts high above the grounds of the facility. Although

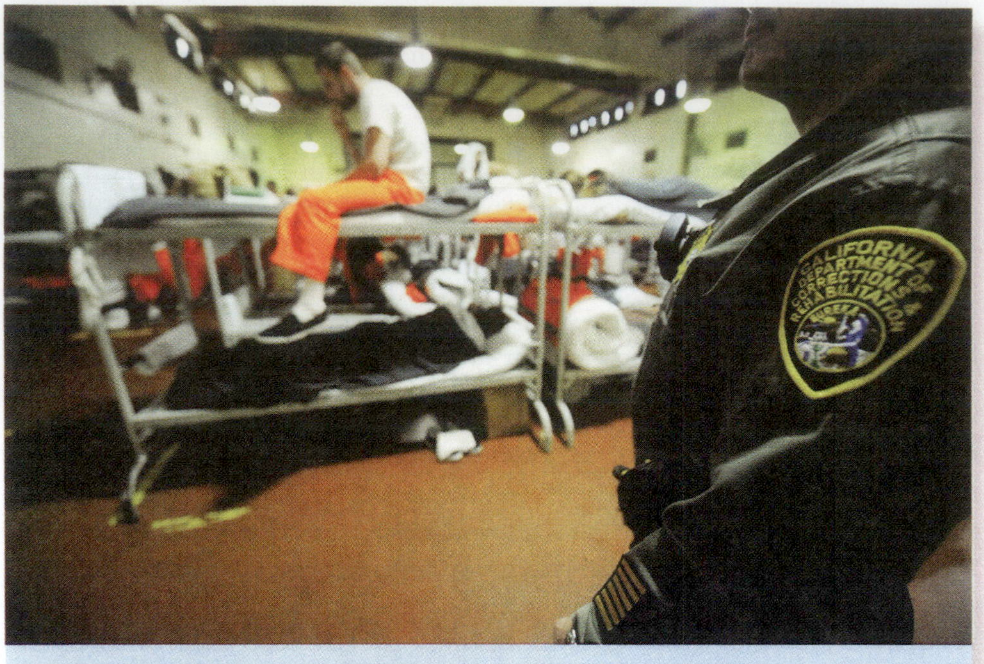

▲ A number of California correctional facilities, including Chino State Prison (pictured here), suffer from chronic overcrowding. How does overcrowding make it more difficult for correctional officers to "keep the peace" in a prison or jail? Kevork Djansezian/Getty Images

their only means of communication are walkie-talkies or cellular devices, the safety benefits of the position can outweigh the loneliness that comes with the job.

6. *Administrative building assignments.* Officers who hold these positions provide security at prison gates, oversee visitation procedures, act as liaisons for civilians, and handle administrative tasks such as processing the paperwork when an inmate is transferred from another institution.

Discipline

Inmate discipline policies have three general goals:

1. To ensure a safe and orderly living environment,
2. To instill respect for authority of correctional officers and administrators, and
3. To teach values and respectful behavior that influence the inmate's attitude when she or he is released from prison.[47]

As Erving Goffman noted in his essay on the "total institution," in the general society adults are rarely placed in a position where they are "punished" as a child would be.[48] Therefore, the strict disciplinary measures imposed on prisoners come as something of a shock and can provoke strong defensive reactions. Correctional officers who must deal with these responses often find that disciplining inmates is the most difficult and stressful aspect of their job.

Sanctioning Prisoners As mentioned earlier, one of the first things that an inmate receives on entering a correctional facility is a manual that details the rules of the prison or jail, along with the punishment that will result from rule violations. These handbooks can be quite lengthy—running one hundred pages in some instances—and specific. Not only will a prison manual prohibit obvious misconduct such as violent or sexual activity, gambling, and possession of drugs or currency, but it also addresses matters of daily life such as personal hygiene, dress codes, and conduct during meals.

Correctional officers enforce the prison rules in much the same way that a highway patrol officer enforces traffic regulations. For a minor violation, the inmate may be "let off easy" with a verbal warning. More serious infractions will result in a "ticket," or a report forwarded to the institution's disciplinary committee. The disciplinary committee generally includes several correctional officers and, in some instances, outside citizens or even inmates. Although, as we shall see, the United States Supreme Court has ruled that an inmate must be given a "fair hearing" before being disciplined, the Court denied inmates the ability to confront adverse witnesses or access to a lawyer during these hearings.[49]

In practice, then, an inmate has very little ability to challenge the committee's decision. Depending on the seriousness of the violation, sanctions can range from a loss of privileges such as visits from family members to the unpleasantness of solitary confinement, discussed in the previous chapter. Most correctional officers prefer to rely on the "you scratch my back and I'll scratch yours" model for controlling inmates. In other words, as long as the prisoner makes a reasonable effort to conform to institutional rules, the correctional officer will refrain from taking disciplinary steps. (To learn more about the potential hazards for correctional officers in dealing with inmates, see the feature *Discretion in Action—"Downing a Duck."*)

Discretion in ACTION

Downing a Duck

Rachel Donahue/Shutterstock.com

The Situation You have just been hired as a correctional officer at a maximum-security prison. Most of the inmates at the facility are violent criminals serving lengthy sentences. During your first week, the inmates in your cell block do a poor job keeping their living quarters clean, causing you to get a negative performance review and a tongue-lashing from your supervisor. An inmate named Rick consoles you, and promises that he will use his influence to ensure that the other inmates "make you look good." He does so. Later, you are threatened by two inmates who vow to "get" you. Rick steps in and defuses the situation. You are grateful, and begin to look at Rick as something of a friend. When another inmate dies of a heart attack, Rick comes to you and asks for a favor. He and the other inmates have taken up a collection for the inmate's widow, and he wants you to deliver the money, with a sympathy card, to her on the outside.

The Law Prison regulations strictly prohibit inmates from possessing any form of money or currency. State law prohibits correctional officers from transporting any contraband outside the prison.

What Would You Do? Clearly, you are legally required not only to refuse Rick's request, but also to report him and the other inmates for possession of cash. You also remember advice from a colleague, who warned that inmates are skilled at manipulating inexperienced correctional officers, a strategy called "downing a duck." At the same time, Rick has made your job much easier and it is possible that he saved your life. While Rick's request may technically be against the rules, he is hardly asking you to do something immoral or unethical. How do you respond?

To see how prison employees in upstate New York reacted to friendly overtures from a pair of inmates, go to Example 12.1 in Appendix B.

Use of Force Generally, courts have been unwilling to put too many restrictions on the use of force by correctional officers. As we saw with police officers in Chapter 5, correctional officers are given great leeway to use their experience to determine when force is warranted. In *Whitley v. Albers* (1986),[50] the Supreme Court held that the use of force by prison officials violates an inmate's Eighth Amendment protections only if the force amounts to "the unnecessary and wanton infliction of pain." Excessive force can be considered "necessary" if the legitimate security interests of the penal institution are at stake. Consequently, an appeals court ruled that when officers at a Maryland prison formed an "extraction team" to remove the leader of a riot from his cell, beating him in the process, the use of force was justified given the situation.[51]

Legitimate Security Interests Courts have found that the "legitimate security interests" of a prison or jail justify the use of force when the correctional officer is:

Learning Objective 4

List the circumstances in which courts have found that the "legitimate security interests" of a jail or prison justify the use of force by correctional officers.

1. Acting in self-defense.
2. Acting to defend the safety of a third person, such as a member of the prison staff or another inmate.
3. Upholding the rules of the institution.
4. Preventing a crime such as assault, destruction of property, or theft.
5. Preventing an escape effort.[52]

In addition, most prisons and jails have written policies that spell out the situations in which their employees may use force against inmates.

The "Malicious and Sadistic" Standard The judicial system has not, however, given correctional officers total freedom of discretion to apply force. In *Hudson v. McMillan* (1992),[53] the Supreme Court ruled that minor injuries suffered by a convict at the hands of a correctional officer following an argument did violate the inmate's rights, because there was no security concern at the time of the incident. In other words, the issue is not *how much* force was used, but whether the officer used the force as part of a good faith effort to restore discipline or acted "maliciously and sadistically" to cause harm.

Furthermore, correctional officers are subject to being sued for violating the *civil rights* of inmates by depriving them of their constitutional rights.[54] In 2015, the Supreme Court made it more likely that such civil lawsuits against correctional officers would succeed. The case involved the use, by Wisconsin jail officials, of a stun gun on an inmate who was handcuffed and removed from his cell for refusing to take off a piece of paper covering a light fixture. The Court held that, to succeed in his suit, the inmate did not need to show that the correctional officers were *aware* that their use of force was unjustified under the circumstances. Instead, the inmate need only prove that the use of force was "objectively unreasonable," a much easier standard to meet.[55]

Female Correctional Officers

Security concerns were the main reason that, for many years, prison administrators refused to hire women as correctional officers in men's prisons. The consensus was that women were not physically strong enough to subdue violent male inmates and that their mere presence in the predominantly masculine prison world would cause disciplinary breakdowns.[56] As a result, in the 1970s a number of women brought lawsuits against state corrections systems, claiming that they were being discriminated against on the basis of their gender. For the most part, these legal actions were successful in opening the doors to men's prisons for female correctional officers (and vice versa).[57]

Today, more than 150,000 women work in correctional facilities, many of them in constant close contact with male inmates.[58]

As it turns out, female correctional officers have proved just as effective as their male counterparts in maintaining discipline in men's prisons. Furthermore, evidence shows that women prison staff can have a calming influence on male inmates, thus lowering levels of prison violence.[59] The primary problem caused by women working in male prisons, it seems, involves sexual misconduct. According to the federal government, nearly 55 percent of prison staff members who engage in sexual misconduct are female, with 84 percent of those sexual encounters considered consensual.[60] As we will see in the next section, similar issues exist between male correctional officers and female inmates, though in those cases the sexual contact is much more likely to be coerced.

▲ Women make up a small—if not tiny—percentage of the security staff at most jails in the United States, including the Baltimore County (Maryland) Detention Center shown here. What are some of the challenges that face female correctional officers in men's prisons and jails? Baltimore Sun/Getty Images

Protecting Prisoners' Rights

The general attitude of the law toward inmates is summed up by the Thirteenth Amendment to the U.S. Constitution:

> Neither slavery nor involuntary servitude, except as a punishment for crime whereof the party shall have been duly convicted, shall exist within the United States.

In other words, inmates do not have the same guaranteed rights as other Americans. For most of the nation's history, courts have followed the spirit of this amendment by applying the **"hands-off" doctrine** of prisoner law. This (unwritten) doctrine assumes that the care of inmates should be left to prison officials and that it is not the place of judges to intervene in penal administrative matters.

Learning Objective

5 Describe the hands-off doctrine of prisoner law and indicate two standards used to determine if prisoners' rights have been violated.

At the same time, the United States Supreme Court has stated that "[t]here is no iron curtain between the Constitution and the prisons of this country."[61] Consequently, like so many other areas of the criminal justice system, the treatment of prisoners is based on a balancing act—here, between the rights of prisoners and the security needs of the correctional institutions. Of course, as just noted, inmates do not have the same civil rights as do other members of society. In 1984, for example, the Supreme Court ruled that arbitrary searches of prison cells are allowed under the Fourth Amendment because inmates have no reasonable expectation of privacy.[62] (See Chapter 6 for a review of this expectation.)

The "Deliberate Indifference" Standard As for those constitutional rights that inmates do retain, in 1976 the Supreme Court established the **"deliberate indifference"** standard. In the case in question, *Estelle v. Gamble*,[63] an inmate had claimed to be the victim of medical malpractice. In his majority opinion, Justice Thurgood Marshall wrote that prison officials violated a convict's Eighth Amendment rights if they "deliberately" failed to provide him or her with necessary medical care. At the time, the decision was hailed as a victory for prisoners' rights, and it continues to ensure that a certain level of health care is provided. Several years ago, for example, a U.S. district court ruled that prison officials at the Louisiana State Penitentiary were "deliberately

"hands-off" doctrine The unwritten judicial policy that favors noninterference by the courts in the administration of prisons and jails.

"deliberate indifference" The standard for establishing a violation of an inmate's Eighth Amendment rights, requiring that prison officials were aware of harmful conditions in a correctional institution *and* failed to take steps to remedy those conditions.

"identifiable human needs" The basic human necessities that correctional facilities are required by the Constitution to provide to inmates.

indifferent" by allowing the heat in that facility's death row to reach levels causing "cruel and unusual" punishment.[64]

In general, however, courts have found it difficult to define "deliberate" in this context. Does it mean that prison officials "should have known" that an inmate was placed in harm's way, or does it mean that officials purposefully placed the inmate in that position?

The Supreme Court seems to have taken the latter position. In *Wilson v. Seiter* (1991),[65] for example, inmate Pearly L. Wilson filed a lawsuit alleging that certain conditions of his confinement—including overcrowding; excessive noise; inadequate heating, cooling, and ventilation; and unsanitary bathroom and dining facilities—were cruel and unusual. The Court ruled against Wilson, stating that he had failed to prove that these conditions, even if they existed, were the result of "deliberate indifference" on the part of prison officials.

"Identifiable Human Needs" In its *Wilson* decision, the Supreme Court created the **"identifiable human needs"** standard for determining Eighth Amendment violations. The Court asserted that a prisoner must show that the institution has denied her or him a basic need such as food, warmth, or exercise.[66] The Court mentioned only these three needs, however, forcing the lower courts to determine for themselves what other needs, if any, fall into this category.

Because of the Supreme Court's *Estelle* decision described above, prisoners do have a well-established right to "adequate" medical care. "Adequate" has been interpreted to mean a level of care comparable to what the inmate would receive if he or she were not behind bars.[67] So, for example, in 2015 California agreed to provide sex reassignment surgery for transgender inmate Shiloh Quine, who is serving a life sentence without parole for murder. The state's medical expert had ruled that the procedure was necessary to "alleviate severe pain caused by her gender dysphoria."[68] Furthermore, as noted earlier in the chapter, several years ago the Supreme Court asserted, controversially, that the overcrowding of California's state prisons was so severe that it denied inmates satisfactory levels of health care.[69]

CJ Policy—Your Take

In 2015, the United States Supreme Court ruled that the state of Arkansas violated an inmate's **First Amendment rights** by refusing him the ability to grow a half-inch beard as required by his Muslim faith. Arkansas prison officials had argued that the policy was necessary because such beards could be used to hide drugs or razor blades. **Do you agree with the Court's decision? Should inmates be allowed to grow beards of *any* length for religious reasons, or would lengthy facial hair pose an obvious security risk? Explain your answers.**

The First Amendment in Prison The First Amendment reads, in part, that the federal government "shall make no law respecting an establishment of religion, or prohibiting the free exercise thereof; or abridging the freedom of speech." In the 1970s, the prisoners' rights movement forced open the "iron curtain" to allow the First Amendment behind bars. In 1974, for example, the Supreme Court held that prison officials can censor inmate mail only if doing so is necessary to maintain prison security.[70] The decade also saw court decisions protecting inmates' access to group worship, instruction by clergy, special dietary requirements, religious publications, and other aspects of both mainstream and nonmainstream religions.[71]

Judges will limit some such protections when an obvious security interest is at stake. In 2010, for example, a Pennsylvania prison was allowed to continue banning religious headscarves because of legitimate concerns that the scarves could be used to conceal drugs or strangle someone.[72] Such was not the case in 2015, however, when a federal judge ruled that jail inmates in Chicago have a First Amendment right to read newspapers. The Cook County sheriff's department had banned these items in city jails over concerns that they could be used to fashion paper-mache weapons, fuel fires, and clog toilets.[73] (This chapter's *CJ Policy—Your Take* examines the First Amendment issues raised by religion and inmate facial hair.)

EthicsChallenge

As part of the Angola Prison Rodeo, celebrated annually at the Louisiana State Penitentiary, inmates risk serious injury trying to grab a $500 poker chip tied to the forehead of an enraged, two-thousand-pound bull. Are there any ethical problems with allowing prisoners to participate in such a dangerous competition in front of paying customers? Explain your answer.

Inside a Women's Prison

When the first women's prison in the United States opened in 1839 on the grounds of New York's Sing Sing institution, the focus was on rehabilitation. Prisoners were prepared for a return to society with classes on reading, knitting, and sewing. Early women's reformatories had few locks or bars, and several included nurseries for the inmates' young children. Today, the situation is dramatically different. "Women's institutions are literally men's institutions, only we pull out the urinals," remarks Meda Chesney-Lind, a criminologist at the University of Hawaii.[74] Following a decade-long study of conditions in women's prisons, researchers at the University of Cincinnati identified six specific concerns relating to female inmates:

1. They often suffer from lack of *self-efficacy,* meaning that they do not feel able to meet personal goals and believe that they are not in control of their own lives.
2. Their criminal behavior is linked to *parental stress*—specifically, the financial strain of raising children and the possibility of losing custody of children due to antisocial behavior such as crime and substance abuse.
3. They are more likely than male offenders to suffer from *mental health problems* such as depression, anxiety, and self-injurious behaviors.
4. They are more likely than male offenders to have been *victims of physical and sexual abuse* as children and adults.
5. Before arrest, they were involved in *unhealthy relationships* with family members, spouses, or romantic partners that contributed to their criminal behavior.
6. Their lives are marked by *poverty and homelessness,* often brought on by substance abuse, child care responsibilities, and lack of educational and work skills.[75]

These concerns—when combined with the fact that most female inmates are nonviolent offenders—suggest that women's prisons require a different management style than men's prisons.

Characteristics of Female Inmates

Male inmates outnumber female inmates by approximately nine to one, and there are only about a hundred women's correctional facilities in the United States. Consequently, most research concerning the American corrections system focuses on male inmates and men's prisons. Enough data exist, however, to provide a useful portrait of women behind bars. Female inmates are typically low income and undereducated, and have a history of unemployment. Female offenders are much less likely than male offenders to have committed a violent offense. Most are incarcerated for a nonviolent drug or property crime.[76] As Figure 12.3 shows, the demographics of female prisoners are similar to those of their male counterparts. That is, the majority of female inmates are under the age of forty, and the population is disproportionately African American.

FIGURE 12.3 Female Prisoners in the United States by Race, Ethnicity, and Age

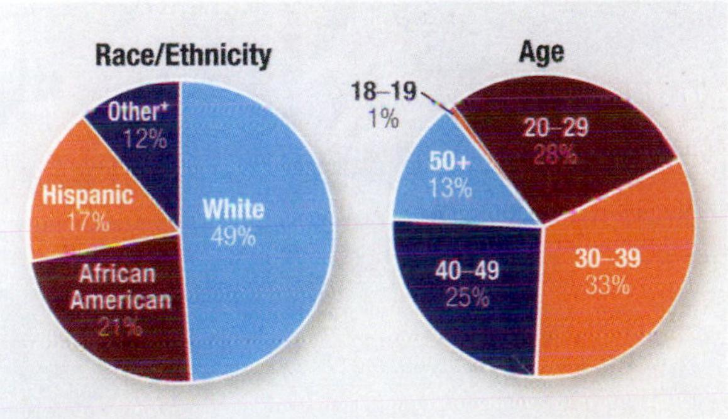

*Includes American Indians, Alska Native, Native Hawaiians, other Pacific Islanders, and persons indentifying two or more races.

Source: Bureau of Justice Statistics, *Prisoners in 2014* (Washington, D.C.: U.S. Department of Justice, September 2015) Appendix table 3, page 29.

The single factor that most distinguishes female prisoners from their male counterparts is a history of physical or sexual abuse. A self-reported study conducted by the federal government indicates that 55 percent of female jail inmates have been abused at some point in their lives, compared with only 13 percent of male jail inmates.[77] Fifty-seven percent of women in state prisons and 40 percent of women in federal prisons report some form of past abuse—both figures are significantly higher than those for male prisoners.[78] Health experts believe that these levels of abuse are related to the significant amount of drug and/or alcohol addiction that plagues the female prison population, as well as to the mental illness problems that such addictions can cause or exacerbate.[79]

The Motherhood Problem

Learning Objective 6

Explain the aspects of imprisonment that prove challenging for incarcerated mothers and their children.

Drug and alcohol use within a women's prison can be a function of the anger and depression many inmates experience due to being separated from their children. An estimated 147,000 American children have a mother in state prison, and the problem is much more pronounced for African American and Latino children than for white ones.[80] One study found that almost two-thirds of women in federal prison are more than five hundred miles from their homes.[81]

Further research indicates that an inmate who serves her sentence more than fifty miles from her residence is much less likely to receive phone calls or personal visits from family members. For most inmates and their families, the costs of "staying in touch" are too high.[82] This kind of separation can have serious consequences for the children of inmates. When a father goes to prison, his children are likely to live with their mother. When a mother is incarcerated, however, her children are likely to live with other relatives or, in about 11 percent of the cases, be sent to foster care.[83] Only nine states provide facilities where inmates and their infant children can live together, and even in these facilities nursery privileges generally end once the child is eighteen months old.

▼ An inmate at the Decatur Correctional Center in Decatur, Illinois, plays with her three-month-old daughter. As part of the Moms with Babies program at this minimum security facility, incarcerated mothers can live with their infant children for up to two years while serving their sentences. **Why might this type of program reduce recidivism rates among participating inmates?**
Scott Olson/Getty Images

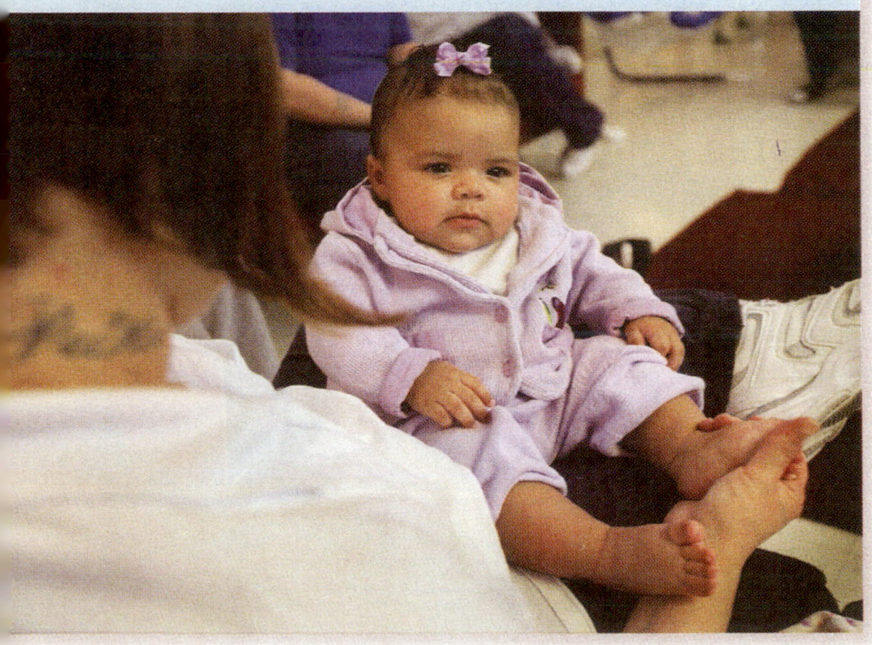

The Culture of Women's Prisons

After spending five years visiting female inmates in the Massachusetts Correctional Institution (MCI) at Framingham, journalist Cristina Rathbone observed that the medium-security facility seemed "more like a high school than a prison."[84] The prisoners were older and tougher than high school girls, but they still divided into cliques, with the "lifers" at the top of the hierarchy and "untouchables" such as child abusers at the bottom. Unlike in men's prisons, where the underground economy revolves around drugs and weapons, at MCI-Framingham the most treasured contraband items are clothing, food, and makeup.[85]

The Pseudo-Family Although both men's and women's prisons are organized with the same goals of control and discipline, the cultures within the two institutions are generally very different. As we have seen, male prison society operates primarily on the basis of power. Deprived of the benefits of freedom, male prisoners tend to create a violent environment that bears little relation to life on the outside.[86] In contrast, researchers have found that women prisoners prefer to re-create their outside identities by forming social networks that resemble, as noted earlier, high school cliques or, more commonly, the traditional family structure.[87] In these pseudo-families, inmates often play specific roles, with the more experienced convicts acting as "mothers" to younger, inexperienced "daughters." As one observer noted, the younger women rely on their "moms" for emotional support, companionship, loans, and even discipline.[88]

Sexual Violence and Prison Staff Compared with men's prisons, women's prisons have extremely low levels of race-based, gang-related physical aggression.[89] Furthermore, though rates of sexual victimization can be high, most such episodes involve abusive sexual contacts such as unwanted touching rather than sexual assault or rape.[90]

One form of serious prison violence that does plague women prisoners, however, is sexual misconduct by prison staff. Although no large-scale study on sexual abuse of female inmates by male correctional officers exists, a number of state-level studies suggest that it is widespread.[91] Dr. Kerry Kupers, who has studied the effects of prison sexual assault, believes that it contributes to the PTSD, depression, anxiety, and other mental illnesses suffered by so many women prisoners.[92]

EthicsChallenge

A number of states place pregnant inmates in handcuffs or other forms of restraint as part of the procedure for childbirths that take place while the inmates are incarcerated. What might be some of the reasons for this practice? Do you feel it is an ethical way to treat these women during and after labor? Why or why not?

Return to Society

On May 26, 2015, Jeremiah Smith broke into a North Spokane, Washington, tattoo parlor and, according to police, fatally shot a seventeen-year-old. Smith had been released from prison less than two weeks earlier after serving five years for robbery, burglary, and assault convictions. In contrast, two years after serving a decade in federal prison for drug distribution, Dquan Rosario earned a job as an emergency medical technician in Essex County, New Jersey. "Instead of peddling drugs that are destroying lives, he's saving lives," said one of Rosario's supporters. "He's making the community better."[93]

Each year, about 630,000 inmates are released from American prisons. The challenge for ex-inmates is to ensure that their post-release experience mirrors that of Dquan Rosario rather than that of Jeremiah Smith. More so than in the past, however, ex-convicts are not facing this challenge alone. Given the benefits to society of reducing recidivism, corrections officials and community leaders are making unprecedented efforts to help newly released prisoners establish crime-free lives.

Types of Prison Release

The majority of all inmates leaving prison—about two-thirds—do so through one of the parole mechanisms discussed in Chapter 10. Of the remaining third, most are given an **expiration release**.[94] Also known as "maxing out," expiration release occurs when an

expiration release The release of an inmate from prison at the end of his or her sentence without any further correctional supervision.

Learning Objective

7 Contrast parole, expiration release, pardon, and furlough.

inmate has served the maximum amount of time on the initial sentence, minus reductions for good-time credits, and is not subjected to community supervision. Another, quite rare unconditional release is a **pardon**, a form of executive clemency. The president (on the federal level) and the governor (on the state level) can grant a pardon, or forgive a convict's criminal punishment. Most states have a board of pardons—affiliated with the parole board—that makes recommendations to the governor in cases in which it believes a pardon is warranted. The majority of pardons involve obvious miscarriages of justice, though sometimes a governor will pardon an individual to remove the stain of conviction from her or his criminal record.

Certain temporary releases also exist. Some inmates, who qualify by exhibiting good behavior and generally proving that they do not represent a risk to society, are allowed to leave the prison on **furlough** for a certain amount of time, usually between a day and a week. At times, a furlough is granted because of a family emergency, such as a funeral. Furloughs can be particularly helpful for an inmate who is nearing release and can use them to ease the readjustment period. Finally, *probation release* occurs following a short period of incarceration at the back end of shock probation, which we discussed in Chapter 10. Generally, however, as you have seen, probationers experience community supervision in place of a prison term.

The Challenges of Reentry

What steps can corrections officials take to lessen the possibility that ex-convicts will reoffend following their release? Efforts to answer that question have focused on programs that help inmates make the transition from prison to the outside. In past years, these programs would have come under the general heading of "rehabilitation," but today corrections officials and criminologists refer to them as part of the strategy of **prisoner reentry**.

The concept of reentry has come to mean many things to many people. For our purposes, keep in mind the words of Joan Petersilia of the University of California, Irvine, who defines *reentry* as encompassing "all activities and programming conducted to prepare ex-convicts to return safely to the community and to live as law abiding citizens."[95] In other words, whereas rehab is focused on the individual offender, *reentry* encompasses the released convict's relationship with society.

Barriers to Reentry Perhaps the largest obstacle to successful prisoner reentry is the simple truth that life behind bars is very different from life on the outside. As one inmate explains, the "rules" of prison survival are hardly compatible with good citizenship:

> An unexpected smile could mean trouble. A man in uniform was not a friend. Being kind was a weakness. Viciousness and recklessness were to be respected and admired.[96]

The prison environment also insulates inmates. They are not required to make the day-to-day decisions that characterize a normal existence beyond prison bars. Bruce Western, a Harvard sociologist, describes one freed female offender who "frequently forgot to eat breakfast or lunch for several months because she was used to being called to meals in prison."[97]

Depending on the length of incarceration, a released inmate must adjust to an array of economic, technological, and social changes that took place while she or he was behind bars. Common acts such as using an ATM or a smartphone may be completely alien to someone who has just completed a long prison term. According to Ann Jacobs, director of the Prisoner Reentry Institute at New York's John Jay College of Criminal Justice, ex-convicts often perceive themselves as "impostors" who are "incapable of living a normal life."[98]

pardon An act of executive clemency that overturns a conviction and erases mention of the crime from the person's criminal record.

furlough Temporary release from a prison for purposes of vocational or educational training, to ease the shock of release, or for personal reasons.

prisoner reentry A corrections strategy designed to prepare inmates for a successful return to the community and to reduce the possibility of criminal activity after release.

Challenges of Release Other obstacles hamper reentry efforts. Released offenders generally have no means of transportation. Housing can be difficult to secure, as many private property owners refuse to rent to someone with a criminal record, and federal and state laws restrict public housing options for ex-convicts. Crucially, a criminal past also limits the ability to find employment.

The American Bar Association has tabulated more than 46,000 federal and state restrictions imposed on convicted felons, about three-quarters of which are employment related.[99] One survey shows that more than 50 percent of private corporations conduct background checks because they are concerned about getting sued for the actions of an employee with a criminal record.[100] As a result, according to research conducted by the Ella Baker Institute, about a quarter of former inmates remain unemployed five years after their release, with the vast majority of the rest only able to find part-time or temporary work.[101]

These economic barriers can be complicated by the physical and mental conditions of the freed convict. We have already discussed the high incidence of substance abuse among prisoners and the health-care needs of aging inmates. In addition, one study concluded that as many as one in five Americans leaving jail or prison is seriously mentally ill.[102] (See Figure 12.4 for a list of the issues commonly faced by former inmates in their first year out of prison.)

Promoting Desistance One ex-inmate compared the experience of being released to entering a "dark room, knowing that there are steps in front of you and waiting to fall."[103] The goal of reentry is to act as a flashlight for convicts by promoting **desistance**, a general term used to describe the continued abstinence from offending and the reintroduction of offenders into society. Certainly, the most important factor in the process is the individual convict. She or he has to *want* to desist and take steps to do so. In most

desistance The process through which criminal activity decreases and reintegration into society increases over a period of time.

Figure 12.4 Prisoner Reentry Issues

Researchers from the Urban Institute in Washington, D.C., asked nearly three hundred former prisoners (all male) in the Cleveland, Ohio, area about the most pressing issues they faced in their first year after release. The answers provide a useful snapshot of the many challenges of reentry.

1. **Housing.** Nearly two-thirds of the men were living with family members, and about half considered their housing situation "temporary." Many were concerned about their living environment: half said that drug dealing was a major problem in their neighborhoods, and almost 25 percent were living with drug and alcohol abusers.
2. **Employment.** After one year, only about one-third of the former inmates had a full-time job, and another 11 percent were working part-time.
3. **Family and friends.** One in four of the men identified family support as the most important thing keeping them from returning to criminality. Another 16 percent said that avoiding certain people and situations was the most crucial factor in their continued good behavior.
4. **Programs and services.** About two-thirds of the former inmates had taken part in programs and services such as drug treatment and continuing education.
5. **Health.** More than half of the men reported suffering from a chronic health condition, and 29 percent showed symptoms of depression.
6. **Substance use.** About half of the men admitted to weekly drug use or alcohol intoxication. Those who had strong family ties and those who were required to maintain telephone contact with their parole officers were less likely to engage in frequent substance use.
7. **Parole violation and recidivism.** More than half of the former inmates reported that they had violated the conditions of their parole, usually by using drugs or having contact with other parolees. Fifteen percent of the men returned to prison in the year after release. Four out of five of the returns were the result of a new crime.

Source: Christy A. Visher and Shannon M. E. Courtney, *One year Out: Experience of Prisoners Returning to Cleveland* (Washington, D.C.: Urban Institute, April 2007, 2.

work release program Temporary release of convicts from prison for purposes of employment. The offenders may spend their days on the job, but must return to the correctional facility at night and during the weekend.

halfway house A community-based form of early release that places inmates in residential centers and allows them to reintegrate with society.

cases, however, ex-inmates are going to need help—help getting an education, help finding and keeping a job, and help freeing themselves from harmful addictions to drugs and alcohol. Corrections officials are in a good position to offer this assistance, and their efforts in doing so form the backbone of the reentry movement.

Reentry planning starts behind bars. In addition to the rehabilitation-oriented prison programs discussed earlier in the chapter, most correctional facilities offer "life skills" classes to inmates. This counseling covers topics such as finding and keeping a job, locating a residence, understanding family responsibilities, and budgeting. After release, however, former inmates often find it difficult to continue with educational programs and counseling as they struggle to readjust to life outside prison. Consequently, parole supervising agencies operate a number of programs to facilitate offenders' desistance efforts while, at the same time, protecting the community to the greatest extent possible.

Learning Objective 8

Explain the goal of prisoner reentry programs.

Community-Based Reentry Programs As is made clear in Figure 12.4, work and lodging are crucial components of desistance. Corrections officials have several options in helping certain parolees—usually low-risk offenders—find employment and a place to live during the supervision period. Nearly a third of correctional facilities offer **work release programs**, in which prisoners nearing the end of their sentences are given permission to work at paid employment in the community.[104]

Inmates on work release either return to the correctional facility in the evening or, under certain circumstances, live in community residential facilities known as **halfway houses.** These facilities, also available to other parolees and those who have finished their sentences, are often remodeled hotels or private homes. They provide a less institutionalized living environment than a prison or jail for a small number of offenders (usually between ten and twenty-five). Halfway houses can be tailored to the needs of the former inmate. Many communities, for example, offer substance-free transitional housing for those whose past criminal behavior was linked to drug or alcohol abuse.

▼ Homeboy Industries, which operates this bakery in downtown Los Angeles, provides former gang members and recently released ex-convicts with job training opportunities and other reentry programs. Why is finding employment such an important part of any desistance program? AP Images/ Damian Dovaganes

What Works in Reentry Research conducted by the Pew Center on the States found that 43 percent of ex-prisoners are back in prison or jail within three years of their release dates.[105] According to a study carried out by professors Alfred Blumstein of Carnegie Mellon University and Kiminori Nakamura of the University of Maryland, however, after ten to thirteen years in the community, ex-inmates pose the same risk of offending as do those without a criminal record.[106]

How can society help released prisoners go at least a decade without reoffending? In general, reentry planning is most effective when it focuses on reducing substance abuse and promoting employment. To that end, a number of jurisdictions have established *reentry courts,* in which a judge ensures that the inmate has been following her or his reentry requirements.

Careers in CJ

Photo courtesy of Julie Howe

Julie Howe
Halfway House Program Manager

Early on in my career, I felt a bit intimidated by the clients simply because of my discomfort, not by their behavior. I started out very stern and learned later that it was better to start strong and to lighten up later rather than the reverse. The clients respect you more and know to take you seriously. My first client as a case manager was a real eye-opener. He was in his fifties, and I was in my early twenties. Earning his trust was quite a challenge. In the end, he learned to respect me, and I learned different techniques when working with offenders.

My favorite part of my job is that I know that I have an impact on people's lives. If I can assist someone to become sober, responsible, employed, and self-sufficient, I am also having an impact on the community and those whom my clients' lives touch. I never get tired of hearing clients say thanks and knowing their lives are forever changed when they realize their potential and value. I also love that I have the opportunity to influence the behavior of others and shape their future. What an awesome responsibility!

SOCIAL MEDIA CAREER TIP Don't misrepresent facts or tell lies of omission online. Doing so in front of millions of online viewers virtually ensures you will be caught, and such untruths can permanently damage career possibilities.

FASTFACTS

Halfway house program manager

Job description:

- Coordinate recreational, educational, and vocational counseling and other programs for residents.
- Maintain the security of the house and residents.

What kind of training is required?

- A bachelor's degree or master's degree in social work, career counseling, criminal justice, or psychology.
- Also helpful are internships, volunteer work with a halfway house, and community service work with an agency.

Annual salary range?

- $41,000–$61,000

As noted earlier in the chapter, the reluctance of employers to consider hiring an ex-convict is a severe hurdle for many released inmates. Two policies have emerged to remedy this situation:

1. Expungement laws, which allow low-level criminals to remove offenses from their criminal records so that these crimes will not be uncovered by employer background checks.
2. "Ban the box" laws, which prohibit public employers from inquiring into the criminal backgrounds of potential employees by having a "criminal history box" on their application forms.[107]

Even though companies such as Walmart, Target, and Home Depot have adopted their own "ban the box" policies, the practice is not universally applauded in the private sector. "Does everybody deserve a second chance? Of course," says a spokesman for the National Federation of Independent Businesses. "But it's up to me as the guy taking the risk to decide that this person is worth taking the risk. The fact that they have a criminal record proves that at one point in their lives they weren't trustworthy."[108]

The Special Case of Sex Offenders

Despite the beneficial impact of reentry efforts, one group of wrongdoers has consistently been denied access to such programs: those convicted of sex crimes. The eventual return of these offenders to society causes such high levels of community anxiety that the criminal justice system has not yet figured out what to do with them.

Conditions of Release Although research concerning recidivism rates of sex offenders is often inconclusive,[109] these offenders are subject to extensive community supervision after being released from prison. Generally, they are supervised by parole officers and live under the same threat of revocation as other parolees. Specifically, many sex offenders—particularly child molesters—have the following special conditions of release:

- No contact with children under the age of eighteen.
- Psychiatric treatment.
- Must stay a certain distance from schools or parks where children are present.
- Cannot own toys that may be used to lure children.
- Cannot have a job or participate in any activity that involves children.

Also, more than half of the states and hundreds of municipalities have passed laws limiting housing options for convicted sex offenders, a subject we address in the feature *CJ Controversy—Residency Restrictions.*

Sex Offender Notification Laws Perhaps the most dramatic step taken by criminal justice authorities to protect the public from sex crimes involves *sex offender registries,* or databases that contain sex offenders' names, addresses, photographs, and

CJ Controversy
EQUAL·JUSTICE·UNDER·LAW

M Dogan/Shutterstock.com

Residency Restrictions

In many jurisdictions throughout the United States, residency laws ban sex offenders from living within a certain distance of places where children naturally congregate. In New Jersey, for example, "high-risk" offenders cannot take up residence within 3,000 feet of any school, park or campground, church, theater, bowling alley, library, or convenience store. (For medium- and low-risk offenders, the distances are 2,500 feet and 1,000 feet, respectively.) The overlapping "off-limit zones" created by residency requirements can dramatically restrict where a sex offender is able to find affordable housing.

Residency Restrictions Should Be Encouraged Because . . .

- Forbidding sex offenders from residing near schools and other areas that attract large groups of children decreases their access to these children, thus reducing the risk that they will reoffend.
- The right of convicted sex offenders to choose where they live is less important than the safety of children and other vulnerable members of society.

Residency Restrictions Should Be Discouraged Because . . .

- They push sex offenders into less-populated, rural areas or into homelessness, which makes it much more difficult for law enforcement and corrections agents to stay in contact with them.
- They are inadequate. Strangers commit only about 10 percent of all sexual offenses against children. Sex offenders are much more likely to be family members, friends, or other acquaintances.

Your Assignment

A number of jurisdictions keep track of sex offenders by using GPS monitoring devices, discussed in Chapter 10. To learn more about this strategy, search the Internet for **GPS monitoring and sex offenders**. Also, read ***Grady v. North Carolina*** online to see how the United States Supreme Court regards the practice. Comparing GPS monitoring and residency restrictions, which do you think is more effective in protecting the public from sex offenders? Or, is there a better, third way? Your answer should include at least two full paragraphs.

other information. The movement to register sex offenders started about two decades ago, after seven-year-old Megan Kanka of Hamilton Township, New Jersey, was raped and murdered by a twice-convicted pedophile (an adult sexually attracted to children) who had moved into her neighborhood after being released from prison on parole.

The next year, in response to public outrage, the state passed a series of laws known collectively as the New Jersey Sexual Offender Registration Act, or "Megan's Law."[110] Today, all fifty states and the federal government have their own version of Megan's Law, or a **sex offender notification law**, which requires local law authorities to alert the public when a sex offender has been released into the community.

▲ Residents of Monrovia, California, protest in front of the home of a registered sex offender living nearby. **What are some of the reasons that community members fear the nearby presence of freed sex offenders? Do sex offender registries adequately address these concerns? Why or why not?** Rick Meyer/Getty Images

Active and Passive Notification No two sex offender notification laws have exactly the same provisions, but all are designed with the goal of allowing the public to learn the identities of convicted sex offenders living in their midst. In general, the laws demand that a paroled sex offender notify local law enforcement authorities upon taking residence in a state. In Georgia, for example, paroled sex offenders are required to present themselves to both the local sheriff and the superintendent of the public school district where they plan to live.[111] This registration process must be renewed every time the parolee changes his or her address.

The authorities, in turn, notify the community of the sex offender's presence through the use of one of two models. Under the "active" model, the authorities directly notify the community or community representatives. Traditionally, this notification has taken the form of bulletins or posters, distributed and posted within a certain distance from the offender's home. Now, however, a number of states use e-mail alerts to fulfill notification obligations. In the "passive" model, information on sex offenders is made open and available for public scrutiny.

Prevalence of Sex Offender Registries In 2006, Congress passed the Adam Walsh Child Protection and Safety Act, which established a national registry of sex offenders.[112] In addition, all fifty states operate sex offender registries with data on registered sex offenders in their jurisdictions. (For an idea of how this process works, you can visit the Federal Bureau of Investigation's Sex Offender Registry website.) The total number of registered sex offenders in the United States is about 800,000.

Civil Confinement

To many, any type of freedom, even if encumbered by notification requirements, is too much freedom for a sex offender. "The issue is, what can you do short of putting them all in prison for the rest of their lives?" complained one policymaker.[113]

In fact, a number of states have devised a legal method to keep sex offenders off the streets for, if not their entire lives, then close to it. These **civil confinement** laws allow corrections officials to lock sex offenders up in noncorrectional facilities such as psychiatric hospitals after the conclusion of their prison terms. Under these laws, corrections officials can hold sexual criminals in these institutions for an undetermined amount of time, as long as they are deemed a danger to society. In practice, civil confinement laws essentially give the state the power to detain this class of criminal indefinitely—a power upheld by the United States Supreme Court in 2010.[114]

sex offender notification law Legislation that requires law enforcement authorities to notify people when convicted sex offenders are released into their neighborhood or community.

civil confinement The practice of confining individuals against their will if they present a danger to the community.

Summary

For more information on these concepts, look back to the Learning Objective icons throughout the chapter.

1 Explain the concept of prison as a total institution. Though many people spend time in partial institutions—schools, companies where they work, and religious organizations—only in prison is every aspect of an inmate's life controlled, and that is why prisons are called total institutions. Every detail for every prisoner is fully prescribed and managed.

2 Describe a risk run by corrections officials who fail to provide adequate medical care to the inmates under their control. In the first decade of the 2000s, medical care for inmates in California's prison system was severely compromised by extreme overcrowding. As a result, the U.S. Supreme Court ordered state corrections officials to release 30,000 inmates so that standards of health care in the prison could be more compatible "with the concept of human dignity."

3 Indicate some of the reasons for violent behavior in prisons. (a) To separate the powerful from the weak and establish a prisoner hierarchy; (b) to minimize one's own probability of being a target of assault; (c) to enhance one's self-image; (d) to obtain sexual relief; and (e) to obtain material goods through extortion or robbery.

4 List the circumstances in which courts have found that the "legitimate security interests" of a jail or prison justify the use of force by correctional officers. A correctional officer is justified in using force if she or he is (a) acting in self-defense; (b) protecting another prison employee or inmate; (c) upholding the rules of the correctional facility; (d) preventing an inmate from committing a crime; or (e) preventing an inmate from attempting to escape.

5 Describe the hands-off doctrine of prisoner law and indicate two standards used to determine if prisoners' rights have been violated. The hands-off doctrine assumes that the care of prisoners should be left to prison officials and that it is not the place of judges to intervene. Nonetheless, the Supreme Court has created two standards to be used by the courts in determining whether a prisoner's Eighth Amendment protections against cruel and unusual punishment have been violated. Under the "deliberate indifference" standard, prisoners must show that prison officials were aware of harmful conditions at the facility and failed to remedy them. Under the "identifiable human needs" standard, prisoners must show that they were denied a basic need such as food, warmth, or exercise.

6 Explain the aspects of imprisonment that prove challenging for incarcerated mothers and their children. Besides the anxiety that results from any separation of parent and child, incarcerated mothers often find it difficult to stay in contact with their children due to long distances between the prison and home. Furthermore, when a mother is imprisoned, her children are more likely not only to be separated from their father, but also to wind up in foster care.

7 Contrast parole, expiration release, pardon, and furlough. Parole is an early release program for those incarcerated. Expiration release occurs when the inmate has served the maximum time for her or his initial sentence minus good-time credits. A pardon can be given only by the president or one of the fifty governors. Furlough is a temporary release while in jail or prison.

8 Explain the goal of prisoner reentry programs. Based on the ideals of promoting desistance, these programs have two main objectives: (a) to prepare a prisoner for a successful return to the community, and (b) to protect the community by reducing the chances that the ex-convict will continue her or his criminal activity after release from prison.

Questions for Critical Analysis

1. Can prison treatment and rehabilitation programs be justified for reasons that have nothing to do with their potential cost and safety benefits for society? In other words, does the American criminal justice system have a responsibility to individual inmates to "improve" them during incarceration?

2. Several years ago, an inmate sued the Florida Department of Corrections, claiming that his soy-based diet was cruel and unusual punishment. Under what circumstances, if any, do you think that unpleasant prison food can violate an inmate's constitutional rights?

3. Do you agree with prison policies that prohibit male correctional officers from patting down and strip-searching female inmates? Why or why not? Under what circumstances might such policies be unrealistic?

4. How does the process of prisonization differ between male and female inmates?

5. What is the main justification for legislation that prohibits convicted sex offenders from accessing social media sites such as Facebook, Instagram, and online video games? What is your opinion of such legislation?

Key Terms

civil confinement 375
"deliberate indifference" 365
deprivation model 357
desistance 371
expiration release 369
furlough 370
halfway house 372
"hands-off" doctrine 365
"identifiable human needs" 366
pardon 370
prisoner reentry 370
prison gang 358
prisonization 354
prison programs 355
prison segregation 358
relative deprivation 358
security threat group (STG) 359
sex offender notification law 375
total institution 353
work release program 372

Notes

1. Erving Goffman, "On the Characteristics of Total Institutions," in *Asylums: Essays on the Social Situation of Mental Patients and Other Inmates* (New York: Doubleday, 1961), 6.
2. Donald Clemmer, *The Prison Community* (Boston: Christopher, 1940).
3. John Irwin, *Prisons in Turmoil* (Boston: Little, Brown, 1980), 67.
4. *Old Behind Bars: The Aging Prison Population in the United States* (New York: Human Rights Watch, 2012), 24–42.
5. Bureau of Justice Statistics, *Medical Problems of State and Federal Prisoners and Jail Inmates, 2011–12* (Washington, D.C.: U.S. Department of Justice, February 2015), 1.
6. Bureau of Justice Statistics, *Mortality in Local Jails and State Prisons, 2000–2013—Statistical Tables* (Washington, D.C.: U.S. Department of Justice, August 2015), Table 19, page 21.
7. *Ibid.*
8. Kevin E. McCarthy and Carrie Rose, *State Initiatives to Address Aging Prisoners* (Hartford, Conn.: Connecticut General Assembly, Office of Legislative Research, 2013), 3.
9. *Managing Prison Health Care Spending* (Philadelphia: The Pew Charitable Trusts, October 2013), 11.
10. Katherine Stuart van Wormer and Clemens Bartollas, *Women and the Criminal Justice System*, 3d ed. (Upper Saddle River, N.J.: Pearson Education, 2011), 143.
11. Ian Lovett, "Los Angeles Agrees to Overhaul Jails to Care for Mentally Ill and Curb Abuse," *New York Times* (August 6, 2015), A13.
12. Kevin Johnson, "Mentally Ill Fill Crowded Prisons," *USA Today* (July 25, 2014), 5A.
13. William Kanapaux, "Guilty of Mental Illness," *Psychiatric Times* (January 1, 2004), at **www.psychiatrictimes.com/forensic-psych/content/article/10168/47631.**
14. Bureau of Justice Statistics, *Census of State and Federal Correctional Facilities, 2005* (Washington, D.C.: U.S. Department of Justice, October 2008), 6.
15. Kenneth L. Parker, "The Saint Louis University Prison Program: An Ancient Mission, a New Beginning," *Saint Louis University Public Law Review* 33 (2014), 383–384.
16. Joan Petersilia, "Beyond the Prison Bubble," *Wilson Quarterly* (Winter 2011), 29.
17. Anasseril E. Daniel, "Care of the Mentally Ill in Prisons: Challenges and Solutions," *Journal of the American Academy of Psychiatry and the Law Online* (December 2007), at **www.jaapl.org/content/35/4/406.full.**
18. Robert Johnson, *Hard Time: Understanding and Reforming the Prison*, 2d ed. (Belmont, Calif.: Wadsworth, 1996), 133.
19. Tom Robbins, "A Brutal Beating Wakes Attica's Ghosts," *New York Times* (March 1, 2015), A1.
20. *Mortality in Local Jails and State Prisons, 2000–2013—Statistical Tables, op. cit.*, Table 1, page 7; and Table 16, page 20.
21. Daniel P. Mears et al., "The Code of the Street and Inmate Violence: Investigating the Salience of Imported Belief Systems," *Criminology* (August 2013), 695–728.
22. James E. Robertson, "The Prison Rape Elimination Act of 2003: A Primer," *Criminal Law Bulletin* (May/June 2004), 270–273.
23. Bureau of Justice Statistics, *Sexual Victimization in Prisons and Jails Reported by Inmates, 2011–12* (Washington, D.C.: U.S. Department of Justice, May 2013), 6.
24. Lee H. Bowker, *Prison Victimization* (New York: Elsevier, 1981), 31–33.
25. Stephen C. Light, "The Severity of Assaults on Prison Officers: A Contextual Analysis," *Social Science Quarterly* 71 (1990), 267–284.
26. Randy Martin and Sherwood Zimmerman, "A Typology of the Causes of Prison Riots and

an Analytical Extension to the 1986 Virginia Riot," *Justice Quarterly* 7 (1990), 711–737.

27. Bert Useem, "Disorganization and the New Mexico Prison Riot of 1980," *American Sociological Review* 50 (1985), 677–688.
28. 42 U.S.C. Sections 15601–15609 (2006).
29. Leo Carroll, "Race, Ethnicity, and the Social Order of the Prison," in *The Pains of Imprisonment*, eds. R. Johnson and H. Toch (Beverly Hills, Calif.: Sage, 1982).
30. *Lee v. Washington*, 390 U.S. 333 (1968).
31. *Johnson v. California*, 543 U.S. 499 (2005).
32. *Ibid.*, at 508.
33. Paige St. John, "California Prisons to End Race-Based Policy for Inmate Violence," *Los Angeles Times* (October 23, 2014), at **www.latimes.com/local/lanow/la-me-ln-california-prisons-race-policy-inmate-violence-20141023-story.html.**
34. Craig Haney, "Psychology and the Limits of Prison Pain," *Psychology, Public Policy, and Law* (December 1977), 499.
35. Alan J. Drury and Matt DeLisi, "Gangkill: An Exploratory Empirical Assessment of Gang Membership, Homicide Offending, and Prison Misconduct," *Crime & Delinquency* (January 2011), 130–146.
36. George W. Knox, "The Problem of Gangs and Security Threat Groups (STGs) in American Prisons and Jails Today: Recent Findings from the 2012 NGCRC National Gang/STG Survey" (2012), at **www.ngcrc.com/corr2012.html.**
37. *2013 National Gang Report* (Washington, D.C.: National Gang Intelligence Center, 2013), 15.
38. Knox, *op. cit.*
39. John Winterdyk and Rick Ruddell, "Managing Prison Gangs: Results from a Survey of U.S. Prison Systems," *Journal of Criminal Justice* 38 (2010), 733–734.
40. Alan Gomez, "States Make Prisons Far Less Deadly," *USA Today* (August 22, 2008), 3A.
41. Quoted in John J. DiIulio, Jr., *No Escape: The Future of American Corrections* (New York: Basic Books, 1991), 268.
42. Jack Henry Abbott, *In the Belly of the Beast* (New York: Vintage Books, 1991), 54.
43. Michel Foucault, *Discipline and Punish: The Birth of the Prison* (New York: Pantheon Books, 1977), 128.
44. Todd R. Clear, George F. Cole, and Michael D. Reisig, *American Corrections*, 11th ed (Belmont, Calif.: Wadsworth Cengage Learning, 2016), 340.
45. *Ibid.*, 342.
46. Lucien X. Lombardo, *Guards Imprisoned: Correctional Officers at Work* (Cincinnati, Ohio: Anderson Publishing Co., 1989), 51–71.
47. Clair A. Crip, "Inmate Disciplinary Procedures," in *Prison and Jail Administration: Practice and Theory*, 3rd ed., ed. Peter M. Carlson (Burlington, Mass.: Jones & Bartlett Learning, 2015).
48. Goffman, *op. cit.*, 7.
49. *Wolff v. McDonnell*, 418 U.S. 539 (1974).
50. 475 U.S. 312 (1986).
51. *Stanley v. Hejirika*, 134 F.3d 629 (4th Cir. 1998).
52. Christopher R. Smith, *Law and Contemporary Corrections* (Belmont, Calif.: Wadsworth, 1999), Chapter 6.
53. 503 U.S. 1 (1992).
54. *Cooper v. Pate*, 378 U.S. 546 (1964).
55. *Kingsley v. Hendrickson*, 576 U.S. _____ (2015).
56. Van Wormer and Bartollas, *op. cit.*, 387.
57. Cristina Rathbone, *A World Apart: Women, Prison, and a Life behind Bars* (New York: Random House, 2006), 46.
58. Carl Nink et al., *Women Professionals in Corrections: A Growing Asset* (Centerville, Utah: MTC Institute, August 2008), 1.
59. Michael H. Jaime and Armand R. Burruel, "Labor Relations in Corrections," in *Prison and Jail Administration: Practice and Theory*, 3rd ed., *op. cit.*, 264.
60. Bureau of Justice Statistics, *Sexual Victimization Reported by Adult Correctional Authorities, 2009–11* (Washington, D.C.: U.S. Department of Justice, January 2014), Table 10, page 12; and page 17.
61. *Wolff v. McDonnell*, 539.
62. *Hudson v. Palmer*, 468 U.S. 517 (1984).
63. 429 U.S. 97 (1976).
64. "Judge Orders Air Conditioning for Angola Prison's Death Row," *Associated Press* (May 24, 2014).
65. 501 U.S. 294 (1991).
66. *Wilson v. Seiter*, 501 U.S. 294, 304 (1991).
67. *Woodall v. Foti*, 648 F.2d, 268, 272 (5th Cir. 1981).
68. Paige St. John, "In a First, California Agrees to Pay for Transgender Inmate's Sex Reassignment," *Los Angeles Times* (August 10, 2015), at **www.latimes.com/local/california/la-me-inmate-transgender-20150810-story.html.**
69. *Brown v. Plata*, 563 U.S. ____ (2011).
70. *Procunier v. Martinez*, 416 U.S. 396 (1974).
71. *Cruz v. Beto*, 405 U.S. 319 (1972); *Gittlemacker v. Prasse*, 428 F.2d 1 (3d Cir. 1970); and *Kahane v. Carlson*, 527 F.2d 492 (2d Cir. 1975).
72. Maryclaire Dale, "Court Says Pa. Prison Can Ban Muslim Scarf," *Associated Press* (August 2, 2010).
73. Elizabeth Nolan Brown, "Jail Newspaper Ban Not Justified by Threat of Clogged Toilets and Paper Mâché Weapons," *Reason* (July 8, 2015), at **reason.com/blog/2015/07/08/jail-newspaper-ban-unconstitutional.**
74. Quoted in Alexandra Marks, "Martha Checks in Today," *Seattle Times* (October 8, 2004), A8.
75. Emily M. Wright et al., "Gender-Responsive Lessons Learned and Policy Implications for Women in Prison: A Review," *Criminal Justice and Behavior* (September 2012), 1612–1632.
76. Bureau of Justice Statistics, *Sourcebook of Criminal Justice*, 3d ed. (Washington, D.C.: U.S. Department of Justice, 2003), Table 6.56, page 519; and Bureau of Justice Statistics, *Prisoners in 2014* (Washington, D.C.: U.S. Department of Justice, September 2015), Table 11, page 16.
77. Bureau of Justice Statistics, *Profile of Jail Inmates, 2002* (Washington, D.C.: U.S. Department of Justice, July 2004), 10.
78. Bureau of Justice Statistics, *Prior Abuse Reported by Inmates and Probationers* (Washington, D.C.: U.S. Department of Justice, April 1999), 2.
79. *Caught in the Net: The Impact of Drug Policies on Women and Families* (Washington, D.C.: American Civil Liberties Union, 2004), 18–19.
80. Bureau of Justice Statistics, *Parents in Prison and Their Minor Children* (Washington, D.C.: U.S. Department of Justice, March 2010), 2.
81. Kelly Bedard and Eric Helland, "Location of Women's Prisons and the Deterrent Effect of 'Harder' Time," *International Review of Law and Economics* (June 2004), 152.
82. *Ibid.*
83. Sarah Schirmer, Ashley Nellis, and Marc Mauer, *Incarcerated Parents and Their Children: Trends 1991–2007* (Washington, D.C.: The Sentencing Project, February 2009), 5.
84. Rathbone, *op. cit.*, 4.
85. *Ibid.*, 158.
86. Van Wormer and Bartollas, *op. cit.*, 137–138.
87. Barbara Bloom and Meda Chesney-Lind, "Women in Prison," in *It's a Crime: Women and Justice*, 4th ed., ed. Roslyn Muraskin (Upper Saddle River, N.J.: Prentice Hall, 2007), 542–563.
88. Piper Kerman, *Orange Is the New Black: My Year in a Women's Prison* (New York: Spiegal and Grau, 2011), 131.
89. Barbara Owen et al., *Gendered Violence and Safety: A Contextual Approach to Improving Security in Women's Facilities*, December 2008, 12–14, at **www.ncjrs.gov/pdffiles1/nij/grants/225340.pdf.**
90. Nancy Wolff, Cynthia Blitz, Jing Shi, Jane Siegel, and Ronet Bachman, "Physical Violence inside Prisons: Rates of Victimization," *Criminal Justice and Behavior* 34 (2007), 588–604.
91. Van Wormer and Bartollas, *op. cit.*, 146–148.
92. Cited in Barbara Bloom, Barbara Owen, and Stephanie Covington, *Gender Responsive Strategies: Research, Practice, and Guiding Principles for Women Offenders* (Washington, D.C.: National Institute of Corrections, 2003), 26.
93. Quoted in S. P. Sullivan, "Obama Tells N.J. Inmate's Recovery Story During Newark Stop" *NJ.com* (November 3, 2015), at **www.nj.com/politics/index.ssf/2015/11/obama_highlights_reentry_programs_at_roundtable.html.**
94. Bureau of Justice Statistics, *Prisoners in 2014*, *op. cit.*, Table 7, page 10.

95. Joan Petersilia, *When Prisoners Come Home: Parole and Prisoner Reentry* (New York: Oxford University Press, 2003), 39.

96. Victor Hassine, *Life without Parole: Living in Prison Today*, eds. Thomas J. Bernard and Richard McCleary (Los Angeles: Roxbury Publishing Co., 1996), 12.

97. Bruce Western et al., "Stress and Hardship after Prison," *American Journal of Sociology* (March 2015), 1526.

98. Quoted in Jon Mooallem, "You Just Got Out of Prison. Now What?" *New York Times Sunday Magazine* (July 29, 2015), 38.

99. American Bar Association, "National Inventory of the Collateral Consequences of Conviction," at **www.abacollateralconsequences.org.**

100. Society for Human Resource Management, "Background Checking—The Use of Criminal Background Checks in Hiring Decisions" (July 19, 2012), at **www.shrm.org/research/surveyfindings/articles/pages/criminalbackgroundcheck.aspx.**

101. Saneta deVuono-Powell et al., *Who Pays? The True Cost of Incarceration on Families* (Oakland, Calif: Ella Baker Center (2015), 20.

102. *Ill Equipped: U.S. Prisons and Offenders with Mental Illness* (New York: Human Rights Watch, 2003).

103. Quoted in Kevin Johnson, "After Years of Solitary, Freedom Is Hard to Grasp," *USA Today* (June 9, 2005), 2A.

104. *Census of State and Federal Correctional Facilities, 2005, op. cit.*, Table 6, page 5.

105. Pew Center on the States, *State of Recidivism: The Revolving Door of America's Prisons* (Washington, D.C.: The Pew Charitable Trusts, April 2011), 2.

106. Alfred Blumstein and Kiminori Nakaruma, "Redemption in the Presence of Widespread Criminal Background Checks," *Criminology* (May 2009), 327–359.

107. *The State of Sentencing 2014: Developments in Policy and Practice* (Washington, D.C.: The Sentencing Project, February 2015), 8–9.

108. Quoted in Timothy Williams and Tanzina Vega, "A Plan to Cut Costs and Crime: End Hurdle to Job after Prison," *New York Times* (October 24, 2014), A1.

109. Roger Przybykski, "Recidivism of Adult Sexual Offenders," *Sex Offender Management Assessment and Planning Initiative Research Brief* (July 2015), 1–6.

110. New Jersey Revised Statute Section 2C:7-8(c) (1995).

111. Georgia Code Annotated Section 42-9-44.1 (b)(1).

112. Public Law Number 109-248, Section 116, 120 Statute 595 (2006).

113. Abby Goodnough, "After Two Cases in Florida, Crackdown on Molesters," *Law Enforcement News* (May 2004), 12.

114. *United States v. Comstock*, 560 U.S. 126 (2010).

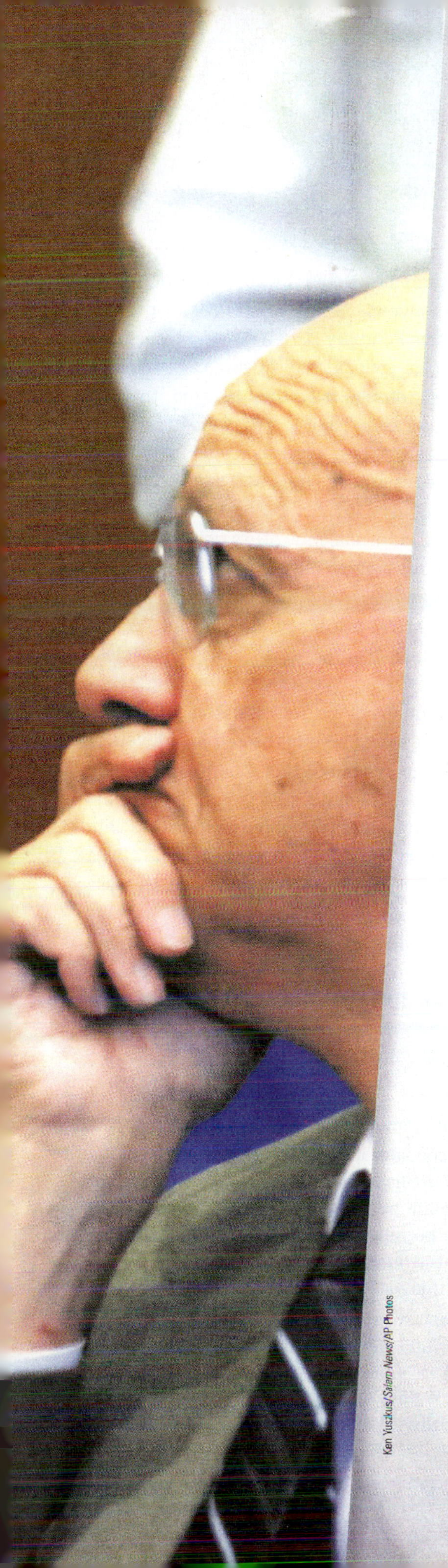

Ken Yuszkus/*Salem News*/AP Photos

13

The Juvenile Justice System

Chapter Outline		Corresponding Learning Objectives
The Evolution of American Juvenile Justice	1	List the four major differences between juvenile courts and adult courts.
	2	Identify and briefly describe the single most important U.S. Supreme Court case with respect to juvenile justice.
Determining Delinquency Today	3	Describe the reasoning behind recent U.S. Supreme Court decisions that have lessened the harshness of sentencing outcomes for violent juvenile offenders.
Trends in Juvenile Delinquency	4	Define *bullying*, and list the four components that are often present in this sort of behavior.
Factors in Juvenile Delinquency	5	Describe the one variable that always correlates highly with juvenile crime rates.
First Contact: The Police and Pretrial Procedures	6	Describe the four primary stages of pretrial juvenile justice procedure.
	7	Detail the three most common methods for transferring juvenile offenders to the adult criminal justice system.
Trying and Punishing Juveniles	8	Explain the distinction between an adjudicatory hearing and a disposition hearing.

To target your study and review, look for these numbered Learning Objective icons throughout the chapter.

a second Chance

fifteen-year-old Nehemiah Griego had been planning the massacre for days. First, early on the morning of January 19, 2013, he shot his mother while she slept in bed. Then, after waking his nine-year-old brother to show him their mother's dead body, he killed the younger boy as well. After taking photos of his victims, Griego went to his sisters' bedroom and fatally shot those two girls, aged five and two. Finally, he waited for his father to return home from an overnight shift at a local homeless shelter and ambushed him with a rifle in the family bathroom.

For two years following this horrific incident, Griego received psychological counseling at the Sequoyah Adolescent Treatment Center in Albuquerque, New Mexico. Because he was charged as a "serious youthful offender," under state law Griego was eventually afforded an inquest to determine whether he should be punished as an adult or as a juvenile for the murders of his parents and siblings. At this February 2016 hearing, prosecutors argued that Griego's actions were "planned," "thought out," and "cruel." Consequently, they insisted, the boy should be sentenced as an adult to 120 years in prison—the terms of an earlier plea bargain. Griego's defense attorneys countered that their client had been physically and emotionally abused by his parents and suffered from a number of mental ailments. "He's getting better," said public defender Jeffrey Buckels, "and deserves a [second] chance."

After seven days of testimony, Judge John Romero ruled that the state had failed to prove by "clear and convincing evidence" that the now eighteen-year-old Griego could not be rehabilitated. Thus, the teenager would be adjudicated as a juvenile. Practically speaking, this meant that Griego would spend another two years in a juvenile treatment center and then be released into society on his twenty-first birthday. "I was in shock. I couldn't believe it," said Vanessa Lightbourne, Griego's older sister. "I love my brother and forgave him a long time ago, but I feel like there has to be consequences for what he did."

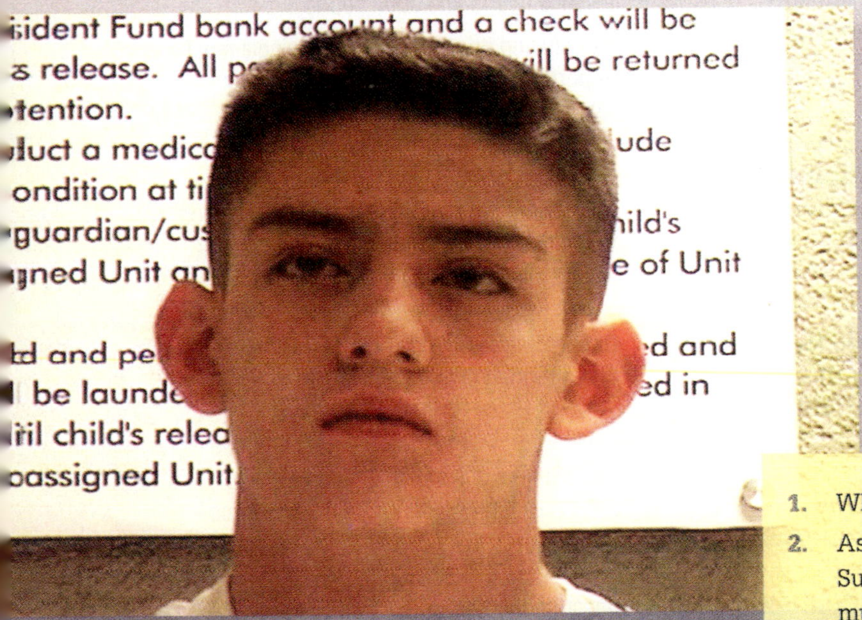

Bernalillo County Sheriff's Department/AP Photos

▲ Nehemiah Griego, shown here as a fifteen-year-old after being arrested for murdering five family members, will be confined in a juvenile treatment center until his twenty-first birthday.

1. What is your opinion of the outcome of this case?
2. As we will see later in the chapter, the United States Supreme Court has ruled that juveniles who commit murder should be given a chance to rehabilitate themselves because they were too young to fully appreciate the magnitude of their crimes. Do you agree with this reasoning? Why or why not?
3. A psychiatrist who interviewed Nehemiah Griego told Judge John Romero that the teenager showed no signs of remorse for killing his family members. How much weight should the judge have given this testimony when determining Griego's punishment? Explain your answer.

The Evolution of American Juvenile Justice

A difficult question—asked every time a younger offender such as Nehemiah Griego commits a heinous act of violence—lies at the heart of the juvenile justice debate: Should such acts by youths be given the same weight as those committed by adults, or should they be seen as "mistakes" that can be corrected by care and counseling?

From its earliest days, the American juvenile justice system has operated as an uneasy compromise between "rehabilitation and punishment, treatment and custody."[1] At the beginning of the 1800s, juvenile offenders were treated the same as adult offenders—they were judged by the same courts and sentenced to the same severe penalties. This situation began to change soon after, as urbanization and industrialization created an immigrant underclass that was, at least in the eyes of many reformers, predisposed to deviant activity. Certain members of the Progressive movement, known as the child savers, began to take steps to "save" children from these circumstances, introducing the idea of rehabilitating delinquents in the process.

parens patriae A doctrine that holds that the state has a responsibility to look after the well-being of children and to assume the role of parent if necessary.

The Child-Saving Movement

In general, the child savers favored the doctrine of ***parens patriae***, which holds that the state has not only a right but also a duty to care for children who are neglected, delinquent, or in some other way disadvantaged. Juvenile offenders, the child savers believed, required treatment, not punishment, and they were horrified at the thought of placing children in prisons with hardened adult criminals. In 1967, then Supreme Court justice Abe Fortas said of the child savers:

> They believed that society's role was not to ascertain whether the child was "guilty" or "innocent," but "What is he, how has he become what he is, and what had best be done in his interest and in the interest of the state to save him from a downward career." The child—essentially good, as they saw it—was made "to feel that he is the object of [the government's] care and solicitude," not that he was under arrest or on trial.[2]

Child-saving organizations convinced local legislatures to pass laws that allowed them to take control of children who exhibited criminal tendencies or had been neglected by their parents. To separate these children from the environment in which they were raised, the organizations created a number of institutions, the best known of which was New York's House of Refuge. Opening in 1825, the House of Refuge implemented many of the same reformist measures popular in the penitentiaries of the time, meaning that its charges were subjected to the healthful influences of hard study and labor. Although the House of Refuge was criticized for its harsh discipline (which caused many boys to run away), similar institutions sprang up throughout the Northeast during the middle of the 1800s.

The Illinois Juvenile Court

The efforts of the child savers culminated with the passage of the Illinois Juvenile Court Act in 1899. The Illinois legislature created the first court specifically for juveniles, guided by the principles of *parens patriae* and based on the belief that children are not fully responsible for criminal conduct and are capable of being rehabilitated.[3]

The Illinois Juvenile Court and those in other states that followed in its path were (and, in many cases, remain) drastically different from adult courts:

Learning Objective

1 List the four major differences between juvenile courts and adult courts.

- *No juries.* The matter was decided by judges who wore regular clothes instead of black robes and sat at a table with the other participants rather than behind a

status offender A juvenile who has engaged in behavior deemed unacceptable for those under a certain statutorily determined age.

juvenile delinquency Behavior that is illegal under federal or state law that has been committed by a person who is under an age limit specified by statute.

bench. Because the primary focus of the court was on the child and not the crime, the judge had wide discretion in disposing of each case.

- *Different terminology.* To reduce the stigma of criminal proceedings, "petitions" were issued instead of "warrants." The children were not "defendants" but "respondents," and they were not "found guilty" but "adjudicated delinquent."
- *No adversarial relationship.* Instead of trying to determine guilt or innocence, the parties involved in the juvenile court worked together in the best interests of the child, with the emphasis on rehabilitation rather than punishment.
- *Confidentiality.* To avoid "saddling" the child with a criminal past, juvenile court hearings and records were kept sealed, and the proceedings were closed to the public.

By 1945, every state had a juvenile court system modeled after the first Illinois court. For the most part, these courts were able to operate without interference until the 1960s and the onset of the juvenile rights movement.

Status Offending

After the first juvenile court was established in Illinois, the Chicago Bar Association described its purpose as, in part, to "exercise the same tender solicitude and care over its neglected wards that a wise and loving parent would exercise with reference to his [or her] own children under similar circumstances."[4] In other words, the state was given the responsibility of caring for those minors whose behavior seemed to show that they could not be controlled by their parents.

As a result, many **status offenders** found themselves in the early houses of refuge and continue to be placed in state-run facilities today. A status offense is an act that, if committed by a juvenile, is considered illegal and grounds for possible state custody. The same act, if committed by an adult, does not warrant law enforcement action. (See Figure 13.1 for an idea of which status offenses are most commonly brought to the attention of authorities.)

Figure 13.1 Status Offenses

About 110,000 status offenses are processed by juvenile courts in the United States each year. The most common, as this graph shows, are truancy (skipping school) and liquor-related offenses.

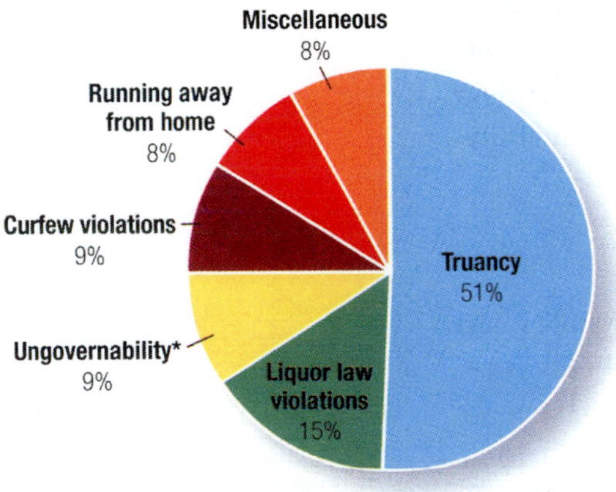

* Being beyond the control of parents, teachers, or other adult authority figures.

Source: Sarah Hockenberry and Charles Puzzanchera, *Juvenile Court Statistics, 2013* (Pittsburgh, Pa.: National Center for Juvenile Justice, July 2015), 66.

Juvenile Delinquency

In contrast to status offending, **juvenile delinquency** refers to conduct that would also be criminal if committed by an adult. According to federal law and the laws of most states, a juvenile delinquent is someone who has not yet reached his or her eighteenth birthday—the age of adult criminal responsibility—at the time of the offense in question. In two states (New York and North Carolina), persons aged sixteen are considered adults, and nine other states confer adulthood on seventeen-year-olds for purposes of criminal law.

Given certain circumstances, discussed later in this chapter, children under these ages can be tried in adult courts and incarcerated in adult prisons and jails. Remember, from the opening of this chapter, that Nehemiah Griego faced the possibility of being charged as an adult and spending 120 years in an adult prison for the crimes he committed when he was fifteen years old. Instead, Griego was adjudicated as a juvenile, meaning that he cannot be incarcerated past his twenty-first birthday per New Mexico law.

Constitutional Protections and the Juvenile Court

Though the ideal of the juvenile court seemed to offer the "best of both worlds" for juvenile offenders, in reality the lack of procedural protections led to many children being arbitrarily punished not only for crimes, but for status offenses as well. Juvenile judges were treating all violators similarly, which led to many status offenders being incarcerated in the same institutions as violent delinquents. In response to a wave of lawsuits demanding due process rights for juveniles, the United States Supreme Court issued several rulings in the 1960s and 1970s that significantly changed the juvenile justice system.

▲ Students at Simon Elementary School in Washington, D.C., show off numbered index cards that can be turned in for various prizes such as pencils, snacks, or backpacks. This daily raffle is part of an effort to combat truancy in the city's school system. **What is the primary difference between a status offense such as truancy and an act of juvenile delinquency?**

Washington Post/Getty Images

Kent v. United States The first decision to extend due process rights to children in juvenile courts was *Kent v. United States* (1966).[5] The case concerned sixteen-year-old Morris Kent, who had been arrested for breaking into a woman's house, stealing her purse, and raping her. Because Kent was on juvenile probation, the state sought to transfer his trial for the crime to an adult court (a process to be discussed later in the chapter).

Without giving any reasons for his decision, the juvenile judge consented to this strategy, and Kent was sentenced in the adult court to a thirty- to ninety-year prison term. The Supreme Court overturned the sentence, ruling that juveniles have a right to counsel and a hearing in any instance in which the juvenile judge is considering sending the case to an adult court. The Court stated that, in such cases, a child receives "the worst of both worlds," getting neither the "protections accorded to adults" nor the "solicitous care and regenerative treatment" offered in the juvenile justice system.[6]

In re Gault The *Kent* decision provided the groundwork for *In re Gault* one year later. Considered by many to be the single most important case concerning juvenile justice, *In re Gault* involved a fifteen-year-old boy who was arrested for allegedly making a lewd phone call while on probation.[7] In its decision, the Supreme Court held that juveniles facing a loss of liberty were entitled to many of the same basic procedural safeguards granted to adult offenders in this country. (See the feature *Landmark Cases*—In re Gault for more information on this case.)

Other Important Court Decisions Over the next ten years, the Supreme Court handed down three more important decisions concerning juvenile court procedure. The ruling in *In re Winship* (1970)[8] required the government to prove "beyond a reasonable doubt" that a juvenile had committed an act of delinquency, raising the burden of proof from a "preponderance of the evidence." In *Breed v. Jones* (1975),[9] the Court held that the Fifth Amendment's double jeopardy clause prevented a juvenile from being tried in an adult court for a crime that had already been adjudicated in juvenile court. In contrast, the decision in *McKeiver v. Pennsylvania* (1971)[10] represented an instance in which the

Court did not move the juvenile court further toward the adult model. In that case, the Court ruled that the Constitution did not give juveniles the right to a jury trial.

Determining Delinquency Today

In the eyes of many observers, the net effect of the Supreme Court decisions during the 1966–1975 period was to move juvenile justice away from the ideals of the child savers. As a result of these decisions, many young offenders would find themselves in a

Landmark Cases

In re Gault

In 1964, fifteen-year-old Gerald Gault and a friend were arrested for making lewd telephone calls to a neighbor in Gila County, Arizona. Gault, who was on probation, was placed under custody with no notice given to his parents. The juvenile court in his district held a series of informal hearings to determine Gault's punishment. During these hearings, no records were kept, Gault was not afforded the right to counsel, and the complaining witness was never made available for questioning. At the close of the hearing, the judge sentenced Gault to remain in Arizona's State Industrial School until the age of twenty-one. Gault's lawyers challenged this punishment, arguing that the proceedings had denied their client his due process rights. Eventually, the matter reached the United States Supreme Court.

Learning Objective 2

Identify and briefly describe the single most important U.S. Supreme Court case with respect to juvenile justice.

In re Gault
United States Supreme Court
387 U.S. 1 (1967)

In the Words of the Court . . .

Justice Fortas, Majority Opinion

* * * *

From the inception of the juvenile court system, wide differences have been tolerated—indeed insisted upon—between the procedural rights accorded to adults and those of juveniles. In practically all jurisdictions, there are rights granted to adults which are withheld from juveniles.

* * * *

The absence of substantive standards has not necessarily meant that children receive careful, compassionate, individualized treatment. The absence of procedural rules based upon constitutional principle has not always produced fair, efficient, and effective procedures. Departures from established principles of due process have frequently resulted not in enlightened procedure, but in arbitrariness.

* * * *

Ultimately, however, we confront the reality of that portion of the Juvenile Court process with which we deal in this case. A boy is charged with misconduct. The boy is committed to an institution where he may be restrained of liberty for years.* * * His world becomes "a building with whitewashed walls, regimented routine and institutional hours. . . ." Instead of mother and father and sisters and brothers and friends and classmates, his world is peopled by guards, custodians, state employees, and "delinquents" confined with him for anything from waywardness to rape and homicide. In view of this, it would be extraordinary if our Constitution did not require the procedural regularity and the exercise of care implied in the phrase "due process." Under our Constitution, the condition of being a boy does not justify a kangaroo court.

* * * *

Decision

The Court held that juveniles were entitled to the basic procedural safeguards afforded by the U.S. Constitution, including the right to advance notice of charges, the right to counsel, the right to confront and cross-examine witnesses, and the privilege against self-incrimination. The decision marked a turning point in juvenile justice in this country: no longer would informality and paternalism be the guiding principles of juvenile courts. Instead, due process would dictate the adjudication process, much as in an adult court.

For Critical Analysis

What might be some of the negative consequences of the *In re Gault* decision for juveniles charged with committing delinquent acts? Can you think of any reasons why juveniles should not receive the same due process protections as adult offenders?

formalized system that is often indistinguishable from its adult counterpart. At the same time, though the Court has recognized that minors charged with crimes possess certain constitutional rights, it has failed to dictate at what age these rights should be granted. Consequently, the legal status of children in the United States varies depending on where they live, with each state making its own policy decisions on the crucial questions of age and culpability.

The Age Question

On the evening of October 3, 2015, eleven-year-old Benjamin Tiller was talking with three girls through the window of his family's trailer home in White Pine, Tennessee. When one of the girls, eight-year-old MaKayla Dyer, refused to show Tiller her new puppies, Tiller became angry and threated Dyer with his father's twelve-gauge shotgun. As Dyer laughed, saying the weapon was not real, Tiller "made certain the gun was loaded, cocked the hammer on the gun, and shot the victim just above the heart at a downward trajectory," according to court reports.[11] Shortly thereafter, the girl died in her mother's arms.

In Chapter 3, we saw that early American criminal law recognized infancy as a defense against criminal charges. At that time, on attaining fourteen years of age, a youth was considered an adult and treated accordingly by the criminal justice system. Today, as Figure 13.2 shows, every state allows for the prosecution of juveniles under fourteen years old as adults, with the majority of states, including Tennessee, having no age minimum whatsoever. In Tiller's case, a district attorney decided that the boy was too young to be charged in adult court. Subsequently, a juvenile court judge found Tiller guilty of first degree murder and ordered that he be held in state custody until his nineteenth birthday. In general, when young offenders who remain in juvenile court are found guilty, they receive "limited" sentences that, depending on the state, expire before they turn twenty-five.

The Culpability Question

Many researchers believe that by the age of fourteen, an adolescent has the same ability as an adult to make a competent decision. Nevertheless, according to some observers, a juvenile's capacity to understand the difference between "right" and "wrong" does not mean that she or he should be held to the same standards of competency as an adult.

Juvenile Behavior A study released in 2003 by the Research Network on Adolescent Development and Juvenile Justice found that 33 percent of juvenile defendants in criminal courts had the same low level of understanding of legal matters as mentally ill adults who had been found incompetent to stand trial.[12] Legal psychologist Richard E. Redding believes that

Figure 13.2
The Minimum Age at Which a Juvenile Can Be Tried as an Adult

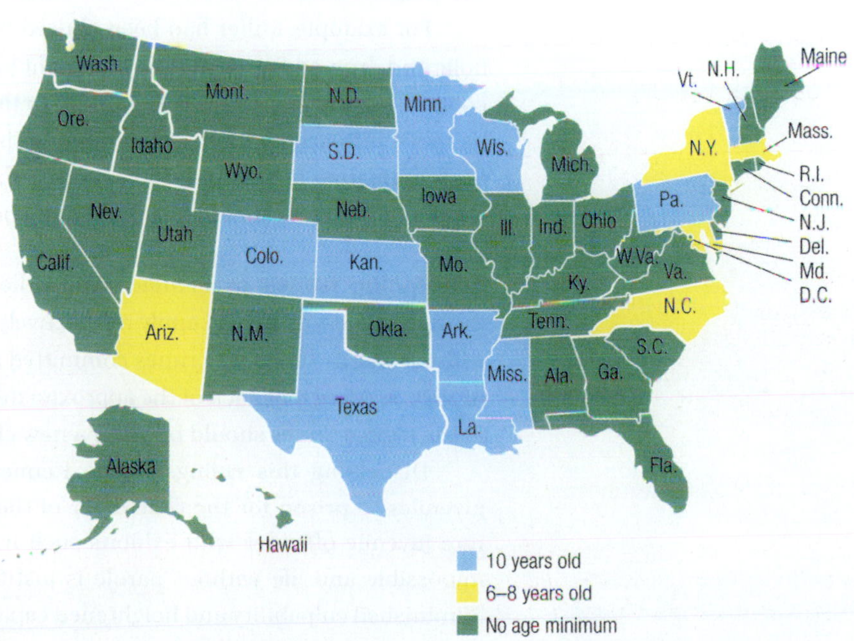

Source: National Criminal Justice Reference Service.

adolescents' lack of life experience may limit their real-world decision-making ability. Whether we call it wisdom, judgment, or common sense, adolescents may not have nearly enough.[13]

Juveniles are generally more impulsive, more likely to engage in risky behavior, and less likely to calculate the long-term consequences of any particular action. Furthermore, adolescents are far more likely to respond to peer pressure than are adults, meaning that they often engage in the same criminal or delinquent behavior as their friends.[14] Furthermore, juveniles are less likely than adults to display remorse immediately following a violent act. As a result, they are often penalized by the courts for showing "less grief than the system demands."[15]

Learning Objective 3

Describe the reasoning behind recent U.S. Supreme Court decisions that have lessened the harshness of sentencing outcomes for violent juvenile offenders.

Diminished Guilt The "diminished culpability" of juveniles was one of the reasons given by the United States Supreme Court in its landmark decision in *Roper v. Simmons* (2005).[16] As we saw in Chapter 9, that case forbade the execution of offenders who were under the age of eighteen when they committed their crimes. In his majority opinion, Justice Anthony Kennedy wrote that because minors cannot fully comprehend the consequences of their actions, the two main justifications for the death penalty—retribution and deterrence—do not "work" with juvenile wrongdoers.[17]

Life Imprisonment Issues The Supreme Court applied the same reasoning in two later cases that have dramatically affected the sentencing of violent juvenile offenders. First, in *Graham v. Florida* (2010),[18] the Court held that juveniles who commit crimes that do not involve murder may not be sentenced to life in prison without the possibility of parole. According to Justice Kennedy, who wrote the majority opinion, state officials must give these inmates "some meaningful opportunity to obtain release based on demonstrated maturity and rehabilitation."[19]

Then, with *Miller v. Alabama* (2012),[20] the Court banned laws in twenty-eight states that made life-without-parole sentences *mandatory* for juveniles convicted of murder. The case focused on the fate of Evan Miller, who was fourteen years old when he killed a neighbor with a baseball bat. The ruling did not signify that juvenile offenders such as Miller could not, under any circumstances, be sentenced to life without parole. Rather, the Court stated that judges must have the discretion to weigh the mitigating factors in each individual case.

For example, Miller had been abused by his stepfather and neglected by his alcoholic and drug-addicted mother, had spent most of his life in foster care, and had tried to commit suicide four times.[21] According to the Court, this type of personal history must be taken into account when determining the proper sentence for a juvenile murderer. Such mitigating factors may indicate that the offender has the potential to be rehabilitated and therefore should be afforded the possibility of parole.

Sentencing Issues In its *Miller* ruling, the Supreme Court failed to indicate whether the new standards should apply retroactively to inmates already serving mandatory life-without-parole terms for crimes committed as juveniles. The Court clarified this matter in 2016, holding that each of the approximately two thousand such offenders imprisoned in the United States should be given a new chance at release.[22]

Discussing this ruling, Justice Kennedy clearly indicated distaste for sending juveniles to prison for the remainder of their lives. "A sentencer might encounter the rare juvenile offender who exhibits such irretrievable depravity that rehabilitation is impossible and life without parole is justified," he argued. But, given young people's "diminished culpability and heightened capacity for change," the "appropriate occasions for sentencing juveniles to this harshest possible penalty will be uncommon."[23] (See this chapter's *CJ Policy—Your Take* to consider another class of juvenile offenders whose levels of punishment are being reconsidered by the criminal justice system.)

Trends in Juvenile Delinquency

When asked, juveniles will admit to a wide range of illegal or dangerous behavior, including carrying weapons, getting involved in physical fights, driving after drinking alcohol, and stealing or deliberately damaging school property. Has the juvenile justice system been effective in controlling and preventing this kind of misbehavior, as well as more serious acts?

Delinquency by the Numbers

According to the Uniform Crime Report, in 2014 juveniles accounted for 10.7 percent of violent crime arrests and 15.1 percent of Part I property crime arrests.[24] As Figure 13.3 shows, juvenile arrest rates for violent crimes have fluctuated dramatically over the past three decades. In the 2000s, with a few exceptions, juvenile crime in the United States has decreased at a rate similar to that of adult crime, as discussed earlier in this textbook. From 1997 to 2013, juvenile court delinquency caseloads declined by 44 percent.[25] Not surprisingly, the drop in juvenile arrests and court appearances has led to fewer incarcerated juveniles. The national population of juvenile inmates decreased 53 percent between 1997 and 2013, allowing officials in some states, including California, Ohio, and Texas, to close juvenile detention facilities.[26]

A number of theories have been put forth to explain this downturn in juvenile offending. Some observers point to the increase in police action against "quality-of-life" crimes such as loitering, which they believe stops juveniles before they have a chance to commit more serious crimes. Similarly, about 80 percent of American municipalities enforce juvenile curfews, which restrict the movement of minors during certain hours, usually after dark.[27] In 2014, law enforcement made about 54,000 arrests for curfew and loitering law violations.[28] Furthermore, hundreds of local programs designed to educate children about the dangers of drugs and crime operate across the country. Though the results of such community-based efforts are difficult, if not impossible, to measure—it cannot be assumed that children would have become delinquent if they had not participated—these programs are generally considered a crucial element of keeping youth crime under control.[29]

Race and Juvenile Delinquency As is the case in the criminal justice system, African Americans are overrepresented in the juvenile justice system. The total delinquency case rate for black juveniles is more than double the total delinquency case rate for white juveniles.[30] African American youths are more likely to be arrested for every major category of crime than are white youths, and more than six in every ten juvenile offenders in state custody belongs to a minority group.[31] Furthermore, black students are 31 percent more likely to face school disciplinary action—discussed later in the chapter—than are white and Hispanic students.[32]

A great deal of research, much of it contradictory, has been done to determine whether these statistics reflect inherent racism in the juvenile justice system or whether social factors are to blame.[33] In general, though, police officers do seem more likely to arrest members of minority groups. Although this may be partially attributed to the social factors discussed in Chapter 2, it also appears that minority youths often fail the "attitude test" during interactions with police officers. After the seriousness of the offense and past

CJ Policy—Your Take

In the previous chapter, you learned that convicted sex offenders are subjected to a number of lifelong legal constraints, such as residency restrictions and inclusion on registries that make it difficult to find employment. For the most part, these conditions are the same for both **juvenile sex offenders** and adult sex offenders. **Is this fair? In other words, do you think that the concept of diminished culpability should apply to juvenile sex offenders in the same manner that it has been applied to juvenile violent offenders? What kind of information would you need to best answer these questions?**

Figure 13.3 Arrest Rates of Juveniles

After rising dramatically in the mid-1990s, juvenile arrest rates for violent crimes have—with a few exceptions—continued to drop steadily in the 2000s.

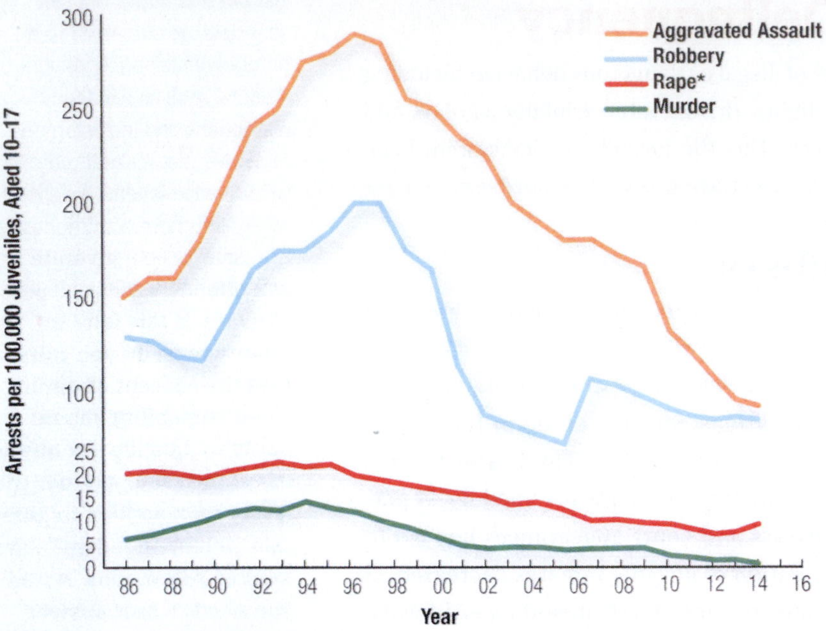

*The recent increase in juvenile arrests for rape can be explained, in part, by an expanded definition of the crime that the federal government began using in 2014.

Source: Office of Juvenile Justice and Delinquency Prevention, *Statistical Briefing Book*, at **ojjdp.gov/ojstatbb/crime/JAR.asp.**

history, the most important factor in the decision of whether to arrest or release appears to be the offender's attitude. An offender who is polite and apologetic generally has a better chance of being released. If the juvenile is hostile or unresponsive, the police are more likely to place him or her in custody for even a minor offense.[34]

Gender and Juvenile Delinquency Although overall rates of juvenile offending have been dropping, arrest rates for girls are declining more slowly than those for boys. Between 1997 and 2013, the number of cases involving males in delinquency courts declined 47 percent, while the female caseload in such courts declined by 34 percent.[35] Self-reported studies show, however, that there has been little change in girls' violent behavior over the past few decades.[36] How, then, do we explain why arrest rates for girls have changed and why the change is different from that for boys?

Detention Trends Evidence shows that law enforcement officers are more likely to apprehend girls than boys for status offenses and nonviolent behavior. In 2013, 37 percent of girls detained by juvenile justice authorities were being held for status offenses and technical violations of probation, compared to 25 percent of boys.[37] Furthermore, 21 percent of girls are taken into custody for simple assault and public order offenses, compared to just 12 percent of boys.[38] Criminologists who focus on issues of gender hypothesize that such behavior is considered normal for boys but is seen as deviant for girls, and therefore more deserving of punishment.[39]

Family- and Sex-Based Delinquency A significant amount of data also suggest that police are much more likely to make arrests in situations involving domestic violence than was the case several decades ago. Experts have found that girls are four times more apt to fight with parents or siblings than are boys, who usually engage in violent encounters with strangers. Consequently, a large percentage of female juvenile arrests for assault arise out of family disputes—arrests that until relatively recently would not have been made.[40] Finally, because girls are more likely to be exploited by sex-trafficking operations, they represent a significant majority of juveniles arrested for prostitution and commercialized vice.[41]

School Violence and Bullying

Just after 10:00 o'clock on the morning of February 29, 2016, fourteen-year-old James Hancock walked into the cafeteria of Madison High School in Middletown, Ohio, carrying a .380-caliber handgun. Hancock opened fire, hitting two other students. The incident was every student's (and teacher's and parent's) worst nightmare. Like other episodes of school violence, it received heavy media coverage, fanning fears that our schools are unsafe.

▲ A police officer interviews two teenage girls who were involved in a fight in Tucson, Arizona. **Do you think that law enforcement is likely to treat girls more harshly than boys for this type of misbehavior? Why?**
Scott Olson/Getty Images

Safe Schools Research does show that juveniles are most likely to be victims of violent crime on school days between 3 P.M. and 4 P.M.—in other words, just after the end of classes.[42] In spite of well-publicized school shootings such as the one carried out by James Hancock in Middletown, Ohio, however, violent crime is not commonplace in American schools. In fact, school-age youths are much more likely to be murdered away from school than on a campus.[43] Furthermore, despite a slight increase in recent years, between 1995 and 2013 victimization rates of students for nonfatal crimes at school declined significantly, meaning that, in general, schools are safer today than they were in the recent past.[44]

For the most part, these statistics mirror the downward trend of all criminal activity in the United States since the mid-1990s. In addition, since the fatal shootings of fourteen students and a teacher at Columbine High School near Littleton, Colorado, in 1999, many schools have improved security measures. From 1999 to 2013, the percentage of American schools using security cameras to monitor their campuses increased from 19 to 64 percent. Today, 88 percent of public schools control access to school buildings by locking or monitoring their doors.[45] Furthermore, many districts rely on law enforcement officers to patrol school grounds, a growing practice that we cover in the feature *CJ Controversy—Police in Schools.*

Learning Objective

4 Define *bullying,* and list the four components that are often present in this sort of behavior.

Bullied Students A disproportionate number of young people who bring guns or other weapons to school report that they have been *bullied* by other students.[46] **Bullying** can be broadly defined as repeated, aggressive behavior that contains at least one of the following elements:

1. *Physical abuse,* such as such as hitting or punching a person or damaging a person's property.
2. *Verbal abuse,* such as teasing, name calling, intimidation, or homophobic or racist remarks.
3. *Social and emotional abuse,* such as spreading false rumors, social exclusion, or playing jokes designed to humiliate.
4. *Cyber abuse,* which includes any form of bullying that takes place online or through the use of devices such as smartphones.

Changing Perspectives Bullying has traditionally been seen more as an inevitable rite of passage among adolescents than as potentially criminal behavior. In recent years, however, society has become more aware of the negative consequences of bullying, underscored by a number of high-profile "bullycides." In September 2013, for example,

bullying Overt acts taken by students with the goal of intimidating, harassing, or humiliating other students.

CJ Controversy

M Dogan/Shutterstock.com

Police in Schools

About 19,000 School-Resource Officers (SROs) are patrolling school hallways in the United States. SROs have the same powers as any other police officer, including the ability to issue criminal citations to students who break the law on school grounds. Although the public often see these officers primarily as protection against mass shootings, SROs are more engaged in disciplinary issues than security issues. According to the National Institute of Justice, SROs spend the majority of their time on law enforcement activities, which include handing out misdemeanor citations for offenses such as acting up in class, getting in fights, or smoking cigarettes.

Police Should Patrol School Grounds Because . . .

- A police presence acts as a deterrent against a school attack. In the words of one commentator, "Rampaging gunmen seek victims at places where they expect no immediate resistance."
- SROs help teachers deal with increasingly dangerous students, who, according to an Austin, Texas, educator, "can be very threatening. The police get called because that way the teacher can go on with teaching instead of wasting half the class dealing with one child, and it sends a message to the other kids."

Police Should Not Patrol School Grounds Because . . .

- Several studies suggest that not only does the presence of SROs have little impact on school safety, but having police officers on campuses also increases the likelihood of certain kinds of student disorder.
- Police in schools lead to a "school-to-prison pipeline," in which minor behavior problems are referred to criminal courts, saddling hundreds of thousands of students with criminal records. As a consequence, these children are more likely to drop out of school and have future interactions with the criminal justice system.

Your Assignment

Go online to find an example of a **police officer using force to arrest a student on school grounds**. Critique the situation: Was the student's behavior worthy of a law enforcement response? Should the student have been arrested? Did the police officer use unnecessary force? Should the officer have been disciplined for his or her actions? Does the incident change your opinion of policies that encourage placing police officers in schools? Your answer should include at least two full paragraphs.

---

twelve-year-old Rebecca Sedwick jumped to her death at an abandoned concrete plant in Lakeland, Florida. Sedwick had been relentlessly bullied online and face-to-face by two other girls who, among other things, told her that she was "ugly" and that she should "drink bleach and die."[47] According to research conducted at Yale University, juveniles who have been bullied are between two and nine times more likely to commit suicide than those who have not been bullied.[48]

Legal Responses According to data gathered by the federal government, 22 percent of students aged twelve to eighteen have been victims of bullying.[49] In particular, gay students are targeted—nine out of ten report being bullied within the previous year.[50] As a response to this problem, nearly every state has passed anti-bullying legislation. These laws focus mostly on "soft" measures, such as training school personnel how to recognize and respond to bullying.[51]

State legislatures have been reluctant to take "harder" measures such as specifically defining bullying as a crime. Returning to our previous example, in October 2013 Polk County sheriff Grady Judd arrested the two girls who had bullied Rebecca Sedwick prior to her death and charged them with felony aggravated stalking. The state attorney's office quickly dropped the charges, however, after determining that the girls' behavior, while reprehensible, was not criminal.

CJ & Technology

Cyberbullying

Cheryl E. Davis/Shutterstock.com

Although it is not clear whether bullying in general is more prevalent now than in the past, one form of bullying is definitely on the rise. As the Internet, texting, and social networking sites such as Snapchat and Instagram have become integral parts of youth culture, so, it seems, has cyberbullying. Apps such as Yik Yak allow young people to make anonymous rude, cruel, and sexually suggestive comments about peers. In a recent poll, 85 percent of American and Canadian students said that they had been subject to cyberbullying at least once during the previous year.

To many, cyberbullying can be even more devastating than "old school" bullying. Not only does the anonymity of cyberspace seem to embolden perpetrators, causing them to be more vicious than they might be in person, but, as one expert points out, when bullying occurs online, "you can't get away from it." Still, as the example of Rebecca Sedwick in the text highlights, criminal law does not yet cover most forms of cyberbullying. The consensus seems to be that children should not be charged with a crime for vicious behavior online unless that behavior contains a "specific threat of bodily harm or death." Another suggestion, that parents be held legally responsible for their child's online bullying, has also been ruled out as an unworkable solution to the problem.

Thinking about Cyberbullying

How should the criminal justice system respond to cyberbullying, if at all?

Factors in Juvenile Delinquency

As we discussed in Chapter 2, an influential study conducted by Professor Marvin Wolfgang and several colleagues in the early 1970s introduced the "chronic 6 percent" to criminology. The researchers found that out of one hundred boys, six will become chronic offenders, meaning that they will be arrested five or more times before their eighteenth birthdays. Furthermore, Wolfgang and his colleagues determined that these chronic offenders are responsible for half of all crimes and two-thirds of all violent crimes within any given cohort (a group of persons who have similar characteristics).[52]

Does this "6 percent rule" mean that no matter what steps society takes, six out of every hundred juveniles are "bad seeds" and will act delinquently? Or does it point to a situation in which a small percentage of children may be more likely to commit crimes under certain circumstances? Most criminologists favor the second interpretation. In this section, we will examine the four factors that have traditionally been used to explain juvenile criminal behavior and violent crime rates: age, substance abuse, family problems, and gangs. Keep in mind, however, that the factors influencing delinquency are not limited to these topics (see Figure 13.4). Researchers are constantly interpreting and reinterpreting statistical evidence to provide fresh perspectives on this very important issue.

For instance, increased attention to the nationwide problem of bullying has led to numerous studies regarding its impact on victims. Generally speaking, this research shows that victims of bullying are at an increased risk of becoming bullies themselves, and of engaging in a variety of other antisocial and criminal behavior.[53] Several years ago, Michael Turner, an associate professor of criminal justice and criminology at the University of North Carolina at Charlotte, released data showing that bullied preteens

Figure 13.4 Risk Factors for Juvenile Delinquency

The characteristics listed here are generally accepted as "risk factors" for juvenile delinquency. In other words, if one or more of these factors are present in a juvenile's life, he or she has a greater chance of exhibiting delinquent behavior—though such behavior is by no means a certainty.

Family	• Single parent/lack of parental role model • Parental or sibling drug/alcohol abuse • Extreme economic deprivation • Family members in a gang or in prison
School	• Academic frustration/failure • Learning disability • Negative labeling by teachers • Disciplinary problems
Community	• Social disorganization (refer to Chapter 2) • Presence of gangs and obvious drug use in the community • Availability of firearms • High crime/constant feeling of danger • Lack of social and economic opportunities
Peers	• Delinquent friends • Friends who use drugs or who are members of gangs • Lack of "positive" peer pressure
Individual	• Mental illness • Tendency toward aggressive behavior • Inability to concentrate or focus/easily bored/hyperactive • Alcohol or drug use • Fatalistic/pessimistic viewpoint

were twice as likely to wind up in prison as those preteens who had not been bullied. Furthermore, Turner found that, regardless of race, exposure to bullying during adolescence correlates strongly with substance abuse and delinquency.[54]

The Age-Crime Relationship

Learning Objective 5

Describe the one variable that always correlates highly with juvenile crime rates.

Crime statistics are fairly conclusive on one point: the older a person is, the less likely he or she will exhibit criminal behavior. Self-reported studies confirm that most people are involved in some form of criminal behavior—however "harmless"—during their early years. In fact, Terrie Moffitt of Duke University has said that "it is statistically aberrant to refrain from crime during adolescence."[55] So, why do the vast majority of us not become chronic offenders?

According to many criminologists, particularly Travis Hirschi and Michael Gottfredson, any group of at-risk persons—regardless of gender, race, intelligence, or class—will commit fewer crimes as they grow older.[56] This process is known as **aging out** (or, sometimes, *desistance,* a term we first encountered in the previous chapter). Professor Robert J. Sampson and his colleague John H. Laub believe that this phenomenon is explained by certain events, such as marriage, employment, and military service, which force delinquents to "grow up" and forgo criminal acts.[57]

Another view sees the **age of onset**, or the age at which the youth begins delinquent behavior, as a consistent predictor of future criminal behavior. One study compared recidivism rates between juveniles first judged to be delinquent before the age of fifteen and those first adjudicated delinquent after the age of fifteen. Of the seventy-one subjects who made up the first group, 32 percent became chronic offenders. Of the sixty-five who made up the second group, none became chronic offenders.[58] Furthermore, according to the Office of Juvenile Justice and Delinquency Prevention, the earlier a youth enters the

aging out A term used to explain the fact that criminal activity declines with age.

age of onset The age at which a juvenile first exhibits delinquent behavior.

juvenile justice system, the more likely he or she will become a violent offender.[59] This research suggests that juvenile justice resources should be concentrated on the youngest offenders, with the goal of preventing crime and reducing the long-term risks for society.

child abuse Mistreatment of children by causing physical, emotional, or sexual damage.

child neglect A form of child abuse in which the child is denied certain necessities such as shelter, food, care, and love.

Substance Abuse

As we have seen throughout this textbook, substance abuse plays a strong role in criminal behavior for adults. The same can certainly be said for juveniles. According to the University of Michigan's Institute for Social Research, 22 percent of American tenth-graders and 25 percent of American twelfth-graders are regular alcohol drinkers, increasing their risks for violent behavior, delinquency, academic problems, and unsafe sexual behavior.[60] Close to 40 percent of high school seniors report using marijuana at least once in the past twelve months, and just under 20 percent admit to using an illegal drug other than marijuana during that time period.[61]

A Strong Correlation As with adults, substance abuse among juveniles seems to play a major role in offending. Drug use is associated with a wide range of antisocial and illegal behaviors by juveniles, from school suspensions to large-scale theft.[62] Nearly all young offenders (94 percent) entering juvenile detention self-report drug use at some point in their lives, and 85 percent have used drugs in the previous six months.[63] According to the Arrestee Drug Abuse Monitoring Program, nearly 60 percent of male juvenile detainees and 46 percent of female juvenile detainees test positive for drug use at the time of their offense.[64] Drug use is a particularly strong risk factor for girls: 75 percent of young women incarcerated in juvenile facilities report regular drug and alcohol use—starting at the age of fourteen—and one study found that 87 percent of female teenage offenders need substance abuse treatment.[65]

Strong Causation? The correlation between substance abuse and offending for juveniles seems obvious. Does this mean that substance abuse *causes* juvenile offending? Researchers make the point that most youths who become involved in antisocial behavior do so before their first experience with alcohol or drugs. Therefore, it would appear that substance abuse is a form of delinquent behavior rather than its cause.[66] Still, a 2011 study of adolescent offenders did find that substance abuse treatment reduces criminal behavior in the short term, suggesting that, at the least, the use of illegal drugs is an integral component of the juvenile delinquent lifestyle.[67]

Child Abuse and Neglect

Abuse by parents also plays a substantial role in juvenile delinquency. **Child abuse** can be broadly defined as the infliction of physical, emotional, or sexual damage on a child. **Child neglect** is a form of abuse that occurs when caregivers deprive a child of necessities such as love, shelter, food, and proper care. According to the National Survey of Children's Exposure to Violence, one in ten children in the United States experience mistreatment at the hands of a close family member before reaching eighteen years of age.[68]

Children in homes characterized by violence or neglect suffer from a variety of physical, emotional, and mental health problems at a much greater rate than their peers.[69] This, in turn, increases their chances of engaging in delinquent behavior. One survey of violent juveniles showed that 75 percent had been subjected to severe abuse by a family member and 80 percent had witnessed violence in their homes.[70] Nearly half of all juveniles—and 80 percent of girls—sentenced to life in prison suffered high rates of abuse.[71]

Getting Linked in™

Given how many children are at risk of being abused and neglected in this country, **child welfare specialists** can have a direct influence on reducing national levels of delinquent behavior. As a search for "child welfare" on LinkedIn shows, hundreds of public and private institutions presently need the services of professionals in this crucial field.

youth gang A self-formed group of youths with several identifiable characteristics, including a gang name and other recognizable symbols, a geographic territory, and participation in illegal activities.

Gangs

When youths cannot find the stability and support they require in the family structure, they will often turn to their peers. This is just one explanation for why juveniles join **youth gangs**. Although jurisdictions may have varying definitions, for general purposes a youth gang is viewed as a group of three or more persons who (1) self-identify as an entity separate from the community by special clothing, vocabulary, hand signals, and names and (2) engage in criminal activity. According to an exhaustive survey of law enforcement agencies, there are probably around 30,000 gangs with approximately 850,000 members in the United States.[72]

Juveniles who have experienced the risk factors discussed in this section are more likely to join a gang, and once they have done so, they are more likely to engage in delinquent and violent behavior than nongang members.[73] Statistics show high levels of gang involvement in most violent criminal activities in the United States.[74] One recent study found that a third of all fatal shootings in Newark, New Jersey, occurred within the city's gang network, which makes up only 4 percent of the city's population.[75] Much of the recent resurgence of violent crime in major cities such as Baltimore, Chicago, and Washington, D.C., is the result of rivalries among street gangs over the sale of illegal drugs.[76]

Furthermore, a study of criminal behavior among juveniles in Seattle found that gang members were considerably more likely to commit crimes than at-risk youths who shared many characteristics with gang members but were not affiliated with any gang (see Figure 13.5). The survey also found that gang members were much more likely to own firearms or have friends who did than nongang members.[77]

Who Joins Gangs? The average gang member is eighteen years old, though members tend to be older in cities with long traditions of gang activity, such as Chicago and

Figure 13.5 Comparison of Gang and Nongang Delinquent Behavior

Taking self-reported surveys of subjects aged thirteen to eighteen in the Seattle area, researchers for the Office of Juvenile Justice and Delinquency Prevention found that gang members were much more likely to exhibit delinquent behavior than nongang members.

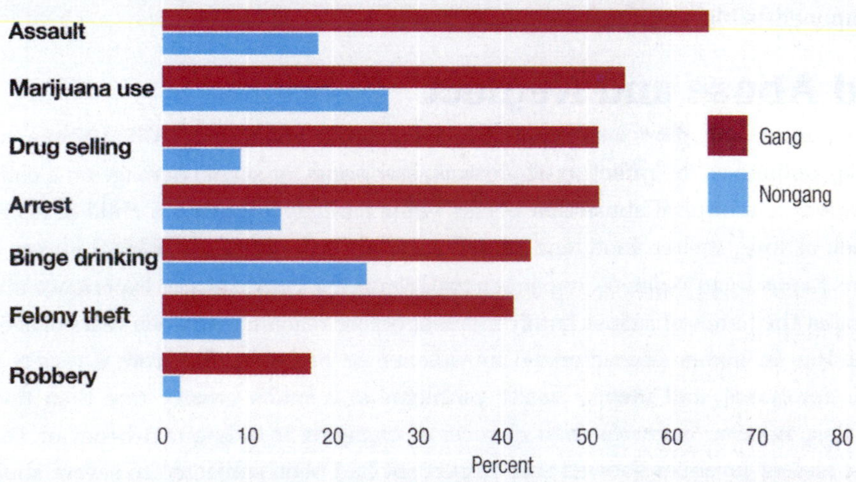

Source: Karl G. Hill, Christina Lui and J. David Hawkins, *Early Precursors of Gang Membership: A Study of Seattle Youth* (Washington, D.C.: Office of Juvenile Justice and Delinquency Prevention, December 2001), Figure 1, page 2.

Los Angeles. Although it is difficult to determine with any certainty the makeup of gangs as a whole, one recent survey found that 53 percent of all gang members in the United States are Hispanic, 32 percent are African American, and 10 percent are white, with the remaining 5 percent belonging to other racial or ethnic backgrounds.[78]

Though gangs tend to have racial or ethnic characteristics—that is, one group predominates in each gang—many researchers do not believe that race or ethnicity is the dominant factor in gang membership. Instead, gang members seem to come from lower-class or working-class communities, mostly in urban areas but with an increasing number from the suburbs and rural counties.

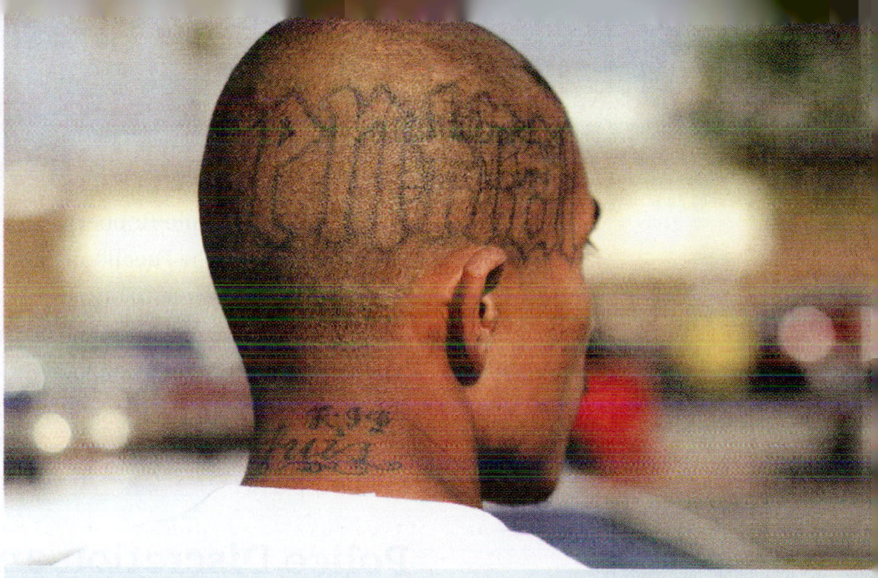

▲ In Los Angeles, a gang member signifies his allegiance to the "Street Villains" through a series of elaborate tattoos. **What role does identity play in a juvenile's decision to join a gang?** Kevork Djansezian/Getty Images

A small percentage of youth gang members are female. In many instances, girls associate themselves with gangs, even though they are not considered members. Generally, girls assume subordinate gender roles in youth gangs, providing emotional, physical, and sexual services for the dominant males.[79] Still, almost half of all youth gangs report having female members, and, according to the most recent data, involvement of girls in gangs is increasing.[80]

Why Join Gangs? The decision to join a gang, as with the decision to engage in any sort of antisocial or criminal behavior, is a complex one, and the factors that go into it vary depending on the individual. Generally, however, the reasons for gang membership involve one or more of the following:

1. *Identity.* Being part of a gang often confers a status that the individual feels he or she could not attain outside the gang.
2. *Protection.* Many gang members live in neighborhoods marked by high levels of crime and violence, and a gang guarantees support and retaliation in case of an attack.
3. *Fellowship.* The gang often functions as an extension of the family and provides companionship that may not be available at home.
4. *Criminal activity.* Many gang members enjoy financial rewards because of the gang's profits and protection.
5. *Intimidation.* Some gang members are pressured or forced to join the gang, often to act as "foot soldiers" in the gang's criminal enterprises.[81]

EthicsChallenge

Suppose your hometown passed an ordinance that makes being a gang member a misdemeanor that carries a maximum penalty of a year in jail and a $5,000 fine. What impact would this law have on local gang membership? What are some of the potential ethical issues raised by this type of law?

low-visibility decision making A term used to describe the discretionary power police have in determining what to do with misbehaving juveniles.

First Contact: The Police and Pretrial Procedures

As part of the Juvenile Robbery Intervention Program, New York City detectives spend hours monitoring the Facebook pages and Twitter accounts of teenagers at risk for gang involvement and violent crime. Most commonly, however, contact between juvenile offenders and law enforcement takes place on the streets, initiated by a police officer on patrol who either apprehends the juvenile while he or she is committing a crime or answers a call for service. (See Figure 13.6 for an overview of the juvenile justice process.) The youth is then passed on to an officer of the juvenile court, who must decide how to handle the case.

Police Discretion and Juvenile Crime

Police arrest about 480,000 youths under the age of eighteen each year.[82] In most cases, police officers must have probable cause to believe that the minor has committed an offense, just as they would if the suspect was an adult. Police power with regard to juveniles is greater than with adults, however, because police can take youths into custody for status offenses, such as possession of alcohol or truancy. In these cases, the officer is acting *in loco parentis,* or in the place of the parent. The officer's role is not necessarily to punish the youths, but to protect them from harmful behavior.

Police officers also have a great deal of discretion in deciding what to do with juveniles who have committed crimes or status offenses. Juvenile justice expert Joseph Goldstein labels this discretionary power **low-visibility decision making** because it relies on factors that the public is not generally in a position to understand or criticize. When a grave offense has taken place, a police officer may decide to formally arrest the juvenile, send him or her to juvenile court, or place the youth under the care of a social-service organization. In less serious situations, the officer may simply issue a warning or take the offender to the police station and release the child into the custody of her or his parents.

Figure 13.6 The Juvenile Justice Process

This diagram shows the possible tracks that a young person may take after her or his first contact with the juvenile justice system (usually a police officer).

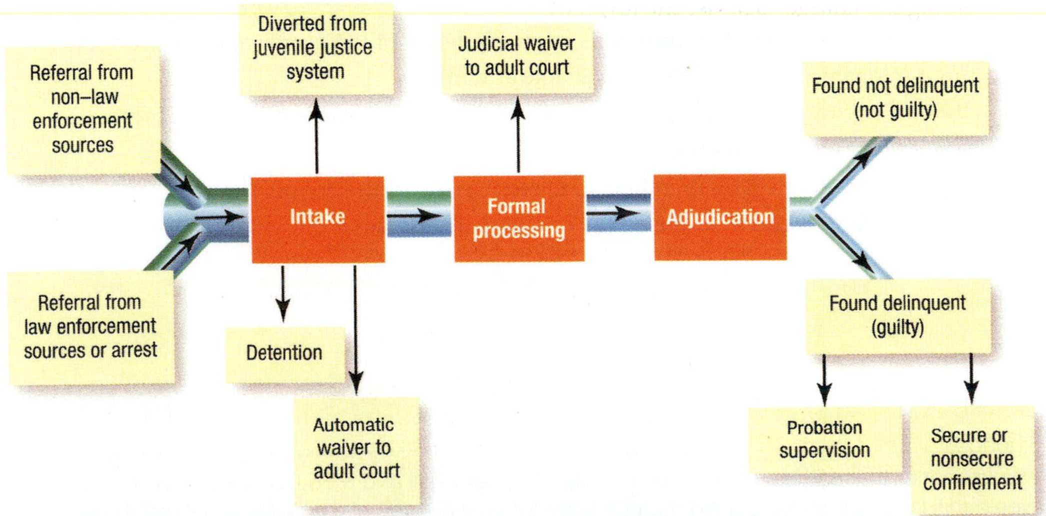

Source: Office of Juvenile Justice and Delinquency Prevention.

In making these discretionary decisions, police generally consider the following factors:

- The nature of the child's offense.
- The offender's past history of involvement with the juvenile justice system.
- The setting in which the offense took place.
- The ability and willingness of the child's parents to take disciplinary action.
- The attitude of the offender.
- The offender's gender.

Law enforcement officers notify the juvenile court system that a particular young person requires its attention through a process known as a **referral**. Anyone with a valid reason, including parents, relatives, welfare agencies, and school officials, can refer a juvenile to the juvenile court. The vast majority of cases in juvenile courts, however, are referred by the police.[83]

Intake

So, if, following arrest, a police officer feels the offender warrants the attention of the juvenile justice process, the officer will refer the youth to juvenile court. Once this step has been taken, a complaint is filed with a special division of the juvenile court, and the **intake** process begins. Intake may be followed by diversion to a community-based program, transfer to an adult court, or detention to await trial in juvenile court. Thus, intake, diversion, transfer, and detention are the four primary stages of pretrial juvenile justice procedure.

During intake, an official of the juvenile court—usually a probation officer, but sometimes a judge—must decide, in effect, what to do with the offender. The intake officer has several options during intake.

1. Simply dismiss the case, releasing the offender without taking any further action. This occurs in about one in five cases, usually because the judge cannot determine a sufficient reason to continue.[84]
2. Divert the offender to a social-services program, such as drug rehabilitation or anger management.
3. File a **petition** for a formal court hearing. The petition is the formal document outlining the charges against the juvenile.
4. Transfer the case to an adult court, where the offender will be tried as an adult.

Learning Objective

6 Describe the four primary stages of pretrial juvenile justice procedure.

With regard to status offenses, judges have sole discretion to decide whether to process the case or *divert* the youth to another juvenile service agency.

Pretrial Diversion

In the context of juvenile justice, diversion refers to the process of removing low-risk offenders from the formal juvenile justice system by placing them in community-based rehabilitation programs.

Diversion programs vary widely, but fall into three general categories:

1. *Probation.* In this program, the juvenile is returned to the community but placed under the supervision of a juvenile probation officer. If the youth breaks the conditions of probation, he or she can be returned to the formal juvenile system.
2. *Treatment and aid.* Many juveniles have behavioral or medical conditions that contribute to their delinquent behavior, and many diversion programs offer

referral The notification process through which a law enforcement officer or other concerned citizen makes the juvenile court aware of a juvenile's unlawful or unruly conduct.

intake The process by which an official of the court must decide whether to file a petition, release the juvenile, or place the juvenile under some other form of supervision.

petition The document filed with a juvenile court alleging that the juvenile is a delinquent or a status offender and requesting that the court either hear the case or transfer it to an adult court.

remedial education, drug and alcohol treatment, and other forms of counseling to alleviate these problems.

3. *Restitution.* In these programs, the offender "repays" her or his victim, either directly or symbolically through community service.[85]

Proponents of diversion programs include many labeling theorists (see Chapter 2), who believe that contact with the formal juvenile justice system "labels" the youth a delinquent, which leads to further delinquent behavior.

Increasingly, juvenile justice practitioners are relying on principles of restorative justice (see Chapter 9) to divert adolescents from formal institutions. For example, in Longmont, Colorado, some delinquents have access to victim-offender conferences, family group conferences, and other methods for determining punishments that range from apologies to counseling to restitution. In 2014, the recidivism rate for participants in Longmont was 8 percent, significantly lower than for most offenders in the juvenile justice system.[86] A number of jurisdictions have also turned to nonprofit *peer courts,* in which other young people determine the proper punishment for status offenders and juveniles charged with minor crimes such as disorderly conduct and vandalism.[87]

Transfer to Adult Court

One side effect of diversionary programs is that the youths who remain in the juvenile courts are more likely to be seen as "hardened" and thus less amenable to rehabilitation. This, in turn, increases the likelihood that the offender will be transferred to an adult court, a process in which the juvenile court waives jurisdiction over the youth. In the 1980s and 1990s, when the American juvenile justice system shifted away from ideals of treatment and toward punishment, transfer to adult court was one of the most popular means of "getting tough" on delinquents.

The proportion of juveniles waived to adult court for property crimes has decreased steadily in the past two decades. About 4,000 delinquent cases are now waived to adult criminal court each year—less than 1 percent of all cases that reach juvenile court. This figure is down significantly from 1994, when the number of such cases peaked at 13,600.[88] As might be expected, the majority of transfer cases involve juveniles who have committed a violent offense.[89] Several years ago, for example, fourteen-year-old Philip Chism killed and raped his high school math teacher in Danvers, Massachusetts. He was tried as an adult and, in 2015, convicted and sentenced to life in prison with eligibility for parole after forty years.

Learning Objective 7

Detail the three most common methods for transferring juvenile offenders to the adult criminal justice system.

Judicial Transfer There are three types of transfer laws, and most states use more than one of them depending on the jurisdiction and the seriousness of the offense. Juveniles are most commonly transferred to adult courts through **judicial waiver**, in which the juvenile judge is given the power to determine whether a young offender's case will be waived to adult court. The judge makes this decision based on the offender's age, the nature of the offense, and any criminal history. All but five states employ judicial waiver.

judicial waiver The process in which the juvenile judge, based on the facts of the case at hand, decides that the alleged offender should be transferred to adult court.

automatic transfer The process by which a juvenile is transferred to adult court as a matter of state law.

prosecutorial waiver A procedure used in situations where the prosecutor has discretion to decide whether a case will be heard by a juvenile court or an adult court.

Other Methods of Transfer Twenty-nine states have taken the waiver responsibility out of judicial hands through **automatic transfer**, also known as *legislative waiver.* In these states, the legislatures have designated certain conditions—usually involving serious crimes such as murder and rape—under which a juvenile case is automatically "kicked up" to adult court. In Rhode Island, for example, a juvenile aged sixteen or older with two prior felony adjudications will automatically be transferred on being accused of a third felony.[90]

Fifteen states also allow for **prosecutorial waiver**, in which prosecutors are allowed to choose whether to initiate proceedings in juvenile or criminal court when certain age and offense conditions are met. (See *Discretion in Action—Juvenile Drunk Driving* for further insight into prosecutorial waiver procedures.) In twenty-five states, criminal court judges also have the freedom to send juveniles who were transferred to adult court back to juvenile court. Known as *reverse transfer* statutes, these laws are designed to provide judges with a measure of discretion even when automatic transfer takes place. This process is popular with those who want to reduce the number of juveniles waived to adult court. For example, Arizona recently expanded the number of offenses eligible for reverse transfer, and gave certain nonviolent juvenile offenders the ability to request a reverse transfer hearing.[91]

detention The temporary custody of a juvenile in a secure facility after a petition has been filed and before the adjudicatory process begins.

detention hearing A hearing to determine whether a juvenile should be detained, or remain detained, while waiting for the adjudicatory process to begin.

Detention

Once the decision has been made that the offender will face adjudication in a juvenile court, the intake official must decide what to do with him or her until the start of the trial. Generally, the juvenile is released into the custody of parents or a guardian—most jurisdictions favor this practice in lieu of setting money bail for youths. The intake officer may also place the offender in **detention**, or temporary custody in a secure facility, until the disposition process begins. Once a juvenile has been detained, most jurisdictions require that a **detention hearing** be held within twenty-four hours. During this hearing, the offender has several due process safeguards, including the right to counsel, the right against self-incrimination, and the right to cross-examine and confront witnesses.

In justifying its decision to detain, the court will usually address one of three issues:

1. Whether the child poses a danger to the community.
2. Whether the child will return for the adjudication process.
3. Whether detention will provide protection for the child.

The Supreme Court upheld the practice of preventive detention (see Chapter 8) for juveniles in *Schall v. Martin* (1984)[92] by ruling that youths can be detained if they are deemed a "risk" to the safety of the community or to their own welfare. About one-third of juveniles involved in violent offenses are detained before trial.[93]

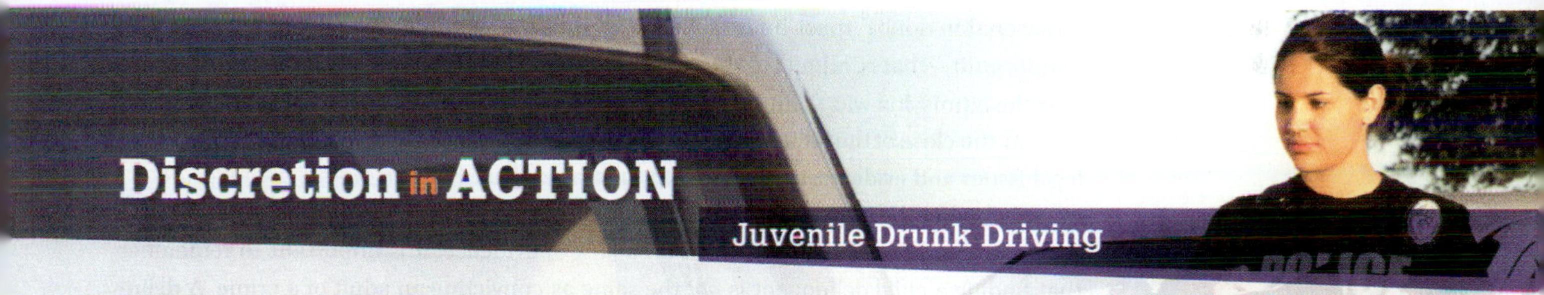

Rachel Donahue/Shutterstock.com

Discretion in ACTION

Juvenile Drunk Driving

The Situation James, a seventeen-year-old high school senior, gets behind the wheel of his father's car with a blood alcohol concentration of .12, well over the state limit for driving under the influence (DUI). He slams headfirst into another car, killing the driver. Initially, he is charged with vehicular homicide as a juvenile.

The Law In this state, prosecutors have the discretion to waive juvenile offenders to adult court if the alleged offender is sixteen years old or older at the time of the alleged offense and is charged with a felony such as vehicular manslaughter.

What Would You Do? You are a prosecutor with the discretionary power to transfer James from juvenile court to adult court. On the one hand, James has no previous criminal record, did not intend to kill his victim, and has shown extreme remorse for his actions. Furthermore, he is a juvenile and, as such, is seen by the law as less culpable than an adult. On the other hand, his careless actions resulted in a homicide, and trying him as an adult might deter other juveniles from committing DUI crimes. Do you keep James in juvenile court or waive him to adult court? Why?

To learn what a prosecutor in Denver, Colorado, did in a similar situation, see Example 13.1 in Appendix B.

EthicsChallenge

Police suspect that a seven-year-old named Patrick has knowledge concerning the murder of an eleven-year-old girl. After Patrick waives his *Miranda* rights, without his parents present, he tells a detective that he threw a rock at the victim's head. Is it ethical for police to treat juveniles the same as adults when it comes to *Miranda* proceedings, which we covered in Chapter 6? At what age can a juvenile be expected to understand the concepts of the right to remain silent and the right to an attorney? Explain your answers. (To learn more about the Supreme Court's approach to this topic, search for *Fare v. Michael C.* [1979] and *J.D.B. v. North Carolina* [2011] online.)

Trying and Punishing Juveniles

In just over half of all referred cases, the juvenile is eventually subject to formal proceedings in juvenile court.[94] As noted earlier, changes in the juvenile justice system since *In re Gault* (1967) have led many to contend that juvenile courts have become indistinguishable, both theoretically and practically, from adult courts.[95] About half the states, for example, permit juveniles to request a jury trial under certain circumstances. As this chapter's *Mastering Concepts* feature explains, however, juvenile justice proceedings may still be distinguished from the adult system of criminal justice, and these differences are evident in the adjudication and disposition of the juvenile trial.

Adjudication

Learning Objective 8

Explain the distinction between an adjudicatory hearing and a disposition hearing.

During the adjudication stage of the juvenile justice process, a hearing is held to determine whether the offender is delinquent or in need of some form of court supervision. Most state juvenile codes dictate a specific set of procedures that must be followed during the **adjudicatory hearing**, with the goal of providing the respondent with "the essentials of due process and fair treatment." Consequently, the respondent in an adjudicatory hearing has the right to notice of charges, counsel, and confrontation and cross-examination, and the privilege against self-incrimination. Furthermore, "proof beyond a reasonable doubt" must be established to find the child delinquent. When the child admits guilt—that is, admits to the charges of the initial petition—the judge must ensure that the admission was voluntary.

At the close of the adjudicatory hearing, the judge is generally required to rule on the legal issues and evidence that have been presented. Based on this ruling, the judge determines whether the respondent is delinquent or in need of court supervision. Alternatively, the judge can dismiss the case based on a lack of evidence. It is important to remember that finding a child delinquent is *not* the same as convicting an adult of a crime. A delinquent does not face the same restrictions imposed on adult convicts in some states, such as limits on the right to vote and to run for political office (discussed in Chapter 11).

Disposition

Once a juvenile has been adjudicated delinquent, the judge must decide what steps will be taken toward treatment and/or punishment. Most states provide for a *bifurcated* process in which a separate **disposition hearing** follows the adjudicatory hearing. Depending on state law, the juvenile may be entitled to counsel at the disposition hearing.

adjudicatory hearing The process through which a juvenile court determines whether there is sufficient evidence to support the initial petition.

disposition hearing Similar to the sentencing hearing for adults, a hearing in which the juvenile judge or officer decides the appropriate punishment for a youth found to be delinquent or a status offender.

Sentencing Juveniles

In an adult trial, the sentencing phase is primarily concerned with protecting the community from the convict. In contrast, a juvenile judge

Mastering**Concepts** The Juvenile Justice System vs. the Criminal Justice System

AP Photo/Columbus Dispatch, James D. DeCamp

When the juvenile justice system was first established in the United States, its participants saw it as being separate from the adult criminal justice system. Indeed, the two systems remain separate in many ways. There are, however, a number of similarities between juvenile and adult justice. Here, we summarize both the similarities and the differences.

Similarities

- The right to receive the *Miranda* warnings.
- Procedural protections when making an admission of guilt.
- Prosecutors and defense attorneys play equally important roles.
- The right to be represented by counsel at the crucial stages of the trial process.
- Access to plea bargains.
- The right to a hearing and an appeal.
- The standard of evidence is proof beyond a reasonable doubt.
- Offenders can be placed on probation by the judge.
- Offenders can be held before adjudication if the judge believes them to be a threat to the community.
- Following trial, offenders can be sentenced to community supervision.

Differences

	Juvenile System	Adult System
Purpose	Rehabilitation of the offender.	Punishment.
Arrest	Juveniles can be arrested for acts (status offenses) that are not criminal for adults.	Adults can be arrested only for acts made illegal by the relevant criminal code.
Wrongdoing	Considered a "delinquent act."	A crime.
Proceedings	Informal; closed to public.	Formal and regimented; open to public.
Information	Courts may NOT release information to the press.	Courts MUST release information to the press.
Parents	Play significant role.	Play no role.
Release	Into parent/guardian custody.	May post bail when appropriate.
Jury trial	In some states, juveniles do NOT have this right.	All adults have this right.
Searches	Juveniles can be searched in school without probable cause.	No adult can be searched without probable cause.
Records	Juvenile records are sealed at age of adult criminal responsibility.	Adult criminal records are, for the most part, permanent.
Sentencing	Juveniles are placed in separate facilities from adults.	Adults are placed in county jails or state or federal prisons.
Death penalty	No death penalty.	Death penalty for certain serious crimes under certain circumstances.

uses the disposition hearing to determine a sentence that will serve the needs of the child. For assistance in this crucial process, the judge will order the probation department to gather information on the juvenile and present it in the form of a **predisposition report**. The report usually contains information concerning the respondent's family background, the facts surrounding the delinquent act, and interviews with social workers, teachers, and other important figures in the child's life.

Judicial Discretion In keeping with the rehabilitative tradition of the juvenile justice system, juvenile judges generally have a great deal of discretion in choosing one of several disposition possibilities. A judge can tend toward leniency, delivering only a stern reprimand or warning before releasing the juvenile into the custody of parents or other legal guardians. Otherwise, the choice is among incarceration in a juvenile correctional

predisposition report A report prepared during the disposition process that provides the judge with relevant background material to aid in the disposition decision.

graduated sanctions The practical theory in juvenile corrections that a delinquent or status offender should receive a punishment that matches in seriousness the severity of the wrongdoing.

facility, probation, or community treatment. In most cases, the seriousness of the offense is the primary factor used in determining whether to incarcerate a juvenile, though history of delinquency, family situation, and the offender's attitude are all relevant.

Juvenile Corrections

In general, juvenile corrections are based on the concept of **graduated sanctions**—that is, the severity of the punishment should fit the crime. Consequently, status and first-time offenders are diverted or placed on probation, repeat offenders find themselves in intensive community supervision or treatment programs, and serious and violent offenders are placed in correctional facilities. (See Figure 13.7 to get a better idea of how graduated sanctions apply to the juvenile justice system.)

As society's expectations of the juvenile justice system have changed, so have the characteristics of its corrections programs. In some cities, for example, juvenile probation officers join police officers on the beat. Because the former are not bound by the same search and seizure restrictions as other law enforcement officials, this interdepartmental teamwork provides more opportunities to fight youth crime aggressively.

Juvenile Probation The most common form of juvenile corrections is probation—33 percent of all delinquency cases disposed of by juvenile courts result in conditional diversion. The majority of all adjudicated delinquents (64 percent) will never receive a disposition more severe than being placed on probation.[96] These statistics reflect a general understanding among juvenile court judges and other officials that a child should normally be removed from her or his home only as a last resort.

The organization of juvenile probation is very similar to adult probation (see Chapter 10), and juvenile probationers are increasingly subjected to electronic monitoring and other supervisory tactics. The main difference between the two programs lies in the attitude toward the offender. Adult probation officers have an overriding responsibility to protect the community from the probationer, while juvenile probation officers are expected to take the role of a mentor or a concerned relative in looking after the needs of the child.

Figure 13.7 The Graduated Sanctions Model

In juvenile corrections, the severity of punishment is, ideally, directly related to the seriousness of the juvenile's delinquent behavior.

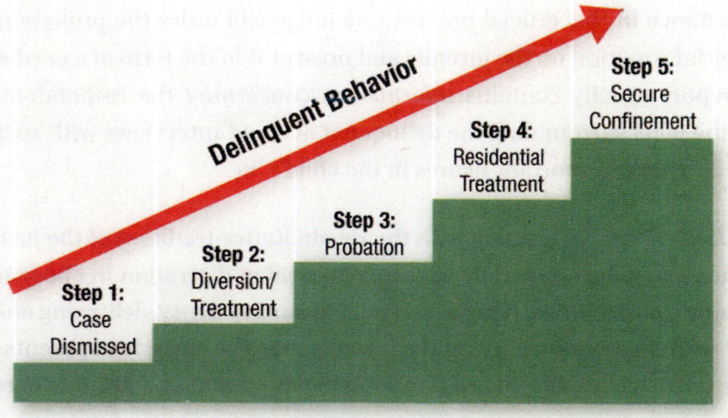

Careers in CJ

Photo courtesy Carl McCullough, Sr.

Carl McCullough, Sr.
Resident Youth Worker

I had a shot in the NFL, playing for the Buffalo Bills and the Minnesota Vikings, but that lasted only a short time. Today, I work at the Hennepin County (Minnesota) Juvenile Detention Center, where I'm responsible for a group of twelve young men, aged thirteen to eighteen, who are awaiting trial, waiting for placements, or just being held in a secure place due to the high-profile nature of their cases. I'm with the kids every day and every other weekend from 6:30 A.M. to 2:30 P.M. I do everything from helping with homework to supervising their leisure time, running group programs, and just being a positive, caring adult with whom to talk.

iStockPhoto.com/Chris Scredon

Having the NFL experience is a huge icebreaker with the residents. "Why are you here?" they always ask me, and I tell them I am here because I care about them, because I want to see a change, and because I'd like to help them believe that something better is possible. To do this job well, you have to be good at building relationships. It helps to know how to work with different cultures as well. Then you have to have patience; without it you won't last long. You know they are going to test you, to see what they can and can't get away with. You also have to be willing to learn a few things from them. You have to be a good listener.

SOCIAL MEDIA CAREER TIP Potential employers want information about you, but they do not want your life story. To capitalize on two primary benefits of social media, personalize your message and be concise.

FASTFACTS

Resident youth worker

Job description:

- Provide safety, security, custodial care, discipline, and guidance. Play a critical role in the rehabilitation of youth and, as a result, have a potentially great impact on a youth's success during and after his or her incarceration.

What kind of training is required?

- A bachelor's degree in human services, behavioral science, or a related field.
- Professional and respectful verbal communication skills.

Annual salary range?

- $30,000–$45,000

Confining Juveniles About 46,000 American youths (down from approximately 92,000 in 1995) are incarcerated in public and private juvenile correctional facilities in the United States.[97] Most of these juveniles have committed crimes against people or property, but a significant number (about 14 percent) have been incarcerated for technical violations of their probation or parole agreements.[98] After deciding that a juvenile needs to be confined, the judge has two sentencing options: nonsecure juvenile institutions and secure juvenile institutions.

Nonsecure Confinement Some juvenile delinquents do not require high levels of control and can be placed in **residential treatment programs**. These programs, run by either probation departments or social-services departments, allow their subjects freedom of movement in the community. Generally, this freedom is predicated on the juveniles following certain rules, such as avoiding alcoholic beverages and returning to the facility for curfew. Residential treatment programs can be divided into four categories:

1. *Foster care programs,* in which the juveniles live with a couple who act as surrogate parents.
2. *Group homes,* which generally house between twelve and fifteen youths and provide treatment, counseling, and education services by a professional staff.

residential treatment program A government-run facility for juveniles whose offenses are not deemed serious enough to warrant incarceration in a training school.

boot camp A variation on traditional shock incarceration in which juveniles (and some adults) are sent to secure confinement facilities modeled on military basic training camps instead of prison or jail.

training school A correctional institution for juveniles found to be delinquent or status offenders.

3. *Family group homes,* which combine aspects of foster care and group homes, meaning that a single family, rather than a group of professionals, looks after the needs of the young offenders.
4. *Rural programs,* which include wilderness camps, farms, and ranches where between thirty and fifty children are placed in an environment that provides recreational activities and treatment programs.

Secure Confinement Secure facilities are comparable to the adult prisons and jails we discussed in Chapters 11 and 12. These institutions go by a confusing array of names depending on the state in which they are located, but the two best known are boot camps and training schools.

A **boot camp** is the juvenile variation of shock probation. As we noted in Chapter 10, boot camps are modeled after military training for new recruits. Boot camp programs are based on the theory that by giving wayward youths a taste of the "hard life" of military-like training for short periods of time, usually no longer than 180 days, they will be "shocked" out of a life of crime. At a typical youth boot camp, inmates are grouped in platoons and live in dormitories. They spend eight hours a day training, drilling, and doing hard labor, and also participate in programs such as basic adult education and job skills training.

No juvenile correctional facility is called a "prison." This does not mean they lack a strong resemblance to prisons. The facilities that most closely mimic the atmosphere at an adult correctional facility are **training schools**, alternatively known as youth camps, youth development centers, industrial schools, and several other similar titles.

▼ Juvenile inmates wait to go into the gym at the Juvenile Detention Center in Toledo, Ohio. **Why might young offenders who are transferred to adult correctional facilities have higher recidivism rates than those who remain in juvenile facilities?** *Christian Science Monitor*/Getty Images

Whatever the name, these institutions claim to differ from their adult countparts by offering a variety of programs to treat and rehabilitate the young offenders. In reality, training schools are plagued by many of the same problems as adult prisons and jails, including high levels of inmate-on-inmate violence, substance abuse, gang wars, and overcrowding.

aftercare The variety of therapeutic, educational, and counseling programs made available to juvenile delinquents (and some adults) after they have been released from a correctional facility.

Aftercare Juveniles leave correctional facilities through an early release program or because they have served the length of their sentences. Juvenile corrections officials recognize that many of these children, like adults, need assistance readjusting to the outside world. In addition, about two-thirds of those youths who come in contact with the juvenile justice system have behavioral health problems such as alcohol abuse, serious depression, trauma related to exposure to violence, risk for suicide, and low self-control disorders.[99] Consequently, released juveniles are often placed in **aftercare** programs. Based on the same philosophy that drives the prisoner reentry movement (discussed in the previous chapter), aftercare programs are designed to offer services for the juveniles, while at the same time supervising them to reduce the chances of recidivism.

The ideal aftercare program includes community support groups, education and employment aid, and continued monitoring to ensure that the juvenile is able to deal with the demands of freedom. Statistics suggest, however, that the aftercare needs of young offenders often go unmet. Criminological research estimates that juvenile incarceration decreases the likelihood of high school graduation by 13 percent and increases the likelihood of adult incarceration by 22 percent.[100] Even more troubling is a recent study showing that youths who had been detained in Cook County (Illinois) were four times more likely to die a violent death than their nondelinquent counterparts.[101] A report on Illinois's juvenile justice system criticized it as "a 'feeder system' to the adult criminal justice system and a cycle of crime, victimization, and incarceration."[102]

EthicsChallenge

Thirteen-year-old Tara, who has no history of trouble with the police, gets into a fight with another girl at school. At the insistence of the other girl's mother, a local prosecutor files second degree assault charges against Tara. In the predisposition report, juvenile court officials recommend that no action be taken in this case. After Tara fails to show up for her trial, however, she is arrested. Would it be ethical for a juvenile court judge to incarcerate Tara under these circumstances? Why or why not? ■

Summary

For more information on these concepts, look back to the Learning Objective icons throughout the chapter.

1 **List the four major differences between juvenile courts and adult courts.** (a) No juries, (b) different terminology, (c) limited adversarial relationship, and (d) confidentiality.

2 **Identify and briefly describe the single most important U.S. Supreme Court case with respect to juvenile justice.** The case was *In re Gault,* decided by the Supreme Court in 1967. In this case a minor was arrested for allegedly making an obscene phone call. His parents were not notified and were not present during the juvenile court judge's decision-making process. In this case, the Supreme Court held that juveniles are entitled to many of the same due process rights granted to adult offenders, including notice of charges, the right to counsel, the privilege against self-incrimination, and the right to confront and cross-examine witnesses.

3 **Describe the reasoning behind recent U.S. Supreme Court decisions that have lessened the harshness of sentencing outcomes for violent juvenile offenders.** In banning capital punishment and limiting the availability of life sentences without parole for offenders who committed their crimes as juveniles, the Supreme Court has focused on the concept of "diminished culpability." This concept is based on the notion that violent juvenile offenders cannot fully comprehend the consequences of their actions and are more deserving of the opportunity for rehabilitation than are adult violent offenders.

4 **Define *bullying,* and list the four components that are often present in this sort of behavior.** Bullying is repeated, aggressive behavior that is characterized by (a) physical abuse, (b) verbal abuse, (c) social and emotional abuse, and/or (d) abuse that take place online or through the use of devices such as smartphones.

5 **Describe the one variable that always correlates highly with juvenile crime rates.** The older a person is, the less likely he or she will exhibit criminal behavior. This process is known as aging out. Thus, persons in any at-risk group will commit fewer crimes as they get older.

6 **Describe the four primary stages of pretrial juvenile justice procedure.** (a) Intake, in which an official of the juvenile court engages in a screening process to determine what to do with the youthful offender; (b) pretrial diversion, which may consist of probation, treatment and aid, and/or restitution; (c) jurisdictional waiver to an adult court, in which case the youth leaves the juvenile justice system; and (d) some type of detention, in which the youth is held until the disposition process begins.

7 **Detail the three most common methods for transferring juvenile offenders to the adult criminal justice system.** (a) Judicial waiver, which requires a judge to make the transfer decision; (b) automatic transfer, in which legislation designates certain crimes that trigger a compulsory transfer; and (c) prosecutorial waiver, which requires a prosecutor to make the transfer decision.

8 **Explain the distinction between an adjudicatory hearing and a disposition hearing.** An adjudicatory hearing is essentially a "trial." Defense attorneys may be present during the adjudicatory hearing in juvenile courts. In many states, once adjudication has occurred, there is a separate disposition hearing that is similar to the sentencing phase in an adult court. At this point, the court, often aided by a predisposition report, determines the sentence that best serves the "needs" of the child.

Questions for Critical Analysis

1. What is the difference between a status offense and a crime? What punishments do you think should be imposed on juveniles who commit status offenses?
2. Do you agree with Supreme Court justice Anthony Kennedy that all juveniles who commit murder "must be given the opportunity to show their crime did not reflect irreparable corruption; and, if it did not, their hope for some years of life outside prison walls must be restored." Or, are mandatory life-without-parole sentences for juvenile killers justified? Explain your answer.
3. Do you think that bullying should be punishable as a felony along the same lines as assault? (For the definition of assault, go back to Chapter 2.) Why or why not?
4. Eight Florida teenagers ranging in age from fourteen to eighteen beat a classmate so badly that she suffered a concussion. According to law enforcement officials, the teenagers recorded the assault so that they could post it on the Internet. If you were a prosecutor and could either waive these teenagers to adult court or refer them to the juvenile justice system, which option would you choose? What other information would you need to make your decision?
5. Forty-four states have enacted parental responsibility statutes, which make parents accountable for the offenses of their children. Seventeen of these states hold parents criminally liable for their children's actions, punishing the parents with fines, community service, and even incarceration. What is your opinion of these laws—particularly those with criminal sanctions for parents?

Key Terms

adjudicatory hearing 402
aftercare 407
age of onset 394
aging out 394
automatic transfer 400
boot camp 406
bullying 391
child abuse 395
child neglect 395
detention 401
detention hearing 401
disposition hearing 402
graduated sanctions 404
intake 399
judicial waiver 400
juvenile delinquency 384
low-visibility decision making 398
parens patriae 383
petition 399
predisposition report 403
prosecutorial waiver 400
referral 399
residential treatment program 405
status offender 384
training school 406
youth gang 396

Notes

1. Jennifer M. O'Connor and Lucinda K. Treat, "Getting Smart about Getting Tough: Juvenile Justice and the Possibility of Progressive Reform," *American Criminal Law Review* 33 (Summer 1996), 1299.
2. *In re Gault*, 387 U.S. 1, 15 (1967).
3. Samuel Davis, *The Rights of Juveniles: The Juvenile Justice System*, 2d ed. (New York: C. Boardman Co., 1995), Section 1.2.
4. Quoted in Anthony Platt, *The Child Savers* (Chicago: University of Chicago Press, 1969), 119.
5. 383 U.S. 541 (1966).
6. *Ibid.*, 556.
7. 387 U.S. 1 (1967).
8. 397 U.S. 358 (1970).
9. 421 U.S. 519 (1975).
10. 403 U.S. 528 (1971).
11. Kellan Howell, "Tennessee Boy, 11, Found Guilty of Murdering 8-Year-Old Girl during Argument over Puppy," *Washington Times* (February 6, 2016), at **www.washingtontimes.com/news/2016/feb/6/benjamin-tiller-11-found-guilty-killing-8-year-old/?page=all.**
12. Research Network on Adolescent Development and Juvenile Justice, *Youth on Trial: A Developmental Perspective on Juvenile Justice* (Chicago: John D. & Catherine T. MacArthur Foundation, 2003), 1.
13. Richard E. Redding, "Juveniles Transferred to Criminal Court: Legal Reform Proposals Based on Social Science Research," *Utah Law Review* (1997), 709.
14. Kyle J. Thomas, "Delinquent Peer Influence on Offending Versatility: Can Peers Promote Specialized Delinquency?" *Criminology* (May 2015), 280–307.
15. Martha Grace Duncan. "'So Young and So Untender': Remorseless Children and the Expectations of the Law," *Columbia Law Review* (October 2002), 1469.
16. 543 U.S. 551 (2005).
17. *Ibid.*, 567.
18. 130 S.Ct. 2011 (2010).
19. *Ibid.*, 2030.
20. 132 S. Ct. 2455 (2012).
21. *Ibid.*, 2463.
22. *Montgomery v. Louisiana*, 577 U.S. ____ (2016).
23. Quoted in Adam Liptak, "Justices Expand Parole Rights for Juveniles Sentenced to Life for Murder," *New York Times* (January 2016), A18.
24. Federal Bureau of Investigation, *Crime in the United States 2014* (Washington, D.C.: U.S. Department of Justice, 2015), Table

38, at **www.fbi.gov/about-us/cjis/ucr/crime-in-the-u.s/2014/crime-in-the-u.s.-2014.**

25. Sarah Hockenberry and Charles Puzzanchera, *Juvenile Court Statistics 2013* (Washington, D.C.: National Center for Juvenile Justice, July 2015), 6.
26. Office of Juvenile Justice and Delinquency Prevention, "One Day Count of Juveniles in Residential Placement Facilities, 1997–2013," at **www.ojjdp.gov/ojstatbb/corrections/qa08201.asp;** and Todd Richmond, "Fewer Young Criminals Push States to Close Prisons," *Associated Press* (June 7, 2010).
27. David McDowell, "Juvenile Curfew Laws and Their Influence on Crime," *Federal Probation* (December 2006), 58.
28. *Crime in the United States, 2014, op. cit.*, Table 29.
29. Office of Juvenile Justice and Delinquency Prevention, "Community Prevention Grants Program," at **https://www.ncjrs.gov/pdffiles1/ojjdp/227345.pdf.**
30. *Juvenile Court Statistics, 2013, op. cit.*, 20.
31. *Juvenile Offenders and Victims: 2014 National Report,* eds. Melissa Sickmund and Charles Puzzancherra (Pittsburgh: National Center for Juvenile Justice, December 2014), 158, 196.
32. Tony Fabelo, Michael D. Thompson, and Martha Plotkin, *Breaking School Rules: A Statewide Study of How School Discipline Relates to Students' Success and Juvenile Justice Involvement* (New York: The Council of State Governments, July 2011), x.
33. Carl E. Pope and Howard N. Snyder, *Race as a Factor in Juvenile Arrests* (Washington, D.C.: Office of Juvenile Justice and Delinquency Prevention, April 2003), 1.
34. National Institute of Justice, *The Code of the Street and African-American Adolescent Violence* (Washington, D.C.: U.S. Department of Justice, February 2009), 7, 10, 14.
35. *Juvenile Court Statistics, 2013, op. cit.*, 12.
36. Sara Goodkind et al., "Are Girls Really Becoming More Delinquent? Testing the Gender Convergence Hypothesis by Race and Ethnicity, 1976–2005," *Children and Youth Services Review* (August 2009), 885–889.
37. Office of Juvenile Justice and Delinquency Prevention, "Girls and the Juvenile Justice System" (2015) at **www.ojjdp.gov/policyguidance/girls-juvenile-justice-system.**
38. *Ibid.*
39. Meda Chesney-Lind, *The Female Offender: Girls, Women, and Crime* (Thousand Oaks, Calif.: Sage Publications, 1997).
40. Margaret A. Zahn et al., "The Girls Study Group—Charting the Way to Delinquency Prevention for Girls," *Girls Study Group: Understanding and Responding to Girls' Delinquency* (Washington, D.C.: Office of Juvenile Justice and Delinquency Prevention, October 2008), 3.
41. *Crime in the United States, 2014, op. cit.*, Table 38 and Table 40.
42. *Juvenile Offenders and Victims: 2014 National Report, op. cit.*, 47.
43. National Center for Education Statistics and Bureau of Justice Statistics, *Indicators of School Crime and Safety: 2014* (Washington, D.C.: U.S. Department of Justice, July 2015), Figure 1.2, page 7.
44. *Ibid.*, Figure 2.1, page 11.
45. *Ibid.*, 86.
46. Lana Shapiro and Andrew Adesman, "Exponential, Not Additive, Increase in Risk of Weapons Carrying by Adolescents Who Themselves Are Frequent and Recurrent Victims of Bullying," *Developmental & Behavioral Pediatrics* (May 2014), at **www.medicalxpress.com/news/2014-05-scores-bullying-victims-weapons-school.html.**
47. Quoted in "Online Bullying: Charging Kids with Felonies," *The Week* (November 1, 2013), 14.
48. Young-Shin Kim and Bennett Leventhal, "Bullying and Suicide: A Review," *International Journal of Adolescent Medicine and Health* (April-June 2008), 133–154.
49. *Indicators of School Crime and Safety: 2014, op. cit.*, 46.
50. Jessica Bennett, "From Lockers to Lockup," *Newsweek* (October 11, 2010), 39.
51. Adam J. Speraw, "No Bullying Allowed: A Call for a National Anti-Bullying Statute to Promote a Safer Learning Environment in American Public Schools," *Valparaiso University Law Review* (Summer 2010), 1151–1198.
52. Marvin E. Wolfgang, *From Boy to Man, from Delinquency to Crime* (Chicago: University of Chicago Press, 1987).
53. Carlos A. Cuevas et al., *Children's Exposure to Violence and the Intersection between Delinquency and Victimization* (Washington, D.C.: Office of Juvenile Justice and Delinquency Prevention, October 2013), 1–2.
54. Michael Turner, "Repeat Bully Victimization and Legal Outcomes in a National Sample: The Impact over the Life Course" (2013), at **www.apa.org/news/press/releases/2013/08/bully-victimizations.pdf.**
55. Quoted in John H. Laub and Robert J. Sampson, "Understanding Desistance from Crime," in *Crime and Justice: A Review of Research* (Chicago: University of Chicago Press, 2001), 6.
56. Travis Hirschi and Michael Gottfredson, "Age and the Explanation of Crime," *American Journal of Sociology* 89 (1982), 552–584.
57. Robert J. Sampson and John H. Laub, "A Life-Course View on the Development of Crime," *Annals of the American Academy of Political and Social Science* (November 2005), 12.
58. David P. Farrington, "Offending from 10 to 25 Years of Age," in *Prospective Studies of Crime and Delinquency,* eds. Katherine Teilmann Van Dusen and Sarnoff A. Mednick (Boston: Kluwer-Nijhoff Publishers, 1983), 17.
59. Office of Juvenile Justice and Delinquency Prevention, *Juveniles in Court* (Washington, D.C.: U.S. Department of Justice, June 2003), 29.
60. Lloyd D. Johnston et al., *Monitoring the Future: National Survey Results on Drug Use, 1975–2015—2015 Overview; Key Findings on Adolescent Drug Use* (Ann Arbor, Mich.: Institute for Social Research, February 2016), 37.
61. *Ibid.*, 10, 12.
62. Carl McCurley and Howard Snyder, *Co-occurrence of Substance Abuse Behaviors in Youth* (Washington, D.C.: Office of Juvenile Justice and Delinquency Prevention, 2008).
63. Gary McClelland, Linda Teplin, and Karen Abram, "Detection and Prevalence of Substance Abuse among Juvenile Detainees," *Juvenile Justice Bulletin* (Washington, D.C.: Office of Juvenile Justice and Delinquency Prevention, June 2004), 10.
64. Arrestee Drug Abuse Monitoring Program, *Preliminary Data on Drug Use and Related Matters among Adult Arrestees and Juvenile Detainees* (Washington, D.C.: National Institute of Justice, 2003).
65. *Mental Health Treatment for Youth in the Juvenile Justice System: A Compendium of Promising Practices* (Alexandria, Va.: National Mental Health Association, 2004), 10.
66. Larry J. Siegel and Brandon C. Welsh, *Juvenile Delinquency: The Core,* 4th ed. (Belmont, Calif.: Wadsworth Cengage Learning, 2011), 268.
67. Edward P. Mulvey, *Highlights from Pathways to Desistance: A Longitudinal Study of Serious Adolescent Offenders* (Washington, D.C.: Office of Juvenile Justice and Delinquency Prevention, March 2011), 1–3.
68. David Finkelhor et al., *Juvenile Justice Bulletin: Children's Exposure to Violence, Crime, and Abuse: An Update* (Washington, D.C.: Office of Juvenile Justice and Delinquency Prevention, September 2015), 7.
69. Kimberly A. Tyler and Katherine A. Johnson, "A Longitudinal Study of the Effects of Early Abuse on Later Victimization among High-Risk Adolescents," *Violence and Victims* (June 2006), 287–291.
70. Grover Trask, "Defusing the Teenage Time Bombs," *Prosecutor* (March/April 1997), 29.
71. Ashley Nellis, *The Lives of Juvenile Lifers: Findings from a National Survey* (Washington, D.C.: The Sentencing Project, March 2012), 2.
72. Arlen Egley, Jr., James C. Howell, and Meena Harris, "Highlights of the 2012 National Youth Gang Survey," *Office of Juvenile Justice and Delinquency Prevention Fact Sheet* (December 2014), 1.
73. Chris Melde and Finn-Aage Esbensen, "Gangs and Violence: Disentangling the Impact of Gang Membership on the Level and Nature of Offending," *Journal of Quantitative Criminology* (June 2013), 143–166.
74. *2013 National Gang Report* (Washington, D.C.: National Gang Intelligence Center, 2014), 3–5.

75. Andrew V. Papachristos et al., "The Company You Keep? The Spillover Effects of Gang Membership on Individual Gunshot Victimization in a Co-Offending Network," *Criminology* (November 2015), 624.

76. Monica Davey and Mitch Smith, "Murder Rates Rising Sharply in Many U.S. Cities," *New York Times* (September 1, 2015), A1.

77. Karl G. Hill, Christina Lui, and J. David Hawkins, *Early Precursors of Gang Membership: A Study of Seattle Youth* (Washington, D.C.: Office of Juvenile Justice and Delinquency Prevention, December 2001).

78. *Juvenile Offenders and Victims: 2014 National Report, op. cit.*, 69.

79. National Alliance of Gang Investigators Alliance, 2005 National Gang Threat Assessment (Washington, D.C.: Bureau of Justice Assistance, 2005), 10–11.

80. *2013 National Gang Report, op. cit.*, 41–42.

81. Los Angeles Police Department, "Why Young People Join Gangs" (2014), at **www.lapdonline.org/top_ten_most_wanted_gang_members/content_basic_view/23473.**

82. *Crime in the United States 2014, op. cit.*, Table 32.

83. *Juvenile Offenders and Victims: 2014 National Report, op. cit.*, 94.

84. Julie Furdella and Charles Puzzanchera, *Delinquency Cases in Juvenile Court, 2013* (Washington, D.C.: Office of Juvenile Justice and Delinquency Prevention, October 2015), 3.

85. S'Lee Arthur Hinshaw II, "Juvenile Diversion: An Alternative to Juvenile Court," *Journal of Dispute Resolution* (1993), 305.

86. Molly R. Leach, "The Political Rise of Restorative Justice," *The Huffington Post* (May 26, 2014), at **www.huffingtonpost.com/molly-rowan-leach/the-political-rise-of-res_b_5029413.html.**

87. Lane Crisler, *Recidivism within Salt Lake Peer Court* (Salt Lake City, Utah: University of Utah, 2013), 6–7.

88. *Juvenile Court Statistics 2013, op. cit.*, 38.

89. Office of Juvenile Justice and Delinquency Prevention, *Delinquency Cases Waived to Criminal Court, 2011* (Washington, D.C.: U.S. Department of Justice, December 2014), 2.

90. Rhode Island General Laws Section 14-1-7.1 (1994 and Supp. 1996).

91. *State Trends: Legislative Victories from 2011–2013* (Washington, D.C.: Campaign for Youth & Justice, 2014), 5.

92. 467 U.S. 253 (1984).

93. *Juvenile Court Statistics, 2013, op. cit.*, 32.

94. *Delinquency Cases in Juvenile Court, 2013, op. cit*, 3.

95. Barry C. Feld, "Criminalizing the American Juvenile Court," *Crime and Justice* 17 (1993), 227–254.

96. *Delinquency Cases in Juvenile Court, 2013, op. cit.*, 3.

97. Office of Juvenile Justice and Delinquency Prevention, "Easy Access to the Census of Juveniles in Residential Placement: 1997–2013" (2015), at **www.ojjdp.gov/ojstatbb/ezacjrp/asp/display.asp.**

98. *Juvenile Offenders and Victims: 2014 National Report, op. cit.*, 194.

99. Thomas Grisso, *Double Jeopardy: Adolescent Offenders with Mental Disorders* (Chicago: University of Chicago Press, 2004), 2–3.

100. Anna Aizer and Joseph J. Doyle, Jr., "Juvenile Incarceration, Human Capital and Future Crime: Evidence from Randomly Assigned Judges," *The National Bureau of Economic Research* (June 2013), at **www.nber.org/papers/w19102.**

101. Linda A. Teplin et al., *Violent Death in Delinquent Youth after Detention* (Washington, D.C.: Office of Juvenile Justice and Delinquency Prevention, September 2015), 4–7.

102. *Youth Reentry Improvement Report* (Springfield, Ill.: Illinois Juvenile Justice Commission, November 2011), 9.

wk1003mike/Shutterstock.com

14

Crucial Issues in Criminal Justice

Chapter Outline		Corresponding Learning Objectives
Security vs. Liberty	1	Summarize the three federal laws that have been particularly influential on our nation's counterterrorism strategies.
	2	Explain why privacy expectations are so important to the federal government's metadata surveillance operations.
	3	Distinguish verbal threats that are protected by the Constitution from verbal threats that can be prosecuted as "true threats."
Cyber Crime	4	Outline the three major reasons why the Internet is conducive to the dissemination of child pornography.
	5	Explain how the Internet has contributed to piracy of intellectual property.
Gun Control Policy	6	Explain how background checks, in theory, protect the public from firearm-related violence.
White-Collar Crime	7	Indicate some of the ways that white-collar crime is different from violent or property crime.
	8	Explain the concept of corporate violence.

To target your study and review, look for these numbered Learning Objective icons throughout the chapter.

two paths **Diverged**

one Wednesday morning in May 2014, eighteen-year-old Abdullahi Yusuf left school early and took the train to the Minneapolis-St. Paul International Airport. His goal: fly to Turkey and then make his way to Syria to join an Islamic fundamentalist organization called the Islamic State. The next day, twenty-year-old Abdi Nur arrived at the same airport with the same objective. Yusuf and Nur are part of a "cluster" of Somali Americans from the Minneapolis area who have become enamored with terrorist organizations operating out of the Middle East and elsewhere. From 2007 to 2009, nearly two dozen of these young individuals ventured to Somalia to take up arms with al-Shabaab, a branch of al Qaeda. More recently, about twice that number, including Yusuf and Nur, are suspected of falling under the influence of the Islamic State.

Nur succeeded in reaching Syria. Soon thereafter, according to U.S. authorities, he sent a Facebook message to a friend in the United States saying that he had "gone to the brothers" and was not coming back. Active on Twitter, Ask.fm, and other social media sites, Nur has become an effective recruiter for the Islamic State. In 2015, officials arrested six Somali Americans, ranging in age from nineteen to twenty-one, from Minneapolis whom he had convinced to follow his path to Syria.

As for Yusuf, he did not make it quite as far. Federal Bureau of Investigation (FBI) agents who had been monitoring the young man's activities apprehended him at the airport before he could board his flight. Yusuf eventually pleaded guilty to several terrorism-related charges. Instead of incarcerating him, however, a judge allowed Yusuf to take part in a halfway house "deradicalization" program designed to reintegrate him back into American society. As part of the program, Yusuf was exposed to the writings of Martin Luther King, Jr., and Native American author Sherman Alexie and asked to write poetry about "who he is [and] what he wants to become." This experiment—the first of its kind in the United States—ended in May 2015, when Yusuf committed an unspecified violation of the terms of his release and was sent to prison.

AP Photo/*Star Tribune*, Leila Navidi

▲ Members of Minneapolis's Muslim and Somali community address the issue of homegrown radicalization during a 2015 press conference.

1. What is your opinion of a program designed to "deradicalize" young terrorist sympathizers? How would society benefit if such a program were to succeed?
2. What are some of the strategies that U.S. authorities could use to lessen the influence of successful terrorist recruiters such as Abdi Nur?
3. Many of the Somali Americans from the Minneapolis area who became involved with al-Shabaab and the Islamic State grew up in the same communities, attended the same schools, and congregated at the same places of worship. Would it be advisable for the FBI and local law enforcement agencies to closely monitor these neighborhoods and institutions for evidence of terrorist activity? Why or why not?

Security vs. Liberty

▲ In 2015, a white rose is placed on the name of one of the victims of the September 11, 2001, terrorist attacks at a memorial in New York City. **Why does large-scale terrorist activity often make citizens of the targeted country more willing to trade certain freedoms for greater security against future attacks?** Jewel Samad/AFP/Getty Images

The Minneapolis cluster of Islamic State supporters is fairly homogenous, mostly consisting of young men from the city's ethnic Somali community. In general, however, American recruits to this terrorist cause are a diverse group. According to a report released by researchers at George Washington University in 2015, Islamic State sympathizers in the United States range in age from the mid-teens to the mid-forties. About 14 percent of those arrested by the FBI on charges related to the terrorist organization are women, and the vast majority are American citizens or legal resident immigrants.[1]

The one thing that many of these "keyboard *jihadists*" do have in common is a presence on the Internet and, in particular, social media. Consequently, homeland security officials have placed paramount importance on tracking communications among suspected terrorists. To do so, since the attacks of September 11, 2001, in New York City, Washington, D.C., and rural Pennsylvania, the federal government has greatly enhanced the capabilities of law enforcement and intelligence agencies to collect and store information on these suspects. At the same time, the federal government has angered many Americans who feel that their privacy rights have been ignored or discarded for the sake of national security. "You can't have 100 percent security and also then have 100 percent privacy," remarked former president Barack Obama,[2] succinctly summarizing an ongoing balancing act that goes to the heart of American ideals of fairness and justice.

National Security and Privacy

As has been noted several times in this textbook, our Constitution upholds the premise that Americans should not be subjected to the unreasonable use of government power. As we have also pointed out, *reasonableness* is a highly subjective concept, and Americans are often willing to give their government more leeway in times of national crisis. When it comes to antiterrorism efforts and homeland security, this flexibility has manifested itself in the form of federal legislation that expands the government's ability to locate, observe, prosecute, and punish suspected terrorists. The first legislative step in this direction, however, took place decades before September 11, 2001, and was designed primarily to weaken the office of the presidency.

Learning Objective

1 Summarize the three federal laws that have been particularly influential on our nation's counterterrorism strategies.

Foreign Surveillance Until the 1970s, policies regarding **surveillance**, or the governmental monitoring of individuals or groups that posed national security threats to the United States, were primarily the domain of the executive branch. That is, the president and his advisers decided whom the federal government would target for its spy operations. Following President Richard Nixon's abuse of this discretion to eavesdrop on political opponents during the 1974 presidential campaign, in 1978 Congress passed the Foreign Intelligence Surveillance Act (FISA).[3] This legislation provided a legal framework for the government's electronic monitoring of suspected criminals or national security threats.

surveillance The close observation of a person or group by government agents, in particular to uncover evidence of criminal or terrorist activities.

Under FISA, federal agents are able to eavesdrop on the communications of foreign persons or foreign entities, without a court order, for up to a year, as long as the purpose of the surveillance is national security and not law enforcement. If this surveillance uncovers wrongdoing by an American citizen, the government has seventy hours to gain judicial authorization to continue monitoring this suspect's activities.[4]

If the target is a "foreign agent" operating within the United States, FISA requires permission from a special court to engage in surveillance. This court, known as the Foreign Intelligence Surveillance Court, or FISA Court, is made up of eleven federal judges assigned by the chief justice of the Supreme Court. The FISA warrant application must identify the target of the surveillance, the nature of the information sought, and the monitoring method. The government agency must also certify that the goal of the surveillance is to "obtain foreign intelligence information."[5]

Material Support Another crucial piece of counterterrorism legislation was passed in response to the 1995 truck bombing of the Alfred P. Murrah Federal Building in Oklahoma City, Oklahoma, which killed 168 people. The primary goal of this legislation, the Antiterrorism and Effective Death Penalty Act (AEDPA), is to hamper terrorist organizations by cutting off their funding. The law prohibits persons from "knowingly providing *material support* or resources" to any group that the United States has designated a "foreign terrorist organization."[6]

Material support is defined very broadly in the legislation, covering funding, financial services, lodging, training, expert advice or assistance, communications equipment, transportation, and other physical assets.[7] For example, Abdullahi Yusuf—discussed at the beginning of this chapter—was charged under the material support statute even though he never actually left the United States or, as far as has been reported, had any personal contact with active terrorists.

Furthermore, the AEDPA does not require that a suspect *intend* to aid the terrorist organization in question.[8] About a decade ago, Javed Iqbal was successfully prosecuted in New York for providing a satellite television package that included a channel operated by Hezbollah, a government-designated terrorist organization based in Lebanon. Even though there was no evidence that Iqbal intended to further the goals of Hezbollah, the fact that his conduct provided material support to the organization was sufficient to allow his prosecution under the law.[9]

The Patriot Act Enacted six weeks after the September 11, 2001, terrorist attacks, the **Patriot Act**[10] greatly strengthened the ability of federal law enforcement agents to investigate and incarcerate terrorist suspects. At 342 pages, the Patriot Act covers numerous areas related to homeland security, including immigration law and border protection, grants to local police departments, and compensation for the victims of the September 11 attacks. Here, we will focus on the legislation's rules regarding surveillance, summarized in Figure 14.1.

Critics of the Patriot Act have focused on Sections 213 and 215, which allow government agents to conduct searches and seizures without many of the Fourth Amendment protections discussed in Chapter 6. Specifically, Section 215 provides the National Security Agency (NSA), a federal agency that focuses on foreign intelligence operations, with the authority to collect the telephone billing records of Americans who have made calls to other countries, as those records are considered reasonably "relevant" to the agency's counterterrorism investigations.[11] Furthermore, the Patriot Act requires third parties such as telephone companies and Internet providers to turn over records of stored electronic communications to the federal government without notice to persons making

material support In the context of federal antiterrorism legislation, the act of helping a terrorist organization by engaging in a wide range of activity that includes providing financial support, training, and expert advice or assistance.

Patriot Act Legislation passed in the wake of the September 11, 2001, terrorist attacks that greatly expanded the ability of government agents to monitor and apprehend suspected terrorists.

Figure 14.1 The Patriot Act and Electronic Surveillance

Under Title II of the Patriot Act, the following sections greatly expanded the ability of federal intelligence operatives and law enforcement agents to conduct electronic surveillance operations on suspected terrorists.

- **Section 201:** Enables government agents to wiretap the communications of any persons suspected of terrorism or the dissemination of chemical weapons.
- **Section 204:** Makes it easier for government agents to get a warrant to search stored e-mail communications held by Internet service providers (ISPs).
- **Section 206:** The "roving wiretap" provision removes the requirement that government agents specify the particular places or things to be searched when obtaining warrants for surveillance of suspected terrorists.
- **Section 210:** Gives government agents enhanced authority to access the duration and timing of phone calls, along with phone numbers and credit cards used to pay for cell phone service.
- **Section 213:** The "sneak and peak" provision removes the requirement that government agents give notice to a target when they have searched her or his property.*
- **Section 214:** Removes the requirement that government agents prove that the subject of a FISA search, discussed earlier in the section, is actually the "agent of a foreign power."
- **Section 215:** The "business records" provision permits government agents to access "business records, medical records, educational records and library records" without showing probable cause of wrongdoing if the investigation is related to terrorism activities.

*In 2012, this rule was revised to rquire notice within thirty days of the search in most circumstances.

those communications. Government agents do not need judicial permission to issue **national security letters**, as such requests are called. The agents only need to show, after the fact, that the targeted communications are relevant to a terrorism investigation.[12] These national security letters can be used to collect:

1. Credit information from banks and loan companies,
2. Telephone and Internet data, including names, call times, physical addresses, and e-mail addresses,
3. Financial records, such as money transfers and bank accounts, and
4. Travel records held by "any commercial entity."[13]

As we will soon see, widespread use of such surveillance tactics has led to a great deal of controversy over the federal government's information-gathering practices.

Mass Surveillance

Following a series of controversies concerning the ability of the NSA to wiretap telephone and e-mail communications of suspected terrorists, in 2008 Congress passed an amended version of FISA. This legislative action did not, however, place greater limits on the NSA, which had amassed a massive database by secretly keeping track of millions of phone calls made by Americans who were not under suspicion of any wrongdoing. Instead, it essentially legalized government surveillance tactics that had previously been illegal by giving the NSA more freedom to act without oversight by the FISA court.[14]

Fourth Amendment and Homeland Security The problem with the original FISA, according to some observers, was that it required a lengthy review process before the FISA court would issue a warrant allowing government agents to monitor a terrorist suspect. In an environment where individuals can rapidly change their e-mail addresses and mode of Internet communication, or use multiple cell phone numbers, this procedure

national security letters Legal notices that compel the disclosure of customer records held by banks, telephone companies, Internet service providers, and other companies to the agents of the federal government.

was seen by these critics as too slow and cumbersome for effective intelligence gathering.[15] The NSA, FBI, and other government agencies argued that they needed more freedom to quickly collect massive amounts of information without judicial oversight.

This need, of course, must be tempered by the Fourth Amendment, which broadly requires that the government have probable cause of wrongdoing before intruding on a citizen's reasonable expectation of privacy. The amended FISA's authorization of large-scale warrantless electronic eavesdropping, in which hundreds of millions of phone and Internet records have been collected and stored in databases, created concerns that the federal government aimed to "write off the Fourth Amendment as technologically obsolete."[16]

Metadata Collection In 2013, an NSA contractor named Edward Snowden revealed that, under the revised FISA, the NSA has monitored the cell phone and Internet activity of approximately 113 million Americans without probable cause or a warrant from the FISA court. Through a program known as Prism, the NSA gained access to the information by sending national security letters to a number of major telephone companies and ISPs, including Apple, AT&T, Facebook, Google, Microsoft, Skype, Verizon, Yahoo, and YouTube.[17] By storing this "metadata," the government agency has gained unprecedented knowledge about whom Americans are communicating with, when these communications are taking place, and for how long.

"Red Flagging" Agents of the federal government had not been listening to actual phone conversations or reading hundreds of millions of e-mails. Rather, warrantless metadata collection and storage—justified, according to the FISA court, under Section 215 of the Patriot Act (see Figure 14.1)[18]—had been designed to retroactively determine communications patterns that might raise a "red flag" of terrorist activity. If the NSA was able to uncover a pattern of communications that suggested such activity, it would apply for a FISA warrant and undertake further investigations of the individuals involved. Using this process, the FISA court was issuing about 1,800 orders each year for domestic surveillance.[19]

Revising the Patriot Act Following the firestorm of criticism that followed Snowden's revelations about "government spying," in 2015 Congress overhauled the NSA's bulk phone record program. This legislative effort specifically targeted Section 215 of the Patriot Act for revision. Now, instead of the federal government storing metadata, phone companies such as AT&T and Verizon have the authority to do so, and government agencies such as the NSA must petition a special court for access to that information.[20] In theory, then, a telephone company could refuse to cooperate with an NSA request for metadata information, subject to the court's review. In practice, it remains to be seen how this partnership will impact federal antiterrorism investigations.

Coincidentally, just weeks before these new rules went into effect on November 29, 2015, Islamic State operatives carried out a series of brutal terrorist attacks that claimed 130 lives in Paris, France. Proponents of the previous NSA metadata program pointed out that this was just the sort of plot this program was designed to thwart, involving communications between multiple actors in multiple locations. "In the wake of Paris, a big stack of metadata doesn't seem to be the scariest thing in the room," said Michael V. Hayden, a former director of the NSA.[21]

Learning Objective 2

Explain why privacy expectations are so important to the federal government's metadata surveillance operations.

Expectations of Privacy Even with the revision of Section 2015, the federal government probably will still have access to large amounts of communications data. (AT&T, in particular, generally has been cooperative in sharing information with the

NSA.[22]) Thus, critics of metadata counterterrorism programs continue to point out that while such tactics may contribute to a small number of homeland security investigations, there is no evidence that they have disrupted any major terrorist organizations or operations.[23] This limited impact, they argue, does not justify the significant *invasion of privacy* involved.

▲ Civil liberties activists hold a rally outside the United States Justice Department building in Washington, D.C., condemning the surveillance of American citizens. Do you think that Internet users have a reasonable expectation of privacy while online? Why or why not? Nicholas Kamm/Getty Images

Privacy Precedents As you may recall from Chapter 6, an individual usually has no expectation of privacy with regard to information voluntarily disclosed to third parties. So, for example, a person does not have an expectation of privacy for writing on the outside of an envelope given to the U.S. Postal Service or garbage left on the curb for collection.[24] As a result, government agents can search and seize that "information" without a warrant.

Several federal appeals courts have held that defendants have no reasonable expectation of privacy over information "voluntarily" provided to a telephone company or an ISP. In 2013, a federal judge refused to grant a new trial to defendants convicted of providing material support in the form of funds to an African terrorist organization. Federal agents admitted that they initially became interested in the defendants' behavior because of telephone records contained in the NSA database. The judge ruled that the agents did not need a warrant to obtain such information from the telephone company because individuals have "no legitimate expectation of privacy" over phone call data.[25]

In general, these judicial decisions rely on the precedent set by the United States Supreme Court in its *Smith v. Maryland* (1979)[26] decision. That case involved the police's warrantless seizure of phone numbers dialed from the home of a robbery suspect. The Court ruled that the defendant had voluntarily turned over the phone numbers to a third party—the phone company—for billing purposes and therefore had no reasonable expectation of privacy in the matter.

Privacy and Technology One federal judge has gone against the tide with regard to metadata and expectations of privacy. In 2013, U.S. District judge Richard Leon of the District of Columbia found that the NSA's phone-data collection program "almost certainly" violated the Fourth Amendment.[27] Judge Leon argued that the Supreme Court's *Maryland* case involved a "one-time" search of phone calls emanating from the home of a single criminal suspect. In contrast, the NSA metadata program is a "daily, all-encompassing indiscriminate dump" of information from "the phones of people who are not suspected of any wrongdoing."[28]

Judge Leon's opinion raises an interesting question: have our reasonable expectations of privacy changed because of technological innovations? The judge referred to the Supreme Court's 2012 decision that it is unconstitutional for the police to use a GPS device to track a suspect's movement without a warrant, which we covered in Chapter 6, as proof that such expectations have changed.[29] He noted that the Supreme Court justices who made the *Maryland* ruling in 1979 could not "have ever imagined how the citizens of [today] would interact with their phones."[30]

Foreign Surveillance Targets Foreign citizens do not enjoy the same protections under the Fourth Amendment as U.S. citizens. This distinction is important to the operation of a separate NSA data-collection program—mandated under the revised FISA of 2008—that gives the government the ability to monitor non–U.S. citizens believed to be located in another country. Section 702 of the FISA Amendment Act permits eavesdropping (not merely metadata collection) without a warrant of foreign persons to obtain information related to:

1. National security, such as details of an "actual or potential attack" or "other grave hostile acts [by a] foreign power or agent of a foreign power,"
2. Foreign "intelligence activities," and
3. "The conduct of the foreign affairs of the United States."[31]

In the event that the target comes to the United States, surveillance without a warrant can continue for seventy-two hours if a lapse would pose a threat of death or bodily harm to U.S. citizens. After this time period, a warrant must be obtained to continue the surveillance on American soil.[32]

The broad language of this amended law allowed the NSA to target nearly 90,000 foreign people and organizations for surveillance in 2013.[33] This figure is significant because the law also permits eavesdropping without a warrant of a person who communicates with the target of foreign surveillance, even if that person is an American citizen. According to a detailed analysis of the NSA's global surveillance practices, the agency intercepts communications of nine incidental "bystanders" for every single "legally targeted" foreigner.[34]

This loophole has allowed the NSA to gather highly personal information such as baby pictures, medical records, and flirtatious Webcam chats from innocent persons, including Americans.[35] At the same time, it provides a valuable tool to uncover terrorist operations on U.S. soil, a growing concern that we have addressed throughout this textbook.

National Security and Speech

In the context of homeland security, FBI director James Comey is careful to distinguish the "mouth runners"—those who merely talk about their anti-American or violent beliefs—from potential terrorists. "This is a great country with lots of traditions of protecting mouth-running," said Comey. "We should continue that. But those who are inclined to cross the line, I've got to focus on them."[36]

How do our federal intelligence and law enforcement agencies tell the "mouth runners," protected by the American tradition of free speech, from the true threats? This question took on added urgency after a series of deadly terrorist attacks in Europe in 2015 and 2016, carried out by citizens of countries such as France and Belgium who had returned home after receiving training and support in the Middle East. This type of "small-scale attack" by a homegrown terrorist is "what keeps me up at night," says U.S. representative Michael McCaul, a Republican from Texas who chairs the House Homeland Security Committee.[37]

True Threat Law The crucial United States Supreme Court case for differentiating "mere speech," which is protected by the First Amendment of the U.S. Constitution, from a *true threat,* which is not, concerned the racially charged issue of cross burning. In *Virginia v. Black* (2003),[38] the Court struck down part of a Virginia law that prohibited *all* forms of cross burning. The statute assumed that any person who would burn a cross would only do so with the intent to frighten or intimidate specific African American targets. The Court ruled that the act of burning a cross was not enough to constitute a crime. The state must also prove that the act was done to place a specific victim "in fear of bodily harm or death."[39]

So, burning a cross on the front lawn of an African American family is a **true threat**, and therefore a crime. By the same measure, burning a cross on one's own property to make a general expression of racial hatred, out of sight of any members of minority groups, is not. (See the feature *Discretion in Action—Bragging about Bombing* for an example of how true threat doctrine works in the context of domestic terrorism.)

true threat An act of speech or expression that is not protected by the First Amendment because it is done with the intention placing a specific victim or group of victims in fear of unlawful violence.

Hidden Threats As a rule, individuals who intend to offer material support to terrorist organizations do not enjoy First Amendment protections. That is, they cannot claim to be harmless "mouth runners." Rather, by statute, many of the activities that constitute material support are considered true threats.[40] Sometimes, the true threat is legally obvious. In 2015, for example, six Bosnian immigrants living in Illinois, Missouri, and New York were indicted for providing material support to terrorist organizations in Syria and Iraq after sending $8,000 worth of U.S. military uniforms, technical gear, and weapons to those countries. It would be difficult, if not impossible, to claim that such behavior was a protected form of free speech.

The vast majority of terrorist sympathizers online, however, behave like political supporters or sports fans, expressing their enthusiasm by posting comments and videos to share with friends. Furthermore, being an Islamic State advocate is not against the law. Neither is expressing hatred for the United States. Consequently, counterterrorism investigators are faced with the nearly impossible task of differentiating between those terrorism suspects who are fantasizing in public and those who are planning actual violence.

Discretion in ACTION

Bragging about Bombing

Rachel Donahue/Shutterstock.com

Learning Objective

3 Distinguish verbal threats that are protected by the Constitution from verbal threats that can be prosecuted as "true threats."

The Situation On his last night in prison after serving a short stint for marijuana distribution, Steven has a long conversation with his cellmate, who is wearing a recording device. First, Steven discusses his skill as a bomb builder, giving as an example an explosive device he designed to be hidden in the face-cream container of an ex-girlfriend. Steven then specifically outlines his plans to pose as a delivery man and blow up the Reuss Federal Plaza in Milwaukee with a truck bomb. His detailed explanation includes the number of detonators and drums of explosives he would use, where he would park, and how he would deflect suspicion. Steven describes his desire to kill as many government agents as possible and, when pressed, tells his cellmate that there is "no doubt" that "someone's gonna get it."

The Law Steven's statements can be considered a "true threat," and therefore a criminal act, if they represent "a serious expression of an intent to commit an act of unlawful violence to a particular individual or group of individuals." There is no requirement that the targets of the action be aware of the threat.

What Would You Do? As soon as he leaves prison, Steven is arrested by police for threatening to use a weapon of mass destruction against a government building. Steven tells police that he was joking and never intended to actually destroy the Reuss Federal Plaza. After hearing a tape of the conversation, Steven's lawyer points out that his client bragged he would carry out the attack after he finished his probation—in eight years. If you are the prosecutor in this case, do you bring charges against Steven for making a "true threat?" Why or why not? What additional information would you need to make this decision?

To see what happened in a similar situation involving an inmate in Milwaukee, Wisconsin, see Example 14.1 in Appendix B.

Following "Known Wolves" In May 2015, the FBI began surveillance of Usaamah Rahim, a twenty-six-year-old Boston man who had been in touch with the Islamic State online. Investigators did not believe Rahim to be an imminent threat, but on June 2, during a telephone conversation on a line that was being tapped, Rahim said that he planned to behead a local police officer. Later that day, when FBI agents tried to apprehend him, Rahim pulled out a knife and was fatally shot.

This example highlights two difficulties for America's homeland security efforts. First, "known wolf," small-scale operators such as Rahim are highly unpredictable. Second, with hundreds, if not thousands, of people in the United States expressing online support for the Islamic State and other terrorist groups, law enforcement authorities do not have the resources to physically track each one. "We don't expect to eradicate crime, but we've made a political promise that we're going to stop every act of terrorism," said one observer. "It's ridiculous."[41]

Limiting Internet Speech Should the government take more dramatic steps to crack down on online terrorist sympathizers? Eric Posner, a professor of law at the University of Chicago, recently proposed legal limits on freedom of speech online to control "ideas that lead directly to terrorist attacks." Specifically, Posner suggests that the mere act of visiting a website that supports the Islamic State or furthers its recruiting operations should be considered a crime. Under Posner's proposal, a first offense would result in a warning letter, with further offenses drawing gradually harsher punishments.[42]

Such a law would almost certainly be struck down by the courts as unconstitutional. Still, France has passed legislation that makes it illegal to use the Internet to disseminate terrorist propaganda, and legal experts can imagine circumstances under which something similar could occur in this country. If America were to be struck by a series of terrorist attacks inspired by Internet recruiting, says Geoffrey Stone, a colleague of Posner at the University of Chicago, "You can imagine a scenario in which things get so terrible that you start watering down the [online free speech] protections."[43]

EthicsChallenge

The federal government maintains a secret "no-fly list" of persons suspected of having ties to terrorism who are not allowed to board a commercial airline flight that originates or terminates in the United States. Even if a person is a U.S. citizen, he or she is not permitted to challenge his or her inclusion on the no-fly list. Is this an ethical governmental policy? Should those on the no-fly list be able to go to court to get their names removed? Explain your answers.

Cyber Crime

In April 2015, visitors to the website of the Lamont Christian Reformed Church near Grand Rapids, Michigan, were automatically diverted to a video message that included the excerpt, "We will conquer your Rome, break your crosses, and enslave your women." The words "hacked by the United Cyber Caliphate," a group affiliated with the Islamic State, also scrolled across the screen.[44]

Homeland security experts worry that such relatively harmless incidents are a precursor to a much more serious **cyberattack** by a terrorist organization. Such attacks are designed to damage a nation's infrastructure, such as power companies, water treatment plants, airports, chemical plants, and oil refineries. In a worst-case scenario, a cyberattack could allow a terrorist organization to seize control of the federal air traffic

cyberattack An attempt to damage or disrupt computer systems or electronic networks operated by computers.

control system, or shut down national power grids. "This is a much bigger threat over time than losing some credit cards to cyber criminals," said one security expert.[45]

Of course, "losing some credit cards" is hardly a small concern, particularly if one of the credit cards in question happens to be your own. Furthermore, the Internet has proved reasonably secure from a "cyber 9/11," while being disturbingly susceptible to financial attacks. Several years ago, for example, a harmful piece of software created in Russia called GameOver Zeus was used to steal login details from computers belonging to thousands of small businesses and drain over $100 million from their bank accounts. "Robbing one person at a time using a knife or a gun doesn't scale well," notes Marc Goodman of the Future Crimes Institute. "But now one person can rob millions at the click of a button."[46]

Peter C. Vey/The New Yorker Collection/The Cartoon Bank

"You know, you can do this just as easily online."

Computer Crime and the Internet

Nearly every business in today's economy relies on computers to conduct its affairs and to provide consumers with easy access to its products and services. Furthermore, more than 3.1 billion people worldwide use the Internet on a daily basis, and the proliferation of handheld Internet devices has made it possible to be online at almost any time or place. In short, the Internet has become a place where large numbers of people interact socially and commercially.

In any such environment, wrongdoing has an opportunity to flourish. Throughout this section, we will be using the broad term **cyber crime** to describe any criminal activity occurring via a computer in the virtual community of the Internet.

Online Crime The example of *child pornography* shows how cyber crime has raised the stakes for the criminal justice system. (Child pornography is the illegal production and sale of material depicting sexually explicit conduct involving a child.) In the late 1970s, about 250 child pornography magazines were circulating in the United States, and it was relatively easy for law enforcement to confiscate hard copies of these publications.[47] With the advent of the Internet, however, child pornography became much easier to disseminate. The reasons for this include:

1. *Speed.* The Internet is a quick means of sending visual material over long distances. Child pornographers can deliver their material faster and more securely online than through regular mail.
2. *Security.* Any illegal material that passes through the hands of a mail carrier is inherently in danger of being discovered. This risk is significantly reduced with e-mail. Furthermore, Internet sites that offer child pornography can protect their

cyber crime A crime that occurs online, in the virtual community of the Internet, as opposed to in the physical world.

Learning Objective 4

Outline the three major reasons why the Internet is conducive to the dissemination of child pornography.

customers with passwords, which keep random Web surfers (or law enforcement agents) from stumbling on the site of chat rooms.

3. *Anonymity.* Obviously, anonymity is the most important protection offered by the Internet for sellers and buyers of child pornography, as it is for any person engaged in illegal behavior in cyberspace.[48]

Because of these three factors, courts and lawmakers have had a difficult time controlling not only child pornography but also a wide variety of other online wrongdoing.

The Incidence of Cyber Crime It is difficult, if not impossible, to determine how much cyber crime actually takes place. Often, people never know that they have been the victims of this type of criminal activity. Furthermore, businesses sometimes fail to report such crimes for fear of losing customer confidence. Nonetheless, in 2014, the Internet Crime Complaint Center (IC3), operated as a partnership between the FBI and the National White Collar Crime Center, received almost 270,000 complaints representing about $530 million in victim losses.[49] According to Juniper, a technology consulting firm, cyber crime will cost businesses $2.1 trillion globally by 2019.[50]

Cyber Crimes against Persons and Property

Most cyber crimes are not "new" crimes. Rather, they are existing crimes in which the Internet is the instrument of wrongdoing. The challenge for law enforcement is to apply traditional laws, which were designed to protect persons from physical harm or to safeguard their physical property, to crimes committed in cyberspace. Here, we look at several types of activity that constitute "updated" crimes against persons and property—online consumer fraud, cyber theft, and cyberstalking.

Cyber Fraud The expanding world of e-commerce has created many benefits for consumers. It has also created some notable drawbacks, including fraud conducted via the Internet. In general, fraud is any misrepresentation knowingly made with the intention of deceiving another person. Furthermore, the victim must reasonably rely on the fraudulent information to her or his detriment. **Cyber fraud**, then, is fraud committed over the Internet. Scams that were once conducted solely by mail or phone can now be found online, and new technology has led to increasingly creative ways to commit fraud.

Online dating scams, for example, have escalated dramatically in recent years, with fraudsters creating fake profiles to deceive unwitting romantic partners. According to the IC3, in 2014 online romance scam artists defrauded victims out of more than $86 million.[51] In one case, the FBI arrested a Houston resident for defrauding numerous older women he met on Internet dating websites out of millions of dollars. First, he would profess to fall into love with his victims. Then, he would offer to take over management of their personal finances, which he would steal as soon as the funds were placed naively in his control. (See Figure 14.2 to learn about the costs associated with other common forms of cyber fraud.)

Cyber Theft A **data breach** is an incident in which an unauthorized person or persons is able to access and steal confidential or protected information. In cyberspace, those who carry out data breaches are not subject to the physical limitations of the "real" world. A thief can steal data stored in a networked computer with online access from anywhere on the globe. Only the speed of the connection and the thief's computer equipment limit the quantity of data that can be stolen.

cyber fraud Any misrepresentation knowingly made over the Internet with the intention of deceiving another and on which a reasonable person would and does rely to his or her detriment.

data breach The act of illegally appropriating protected or confidential information by an individual or group unauthorized to do so.

Identity Theft Such freedom from physical limitations has led to a marked increase in data breaches of personal information, or **identity theft**. This crime occurs when the wrongdoer steals a form of identification—such as a name, date of birth, or Social Security number—and uses the information to access the victim's financial resources. According to the federal government, about 7 percent of Americans aged sixteen and older are victims of identity theft each year.[52]

The vast majority of identity theft victims (86 percent) experience data breaches involving existing bank and credit card accounts.[53] Online, an identity thief can steal financial information by fooling website hosts into thinking that he or she is the true account holder. For example, important personal information such as one's birthday, hometown, or employer that is available on social media sites such as Facebook can be used to convince a third party to reveal the victim's Social Security or bank account number. Offenders are also installing undetectable devices that capture information from a credit card's magnetic stripe in ATM machines. This technique, called *skimming*, allows for the production of counterfeit credit cards that can be used to withdraw cash at an ATM or make a purchase at a store or online.

Figure 14.2 Fraudulent Activity on the Internet

In its most recent annual report on cyber crime, the Internet Crime Complaint Center highlighted five "frequently reported Internet crimes." These crimes, along with the annual total losses reported by their victims, are detailed below.

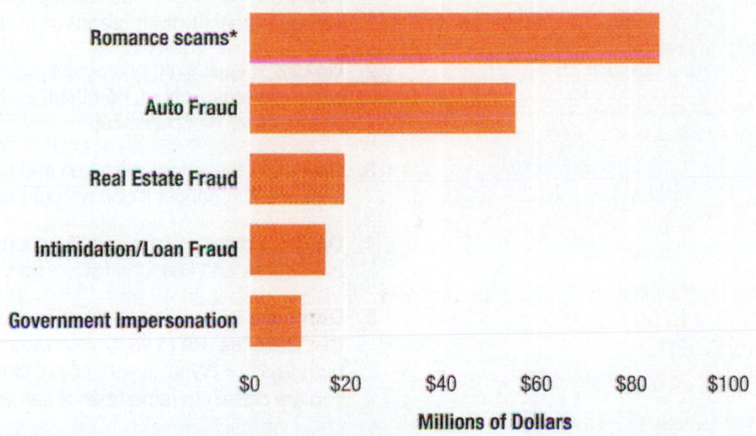

Auto fraud: Victim orders and pays for an automobile that is never delivered.

Real estate fraud: Victim pays first month's rent or makes a down payment on housing that does not exist or is not actually available to live in.

Intimidation/loan fraud: Victim is pressured to repay a loan—which may or may not actually exist—by an impostor pretending to be a representative of a legitimate agency or bank. The victim is threatened with legal action, arrest, or physical violence if the funds are not immediately provided.

Government impersonation: An offender poses as a legitimate government or law enforcement official to gain either personal information or funds from unsuspecting victims.

*See the "Cyber Fraud" section in the text for description.

Source: Internet Crime Complaint Center, *ICE 2014 Internet Crime Report* (Glen Allen, Va: National White Collar Crime Center, 2015) 10–14.

Password Protection The more personal information a cyber criminal obtains, the easier it is for him or her to find a victim's online user name. Once the online user name has been compromised, the easier it is to steal a victim's password, which is often the last line of defense to financial information. Numerous software programs aid identity thieves in illegally obtaining passwords. A technique called *keystroke logging,* for example, relies on software that embeds itself in a victim's computer and records every keystroke made on that computer. User names and passwords are then recorded and sold to the highest bidder. Internet users should also be wary of any links contained within e-mails sent from an unknown source, as these links can sometimes be used to illegally obtain personal information. (See Figure 14.3 for some hints on how to protect your online passwords.)

Phishing A distinct form of identity theft known as **phishing** adds a different wrinkle to this particular form of cyber crime. In a phishing attack, the perpetrators "fish" for financial data and passwords from consumers by posing as a legitimate business such as a bank or credit-card company. The "phisher" sends an e-mail asking the recipient to "update" or "confirm" vital information, often with the threat that an account or some other service will be discontinued if the information is not provided. Once the unsuspecting target enters the information, the phisher can use it to masquerade as the person or to extract funds from his or her bank or credit account.

The preferred method of phishing is through the use of **spam**, or unsolicited "junk e-mails" that flood virtual mailboxes with advertisements, solicitations, and other

identity theft The theft of personal information, such as a person's name, driver's license number, or Social Security number.

phishing Sending an unsolicited e-mail that falsely claims to be from a legitimate organization in an attempt to acquire sensitive information from the recipient.

spam Bulk e-mails, particularly of commercial advertising, sent in large quantities without the consent of the recipient.

Figure 14.3 Protecting Online Passwords

Once an online password has been compromised, the information on the protected website is fair game for identity thieves. By following these simple rules, you can strengthen the protection provided by your online passwords.

1. **Don't** use existing words such as your pet's name or your hometown. Such words are easy for computer identity theft programs to decode.
2. **Do** use at least eight characters in your passwords, with a nonsensical combination of upper- and lower-case letters, numbers, and symbols. A weak password is "scout1312." A strong password is "4X$dQ%3Z9j."
3. **Don't** use the same username and password for different Web accounts. If you do, then each account is in danger if one account is compromised.
4. **Do** use a different password for each Web account. If necessary, write down the various passwords and keep the list in a safe place.
5. **Don't** use information that can be easily found online or guessed at in choosing the questions that websites use to verify your password. That is, don't select questions such as "What is your birthday?" or "What is your city of birth?" Instead, choose questions with obscure answers that you are certain to remember or can easily look up.
6. **Don't** log on to any website if you are connected to the Internet via a wireless network (Wi-Fi) that is not itself password protected.

messages. Although 86 percent of the world's e-mail traffic still involves spam, filter systems are now able to block most unwanted e-mails from entering our digital mailboxes.[54] To get around these filters, phishers are increasingly using tactics that target small groups of recipients rather than blasting fake e-mails to millions of people at a time. Phishing scams have also spread to other areas, such as text messaging and social-networking sites. About 22 percent of all phishing, for example, takes place on Facebook.[55]

Another form of phishing, called *spear phishing,* is much more difficult to detect because the messages seem to have come from co-workers, friends, or family members. In 2015, a cybergang infiltrated the security systems of a number of banks worldwide by sending bank employees e-mails containing links to news clips, apparently sent by colleagues. When the employees clicked on the links, they inadvertently downloaded software onto their computers that allowed the cyber thieves to drain hundreds of millions of dollars from accounts in the affected banks.[56]

Cyber Aggression and Social Media The growing use of mobile devices such as smartphones and tablets has added another outlet for online criminal activity. According to Norton Security, only a quarter of the owners of such devices use security software for protection. As a result, nearly 40 percent of these users have experienced cyber crime such as vishing (phishing by phone) and smishing (phishing by SMS/text message).[57] In particular, widespread smartphone use seems to have exacerbated cyberbullying, which we discussed in the context of school crime in the previous chapter. According to one survey, American teenagers who consider themselves "heavy users" of their cell phones are much more likely to experience cyberbullying than those who consider themselves "normal users" of the devices.[58]

About one in four victims of stalking (discussed in Chapter 2) experiences a form of **cyberstalking**, which occurs when one person uses e-mail, text messages, or some other form of electronic communication to cause a victim to reasonably fear for her or his safety or the safety of the victim's immediate family. According to the most recent federal data on the subject, about 850,000 Americans are targets of cyberstalking each year.[59] Social media also offers sexual predators the opportunity to deceive potential victims. In

cyberstalking The crime of stalking, committed in cyberspace through the use of e-mail, text messages, or another form of electronic communication.

2016, for example, two college students apparently used the messaging app Kik to set up a meeting with thirteen-year-old Nicole Lowell in rural Virginia before kidnapping and murdering the girl. Furthermore, apps such as Kik are commonly used in cases of "sextortion," in which an offender convinces the victim to send nude photos and then threatens to post the images online if more such photos are not forthcoming.

Cyber Crimes in the Business World

Just as cyberspace can be a dangerous place for consumers, it presents a number of hazards for businesses that wish to offer their services on the Internet. The same circumstances that enable companies to reach a large number of consumers also leave them vulnerable to cyber crime. Online criminals are increasingly relying on software known as *crimeware* to engage in large-scale online criminal activity. The spread of crimeware has led to a dramatic increase in the number of *mega-breaches* in which more than 10 million personal records are stolen, almost always from corporate or government websites. In 2015, nine mega-breaches occurred, including the theft of medical records of nearly 100 million clients of Anthem and Premera, two major American health insurers.

Hackers The individuals who breached security at Anthem and Premera are known as *hackers.* A **hacker** is a person who uses one computer to illegally access another. The danger posed by hackers has increased significantly because of **botnets**, or networks of computers that have been appropriated by hackers without the knowledge of their owners. A hacker will secretly install a program on large numbers of personal computer "robots," or "bots," that allows him or her to forward transmissions to an even larger number of systems. The program attaches itself to the host computer when someone operating the computer opens a fraudulent e-mail.

Botnets are particularly effective in performing *distributed denial of service (DDoS) attacks.* During a DDoS attack, hackers flood targeted systems with false service requests. This onslaught of electronic "traffic" causes the systems to crash and become inaccessible, which can frustrate consumers and cost impacted companies large amounts of lost revenue. In April 2016, for example, a hacker group called the Lizard Squad temporarily shut down video game developer Blizzard Entertainment's online systems with a DDos attack, thereby denying thousands of customers access to games such as Starcraft 2, World of Warcraft, and Hearthstone.

Malware Programs that create botnets are forms of *malware,* a term that refers to any program that is harmful to a computer or, by extension, a computer user. A **worm**, for example, is a software program that is capable of reproducing itself as it spreads from one computer to the next. A **virus**, another form of malware, is also able to reproduce itself but must be attached to an "infested" host file to travel from one computer network to another. Worms and viruses can be programmed to perform a number of functions, such as prompting host computers to continually "crash" and reboot, or otherwise infect the system.

Ransomware New variations of malware and crimeware are constantly appearing on the Internet, challenging businesses and law enforcement to continuously play "catch-up" with the new technologies. Several years ago, hackers began employing a form of *ransomware* called CryptoLocker, which *encrypts* all the files on a targeted computer system. As we first saw in Chapter 1, **encryption** is the process of encoding information stored on computers in such a way that only authorized parties have access to it.

hacker A person who uses one computer to break into another.

botnet A network of computers that have been appropriated without the knowledge of their owners and used to spread harmful programs via the Internet; short for *robot network.*

worm A computer program that can automatically replicate itself and interfere with the normal use of a computer. A worm does not need to be attached to an existing file to move from one network to another.

virus A computer program that can replicate itself and interfere with the normal use of a computer. A virus cannot exist as a separate entity and must attach itself to another program to move through a network.

encryption The translation of computer data in a secret code with the goal of protecting that data from unauthorized parties.

intellectual property Property resulting from intellectual, creative processes.

Generally, encryption is used to protect information. When a computer system is infected with ransomware, however, its owners are unable to access their own files and must pay hackers a fee to unlock the data. After authorities shut down CryptoLocker in 2014, a more virulent strain of the malware called CryptoWall emerged, contaminating over 800,000 computers worldwide. According to the Cyber Threat Alliance, in 2015 businesses and individuals paid an estimated $325 million to free their files from CryptoWall encryption.[60]

Learning Objective 5

Explain how the Internet has contributed to piracy of intellectual property.

Pirating Intellectual Property Online Most people think of wealth in terms of houses, land, cars, stocks, and bonds. Wealth, however, also includes **intellectual property**, which consists of the products that result from intellectual, creative processes. The government provides various forms of protection for intellectual property, such as copyrights and patents. These protections ensure that a person who writes a book or a song or creates a software program is financially rewarded if that product is sold in the marketplace.

Intellectual property such as books, films, music, and software is vulnerable to "piracy"—the unauthorized copying and use of the property. In the past, copying intellectual products was time consuming, and the quality of the pirated copies was clearly inferior. In today's online world, however, things have changed. Simply clicking a mouse can now reproduce millions of unauthorized copies, and pirated duplicates of copyrighted works obtained via the Internet are often exactly the same as the original, or close to it. The Business Software Alliance estimates that 43 percent of all business software is pirated, costing software makers more than $62 billion annually.[61]

CJ & Technology

Hacking the "Internet of Things"

Syda Productions/Shutterstock.com

The "Internet of things" (IOT) is set to dominate our daily lives in the near future. The IOT refers to the embedding of tiny computer chips into objects so as to wirelessly connect them to the Internet. The roster of Web-connected items—including automobiles, refrigerators, televisions, pacemakers, and smoke detectors—is already extensive, and the technology will be present in an estimated 50 billion devices worldwide by 2020.

The tiny computers that form the basis of the IOT do not have as much processing power or memory as smartphones or handheld tablets. Consequently, the security software on these systems tends to be unsophisticated and, therefore, easily bypassed. Hackers have already taken advantage of this weakness to infiltrate baby monitors, security cameras, smart televisions, and medical equipment. Disturbingly, Fiat Chrysler recalled 1.4 million vehicles in 2015 after hackers demonstrated the ability to take remote control of a Jeep Cherokee driving 70 mph down a highway in St. Louis.

Thinking about Hacking the "Internet of Things"

How could ransomware (described earlier in the section) be used to take advantage of Web-connected automobiles or medical devices such as heart monitors?

Fighting Cyber Crime

During the 2013 holiday season, hackers used a form of malware called Kaptoxa to steal credit- and debit-card data from at least 70 million customers of the retail giant Target. In response, the company hired private contractors to plug its security holes and erase the malware from its compromised systems. Ideally, of course, corporations should have software already in place to prevent hacking operations, and most do. Businesses spend billions of dollars a year to encrypt their vital information, and encryption is seen as the best strategy for protecting the "Internet of things," whose vulnerabilities were discussed in this chapter's *CJ & Technology* feature.

Companies also hire outside experts to act as hackers and attempt to gain access to their systems, a practice known as "penetration testing." In 2016, the passenger-referral company Uber launched a "bug bounty" program that pays as much as $10,000 to anybody who can find security weaknesses in its mobile app.[62] Even the most thorough private protection services often lag behind the ingenuity of the hacker community, however. In the Target attack, for example, the malware was programmed to constantly erase itself, making it practically impossible to detect. "The dynamics of the Internet and cyberspace are so fast that we have a hard time staying ahead of the adversary," admits former U.S. Secret Service agent Robert D. Rodriguez.[63]

▲ In November 2015, U.S. authorities accused Gery Shalon of hacking into the computer systems of dozens of American businesses, including JPMorgan Chase & Co. and Dow Jones & Co. **Do you think that U.S. law enforcement should have the power to charge Shalon—an Israeli citizen shown here (in a white shirt) arriving at a Jerusalem courtroom—for crimes against American corporations? Why or why not?** Amir Cohen/REUTERS

The "Zero Days" Problem The Internet was designed to promote connectivity, not security. As more and more online threats to companies such as Target have developed, those businesses have had to respond with increasingly novel defenses. Facebook, for example, has constructed ThreatData, a defense system that monitors new worms, viruses, and malicious websites to create a constantly updated "blacklist" of blocked malware. Still, it is virtually impossible to protect against "zero days," the industry term for new vulnerabilities that security software cannot detect and for which there are no defenses. Symantec, an Internet security consulting firm, uncovered an average of one new zero-day vulnerability per week in 2015.[64]

Clearly, private industry needs government help to fight off cyber criminals. With hundreds of millions of users in every corner of the globe transferring unimaginable amounts of information almost instantaneously, however, the Internet has proved resistant to government regulation. In addition, although a number of countries have tried to "control" the Internet (see the feature *Comparative Criminal Justice—The Great Firewall of China*), the U.S. government has generally adopted a hands-off attitude to better promote the free flow of ideas and encourage the growth of electronic commerce. Thus, in this country cyberspace is, for the most part, unregulated, making efforts to fight cyber crime all the more difficult.

Challenges for Law Enforcement "In the eighties, if there was a bank robbery, the pool of suspects was limited to the people who were in the vicinity at the time," says Shawn Henry, former head of the FBI's Cyber Division, in trying to describe the complexities of fighting cyber crime. "Now when a bank is robbed the pool of suspects is limited to the number of people in the world with access to a five-hundred dollar laptop and an Internet connection. Which . . . is two and a half billion people."[65] The difficulty of finding

Comparative Criminal Justice

Pable631/Dreamstime.com

Central Intelligence Agency

The Great Firewall of China

The online anonymity enjoyed by many Americans on the Internet is increasingly hard to come by in China. In 2012, the Chinese government imposed new rules that require Internet users in that country to supply service providers with their real names. The regulations also require the service providers to report suspicious online activity, such as viewing pornography or the use of words such as *freedom* or *democracy,* to the authorities. Observers have little doubt that the changes are designed to restrict freedom of speech on the Internet. In the past, Chinese bloggers have been jailed for making politically sensitive comments or accusing local officials of wrongdoing.

In the United States, the issue of whether the government should regulate the Internet—and, if so, how much—is hotly debated. In China, the question was answered long before the Internet was even imagined. Since the 1950s, the Chinese Communist Party has exercised strict control over all forms of information, including newspapers, television, radio, movies, and books. Today, under the auspices of the Ministry of Information Industry, that control has been extended to the world of cyberspace.

Under broad laws that prohibit, among other things, "destroying the order of society" and "making falsehoods or distorting the truth," Chinese censors have free rein to limit the flow of information through government-controlled Internet service providers. The "Great Firewall," as this system is sometimes called, routinely blocks more than a million websites. Many of the sites are pornographic, but the obstruction also extends to Facebook, Twitter, YouTube, and Evite. These steps anger many Chinese citizens, and a number of blogs in the country are dedicated to "tearing down the Great Firewall." In 2015, after a new round of government restrictions effectively shut down Gmail and made it nearly impossible for those in China to access foreign websites, a naval historian who uses the Internet for academic research complained, "It's like we're living in the Middle Ages."

For Critical Analysis

How would China-style Internet censorship affect cyber crime in the United States? Under what circumstances, if any, would Americans accept such levels of Internet control by the government?

---

suspects is just one of the challenges that law enforcement officers face in dealing with online crime. Another is gathering evidence in cyberspace.

Cyber Forensics Police officers cannot put yellow tape around a computer screen or dust a website for fingerprints. The best, and often the only, way to fight computer crime is with technology that gives law enforcement agencies the ability to "track" hackers and other cyber criminals through the Internet. These efforts are complicated by the fact that digital evidence can be altered or erased even as the cyber crime is being committed. In Chapter 5, we discussed forensics, or the application of science to find evidence of criminal activity. Within the past two decades, a branch of this science known as **cyber forensics** has evolved to gather evidence of cyber crimes.

The main goal of cyber forensics is to gather **digital evidence**, or information of value to a criminal investigation that is stored on, received by, or transmitted by an electronic device such as a computer. Sometimes, this evidence is not particularly difficult to find. In one Social Security identity theft scheme, the offender bragged on her Facebook page about buying a $92,000 car and being the "queen of IRS tax fraud."

Cyber Sleuthing More sophisticated cyber criminals employ technology such as Tor to cover their tracks. Tor is a form of software that allows users to mask their IP addresses (codes that identify individual computers on the Internet) and the IP addresses of anyone with whom they communicate. To counteract such efforts, experts in cyber forensics have created tools such as the search engine Memex, which has the ability to bypass Tor's

cyber forensics The application of computer technology to finding and utilizing evidence of cyber crimes.

digital evidence Information or data of value to a criminal investigation that is either stored or transmitted by electronic means.

encryption codes by tracing past Internet activity. Memex has been particularly helpful in uncovering online sex trafficking operations, as it is able to determine the time and location of the photos that these criminal enterprises use to advertise sex workers on the Internet.[66]

Cyber sleuths can also create a digital duplicate of a targeted hard drive, enabling them to break access codes, determine passwords, and search files. "Short of taking your hard drive and having it run over by a Mack truck," says one expert, "you can't be sure that anything is truly deleted from your computer."[67] The latest challenge to cyber investigators is posed by *cloud computing*, in which data are stored not in a physical location but in a virtual, shared computing platform that is linked simultaneously to a number of different computers. Therefore, law enforcement officers investigating wrongdoing in the "cloud" may not have full control of the "crime scene." (The growing importance of cyber crime has led a number of universities to offer graduate certificates in cyber forensics. To learn about one of these programs, go to the website of the Marshall University Forensic Science Center.)

Getting Linked in

Computer forensic specialists investigate criminal or harmful activity on computer systems by collecting and analyzing computer-related evidence. They also protect commercial data and defend employers against malware. By entering "computer forensics" in LinkedIn's search engine, you will be exposed to dozens of entry-level jobs in this growing field.

Ethics Challenge

As noted earlier in this section, child pornography is illegal, both online and in the real world. Pornography involving adults, however, is legal for adult consumption and has a massive presence on the Internet. What might be some ethical problems with the easy availability of pornography online? What are the arguments for and against legislation that would make it more difficult to view pornography on the Internet?

Gun Control Policy

As was made clear in the previous section, technology often outpaces the ability of the government to regulate it. For example, in May 2013, when Cody Wilson posted instructions online on how to build a gun using a 3D printer, the U.S. State Department immediately ordered him to cease and desist. This order was problematic for several reasons. First, while there are many laws concerning the sale of firearms, it is entirely legal to make them. Second, "the United States Constitution guarantees a right to share truthful speech," as Wilson claimed in a 2015 lawsuit against the federal government.[68]

Other factors further complicate this issue. Being plastic, 3D printer guns can pass through metal detectors at airports, schools, and government buildings without notice. Also, these guns do not look like typical firearms, raising questions of police officer safety. Efforts to ban 3D printed firearms have, however, met resistance. Supporters insist that the plastic gun should be regulated like any other gun, meaning that, eventually, it will become widely available to the public. Thus, this new type of weapon has become another flashpoint in the debate over *gun control*, the shorthand term for policies that the government implements to regulate firearm ownership.

Firearms in the United States

According to the Bureau of Alcohol, Tobacco, Firearms and Explosives, 10.8 million firearms were manufactured in the United States in 2013, up from 5.4 million in 2010.[69] Extrapolating from these numbers, the *Washington Post* estimates that there are approximately 357 million firearms in the United States, not counting illegally owned guns and those weapons used on military bases.[70] Furthermore, there are nearly 130,000 federally licensed firearms dealers in this country, compared with about 144,000 gas stations and 14,000 McDonald's restaurants.[71]

The vast majority of gun owners are law-abiding citizens who use firearms for self-protection or recreational activities. Still, about 32,000 people are killed by gunfire in the United States each year, and firearms are used in 68 percent of the nation's murders and 40 percent of its robberies.[72] Indeed, illegally obtained firearms are a constant concern for law enforcement officials and, apparently, many citizens. A recent poll showed that 55 percent of Americans favor stricter measures by the government to control gun ownership.[73]

Regulating Gun Ownership

The Second Amendment to the U.S. Constitution states, "A well regulated Militia, being necessary to the security of a free State, the right of the people to keep and bear Arms, shall not be infringed." Because this language is somewhat archaic and vague, the United States Supreme Court has attempted to clarify the amendment's modern meaning. Over the course of two separate rulings, the Court stated that the Second Amendment provides individuals with a constitutional right to bear arms and that this right must be recognized at all levels of government—federal, state, and local.[74]

Learning Objective 6

Explain how background checks, in theory, protect the public from firearm-related violence.

Background Checks In both its Second Amendment cases, the Supreme Court emphasized that, to promote public safety, the government could continue to prohibit certain individuals—such as criminals and the mentally ill—from legally purchasing firearms. The primary method for doing so involves **background checks** of individuals who purchase firearms from federally licensed gun dealers.

The mechanics of background checks are regulated by the Brady Handgun Violence Prevention Act, enacted in 1993.[75] Known as the Brady Bill, this legislation requires a person wishing to purchase a gun from a licensed firearms dealer to apply for the privilege of doing so. The application process includes a background check by a law enforcement agency, usually the FBI. The applicant can be prohibited from purchasing a firearm if his or her record contains one of a number of "red flags," including a previous felony conviction, evidence of illegal drug addiction, or wrongdoing associated with domestic violence.[76]

Potential Loopholes The Brady Bill has been criticized for requiring background checks only for those consumers who buy guns from federally licensed firearms dealers. It does not cover purchases made at gun shows or from private citizens, which make up a significant percentage of the market.

Furthermore, under federal law, the FBI has three business days to determine whether there is sufficient evidence to deny a purchase made from a licensed dealer. If the FBI does not respond within this time period, the dealer is free to complete the sale. Dylann Roof, charged with fatally shooting nine people in a Charleston, South Carolina, church in June 2015, took advantage of this three-day "loophole" to purchase the gun he used to commit the murders. Roof's application should have been denied because he had previously admitted to illegal drug possession, a fact not uncovered in a timely manner by the FBI.[77]

background check An investigation of a person's history to determine whether that person should be allowed a certain privilege, such as the ability to possess a firearm.

Mental Health Issues Crucially, any person who has been involuntarily committed to a "mental institution" or "adjudicated as a mental defective" is also barred from purchasing or possessing firearms. The designation of being "mentally defective" is given to a person whom a court or other legal entity determines:

1. Is a danger to herself or himself or others,
2. Lacks the mental capacity to manage her or his own affairs, or
3. Has been found insane or incompetent to stand trial by a criminal or military court.[78]

▲ In late 2015, following a series of well-publicized mass shootings, gun sales in the United States reached record levels. **Can you think of two reasons for this correlation between high-profile violence and firearms purchases?** *Washington Post*/Getty Images

In 2007, a student with mental health issues shot and killed thirty-two people on the Virginia Tech campus in Blacksburg. As a result, most states began providing the federal government with the names of those residents who had been involuntary committed for psychiatric treatment. Over the next seven years, the number of people prohibited from purchasing firearms for reason of mental illness nationwide increased more than twelve-fold, to about 3.8 million.[79]

Even with all these restrictions, a wide range of behavior does not trigger the National Instant Criminal Background Check System's safeguards in this area. In July 2015, for example, John Houser fatally shot two people and injured nine others before killing himself at a movie theater in Lafayette, Louisiana. Seven years earlier, at his family's request, a judge in Georgia had Houser detained and sent to a mental hospital. Because he was quickly released from the hospital, the visit did not count as an "involuntary commitment," and Houser legally was able to walk into an Alabama pawnshop and purchase the .40-caliber handgun he used to commit the mass shooting in Louisiana.[80]

Recent Legislative Gun Control Efforts After John Houser opened fire on the movie theater in Lafayette, Louisiana governor Bobby Jindal called on states to make it more difficult for residents with a history of mental illness to purchase guns. "I think every state should strengthen their laws," said Jindal. "[T]his man should never have been able to buy a gun [in Alabama]."[81] Indeed, because of federal inaction, it largely has been left to the states to determine the direction of gun control in this country. In 2016, for example, California adopted a "gun violence restraining order" strategy that allows judges to seize guns for twenty-one days from someone they believe to be a danger to themselves or others.[82]

Following a 2012 mass shooting at an elementary school in Newtown, Connecticut, thirteen states passed measures tightening the background checks for firearm purchases within their borders. Seven of these states require such checks for private gun sales, which federal law does not. In addition, sixteen states have made it more difficult for the mentally ill to buy firearms, and two dozen states have passed legislation limiting the ability of domestic abusers to own guns.[83]

At the same time, in 2016 Texas became the fortieth state to permit "open carry"—the popular term for allowing people to arm themselves in plain sight.[84] That same year, Idaho, Mississippi, Oklahoma, and West Virginia also enacted legislation that lessened restrictions on gun ownership and use.[85] Between 2008 and 2016, the Supreme Court declined to hear nearly seventy lawsuits involving federal, state, or local firearms regulations,[86] meaning that the fate of gun control will continue to be decided by the voters and their elected representatives. (To express your own opinion on one aspect of this divisive issue, see the feature *CJ Controversy—The Debate over Gun Control.*)

EQUAL·JUSTICE·UNDER·LAW

CJ Controversy

M Dogan/Shutterstock.com

The Debate over Gun Control

Critics of our nation's gun laws have been disappointed that high-profile shooting sprees such as those carried out by Dylann Roof and John Houser, mentioned in the text, have not led to greater gun control in the United States. Opponents of stricter gun control laws point out that firearm massacres are quite rare and, in fact, our gun homicide rates are at historically low levels. They also reject the notion that firearms themselves are to blame for violent crime. Said one gun seller, "That's like pointing a finger at Ford and blaming them for car deaths."

The U.S. Should Make It Harder for People to Own Guns Because . . .

- The importance of guns for self-protection is overstated. Less than 1 percent of all gun deaths involve self-defense, with the rest being accidents, suicides, and homicides.
- Several studies show that stricter gun control laws are strongly correlated with lower gun homicide rates.

The U.S. Should Not Make It Harder for People to Own Guns Because . . .

- Someone who is going to commit a crime with a gun is probably going to obtain that firearm illegally. Consequently, stricter gun control would "prevent only law-abiding citizens from owning handguns."
- Firearms give citizens the ability to protect themselves and their families against criminal attacks when public law enforcement agents are unable to do so.

Your Assignment

In recent years, fifteen states have seen legislative efforts to expand the right to carry concealed weapons on public college campuses. Go online to learn about the issue of **college campus carry**. Specifically, research the details of one such law in **Texas**, which recently went into effect. Are you for or against allowing firearms on college campuses? What is your opinion of the new Texas legislation? Explain your answers in at least two full paragraphs.

White-Collar Crime

A travel agent in Saco, Maine, takes thousands of dollars from clients for trips she never books. A man in Oakland, California, prepares federal loan applications for "straw students" who have no intention of attending school, pocketing $500,000 in the process. Employees of a Framingham, Massachusetts, pharmacy dispense tainted meningitis drugs that cause sixty-four deaths. A member of the United States House of Representatives from Illinois spends eighteen months behind bars for using campaign contributions to buy more than $750,000 worth of personal luxury items.

These cases represent a variety of criminal behavior with different motives, different methods, and different victims. Yet they all fall into the category of *white-collar crime,* an umbrella term for wrongdoing marked by deceit and scandal rather than violence. As we mentioned in Chapter 1, white-collar crime has a broad impact on the global economy, causing American businesses alone hundreds of billions of dollars in losses each year. Despite its global and national importance, however, white-collar crime has consistently challenged a criminal justice system that struggles to define the problem, much less effectively combat it.

What Is White-Collar Crime?

White-collar crime is not an official category of criminal behavior measured by the federal government in the Uniform Crime Report. Rather, it covers a broad range of illegal acts involving "lying, cheating, and stealing," according to the FBI's website on the subject.[87] A more technical definition is that white-collar crimes are financial activities characterized by deceit and concealment that do not involve physical force or violence. Figure 14.4 lists and describes some common types of white-collar crime.

Figure 14.4 White-Collar Crimes

Embezzlement
Embezzlement is a form of employee fraud in which an individual uses his or her position within an organization to *embezzle*, or steal, the employer's funds, property, or other assets. Pilferage is a less serious form of employee fraud in which the individual steals items from the workplace.

Tax Evasion
Tax evasion occurs when taxpayers underreport (or do not report) their taxable income or otherwise purposely attempt to evade a tax liability.

iStockPhoto.com/skodonnell

iStockPhoto.com/oztasbc

Credit-Card and Check Fraud
Credit-card fraud involves obtaining credit-card numbers through a variety of schemes (such as stealing them from the Internet) and using the numbers for personal gain. Check fraud includes writing checks that are not covered by bank funds, forging checks, and stealing traveler's checks.

Mail and Wire Fraud
This umbrella term covers all schemes that involve the use of mail, radio, television, the Internet, or a telephone to intentionally deceive in a business environment.

Securities Fraud
Securities fraud covers illegal activity in the stock market. Stockbrokers who steal funds from their clients are guilty of securities fraud, as are those who engage in *insider trading*, which involves buying or selling securities on the basis of information that has not been made available to the public.

Bribery
Also known as *influence peddling*, bribery occurs in the business world when somebody within a company or government sells influence, power, or information to a person outside the company or government who can benefit. A county official, for example, could give a construction company a lucrative county contract to build a new jail. In return, the construction company would give some of the proceeds, known as a *kickback*, to the official.

Consumer Fraud
This term covers a wide variety of activities designed to defraud consumers, from selling counterfeit art to offering "free" items, such as electronic devices or vacations, that include a number of hidden charges.

Insurance Fraud
Insurance fraud involves making false claims in order to collect insurance payments. Faking an injury in order to receive payments from a workers' compensation program, for example, is a form of insurance fraud.

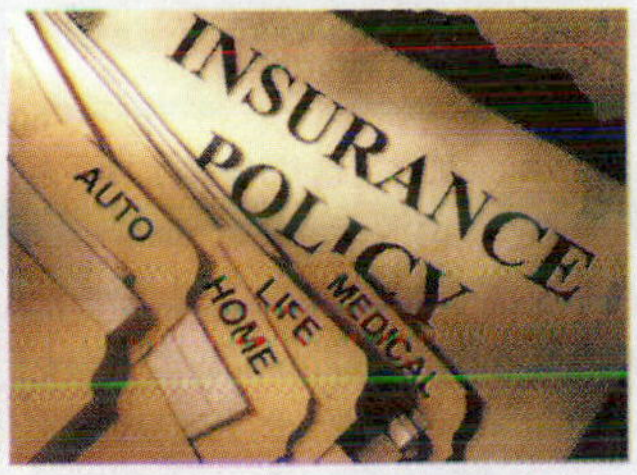

iStockPhoto.com/DNY59

Different Techniques To differentiate white-collar crime from "regular" crime, criminologists Michael L. Benson of the University of Cincinnati and Sally S. Simpson of the University of Maryland focus on technique. For example, in an ordinary burglary, a criminal uses physical means, such as picking a lock, to get somewhere he or she should not be—someone else's home—to do something that is clearly illegal. Furthermore, the victim is a specific identifiable individual—the homeowner. In contrast, white-collar criminals usually (1) have legal access to the place where the crime occurs; (2) are spatially separated from the victim, who is often unknown; and (3) behave in a manner that is, at least superficially, legitimate.[88]

Learning Objective

7 Indicate some of the ways that white-collar crime is different from violent or property crime.

Benson and Simpson also identify three main techniques used by white-collar criminals to carry out their crimes:[89]

1. *Deception.* White-collar crime almost always involves a party who deceives and a party who is deceived. The nation's federal Medicare system, which provides health insurance for those sixty-five years of age and older, is a frequent target of deceptive practices. For example, from 1999 to 2014, the federal government paid billions of dollars to medical-supply companies as reimbursement for expensive wheelchairs that the companies ostensibly provided to Medicare patients. Because the patients either did not exist or did not actually need wheelchairs, employees at the companies kept the reimbursed funds for themselves.[90]
2. *Abuse of trust.* A white-collar criminal often operates in a position of trust and misuses that trust for personal benefit. In 2015, for example, a financial adviser from Rockville, Maryland, was sentenced to forty-two months in prison for secretly withdrawing $1.2 million from the bank account of an elderly client to deposit in various personal accounts.

CJ Policy—Your Take

In Chapter 12, you learned about registries for sex offenders. Recently, Utah became the first state to create a **registry for white-collar criminals**, which includes anyone convicted of second-degree fraud or other financial felonies since 2006. According to state officials, the registry serves two purposes: offering investors information about con artists, and providing incentives for felons to pay restitution to their victims—a prerequisite for removal from the list. **What is your opinion of this strategy to "shame" white-collar criminals? Is it fair to add this punishment to the sanctions such as fines and incarceration already handed down by a court? Why or why not?**

3. *Concealment and conspiracy.* To continue their illegal activities, white-collar criminals need to conceal those activities. In *odometer fraud,* for example, an automobile dealership "rolls back" the odometers of used cars so that a higher price can be charged for the vehicles. As soon as the fraud is discovered, the scheme can no longer succeed.

Victims of White-Collar Crime As the above examples show, sometimes the victim of a white-collar crime is obvious. A dishonest financial adviser is stealing directly from his or her clients, and odometer fraud denies consumers the actual value of their purchased automobiles. But who was victimized in the fraudulent Medicare wheelchair scheme? In that instance, the "victims" were the U.S. taxpayers, who collectively had to cover the cost of the unwarranted items. Such health-care scams defraud U.S. taxpayers out of about $60 billion each year.[91] Often, white-collar crime does not target individuals but rather large groups or even abstract concepts such as "society" or "the environment." (This chapter's *CJ Policy—Your Take* addresses a novel approach taken by one state to protect potential and actual victims from white-collar crime.)

Regulating and Policing White-Collar Crime

For legal purposes, a corporation can be treated as a person capable of forming the intent necessary to commit a crime. Thus, in September 2015, General Motors Co. (GM) admitted criminal wrongdoing related to flawed ignition switches in its automobiles and paid a $900-million fine to the federal government. The faulty switches would cause the cars' engines to shut off for no apparent reason, putting drivers and passengers at considerable risk. GM employees were aware of the defect—which has been linked to at least 124 deaths and numerous injuries—for nearly a decade before addressing the problem.

Learning Objective

Explain the concept of corporate violence. **8**

The deaths and injuries caused by GM's deception and negligence are an example of *corporate violence.* In contrast to assaults committed by individual people, **corporate violence** is a result of policies or actions undertaken by a corporation. In the United States, parallel regulatory and criminal justice systems have evolved to prevent corporate violence and other forms of white-collar crime.

The Regulatory Justice System Although most white-collar crimes cause harm, these harms are not necessarily covered by criminal statutes. Indeed, more often they are covered by *administrative* laws, which we first encountered in Chapter 3. Such laws make up the backbone of the U.S. regulatory system, through which the government attempts to control the actions of individuals, corporations, and other institutions. The goal of **regulation** is not prevention or punishment as much as **compliance**, or the following of regulatory guidelines.

For example, in 2012, the appliance manufacturer Gree sold thousands of defective humidifiers that were prone to overheating and catching fire. Incidents involving this malfunction caused nearly $4.5 million in property damage, yet Gree failed to recall the products until September 2013. Furthermore, Gree neglected to report the defect to the U.S. Consumer Product Safety Commission (CPSC) as required by federal law, and the company's employees lied to CPSC staff members during the investigation of the humidifiers that followed. In 2016, Gree agreed to pay $15.45 million in penalties stemming from its lack of compliance with federal product-safety regulations.

The CPSC—which protects the public from unreasonable risk of injury or death associated with consumer products—is one of the federal administrative agencies whose

corporate violence Physical harm to individuals or the environment that occurs as the result of corporate policies or decision making.

regulation A governmental order or rule having the force of law that is usually implemented by an administrative agency.

compliance The state of operating in accordance with governmental standards.

Careers in CJ

Photo courtesy Paul Morris

Paul Morris
Customs and Border Protection Agent

The most memorable day of my career was, without a doubt, September 11, 2001. That morning, as I watched the fall of the Twin Towers, I knew that things were going to be different. Personally, the attacks left me with a resolve to ensure, to the maximum extent possible, that nothing similar ever happens again. Professionally, that day marked a sea change with respect to how the federal border agencies viewed border security. Ever since, our antiterrorism mission has been elevated above our other responsibilities, such as controlling illegal immigration, protecting our agricultural interests, and stopping the flow of illegal narcotics into this country.

www.dhs.gov

To be sure, as each of these tasks is crucially important, the extra burdens of antiterrorism pose a significant challenge. With the volume of vehicles, cargo, and persons crossing our borders, there can be no guarantees that a potential terrorist or weapon of mass destruction cannot slip across the border. Nevertheless, with advanced identification technology, increased personnel, and a more efficient infrastructure, I am confident that the possibility of such a breach is low.

SOCIAL MEDIA CAREER TIP Consider setting up personal and career-oriented Facebook pages or Twitter accounts and keeping your posts on each separated. Remember, though, that just because material is on your "personal" page or account, it still may be seen by others outside your network.

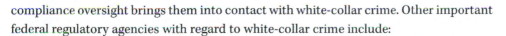

FAST FACTS

Customs and border protection agent

Job description:

- Make sure that laws are observed when goods or people enter the United States. Work at ports of entry and all along the border to prevent smuggling and the entrance of unauthorized immigrants.

What kind of training is required?

- Be under age 40, be a U.S. citizen and resident of the United States, and possess a valid state driver's license.
- Be fluent in Spanish or be able to learn the Spanish language.

Annual salary range?

- $38,000–$93,000

compliance oversight brings them into contact with white-collar crime. Other important federal regulatory agencies with regard to white-collar crime include:

1. The Environmental Protection Agency (EPA), which regulates air quality, water quality, and toxic waste.
2. The Food and Drug Administration (FDA), which protects the public health by regulating food products and a wide variety of drugs and medical practices.
3. The Occupational Safety and Health Administration (OSHA), which enforces workplace health and safety standards.
4. The Securities and Exchange Commission (SEC), which ensures that financial markets such as the New York Stock Exchange operate in a fair manner.

In 2015, the Federal Communications Commission voted to regulate the Internet as a *public utility* (a company that provides a public service, such as electricity or telephone communications). This move may eventually impact federal law enforcement efforts to combat the various forms of cyber crime we discussed in a previous section.

Law Enforcement and White-Collar Crime In general, when officials at a regulatory agency find that criminal prosecution is needed to punish a particular violation, they will refer the matter to the U.S. Department of Justice. Either through such referrals or at their own discretion, federal officials prosecute white-collar crime using

▲ In 2015, the New York State attorney general's office began investigating claims that store-brand dietary supplements sold at "big-box" stores such as Walmart and Walgreens contained ingredients that cause allergies without listing such "allergens" on their labels. **If true, does this behavior fall into the category of white-collar crime? Why or why not?**

Scott Olson/Getty Images News/Getty Images

the investigatory powers of several different federal law enforcement agencies. The FBI has become the lead agency when it comes to white-collar crime, particularly in response to financial scandals, as we shall soon see. The U.S. Postal Inspection Service is also quite active in such investigations, as fraudulent activities often involve the U.S. mail. In addition, the Internal Revenue Service's Criminal Investigative Division has jurisdiction over a wide variety of white-collar crimes, including tax fraud, and operates perhaps the most effective white-collar crime lab in the country.[92]

Local and state agencies also investigate white-collar crimes, but because of the complexity and costs of such investigations, most are handled by the federal government. Federal prosecutors are also in a unique position to enforce the federal Racketeer Influenced and Corrupt Organizations Act (RICO), which we discussed briefly in Chapter 10. Originally designed to combat organized crime, RICO makes it illegal to receive income through a pattern of *racketeering*.[93] The definition of **racketeering** is so inclusive—basically covering any attempt to earn illegal income involving more than one person—that it can be used against a broad range of criminal activity, white-collar or otherwise. In March 2016, for example, federal prosecutors used RICO to convict four members of the West Coast Crips street gang for working "together as a criminal enterprise to commit six murders, to use a 15-year-old girl and another female as prostitutes, and to commit robbery."[94]

White-Collar Crime in the 2000s

racketeering The criminal action of being involved in an organized effort to engage in illegal business transactions.

The decade that ended in 2010 was marked by two periods of financial scandal. First, in 2001 and 2002, fraudulent accounting practices led to the demise of giant corporations such as Enron and Worldcom, costing investors tens of billions of dollars. Then, near the end of the decade, the collapse of the subprime mortgage market caused millions of Americans to lose their homes to foreclosure and led to the collapse of major financial institutions such as Lehman Brothers and Washington Mutual. In the latter period, headlines focused on widespread *mortgage fraud,* or dishonest practices relating to home loans, along with the misdeeds of Bernard Madoff. Before his 2008 arrest, Madoff managed to defraud thousands of investors out of approximately $65 billion.

As has often occurred in U.S. history, these scandals and the concurrent economic downturns led to greater regulation and criminalization of white-collar crime. In 1934, for example, in the wake of the Great Depression, Congress established the SEC to watch over the American economy.[95] Similarly, in 2002 Congress passed legislation which, among other things, enhanced the penalties for those convicted of white-collar crimes.[96] Furthermore, in response to the "Great Recession" of 2008 and 2009, the FBI created the National Mortgage Fraud Team and began to crack down on a variety of white-collar crimes. Indeed, FBI agents are increasingly using aggressive tactics such as going undercover, planting wiretaps, and raiding offices—methods previously reserved for drug dealers, mobsters, and terrorists—against white-collar criminals.

EthicsChallenge

No individual employees of GM were criminally charged as a result of the flawed ignition-switch scandal discussed in this section. Do you think fines, civil lawsuits, and the financial ramifications of a damaged reputation are enough to ensure that corporations behave ethically? Or, do you agree with the mother of one GM crash victim who said that "jail time" for executives is the only "serious deterrent" against corporate wrongdoing? Explain your answer. ■

Summary

For more information on these concepts, look back to the Learning Objective icons throughout the chapter.

1 **Summarize the three federal laws that have been particularly influential on our nation's counterterrorism strategies.** (a) The Foreign Intelligence Surveillance Act (FISA) lays the groundwork for electronically monitoring national security threats. (b) The Antiterrorism and Effective Death Penalty Act (AEDPA) prohibits the providing of material support to terrorist organizations. (c) The Patriot Act greatly strengthened the ability of law enforcement agents to investigate and prosecute suspected terrorists.

2 **Explain why privacy expectations are so important to the federal government's metadata surveillance operations.** Under the Fourth Amendment, the government needs a warrant to eavesdrop on or record communications made by U.S. citizens, who have a reasonable expectation that those communications are private. Because a number of federal courts have ruled that there is no reasonable expectation of privacy with regard to communications involving cell phone calls and Internet use, the government has more leeway in "searching and seizing" information relating to that activity.

3 **Distinguish verbal threats that are protected by the Constitution from verbal threats that can be prosecuted as "true threats."** The First Amendment protects speech, including threats, that should not cause a person or group of people reasonably to fear for their safety. A "true threat," by contrast, expresses the viable intent of the speaker to harm potential victims, or to place those victims in reasonable fear of danger.

4 **Outline the three major reasons why the Internet is conducive to the dissemination of child pornography.** The Internet provides (a) a quick way to transmit child pornography from providers to consumers; (b) security such as untraceable e-mails and password-protected websites and chat rooms; and (c) anonymity for buyers and sellers of child pornography.

5 **Explain how the Internet has contributed to piracy of intellectual property.** In the past, copying intellectual property such as films and music was time consuming, and the quality of the pirated copies was vastly inferior to that of the originals. On the Internet, however, millions of unauthorized copies of intellectual property can be reproduced at the click of a mouse, and the quality of these items is often the same as that of the original, or close to it.

6 **Explain how background checks, in theory, protect the public from firearm-related violence.** Any person who wants to buy a firearm from a federally licensed dealer must go through an application process that includes a background check. This process is designed to keep firearms out of the hands of individuals who are deemed safety risks. Consequently, a person will fail the background check—and have the gun purchase denied—if he or she exhibits any one of a number of dangerous tendencies, including showing signs of mental illness, having a felony conviction, being addicted to illegal drugs, or engaging in domestic violence.

7 **Indicate some of the ways that white-collar crime is different from violent or property crime.** A wrongdoer committing a standard crime usually uses physical means to get somewhere he or she legally should not be in order to do something clearly illegal. Also, the victims of violent and property crimes are usually easily identifiable. In contrast, a white-collar criminal usually has legal access to the crime scene where he or she is doing something seemingly legitimate. Furthermore, victims of white-collar crimes are often unknown or unidentifiable.

8 **Explain the concept of corporate violence.** Corporate violence occurs when a corporation implements policies that ultimately cause harm to individuals or the environment.

Questions for Critical Analysis

1. Suppose a member of al Qaeda posts a video on YouTube that shows how to make an IED (improvised explosive device) out of common household cleaning detergents and a piece of pipe. Before YouTube can take down the video, a young man uses the instructions to carry out a terrorist attack during a high school basketball game. Do you think YouTube, as a corporate "person," could be charged with providing material support to al Qaeda, a terrorist organization? *Should* the company be so charged? Explain your answers.
2. Should the federal government make it a crime to publish bomb-making instructions online? Why or why not?
3. Consider the following proposed state law: *It is unlawful for any person, with intent to terrify, intimidate, threaten, harass, annoy, or offend, to use ANY ELECTRONIC OR DIGITAL DEVICE and use any obscene, lewd, or profane language.* What is your opinion of this statute? What might be some of its unforeseen consequences?
4. In 2015, Virginia's attorney general announced that the state would no longer recognize concealed handgun permits issued by other states, meaning that citizens of those states would no longer be permitted to carry concealed weapons in Virginia. What is your opinion of Virginia's new policy?
5. Using your own words, define *white-collar crime.*

Key Terms

background check 432
botnet 427
compliance 436
corporate violence 436
cyberattack 422
cyber crime 423
cyber forensics 430
cyber fraud 424
cyberstalking 426
data breach 424
digital evidence 430
encryption 427
hacker 427
identity theft 425
intellectual property 428
material support 416
national security letters 417
Patriot Act 416
phishing 425
racketeering 438
regulation 436
spam 425
surveillance 415
true threat 421
virus 427
worm 427

Notes

1. Lorenzo Vidino and Seamus Hughes, *ISIS in America: From Retweets to Raqqa* (Washington, D.C.: GWU Program on Extremism, 2015), 5.
2. Quoted in Anita Kumar and Michael Doyle, "Federal Watching Is Rampant These Days," *Arizona Daily Star* (June 8, 2013), A1.
3. 50 U.S.C. Sections 1801–1811.
4. 50 U.S.C. Sections 1801(a)(1)–(3).
5. 50 U.S.C. Section 1804(a)(6).
6. 18 U.S.C. Section 2339B(a)(1) (1996).
7. 18 U.S.C. Section 2339A(b) (Supp. I 2001).
8. 18 U.S.C. Section 2339B(a)(1) (2006).
9. William K. Rashbaum, "Law Put to Unusual Use in Hezbollah TV Case, Some Say," *New York Times* (August 26, 2006), B2.
10. Uniting and Strengthening America by Providing Appropriate Tools Required to Intercept and Obstruct Terrorism (USA PATRIOT) Act of 2001, Pub. L. No. 107-56, 115 Stat. 272 (2001).
11. 50 U.S.C. Section 1861(b)(2)(A) (2006).
12. 18 U.S.C. Section 2709 (2012).
13. John S. Dempsey and Linda S. Forst, *An Introduction to Policing,* 7th ed. (Clifton Park, N.Y.: Delmar Cengage Learning, 2014), 537.
14. FISA Amendment Act of 2008, Pub. L. No. 110-261, 122 Stat. 2436 (2008).
15. John Yoo, "The Legality of the National Security Agency's Bulk Data Surveillance Programs," *Harvard Journal of Law and Public Policy* (Summer 2014), at **papers.ssrn.com/sol3/papers.cfm?abstract_id=2369192.**
16. Jay Bookman, "Which Do You Value? Privacy, or the Illusion of Security?" *AJC.com* (December 17, 2013), at **www.ajc.com/weblogs/jay-bookman/2013/dec/17/which-do-you-value-privacy-or-illusion-security/#__federated=1.**
17. Timothy B. Lee, "Here's Everything We Know about PRISM to Date," *Washington Post WonkBlog* (June 12, 2013), at **www.washingtonpost.com/blogs/wonkblog/wp/2013/06/12/heres-everything-we-know-about-prism-to-date/.**
18. Steven G. Bradbury, "Understanding the NSA Programs: Bulk Acquisition of Telephone Metadata under Section 215 and Foreign-Targeted Collection under Section 702," *Lawfare Research Paper Series* (September 1, 2013), 2.
19. Charlie Savage and Matt Apuzzo, "U.S. Spied on 5 American Muslims, a Report Says," *New York Times* (July 10, 2014), A17.
20. Jennifer Steinhauer and Jonathan Weisman, "U.S. Surveillance in Place since 9/11

Is Sharply Limited," *New York Times* (June 2, 2015), A1.

21. Quoted in Scott Shane, "After Paris Attacks, C.I.A. Director Rekindles Debate over Surveillance," *New York Times* (November 17, 2015), A1.
22. Julia Angwin et al., "AT&T Helped U.S. Spy on Internet on a Vast Scale," *New York Times* (August 26, 2015), A1.
23. Steinhauer and Weisman, *op. cit.*
24. *Katz v. United States*, 389 U.S. 347, 351 (1967); and *California v. Greenwood*, 486 U.S. 35 (1988).
25. *United States v. Moalin et al.*, at **www.documentcloud.org/documents/902291-moalin-131114-deny-new-trial.html.**
26. 442 U.S. 735 (1979).
27. *Klayman v. Obama*, 957 F.Supp.2d 825 (D.D.C. December 16, 2013).
28. Quoted in "A Powerful Rebuke of Mass Surveillance," *New York Times* (December 17, 2013).
29. *United States v. Jones*, 565 U.S. ____ (2012).
30. Quoted in "A Powerful Rebuke of Mass Surveillance," *op. cit.*
31. 50 U.S.C. Section 1881a (2011).
32. Edward C. Liu, *Surveillance of Foreigners outside the United States under Section 702 of the Foreign Intelligence Surveillance Act (FISA)* (Washington, D.C.: Congressional Research Service, April 13, 2016), 1.
33. Ellen Nakashima, "Feds Report 90,000 Foreign Surveillance Targets," *Dallas Morning News* (June 28, 2014), 11A.
34. David E. Sanger and Matt Apuzzo, "Officials Defend N.S.A. after New Privacy Details Are Reported," *New York Times* (July 7, 2014), A9.
35. *Ibid.*
36. Quoted in "Colorado Teen Shannon Conley's Support of ISIS Raises Alarm about American *Jihadists*," *Associated Press* (September 10, 2014).
37. Quoted in Stephen Collinson, "Paris Attack: The New Terror," *CNN.com* (January 8, 2015), at **www.cnn.com/2015/01/08/politics/paris-new-terror/.**
38. 538 U.S. 343 (2003).
39. *Ibid.*, 358.
40. 18 U.S.C. Section 2339A(b)(1).
41. Quoted in Matt Apuzzo and Michael S. Schmidt, "F.B.I. Emphasizes Speed as ISIS Exhorts Individuals to Attack," *New York Times* (July 28, 2015), A11.
42. Eric Posner, "ISIS Gives Us No Choice but to Consider Limits on Speech," *Slate* (December 15, 2016), at **www.slate.com/articles/news_and_politics/view_from_chicago/2015/12/isis_s_online_radicalization_efforts_present_an_unprecedented_danger.html.**
43. Quoted in Erik Eckholm, "ISIS Influence on Web Prompts Second Thoughts on First Amendment," *New York Times* (December 28, 2015), A10.
44. Andrew Blake, "Michigan Church's Website Hacked to Play Islamic State Video," *Washington Times* (April 25, 2016), at **www.washingtontimes.com/news/2016/apr/25/michigan-church-website-hacked-to-play-islamic-sta.**
45. Derek Harp, quoted in Erin Kelly, "As Cyberthreats Rise, Push for Intelligence Heightened," *USA Today* (December 24, 2014), 3A.
46. Quoted in "Special Report Cyber-Security: Hackers Inc.," *The Economist* (July 12, 2014), 5.
47. William R. Graham, Jr., "Uncovering and Eliminating Child Pornography Rings on the Internet," *Law Review of Michigan State University Detroit College of Law* (Summer 2000), 466.
48. Richard Wortley and Stephen Smallbone, "The Problem of Internet Child Pornography," Center for Problem Oriented Policing (2006), at **www.popcenter.org/problems/child_pornography.**
49. Internet Crime Complaint Center, *IC3 2014 Internet Crime Report* (Glen Allen, Va.: National White Collar Crime Center, 2015), 8.
50. Juniper Research, "Cybercrime Will Cost Businesses over $2 Trillion by 2019" (May 12, 2015), at **www.juniperresearch.com/press/press-releases/cybercrime-cost-businesses-over-2trillion.**
51. Internet Crime Complaint Center, *op. cit.*, 14.
52. Bureau of Justice Statistics, *Victims of Identity Theft*, 2014 (Washington, D.C.: U.S. Department of Justice, September 2015), 1.
53. *Ibid.*
54. Jordan Robertson, "E-Mail Spam Goes Artisanal," *Bloomberg Technology* (January 19, 2016), at **www.bloomberg.com/news/articles/2016-01-19/e-mail-spam-goes-artisanal.**
55. Nadezhda Demidova, "Social Network Frauds," *SecureList.com* (June 11, 2014), at **securelist.com/analysis/publications/63855/social-network-frauds/.**
56. David E. Sanger and Nicole Perloth, "Bank Hackers Steal Millions via Malware," *New York Times* (February 14, 2015), A1.
57. *2013 Norton Report* (Mountain View, Calif.: Symantec, 2014), 7.
58. Openet, press release, "Openet-Sponsored Study Reveals 41 Percent of Teenagers Experience Cyber-bullying" (January 18, 2012), at **www.openet.com/about-us/press-room/press-releases/openet-sponsored-study-reveals-41-percent-teenagers-experience.**
59. Bureau of Justice Statistics, *Stalking Victimization in the United States* (Washington, D.C.: U.S. Department of Justice, January 2009), 1.
60. Cyber Threat Alliance, "Lucrative Ransomware Attacks: Analysis of the CryptoWall Version 3 Threat" (2016), at **cyberthreatalliance.org/cryptowall-executive-summary.pdf.**
61. *The Compliance Gap: BSA Global Software Survey* (Washington, D.C.: Business Software Alliance, June 2014), 2.
62. Uber Newsroom, "Welcome All Bug Bounty Hunters" (March 22, 2016), at **newsroom.uber.com/bug-bounty-program.**
63. Quoted in Marc Santora, "In Hours, Thieves Took $45 Million in A.T.M. Scheme," *New York Times* (May 10, 2013), A1.
64. *2016 Internet Security Threat Report* (Mountain View, Calif.: Symantec, April 2016), 5.
65. Quoted in John Seabrook, "Network Insecurity," *The New Yorker* (May 20, 2013), 64.
66. Elizabeth Dwoskin, "Sleuthing Search Engine: Even Better than Google?" *Wall Street Journal* (February 11, 2015), at **www.wsj.com/articles/sleuthing-search-engine-even-better-than-google-1423703464.**
67. Quoted in "Cybersleuths Find Growing Role in Corporate Crime Fighting," *Associated Press* (April 7, 2001).
68. Alan Feuer, "Cody Wilson, Who Posted Gun Instructions Online, Sues State Department," *New York Times* (May 2, 2015), A18.
69. Bureau of Alcohol, Tobacco, Firearms and Explosives, "ATF Releases 2015 Report on Firearms Commerce in the U.S." (July 22, 2015), at **www.atf.gov/news/pr/atf-releases-2015-report-firearms-commerce-us-0.**
70. Christopher Ingraham, "There Are Now More Guns than People in the United States," *Washington Post* (October 5, 2015), at **www.washingtonpost.com/news/wonk/wp/2015/10/05/guns-in-the-united-states-one-for-every-man-woman-and-child-and-then-some.**
71. Mathias H. Heck, Jr., "Section Offers Forum for Discussion of Gun Policy," *Criminal Justice* (Winter 2014), 1.
72. Federal Bureau of Investigation, *Crime in the United States 2014* (Washington, D.C.: U.S. Department of Justice, 2014), at **www.fbi.gov/about-us/cjis/ucr/crime-in-the-u.s/2014/crime-in-the-u.s.-2014,** Expanded Homicide Table 7 and Robbery Table 3.
73. Art Swift, "American's Desire for Stricter Gun Laws Up Sharply," *Gallup.com* (October 19, 2015), at **www.gallup.com/poll/186236/americans-desire-stricter-gun-laws-sharply.aspx.**
74. *District of Columbia v. Heller*, 554 U.S. 570 (2008); and *McDonald v. Chicago*, 561 U.S. 3025 (2010).
75. 18 U.S.C. 922(t).
76. Ronald J. Frandsen et al., *Background Checks for Firearm Transfers, 2010—Statistical Tables* (Washington, D.C.: U.S. Department of Justice, February 2013), 1.
77. Michael S. Schmidt, "Background Check Flaw Let Dylann Roof Buy Gun, F.B.I. Says," *New York Times* (July 11, 2015), A1.
78. 27 C.F.R. Section 478.11 (2010).

79. Richard Pérez-Peña, "Problems Plague System to Check Gun Buyers," *New York Times* (July 28, 2015), A1.

80. *Ibid.*

81. Quoted in Ashley Southall, "Bobby Ji[illegible] Calls for States to Follow Louisiana's Exa[illegible]ple in Toughening Gun Laws," *New York Times* (July 27, 2015), A10.

82. California Legislative Information, "AB-1014 Gun Violence Restraining Orders (2013-2014)," at **leginfo .legislature.ca.gov/faces/billNavClient .xhtml?bill_id=201320140AB1014.**

83. "Gun Laws," *The Economist* (May 3, 2014), 28.

84. Texas Department of Public Safety, "New Laws for Handgun Licensing Program (Formerly Known as Concealed Handgun Licensing): Effective January 1, 2016," at **www.txdps.state.tx.us/rsd/chl/legal /newlegislation.htm.**

85. Campbell Robertson and Timothy Williams, "As States Expand Gun Rights, the Police Object," *New York Times* (May 4, 2016), A10.

86. [illegible]ce, "Pro-[illegible]Gun [illegible]me Court [illegible]ower C[illegible]ntouched," [illegible]gust 26, [illegible] **[illegible]martgunlaws .org/prote[illegible]gun-laws-the -suprem[illegible]es-lower-court -victori[illegible]**nd author research.

87. The F[illegible] Investigation, "White-Col[illegible] **www.fbi.gov/about-us /inve[illegible]hite_collar/whitecollar crime.**

88. Michael L. Benson and Sally S. Simpson, *White-Collar Crime: An Opportunity Perspective* (New York: Routledge, 2009), 79–80.

89. *Ibid.*, 81–87.

90. David A. Fahrenthold, "A Medicare Scam That Just Kept Rolling," *Washington Post* (August 16, 2014), at **www.washingtonpost .com/sf/national/2014/08/16/a -medicare-scam-that-just-kept-rolling/.**

91. *High-Risk Series: An Update* (Washington, D.C.: United States Government Accountability Office, February 2015), 57.

92. David O. Friedrichs, *Trusted Criminals: White Collar Crime in Contemporary Society,* 4th ed. (Belmont, Calif.: Wadsworth Cengage Learning, 2010), 278–283.

93. Lawrence Salinger, *Encyclopedia of White-Collar and Corporate Crime,* 2d ed. (Thousand Oaks, Calif.: Sage, 2004), 361.

94. United States Attorney's Office, Southern District of California, "Federal Jury Convicts Four West Coast Crips Street Gang Members of Racketeering Conspiracy Involving Murders, Sex Trafficking and Robbery" (March 11, 2016), at **www.justice.gov/usao-sdca /pr/federal-jury-convicts-four-west -coast-crips-street-gang-members -racketeering-conspiracy.**

95. 15 U.S.C. Sections 78a *et seq.*

96. White-Collar Crime Penalty Enhancement Act of 2002, 18 U.S.C. Sections 1341, 1343, 1349–1350.

Appendix A

The Constitution of the United States

Preamble

We the People of the United States, in Order to form a more perfect Union, establish Justice, insure domestic Tranquility, provide for the common defence, promote the general Welfare, and secure the Blessings of Liberty to ourselves and our Posterity, do ordain and establish this Constitution for the United States of America.

Article I

Section 1. All legislative Powers herein granted shall be vested in a Congress of the United States, which shall consist of a Senate and House of Representatives.

Section 2. The House of Representatives shall be composed of Members chosen every second Year by the People of the several States, and the Electors in each State shall have the Qualifications requisite for Electors of the most numerous Branch of the State Legislature.

No Person shall be a Representative who shall not have attained to the Age of twenty five Years, and been seven Years a Citizen of the United States, and who shall not, when elected, be an Inhabitant of that State in which he shall be chosen.

Representatives and direct Taxes shall be apportioned among the several States which may be included within this Union, according to their respective Numbers, which shall be determined by adding to the whole Number of free Persons, including those bound to Service for a Term of Years, and excluding Indians not taxed, three fifths of all other Persons. The actual Enumeration shall be made within three Years after the first Meeting of the Congress of the United States, and within every subsequent Term of ten Years, in such Manner as they shall by Law direct. The Number of Representatives shall not exceed one for every thirty Thousand, but each State shall have at Least one Representative; and until such enumeration shall be made, the State of New Hampshire shall be entitled to chuse three, Massachusetts eight, Rhode Island and Providence Plantations one, Connecticut five, New York six, New Jersey four, Pennsylvania eight, Delaware one, Maryland six, Virginia ten, North Carolina five, South Carolina five, and Georgia three.

When vacancies happen in the Representation from any State, the Executive Authority thereof shall issue Writs of Election to fill such Vacancies.

The House of Representatives shall chuse their Speaker and other Officers; and shall have the sole Power of Impeachment.

Section 3. The Senate of the United States shall be composed of two Senators from each State, chosen by the Legislature thereof, for six Years; and each Senator shall have one Vote.

Immediately after they shall be assembled in Consequence of the first Election, they shall be divided as equally as may be into three Classes. The Seats of the Senators of the first Class shall be vacated at the Expiration of the second Year, of the second Class at the Expiration of the fourth Year, and of the third Class at the Expiration of the sixth Year, so that one third may be chosen every second Year; and if Vacancies happen by Resignation, or otherwise, during the Recess of the Legislature of any State, the Executive thereof may make temporary Appointments until the next Meeting of the Legislature, which shall then fill such Vacancies.

No Person shall be a Senator who shall not have attained to the Age of thirty Years, and been nine Years a Citizen of the United States, and who shall not, when elected, be an Inhabitant of that State for which he shall be chosen.

The Vice President of the United States shall be President of the Senate, but shall have no Vote, unless they be equally divided.

The Senate shall chuse their other Officers, and also a President pro tempore, in the Absence of the Vice President, or when he shall exercise the Office of President of the United States.

The Senate shall have the sole Power to try all Impeachments. When sitting for that Purpose, they shall be on Oath or Affirmation. When the President of the United States is tried, the Chief Justice shall preside: And no Person shall be convicted without the Concurrence of two thirds of the Members present.

Judgment in Cases of Impeachment shall not extend further than to removal from Office, and disqualification to hold and enjoy any Office of honor, Trust, or Profit under the United States: but the Party convicted shall nevertheless be liable and subject to Indictment, Trial, Judgment, and Punishment, according to Law.

Section 4. The Times, Places and Manner of holding Elections for Senators and Representatives, shall be prescribed in each State by the Legislature thereof; but the Congress may at any time by Law make or alter such Regulations, except as to the Places of chusing Senators.

The Congress shall assemble at least once in every Year, and such Meeting shall be on the first Monday in December, unless they shall by Law appoint a different Day.

Section 5. Each House shall be the Judge of the Elections, Returns, and Qualifications of its own Members, and a Majority of each shall constitute a Quorum to do Business; but a smaller Number may adjourn from day to day, and may be authorized to compel the Attendance of absent Members, in such Manner, and under such Penalties as each House may provide.

Each House may determine the Rules of its Proceedings, punish its Members for disorderly Behavior, and, with the Concurrence of two thirds, expel a Member.

Each House shall keep a Journal of its Proceedings, and from time to time publish the same, excepting such Parts as may in their Judgment require Secrecy; and the Yeas and Nays of the Members of either House on any question shall, at the Desire of one fifth of those Present, be entered on the Journal.

Neither House, during the Session of Congress, shall, without the Consent of the other, adjourn for more than three days, nor to any other Place than that in which the two Houses shall be sitting.

Section 6. The Senators and Representatives shall receive a Compensation for their Services, to be ascertained by Law, and paid out of the Treasury of the United States. They shall in all Cases, except Treason, Felony and Breach of the Peace, be privileged from Arrest during their Attendance at the Session of their respective Houses, and in going to and returning from the same; and for any Speech or Debate in either House, they shall not be questioned in any other Place.

No Senator or Representative shall, during the Time for which he was elected, be appointed to any civil Office under the Authority of the United States, which shall have been created, or the Emoluments whereof shall have been increased during such time; and no Person holding any Office under the United States, shall be a Member of either House during his Continuance in Office.

Section 7. All Bills for raising Revenue shall originate in the House of Representatives; but the Senate may propose or concur with Amendments as on other Bills.

Every Bill which shall have passed the House of Representatives and the Senate, shall, before it become a Law, be presented to the President of the United States; If he approve he shall sign it, but if not he shall return it, with his Objections to the House in which it shall have originated, who shall enter the Objections at large on their Journal, and proceed to reconsider it. If after such Reconsideration two thirds of that House shall agree to pass the Bill, it shall be sent together with the Objections, to the other House, by which it shall likewise be reconsidered, and if approved by two thirds of that House, it shall become a Law. But in all such Cases the Votes of both Houses shall be determined by Yeas and Nays, and the Names of the Persons voting for and against the Bill shall be entered on the Journal of each House respectively. If any Bill shall not be returned by the President within ten Days (Sundays excepted) after it shall have been presented to him, the Same shall be a Law, in like Manner as if he had signed it, unless the Congress by their Adjournment prevent its Return in which Case it shall not be a Law.

Every Order, Resolution, or Vote, to which the Concurrence of the Senate and House of Representatives may be necessary (except on a question of Adjournment) shall be presented to the President of the United States; and before the Same shall take Effect, shall be approved by him, or being disapproved by him, shall be repassed by two thirds of the Senate and House of Representatives, according to the Rules and Limitations prescribed in the Case of a Bill.

Section 8. The Congress shall have Power To lay and collect Taxes, Duties, Imposts and Excises, to pay the Debts and provide for the common Defence and general Welfare of the United States; but all Duties, Imposts and Excises shall be uniform throughout the United States;

To borrow Money on the credit of the United States;

To regulate Commerce with foreign Nations, and among the several States, and with the Indian Tribes;

To establish an uniform Rule of Naturalization, and uniform Laws on the subject of Bankruptcies throughout the United States;

To coin Money, regulate the Value thereof, and of foreign Coin, and fix the Standard of Weights and Measures;

To provide for the Punishment of counterfeiting the Securities and current Coin of the United States;

To establish Post Offices and post Roads;

To promote the Progress of Science and useful Arts, by securing for limited Times to Authors and Inventors the exclusive Right to their respective Writings and Discoveries;

To constitute Tribunals inferior to the supreme Court;

To define and punish Piracies and Felonies committed on the high Seas, and Offenses against the Law of Nations;

To declare War, grant Letters of Marque and Reprisal, and make Rules concerning Captures on Land and Water;

To raise and support Armies, but no Appropriation of Money to that Use shall be for a longer Term than two Years;

To provide and maintain a Navy;

To make Rules for the Government and Regulation of the land and naval Forces;

To provide for calling forth the Militia to execute the Laws of the Union, suppress Insurrections and repel Invasions;

To provide for organizing, arming, and disciplining, the Militia, and for governing such Part of them as may be employed in the Service of the United States, reserving to the States respectively, the Appointment of the Officers, and the Authority of training the Militia according to the discipline prescribed by Congress;

To exercise exclusive Legislation in all Cases whatsoever, over such District (not exceeding ten Miles square) as may, by Cession of particular States, and the Acceptance of Congress, become the Seat of the Government of the United States, and to exercise like Authority over all Places purchased by the Consent of the Legislature of the State in which the Same shall be, for the Erection of Forts, Magazines, Arsenals, dock-Yards, and other needful Buildings;—And

To make all Laws which shall be necessary and proper for carrying into Execution the foregoing Powers, and all other Powers vested by this Constitution in the Government of the United States, or in any Department or Officer thereof.

Section 9. The Migration or Importation of such Persons as any of the States now existing shall think proper to admit, shall not be prohibited by the Congress prior to the Year one thousand eight hundred and eight, but a Tax or duty may be imposed on such Importation, not exceeding ten dollars for each Person.

The privilege of the Writ of Habeas Corpus shall not be suspended, unless when in Cases of Rebellion or Invasion the public Safety may require it.

No Bill of Attainder or ex post facto Law shall be passed.

No Capitation, or other direct, Tax shall be laid, unless in Proportion to the Census or Enumeration herein before directed to be taken.

No Tax or Duty shall be laid on Articles exported from any State.

No Preference shall be given by any Regulation of Commerce or Revenue to the Ports of one State over those of another: nor shall Vessels bound to, or from, one State be obliged to enter, clear, or pay Duties in another.

No Money shall be drawn from the Treasury, but in Consequence of Appropriations made by Law; and a regular Statement and Account of the Receipts and Expenditures of all public Money shall be published from time to time.

No Title of Nobility shall be granted by the United States: And no Person holding any Office of Profit or Trust under them, shall, without the Consent of the Congress, accept of any present, Emolument, Office, or Title, of any kind whatever, from any King, Prince, or foreign State.

Section 10. No State shall enter into any Treaty, Alliance, or Confederation; grant Letters of Marque and Reprisal; coin Money; emit Bills of Credit; make any Thing but gold and silver Coin a Tender in Payment of Debts; pass any Bill of Attainder, ex post facto Law, or Law impairing the Obligation of Contracts, or grant any Title of Nobility.

No State shall, without the Consent of the Congress, lay any Imposts or Duties on Imports or Exports, except what may be absolutely necessary for executing its inspection Laws: and the net Produce of all Duties and Imposts, laid by any State on Imports or Exports, shall be for the Use of the Treasury of the United States; and all such Laws shall be subject to the Revision and Controul of the Congress.

No State shall, without the Consent of Congress, lay any Duty of Tonnage, keep Troops, or Ships of War in time of Peace, enter into any Agreement or Compact with another State, or with a foreign Power, or engage in War, unless actually invaded, or in such imminent Danger as will not admit of delay.

Article II

Section 1. The executive Power shall be vested in a President of the United States of America. He shall hold his Office during the Term of four Years, and, together with the Vice President, chosen for the same Term, be elected, as follows:

Each State shall appoint, in such Manner as the Legislature thereof may direct, a Number of Electors, equal to the whole Number of Senators and Representatives to which the State may be entitled in the Congress; but no Senator or Representative, or Person holding an Office of Trust or Profit under the United States, shall be appointed an Elector.

The Electors shall meet in their respective States, and vote by Ballot for two Persons, of whom one at least shall not be an Inhabitant of the same State with themselves. And they shall make a List of all the Persons voted for, and of the Number of Votes for each; which List they shall sign and certify, and transmit sealed to the Seat of the Government of the United States, directed to the President of the Senate. The President of the Senate shall, in the Presence of the Senate and House of Representatives, open all the Certificates, and the Votes shall then be counted. The Person having the greatest Number of Votes shall be the President, if such Number be a Majority of the whole Number of Electors appointed; and if there be more than one who have such Majority, and have an equal Number of Votes, then the House of Representatives shall immediately chuse by Ballot one of them for President; and if no Person have a Majority, then from the five highest on the List the said House shall in like Manner chuse the President. But in chusing the President, the Votes shall be taken by States, the Representation from each State having one Vote; A quorum for this Purpose shall consist of a Member or Members from two thirds of the States, and a Majority of all the States shall be necessary to a Choice. In every Case, after the Choice of the President, the Person having the greater Number of Votes of the Electors shall be the Vice President. But if there should remain two or more who have equal Votes, the Senate shall chuse from them by Ballot the Vice President.

The Congress may determine the Time of chusing the Electors, and the Day on which they shall give their Votes; which Day shall be the same throughout the United States.

No person except a natural born Citizen, or a Citizen of the United States, at the time of the Adoption of this Constitution, shall be eligible to the Office of President; neither shall any Person be eligible to that Office who shall not have attained to the Age of thirty five Years, and been fourteen Years a Resident within the United States.

In Case of the Removal of the President from Office, or of his Death, Resignation or Inability to discharge the Powers and Duties of the said Office, the same shall devolve on the Vice President, and the Congress may by Law provide for the Case of Removal, Death, Resignation or Inability, both of the President and Vice President, declaring what Officer shall then act as President, and such Officer shall act accordingly, until the Disability be removed, or a President shall be elected.

The President shall, at stated Times, receive for his Services, a Compensation, which shall neither be increased nor diminished during the Period for which he shall have been elected, and he shall not receive within that Period any other Emolument from the United States, or any of them.

Before he enter on the Execution of his Office, he shall take the following Oath or Affirmation: "I do solemnly swear (or affirm) that I will faithfully execute the Office of President of the United States, and will to the best of my Ability, preserve, protect and defend the Constitution of the United States."

Section 2. The President shall be Commander in Chief of the Army and Navy of the United States, and of the Militia of the several States, when called into the actual Service of the United States; he may require the Opinion, in writing, of the principal Officer in each of the executive Departments, upon any Subject relating to the Duties of their respective Offices, and he shall have Power to grant Reprieves and Pardons for Offenses against the United States, except in Cases of Impeachment.

He shall have Power, by and with the Advice and Consent of the Senate to make Treaties, provided two thirds of the Senators present concur; and he shall nominate, and by and with the Advice and Consent of the Senate, shall appoint Ambassadors, other public Ministers and Consuls, Judges of the supreme Court, and all other Officers of the United States, whose Appointments are not herein otherwise provided for, and which shall be established by Law; but the Congress may by Law vest the Appointment of such inferior Officers, as they think proper, in the President alone, in the Courts of Law, or in the Heads of Departments.

The President shall have Power to fill up all Vacancies that may happen during the Recess of the Senate, by granting Commissions which shall expire at the End of their next Session.

Section 3. He shall from time to time give to the Congress Information of the State of the Union, and recommend to their Consideration such Measures as he shall judge necessary and expedient; he may, on extraordinary Occasions, convene both Houses, or either of them, and in Case of Disagreement between them, with Respect to the Time of Adjournment, he may adjourn them to such Time as he shall think proper; he shall receive Ambassadors and other public Ministers; he shall take Care that the Laws be faithfully executed, and shall Commission all the Officers of the United States.

Section 4. The President, Vice President and all civil Officers of the United States, shall be removed from Office on Impeachment for, and Conviction of, Treason, Bribery, or other high Crimes and Misdemeanors.

Article III

Section 1. The judicial Power of the United States, shall be vested in one supreme Court, and in such inferior Courts as the Congress may from time to time ordain and establish. The Judges, both of the supreme and inferior Courts, shall hold their Offices during good Behaviour, and shall, at stated Times, receive for their Services a Compensation, which shall not be diminished during their Continuance in Office.

Section 2. The judicial Power shall extend to all Cases, in Law and Equity, arising under this Constitution, the Laws of the United States, and Treaties made, or which shall be made, under their Authority;—to all Cases affecting Ambassadors, other public Ministers and Consuls;—to all Cases of admiralty and maritime Jurisdiction;—to Controversies to which the United States shall be a Party;—to Controversies between two or more States;—between a State and Citizens of another State;—between Citizens of different States;—between Citizens of the same State claiming Lands under Grants of different States, and between a State, or the Citizens thereof, and foreign States, Citizens or Subjects.

In all Cases affecting Ambassadors, other public Ministers and Consuls, and those in which a State shall be a Party, the supreme Court shall have original Jurisdiction. In all the other Cases before mentioned, the supreme Court shall have appellate Jurisdiction, both as to Law and Fact, with such Exceptions, and under such Regulations as the Congress shall make.

The Trial of all Crimes, except in Cases of Impeachment, shall be by Jury; and such Trial shall be held in the State where the said Crimes shall have been committed; but when not committed within any State, the Trial shall be at such Place or Places as the Congress may by Law have directed.

Section 3. Treason against the United States, shall consist only in levying War against them, or, in adhering to their Enemies, giving them Aid and Comfort. No Person shall be convicted of Treason unless on the Testimony of two Witnesses to the same overt Act, or on Confession in open Court.

The Congress shall have Power to declare the Punishment of Treason, but no Attainder of Treason shall work Corruption of Blood, or Forfeiture except during the Life of the Person attainted.

Article IV

Section 1. Full Faith and Credit shall be given in each State to the public Acts, Records, and judicial Proceedings of every other State. And the Congress may by general Laws prescribe the Manner in which such Acts, Records and Proceedings shall be proved, and the Effect thereof.

Section 2. The Citizens of each State shall be entitled to all Privileges and Immunities of Citizens in the several States.

A Person charged in any State with Treason, Felony, or other Crime, who shall flee from Justice, and be found in another State, shall on Demand of the executive Authority of the State from which he fled, be delivered up, to be removed to the State having Jurisdiction of the Crime.

No Person held to Service or Labour in one State, under the Laws thereof, escaping into another, shall, in Consequence of any Law or Regulation therein, be discharged from such Service or Labour, but shall be delivered up on Claim of the Party to whom such Service or Labour may be due.

Section 3. New States may be admitted by the Congress into this Union; but no new State shall be formed or erected within the Jurisdiction of any other State; nor any State be formed by the Junction of two or more States, or Parts of States, without the Consent of the Legislatures of the States concerned as well as of the Congress.

The Congress shall have Power to dispose of and make all needful Rules and Regulations respecting the Territory or other Property belonging to the United States; and nothing in this Constitution shall be so construed as to Prejudice any Claims of the United States, or of any particular State.

Section 4. The United States shall guarantee to every State in this Union a Republican Form of Government, and shall protect each of them against Invasion; and on Application of the Legislature, or of the Executive (when the Legislature cannot be convened) against domestic Violence.

Article V

The Congress, whenever two thirds of both Houses shall deem it necessary, shall propose Amendments to this Constitution, or, on the Application of the Legislatures of two thirds of the several States, shall call a Convention for proposing Amendments, which, in either Case, shall be valid to all Intents and Purposes, as part of this Constitution, when ratified by the Legislatures of three fourths of the several States, or by Conventions in three fourths thereof, as the one or the other Mode of Ratification may be proposed by the Congress; Provided that no Amendment which may be made prior to the Year One thousand eight hundred and eight shall in any Manner affect the first and fourth Clauses in the Ninth Section of the first Article; and that no State, without its Consent, shall be deprived of its equal Suffrage in the Senate.

Article VI

All Debts contracted and Engagements entered into, before the Adoption of this Constitution shall be as valid against the United States under this Constitution, as under the Confederation.

This Constitution, and the Laws of the United States which shall be made in Pursuance thereof; and all Treaties made, or which shall be made, under the Authority of the United States, shall be the supreme Law of the Land; and the Judges in every State shall be bound thereby, any Thing in the Constitution or Laws of any State to the Contrary notwithstanding.

The Senators and Representatives before mentioned, and the Members of the several State Legislatures, and all executive and judicial Officers, both of the United States and of the several States, shall be bound by Oath or Affirmation, to support this Constitution; but no religious Test shall ever be required as a Qualification to any Office or public Trust under the United States.

Article VII

The Ratification of the Conventions of nine States shall be sufficient for the Establishment of this Constitution between the States so ratifying the Same.

Amendment I [1791]

Congress shall make no law respecting an establishment of religion, or prohibiting the free exercise thereof; or abridging the freedom of speech, or of the press; or the right of the people peaceably to assembly, and to petition the Government for a redress of grievances.

Amendment II [1791]

A well regulated Militia, being necessary to the security of a free State, the right of the people to keep and bear Arms, shall not be infringed.

Amendment III [1791]

No Soldier shall, in time of peace be quartered in any house, without the consent of the Owner, nor in time of war, but in a manner to be prescribed by law.

Amendment IV [1791]

The right of the people to be secure in their persons, houses, papers, and effects, against unreasonable searches and seizures, shall not be violated, and no Warrants shall issue, but upon probable cause, supported by Oath or affirmation, and particularly describing the place to be searched, and the persons or things to be seized.

Amendment V [1791]

No person shall be held to answer for a capital, or otherwise infamous crime, unless on a presentment or indictment of a Grand Jury, except in cases arising in the land or naval forces, or in the Militia, when in actual service in time of War or public danger; nor shall any person be subject for the same offence to be twice put in jeopardy of life or limb; nor shall be compelled in any criminal case to be a witness against himself, nor be deprived of life, liberty, or property, without due process of law; nor shall private property be taken for public use, without just compensation.

Amendment VI [1791]

In all criminal prosecutions, the accused shall enjoy the right to a speedy and public trial, by an impartial jury of the State and district wherein the crime shall have been committed, which district shall have been previously ascertained by law, and to be informed of the nature and cause of the accusation; to be confronted with the witnesses against him; to have compulsory process for obtaining witnesses in his favor, and to have the Assistance of Counsel for his defence.

Amendment VII [1791]

In Suits at common law, where the value in controversy shall exceed twenty dollars, the right of trial by jury shall be preserved, and no fact tried by jury, shall be otherwise reexamined in any Court of the United States, than according to the rules of the common law.

Amendment VIII [1791]

Excessive bail shall not be required, nor excessive fines imposed, nor cruel and unusual punishments inflicted.

Amendment IX [1791]

The enumeration in the Constitution, of certain rights, shall not be construed to deny or disparage others retained by the people.

Amendment X [1791]

The powers not delegated to the United States by the Constitution, nor prohibited by it to the States, are reserved to the States respectively, or to the people.

Amendment XI [1798]

The Judicial power of the United States shall not be construed to extend to any suit in law or equity, commenced or prosecuted against one of the United States by Citizens of another State, or by Citizens or Subjects of any Foreign State.

Amendment XII [1804]

The Electors shall meet in their respective states, and vote by ballot for President and Vice-President, one of whom, at least, shall not be an inhabitant of the same state with themselves; they shall name in their ballots the person voted for as President, and in distinct ballots the person voted for as Vice-President, and they shall make distinct lists of all persons voted for as President, and of all persons voted for as Vice-President, and of the number of votes for each, which lists they shall sign and certify, and transmit sealed to the seat of the government of the United States, directed to the President of the Senate;—The President of the Senate shall, in the presence of the Senate and House of Representatives, open all the certificates and the votes shall then be counted;—The person having the greatest number of votes for President, shall be the President, if such number be a majority of the whole number of Electors appointed; and if no person have such majority, then from the persons having the highest numbers not exceeding three on the list of those voted for as President, the House of Representatives shall choose immediately, by ballot, the President. But in choosing the President, the votes shall be taken by states, the representation from each state having one vote; a quorum for this purpose shall consist of a member or members from two-thirds of the states, and a majority of all states shall be necessary to a choice. And if the House of Representatives shall not choose a President whenever the right of choice shall devolve upon them, before the fourth day of March next following, then the Vice-President shall act as President, as in the case of the death or other constitutional disability of the President.—The person having the greatest number of votes as Vice-President, shall be the Vice-President, if such number be a majority of the whole number of Electors appointed, and if no person have a majority, then from the two highest numbers on the list, the Senate shall choose the Vice-President; a quorum for the purpose shall consist of two-thirds of the whole number of Senators, and a majority of the whole number shall be necessary to a choice. But no person constitutionally ineligible to the office of President shall be eligible to that of Vice-President of the United States.

Amendment XIII [1865]

Section 1. Neither slavery nor involuntary servitude, except as a punishment for crime whereof the party shall have been duly convicted, shall exist within the United States, or any place subject to their jurisdiction.

Section 2. Congress shall have power to enforce this article by appropriate legislation.

Amendment XIV [1868]

Section 1. All persons born or naturalized in the United States, and subject to the jurisdiction thereof, are citizens of the United States and of the State wherein they reside. No State shall make or enforce any law which shall abridge the privileges or immunities of citizens of the United States; nor shall any State deprive any person of life, liberty, or property, without due process of law; nor deny to any person within its jurisdiction the equal protection of the laws.

Section 2. Representatives shall be apportioned among the several States according to their respective numbers, counting the whole number of persons in each State, excluding Indians not taxed. But when the right to vote at any election for the choice of electors for President and Vice President of the United States, Representatives in Congress, the Executive and Judicial officers of a State, or the members of the Legislature thereof, is denied to any of the male inhabitants of such State, being twenty-one years of age, and citizens of the United States, or in any way abridged, except for participation in rebellion, or other crime, the basis of representation therein shall be reduced in the proportion which the number of such male citizens shall bear to the whole number of male citizens twenty-one years of age in such State.

Section 3. No person shall be a Senator or Representative in Congress, or elector of President and Vice President, or hold any office, civil or military, under the United States, or under any State, who having previously taken an oath, as a member of Congress, or as an officer of the United States, or as a member of any State legislature, or as an executive or judicial officer of any State, to support the Constitution of the United States, shall have engaged in insurrection or rebellion against the same, or given aid or comfort to the enemies thereof. But Congress may by a vote of two-thirds of each House, remove such disability.

Section 4. The validity of the public debt of the United States, authorized by law, including debts incurred for payment of pensions and bounties for services in suppressing insurrection or rebellion, shall not be questioned. But neither the United States nor any State shall assume or pay any debt or obligation incurred in aid of insurrection or rebellion against the United States, or any claim for the loss or emancipation of any slave; but all such debts, obligations and claims shall be held illegal and void.

Section 5. The Congress shall have power to enforce, by appropriate legislation, the provisions of this article.

Amendment XV [1870]

Section 1. The right of citizens of the United States to vote shall not be denied or abridged by the United States or by any State on account of race, color, or previous condition of servitude.

Section 2. The Congress shall have power to enforce this article by appropriate legislation.

Amendment XVI [1913]

The Congress shall have power to lay and collect taxes on incomes, from whatever source derived, without apportionment among the several States, and without regard to any census or enumeration.

Amendment XVII [1913]

Section 1. The Senate of the United States shall be composed of two Senators from each State, elected by the people thereof, for six years; and each Senator shall have one vote. The electors in each State shall have the qualifications requisite for electors of the most numerous branch of the State legislatures.

Section 2. When vacancies happen in the representation of any State in the Senate, the executive authority of such State shall issue writs of election to fill such vacancies: *Provided,* That the legislature of any State may empower the executive thereof to make temporary appointments until the people fill the vacancies by election as the legislature may direct.

Section 3. This amendment shall not be so construed as to affect the election or term of any Senator chosen before it becomes valid as part of the Constitution.

Amendment XVIII [1919]

Section 1. After one year from the ratification of this article the manufacture, sale, or transportation of intoxicating liquors within, the importation thereof into, or the exportation thereof from the United States and all territory subject to the jurisdiction thereof for beverage purposes is hereby prohibited.

Section 2. The Congress and the several States shall have concurrent power to enforce this article by appropriate legislation.

Section 3. This article shall be inoperative unless it shall have been ratified as an amendment to the Constitution by the legislatures of the several States, as provided in the Constitution, within seven years from the date of the submission hereof to the States by the Congress.

Amendment XIX [1920]

Section 1. The right of citizens of the United States to vote shall not be denied or abridged by the United States or by any State on account of sex.

Section 2. Congress shall have power to enforce this article by appropriate legislation.

Amendment XX [1933]

Section 1. The terms of the President and Vice President shall end at noon on the 20th day of January, and the terms of Senators and Representatives at noon on the 3d day of January, of the years in which such terms would have ended if this article had not been ratified; and the terms of their successors shall then begin.

Section 2. The Congress shall assemble at least once in every year, and such meeting shall begin at noon on the 3d day of January, unless they shall by law appoint a different day.

Section 3. If, at the time fixed for the beginning of the term of the President, the President elect shall have died, the Vice President elect shall become President. If the President shall not have been chosen before the time fixed for the beginning of his term, or if the President elect shall have failed to qualify, then the Vice President elect shall act as President until a President shall have qualified; and the Congress may by law provide for the case wherein neither a President elect nor a Vice President elect shall have qualified, declaring who shall then act as President, or the manner in which one who is to act shall be selected, and such person shall act accordingly until a President or Vice President shall have qualified.

Section 4. The Congress may by law provide for the case of the death of any of the persons from whom the House of Representatives may choose a President whenever the right of choice shall have devolved upon them, and for the case of the death of any of the persons from whom the Senate may choose a Vice President whenever the right of choice shall have devolved upon them.

Section 5. Sections 1 and 2 shall take effect on the 15th day of October following the ratification of this article.

Section 6. This article shall be inoperative unless it shall have been ratified as an amendment to the Constitution by the legislatures of three-fourths of the several States within seven years from the date of its submission.

Amendment XXI [1933]

Section 1. The eighteenth article of amendment to the Constitution of the United States is hereby repealed.

Section 2. The transportation or importation into any State, Territory, or possession of the United States for delivery or use therein of intoxicating liquors, in violation of the laws thereof, is hereby prohibited.

Section 3. This article shall be inoperative unless it shall have been ratified as an amendment to the Constitution by conventions in the several States, as provided in the Constitution, within seven years from the date of the submission hereof to the States by the Congress.

Amendment XXII [1951]

Section 1. No person shall be elected to the office of the President more than twice, and no person who has held the office of President, or acted as President, for more than two years of a term to which some other person was elected President shall be elected to the office of President more than once. But this Article shall not apply to any person holding the office of President when this Article was proposed by the Congress, and shall not prevent any person who may be holding the office of President, or acting as President, during the term within which this Article becomes operative from holding the office of President or acting as President during the remainder of such term.

Section 2. This article shall be inoperative unless it shall have been ratified as an amendment to the Constitution by the legislatures of three-fourths of the several States within seven years from the date of its submission to the States by the Congress.

Amendment XXIII [1961]

Section 1. The District constituting the seat of Government of the United States shall appoint in such manner as the Congress may direct:

A number of electors of President and Vice President equal to the whole number of Senators and Representatives in Congress to which the District would be entitled if it were a State, but in no event more than the least populous state; they shall be in addition to those appointed by the states, but they shall be considered, for the purposes of the election of President and Vice President, to be electors appointed by a state; and they shall meet in the District and perform such duties as provided by the twelfth article of amendment.

Section 2. The Congress shall have power to enforce this article by appropriate legislation.

Amendment XXIV [1964]

Section 1. The right of citizens of the United States to vote in any primary or other election for President or Vice President, for electors for President or Vice President, or for Senator or Representative in Congress, shall not be denied or abridged by the United States, or any State by reason of failure to pay any poll tax or other tax.

Section 2. The Congress shall have power to enforce this article by appropriate legislation.

Amendment XXV [1967]

Section 1. In case of the removal of the President from office or of his death or resignation, the Vice President shall become President.

Section 2. Whenever there is a vacancy in the office of the Vice President, the President shall nominate a Vice President who shall take office upon confirmation by a majority vote of both Houses of Congress.

Section 3. Whenever the President transmits to the President pro tempore of the Senate and the Speaker of the House of Representatives his written declaration that he is unable to discharge the powers and duties of his office, and until he transmits to them a written declaration to the contrary, such powers and duties shall be discharged by the Vice President as Acting President.

Section 4. Whenever the Vice President and a majority of either the principal officers of the executive departments or of such other body as Congress may by law provide, transmit to the President pro tempore of the Senate and the Speaker of the House of Representatives their written declaration that the President is unable to discharge the powers and duties of his office, the Vice President shall immediately assume the powers and duties of the office as Acting President.

Thereafter, when the President transmits to the President pro tempore of the Senate and the Speaker of the House of Representatives his written declaration that no inability exists, he shall resume the powers and duties of his office unless the Vice President and a majority of either the principal officers of the executive department or of such other body as Congress may by law provide, transmit within four days to the President pro tempore of the Senate and the Speaker of the House of Representatives their written declaration that the President is unable to discharge the powers and duties of his office. Thereupon Congress shall decide the issue, assembling within forty-eight hours for that purpose if not in session. If the Congress, within twenty-one days after receipt of the latter written declaration, or, if Congress is not in session, within twenty-one days after Congress is required to assemble, determines by two-thirds vote of both Houses that the President is unable to discharge the powers and duties of his office, the Vice President shall continue to discharge the same as Acting President; otherwise, the President shall resume the powers and duties of his office.

Amendment XXVI [1971]

Section 1. The right of citizens of the United States, who are eighteen years of age or older, to vote shall not be denied or abridged by the United States or by any State on account of age.

Section 2. The Congress shall have power to enforce this article by appropriate legislation.

Amendment XXVII [1992]

No law, varying the compensation for the services of the Senators and Representatives, shall take effect, until an election of Representatives shall have intervened.

the office of President, or acted as President, for more than two years of a term to which some other person was elected President shall be elected to the office of President more than once. But this Article shall not apply to any person holding the office of President when this Article was proposed by the Congress, and shall not prevent any person who may be holding the office of President, or acting as President, during the term within which this Article becomes operative from holding the office of President or acting as President during the remainder of such term.

Section 2. This article shall be inoperative unless it shall have been ratified as an amendment to the Constitution by the legislatures of three-fourths of the several States within seven years from the date of its submission to the States by the Congress.

Amendment XXIII [1961]

Section 1. The District constituting the seat of Government of the United States shall appoint in such manner as the Congress may direct:

A number of electors of President and Vice President equal to the whole number of Senators and Representatives in Congress to which the District would be entitled if it were a State, but in no event more than the least populous State; they shall be in addition to those appointed by the States, but they shall be considered, for the purposes of the election of President and Vice President, to be electors appointed by a State; and they shall meet in the District and perform such duties as provided by the twelfth article of amendment.

Section 2. The Congress shall have power to enforce this article by appropriate legislation.

Amendment XXIV [1964]

Section 1. The right of citizens of the United States to vote in any primary or other election for President or Vice President, for electors for President or Vice President, or for Senator or Representative in Congress, shall not be denied or abridged by the United States or any State by reason of failure to pay any poll tax or other tax.

Section 2. The Congress shall have power to enforce this article by appropriate legislation.

Amendment XXV [1967]

Section 1. In case of the removal of the President from office or of his death or resignation, the Vice President shall become President.

Section 2. Whenever there is a vacancy in the office of the Vice President, the President shall nominate a Vice President who shall take office upon confirmation by a majority vote of both Houses of Congress.

Section 3. Whenever the President transmits to the President pro tempore of the Senate and the Speaker of the House of Representatives his written declaration that he is unable to discharge the powers and duties of his office, and until he transmits to them a written declaration to the contrary, such powers and duties shall be discharged by the Vice President as Acting President.

Section 4. Whenever the Vice President and a majority of either the principal officers of the executive departments or of such other body as Congress may by law provide, transmit to the President pro tempore of the Senate and the Speaker of the House of Representatives their written declaration that the President is unable to discharge the powers and duties of his office, the Vice President shall immediately assume the powers and duties of the office as Acting President.

Thereafter, when the President transmits to the President pro tempore of the Senate and the Speaker of the House of Representatives his written declaration that no inability exists, he shall resume the powers and duties of his office unless the Vice President and a majority of either the principal officers of the executive department or of such other body as Congress may by law provide, transmit within four days to the President pro tempore of the Senate and the Speaker of the House of Representatives their written declaration that the President is unable to discharge the powers and duties of his office. Thereupon Congress shall decide the issue, assembling within forty-eight hours for that purpose if not in session. If the Congress, within twenty-one days after receipt of the latter written declaration, or, if Congress is not in session, within twenty-one days after Congress is required to assemble, determines by two-thirds vote of both Houses that the President is unable to discharge the powers and duties of his office, the Vice President shall continue to discharge the same as Acting President; otherwise, the President shall resume the powers and duties of his office.

Amendment XXVI [1971]

Section 1. The right of citizens of the United States, who are eighteen years of age or older, to vote shall not be denied or abridged by the United States or by any State on account of age.

Section 2. The Congress shall have power to enforce this article by appropriate legislation.

Amendment XXVII [1992]

No law, varying the compensation for the services of the Senators and Representatives, shall take effect, until an election of Representatives shall have intervened.

Discretion in Action Case Studies

Appendix B

1.1 In 2015, prosecutor Thom LeDoux decided that no charges would be filed in a "sexting" scandal that involved about one hundred Cañon City High School students. Because nobody had been coerced to share or view the inappropriate images, LeDoux decided that the students were merely "doing stupid things" and did not deserve to be punished under Colorado criminal law. On a practical level, it would be unreasonable to rely solely on the criminal justice system for a resolution to the issue of "sexting" in the United States. According to one study, about 30 percent of American teenagers have shared a nude photo of themselves with another teenager. As one expert puts it, the child pornography laws under which this behavior often falls "are not meant to deal with a privacy violation but a really horrific form of abuse."

Most prosecutors agree with Peter Weir, a district attorney in Jefferson County, Colorado, who believes that the goal in most teen sexting cases should be "educate" rather than "prosecute." Exceptions do, however, occur. Recently, two sixteen-year-old sweethearts who traded nude photos were charged with the felony of "exploiting a minor" by authorities in Fayetteville, North Carolina. The charges, which could have resulted in lengthy prison sentences, caused such a community outcry that the penalty was eventually reduced to a year's probation. Because of the possibility that prosecutors will use their discretion to severely punish young "sexters," approximately twenty states have passed laws mandating a softer approach to the problem in cases involving willing participants.

3.1 After University of Virginia senior George Huguely was arrested for the death of his twenty-two-year-old ex-girlfriend Yeardley Love in 2010, prosecutors charged him with first degree murder, punishable by life in prison. The prosecutors asserted that Huguely was enraged because Love was dating someone else, and that he intended to kill her in a premeditated act. Huguely's lawyers insisted that, at worst, their client was guilty of involuntary manslaughter. At the time of the crime, they pointed out, he was drunk and had no intent to harm Love, much less kill her. Furthermore, they argued, Love died from suffocation well after Huguely left her apartment.

In 2012, a Charlottesville, Virginia, jury found Huguely guilty of second degree murder, reasoning that although he did not intend to kill Love, he did act with malice aforethought, and his violent behavior was the cause of her death. A judge later sentenced Huguely to twenty-three years in prison.

4.1 The two officers, Holder and Reynolds, believing that the matter required their "immediate attention," forced their way back into Teresa Sheehan's room. When Sheehan continued to wave the knife in a threatening manner, Officer Reynolds pepper-sprayed her in the face. Sheehan still refused to drop the knife. Holder then shot her twice.

Sheehan survived her resulting injuries and eventually brought a lawsuit against the city of San Francisco. In the suit, she alleged that the police officers, acting on behalf of the city government, had violated her rights under the Americans with Disability Act by subduing her in a way that did not take into account her mental illness. The case eventually made its way to the United States Supreme Court, where the justices ruled against Sheehan. According to the Supreme Court, the officers' use of force was reasonable under the circumstances, regardless of whether Sheehan suffered from a mental illness or not.

5.1 In December 2015, Cuyahoga County prosecutor Timothy J. McGinty recommended that the grand jury not bring any criminal charges against Cleveland police officer Timothy Loehmann for the death of twelve-year-old Tamir Rice. When the grand jury followed McGinty's recommendation, the decision was met with outrage, particularly in the city's African American community, where many believed that Loehmann, who is white, fired without hesitation on Rice because Rice was black. For his part, McGinty called the incident a "perfect storm of human error, mistakes, and miscommunications," and argued that Loehmann could not be charged because there was no way the officer could have known that Tamir was holding a pellet gun instead of a real one. Under those circumstances, a police officer could reasonably have feared for his own life or the lives of those nearby.

6.1 In 1996, two Washington, D.C., police officers pulled over Michael J. Wren—a young African American male who was driving a truck with temporary plates in a high-crime neighborhood—for failing to signal while making a right turn. They found two large bags of crack cocaine in Wren's possession and arrested him. The United States Supreme Court upheld Wren's conviction, ruling that as long as police officers have probable cause to believe that a traffic violation has occurred, the "real" reason for making the stop is irrelevant.

As Justice Antonin Scalia put it, "Subjective intentions play no role in ordinary, probable-cause, Fourth Amendment analysis." In practical terms, this ruling gives law enforcement agents the ability to confirm "hunches" about serious illegal behavior as long as the target of these hunches commits even the most minor traffic violation. Such violations could include failing to properly signal during a turn, or making a rolling stop at a stop sign, or driving five miles over the posted speed limit.

7.1 Gerard Marrone decided that his conscience prevented him from representing Levi Aron, and he withdrew from the case. His replacement, Jennifer McCann, criticized Marrone's actions. "To sit there and say, 'This is a hard case, I don't want to take it,'" McCann said, "That's for somebody else, that's not who I am." She added, "It's not about defending [Aron's] actions. It's about defending his rights." In 2012, Aron pleaded guilty to charges of second degree murder and kidnapping, and was sentenced to forty years to life in prison.

8.1 The North Carolina prosecutor in this case charged Judy Norman with first degree murder, reasoning that self-defense did not apply because Judy did not face any *imminent* danger from her husband, John. Despite his threats and the years of abuse, John was, at the time of his murder, asleep and thus incapable of harming her. A jury in the case, however, found Judy guilty of voluntary manslaughter only, and she was sentenced to six years in prison.

This case gained national attention because the trial court refused to allow evidence of *battered woman syndrome (BWS)* to be presented to the jury. The term describes the psychological state a person descends into following a lengthy period of physical and mental abuse. In a courtroom, an expert might argue that anyone suffering from this syndrome is in a constant, and reasonable, fear for her or his life. Some states do allow evidence of BWS to support the defendant's claim of self-defense in these sorts of cases, and it has been effective. A New York woman who shot her abusive husband as he slept, for example, was acquitted after a jury accepted her self-defense claims, bolstered by expert testimony on BWS.

9.1 On April 15, 2015, Fulton County Superior Court Judge Jerry Baxter sentenced the three defendants to seven years behind bars each, as well as thirteen years of probation, a $25,000 fine, and 2,000 hours of community service. Two weeks later, however, Judge Baxter reduced the sentences to three years in prison for each defendant. "When a judge goes home and he keeps thinking over and over that something's wrong, something is usually wrong," explained Baxter. "And anyway, I want to modify the sentence so that I can live with it."

10.1 Susan Atkins was a disciple of cult leader Charles Manson and, in the summer of 1969, participated in one of the most sensationalized mass murders in American history. The woman Atkins stabbed sixteen times was Sharon Tate, an actress and the wife of film director Roman Polanski. On September 2, 2009, the California Board of Parole unanimously denied compassionate release for Atkins, marking the eighteenth time she had been refused parole. Three months later, Atkins died of brain cancer. Her case highlights the extent to which parole boards are often swayed by the nature of the crime above all other considerations.

12.1 The example given here is loosely taken from an online account of an inmate describing how he "downed a duck." In this account, after the correctional officer delivered the sympathy card with the funds, the inmate eventually turned the officer into a "golden goose" who helped with an escape attempt.

Although this account is impossible to verify, there have been real-life examples of prison employees being duped into conspiring with inmates. In the summer of 2015, for example, prisoners Richard Matt and David Sweat escaped the Clinton Correctional Facility in upstate New York with the help of correctional officer Gene Palmer and civilian prison employee Joyce Mitchell. Matt gave Palmer a series of paintings the inmate had done while behind bars, and in return Palmer apparently smuggled the tools into the prison used by Matt and Sweat for their escape. For her part, Mitchell told investigators that she talked with Matt "every day and he treated me with respect and was nice to me. He made me feel special." Mitchell eventually procured two pairs of spectacles, equipped with lights, for the inmates, so that they could work on their escape route at night. (After a three-week manhunt, Matt was shot and killed and Sweat was shot and captured. Both Palmer and Mitchell received prison sentences for their misconduct.)

13.1 In 2008, a Denver, Colorado, prosecutor chose to charge seventeen-year-old James Stewart as an adult for vehicular homicide. After Stewart was moved to an adult jail, he tightened several bed sheets around his neck and hung himself. Stewart's suicide led to a change in state law that requires judges to review prosecutorial waivers in certain situations and makes it much less likely that a juvenile offender awaiting trial will be held in an adult jail.

In the first year after this law was passed, the number of juvenile offenders waived to state adult court dropped by nearly 85 percent. Nonetheless, Colorado prosecutors dislike the new law. One claims that he and his colleagues are in a better position than judges to decide whether a juvenile should be tried in adult court, due to a prosecutor's "experience" and "years and years of weighing one case against similarly situated cases."

14.1 In 2004, Steven Parr was convicted of threatening to blow up the Reuss Federal Plaza in Milwaukee and was sentenced to ten years in prison. Before finding that Parr's bragging was a "true threat" and therefore not protected by the First Amendment, the jury heard a great deal of evidence in addition to the recording made by the prison whistleblower. A number of witnesses—including three ex-girlfriends and two former neighbors—testified that not only was Parr skilled in explosives, but also that he often spoke of his hatred for the federal government and his admiration for domestic terrorists such as Timothy McVeigh, whose 1995 bombing of the Alfred P. Murrah Federal Building in Oklahoma City is mentioned in the text.

Prosecutors also showed the jury a number of books and notebooks in Parr's possession that indicated his obsession with bomb building. Because of this evidence, in 2008 an appeals court ruled that a reasonable jury could have found that Parr's words constituted a "true threat" and upheld his conviction.

Appendix C

Table of Cases

Glossary

A

acquittal A declaration following a trial that the individual accused of the crime is innocent in the eyes of the law and thus is absolved from the charges.

actus reus (pronounced *ak*-tus *ray*-uhs). A guilty (prohibited) act.

adjudicatory hearing The process through which a juvenile court determines whether there is sufficient evidence to support the initial petition.

administrative law The body of law created by administrative agencies (in the form of rules, regulations, orders, and decisions) in order to carry out their duties and responsibilities.

affidavit A written statement of facts, confirmed by the oath or affirmation of the party making it and made before a person having the authority to administer the oath or affirmation.

affirmative action A hiring or promotion policy favoring those groups, such as women, African Americans, or Hispanics, who have suffered from discrimination in the past or continue to suffer from discrimination.

aftercare The variety of therapeutic, educational, and counseling programs made available to juvenile delinquents (and some adults) after they have been released from a correctional facility.

age of onset The age at which a juvenile first exhibits delinquent behavior.

aggravating circumstances Any circumstances accompanying the commission of a crime that may justify a harsher sentence.

aging out A term used to explain the fact that criminal activity declines with age.

alibi Proof that the suspect was somewhere other than the scene of the crime at the time of the crime, typically offered to demonstrate that he or she was not guilty of that particular crime.

***Allen* charge** An instruction by a judge to a deadlocked jury with only a few dissenters that asks the jurors in the minority to reconsider the majority opinion.

appeal The process of seeking a higher court's review of a lower court's decision for the purpose of correcting or changing this decision.

appellate courts Courts that review decisions made by lower courts, such as trial courts; also known as *courts of appeals*.

arraignment A court proceeding in which the suspect is formally charged with the criminal offense stated in the indictment.

arrest To deprive the liberty of a person suspected of criminal activity.

arrest warrant A written order, based on probable cause and issued by a judge or magistrate, commanding that the person named on the warrant be arrested by the police.

assault A threat or an attempt to do violence to another person that causes that person to fear immediate physical harm.

attempt The act of taking substantial steps toward committing a crime while having the ability and the intent to commit the crime, even if the crime never takes place.

attendant circumstances The facts surrounding a criminal event that must be proved to convict the defendant of the underlying crime.

attorney-client privilege A rule of evidence requiring that communications between a client and his or her attorney be kept confidential, unless the client consents to disclosure.

attorney general The chief law officer of a state; also, the chief law officer of the nation.

authority The power designated to an agent of the law over a person who has broken the law.

automatic transfer The process by which a juvenile is transferred to adult court as a matter of state law.

B

background check An investigation of a person's history to determine whether that person should be allowed a certain privilege, such as the ability to possess a firearm.

bail The dollar amount or conditions set by the court to ensure that an individual accused of a crime will appear for further criminal proceedings.

bail bond agent A businessperson who agrees, for a fee, to pay the bail amount if the accused fails to appear in court as ordered.

ballistics The study of firearms, including the firing of a weapon and the flight of a bullet.

ballot initiative A procedure in which the citizens of a state, by collecting enough signatures, can force a public vote on a proposed change to state law.

battery The act of physically contacting another person with the intent to do harm, even if the resulting injury is insubstantial.

bench trial A trial conducted without a jury, in which a judge makes the determination of the defendant's guilt or innocence.

beyond a reasonable doubt The degree of proof required to find the defendant in a criminal trial guilty of committing the crime. The defendant's guilt must be the only reasonable explanation for the criminal act before the court.

Bill of Rights The first ten amendments to the U.S. Constitution.

biology The science of living organisms, including their structure, function, growth, and origin.

biometrics Methods to identify a person based on his or her unique physical characteristics, such as fingerprints or facial configuration.

blue curtain A metaphorical term used to refer to the value placed on secrecy and the general mistrust of the outside world shared by many police officers.

boot camp A variation on traditional shock incarceration in which juveniles (and some adults) are sent to secure confinement facilities modeled on military basic training camps instead of prison or jail.

botnet A network of computers that have been appropriated without the knowledge of their owners and used to spread harmful programs via the Internet; short for *robot network*.

***Boykin* form** A form that must be completed by a defendant who pleads guilty. The defendant states that she or he has done so voluntarily and with full comprehension of the consequences.

broken windows theory Wilson and Kelling's theory that a neighborhood in disrepair signals that criminal activity is tolerated in the area. By cracking down on quality-of-life crimes, police can reclaim the neighborhood and encourage law-abiding citizens to live and work there.

bullying Overt acts taken by students with the goal of intimidating, harassing, or humiliating other students.

bureaucracy A hierarchically structured administrative organization that carries out specific functions.

burglary The act of breaking into or entering a structure (such as a home or office) without permission for the purpose of committing a felony.

burnout A mental state that occurs when a person suffers from exhaustion and has difficulty functioning normally as a result of overwork and stress.

C

capital crime A criminal act that makes the offender eligible to receive the death penalty.

capital punishment The use of the death penalty to punish wrongdoers for certain crimes.

case attrition The process through which prosecutors, by deciding whether to prosecute each person arrested, effect an overall reduction in the number of persons prosecuted.

case law The rules of law announced in court decisions.

caseload The number of individual probationers or parolees under the supervision of a probation or parole officer.

causation The relationship in which a change in one measurement or behavior creates a recognizable change in another measurement or behavior.

challenge for cause A *voir dire* challenge for which an attorney states the reason why a prospective juror should not be included on the jury.

charge The judge's instructions to the jury following the attorneys' closing arguments.

child abuse Mistreatment of children by causing physical, emotional, or sexual damage.

child neglect A form of child abuse in which the child is denied certain necessities such as shelter, food, care, and love.

circumstantial evidence Indirect evidence that is offered to establish, by inference, the likelihood of a fact that is in question.

citizen oversight The process by which citizens review complaints brought against individual police officers or police departments.

civil confinement The practice of confining individuals against their will if they present a danger to the community.

civil law The branch of law dealing with the definition and enforcement of all private or public rights, as opposed to criminal matters.

civil liability The potential responsibility of police officers, police departments, or municipalities to defend themselves against civil lawsuits.

civil liberties The basic rights and freedoms guaranteed by the U.S. Constitution, particularly in the Bill of Rights.

civil rights violation Any interference with a citizen's constitutional rights by a civil servant, such as a police officer.

classification The process through which prison officials screen each incoming inmate to best determine that inmate's security and treatment needs.

clearance rate A comparison of the number of crimes cleared by arrest and prosecution with the number of crimes reported during any given time period.

closing arguments Arguments made by each side's attorney after the cases for the plaintiff and defendant have been presented.

coercion The use of physical force or mental intimidation to compel a person to do something—such as confess to committing a crime—against her or his will.

cold case A criminal investigation that has not been solved after a certain amount of time.

cold hit The establishment of a connection between a suspect and a crime, often through the use of DNA evidence, in the absence of an ongoing criminal investigation.

community corrections The correctional supervision of offenders in the community as an alternative to sending them to prison or jail.

community policing A policing philosophy that emphasizes community support for and cooperation with the police in preventing crime.

competency hearing A court proceeding to determine whether the defendant is mentally well enough to understand the charges filed against him or her and cooperate with a lawyer in presenting a defense.

compliance The state of operating in accordance with governmental standards.

computer-aided dispatch (CAD) A method of dispatching police patrol units to the site of 911 emergencies with the assistance of a computer program.

concurrent jurisdiction The situation that occurs when two or more courts have the authority to preside over the same criminal case.

concurring opinions Separate opinions prepared by judges who support the decision of the majority of the court but who want to make or clarify a particular point or to voice disapproval of the grounds on which the decision was made.

confidential informant (CI) A human source for police who provides information concerning illegal activity in which he or she is involved.

conflict model A criminal justice model in which the content of criminal law is determined by the groups that hold economic, political, and social power in a community.

confrontation clause The part of the Sixth Amendment that guarantees all defendants the right to confront witnesses testifying against them during the criminal trial.

congregate system A nineteenth-century penitentiary system developed in New York in which inmates were kept in separate cells during the night but worked together in the daytime under a code of enforced silence.

consensus model A criminal justice model in which the majority of citizens in a society share the same values and beliefs. Criminal acts are acts that conflict with these values and beliefs and that are deemed harmful to society.

consent searches Searches by police that are made after the subject of the search has agreed to the action. In these situations, consent, if given of free will, validates a warrantless search.

conspiracy A plot by two or more people to carry out an illegal or harmful act.

constitutional law Law based on the U.S. Constitution and the constitutions of the various states.

control theory A series of theories that assume that all individuals have the potential for criminal behavior, but are restrained by the damage that such actions would do to their relationships with family, friends, and members of the community.

coroner The medical examiner of a county, usually elected by popular vote.

corporate violence Physical harm to individuals or the environment that occurs as the result of corporate policies or decision making.

corpus delicti The body of circumstances that must exist for a criminal act to have occurred.

correlation The relationship between two measurements or behaviors that tend to move in the same direction.

courtroom work group The social organization consisting of the judge, prosecutor, defense attorney, and other court workers.

crime An act that violates criminal law and is punishable by criminal sanctions.

crime control model A criminal justice model that places primary emphasis on the right of society to be protected from crime and violent criminals.

crime mapping Technology that allows crime analysts to identify trends and patterns of criminal behavior within a given area.

criminal justice system The interlocking network of law enforcement agencies, courts, and corrections institutions designed to enforce criminal laws and protect society from criminal behavior.

criminology The scientific study of crime and the causes of criminal behavior.

cross-examination The questioning of an opposing witness during trial.

custodial interrogation The questioning of a suspect after that person has been taken into custody. In this situation, the suspect must be read his or her *Miranda* rights before interrogation can begin.

custody The forceful detention of a person, or the perception that a person is not free to leave the immediate vicinity.

cyberattack An attempt to damage or disrupt computer systems or electronic networks operated by computers.

cyber crime A crime that occurs online, in the virtual community of the Internet, as opposed to in the physical world.

cyber forensics The application of computer technology to finding and utilizing evidence of cyber crimes.

cyber fraud Any misrepresentation knowingly made over the Internet with the intention of deceiving another and on which a reasonable person would and does rely to his or her detriment.

cyberstalking The crime of stalking, committed in cyberspace through the use of e-mail, text messages, or another form of electronic communication.

D

dark figure of crime A term used to describe the actual amount of crime that takes place. The "figure" is "dark," or impossible to detect, because a great number of crimes are never reported to the police.

data breach The act of illegally appropriating protected or confidential information by an individual or group unauthorized to do so.

day reporting center (DRC) A community-based corrections center to which offenders report on a daily basis for treatment, education, and rehabilitation.

deadly force Force applied by a police officer that is likely or intended to cause death.

defendant In a civil court, the person or institution against whom an action is brought. In a criminal court, the person or entity who has been formally accused of violating a criminal law.

defense attorney The lawyer representing the defendant.

delegation of authority The principles of command on which most police departments are based, in which personnel take orders from and are responsible to those in positions of power directly above them.

"deliberate indifference" The standard for establishing a violation of an inmate's Eighth Amendment rights, requiring that prison officials were aware of harmful conditions in a correctional institution *and* failed to take steps to remedy those conditions.

departure A stipulation in many federal and state sentencing guidelines that allows a judge to adjust his or her sentencing decision based on the special circumstances of a particular case.

deprivation model A theory that inmate aggression is the result of the frustration inmates feel at being deprived of freedom, consumer goods, sex, and other staples of life outside the institution.

desistance The process through which criminal activity decreases and reintegration into society increases over a period of time.

detective The primary police investigator of crimes.

detention The temporary custody of a juvenile in a secure facility after a petition has been filed and before the adjudicatory process begins.

detention hearing A hearing to determine whether a juvenile should be detained, or remain detained, while waiting for the adjudicatory process to begin.

determinate sentencing Imposition of a sentence that is fixed by a sentencing authority and cannot be reduced by judges or other corrections officials.

deterrence The strategy of preventing crime through the threat of punishment.

deviance Behavior that is considered to go against the norms established by society.

differential response A strategy for answering calls for service in which response time is adapted to the seriousness of the call.

digital evidence Information or data of value to a criminal investigation that is either stored or transmitted by electronic means.

directed patrol A patrol strategy that is designed to focus on a specific type of criminal activity in a specific geographic area.

direct evidence Evidence that establishes the existence of a fact that is in question without relying on inference.

direct examination The examination of a witness by the attorney who calls the witness to the stand to testify.

direct supervision approach A process of prison and jail administration in which correctional officers are in continuous visual contact with inmates during the day.

discovery Formal investigation by each side prior to trial.

discretion The ability of individuals in the criminal justice system to make operational decisions based on personal judgment instead of formal rules or official information.

discretionary release The release of an inmate into a community supervision program at the discretion of the parole board within limits set by state or federal law.

discrimination The illegal use of characteristics such as gender or race by employers when making hiring or promotion decisions.

disposition hearing Similar to the sentencing hearing for adults, a hearing in which the juvenile judge or officer decides the appropriate punishment for a youth found to be delinquent or a status offender.

dissenting opinions Separate opinions in which judges disagree with the conclusion reached by the majority of the court and expand on their own views about the case.

diversion An effort to keep offenders out of prison or jail by diverting them into programs that promote treatment and rehabilitation rather than punishment.

DNA fingerprinting The identification of a person based on a sample of her or his DNA, the genetic material found in the cells of all living things.

docket The list of cases entered on a court's calendar and thus scheduled to be heard by the court.

domestic terrorism Acts of terrorism that take place on U.S. territory.

domestic violence The act of willful neglect or physical violence that occurs within a familial or other intimate relationship.

double jeopardy To twice place at risk (jeopardize) a person's life or liberty. Constitutional law prohibits a second prosecution in the same court for the same criminal offense.

double marginality The double suspicion that minority law enforcement officers face from their white colleagues and from members of the minority community to which they belong.

drug Any substance that modifies biological, psychological, or social behavior. In particular, an illegal substance with those properties.

drug abuse The use of drugs that results in physical or psychological problems for the user, as well as disruption of personal relationships and employment.

Drug Enforcement Administration (DEA) The federal agency responsible for enforcing the nation's laws and regulations regarding narcotics and other controlled substances.

dual court system The separate but interrelated court system of the United States, made up of the courts on the national level and the courts on the state level.

due process clause The provisions of the Fifth and Fourteenth Amendments to the Constitution that guarantee that no person shall be deprived of life, liberty, or property without due process of law.

due process model A criminal justice model that places primacy on the right of the individual to be protected from the power of the government.

duress Unlawful pressure brought to bear on a person, causing the person to perform an act that he or she would not otherwise perform.

duty The moral sense of a police officer that she or he should behave in a certain manner.

duty to retreat The requirement that a person claiming self-defense prove that she or he first took reasonable steps to avoid the conflict that resulted in the use of deadly force.

E

electronic monitoring A supervision technique in which the offender's whereabouts are kept under surveillance by an electronic device.

electronic surveillance The use of electronic equipment by law enforcement agents to record private conversations or observe conduct that is meant to be private.

encryption The translation of computer data in a secret code with the goal of protecting that data from unauthorized parties.

entrapment A defense in which the defendant claims that he or she was induced by a public official—usually an undercover agent or police officer—to commit a crime that he or she would otherwise not have committed.

ethics The moral principles that govern a person's perception of right and wrong.

evidence Anything that is used to prove the existence or nonexistence of a fact.

evidence-based practices Approaches or strategies that have been extensively researched and shown consistently to produce the desired outcomes.

exclusionary rule A rule under which any evidence that is obtained in violation of the accused's rights, as well as any evidence derived from illegally obtained evidence, will not be admissible in criminal court.

exigent circumstances Situations that require extralegal or exceptional actions by the police.

expert witness A witness with professional training or substantial experience qualifying her or him to testify on a certain subject.

expiration release The release of an inmate from prison at the end of his or her sentence without any further correctional supervision.

extradition The process by which one jurisdiction surrenders a person accused or convicted of violating another jurisdiction's criminal law to the second jurisdiction.

F

false confession An admission of guilt when the confessor did not, in fact, commit the crime.

Federal Bureau of Investigation (FBI) The branch of the Department of Justice responsible for investigating violations of federal law.

federalism A form of government in which a written constitution provides for a division of powers between a central government and several regional governments.

fee system A system in which the sheriff's department is reimbursed by a government agency for the costs of housing jail inmates.

felony A serious crime, usually punishable by death or imprisonment for a year or longer.

felony-murder An unlawful homicide that occurs during the attempted commission of a felony.

field training The segment of a police recruit's training in which he or she is removed from the classroom and placed on the beat, under the supervision of a senior officer.

forensics The application of science to establish facts and evidence during the investigation of crimes.

forfeiture The process by which the government seizes private property attached to criminal activity.

formal criminal justice process The model of the criminal justice process in which participants follow formal rules to create a smoothly functioning disposition of cases from arrest to punishment.

frisk A pat-down or minimal search by police to discover weapons.

fruit of the poisoned tree Evidence that is acquired through the use of illegally obtained evidence and is therefore inadmissible in court.

furlough Temporary release from a prison for purposes of vocational or educational training, to ease the shock of release, or for personal reasons.

G

genetics The study of how certain traits or qualities are transmitted from parents to their offspring.

"good faith" exception The legal principle that evidence obtained with the use of a technically invalid search warrant is admissible during trial if the police acted in good faith when they sought the warrant from a judge.

"good time" A reduction in time served by prisoners based on good behavior, conformity to rules, and other positive behavior.

graduated sanctions The practical theory in juvenile corrections that a delinquent or status offender should receive a punishment that matches in seriousness the severity of the wrongdoing.

grand jury The group of citizens called to decide whether probable cause exists to believe that a suspect committed the crime with which she or he has been charged.

gun control Efforts by the federal government or state governments to regulate the sale of firearms.

H

habeas corpus An order that requires corrections officials to bring an inmate before a court or a judge and explain why he or she is being held in prison.

habitual offender laws Statutes that require lengthy prison sentences for those who are convicted of multiple felonies.

hacker A person who uses one computer to break into another.

halfway house A community-based form of early release that places inmates in residential centers and allows them to reintegrate with society.

"hands-off" doctrine The unwritten judicial policy that favors noninterference by the courts in the administration of prisons and jails.

hate crime law A statute that provides for greater sanctions against those who commit crimes motivated by bias against an individual or a group based on race, ethnicity, religion, gender, sexual orientation, disability, or age.

hearsay An oral or written statement made by an out-of-court speaker that is later offered in court by a witness (not the speaker) concerning a matter before the court.

home confinement A community-based sanction in which offenders serve their terms of incarceration in their homes.

homeland security A concerted national effort to prevent terrorist attacks within the United States and reduce the nation's vulnerability to terrorism.

hot spots Concentrated areas of high criminal activity that draw a directed police response.

hung jury A jury whose members are so irreconcilably divided in their opinions that they cannot reach a verdict.

hypothesis A possible explanation for an observed occurrence that can be tested by further investigation.

I

"identifiable human needs" The basic human necessities that correctional facilities are required by the Constitution to provide to inmates.

identity theft The theft of personal information, such as a person's name, driver's license number, or Social Security number.

incapacitation A strategy for preventing crime by detaining wrongdoers in prison, thereby separating them from the community and reducing criminal opportunities.

inchoate offenses Conduct deemed criminal without actual harm being done, provided that the harm that would have occurred is one the law tries to prevent.

incident-driven policing A reactive approach to policing that emphasizes a speedy response to calls for service.

indeterminate sentencing Imposition of a sentence that prescribes a range of years rather than a definite period of years to be served.

indictment A charge or written accusation, issued by a grand jury, that probable cause exists to believe that a named person has committed a crime.

"inevitable discovery" exception The legal principle that illegally obtained evidence can be admissible in court if police using lawful means would have "inevitably" discovered it.

infancy A condition that, under early American law, excused young wrongdoers of criminal behavior because presumably they could not understand the consequences of their actions.

informal criminal justice process A model of the criminal justice system that recognizes the informal authority exercised by individuals at each step of the criminal justice process.

information The formal charge against the accused issued by the prosecutor after a preliminary hearing has found probable cause.

infraction In most jurisdictions, a noncriminal offense for which the penalty is a fine rather than incarceration.

infrastructure The services and facilities that support the day-to-day needs of modern life, such as electricity, food, transportation, and water.

initial appearance An accused's first appearance before a judge or magistrate following arrest.

insanity A defense for criminal liability that asserts a lack of criminal responsibility due to mental instability

intake The process by which an official of the court must decide whether to file a petition, release the juvenile, or place the juvenile under some other form of supervision.

intellectual property Property resulting from intellectual, creative processes.

intelligence-led policing An approach that measures the risk of criminal behavior associated with certain individuals or locations so as to predict when and where such criminal behavior is most likely to occur in the future.

intensive supervision probation (ISP) A punishment-oriented form of probation in which the offender is placed under stricter and more frequent surveillance and control than in conventional probation.

intermediate sanctions Sanctions that are more restrictive than probation and less restrictive than imprisonment.

internal affairs unit (IAU) A division within a police department that receives and investigates complaints of wrongdoing by police officers.

interrogation The direct questioning of a suspect to gather evidence of criminal activity and to try to gain a confession.

intoxication A defense for criminal liability in which the defendant claims that the taking of intoxicants rendered him or her unable to form the requisite intent to commit a criminal act.

involuntary manslaughter A homicide in which the offender had no intent to kill her or his victim.

irresistible-impulse test A test for the insanity defense under which a defendant who knew his or her action was wrong may still be found insane if he or she was unable, as a result of a mental deficiency, to control the urge to complete the act.

J

jail A facility, usually operated by the county government, used to hold persons awaiting trial or those who have been found guilty of less serious felonies or misdemeanors.

judicial review The power of a court—particularly the United States Supreme Court—to review the actions of the executive and legislative branches and, if necessary, declare those actions unconstitutional.

judicial waiver The process in which the juvenile judge, based on the facts of the case at hand, decides that the alleged offender should be transferred to adult court.

jurisdiction The authority of a court to hear and decide cases within an area of the law or a geographic territory.

jury trial A trial before a judge and a jury.

just deserts A sanctioning philosophy based on the assertion that criminal punishment should be proportionate to the severity of the crime.

justice The quality of fairness that must exist in the processes designed to determine whether individuals are guilty of criminal wrongdoing.

justice reinvestment A corrections policy that promotes (a) a reduction in spending on prisons and jails and (b) reinvestment of the resulting savings into programs that decrease crime and reduce reoffending.

juvenile delinquency Behavior that is illegal under federal or state law that has been committed by a person who is under an age limit specified by statute.

L

larceny The act of taking property from another person without the use of force with the intent of keeping that property.

lay witness A witness who can truthfully and accurately testify on a fact in question without having specialized training or knowledge.

learning theory The theory that delinquents and criminals must be taught both the practical and the emotional skills necessary to participate in illegal activity.

legalization The process of making a formerly illegal product or action lawful. In the context of marijuana, the process includes strict regulation, including a ban on sale to or use by minors.

liability In a civil court, legal responsibility for one's own or another's actions.

life course criminology The study of crime based on the belief that behavioral patterns developed in childhood can predict delinquent and criminal behavior later in life.

lockdown A disciplinary action taken by prison officials in which all inmates are ordered to their quarters, and nonessential prison activities are suspended.

low-visibility decision making A term used to describe the discretionary power police have in determining what to do with misbehaving juveniles.

M

magistrate A public civil officer or official with limited judicial authority within a particular geographic area, such as the authority to issue an arrest warrant.

mala in se A descriptive term for acts that are inherently wrong, regardless of whether they are prohibited by law.

mala prohibita A descriptive term for acts that are made illegal by criminal statute and are not necessarily wrong in and of themselves.

mandatory release Release from prison that occurs when an offender has served the full length of his or her sentence, minus any adjustments for good time.

mandatory sentencing guidelines Statutorily determined punishments that must be applied to those who are convicted of specific crimes.

master jury list The list of citizens in a court's district from which a jury can be selected; compiled from voter-registration lists, driver's license lists, and other sources.

material support In the context of federal antiterrorism legislation, the act of helping a terrorist organization by engaging in a wide range of activity that includes providing financial support, training, and expert advice or assistance.

maximum-security prison A correctional institution designed and organized to control and discipline dangerous felons, as well as prevent escape.

medical model A model of corrections in which the psychological and biological roots of an inmate's criminal behavior are identified and treated.

medium-security prison A correctional institution that houses less dangerous inmates and therefore uses less restrictive measures to prevent violence and escapes.

mens rea (pronounced mehns *ray*-uh). Wrongful mental state, or intent; usually as necessary as a wrongful act to establish criminal liability.

minimum-security prison A correctional institution designed to allow inmates, most of whom pose low security risks, a great deal of freedom of movement and contact with the outside world.

***Miranda* rights** The constitutional rights of accused persons taken into custody by law enforcement officials, such as the right to remain silent and the right to counsel.

misdemeanor A criminal offense that is not a felony; usually punishable by a fine and/or a jail term of less than one year.

Missouri Plan A method of selecting judges that combines appointment and election.

mitigating circumstances Any circumstances accompanying the commission of a crime that may justify a lighter sentence.

***M'Naghten* Rule** A common law test of criminal responsibility, derived from *M'Naghten's* Case in 1843, that relies on the defendant's inability to distinguish right from wrong.

morals Principles of right and wrong behavior, as practiced by individuals or by society.

murder The unlawful killing of one human being by another.

N

national security letters Legal notices that compel the disclosure of customer records held by banks, telephone companies, Internet service providers, and other companies to the agents of the federal government.

necessity A defense against criminal liability in which the defendant asserts that circumstances required her or him to commit an illegal act.

negligence A failure to exercise the standard of care that a reasonable person would exercise in similar circumstances.

new-generation jail A type of jail that is distinguished architecturally from its predecessors by a design that encourages interaction between inmates and jailers and that offers greater opportunities for treatment.

night watch system An early form of American law enforcement in which volunteers patrolled their community from dusk to dawn to keep the peace.

nolo contendere Latin for "I will not contest it." A criminal defendant's plea, in which he or she chooses not to challenge, or contest, the charges brought by the government.

nonpartisan elections Elections in which candidates are presented on the ballot without any party affiliation.

O

opening statements The attorneys' statements to the jury at the beginning of the trial.

opinions Written statements by appellate judges expressing the reasons for the court's decision in a case.

oral arguments The verbal arguments presented in person by attorneys to an appellate court. Each attorney presents reasons why the court should rule in his or her client's favor.

organized crime Illegal acts carried out by illegal organizations engaged in the market for illegal goods or services, such as illicit drugs or firearms.

P

pardon An act of executive clemency that overturns a conviction and erases mention of the crime from the person's criminal record.

parens patriae A doctrine that holds that the state has a responsibility to look after the well-being of children and to assume the role of parent if necessary.

parole The conditional release of an inmate before his or her sentence has expired.

parole board A body of appointed civilians that decides whether a convict should be granted conditional release before the end of his or her sentence.

parole contract An agreement between the state and the offender that establishes the conditions of parole.

parole grant hearing A hearing in which the entire parole board or a subcommittee reviews information, meets the offender, and hears testimony from relevant witnesses to determine whether to grant parole.

parole guidelines Standards that are used in the parole process to measure the risk that a potential parolee will recidivate.

Part I offenses Crimes reported annually by the FBI in its Uniform Crime Report. Part I offenses include murder, rape, robbery, aggravated assault, burglary, larceny, and motor vehicle theft.

Part II offenses All crimes recorded by the FBI that do not fall into the category of Part I offenses. These crimes include both misdemeanors and felonies.

partisan elections Elections in which candidates are affiliated with and receive support from political parties.

Patriot Act Legislation passed in the wake of the September 11, 2001, terrorist attacks that greatly expanded the ability of government agents to monitor and apprehend suspected terrorists.

patronage system A form of corruption in which the political party in power hires and promotes police officers and receives job-related "favors" in return.

penitentiary An early form of correctional facility that emphasized separating inmates from society and from each other.

peremptory challenges *Voir dire* challenges to exclude potential jurors from serving on the jury without any supporting reason or cause.

petition The document filed with a juvenile court alleging that the juvenile is a delinquent or a status offender and requesting that the court either hear the case or transfer it to an adult court.

phishing Sending an unsolicited e-mail that falsely claims to be from a legitimate organization in an attempt to acquire sensitive information from the recipient.

plaintiff The person or institution that initiates a lawsuit in civil court proceedings by filing a complaint.

plain view doctrine The legal principle that objects in plain view of a law enforcement agent who has the right to be in a position to have that view may be seized without a warrant and introduced as evidence.

plea bargaining The process by which the accused and the prosecutor work out a mutually satisfactory conclusion to the case, subject to court approval.

police corruption The abuse of authority by a law enforcement officer for personal gain.

police subculture The values and perceptions that are shared by members of a police department and, to a certain extent, by all law enforcement agents.

precedent A court decision that furnishes an example of authority for deciding subsequent cases involving similar facts.

predisposition report A report prepared during the disposition process that provides the judge with relevant background material to aid in the disposition decision.

preliminary hearing An initial hearing in which a magistrate decides if there is probable cause to believe that the defendant committed the crime with which he or she is charged.

preponderance of the evidence The degree of proof required to decide in favor of one side or the other in a civil case. In general, this requirement is met when a plaintiff proves that a fact more likely than not is true.

prescription drugs Medical drugs that require a physician's permission for purchase.

presentence investigative report An investigative report on an offender's background that assists a judge in determining the proper sentence.

pretrial detainees Individuals who cannot post bail after arrest and are therefore forced to spend the time prior to their trial incarcerated in jail.

pretrial diversion program An alternative to trial offered by a judge or prosecutor, in which the offender agrees to participate in a specified counseling or treatment program in return for withdrawal of the charges.

preventive detention The retention of an accused person in custody due to fears that she or he will commit a crime if released before trial.

prisoner reentry A corrections strategy designed to prepare inmates for a successful return to the community and to reduce the possibility of criminal activity after release.

prison gang A group of inmates who band together within the corrections system to engage in social and criminal activities.

prisonization The socialization process through which a new inmate learns the accepted norms and values of the prison culture.

prison programs Organized activities for inmates that are designed to improve their physical and mental health, provide them with vocational skills, or simply keep them busy while incarcerated.

prison segregation The practice of separating inmates based on a certain characteristic, such as ethnicity or race.

private prisons Correctional facilities operated by private corporations instead of the government and, therefore, reliant on profits for survival.

private security The practice of private corporations or individuals offering services traditionally performed by police officers.

proactive arrests Arrests that occur because of concerted efforts by law enforcement agencies to respond to a particular type of criminal behavior.

probable cause Reasonable grounds to believe the existence of facts warranting certain actions, such as the search or arrest of a person.

probation A criminal sanction in which a convict is allowed to remain in the community rather than be imprisoned.

probationary period A period of time at the beginning of a police officer's career during which she or he may be fired without cause.

problem-oriented policing A policing philosophy that requires police to identify potential criminal activity and develop strategies to prevent or respond to that activity.

problem-solving courts Lower courts that have jurisdiction over one specific area of criminal activity, such as illegal drugs or domestic violence.

procedural criminal law Rules that define the manner in which the rights and duties of individuals may be enforced.

procedural due process A provision in the Constitution that states that the law must be carried out in a fair and orderly manner.

professional model A style of policing advocated by August Vollmer and O. W. Wilson that emphasizes centralized police organizations, increased use of technology, and a limitation of police discretion through regulations and guidelines.

property bond An alternative to posting bail in cash, in which the defendant gains pretrial release by providing the court with property as assurance that he or she will return for trial.

prosecutorial waiver A procedure used in situations where the prosecutor has discretion to decide whether a case will be heard by a juvenile court or an adult court.

psychoactive drugs Chemicals that affect the brain, causing changes in emotions, perceptions, and behavior.

psychology The scientific study of mental processes and behavior.

public defenders Court-appointed attorneys who are paid by the state to represent defendants who cannot afford private counsel.

public order crime Behavior that has been labeled criminal because it is contrary to shared social values, customs, and norms.

public prosecutors Individuals, acting as trial lawyers, who initiate and conduct cases in the government's name and on behalf of the people.

Q

qualified immunity A doctrine that shields law enforcement officers from damages for civil liability so long as they have not violated an individual's statutory or constitutional rights.

R

racial profiling The practice of targeting people for police action based solely on their race, ethnicity, or national origin.

racketeering The criminal action of being involved in an organized effort to engage in illegal business transactions.

random patrol A patrol strategy that relies on police officers monitoring a certain area with the goal of detecting crimes in progress or preventing crime due to their presence. Also known as *general* or *preventive patrol.*

rational choice theory A school of criminology that holds that wrongdoers weigh the possible benefits of criminal or delinquent activity against the expected costs of being apprehended.

reactive arrests Arrests that come about as part of the ordinary routine of police patrol and responses to calls for service.

real evidence Evidence that is brought into court and seen by the jury, as opposed to evidence that is described for a jury.

"real offense" The actual offense committed, as opposed to the charge levied by a prosecutor as the result of a plea bargain.

reasonable force The degree of force that is appropriate to protect the police officer or other citizens and is not excessive.

rebuttal Evidence given to counteract or disprove evidence presented by the opposing party.

recidivism The act of committing a new crime after a person has already been punished for a previous crime by being convicted and sent to jail or prison.

recklessness The state of being aware that a risk does or will exist and nevertheless acting in a way that consciously disregards this risk.

recruitment The process by which law enforcement agencies develop a pool of qualified applicants from which to select new employees.

referral The notification process through which a law enforcement officer or other concerned citizen makes the juvenile court aware of a juvenile's unlawful or unruly conduct.

regulation A governmental order or rule having the force of law that is usually implemented by an administrative agency.

rehabilitation The philosophy that society is best served when wrongdoers are provided the resources needed to eliminate criminality from their behavioral pattern.

reintegration A goal of corrections that focuses on preparing the offender for a return to the community unmarred by further criminal behavior.

relative deprivation The theory that inmate aggression is created when freedoms and services that the inmate has come to accept as normal are decreased or eliminated.

release on recognizance (ROR) A judge's order that releases an accused from jail with the understanding that he or she will return of his or her own will for further proceedings.

relevant evidence Evidence tending to make a fact in question more or less probable than it would be without the evidence. Only relevant evidence is admissible in court.

repeat victimization The theory that certain people and places are more likely to be subject to repeated criminal activity and that past victimization is a strong indicator of future victimization.

residential treatment program A government-run facility for juveniles whose offenses are not deemed serious enough to warrant incarceration in a training school.

response time The speed with which calls for service are answered.

restitution Monetary compensation for damages done to the victim by the offender's criminal act.

restorative justice An approach to punishment designed to repair the harm done to the victim and the community by the offender's criminal act.

retribution The philosophy that those who commit criminal acts should be punished for breaking society's rules to the extent required by just deserts.

revocation The formal process that follows the failure of a probationer or parolee to comply with the terms of his or her probation or parole, often resulting in the probationer's or parolee's incarceration.

robbery The act of taking property from another person through force, threat of force, or intimidation.

rule of four A rule of the United States Supreme Court that the Court will not issue a writ of *certiorari* unless at least four justices approve of the decision to hear the case.

rule of law The principle that the rules of a legal system apply equally to all persons, institutions, and entities—public or private—that make up a society.

S

search The process by which police examine a person or property to find evidence that will be used to prove guilt in a criminal trial.

searches and seizures The legal term, as found in the Fourth Amendment to the U.S. Constitution, that generally refers to the searching for and the confiscating of evidence by law enforcement agents.

searches incidental to arrests Searches for weapons and evidence that are conducted on persons who have just been arrested.

search warrant A written order, based on probable cause and issued by a judge or magistrate, commanding that police officers or criminal investigators search a specific person, place, or property to obtain evidence.

secondary policing The situation in which a police officer accepts off-duty employment from a private company or government agency.

security threat group (STG) A group of three or more inmates who engage in activity that poses a threat to the safety of other inmates or the prison staff.

seizure The forcible taking of a person or property in response to a violation of the law.

self-defense The legally recognized privilege to protect one's self or property from injury by another.

self-reported survey A method of gathering crime data that relies on participants to reveal and detail their own criminal or delinquent behavior.

sentencing discrimination A situation in which the length of a sentence appears to be influenced by a defendant's race, gender, economic status, or other factor not directly related to the crime he or she committed.

sentencing disparity A situation in which those convicted of similar crimes do not receive similar sentences.

sentencing guidelines Legislatively determined guidelines that judges are required to follow when sentencing those convicted of specific crimes.

separate confinement A nineteenth-century penitentiary system developed in Pennsylvania in which inmates were kept separate from each other at all times, with daily activities taking place in individual cells.

sequestration The isolation of jury members during a trial to ensure that their judgment is not tainted by information other than what is provided in the courtroom.

sex offender notification law Legislation that requires law enforcement authorities to notify people when convicted sex offenders are released into their neighborhood or community.

sexual assault Forced or coerced sexual intercourse (or other sexual acts).

sheriff The primary law enforcement officer in a county, usually elected to the post by a popular vote.

shock incarceration A short period of incarceration that is designed to deter further criminal activity by "shocking" the offender with the hardships of imprisonment.

social conflict theories A school of criminology that views criminal behavior as the result of class conflict.

social disorganization theory The theory that deviant behavior is more likely in communities where social institutions such as the family, schools, and the criminal justice system fail to exert control over the population.

socialization The process through which a police officer is taught the values and expected behavior of the police subculture.

social process theories A school of criminology that considers criminal behavior to be the predictable result of a person's interaction with his or her environment.

sociology The study of the development and functioning of groups of people who live together within a society.

spam Bulk e-mails, particularly of commercial advertising, sent in large quantities without the consent of the recipient.

split sentence probation A sentence that consists of incarceration in a prison or jail, followed by a probationary period in the community.

stalking The criminal act of causing fear in a person by repeatedly subjecting that person to unwanted or threatening attention.

stare decisis (pronounced *ster*-ay dih-*si-ses*). A legal doctrine under which judges are obligated to follow the precedents established under prior decisions.

status offender A juvenile who has engaged in behavior deemed unacceptable for those under a certain statutorily determined age.

statute of limitations A law limiting the amount of time prosecutors have to bring criminal charges against a suspect after the crime has occurred.

statutory law The body of law enacted by legislative bodies.

statutory rape A strict liability crime in which an adult engages in a sexual act with a minor.

stop A brief detention of a person by law enforcement agents for questioning.

strain theory The assumption that crime is the result of frustration felt by individuals who cannot reach their financial and personal goals through legitimate means.

stressors The aspects of police work and life that lead to feelings of stress.

strict liability crimes Certain crimes, such as traffic violations, in which the defendant is guilty regardless of her or his state of mind at the time of the act.

substantial-capacity test (ALI/MPC test) A test for the insanity defense that states that a person is not responsible for criminal behavior when he or she "lacks substantial capacity" to understand that the behavior is wrong or to know how to behave properly.

substantive criminal law Law that defines the rights and duties of individuals with respect to one another.

substantive due process The constitutional requirement that laws used in accusing and convicting persons of crimes must be fair.

supermax prison A highly secure, freestanding correctional facility—or such a unit within a correctional facility—that manages offenders who would pose a threat to the security and safety of other inmates and staff members if housed in the general inmate population.

supremacy clause A clause in the U.S. Constitution establishing that federal law is the "supreme law of the land" and shall prevail when in conflict with state constitutions or statutes.

surveillance The close observation of a person or group by government agents, in particular to uncover evidence of criminal or terrorist activities.

suspended sentence A judicially imposed condition in which an offender is sentenced after being convicted of a crime, but is not required to begin serving the sentence immediately.

system A set of interacting parts that, when functioning properly, achieve a desired result.

T

technical violation An action taken by a probationer or parolee that, although not criminal, breaks the terms of probation or parole as designated by the court.

terrorism The use or threat of violence to intimidate civilian populations or achieve political objectives.

testimony Verbal evidence given by witnesses under oath.

theory An explanation of a happening or circumstance that is based on observation, experimentation, and reasoning.

time served The period of time a person denied bail (or unable to pay it) has spent in jail prior to his or her trial.

total institution An institution, such as a prison, that provides all of the necessities for existence to those who live within its boundaries.

toxicology The branch of forensic science concerned with the effects and detection of foreign chemicals in the human body.

trace evidence Evidence such as a fingerprint, blood, or hair found in small amounts at a crime scene.

training school A correctional institution for juveniles found to be delinquent or status offenders.

trial courts Courts in which most cases begin and in which questions of fact are examined.

true threat An act of speech or expression that is not protected by the First Amendment because it is done with the intention placing a specific victim or group of victims in fear of unlawful violence.

truth-in-sentencing laws Legislative attempts to ensure that convicts will serve approximately the terms to which they were initially sentenced.

U

Uniform Crime Report (UCR) An annual report compiled by the FBI to give an indication of criminal activity in the United States.

U.S. Customs and Border Protection (CBP) The federal agency responsible for protecting U.S. borders and facilitating legal trade and travel across those borders.

U.S. Immigration and Customs Enforcement (ICE) The federal agency that enforces the nation's immigration and customs laws.

U.S. Secret Service A federal law enforcement organization with the primary responsibility of protecting the president, the president's family, the vice president, and other important political figures.

V

venire The group of citizens from which the jury is selected.

verdict A formal decision made by the jury.

victim Any person who suffers physical, emotional, or financial harm as the result of a criminal act.

victim impact statement (VIS) A statement to the sentencing body (judge, jury, or parole board) in which the victim is given the opportunity to describe how the crime has affected her or him.

victim surveys A method of gathering crime data that directly surveys participants to determine their experiences as victims of crime.

virus A computer program that can replicate itself and interfere with the normal use of a computer. A virus cannot exist as a separate entity and must attach itself to another program to move through a network.

visa Official authorization allowing a person to travel to and within the issuing country.

voir dire The preliminary questions that the trial attorneys ask prospective jurors to determine whether they are biased or have any connection with the defendant or a witness.

voluntary manslaughter A homicide in which the intent to kill was present in the mind of the offender, but malice was lacking.

W

warden The prison official who is ultimately responsible for the organization and performance of a correctional facility.

warrantless arrest An arrest made without first seeking a warrant for the action.

white-collar crime Nonviolent crimes committed by business entities or individuals to gain a personal or business advantage.

widen the net The criticism that intermediate sanctions designed to divert offenders from prison actually increase the number of citizens who are under the control and surveillance of the American corrections system.

work release program Temporary release of convicts from prison for purposes of employment. The offenders may spend their days on the job, but must return to the correctional facility at night and during the weekend.

worm A computer program that can automatically replicate itself and interfere with the normal use of a computer. A worm does not need to be attached to an existing file to move from one network to another.

writ of *certiorari* A request from a higher court asking a lower court for the record of a case. In essence, the request signals the higher court's willingness to review the case.

wrongful conviction The conviction, either by verdict or by guilty plea, of a person who is factually innocent of the charges.

Y

youth gang A self-formed group of youths with several identifiable characteristics, including a gang name and other recognizable symbols, a geographic territory, and participation in illegal activities.

Name Index

G

H

I

J

K

L

M

U

V

W

Y

Z

Subject Index

D

E

F

Fruit of the poisoned tree, 169
Furlough, 370

G

Gambling, 36
Gang investigator, 8
Gangs
  defined, 396
  girls in, 397
  prison, 358–360
  reasons for joining, 397
  as risk factor for juvenile delinquency, 396–397
Garbage, privacy and, 170–171
Gender
  jury selection, 245
  juvenile delinquency and, 390
  sentencing discrimination, 276
General deterrence, 263
General (unlimited) jurisdiction, 200, 203–204
General Motors (GM), 436
General strain theory, 50
General Theory of Crime, A (Gottfredson & Hirschi), 52
Genetics, crime and, 46
Genetic witness, 139
GEO Group, Inc., 338
Germany, hate speech laws, 6
Good faith exception, 170
Good time, 267–268
GPS
  electronic monitoring and, 317
  privacy and electronically following automobiles, 171–172
Graduated sanction, 404
Grand Forks (North Dakota) Police Department, 131
Grand jury, 228, 232
Great Britain, hate speech laws, 6
Great Law (of Pennsylvania), 325
Gross misdemeanor, 75
Group homes, 405
Guilty/guilty plea, 228
  beyond a reasonable doubt, 241
  criminal law and, 74
  defense attorneys defending, 217, 219–220
  guilty but mentally ill statutes, 87
  misdemeanor cases at initial appearance, 227
  plea bargaining, 235–238
  pleading, 235–238
Guns
  AFT responsibilities and, 123
  building with 3D printer, 431
  deaths from, 19
  increase prison population and weapon crimes, 336
  mass shooting, 19
Gun control
  background checks and, 19, 432–433
  debate over, 434
  defined, 19, 431
  firearms sales in U.S., 431–432
  gun shows and private sales of, 432
  mental health issues, 432–433
  recent legislative efforts at, 433
Gun Control Act, 123
Gun courts, 203

H

Habeas corpus, petition, 255
Habitual Criminal Sterilization Act, 93
Habitual offender laws, 279
Hackers, 427, 428
Halfway house program manager, 373
Halfway houses, 12, 372
Hallcrest Report II, 124
Hallucinogens, use of, in United States, 58
Hand geometry scanners, 18
Hands-off doctrine, 365
Harm, 83
Hate crime laws, 82, 83
Hate speech laws, in various countries, 6
Hawaii's Opportunity Probation with Enforcement (HOPE), 306
Hearsay, 250
Heroin
  crime rate and, 41
  naloxone for overdose, 102
  prescription drug abuse and, 60
  use of, in United States, 58
High-tech crimes. *See* Cyber crimes
Highway patrol, 11
  number of agencies, 118
  purpose of, 118
  vs. state police, 118
Hispanics
  biases in policing and, 156–157
  crime and, 43
  death penalty and, 288
  female prisoners, 367
  gang membership, 397
  incarceration rate of, 26
  as judges, 211
  as law enforcement officers, 112–116
  prison violence and, 358
  on probation, 300
  racial profiling and S.B. 1070, 182
  sentencing discrimination and, 275–276
  stops and, 181–182
Home confinement, 316–317
  defined, 316
  levels of, 316
  number of offenders under, 316
Home detention, 316
Home incarceration, 316
Homeland security. *See also* National security
  crime control model and, 16–17
  cyberattacks, 422–423
  defined, 22
  infrastructure security, 422–423
  metadata surveillance, 23
Homeland Security, Department of (DHS), 11
  Customs and Border Protection (CBP), 119–120
  Immigration and Customs Enforcement (ICE), 120
  overview, 119
  Secret Service, 119, 120–121
Homicide. *See also* Murder
  black on black violence, 42
  justifiable, 90
  mens rea, 79
  race and, 42
  by relative or acquaintance, 38
Honesty, ethical dilemmas of, 158
Honor killings, 76
Hot spots, 41, 142–143
  policing, 17
  technology for, 107–108
House of Refuge, 383
Hung jury, 240, 250, 253
  double jeopardy and, 255
Hypothesis, 45

I

Identifiable human needs, 366
Identity theft, 37, 425
Illinois Juvenile Court Act, 383–384
Immigration
  Arizona law on, 182
  increase in prison population and violations of, 336
  racial profiling and, 182
  undocumented immigrants and risk of victimization, 55
Immigration and Customs Enforcement (ICE)
  under Homeland Security Department, 120
  responsibilities of, 12, 119
Impact incarceration programs, 315
Imprisonment, as form of punishment, 269
Incapacitation
  impact of, 264
  as purpose of sentencing, 264
Incarceration
  crime rate and, 41
  decrease in, 24–25
  deincarceration movement, 24–25
  economics of, 24
  effectiveness of reducing crime, 337–338
  high rate of, in U.S., 325, 328, 338
  increased probability of, 335–336
  increase in rate of, 24
  justice reinvestment, 24
  of juveniles, 404–407
  recent drop in rate, 324
  shock, 299
Incident-driven policing, 140–141
Income
  crime and, 43
  risk of victimization, 55
Indeterminate sentencing
  defined, 267
  discretionary release, 308–310
  individualized justice, 269
  rehabilitation and, 269
Indictment, 228
  defined, 232
  grand jury and, 232
Individualized justice, 269
Industrial schools, 406
Industrial shop and school correctional officers, 361
Inevitable discovery exception, 170
Infancy defense, 84, 387
Informal criminal justice process, 14–15
Informants, probable cause based on, 168
Information
  defined, 231
  issued by prosecutor, 231
  probable cause based on, 168
Infraction, 75–76
Infrastructure, 121
  cyberattacks on, 422–423
Inherent coercion, 186
Initial appearance, 227
In loco parentis, 398
Inmates. *See* Prisoners
Innocence, presumption of, 241
Innocence Project, 256
Insanity
  death penalty and, 285
  as defense under criminal law, 84–86, 251
  determining competency, 86
  guilty but mentally ill, 87
  measuring sanity, 85–86
  myth and reality of, 87
Insanity defense, 84–86, 251
Instagram, 110
Insurance fraud, 435
Intake, 399
Intellectual property theft, 428
Intelligence-based policing techniques, 41
Intelligence-led policing, 17, 107–108
  counterterrorism and, 108
  technology and, 109
Intensive supervision probation, 314–315
Intent, 77
  attendant circumstances, 82
  dual intent, 80–81
  as element of arrest, 183–184
Intermediate sanctions, 311–318
  boot camp, 315
  community service, 312
  day-fines, 312
  day reporting centers, 313–314
  defined, 311
  drug courts, 313
  electronic monitoring, 316–317
  fines, 312
  forfeiture, 312, 313, 314

Q

R

T

Terrorism
counterterrorism
Antiterrorism and Effective Death Penalty Act (AEDPA), 416
foreign surveillance, 415–416, 420
mass surveillance, 417–420
Patriot Act, 416–417
counterterrorism strategies
airport security and ethnic profiling, 183
FBI and, 122
hard and soft power, 108
intelligence-led policing, 108
Internet for gathering information, 109
private security and, 124
crowdsourcing, 22–23
defined, 21–22
domestic
anti-government extremists, 22
causes of, 22
defined, 22
lone wolf terrorists, 23
echo chamber of recruitment, 4
encryption and, 24
entrapment issues, 136
known wolves, 422
material support for, 416
metadata surveillance, 23
police academy training in, 112
preventive policing and domestic terrorism, 135–136
terrorist Internet recruiting operations, 422
true threat laws, 420–421
Testimony
defined, 246
as evidence, 246–247
wrongful convictions and false, 256
Theft
cyber, 424–427
defined, 38
gangs and, 396
identity, 425
as misdemeanor or felony, 82
motor vehicle, 35
as property crime, 35
Theory. *See* Crime theories
Thermal imagers, 177–178
Thirteenth Amendment, prisoners' rights, 365
Three-strike laws, 279
Thrill offenders, 45–46
Time served, 342–343
Tokenism, 114
Topeka Correctional Facility, 332
Tor, 430
Tort, 74
Total institution, 353
Totality of the circumstances, 180
Touch DNA, 139
Tours, 132
Tower guards, 361–362
Trace evidence, 137
Traditional jail design, 344–345
Traffic laws, 73
Training schools, 406–407
Trait theory, 46, 48
Transportation Security Administration (TSA), 121
Treasury Department, 119, 123
Trial court administrator, 244
Trial courts
defined, 200
jurisdiction and, 200–201
Trial judges
administrative role of, 209
roles and responsibilities of, 208–209
before trial, 208–209
during trial, 209
Trials
bench, 240
change of venue, 241
elements of
appeals, 253–255
closing arguments, 252
cross-examination, 249–250
defendant's case, 250–251
jury deliberation, 252
jury instructions, 252
opening statements, 246
prosecution's case, 248–249
rebuttal and surrebuttal, 252
role of evidence, 246–248
verdict, 253
jury selection, 242–245
pleading guilty, 235–238
pretrial procedures
establishing probable cause, 231–232
grand jury, 232
pleading guilty, 235–238
preliminary hearing, 231
pretrial detention, 227–231
prosecutorial screening process, 232–234
special features of criminal trials, 238–241
presumption of innocence, 241
privilege against self-incrimination, 240–241
role of jury, 240
speedy trial, 238–240
strict standard of proof, 241
speedy, 238–240
statute of limitations, 239–240
steps leading to, 228
Tribal jurisdiction, 199
True threat, 420–421
Truth-in-sentencing laws, 268
increased length of prison terms, 336
mandatory release and, 310
Tucson (Arizona) Police Department, mental illness calls, 102
Twitter, 110
Two Rivers Correctional Institution, 332

U

UCR. *See* Uniform Crime Report (UCR)
Undercover officers, 135
Uniform Code of Military Justice, 200
Uniform Crime Report (UCR), 37–39, 101
compared to NIBRS, 39
defined, 37
information based on, 37
juvenile delinquency and, 389–390
Part II offenses, 38–39
Part I offenses, 38
timeliness of data, 41
United States Reports, 31
Unmanned aerial vehicles (UAVs), 72
USA Freedom Act, 23
USA Patriot Act. *See* Patriot Act
U.S. attorney, 213
Use of force. *See* Force
Use of force matrix, 150
U.S. Coast Guard, 118, 121
U.S. Marshals Service
creation of, 123
responsibilities of, 119, 123

V

Vehicles, searches of, 175–176
Venire, 242
Verdict, 253
Victim advocate, 55
Victim impact statement (VISs), 280–281
Victimization
alcohol use and, 57–58
mental illness as risk factor for, 57
repeat, 55
risks of, 54–56
Victimless crimes, 36
Victimology, 54
Victims of crime, 54–57
chastity requirement, 251
civil lawsuits brought by, 255
compensating, 265, 266–267
creating reasonable doubt about credibility, 251
defined, 27
impact evidence and sentencing, 280–281
listening to, 265–266
parole and rights of, 311
plea bargaining and, 238
prosecutors and, 215
repeat victimization, 55
restorative justice, 266–267
rights of
advocating for victims, 27
emergence of, 27, 93–94
enforceability, 94
legislative efforts, 27, 94
risks of victim evidence, 281
risks of victimization, 54–56
routine activities theory, 54
surveys of, 40
uncooperative, 234
unreliable, 234
victim-offender connection, 55–56
of white-collar crime, 436
women as, 56
Victims of Crime Act, 266
Victims' Rights Amendment, 93
Victim surveys, 40
Video cameras
body-worn cameras, 21, 130, 153–154
citizen videos, 155–156
Ferguson effect, 19–20
police credibility and, 20–21
race issues and public trust, 21
Video games, violence in, and crime, 51
Video surveillance, 178
Violence
corporate violence, 436
in prisons, 357–358
in schools, 390–392
on television and crime, 51
Violent crimes
average length of sentence, 300
black on black violence, 42
categories of, 35
decrease in rate, 37, 41
defined, 35
disadvantaged neighborhoods and, 42–43
juveniles, 389
mental illness and risk factors for, 47
Virus, 427
Visa, 120
Vocational training, for prisoners, 355
Voir dire, 242–243
Voluntary manslaughter, 79

W

Waiver
automatic, 400
judicial, 400
legislative, 400
prosecutorial, 400–401
Walnut Street Jail, 325–326
Warden, 329–330
War on crime, 102–103
Warrantless arrest, 185–186
Warrants
arrests with, 184–185
arrests without, 185–186
Washington, D.C. police department (Metropolitan Police Department), 116–117
Washington Mutual, Inc., 439
Weapons crimes, increase in prison population, 336
Wedding cake model of criminal justice, 277
Western Penitentiary, 326
White-collar crime, 434–439
in the 2000s, 438–439
characteristics of, 435
corporate violence, 436
by corporations, 436–438
cost of, to businesses worldwide, 36
defined, 36, 434

Y

Z